Lebanon

Why has secularism faced such challenges in the Middle East and in Lebanon in particular? In light of dominating headlines about the spread of sectarianism and the so-called death of Arab secularism, Mark Farha addresses the need for a thorough examination of the history of secular thought and practice in the region. By offering a comprehensive, systematic account of the underlying ideological, socioeconomic, and political factors involved, Farha provides a new understanding of the historical roots of secularism as well as the potential causes for the continued resistance a fully deconfessionalized state faces both in Lebanon and in the region at large. Drawing on a vast corpus of primary and secondary sources to examine the varying political parties and ideologies involved, this book provides a fresh approach to the study of religion and politics in the Arab world and beyond.

MARK FARHA was Assistant Professor of Politics and International Relations at the Doha Institute for Graduate Studies from 2015 to 2018, and Assistant Professor of Government at Georgetown University's School of Foreign Service in Qatar from 2008 to 2015. He has written numerous scholarly articles on the modern history and politics of secularism and sectarianism in Lebanon and the Middle East, and is the contributing editor of *Overcoming Sectarian Faultlines after the Arab Uprisings* (2016). He serves as a member of the Century Foundation's project on minorities, citizenship, and inclusion in the Middle East.

Lebanon

The Rise and Fall of a Secular State under Siege

Mark Farha

Georgetown University in Qatar

CAMBRIDGE
UNIVERSITY PRESS

CAMBRIDGE
UNIVERSITY PRESS

University Printing House, Cambridge CB2 8BS, United Kingdom

One Liberty Plaza, 20th Floor, New York, NY 10006, USA

477 Williamstown Road, Port Melbourne, VIC 3207, Australia

314–321, 3rd Floor, Plot 3, Splendor Forum, Jasola District Centre, New Delhi – 110025, India

79 Anson Road, #06–04/06, Singapore 079906

Cambridge University Press is part of the University of Cambridge.

It furthers the University's mission by disseminating knowledge in the pursuit of education, learning, and research at the highest international levels of excellence.

www.cambridge.org
Information on this title: www.cambridge.org/9781108471459
DOI: 10.1017/9781108558846

First published 2019

Printed in the United Kingdom by TJ International Ltd. Padstow Cornwall

A catalogue record for this publication is available from the British Library.

ISBN 978-1-108-47145-9 Hardback
ISBN 978-1-108-45801-6 Paperback

My primary thanks go to my parents Alfred and Klara Farha without whom nothing would have come to pass. Their marriage of East and West and exceptional cosmopolitan paradigm no doubt served as a touchstone for my academic quest to bridge barriers. Their unstinting support and sacrifice allowed me to pursue my research. My experience at Harvard would not have been what it was without the presence (and gentle prodding) of my mentor, Professor Nur Yalman, the emblematic embodiment of an (Ottoman) gentleman and source of "enlightened" joy to all and sundry.

Contents

Figures

Preface

Why Lebanon? Why Secularism?

> If peace and stability reign in the Lebanon, then peace and stability will also pervade in the regimes surrounding Lebanon.
>
> Count Clemens von Metternich

One would be hard-pressed to find a country of a similar (or even larger) size to Lebanon that has occupied a more preeminent place in international diplomacy. Among Middle Eastern states, only Israel (and more recently Iraq and Syria) can compete with this small state when it comes to the time devoted to the Lebanese file at the United Nations or in the disproportionate coverage given to this tiny country in the global press.

From the intercommunal massacres of 1860 to the devastating famine of World War II to the civil war of 1975, from the seismic 2005 assassination of Rafīq al-Ḥarīrī to the record number of refugees streaming into Lebanon after the destruction of Iraq and Syria, repeatedly the world's attention would be forced to turn to this state situated at several critical faultlines. Even junior Lebanese diplomats are often extended a ready welcome in the major capitals; from Washington to Moscow, from Riyadh to Tehran. What may be the cause for such global preoccupation with a country of some 4 million inhabitants and with, until recently,[1] no significant natural resources to be exploited?

Lebanon's prominence is not a new phenomenon. In part, Lebanon's internal diversity – coupled to a system of competitive political patronage – was, and is, a natural magnet for external interests. Moreover, Lebanon, if only by dint of its geographic location at the faultline between the Mediterranean Sea and Arab hinterland, has always found itself in the crosshairs of geopolitical conflicts, pitting Egypt against Babylon, Greece against Persia, Rome against Arabia, Christendom

[1] The massive gas fields that were discovered in the Eastern Mediterranean basin in 2009 have created an explosive potential for conflict with Israel, with direct military threats being issued by Israel against Lebanon should the state proceed with its exploration of the contested gas fields. A struggle over natural resources was also an important component of past conflicts as Lebanon retains the largest water reservoir in the Eastern Mediterranean. Competition over oil and gas fields has also helped to stoke the geopolitical conflict in Iraq, Libya, and Syria. See Ali Ahmed and Félicité Barrier, "The Geopolitics of Oil and Gas Development in Lebanon," American University of Beirut Policy Brief, 1/2018.

against Islam, Catholicism against Orthodoxy, Sunni against Shia, American-sponsored capitalism against Soviet communism, and, most recently, Arabism against Zionism. Ideologically, Lebanon, as we shall see in this book, served simultaneously as the cradle for both a stultifying sectarianism and a path-breaking secularism.

These dialectical, polar tensions could thus resolve themselves in creative hybridities or ignite devastating animosities. Lebanon's melting pot bears a potential to unleash cross-cultural synergies that can be put to both constructive and destructive uses. Lebanon has been a vanity fair of the rich, a haven for hedonism, but also a most fertile ground for cultural innovation, intellectual, and political activism, and a laboratory of Arab liberalism. It was in Lebanon that the first political parties, journals, newspapers, and nongovernmental organizations of the Arab world were founded during the nineteenth century. On the other hand, it was in Lebanon during the 1930s that the car bomb was pioneered as a means of targeted political assassination, a spectre which was to proliferate and haunt the region until the present day.

The infernal image of a burning Beirut after the Israeli assault of 1982 allegedly provided Usāma Bin Lādin's inspiration for his vengeful Jihad,[2] only a decade after he had left his Quaker high school in liberal Lebanon for conservative Saudi Arabia. And it was in Lebanon that US troops landed twice – in 1958 and 1982 – and where the first Islamic suicide bombers attacked American troops in the gruesome Marine Barracks in 1983 in what was arguably the baptismal fire for Hizballah. Yet, it was also in Lebanon that reform of religious discourse was taken farthest by some of the most innovative thinkers, some of whom are covered in this book. Indeed, few, if any, countries can lay claim to have a longer, more sustained engagement with political pluralism and inter-religious dialogue, and few can show a history as full with lessons for this, our age of global diversity.

Lebanon has shaped its environment as much as its environment has impinged upon its destiny. For every reputable expert accusing foreign powers of having meddled in and caused Lebanon's travails, you will find the sober retort of no less erudite scholars that this quarreling country needs some form of foreign tutelage – or, at minimum, an international consensus – to settle its domestic disputes. A valid case can be made for both theses, although history suggests the most successful and lasting

[2] In the summer of 1982, some 15,000 Lebanese were killed, 40,000 wounded, and 300,000 made homeless. Michael Johnson, *Class & Client in Beirut: The Sunni Muslim Community and the Lebanese State, 1840–1985*, vol. 28 (New York: Ithaca Press, 1986), 204.

efforts at intercommunal mediation were in fact led by fair-minded local leaders who evinced an ability to rise above the fray of confessional pride and prejudice. Yet, the stubborn enigma remains: Were Lebanon's periodic descents into conflict tinged by both confessional identity and class interests, self-induced suicides, or carefully planned assassinations by foreign actors? Or has Lebanon, as this book is inclined to argue, been complicit in repeated attempts of "assisted suicide"?

In revisiting the formative stages of Lebanon's political system, this book shall examine and reexamine these questions, cognizant of the multiple responsibilities and causalities of conflict and coexistence. This book attempts to weigh *both* material and ideological factors accounting for the stunning successes and lethal failures of this diverse country and its democratic political system, the oldest and, arguably, most pluralistic and secular one in the Middle East.[3] As one of the Arab world's leading poet and intellectuals has emphasized, if secularism is to succeed anywhere in the region, it must be in Lebanon.[4] Conversely, if this last haven of liberalism succumbs to the raging sectarian showdown in the region, the repercussions of the demise of an interreligious mosaic will have repercussions for the entire world. As more authoritarian models of semi-secular Arabism crumble under the onslaught of foreign-sponsored Jihadist rebellions ravaging Iraq, Libya, and Syria,[5] Lebanon remains the last rampart of an Arab secularism under siege.

To be sure, there never was a fully-fledged secular state in Lebanon; its establishment was repeatedly resisted by domestic, regional, and global powers who very often were more content to exploit religious radicalisms to further their personal and political ends.[6] Yet, core political principles of nondiscrimination did find entry in the Lebanese constitution and consciousness. Should this pluralistic state and interreligious mosaic succumb to the raging fire of communalism, its demise is sure to be felt far beyond the shores of the Eastern Mediterranean.

[3] According to a 2002 data set, Lebanon shows the lowest level of government interference in religious affairs (GIR) of all states in the Middle East. With 0 denoting the least regulation and 100 maximum restriction of religious freedom, Saudi Arabia's GIR score was 77.56, while Lebanon's stood at 22.17, followed by Israel with a GIR of 36.84. Jonathan Fox, *A World Survey of Religion and the State* (Cambridge University Press, 2008), 219.

[4] See Adūnīs, "al-Khatf," *Al-Hayat*, London, February 24, 2010.

[5] See Mark Farha, "Searching for Sectarianism in the Arab Spring: Colonial Conspiracy or Indigenous Instinct?" *The Muslim World* 106.1 (2016): 8–61 and Christopher Davidson, *Shadow Wars: The Secret Struggle for the Middle East* (Oneworld Publications, 2016).

[6] We thus find Barack Obama, Thomas Friedman, David Petraeus, and Israeli officials advocating, and administering, collusion with ISIS- and Al-Qaida-linked militia. See the Epilogue.

Acknowledgments

Thanks go to multiple people for their help during the writing of this book. During my sojourn at Harvard, which laid the groundwork for this book, Cemil Aydin, Nilufer Shaykh, Dominic Sachsenmeier, Han-Pu Tung, Shady Hikmet Nasser, Himmet Taskomür, Hussein Yilmaz, Hikmet Yaman, Tim Fitzgerald, Tom DeGeorges, and Michael Hall were among the many colleagues who helped me hone my thoughts. The same goes for the late Bill Kennedy who epitomized the best of Bostonian humor and wit, and a good antidote to "Hubris Harvardensiae." During my doctoral years, I incurred a great debt with the late Roger Owen and Aziz al-Azmeh who afforded me maximum freedom and diligent supervision in my most unusual (ad)venture. Next door at MIT, I thank Nasser Rabbat for his ever open doors and mastery of the art of dialogue, so greatly needed in this day and age of haste and superficiality. With his verve and passion, Professor Tu Wei-Ming at the Harvard–Yenching Institute allowed me to gain a quick yet astonishingly deep understanding of China's incredibly rich intellectual history. Allen Callahan and the late Jim Walsh remain my favorite, most erudite sources for the history of (early) Christianity, while Luis Giron-Negron and Steven Ozment allowed me to understand some of the societal dynamics of the medieval and pre-modern periods. The brilliant Marcus Moseley allowed me to probe the depths of Jewish literature and Haskalah enlightenment. Houchang Chehabi remains indispensable to gain insight into Iran. At Tufts University, Ibrahim Warde always stayed above the fray of fratricidal politics with his congenial nature. I thank Cemal Kafadar, the late director of the Center for Middle Eastern studies, for setting a tone of thoughtful inquiry. Also in Boston and New Hampshire, Dean LeBaron over the years was a constant source of support and insight.

In Harvard, and later in Singapore, Doha, and Abu Dhabi, I would like to thank Umej Bhatia and his wife Shireen for their hospitality, feedback and friendship. In Beirut and now Wichita, I owe a debt of gratitude to Adib Farha for having introduced me to a host of invaluable

Lebanese contacts, above all Professor Safiyye Saadeh, whose singularly nonpartisan scholarship, expertise, and unfailing help proved invaluable until this day. The same might be said of Imad Salamey and his wife Maysoun Chehab. My debt also goes to Firas Abi Nassif, Youssef Heneine, Loai Naamani, Nawaf Salam and his brilliant son Abdullah, Rudy Jaafar, Maha Shuayb and Adib Saab for his generous gift of the entire collection of his journal al Azmina. At an-Nahar, I thank the late Gibran Tueni for opening all doors and allowing me – and anyone who knocked on his door – to access the archives and engage in many a heated debate with him. The polymath Yahya Hakim bears testimony to the often superior erudition of non-academics. Cok memnunum hocam. Saad Mehio embodied the best of Lebanese generosity and hospitality, while sharing with me some of his well-measured insights. The genteel Walid Butrus and his family were exceptionally hospitable. Segments of this book were written in their house in Bhamdun, which they kindly offered to me as a refugium. The inimitable Ziad Moussa and his lovely wife Layla al Jisr were and remain an inspiration. Their intercommunal marriage shines as a beacon of hope in bridging all the classic "Lebanese" chasms with a loving light-heartedness. Love (and humor) does conquer all, after all.

I thank Asad Abu Khalil for his indefatigable dedication to scholarship, for generously sharing his expertise on various fine points and for remaining the most prolific critical writer on Lebanon today. Jawad al Adra remains a beacon of hope in Lebanon with his dedication. The doors of his office were always open to me, and this book was greatly aided by the research of him and his team at Information International. Badr al Hage likewise was indispensable in alerting me to several historical sources hitherto neglected that he has unearthed. I thank him for all his help and uplifting spirit.

In Beirut, Bsous, and London, I thank George and Alexandra Asseily for their effortless hospitality and sincere love for Lebanon. In Broumanna, I remain indebted to Bishop Georges Khidr. I thank for his time to discuss my research on his life's work, which I hope to publish independently. I have not missed one of his editorials. I thank the late (Père) Gregoire Haddad for sharing his time, but, more importantly, for his humility and his unstinting fight against sectarianism. His practical service to the poor stands in contrast to the mouthing of pious proclamations (of which there is no shortage). At the Tayyar al Madani, Bishop Haddad's erstwhile right-hand Rami Jibai was an inspiration in commitment to the cause. Through him I got to meet activists such as Hanaa al Yahya whom I thank for sharing her unique story and for her courage to stand apart in defense of justice in Lebanon.

Like so many Lebanese of all ranks, the late Sayyid Hani Fahs, Hussein al Husseini, Mohammad Hassan al Amin, Nemer Freyha, Luqman Slim, Masoud Daher, Radwan al Sayyid, Tawfiq Muhanna, Walid Slaibi, Augarite Yunan, Ahmad Moussali, Jad Shaaban, Ussama Makdisi, Elias Nassour, Ghassan Salaame, Albir Farhat, Hikmet Farha, Salah Salman, and Tarek Mitri all adhered to an "open door" policy and invited me to fruitful dialogues and provided me with many useful suggestions and sources.

In my native Zurich, I thank my friend and mentor the late Obeid Obeid, a true (Arab) gentleman of the old school in act and word who introduced me to some of the gems of Arabic, Arnold Hottinger, and my godfather Prof. Heini Feichtinger for providing me some rare historical sources along with his razor sharp analytical acumen, which aided me in composing the chapter comparing the trajectory of Switzerland and Lebanon.

In Doha, I would like to extend a special thank you to my research assistants Leena Zahir, Salma Mousa, and Jana Okar who did so much of the necessary spadework. At Georgetown, I thank my dear colleagues Mohammad Zayani, Patrick Laude, Herb Howe, Alexis Antoniades, Akintunde Akinade, Amira al Zein, Amira Sonbol, Mehran Kamrava, Rogaia AbuSharaf, Joshua Mitchell, Hana Jabara, Robert Wirsing, and the late Adhip Chaudhuri and Faruk Tabak, two brilliant minds whose cordial demeanor left behind a lasting legacy of admiration and inspiration. Birol Baskan remains a constant source of paradigmatic scholarly inquisitiveness and creativity. In Irvine and now Manchester, Pierre Fuller and his wife Eleanor have been exemplars of scholarly integrity. Whether it be in workshops held in Florence, Bellagio, Istanbul, or Onati, Asli Bali, Miryam Künkler, James Madeley, Shylashri Shankar, Khaled Helmy, Hanna Lerner, and Nathan Brown provided incisive feedback on many of the chapters and concepts expounded in this book. My fellow colleagues from IPSA Research Council 37, above all Zillur Rahman Khan and Yan Vaslavsky, provided inspiration and motivation over the past years.

In Doha, Raed Habayeb at the Doha Institute kindly gave the green light to extend support for the last edits of the manuscript. I further am grateful for all of the useful scholarly debates I was fortunate to enjoy with Youssef Choueiri, Amir Abouelkhair, and Samer Shahata as well as Fahad and H. E. Abdullah bin Hamad al-Attiyah. I also want to thank Wadih Jordan for sharing his incomparable memory, for his humor and for his hospitality in Beirut and New York.

Lastly, I want to thank the editors at Cambridge University Press, Maria Marsh, Natasha Whelan, Vinithan Sethumadhavan and Abigail Neale, for shepherding this manuscript through to final publication. The errors that remain are my own, and I hope to address any lacunae and new avenues in future publications and discussions.

Zürich, Switzerland, March 13, 2019.

Introduction and Conceptual Framework

Political Confessionalism: Modern Blessing or Ancient Bane?

> The superiority of the Carthaginians' constitution is proved by the fact that the common people remain loyal to the constitution. The Carthaginians have never had any rebellion worth speaking of, and have never been under the rule of a tyrant. Aristotle[1]

> The most excellent fair city of Berytus, which may be styled as the nursing mother of the law (*nutris legum*). *Codex Justinianus*[2]

> We are the Arab world's guarantee of secularism. Kamāl Salībī[3]

> I greatly fear history because it is based on pride. Jurj Khidr[4]

This book seeks to discern possible answers to a set of seemingly straightforward questions. First, why has secularism, both as an ideological cornerstone of a non-confessional state and as a practice of state governance and law, been stillborn in the Arab world in general and twentieth-century Lebanon in particular? Second, why is secularism so often prematurely discarded as inimical atheism or feared as a mortal danger rather than apprized as a pragmatic, political principle of statecraft particularly pertinent to pluralistic societies?

In embarking on this inquiry, I distinguish between the *political principle* of secularism (Arabic: *'almanīya*) and the broader, ramified historical and *societal process* of secularization (*'almana*), cognizant of the fact that the two categories are liable to be mixed and melded. In its most threadbare definition secularism shall designate the absence of

[1] Aristotle, *The Politics of Aristotle*, trans. Benjamin Jowett (London: Colonial Press, 1900), 49–51.
[2] *The Digest of Justinian*, trans. C. H. Murno (Cambridge: Cambridge University Press, 1904), viii.
[3] Cited in William Dalrymple, *From the Holy Mountain: A Journey into the Shadow of Byzantium* (New Delhi: Penguin Books India, 2004), 214.
[4] "Naḥnu wa Al-Muslimīn," *an-Nahār*, March 22, 2003.

any discrimination of the state's institutions and legal administration toward the religious/confessional identity of the individual citizen. The use of communalized religion as a (state-sanctioned) exclusionary or hierarchical marker of identity is the issue. This functionalist, negative definition of secularism allows space for civic expressions of religion within the bounds of a constitutive legal framework in which the full freedom of conscience of the individual citizen is unconditionally preserved.[5] Secularism here may also be associated with a certain brand of liberalism, if we define the latter as the state's rigorous impartiality toward its citizens regardless of confessional identity or demographic status.[6]

The issue of secularism looms particularly large in Lebanon, a country that, with its eighteen officially recognized Christian and Muslim denominations, displays unequaled religious diversity. It is by no means apparent why secularism should have faced resistance in Lebanon. Both its role as a beachhead of secular thought in modern Arab intellectual history and the predictions of modernization theory might lead us to suspect that Lebanon should be fertile ground for secularism, as David Lerner, Charles Issawi, and the late Shaykh ʿAbdullāh al-ʿAlāylī all have concluded.[7] Yet, Lebanon has only partially succeeded in finding a Rawlsian "overlapping consensus" across the country's multiple confessions.[8] Secularism in this sense would require a broad accord on the fundamental rights and common measures of justice to be enjoyed by each individual, irrespective of religion, class, or creed. This book will seek to explain why Lebanon's consensual democracy has only established a rudimental framework for egalitarian civil liberties.

From the beginnings of the Arab Renaissance in the nineteenth century until this day, Lebanon has managed to retain its historic vanguard position as the front-runner of all Middle Eastern countries in terms of

[5] Perhaps the earliest Arabic invocation of the vocabulary of civil rights, including the explicit reference to freedom of conscience (*hurrīyat ad-damīr*), is found in Buṭrus al-Bustānī, *Nafīr Sūrīyā* (Beirut: Dawāfir lil-Abhāth, 1990), 22.

[6] "Liberalism is the supreme form of generosity; it is the right which the majority concedes to minorities and hence it is the noblest cry that has ever resounded on this planet. It announces the determination to share existence with the enemy." José Ortega y Gasset, *The Revolt of the Masses* (New York: W. W. Norton & Co., 1994), 24. "La liberté n'est pas autre chose que l'idéology de l'égalité devant la loi." François Châtelet, *Histoire des Idéologies* (Paris: Hachette, 1978), 93.

[7] Charles Issawi, "Economic Development and Political Liberalism in Lebanon," in *Politics in Lebanon*, ed. Leonard Binder (New York: Wiley-Blackwell, 1966), 69–83; ʿAbdullāh al-ʿAlāylī, "Hawl Kalimat ʿAlmana," *al-Āfāq*, 2, June 1978, 1–2; David Lerner, *The Passing of Traditional Society* (Glencoe: The Free Press, 1958), 84–89.

[8] John Rawls, *Political Liberalism* (New York: Columbia University Press, 1993).

levels of education,[9] press freedom, and gross number of publications.[10] However, for all its vaunted liberalism, the Lebanese press can neither be considered "wholly free" nor unambiguously "secular" in its orientation.[11] From the seventeenth century until the present, Lebanon has retained the highest number of universities and secondary schools per capita in the Middle East. It boasted one of the world's lowest student-to-teacher ratios in 1996 and 2010.[12] Although in 2005 Lebanon ranked only at 110th worldwide in terms of the percentage of GDP spent on education,[13] its cumulative public and private expenditure on education (11.4 percent) still outstripped that of Japan (4.8 percent), France (6.2 percent), and the United States (7.1 percent of GDP).[14]

With regard to the media, Levantine intellectuals were among the first to protest the censorship and crackdown on political expression and anti-imperial publications under Ottoman Sultan 'Abdul Hamīd II (1876–1908),[15] thereby laying the foundation for the modern Arab press. This legacy of a free press has weathered the ravages of the last civil war (1975–1990), even as media outlets were shut and dozens of journalists assassinated. According to the Annual Worldwide Press Freedom Index, as of 2018 Lebanon ranked 100th, well above other Middle Eastern countries, including Turkey (157th).[16] In 2009, Lebanon (61st) was neck and neck with Kuwait (60th) as the regional front-runner, ahead

[9] Mark Farha, "Historical Legacy and Political Implications of State and Sectarian Schools in Lebanon," in *Rethinking Education for Social Cohesion: International Case Studies*, ed. Maha Shuayb (London: Palgrave Macmillan, 2012), 64–85.

[10] In 1999, 1,358 titles were printed in Lebanon out of a total of 2,714 in the entire Arab world. This means that Lebanon boasts six times more periodicals than Egypt, the largest Arab country. Egypt, whose population outstrips that of Lebanon by a factor of twenty, lost ground in the publication race with Lebanon due to the boycott that was imposed by the Arab states on Egypt after President Sadat signed the Camp David Accords. Franck Mermier, "Beyrouth, Capitale du Livre Arabe?" *Monde Arabe Maghreb-Machrek* 169 (2000): 100.

[11] The readership of Lebanese dailies is largely divided along confessional lines and, since 2005, partisan camps of March 14 and March 8. Moreover, critical debates on religion remain scarce and are quickly mooted.

[12] Lebanon's ratio was 8.3, while France's ratio was 19, Germany's 17, and Turkey's 28. Riyād Tabbāra, *The Educational System in Lebanon* (Beirut: Center for Development Studies and Projects (MADMA), 2000), 18; Nimr Frayḥa, "Education and Social Cohesion in Lebanon," *Prospects* 23.1 (2003): 87; UNESCO Institute for Statistics, *Global Education Digest* (Montreal: UNESCO Institute for Statistics, 2004), http://unesdoc.unesco.org/images/0021/002184/218449e.pdf.

[13] UNESCO Institute for Statistics, *Global Education Digest*, 126.

[14] UNDP, *Toward a Citizen's State* (Beirut: UNDP, 2009), 131.

[15] 'Abdul Ḥamīd's main target was "subversive" publications aiming at a restoration of the 1876 constitution. Seemingly innocuous books such as Milton's *Paradise Lost* however also were put on the Index. See Ra'īf Khūrī, *Modern Arab Thought: Channels of the French Revolution to the Arab East* (Princeton: The Kingston Press, 1983), 8.

[16] https://rsf.org/en/ranking, last accessed on June 2, 2018.

of the United Arab Emirates (86th) and Israel (93rd).[17] By 2018, however, Lebanon had fallen back to the hundredth position.

Openness has long marked Lebanese politics as well. In 1875, what is often considered as the first organized national political party in the Middle East was established in Beirut,[18] inaugurating a proliferation of vibrant political activism. A near two decades before the Helvetian Confederation, the "Switzerland of the Middle East" was the first Arab country, concurrently with Syria,[19] to grant women suffrage in 1953, three years before Nāṣir's Egypt followed suit.[20] Most significantly with regard to the issue of secularism, full freedom of religion is nominally enshrined in Article 9 of the Lebanese Constitution, which stipulates that "freedom of belief is absolute."

Since the promulgation of its constitution in 1926, Lebanon remains the first and sole state in the Middle East – with the exception of Kemalist Turkey after 1928 – that does not stipulate Islam (or Judaism) as the religion of the state.[21] According to a 2002 data set, Lebanon shows the lowest level of government interference in religious affairs (GIR) of all states in the Middle East. With 0 denoting the least regulation and

17 2018 World Press Freedom Index (Reporters Without Borders, 2018), https://rsf.org/en/lebanon, last accessed February 1, 2019. In 2005, Lebanon for the first time lost its pole position due to a series of assassinations of journalists. Cf. footnote 20.

18 The "Secret Society of Beirut" (Jamīʿat Bayrūt al-Sirrīya) was established at the Syrian Protestant College by the Francophile Ilyās Habbalin and Fāris Nimr. Jurj Antonius, *The Arab Awakening* (London: H. Hamilton, 1938), 79.

19 In 1949, under Ḥusnī al-Zaʿīm a new law was passed that – with restrictions placed on age and education – allowed women to vote. In 1953, under the initiative of Syrian Socialist Nationalist Party (SSNP) member Adīb ash-Shishaklī, the first elections were held with one woman, Thuraya al-Ḥāfiẓ, unsuccessfully running for parliament. In 1963, the Ba'athists dissolved parliament but appointed a revolutionary council, which included women such as ʿĀdīla Bayḥūm. I would like to express my sincere thanks to Saffīya Saʿāda and Sāmī Mubayyid for kindly sharing their expertise.

20 There had been a motion in the 1920s for women's suffrage in Beirut (and Damascus), but of thirty deputies in the Lebanese parliament only Yūsuf al-Khāzin, Fu'ād Arslān, and Ibrāhīm Munthir supported it. We might also add that over a decade before Huda Shaʿrāwī in Egypt, Nāzik al-ʿAbīd shed the veil in battle with General Yūsuf al-ʿAẓma at Maysalūn in 1920. Elisabeth Thompson, *Colonial Citizens* (New York: Columbia University Press, 2000), 123.

21 The first modern Arab state to pronounce Islam as the official religion of the state was Egypt in its constitution of 1923, a result of a deal struck between the British and the Khedeve Ismāʿīl to quell the latter's caliphal ambitions. The Syrian Arab Kingdom of 1920 under Faysal spelled out a "civil government," but likewise insisted on Islam as the religion of the kingdom. In Egypt, law no. 40 of 1977 prohibits the establishment of any party whose tenets challenge any principle of sharīʿa legislation, while Article 2 of the 1980 constitution reaffirmed the sharīʿa as the principle source of legislation, a clause that was also added to the Syrian constitution after it had been briefly removed in 1956. The constitution of 1938, and under Ḥāfiẓ al-Asad in 1973, stipulates that the religion the president, although not the state, is Islam. Joseph Mughayzil, *Kitābāt Joseph Mughayzil*, vol. II (Beirut: Mua'ssasat Mughayzil wa Dār an-Nahār, 1997), 249.

100 maximum restriction of religious freedom, Saudi Arabia's GIR score was 77.56, while Lebanon's stood at 22.17, followed by Israel with a GIR of 36.84.[22] Despite this assessment, the codification of secularism as a full-fledged political system has eluded Lebanon. Almost a century ago ʻAbdul Rahmān al-Kawākibī, the nineteenth-century Syrian reformist, set a phase of seventy-five years for the incubation for secularism in Lebanon and yet – on the surface – little progress seems to have been made.

Indeed, the 2005 parliamentary elections saw perhaps the most overt direct politicized meddling of the clergy in the nation's modern history, with clerics issuing binding religious edicts to compel their constituency to cast votes *en bloc*. The most overt cases involved Hizballāh's issuing a "*taklīf sharʻī*," or a religiously binding edict, in support of the party's coalition with Sunni (Future) and Christian parties (Lebanese Forces), otherwise, rather unlikely favorites among religious Shia. Likewise, the Mufti of Tripoli made use of his Friday and Sunday sermons to demand a vote for the Future electoral list. The Maronite patriarch made his preference public during his politicized Sunday sermon, albeit in a slightly more subtle fashion.

Legally speaking, the Muslim and Christian clergy were not in fact overstepping their bounds in pontificating on political matters. For the same aforementioned Article 9 of the constitution that establishes freedom of speech "guarantees to the people, regardless of their denomination, respect for the system of personal status laws and the religious interests." It is further contradicted by Article 10, which allows the sects to establish confessional schools and Article 473 of the penal code, which stipulates that one who "blasphemes God publicly" may face imprisonment for up to one year. This clause has been subjected to at times arbitrary – and highly politicized – interpretations against artists in particular.[23]

Since 1926, the Republic of Lebanon has adopted a hybrid, "adulterated" constitution that fuses a secular character with special sectarian prerogatives. Designed as a safeguard for the adequate political representation of the nation's confessional communities or "spiritual families," the constitution has equally served to render religious identities an inviolable part of political organization. Far from seeing a neat and tidy separation of religion and state, political mobilization in post-independence Lebanon tends to draw on confessional symbolisms and

[22] Jonathan Fox, *A World Survey of Religion and the State* (Cambridge: Cambridge University Press, 2008), 219.

[23] See *Al-Dustūr Al-Lubnānī*, ed. Shafīq Juḥā (Beirut: Dār al-ʻĀlam, 1991).

is all too often predicated on a "sacralization" of the paternalistic leaders of the various religious communities.[24] The individual citizen for his or her part cannot vote, marry, inherit, or run for office save as a registered member of one of the eighteen sects officially recognized by the Lebanese state.

However, the mere plurality of communal identities is not, *ipso facto,* a necessary nemesis of a secular, democratic state. After all, Lebanon's religious diversity did not only instigate a series of civil wars, but could also countervail the exercise of autocratic power. Arguably, the country's jostling factions and extraordinarily vibrant civil society with 6,032 registered nongovernmental organizations (NGOs) helped mitigate the curbing of freedom of expression to a degree not matched by any of the surrounding Arab states.[25] Significantly, no military coup punctuated Lebanon's entire twentieth-century history, setting the country apart from most Arab regimes whose political power is intimately associated with – if not directly predicated on – the armed forces. To be sure, critics have attributed the weakness of the latter as further evidence of the primacy of confessional substates, which, in turn, may all the more quickly undercut the monopoly of violence and authority vested in the central state.

Defenders of the confessional system and its sectarian quotas have dismissed secularism in the sense of absolute state neutrality vis-à-vis

24 The civil wars have only exacerbated this trend. Examples include: Bashīr Jummayil's associations with Jesus Christ, the divinization of General ʿAwn in the slogans of some of his more ardent followers, Kamāl Janbulāṭ's veneration as quasi-prophetic philosopher, Mūsā Ṣadr's canonization as the Imām Mahdī, Ḥāfiẓ al-Assad's cult of personality among Lebanese members of the Syrian Baʿath Party, and Rafīq al-Ḥarīrī's monumental martyr's shrine filling the central square of Beirut. Even Anṭūn Saʿāda, the staunchly secular head of the SSNP, would find himself venerated as the omniscient leader (zaʿīm) by his party followers who thereby subjected themselves to charges of being victims of a fascist führer cult. The latter charge, however, may fit many a Lebanese party exhibiting martial and authoritarian cultures. Ḥizballāh's fastidious military parades are marked by the troops "Hitler" salute, a Roman gesture that may, in fact, have found local inspiration in the Katāʾib's paramilitary processions and that is still visible among segments of other Lebanese parties, including the Lebanese Forces and the Future Movement. Both the founder of the Katāʾib, Pierre Jummayyil, and of the rival Najjāda Sunni militia, Ḥusayn Siʿjān, were enthralled by the Nazi discipline displayed at the Berlin Olympics of 1936. Stefan Wild, "National Socialism in the Arab Near East between 1933 and 1939," *Die Welt des Islams* 25.1/4 (1985): 126–173. The *locus classicus* for the sociology of clientelistic leader cults in Lebanon is Arnold Hottinger, "Zu'ama in Historical Perspective," in *Politics in Lebanon*, ed. Leonard Binder (New York: Wiley, 1966), 85–105. Also see Michael Johnson, *All Honorable Men: The Social Origins of the War in Lebanon* (London: I. B. Tauris, 2001).

25 At 53 on a scale of 0–100, with 0 denoting full freedoms, Lebanon scored better than regional rival Kuwait (60) in 2017. https://freedomhouse.org/report/freedom-press/2017/lebanon, last accessed February 4, 2019.

religious and ethnic identities, claiming that this remains an untenable mirage in pluralistic societies. Such societies, they argue, are in fact better served by a consortium of sects, even if the latter may subvert the balance of constitutional branches of government. Cultural and religious diversity in Lebanon, it is contended, constitute even greater an obstacle to national integration and cultural homogenization than either in Turkey or the United States, both countries with clear confessional majorities. As we shall see repeatedly in the course of this book, in the Lebanese scenario, the slogan of "deconfessionalization" could indeed be used as a code word for the supremacist, communalist designs of the demographically dominant communities. A useful and fecund analogy can be drawn to India, where the Bharatiya Janata Party (BJP)'s and Rashtriya Swayamsevak Sangh (RSS)'s diatribe against "pseudo-secularism" and "minoritism" is ostensibly waged in defense of the secular Indian state. In reality, the *Hindutva* chauvinists – whose origins, like those of the Syrian Steel Shirts, the Lebanese Phalange, or the Chinese Blue Shirts, stretch back to the 1920s – are craving control over the democratic state apparatus in order to gain domination over the largely Muslim and Christian minorities within India.[26]

In current-day Lebanon, Ḥizballāh stands accused of a similar charge of harboring hegemonic ambitions, the disavowals of its secretary general notwithstanding.[27] "Deconfessionalization" can thus gain a dubious meaning in the context of demographic majorities intent on usurping the discourse of the secular state for ulterior aims. Conversely, secularism has again been reduced by some of its detractors and partisans to a defensive strategy of besieged minorities facing the threat of subjugation. The Lebanese Christians, in this context, are often – rather simplistically – grouped together with the Egyptian Copts, the Iraqi Chaldeans, the Indian Muslims, or the Israeli Jews, the latter, of course, having succeeded in establishing an ethno-religious state unlike any of the former. In fact, despite the common Levantine and Arab environment, Lebanon is a case unto itself.

As the only Arab country with a sizable non-Muslim demographic minority, Lebanon has always been singled out as both a paradigm and villain. The country has already gone through its baptisms of fire as regards the "clash of civilizations." It has also reaped the fruits – sweet

[26] This is the benign reading somewhat confirmed by the pragmatism displayed by the BJP over the past decade. The concern was that the BJP might use the democratic process to "systematically persecute and terrorize" minorities. Partha Chatterjee, "Secularism and Toleration," *Economic and Political Weekly* (1994): 1768–1777.

[27] "The Shia never were the leading sect (*tā'ifa*) … and we do not intend to become the leading one." Hasan Nasrallāh cited in as-Safīr, April 24, 2006.

and bitter – of a premature experiment with ultraliberalism between 1964 and 1975, one which was once again pursued from 1992 onward, albeit with somewhat different players and within different parameters.

It has become a truism to state that Lebanon has always been, by virtue of its geographical position and demographic constitution, particularly susceptible to the whims of external machinations. In his inaugural ministerial declaration of 1943,[28] Premier Riyāḍ al-Sulh announced his solemn intention to abolish sectarianism in Lebanon. Yet, only five years thereafter, he collaborated with the Syrian military leader Ḥusnī al-Zaʿīm and President Bishāra al-Khūrī in the abduction and summary execution of arguably the most notable secular political leader in modern Lebanese history, the late Anṭūn Saʿāda. The latter stood accused of preparing a coup d'état to erect a secular pan-Syrian state.[29] Premier Ṣulḥ may have grandly announced that Lebanon would hitherto not serve as a stalking horse for imperialism, yet he himself would evince himself as one of many Lebanese leaders who adeptly sought political capital from outside powers.[30]

In the post–World War II period of independence, Lebanon has not been able to isolate itself from the regional environment where secularism has progressively been losing its shine amid the ascent of two, mutually reinforcing religious tribalisms: Zionism and Islamism. As the recipient of officially 425,000[31] Palestinian refugees in 1948, 1967, and 1970, Lebanon has been exposed to direct demographic, military, and ideological pressures emerging from an increasingly religiously defined, ever intensifying struggle for land and resources in Israel-Palestine, the

[28] The ministerial declaration is reprinted in Bāsim al-Jisr, *Mithāq 1943* (Beirut: Dār an-Nahār, 1978), 475–495.

[29] It is rarely mentioned that the Syrian premier at the time, Muḥsin al-Barazī, was the brother-in-law of Riyāḍ al-Ṣulḥ, the Lebanese premier. Together they coordinated the arrest and execution of Saʿāda with the head of the Lebanese security forces. Both Pierre Jummayyil and Kamāl Janbulāṭ entreated Ṣulḥ to relent and spare Sa'āda until the end. ʿĀdil, Bishāra, *Lebanon: Politics of Frustration – The Failed Coup of 1961* (London: Routledge, 2005), 181.

[30] A recent work by Raghīd al-Ṣulḥ seeks to corroborate the Lebanese nationalism and loyalty of the late premier who entertained close relations with Chaim Weizmann in the 1920s. Riyāḍ al-Ṣulḥ's attempts to win Arab recognition for a Jewish state failed. Yehoshua Porath, *The Emergence of the Palestinian-Arab National Movement, 1918–1929* (London: Frank Cass, 1974), 112–114.

[31] Of this cumulative number of refugees registered in 1948 with the United Nations Relief and Works Agency for Palestine Refugees in the Near East (UNRWA), 260,000 live in the twelve refugee camps spread across Lebanon. An unabated wave of immigration and the 1994 naturalization decree lessened the number of refugees divested of Lebanese civil rights. See Jad Chaaban, Hala Ghattas, Rima Habib, et al., *Socio-economic Survey of Palestinian Refugees in Lebanon* (Beirut: American University of Beirut, 2010), x, www.pvelebanon.org/Resources/PVE_English.pdf, last accessed February 4, 2019.

chief fulcrum for most noxious fundamentalist movements in the region. Virtually all Islamist fundamentalist groups in Lebanon, both Shia and Sunni, define their foundational struggle in response to the Zionist colonies and later establishment of the state of Israel.[32] The Christian militias during the 1975 civil war, in turn, justified their call to arms in order to ward off the danger of immersion in an Islamic state facilitated by the settlement of Palestinian refugees in Lebanon. This fear was only amplified after 2011 when Lebanon was once again the recipient of a record number of refugees, this time from Syria. Israel and the Gulf States refused to take in refugees, despite having stoked the Syrian conflict, siding with jihadist opposition against a quasi-secular regime.

The blatant hijacking of British and US Middle East policy to prop up an ethnocracy – in repeated contravention of international law – has further besmirched the reputation of secularism and Western democracy in general.[33] The father of the Lebanese constitution, Michel Shīhā, would voice a premonition in 1947 that proved uncannily clairvoyant in this respect:

La décision de partage de la Palestine par la création de l'état juif, est une des erreurs les plus considérables de la politique universelle. D'une chose apparemment petite, les conséquences les plus surprenantes vont sortir. Et ce n'est pas offenser la raison que d'écrire que cette petite histoire contribuera à ébranler la terre dans ses fondements ... Une erreur de cette taille, commise au milieu de ce siècle, nos petits-neveux la retrouveront au milieu de siècle prochain.[34]

[The decision to partition Palestine to make way for the creation of a Jewish state must be considered one of the gravest errors of global politics. From an ostensibly small matter, the most surprising consequences are bound to emerge. And it is not unreasonable to state that this small story will one day shake the earth in its

[32] For a good study on how Israel has undermined secular forces in Palestine, see Loren Diller-Lybarger, "Between Sacred and Secular: Religion, Generations, and Collective Memory among Muslim and Christian Palestinians in the Post-Oslo Period," PhD dissertation, The University of Chicago, 2002.

[33] The forty-two US single Security Council vetoes since 1970 shielding the Jewish state from recriminations have severely undermined trust in international law and encouraged a retreat to parochial identities. Such unilaterism – also evident in the US decision to embark on a regime change in Iraq in 2003 and Syria in 2012 – has ratified a recourse to brute force as the most viable means to settle disputes. For the list of US vetoes in the Security Council, including those directly pertaining to transgressions in Lebanon, see www.jewishvirtuallibrary.org/jsource/UN/usvetoes.html. For the sixty-five UN resolutions Israel stands in direct violation of, see www.jerusalemites.org/new/index.php/2015-12-05-10-43-47/2015-12-05-10-46-39, last accessed on February 4, 2019. For an early critique, see A. Lilienthal, *At What Price Israel?* (Chicago: Henry Regnery Co., 1953).

[34] Shīhā, "Une politique aberrante"; "L'école du racisme", *Le Jour*, December 3, 1947. Lebanon voted against the imposed partition plan (UN 181) for Palestine in the Grand Assembly on November 29, 1947.

foundations … An error of this magnitude, committed in the middle of this century, is bound to be reencountered by our grand-nephews in the middle of the next.]

Given the country's strategic and geographic location bordering the Mediterranean, between the Jewish state and the Arab heartland, Lebanon has been allotted a historical role far surpassing its size, particularly as concerns the issue of secularism and the latent potential "message" the country may carry for interreligious political cohabitation, conflict, and comity. In terms of its exceptionally high literacy rates and levels of education, vibrant political activism as well as its long-established interconfessional networks of business, commerce, and professional unions, Lebanon was a model for Muslim–Christian coexistence and the ostensibly prime candidate for a separation of religion and state in the Arab world.

Yet, Lebanon, the self-same haven of free thought and free trade,[35] has also witnessed the worst of sectarian bickering and bloodshed galore at periodic points in its history. This has generated ideological fodder for militant ideologies, which have come to haunt the world. Ḥizballāh's formation in the throes of the Israeli invasion and brutal bombardment of Beirut in 1982 has been well documented. More recently, Lebanon stood in violation of the injunctions of the National Pact of 1943 wherein the country was neither to serve as "a passage way nor a staging ground" for foreign powers ("*la mamar wa la maqarr*").[36] Instead, from the onset of the Syrian crisis, Lebanon became a transit point for fighters flocking to the proxy battleground, and, conversely, the place of settlement for a record number of refugees fleeing the civil war in its neighbor state. Having alternatively afforded the milieu for repeated "springs" of Arab secularism and the seedbed for insidious sectarianism, Lebanon serves as a singularly emblematic barometer underscoring the ebb and flow of reformist and reactionary currents in the region over time.

[35] From 2001 to 2005, Lebanon was continually ranked first on the Fraser Institute's "Index of Economic Freedoms in the Arab World," yet, by 2016 Lebanon had been overtaken by Bahrain, the UAE, Jordan, Qatar, and Kuwait and was relegated to the sixth position. See page 12 of www.fraserinstitute.org/sites/default/files/economic-freedom-of-the-arab-world-2018.pdf, last accessed on February 4, 2018. The Beiruti mercantile elite's slogans of *laissez-faire* in Lebanon did not entail competition in the internal markets. Such hypocrisy is, of course, common to oligopolies around the Middle East and indeed the globe: "While powerful merchants and bankers hailed the Smithian invisible hand, they were also engaging in price-fixing and manipulation made possible by their market power," Carolyn Gates, *The Merchant Republic* (London: Centre for Lebanese Studies in Association with I. B. Tauris, 1998), 96.

[36] al-Jisr, *Mithāq 1943*, 84, 114.

Despite the "extenuating circumstances" already enumerated, the questions persist: How are we to reconcile the image of a highly developed country still clinging to sectarian mentalities? Can we ascribe the difficulties of secularism in the Middle East in general and Lebanon in particular to a lagging behind in the pace of democratic progress?[37] Is Lebanon, to paraphrase Helmuth Plessner, a "retarded, belated nation," a nation "stuck" in a premodern set of mind and mode of governance?[38] Or, may we, on the contrary, view Lebanon's idiosyncratic "consociational" constitution as an example *par excellence* of "multiple modernities?"[39]

Whether the consensus democracy (*al-dimuqrātīya al- tawāfuqīya*) that has struck root in Lebanon in fact constitutes the best formula to advance national integration and forestall the resurgence of interconfessional feuds remains a conundrum. Lijphart's sanguine prediction that consociationalism by its very success will render itself superfluous has been borne out to a large extent by the Dutch and Swiss, but not by the Lebanese case.[40] There has been a marked inclination – or, perhaps, "temptation" – to attribute this stillbirth of the secular state to "ancient," ostensibly inextricable, sociological roots that are claimed to render political confessionalism a permanent feature of any Lebanese social contract. In what follows, we shall examine the premises of this widespread thesis.

Characteristics of Lebanon's Castes and Client Groups: *Ṭā'ifīyā*

Ṭāi'fīya is the complex of all Lebanese complexes.[41] Nāṣīf Naṣṣār

The study of secularism proper has been somewhat neglected in the historiography of Lebanon. Instead, the predominant study of Lebanese

[37] Ernst Bloch coined the term "Ungleichzeitigkeit," defined as a "disparity of non-synchronic temporal structures," a reference to Germany's lagging behind in developing the institutions and social environment of bourgeois democracy: "*Deutschland … dem bis 1918 keine bürgerliche Revolution gelungen war, ist zum Unterschied von England, oder gar Frankreich, das klassische Land der Ungleichzeitigkeit, das ist, der unüberwundenen Reste älteren ökonomischen Seins und Bewusstseins.*" Ernst Bloch, *Erbschaft dieser Zeit: Gesamtausgabe*, vol. IV (Frankfurt am Main: Suhrkamp, 1977), 114.

[38] Helmuth Plessner, *Die Verspätete Nation: Über die politische Verführbarkeit des Bürgerlichen Geistes* (Stuttgart: W. Kohlhammer Verlag, 1959).

[39] Dominic Sachsenmaier, Jens Riedl, and Shmuel Eisenstadt, eds., *Reflections on Multiple Modernities: European, Chinese and Other Interpretations* (Leiden: Brill, 2002).

[40] Arend Lijphart, *Democracy in Plural Societies: A Comparative Exploration* (New Haven, CT: Yale University Press, 1977), 2.

[41] Nāṣīf Naṣṣār, *Naḥwa Mujtama' Jadīd* (Beirut: Dār al-Talī'a, 1970), 127.

history has been through the prism of the virtually omnipresent notion of *ṭā'ifīya*. Usually rendered into English as "sectarianism," the concept in Lebanon carries a particularly negative power given the maelstrom of confessional conflict out of which it emerged.[42] Some scholars have sought to de-emphasize religious identity and limit *ṭā'ifīya* to a marker of social rank, not religion, a problematic revisionism in more than one way, as we will see.[43] Historically, for one, such a strictly *laïcist* reading of *ṭā'ifīya* neatly denuded of its sectarian component seems untenable. While the etymological origins of the particular adjectival noun indeed seem to lay in the late nineteenth century,[44] seventeenth-century historians such as Isṭfān Duwayhī (1603–1704) already employed the term *ṭā'ifa* denoting the (Maronite) sect alongside the now outdated term *milla*.[45] Likewise, premodern official Ottoman documents refer to the Druze and Maronite Lebanese *ṭā'ifa*.[46] The term has an even older, Quranic lineage.[47]

42 The low associations made with ṭāi'fīya are illustrated by the idiom of "n'arat ṭai'fīya" used to describe a fanatical sectarian instinct. "N'ara" denotes the grunt of a swine or a nasal twang.

43 A more recent example is Usāma Maqdisī, *The Culture of Sectarianism* (Berkeley: University of California Press, 2000). For a Marxist critique see Mas'ūd Ḍāhir, *al-Judhūr al-Tārīkhīya lil-Mas'ala al-Zirā'īya al-Lubnānīya, 1900–1950* (Beirut, 1984). For an overview of historiographies see Axel Havemann, *Geschichte Und Geschichtsschreibung Im Libanon Des 19. und 20. Jahrhunderts* (Beirut: Ergon Verlag Wurzburg, 2002).

44 G. W. Badger in his English–Arabic dictionary translates "sectarianism" indirectly with the Khaldunian notion of "*ta'aṣṣub lil-firqa*." *An English–Arabic Lexicon, in Which the Equivalents for English Words and Idiomatic Sentences Are Rendered into Literary and Colloquial Arabic* (Beirut: Reprinted by Librairie du Liban, [1881] 1967), 937. Likewise, Buṭrus al-Bustānī speaks of "al-ta'aṣṣub al-madhhabī." al-Bustānī, *Nafīr Sūrīyā*, 22.

45 Isṭfān Duwayhī, *Tārīkh al-Azmina: 1095 M–1699 M 425* (Beirut: al-Matb'a al-Kāthūlīkīya, 1951).

46 Abū Raḥmān Abū-Ḥusayn, ed., *The View from Istanbul: Lebanon and the Druze Emirate in the Ottoman Chancery Documents: 1546–1711* (London: I. B. Tauris, 2004), 64.

47 The term is found in the Lisān al-'Arab, albeit in a more generic sense, where it is defined as any aggregation of people or even animals such as a "flock of birds." In medieval Andalusia the *ṭā'ifa* of course referred to the emirates that succeeded the collapse of the Umayyad Caliphate at Cordova in 1031. In the Qur'ān, *ṭā'ifa* is sometimes used as a neutral synonym for a group of people. It is also invoked negatively to denote a "group" of deceivers or dividers from a different faith. "It is the wish of a ṭā'ifa (party) of the People of the Book to lead you astray. But they shall lead astray (Not you), but themselves, and they do not perceive" [3:69; see also 3:72]. In less frequent cases, *ṭā'ifa* is used in reference to upright believers: "and let a party of the believers witness their punishment [for adultery]." [24:2; also see 61:14]. As in today's usage, *ṭawā'if*, is used to denote the scourge of disunity: "Truly the Pharaoh elated himself in the land and broke up its people into ṭawā'if ... for he was indeed a maker of mischief" [28:4].

Sectarianism has as often been diagnosed as an ineffable, malicious spirit [*rūḥ al-ṭā'ifīya*][48] as it has been decried as an all too palpable, stifling political system. The much-disputed nature of the causal relation between the two will recur as a source of debate. Moreover, we will repeatedly encounter efforts to ascribe sectarianism to a foreign plot extraneous to a fluid, trans-sectarian culture allegedly indigenous to precolonial (Mount) Lebanon.

Even as we shall attempt to identify and trace *ṭā'ifīya* as a malleable product of history rather an ontological state, there is no gainsaying that the roots of sectarianism in state policies stretch back further than the age of Western colonialism. In contradistinction to the assertion that "European imagination invented the tribes of Lebanon,"[49] historians such as Jawād Būlus and Kamāl Ṣalībī have traced the tribal origins of most of Lebanon's religious sects and family clans all the way back to the southern Arabian Peninsula.[50] In a similar vein, Waḍḍāḥ Sharāra has contested the extraneous origins of Lebanese confessionalism by documenting its gradual formation among the Shia community of his native Jabal 'Āmil.[51] Confessionalism (*ṭā'ifīya*) to Sharāra is nothing less than the organizing principle of Lebanese society, the "real religion" of the Lebanese, in the words of the late Maxime Rodinson.[52]

[48] Such was the vocabulary used by Khayr ad-Dīn al-'Adra during the elaboration of the Lebanese constitution in 1926 when he described sectarianism as a "mental affliction" [*ḥāla nafsīya*]. See *al-Ṭā'ifīya fī Lubnān Min Khilāl Munāqashāt Majlis al-Nuwwāb, 1923–1987* (Beirut: Dār al-Ḥamrā, 1989), 16.

[49] Maqdisī, *The Culture of Sectarianism*, 23. Maqdisī attempts to qualify his generalization, denying that he is "suggesting that these religious communities did not exist or that travelers' accounts were false or fabricated, but instead that they were conceptualized in certain terms (tribal, free, stagnant, separate) that did not correspond to the way the inhabitants of Mount Lebanon perceived themselves." The available primary accounts, however, such as the premodern Maronite historiography of Ibn al-Qilā'ī or that of the Druze Ṣāliḥ ibn Yaḥyā, display strident communal prejudices and portray a society in which bold sectarian divisions are a salient feature of daily life. Ṣāliḥ Ibn Yaḥyā, *Tārīkh Bayrūt, wa-huwa akhbār al-salaf min dhurriyat BuḤtur ibn 'Alī Amīr al-Gharb bi-Bayrūt*, ed. Kamāl Salībī (Beirut: Dār al-Mashrik, 1969).

[50] Ṣalībī has provocatively labeled the Lebanese sects "tribes in disguise," thereby offering a sociohistorical sub-context to the evolution of confessional cleavages and *ṭā'ifīya*. While acknowledging that Lebanese sects do not constitute separate races, Abū Khalīl As'ad claims that the subjective stress on distinctions, however concocted and artificial, is so strong as to warrant the designation of "sectarian ethnicities." Abū Khalīl As'ad, "The Politics of Sectarian Ethnicity: Segmentation in Lebanese Society," PhD thesis, Georgetown University, 1988, 87ff.

[51] Waḍḍāḥ Sharāra, *Al-Umma Al-Qaliqa Al-'Āmiliyūn wa al-'Aṣabīya Al-'Āmilīya* (Beirut: Riyāḍ al-Rayyis lil-Kutub wa-al-Nashr, 1996).

[52] Maxime Rodinson, "Aux Origines du 'Pacte National': Contribution à l'Histoire de la Crise Franco-Libanaise de Novembre 1943," *Die Welt des Islams* 28.1/4 (1988): 470. Secularism in Lebanon in this reading becomes contingent on the inculcation of a new, civic mentality. We shall revisit this theme in the conclusion to this book.

To be sure, there has been a powerful strand in Lebanese historiography and political science that has sought to deny the very applicability of the terminology of "sectarianism." According to one Francophone scholar, sectarianism is nothing more than a pejorative tag "*en vogue*" among American political scientists woefully ignorant of prior decades of research on the topic.[53] In a sense, the visceral rejection of the very designation of sectarianism, and the insistence on the radical uniqueness of the Lebanese predicament, may both reflect a thinly concealed discomfort with the "Western" paradigm of secularism and the resultant full deconfessionalization of the Lebanese political system it might imply.

Not all Lebanese scholars, however, have been so averse to drawing comparisons to other contexts. The sociologist Saffīya Sa'āda has rendered *ṭā'ifīya* as a form of (religious) "caste," akin to the Indian notion signifying hereditary identities and occupations of closed, endogamous groups.[54] While such an analog to a consanguineous caste system arguably may convey too great a sense of a frozen socioeconomic hierarchy – after all, conversion from one "caste" to another is always an (remote) option in Lebanon – Sa'āda's translation does capture the multiple connotations of the term, incorporating its dual social and sectarian dimensions in Lebanon. As Nur Yalman has noted, communal and kinship loyalties in the Middle East have been as powerful a curb to individualism as Indian concepts of caste hierarchy.[55] In Lebanon, Buṭrus al Bustānī was painfully aware that the eruption of confessional strife in the nineteenth century came as a consequence of unaddressed latent sectarian animosities that he says well preceded 1860. One could well argue that rule in premodern Lebanon (and thereafter) was held by families (the 'Assāfs, the Tanūkhids, the Ma'nids), yet, conversions notwithstanding, family and kinship ties almost always entailed distinct sectarian identities.[56]

53 Antoine Massara, *La Gouvernance D'un Système Consensuel* (Beirut: Librairie Orientale, 2003), 389. Massara does draw parallels between Lebanon and similar states (such as Yugoslavia), but rejects the conventional, binary dichotomy of secularism and sectarianism, confessionalists versus anti-confessionalists.

54 Saffīya Sa'āda, *Social Structure of Lebanon* (Beirut: Dār an-Nahār, 1993), 22. Sa'āda ultimately bases her argument on the dictionary of Zakī Badawī, *A Dictionary of Social Sciences* (Beirut: Librairie du Liban, 1986). Even though real and perceived associations of individual sects with specific occupations are legion, it goes without saying that professional and confessional demarcations do not neatly overlap in Lebanon. Then again, very much the same pertains to urban centers in India where capitalist concerns could override the caste system.

55 Nur Yalman, "De Toqueville in India: An Essay on the Caste System," *Man* 4.1 (1969): 125.

56 al-Bustānī, *Nafīr Sūrīyā*, 36–37.

In the final analysis, to try and sift through and separate the religious and secular connotations of the term *ṭawā'if*, or to privilege one over the other, seems quixotic as the term is laden with at once communal connotations, religious identities, *and* politico-economic interests.

Lebanon's dominant societal infrastructure and political organization along the lines of the *ṭawā'if* deserves further discussion as it is commonly singled out by the opponents of the consociational system as the greatest stumbling block preventing the solidification of a strong notion of secular citizenship in Lebanon. Conversely, the seemingly insurmountable persistence of the *ṭawā'if* as a sociological reality has been identified as the underlying raison d'être justifying Lebanon's peculiar confessional system. Shīḥā refers positively to the plurality of sects, defining Lebanon as "*un pays de minoritiés associées.*"[57] His open *francophilia* notwithstanding, Shīḥā firmly rejected a wholesale import of French laicism as a dangerous delusion, a "*cacophonie qui nous met intellectuellement aux confines de l'anarchie.*"[58] Shīḥā's disciples would continue to exhibit this same fear and disdain for promoters of a "Jacobin," deconfessionalized state.[59]

Far from being a hindrance to be removed, then, Lebanon's denominational diversity in this reading is extolled as the secret elixir that undergirds the state's democratic features. Since the *ṭawā'if* could not be wished away, and since no one *ṭā'ifa* has ever been able to claim a decisive demographic preponderance, the recurring challenge was to find an – ever elusive – equilibrium, a formula that could adequately recognize and represent the communal groups and identities – without summoning their violent side. Both detractors and champions of political confessionalism might concur that the political dilemma of Lebanon need not be cast as a generic, antagonism of *religious versus* secular governance per se. A more important dichotomy could be posited between the fledgling supra-confessional agencies, both state and nonstate, versus the sociological paradigm of the *ṭawā'if*, which are properly conceived as communal, "clientistic interest groups," *Klientelgruppen*, represented by political bosses, the *zu'amā'*.

As Arnold Hottinger puts it:

> The *ṭawā'if* are the actual institutions of Lebanon. Secularism is merely a perfunctory matter of etiquette and showcased acculturation. Just as one might

[57] Michel Shīḥā, *Politique Intérieure* (Beirut: Editions du Trident, 1964), 232.
[58] Shīḥā, *Politique Intérieure*, 288.
[59] Among the more prominent legal scholars who have rephrased Shīḥā's argument are Joseph Mayla and Antoine Masarra, *Le Pacte Libanais: Le Message d'Universalité et ses Contraintes* (Beirut: Librairie Orientale, 1997).

resort to speaking French in the *haute bourgeoisie*, so one would claim to be *'séculaire'* since the *ṭawāʾif* were seen as un-modern, backward and orientals.[60]

Bound by the potent and prolonged ties of endogamy, dynastic families and clannish politicians (more so than any politicized clergy) representing the *ṭawāʾif* have time and again been able to seize the levers of power in the state patronage network and infiltrate its last recesses to their advantage. Moreover, the temptation for these clientistic groups to solicit outside support in their domestic ventures has proven too potent to be withstood, time and again drawing Lebanon into the vortex of clashing global powers.[61] While there is no doubt that these international dependencies have compounded and fueled sectarianism in Lebanon, the principal focus of this book will rest on the inability and unwillingness of the Lebanese to tackle the *domestic* roots of sectarianism in both its material and nonmaterial manifestations. This book therefore refutes the apologetic denial of the indigenous roots of confessionalism in the Arab world and shall resist the facile bracketing of sectarianism as a modern fabrication ascribed to extraneous interventions, while not ignoring the latter's effect on fueling – and at times even financing – sectarian factions in the region.

Before focusing in further on the particular Arab and Lebanese trajectories of secularism, however, we begin by adopting a wide, bird's-eye perspective, which shall enable us to draw parallels to the evolution of secular forms of administration in Europe, as well as other, multiconfessional countries comparable to Lebanon.

Conceptual and Analytic Approach

> The human being can only be understood from the macro cosmos.
>
> Paracelsus

By deliberately laying its primary focus on secularism – rather than the more circumscribed antonym sectarianism – this comprehensive study

[60] Interview and correspondence with the author, Zurich, August 20, 2003 and July 14, 2006.

[61] The Maronites traditionally sought succor from France, the Druze from Tuscany and England, the Orthodox from Russia, the Shia from the Persian empires and Iran, the Sunnis from the Sunni dynasties, and the Ottomans, Saudi Arabia, Egypt, and Syria. This is somewhat of a simplification, particularly as regards the twentieth century and the civil war of 1975–1990. The alliances entered during the civil war did not always follow a strict sectarian logic. For instance, Christian militias – such as the Katāʾib – received assistance not just from the United States and Israel, but also from Saudi Arabia, Jordan, Egypt, and, in the case of General ʿAwn in particular, Saddam Hussein's Iraq. Moreover, before the Iranian revolution, SAVAK gave anti-Nasserist parliamentarians $330,000 in the 1960 elections. Houchang Chehabi and Ḥassan Mneimeh, "Five Centuries of Lebanese-Iranian Relations," in *Distant Relations*, ed. Houchang Chehabi (London: I. B. Tauris, 2006), 170.

seeks to broaden the frame of reference and eschew essentialisms, analytic myopia, and solipsisms. The intent is to refute the forgone conclusion of the endemic, ostensibly congenital nature of sectarianism in Lebanon by demonstrating that the Levant passed through similar classical stages of history – including a premodern Renaissance and Revolutionary Enlightenment – that presaged secularization in the West. Even so, history's course in Lebanon (as elsewhere) can and will not be plotted as a teleological ascent toward inexorable, steadily increasing secularization.

In order to avoid the twin analytic pitfalls of positivist predeterminism on one end, and primordialist prejudice on the other, a comprehensive, comparative and multiangular approach is requisite. Figure I.1 provides a comprehensive illustration for the key conceptual references that inform the structure and rationale of this book. It depicts a select sample of historical models of secularism and places them in their relation to the dynamic, dialectical interplay of a triad of spheres of influence: religion, state, and society, which, alternatively, might be related to the respective realms of ideologies, institutions, and interests. These three principal circles are not left in static isolation, but plotted against the two major variables of state authority on the y-axis and the extent of individual freedoms on the x-axis.[62]

The core premise of this study is visualized in the diagram: If the secular nation-state is to extend to each of its individual citizens an equal measure of civic rights, it must assert the latter's supremacy against the "pull" of potentially exclusionary religious identities (depicted in the bottom-left corner of the following graph), and the no less centripetal individual and communal competition for resources (depicted in the bottom-right corner).[63]

The rigid etatisms of the sister Republics of Turkey and France arguably represent two of the most express concrete endeavors to prevent such devolution of state authority,[64] even though Kemalist *laiklik*, unlike

[62] Ronald Inglehardt and Christian Welzel relate traditional/secular-rationality on the y-axis to the variable of survival/self-expression on the x-axis. *Modernization, Cultural Change and Democracy* (Cambridge: Cambridge University Press, 2005), 79.

[63] Rousseau's benchmark for the limits of tolerance is: "On doit tolérer toutes celles qui tolèrent les autres, autant que leurs dogmes n'ont rien de contraire aux devoirs du Citoyen," *Du Contrat Sociale* (Beirut: L'Academie Rhodanienne des Lettres, 1949), 367.

[64] As we shall later see, secularism in Kemalist Turkey never denoted the separation of state and religion, but rather the submission of the latter under the stiffened and expanded control of the former. Diyanet İşleri See Alfred Stepan, "Religion, Democracy and the Twin Tolerations," *Journal of Democracy* 11.4 (2000): 51–52; Birol Başkan, *From Religious Empires to Secular States: State Secularization in Turkey, Iran and Russia* (Abingdon: Routledge, 2014).

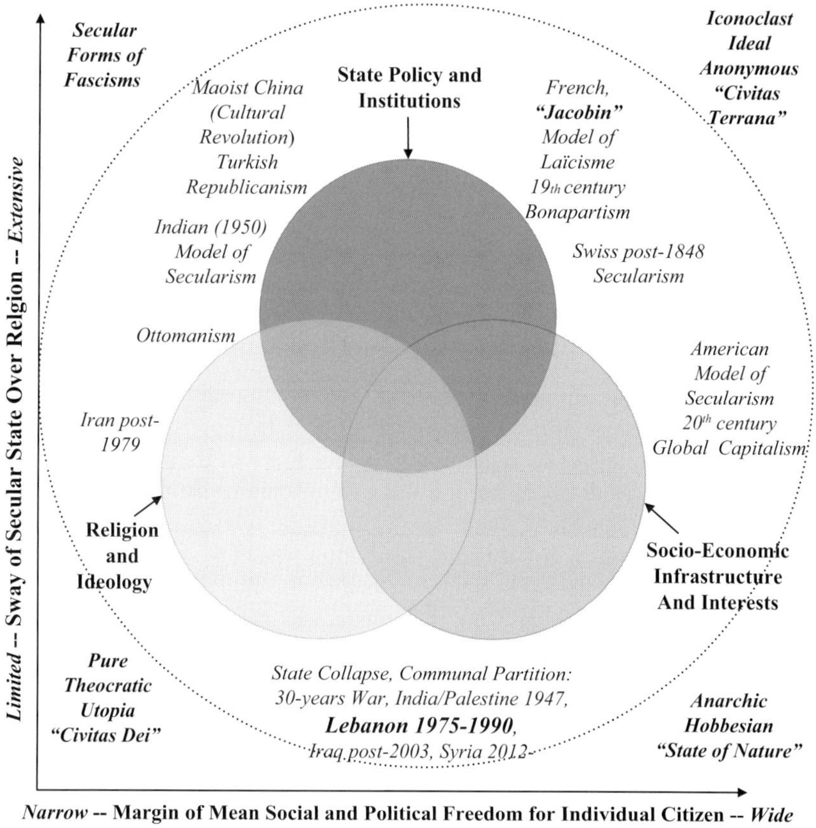

Figure I.1 Reference diagram: Global permutations of secularism

anti-clerical French *laïcité*, retained an undercurrent of (Sunni) communalism both in state and society, thus placing its political system somewhere between Ottomanism and French *laïcisme*.

Before we proceed to situate Lebanon within this panoramic framework,[65] several conceptual assumptions underlying the foregoing diagram should be clarified with historical references. First, a positivist

[65] For a wider elaboration of the premises and cross-national, global implications, see the appendix in Mark Farha, "Global Gradations of Secularism: The Consociational, Communal and Coercive Paradigms," *Comparative Sociology* 11 (2012), 386. The plotting of the countries roughly corresponds to Inglehardt and Welzel, Modernization, Cultural Change and Democracy, 79, figure 2.1, 57. The authors relate traditional/secular-rationality on the y-axis to the variable index of survival/self-expression on the x-axis. The hypothesis is that affluent, "post-materialist" societies tend to prioritize self-expression and political freedoms over (materialist) concerns with survival and sustenance.

might be given to identify the x-axis with the progress of history pure and simple. Such a reading would be consonant with the classical modernization and secularization theses that predict that, as a given society moves to greater social differentiation, higher levels of income and economic development, attachment to tradition should wane accordingly. This is mostly, but not invariably, the case. While recent studies have confirmed the suspected relation between increasing attachments to secular-rational (as opposed to religious) values and higher GDP (or existential security),[66] and while postindustrial European countries have seen a marked decline in religious observance and belief,[67] percentages of agnostics and atheists in Lebanon range between 5 and 8 percent and thus pale in comparison with most Western countries.[68]

Besides the unique cases of Ireland and Poland in which (Catholic) confessional identities were integrally wed to nationalism, the notable exception in the West remains the United States.[69] Depicted on the far right of Figure I.1, America constitutes the classic (counter-)example of a postindustrial society in which personal belief remains high despite secular state institutions and wide margins of personal and economic freedoms. One factor explaining why the United States may have followed such a deviant "*Sonderweg*" may lay in the nation's wider

[66] See figure 2.3.a. in Inglehardt and Welzel, *Modernization, Cultural Change and Democracy*, 58–60. Rather, the expanse of the service sector stands in an almost direct correlation to the identification with autonomous agency on the individual level. The authors conclude that the first phase of a transition from an agrarian to an industrial society did spawn secular-rational attitudes, but not necessarily promote increased individual freedoms of expression.

[67] According to the 2004 European Values Study, just 21 percent of Europeans say religion is "very important" to them. Cited in Chris Young, "What Place of God in Europe?" *Christian Science Monitor*, February 21, 2005. A more recent survey showed a precipitous decline in religiousity across most Western nations, with religiousity dropping by 21 percent in Switzerland and 13 percent in the United States between 2005 and 2011. The ratio of self-identified religious (64 percent) to nonreligious people (33 percent) in Lebanon mirrors that of a country like Germany (54/33 percent). Even Italy shows a larger number of religious people (73 percent) and over half as few nonreligious people (15 percent). See "Global Index of Religiousity and Atheism" (Washington, DC: Win-Gallup International, 2014) last accessed February 16, 2016 at: https://sidmennt.is/wp-content/uploads/Gallup-International-um-tr%C3%BA-og-tr%C3%BAleysi-2012.pdf, last accessed February 4, 2019, 14.

[68] "Youth and Religion," *Ii-Monthly*, 44 (February 2006), 6. Another survey in 1989 revealed a low of 5 percent agnostics. See ʿAbdu al-KāḤī, Aîda Boudjikanian and Joseph Khūrī, *Orientations Culturelles et Valeurs Religieuses au Liban* (Beirut: Centre d'Etudes et de Recherches sur l'Orient Chrétien, 1991), 33, 57, 66.

[69] A survey by the Pew Forum on Religion and Public Life found that nearly three times as many Americans (59 percent) called their faith "very important." Cited in Young, "What Place of God in Europe?"

economic disparities and stronger social anxieties compared with European counterparts.[70] Another consideration omitted from many analyses are *intra*-societal disparities that split the United States into liberal, more agnostic "Blue," and more religious and morally conservative "Red" states. Any in-depth evaluation of individual countries must take due account of such internal heterogeneity. Thus, the aforementioned countries are plotted according to mean aggregate estimates.

Second, none of the associated political extremes delineated in the four peripheral corners of Figure I.1, namely the *utopias* of unmitigated "theocracy, iconoclasm, fascism, and anarchy," can be said to find their full realization in pure, absolute form. This, at any rate, is what the historical record suggests. In post-Revolutionary France, surrogate saints filled the void of anticlerical purges. The revolutionary cults of "Eternal Reason," "Saint Liberty," and the mass dedicated to the "Cult of the Supreme Being" in Notre Dame of 1793 immediately come to mind.[71] The Revolution, with its apostles, militants, and martyrs, assumed a religious form.[72] Similarly, the twentieth-century corporate, fascist state has exhibited an abhorrence of any ideological vacuum to such a degree that it has shown a penchant to concoct its own, carefully choreographed civil religion. If Saint-Simeon and Comte hailed the imminent apotheosis of a "scientific priesthood," Hitler envisaged a "secular priesthood" in *lieu* of the "Church and the Freemasons" in his own conception of a new hierarchical order.[73] The cults of personality cultivated by Arab regimes and dictators around the world also come to mind.

[70] "The United States is exceptionally high in religiosity in large part, we believe, because it is also one of the most unequal post-industrial societies under comparison ... Americans face greater anxieties than citizens in other advanced industrialized countries about whether or not they will be covered by medical insurance, be fired arbitrarily, or be forced to choose between losing their jobs and devoting themselves to their newborn children ... By comparison, despite recent pressures on restructuring, the secular Scandinavian and West European states remain some of the most egalitarian societies, with relatively high levels of personal taxation but also an expansive array of welfare services in the public sector, including comprehensive healthcare, social services, and pensions." Pippa Norris and Ronald Inglehart, *Sacred and Secular: Religion and Politics Worldwide* (Cambridge: Cambridge University Press, 2005), 103. From a global perspective, Europe has been characterized as the "secular exception" to the "religious rule." Hartmut Lehmann, *Säkularisierung: Der Europäische Sonderweg in Sachen Religion* (Göttingen: Wallstein Verlag, 2004), 20.

[71] To historians such as Edgar Quinet, Robespierre was a pope reinstating the scaffolds of Richelieu. Patrice Higonnet, "Terror, Trauma and the 'Young Marx' Explanation of Jacobin Politics," *Past and Present* 191 (2006): 126.

[72] This, at any rate, was the estimate of Alexis De Tocqueville and Alexis Charles Henri Maurice Clérel Tocqueville, "The Old Regime and the French Revolution," *Anchor* 60 (1955): 11–13.

[73] "Ourselves or the Freemasons or the Church – there is room for one of the three and no more ... We are the strongest and shall get rid of the other two ... I am founding an

Bringing these cases to attention is significant insofar as discreditors of secularism have been eager to pinpoint the bleak legacy of ideological intolerance left by communism and Nazism as conclusive proof of the inherent tyranny of all secular regimes.[74] Such a hasty, denunciatory linkage, however, rests on a causal fallacy. More discerning in his analysis, Arnold Toynbee unmasked a familiar theology behind the atheistic facade of communism: God is replaced with "historical necessity," the "chosen people" find themselves reincarnated in Marx's "Proletariat" and Lenin's "vanguard," and, in place of the eschatological fervor for the savior, we find a no less eager anticipation for the "withering of the state" at the liberating end of time.[75] The demarcations of Figure I.1 – and secularism in general – should then be read with due acknowledgment of their inherent dynamism and fluidity. If secular totalitarianisms have lapsed into quasi-religious inquisitorial regimes, on the opposite pole, pursuers of lofty theocratic designs have, conversely, found it all but impossible to avoid contamination – witting and unwitting – with worldly snares and symbols. One of the reasons for fundamentalism's penchant for violence is the frustrating impotence to resolve the irresolvable tension between unattainable absolutes and unavoidable political exigencies.[76] To the purist, the closest approximation to the sublime ideal of the theocratic *civitas dei* might lay not in the politician posing as a prophet, but in the radical indifference to worldly affairs, that is the quiestist

Order ... the stage of the Man-God, when man will be the measure and center of all things." Cited in Gerald Suster, *Hitler and the Age of Horus* (London: Sphere, 1981), 138. Both Hitler and Stalin incidentally dabbled with entering the priesthood as adolescents.

74 One such anti-secular polemicist in the Arab world is 'Abdul Wahāb al-Masīrī who rephrases many of the earlier anti-secular tirades formulated in the aftermath of the 1967 defeat. 'Abdul Wahāb al-Masīrī, *al-'Almānīya al-Shāmila wa al-'Almānīya al-Juzīya*, vol. II (Cairo: Dār al-Shurūq, 2002).

75 Arnold Toynbee, "A Centenary View of Lenin," *International Affairs* 46.3 (1970): 490–500.

76 Thomas Müntzer's words epitomize the perennial promise of theocracy: "As Christ says in Matthew 10: 'I am not come to send peace, but a sword.' But what is one to do with the sword? Exactly this: sweep aside those evil men who obstruct the gospel! Take them out of circulation! Otherwise you will be devils ... Now if you are to be true rulers, you must seize the very roots of government, following the command of Christ. Drive his enemies away from the elect; you are the instruments to do this. My friend, don't let us have any of these hackneyed posturings, about the power of God achieving everything without any resort to your sword; otherwise it may rust in its scabbard ... Hence the sword, too, is necessary to eliminate the godless." Thomas Müntzer, "Sermon to the Princes," in *The Collected Works of Thomas Müntzer*, ed. Peter Matheson (Edinburgh: T & T Clark, 1988). 'Azīz al-'Azma elaborates a suggestive synthesis of the inflections of divine kingship in multiple temporal and cultural modulations. See, in particular, his discussion on the *khalīfat Allāh*. 'Azīz al-'Azma, *Muslim Kingship: Power and the Sacred in Muslim, Christian and Pagan Polities* (London: I. B. Tauris, distributed by St. Martin's Press, 1997), 65ff.

"*Göttliche Gelassenheit*" of the desert anchorite, the divine intoxication of the Sufi dervish, or the utter renouncement of the *sannyasi* savant.[77]

Lastly, in its bottom-most ranges, Figure I.1 lists those extreme cases in which state legitimacy has evaporated entirely and societies plunge headlong into what seems at first a bottomless abyss of anarchy. Such states of lawlessness, too, are not given to endure as tightly structured cells and social constellations are quick to emerge on the microlevel. Case in point are the myriad militia that divided the derelict state of Lebanon into cantons from 1975 to 1990,[78] or indeed the similar sectarian dissolution of Iraq after 2003 and Syria post-2011. Alternatively, the sudden breakdown of central authority may be followed by a no less abrupt genesis of new nation-states along preexisting and newly "imagined" communal lines. Examples of this include the partition of the Indian subcontinent into Pakistan and India, Palestine after the departure of the British authorities in 1947, and the dismemberment of the Ottoman Empire into ethnically and confessionally defined nation-states. Sectarian solidarity in these cases might foist itself as the most ready and potent mobilizing force on even the most agnostic of decision-makers.[79] Thus, a thoroughly agnostic Jinnah saw it opportune to advertise his conversion to a separatist, anti-Hindu jihadism at his Lahore speech of 1940, while Mustafa Kemal would briefly avail himself of the popular aura of a *ghāzī* to rally his followers.

This broad, comprehensive overview should aid the reader in understanding the subsequent treatment of the multiple facets of the Lebanese engagement with secularism. The individual chapters, and their modulation by the previously introduced determinant variables, are depicted in the next diagram (Figure I.2), which is followed by a guide to the sequence of chapters.

As it turns out, the Lebanese case corresponds to none of the individual typologies listed in Figure I.1. Rather, as we shall elaborate, Lebanon combines elements from *Ottoman and Indian communalism* (in its retention of confessional personal status laws), *French republicanism* (in the egalitarian, laic clauses of its 1926 constitution), and features of *(American) economic ultraliberalism* in a single, heterogeneous social, and political spectrum.

Therein lies Lebanon's complexity, and thence its fascination.

[77] Also see Rousseau's classic critique of the bigotry and oppression that tend to taint the rule of the prophetic pontiff who arrogates to himself the role of prince. Rousseau, *Du Contrat Sociale*, 367.

[78] Jurj Qurm has accordingly spoken of communalism as inherently "fascistic and totalitarian." Jurj Qurm, *Le Liban Contemporain: Histoire et Société* (Paris: Le Découverte, 2003), 62.

[79] That sectarian solidarities are by no means a guarantee of unity became evident in the partition of Pakistan and Bangladesh in 1970.

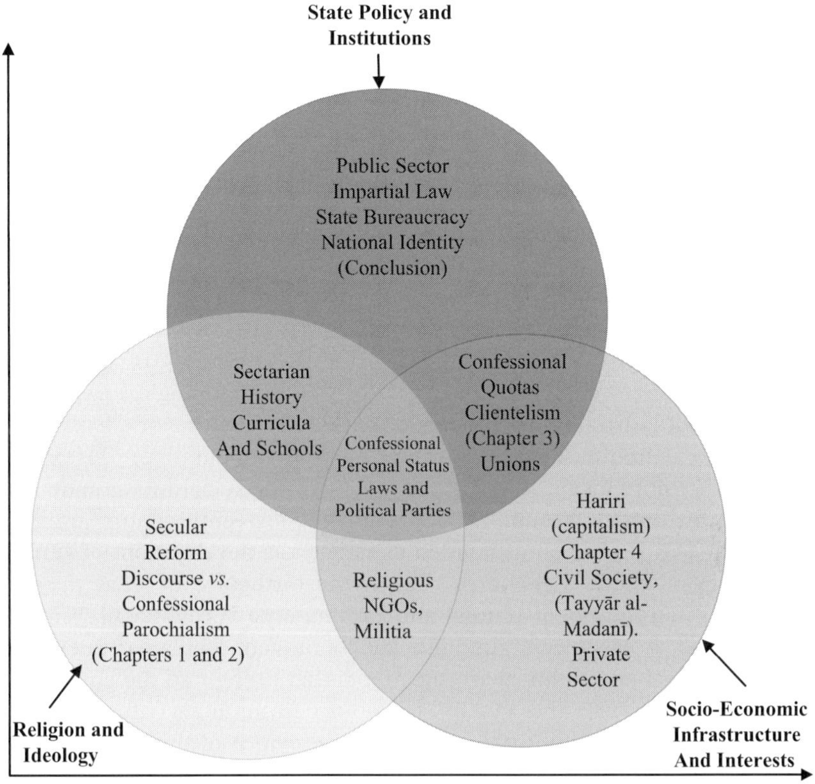

Figure I.2 Situating the Lebanese predicament and individual chapters[80]

Structure and Outline

This study departs from the domain of *Geistesgeschichte*, which is the realm of ideas and ideals demarcated within the bounds of the bottom-left circle of Figure I.2. The underlying premise is that the woes of secularism in Lebanon – and its besieged status in Arab political discourse at large – must be related to the wider set of dominant philosophical and ideological presuppositions, which have hindered the evolution of a

[80] One might note that in Figure I.2, education is placed at the intersection of the circles of (communal narratives of) religion and (state) politics, in contradistinction to administrative quotas that concern the demographic and sociological, but not the ideological and confessional dimensions of the sects *ṭawāʾif*. Lastly, confession-specific personal status laws are placed at the interface of all three circles as they involve the dogma and laws of each confession in addition to prejudicing the state's interaction with each of the sectarian communities.

secular state across the region. Since the reception accorded to secularism in the Arab world has been shaded by a (mis)understanding of its European provenance and significance, Chapter 1 commences with a brief review of the genesis, transmutations, and historical semantics of political secularism in the Western tradition and Arab intellectual history to set the parameters of the subsequent debate. Intellectually and ideologically, I propose that the perception of secularism in Lebanon has been skewed by an often polemicized understanding of European history, a phobia-plagued, apologetic discourse on religion, and an essentially premodern patron–client (*zaʿīm-zilm*) paradigm of social and political relationships.[81] I then proceed to offer my own working definition of secularism as "nondiscrimination" for the purposes of this book. A broadly conceived summary review of the epistemological underpinnings of secularism and sectarianism marks the capstone of Chapter 1.

Chapter 2 marks a move from the (global-comparative) "history of ideas" to a more localized historical review of the social topography and political features of Mount Lebanon and the sixteenth-century emirate Fakhr ad-Dīn II in so far as it aided or stalled the development of secular governance. Mount Lebanon's role as the birthplace of what may be deemed as structures of (feudal and premodern) "proto-secularism" is reexamined. It has been argued that such a nascent secularism is evident in institutional and political arrangements that prefigured the equality of Lebanon's Christian and Muslim religious communities before the law, a development unbeknownst to any other province of the early modern Ottoman Empire, or, indeed, continental Europe. I devote particular attention to the premodern transformations that not only laid the basis for political secularism, but also for the linkage of early modern capitalism[82] with secularism, a theme which gains particular relevance in light

[81] Ayşe Güneş-Ayata has defined clientelism as a holdover from traditional societies. "The dyadic, hierarchical, personalistic nature of clientelistic relations has been associated with ritual kinship, Sufism, and feudalism, all of which enact forms of social interaction and commitments with roots in premodern times." Needless to say, such absolutist appellations of "traditional" or "pre-modern" warrant greater contextualization. Thus, Güneş qualifies her thesis by acknowledging that, from another perspective, "clientelistic relations can be seen as a form of domination that, although not necessarily modern, is used by modern political and economic elites to channel resources for their own benefit." Ayşe Güneş-Ayata, "Clientelism: Premodern and Modern," in *Democracy, Clientelism, and Civil Society*, eds. L. Roniger and Ayşe Güneş-Ayata (Boulder, CO: L. Rienner Publishers, 1994), 21.

[82] The definition for capitalism offered by the Anglican clergyman John Wesley is cited by Weber: "We must exhort all Christians to gain all they can, and to save all they can; that is, in effect, to grow rich." Max Weber, *The Protestant Ethic and the Spirit of Capitalism* (New York: Dover Publications, 2003), 175.

of Lebanon's historical role as a "Merchant Republic."[83] The contested readings of premodern Lebanon are surveyed as they form the backdrop for the contemporary debate on secularism.

I follow a similar line of inquiry in plotting the trajectory of secularism in the subsequent period of the nineteenth-century emirate. By relating the transformations in the Eastern Mediterranean to the global spread of Napoleonic reform, I seek to show that the eruption of sectarian strife in Mount Lebanon and Syria can in part be read as an unintended consequence of secularizing and centralizing republican reform that wrought political dislocation and kindled ethno-religious nationalisms. To further underscore this dynamic, a brief, yet indicative, comparison with the genesis of the Swiss Confederation is adduced. I investigate the origins of Lebanon as a "federation of minorities" by comparing the evolution of its political system to that of its distant Swiss cousin in an attempt to gauge the disparate degrees of success of consocialitionism in establishing the foundation for secularism in these "mountain republics."

The checkered record of success of Napoleonic reforms leads me back to a broad sketch of the evolution of nationalism and secularism as staples of Arab political discourse during the (Arab) Enlightenment. This kaleidoscopic exposition of Arab and Lebanese intellectual history is intended to highlight the principal sociological and historical impediments that have either distorted or defeated secularism as a viable political arrangement of governance in the nineteenth century. The debate is critical to show why the term has gained such a negative reputation, one compounded by its association with European colonial powers, missionary institutions, and clandestine networks. This conceptual confusion has manifested itself in the subsumption of secularism in an undifferentiating attitude of wholesale rejection and totalizing "anti-Westernism," or a no less stultifying posture of "Occidentalism," the rhetorical and epistemological contours of which I sketch in greater detail. I end with the tumultuous period of World War I, the twilight zone out of which would emerge a trans-sectarian solidarity and the first Lebanese nationalists proper.[84]

In its second segment, the book follows the evolution of the Lebanese consociational political system from its origins to its last constitutional recalibration in 1989. I outline the process of the drafting of the constitution under the auspices of the French mandatory powers and trace the

[83] The expression "République Marchande" was coined by Michel Shīḥā, one of the key architects of the 1926 constitution, as we shall see in Chapter 3. Shīḥā, *Politique Intérieure*.

[84] Mark Farha, "From Anti-Imperial Dissent to National Consent: The Formation of a Trans-Sectarian National Consciousness in Lebanon," in *The First World War and Its Aftermath: The Shaping of the Middle East*, ed. T. G. Fraser (Chicago: Gingko/Chicago University Press, 2015), 91–110.

successive accommodation of the Lebanese system to the country's major sects, posing the question why this nationalization only partly induced a concomitant political secularization in the Lebanese case.

The secular and confessional elements of Lebanese constitutional history are traced up until the last amendment of the constitution in the wake of the 1989 *Ṭā'if* Accords. I attempt to show how this watershed agreement still held the Lebanese system hostage to communal dispositions and demographics. Since the latter have gained additional importance due to the dearth of secular political parties, I give a thumbnail sketch of the notion of secularism in Lebanese party discourse and shed light on the changing epicenters of paternalistic leaders (*Za'īm*) before turning to examine the salient role of the late Lebanese prime minister Rafīq al-Harīrī (1944–2005) in Chapter 4. In reviewing the post-*Tā'if* era after 1990, I place a particular focus on the socioeconomic backdrop to secularism. In particular, in light of his return to Lebanon as the preeminent patron, Harīrī's Saudi-sponsored business and development agenda is investigated insofar as it harnessed and/or stifled secular forces in the Lebanese private and public spheres. In a nutshell, the question I pose is whether the embrace of neoliberal privatization and a rentier economy can act as a catalyst for the secular state in the political sphere. To what degree, in other words, do the Lebanese have reason to share Voltaire's Panglossian faith in the integrative, secularizing power of capitalism and the profit motive?[85]

Making the case for a broader base for comprehensive secularism, the book subsequently presents individual case studies that exemplify the concrete instances in which the malaise of secularism is manifested. Due to constraints of space, this book had to omit the (failed) state supervision and secularization of the nation's confessionally administrated educational institutions and personal status laws, cognizant that this topic has been treated in a previous publication.[86] The same entrenched interest groups preventing a deconfessionalization and standardization of history curricula in education stood in the way of the numerous and periodic attempts to secularize personal status laws in Lebanon. As in all Arab countries, the laws and juridical procedure for marriage, divorce, and inheritance in Lebanon fall under the legal remit of Lebanon's

[85] "Go into the Exchange in London, that place more venerable than many a court, and you will see representatives of all nations assembled there for the profit of mankind. There the Jew, the Mahometan, and the Christian deal with one another as if they were of the same religion, and reserve the name of the infidel for those who go bankrupt … On leaving these peaceable and free assemblies, some go to the synagogue, others in search of drink … in the end all are satisfied." Voltaire, *Philosophical Letters* (New York: Macmillan Publishing Company, 1962), 26.

[86] Farha, "Historical Legacy and Political Implications of State and Sectarian Schools in Lebanon" and Mark Farha, "Stumbling Blocks to the Secularization of Personal Status Laws in the Lebanese Republic (1926–2013)," *Arab Law Quarterly* 29 (2015): 31–55.

eighteen confessional denominations. A series of attempts in the twentieth century to push forward a unified secular civil code of family law won support from a large segment of the citizenry, while ultimately being thwarted time and again by a joint Muslim–Christian phalanx of religious and political leaders who drew on the same popular polemical prejudices against secularism discussed in Chapters 1 and 3.

To wit, a number of Arab "Occidentalist" and Western "Orientalist" scholars have categorically dismissed even entertaining the very possibility of secularization in the Muslim world of which Lebanon partakes. Yet, while scholars such as Ernest Gellner summarily rejected the applicability of secularization in Islam,[87] Albert Hourani expressed his hope for a gradual synthesis of secular and religious principles of justice.[88] Indeed, just as we may speak of an (expanding) "informal economy,"[89] so too we may discern an "informal," "implicit" secularism (*'almānīya ḍimnīya*) that pervades even the most (outwardly) religious societies.[90] The nativist's shrill denial of this observation, the crying afoul of the "deleterious infatuation with modernity," only serves to confirm, however inadvertently, the presence of these surreptitious streams of secular premises that permeate the modern Arab world in general and Lebanon in particular. Despite all the obstacles, and despite the searing experience of the civil war, identification with a national, civic identity remains stronger in contemporary Lebanon than in any other Arab country.[91] Meanwhile, Hourani's aspired hybridization of elements of religious morality with exigencies of quotidian secular life is quietly lived by many an Arab family, civil administrator, businessman, and professional, even as the perilous push for phantom theocracies is thriving on the debris of collapsing states across the Arab world.

87 "To say that secularization prevails in Islam is not contentious. It is simply false. Islam is as strong now as it was a century ago. In some ways it is probably much stronger." Ernest Gellner, *Postmodernism, Reason and Religion* (London: Routledge, 1992), 17.

88 Albert Hourani, *A History of the Arab Peoples* (New York: Faber & Faber, 2013), 458.

89 According to one estimate, the size of the informal economy during the war years (1975–1990) was close to $15 billion. Approximately half the Lebanese labor force was employed in the informal sector since 1950. Tawfīq Gaspard, *A Political Economy of Lebanon* (Leiden: Brill, 2004), 86–99.

90 'Azīz al-'Aẓma, *al-'Ilmānīya min Manẓūr Mukhtalif* (Beirut: CAU, 1993), 176.

91 A Zogby poll has revealed that 77 percent of Lebanese view themselves as citizens of their own country, rather than "Arab," Muslim," or "Citizen of the World." The strongest adherence to religion as a principal form of nationality identity is found in Saudi Arabia. A subsequent survey conducted by the Pew Research Center revealed that 81 percent of British, 69 percent of Spanish, 66 percent of German, and 46 percent of French Muslims consider themselves as Muslim first (rather than a citizen of their country), while only a (world) record low 30 percent of Lebanese Muslims did. A total of 42 percent of US Christians and only 14 percent of French and Spanish Christians think of themselves as Christians (rather than citizens) first. See Pew study as cited in David Rampe, "Muslims and Europe," *International Herald Tribune*, July 7, 2006, 4. Six Arab Nation Survey Report, Zogby International, World Economic Forum, Davos, November 2005.

1 Definitions and Genealogies of Secularism

Working Definition of Secularism for the Purposes of This Book

It is important to emphasize from the outset that the suggested definition of secularism proposed in this book does *not directly* address the hold or absence of religious beliefs and orientations in civil society at large or individual consciousness.[1] Nor does it address the barren debate over the compatibility of "secular" science with religious texts. Rather, the notion of secularism shall *instead pertain to the legal, political, and administrative principles that predicate the relation between the citizen and his religious identity on the one hand, and the (religiously neutral, nondiscriminatory) state laws and institutions on the other hand.* The allegedly "inherently atheistic" nature of secularism thus shall be contested, just as no *a priori* antagonistic relation between free exercise of religion and a religiously neutral, laic state shall be admitted.

More specifically, and with regards to the Lebanese predicament, the working definition of – and benchmark for – secularism shall designate *the elimination of any confessional consideration from of all aspects of the administrative and juridical levels of the (Lebanese) body politic.* While this is admittedly a negative definition of secularism, it is comprehensive in that it does encompass both the de-confessionalization of personal status laws and the political system at large. If strictly applied, this definition necessitates a relatively strong state oversight of potential infringements and coordination of legislation. As such, the dichotomy between a secularism predicated on state control versus a secularism based on separation is resolved in favor of the former.[2]

One might also add that this suggested definition of secularism as state equidistance and neutrality vis-à-vis religious affairs had already

[1] See, for instance, Peter Berger, *La Religion dans la Conscience Moderne* (Paris: Editions du Centurion, 1971), 175.

[2] See the introduction to Mirjam Künkler, John Madeley, and Shylashri Shankar, eds., *A Secular Age Beyond the West* (Cambridge: Cambridge University Press, 2018).

been – *mutatis mutandis* – passionately defended by Buṭrus al-Bustānī amid the sectarian bloodshed of 1860. It was also tabled by the select few secular parties of Lebanon, including: the Lebanese Communist Party,[3] Anṭūn Sa'āda's SSNP, the short-lived Democratic Secular Party,[4] and the "Social Movement," as well as the other secular groups I shall allude to in the course of this work. Buṭrus Bustānī defined such secularism as resting on the state's safeguarding of civil and human rights (*al-ḥuqūq al-madanīya wa al-insānīya*) and on the non-mixture of "civil and religious matters."[5] In sum, secularism according to this understanding denotes at once a normative, prescriptive, and a descriptive, historically traceable model of governance.

Before I delve into the idiosyncrasies of the Lebanese experience beginning in Chapter 2, I feel obliged to take stock of the broader regional historical backdrop and discursive context within which the Lebanese debate on secularism has taken place in a brief diachronic sketch.

As I shall try to show, any suggestion of secular governance in modern Lebanon – as in the Arab world as a whole – must wrestle with the deep-seated fear of an undifferentiated, holistic "ideal-type" of a fully secularized, irreligious, and industrial European incubus, an image that has been canonized and perpetuated by a host of nineteenth- and twentieth-century Arab scholars of European history.[6] Whether the particular assessment of

[3] The Communist Party, founded in 1925, retained its secular credentials until the civil war when it was drawn into the vortex of confessional politics and polemics. In an August 18, 1975 declaration that the Communist Party coauthored with the Leftist–Islamist coalition of the National Movement "a full secularization of the political system" is spelled out as the ultimate goal, but with the glaring omission of the secularization of personal status laws on which the Christian counterpart had conditioned political secularization. The ensuing "dialogue of the deaf" between Muslim and Christian political forces constituted the prelude to the civil war and continues to paralyze progress. See Abd al-Azīz Nawwār, *Silsila al-Wathā'iq Asāsīya min Tārīkh Lubnān al-Ḥadīth, 1517–1920* (Beirut: Arab University of Beirut, 1974). Ṭarābulsī suggested an exit from this "inane debate" by calling for a complete secularization during the war. Michele Salkind and Trabulsi Fawwaz, "Organization for Communist Action," *Middle East Research and Information Project* 61 (1977): 5.

[4] The head of this short-lived secular party, the late attorney Joseph Mughayzil, refers to the definition of secularism as it was formulated in the sessions of the French constitutional committee in 1946: "A secular system guarantees freedom of religion, the freedom to move from one religion to another as well as the practice of religious rites and the free expression of beliefs of believers and non-believers"; Mughayzil, *Kitābāt Joseph Mughayzil*, vol. II, 372.

[5] Bustānī, *Nafīr Sūrīyā*, 22.

[6] This "Spenglerian" image of a materialist, soulless West is found both among detractors (such as Jamāl ad-Dīn, Afghānī, Rashīd Riḍā, and Muḥammad Faḍlallāh) as well as among some proponents of the Western, secular paradigm such as Ṣāṭī al-Ḥusrī. Even the late Qunstanṭīn Zurayk, a seasoned scholar and champion of secular Arabism, at one point posited a "spiritual unity," which allegedly united the divergent writings of Plato,

the European model(s)[7] of secularism is positive or negative, ecstatic or dismissive, we find a persistent failure to take account of the fluidity of sacred and mundane forms of authority across European history, rendering the ready trope of a "Christian Secular West" ambiguous at best.[8] The debate on secularism is thus prejudiced by a skewed perception of the trajectory of European history as either a descent into unadulterated, atheistic materialism and predatory imperialism, or, conversely, as a straight ascent to a paradise of secular scientism and democracy. Needless to say, neither reading takes due account of the dynamic of social changes and the (im)balance of power that characterized each particular epoch.

While the French Revolution and Enlightenment have usually served as the standard reference point for discussions on secularism, some scholars have harked back to the Reformation and raised the clarion call for a similar reform movement in the Arab and Islamic worlds from the nineteenth century onward. One prominent pioneer in this respect was the Lebanese author Shiblī Shumayyil (1850–1917) who was one of the first Arab writers to adopt a more sophisticated reading of European history in which the "ideological revolution" of the Reformation was tied directly to the subsequent institutionalization of secularism. Accordingly, "everything which Europe achieved in terms of wealth, power, trade and industry was preceded by a religious revolt which freed the mind and prepared the way for the political revolution."[9]

To be sure, Shumayyil's assessment of a smooth, linear European march to "secular modernity" – defined in the previous quote reductively as a symbol of material prowess – is of course somewhat reified. Clearly, Europe meandered through various baptisms of fire before it arrived at a

Aristotle, Augustine, Descartes, Nietzsche, and Hegel. Cited in ʿAzīz al-ʿAẓma, *Qunstanīn Zurayk: ʿArabī lil-Qarn al ʿAshrīn* (Beirut: Mu'assasat lil-Dirāsāt, 2003), 107.

7 For a succinct comparative study examining the country-specific variant arrangements and the different degrees of establishment and disestablishment of state churches, see Khālid Hilmī, "The Contrasting Fates of Middle Eastern Politicized Islam & European Politicized Christianity: Historical Divergence in Configurations of Religious Contention and Democratization," PhD dissertation, Harvard University, 2006.

8 The same deficiency has conversely afflicted European characterizations of Middle Eastern history. See Anwar ʿAbdul-Mālik, "Orientalism in Crisis," *Diogenes* 44 (Winter 1963): 103–140; Cemal Kafadar, "The Ottomans and Europe," in *Handbook of European History 1400–1600*, vol. 1 (Leiden: Brill, 1994), 589–627; Edward Saʿīd, *Orientalism* (New York: Random House, 1978).

9 Shiblī Shumayyil, *Magmu'at, vol. I, Falsafat an-nushu' wa-l-'irtiqa'* (Cairo: Matb'a, al-Muqtataf, 1910), 40. Shumayyil translated Ludwig Büchner's lectures on materialism into Arabic.

rapprochement and a relatively peaceable *modus vivendi* between religious and secular power brokers as the modern, bureaucratic nation-state gradually supplanted the *ancien régime.*[10] To put matters into perspective, we might also note that at the time the previous analysis was penned and throughout much of the nineteenth-century non-Christians were (still) legally barred from holding public office in England and other European nations. Such pioneering secularists as George Holyoake and Charles Bradlaugh were engaged in a struggle against the privileges of the Anglican Church and Victorian England's blasphemy laws, just as reformers in the Arab world were challenging the rulings of the Azhar establishment in the self-same nineteenth century.

The prevalent image of a "retarded" Middle East lagging behind the West both economically and politically regarding the development of civil rights and religious freedoms is not a baseless preconception. However, this does not warrant exaggerated, normative claims, particularly if we consider that native Jews were only allowed to sit in the English parliament in 1858, or that full civil rights were not extended to African Americans in the United States until 1964, while universal suffrage granting women the right to vote was introduced in Switzerland only in 1970, almost two decades after most Arab states, including Lebanon.[11] As Roger Owen points out, both regions were simultaneously affected by the successive waves of globalization. To be sure, the social and political repercussions did vary, also with respect to the spread of secular principles to the political arena.[12] While all European nations, for instance, eventually allowed nonbelievers to hold public office, they remained

[10] Suffice it to recall the Thirty Years' War, the persecution of the Huguenots in France, the Edict of Nantes and its revocation, the civil strife and terror that marked the French Revolution, the Sonderbund War in Switzerland, or Bismark's Kulturkampf in Prussia, to name but a few historical flash points. The term "nationalism" was first used by Lamartine in the 1830s. Perry Anderson, "Internationalism: A Breviary," *New Left Review* 14 (2002): 5–25.

[11] One might argue, for instance, that the broad suppression of reforming and liberal ideas that the Arab world has witnessed in the twentieth-century mirror similar government crackdowns in nineteenth-century Europe. Rousseau, after all, saw his *Émile* banned in both France and Switzerland. The French parliament ordered the book to be burned, and in 1762 Rousseau was condemned for religious unorthodoxy. Across the Atlantic, Ralph Waldo Emerson was all but expelled from Harvard University for espousing an unorthodox theology at odds with the Unitarian establishment in 1836. It was not until 1843 that non-Congregationalists were eligible for election as overseers of Harvard College and not until 1912 that the first Irish, Boston-born Catholic would graduate from Harvard College, by the name of Joseph P. Kennedy, the father of John F. Kennedy.

[12] Roger Owen, "Using Present Day Notions of Imperialism, Globalization and Internationalism to Understand the Middle East's Late Nineteenth Century Early Twentieth Century Past," *MIT Electronic Journal of Middle Eastern Studies* 3 (2003): 4–16.

barred by law in the Mount Lebanon of Shumayyil's time and indeed the Second Lebanese Republic of today.[13]

Nonetheless, Shumayyil's suggestion of a historical link binding the sixteenth to the nineteenth century deserves further consideration as the trajectory of Western European history from the Reformation to the French Revolution figures as a paradigm for the debate on secularism in the Middle East until this present day. The late liberal Lebanese Shia cleric Sayyid Hānī Faḥṣ, for instance, has likened the situation in the Islamic world today to what transpired in sixteenth-century Europe in terms of the rapid pace of change and the parallel rise of extremist and reformist wings.[14] This transformed premodern zeitgeist eventually found its corollary in a set of newly elaborated treatises promulgating a squarely secular political philosophy. Famously, it was Machiavelli who was the first political theorist to fully and openly divorce *Civitas Dei* from *Civitas Mundi*, that is to say to sever the umbilical cord that had, at least nominally and symbolically, bound statecraft to ethics and authority to religion.[15] *The Prince* then may be seen as a product of the sixteenth-century secularizing impulse, heralding a shift of the dominant political paradigm from a *Corpus Christianum* to a *Res publica*.[16]

This process was not a European but a global one. Simply put, the argument here is that religious law had to be reinterpreted and remolded during the age of commerce. Just as many a "medieval" tenet of Catholicism ran up against many a socioeconomic exigency and was compromised, rewritten, or ignored altogether, so too a similar reactionary stream in the sixteenth-century Ottoman Empire was no match for the less sentimental forces of burgeoning trade and finance, the encroaching "invisible hands," that increasingly eluded the clutches of religious dogma. The latter suffered a retreat insofar as premodern proto-secularism meant that the absolute state was to become the lynchpin of a new social order; the strictures of religion, which may have acted as a

[13] The last US state to abolish a "declaration in the belief in God" as a prerequisite for holding public office was Maryland in 1961. In *Torcaso* v. *Watkins*, 367 US 488 (1961) the US Supreme Court reaffirmed that the US Constitution – chiefly by dint of the Establishment Clause – prohibited the states from requiring any kind of religious test for public office.

[14] Hānī Faḥṣ, *as-Shī'a wa-al-Dawlah fī Lubnān: Malāmiḥ fī al-Ru'ya Wa al-Dhākira* (Beirut: Dār al-Andalus, 1996), 44.

[15] Prior to Machiavelli, Marsile of Padua and Jan Huss began to elaborate a social theory and theology that prepared the way for an autonomous, non-sacral understanding of the political sphere. Châtelet, *Histoire des Idéologies*, 291.

[16] See Heiko Obermann, *The Reformation: Roots and Ramifications* (Edinburgh: T & T Clark, 1994).

restraint, had to be relegated, be it forcibly or by a cardinal's fiat.[17] To be sure, confessional identity remained a pillar of premodern empires and principalities, but it became a new, more sober creature. Militant and millenarian dissidents were eliminated[18]; idealists and religious reactionaries who failed to submit to the supremacy of the state were sidelined, or worse,[19] as Thomas Moore's tragic fate illustrates.[20]

On the other hand, the privileging of sound government over orthodox religious dogma could open up the door for tolerant state policies in religiously pluralistic societies, as exemplified in the sixteenth and seventeenth centuries by the emperors Akbar (1542–1605) and Dara Shoko in the Mughal Empire or, indeed, as we shall now examine, in Fakhr Ad-Dīn II's (1585–1635) contemporaneous Lebanese emirate.[21]

[17] When in 1626 a Jesuit book affirmed the right of the popes to depose kings for wrongdoing, heresy, or incapacity, it was burned in the Place de Grève at the behest of Cardinal Richelieu (1585–1624) who forced the authors to repudiate the work.

[18] Other examples being the apocalyptic dreams and millenarian delusions of Thomas Müntzer or Shabbatai Zevi in the Ottoman Empire, which were brutally crushed by the new powers that be.

[19] To take one example: when the politically powerful pietist Hans Heinrich Bodmer called for a return to the Gospels in order to cleanse corruption, he was banned and exiled to Neuchatel in 1722.

[20] Prior to his execution by Cromwell, the author of *Utopia* dared to defy the absolutist claims of Henry VIII with the famous, but costly, words: "I am the King's good servant, but God's first," cited in R. H. Tawney, *Religion and the Rise of Capitalism* (London: J. Murray, 1926), 135.

[21] Fakhr Ad-Dīn's contemporary, the Mughal Emperor Akbar (1542–1605) embraced a religious syncretism that to a certain degree resembled the amir's "open door policy" toward religion. In many ways Akbar had even more leeway in abolishing the jizya and declaring himself "infallible" in all matters, religious and secular, in 1579. Akbar's liberalism, however, was successfully resisted by Shaykh Aḥmad al-Sirhindi's (1564–1624) subsequent Islamist polemics, which culminated in the harsh rule of Aurangzeb. See Eugene Smith, *India as a Secular State* (Princeton, NJ: Princeton University Press, 1963), 435; T. N. Madan, *Modern Myths: Locked Minds: Secularism and Fundamentalism in India* (New York: Oxford University Press, 1987).

2 Prototypes of Secularism in Lebanon

This chapter departs from the premodern period, focusing on (Mount) Lebanon's inherited *sociopolitical structure* insofar as it prefigured – or foreclosed – the development of a secular state.

One of the guiding hypotheses of this inquiry is that the travails and traces of secularism in twentieth century Lebanon (as elsewhere) cannot solely be explained from the vantage point of intellectual history. Rather, we must leave the level of discursive analysis and turn our attention to the premodern and modern political entities in the Levant in an attempt to gauge to what degree they accommodated and/or resisted secularism as a pragmatic mode of governance especially suited for pluri-communal societies.

The Premodern Identity and Social Structure of Lebanon: In Search of Proto-Secularism

> One of the central arguments of my book *Imagined Communities* is that nationalisms of all varieties cannot be understood without reflecting on the older political forms out of which they emerged: kingdoms, and especially empires of the pre-modern and modern sort.[1]

> Having set before our eyes a goal toward which shall unswervingly move – the goal being full independence of our country and its complete sovereignty – we are resolved that no promise of reward or threat of punishment shall in the least dissuade us. Fakhr ad-Dīn II al-Ma'an[2]

> Lebanon exists ever since the Amir Fakhr ad-Dīn. Raymond 'Iddih[3]

> *C'est au Liban qu'est née l'idee nationaliste.* Sāṭi' 'Abū al-Khaldūn al-Ḥuṣrī[4]

[1] Benedict Anderson, "Western Nationalism, Eastern Nationalism: Is There a Difference?" *New Left Review* 9 (2001): 33.

[2] Phillip Ḥittī, *Lebanon in History* (London: Macmillan Press, 1957), 380; citing Anīs an-Nuṣūlī, *Rasā'il al-Amīr Fakhr al-Dīn min al-Tūskānā* (Beirut: Manshurāt, 1946).

[3] Cited in *Maghreb-Machrek*, no. 14, 1989, 22.

[4] Cited in Michael Hudson, *The Precarious Republic* (New York: Random House, 1968), 50.

Figure E2.1 This portrait has been authenticated as the only contemporaneous, original depiction of Fakhr ad-Dīn II.
Source: Hāfiz Shihāb, "Reconstructing the Medici Portrait of Fakhr ad-Dīn al-Ma'an," *Muqarnas* 11 (1994): 117–124.

Trans-sectarian political trends antedated the appearance of secularism as a full-fledged ideological component in the discourse of nineteenth-century nationalism. It is therefore by no means fortuitous that it was in the self-same premodern period that the first precursors of proto-national consolidation and secularism should appear in the emirate of Lebanon where the Druze prince Fakhr ad-Dīn II al-Ma'an (1585–1635) would freely shed the sectarian straightjacket, choosing instead to focus on securing vital trade networks running through Mount Lebanon and Palestine, and building a formidable army composed – for the first time – of Maronite, Druze, Sunni, and Shia soldiers alike.

In recompense for his aid dispensed to Selim I during the invasion of the Shām in 1516, Fakhr ad-Dīn II's eponymous grandfather, Fakhr ad-Dīn I, was bestowed the title of "Grand Emir of Lebanon" by the sultan himself.[5] This moment in history has been identified as the beginning of

[5] Kamāl Ṣalībī has cast doubt on this geneology, claiming that Fakhr ad-Dīn's real grandfather Fakhr ad-Dīn 'Uthmān (not 'Ibn 'Uthmān) in fact died ten years before the Ottoman entry at the battle of Marj Dābiq in 1516. Ṣalībī's hypothesis, however, would presuppose an inordinately – if not impossibly – long reign for Fakhr ad-Dīn's father from 1511 to 1585, whom Ṣalībī identifies as the amir qurkmāz. The latter is identified by Duwayhī as the amir who received the investiture from Sultan Selim. See Kamāl Ṣalībī,

the emirate regime, characterized by an administrative autonomy under the authorities of the feudal *seigneurs* headed by Fakhr ad-Dīn I, who constrained the power of the (Sunni) Sayfa and (Shia) Ḥamāda lords while supporting the Ḥarfush and Shihāb dynasties in their stead, extending his suzerainty over "Arabistān from Jaffa to Tripoli."[6] Nonetheless, Fakhr ad-Dīn I fell out with the porte and was executed by the *wālī* of Damascus in 1544.[7] Under the reign of Fakhr ad-Dīn II's father, the amir Qurkmāz, the Ottomans were unable to levy any taxes in the insubordinate Druze areas until a massive campaign in 1585 followed by the amir's execution temporarily redressed this matter. At this point, Fakhr ad-Dīn II, who had been hidden and raised by the Maronite Khāzin lords in Kisirwān, was introduced by his mother to the Druze community at the tender age of seven, winning broad support over the other competing Druze amirs who had lost credibility in the mountain due to their "desire to flatter the Ottoman Porte."[8]

The subsequent period of Druze–Christian comity has been attributed to Fakhr ad-Dīn's upbringing by Abū Saqr al-Khāzin, whom Fakhr ad-Dīn called his "father." The amir's "indebtedness" (*Erkenntlichkeit*)[9] toward the Khāzins was shown when Fakhr ad-Dīn tapped Abū Safī al-Khāzin and Abū Nādir al-Khāzin to accompany and advise him during his Ottoman-imposed exile in Tuscany from 1613 to 1618. Abū Nādir came to serve as Fakhr ad-Dīn's prime minister and right-hand man in

"The Secret of the House of Ma'an," *International Journal of Middle East Studies* 4 (1973): 279.

6 Shihāb, as cited in Ṣalībī "The Secret of the House of Ma'an," 275. The terms Barr al-Shām was used interchangeably with 'Arabistān and Sūryīya up until the end of Ibrāhīm Pasha's reign in 1840. See Bustānī, *Nafīr Sūrīyā*, 21. Ibrāhīm Pasha in his letter to Bashīr Shihāb in 1832 uses the same terms as synonyms. See al-Azīz Nawwār, *Wathā'iq Asāsīya min Tārīkh Lubnān al-Ḥadīth, 1517–1920*, doc. no. 75, 289.

7 See Khalīl Arzūnī, *Ilghā al-tā'ifīya fī Lubnān wa-fasl al-tawā'if 'an al-Dawla: Dirāsa fī al-Tārīkh al-Ijtimā'ī* (Beirut: Khalīl Arzūnī, 1997), 94; Edmond Rabbāth, *La Formation Historique du Liban Politique et Constitutionelle* (Beirut: Librairie Orientale, 1973), 181.

8 Cited in Giovanni Mariti, *Des Herrn Mariti Geschichte F'AkkarDin's wie auch der Uebrigen Gross-Emire bis auf das Jahre 1773* (Gotha: Ettinger, 1790), 85. See Ristelhuber, Traditions Francaises au Liban, 132. Hammer-Purgstall, Geschichte des Osmanischen Reiches, Graz. 1963, vol. IX, 225. Despite these multiple sources, Yūsuf al-Shuwayrī, taking his cue from Kamāl Ṣalībī, contests the story is a fabrication not found in the early biographers of Fakhr ad-Dīn, with the inventor surmised to be Shaybān al-Khāzin (d. 1850). Shuwayrī and Ṣalībī neglect to mention the Florentine Mariti, who preceded Shaikh Shaybān by a generation and who describes the years of Fakhr ad-Dīn's childhood with the Khāzins in great detail. Another contemporary source in which the close relationship of Abū Nādir with Fakhr ad-Dīn is related is Carsten Niebuhr, *Reisebeschreibung Nach Arabien* (Zurich: Manesse Verlag, 1992), 744; Kamāl Ṣalībī, "Fakhr ad-Dīn al-Thānī wa al-Fikra al-Lubnānīya," in *Ab'ād al-Qawmīyā al-Lubnānīya* (Beirut, 1970), 95; Yūssuf al-Shuwayrī, *Modern Arab Historiography* (London: Routledge, 2003), 207ff.

9 Mariti, *Des Herrn Mariti Geschichte F'AkkarDin's*, 7ff.

the course of more than three decades, an unprecedented executive role accorded to a non-Muslim in Mount Lebanon.

To this day, Christian and Muslim Lebanese may be unable to reach a consensus on the specificities of the amir's eclectic personal faith (or lack thereof); yet few would doubt his less enigmatic shrewdness and political acumen in wresting sovereignty from Istanbul and Damascus, a measure of autonomy that – in fiscal and administrative terms – de facto had already been achieved earlier, and was continued after Fakhr ad-Dīn II in Mount Lebanon.[10]

While the late Kamāl Janbulāṭ famously quipped that Fakhr ad-Dīn was "born Druze, lived as a Christian and died as a Muslim," and while a contemporary source described him as an agnostic "not a little inclining to the tyrant,"[11] and another casts doubt on the "Christianity" of the prince's polygamy,[12] he is best remembered today for reinforcing a preexistent policy of religious nondiscrimination and equality between Muslims and Christians[13] within an emirate whose confines would overlap and slightly exceed the borders of Bashīr II emirate and the republic of Lebanon, which came into being after 1920.[14] In fact, one of the early French

[10] Fakhr ad-Dīn's nephew Milḥim defeated the beylerbey of Damascus, Muṣṭafa Pasha, but generally seems to have been more subservient to Istanbul. By contrast, the last Ma'an amir Aḥmad Ma'n refused to obey Ottoman orders.

[11] George Sandys, *A Relation of a Journey* (London: Printed for Andrew Crooke, 1637), 89. Sandys rehashes a current rumor and mistakes the Druze for a French contingent brought by Geofrey during the Crusades, which "fell from the knowledge of Christ."

[12] During his five-year exile in Florence, Fakhr ad-Dīn lived in the company of four wives and numerous consorts, leading d'Arvieux to remark laconically: "*Ce nombre des femmes fait voir que l'Emir n'était pas encore chéretien comme on dit qu'il a été dans la suite, ou que s'était, il vivait tres mal dans sa religion.*" Laurent d'Arvieux, *Mémoires*, ed. Antoine Abdelnour (Beirut: Editions Dar Lahad Khater, 1982), 73.

[13] Ṣalībī notes that the ruling 'Assāfs, who were Sunni Muslims, governed according to feudal usage, customs, and local traditions, which were very different from Islamic Law. Kamāl Ṣalībī, "The Maronites' Historic Insight," *An-Nahār dossier*, 40 (January 9, 1973): 25. Reversing the policy of the prior Mamlūk overlords, Fakhr ad-Dīn inaugurated a policy allowing Maronites and other Christian groups to build churches and toll bells.

[14] The Maronite Patriarchate during the *Mutaṣarrifīya* (1864–1914) periodically raised the call for a return to the borders of the Ma'anite emirate (minus Palestine), as did the first Ottoman Mutassarif, Dāūd Pasha. The vital port-cities of Beirut and Tripoli were not part of the *Réglement*. According to one account, the first explicit mention to a "Greater Lebanon" is made by Paul Juplain/Nujaym (1880–1931) in his *La Question du Liban* (Paris, 1908), although the Otttoman governor Dāūd Pasha himself strove to include the Biqā' and Beirut into the *Mutaṣarrifīya* in 1861. Lebanon's present borders were first drawn in December of 1918 by the Administrative Council under Ḥabīb Pasha al-Sa'd. At the insistence of Patriarch Ḥuwayyik – and Bishara al-Khūrī – Tripoli, Beirut, Sidon, and Tyre, their respective hinterlands, and the fertile valley of the Biqā' (comprising of the four qaḍās Baalbek, the Biqā, Rāshayā, and Hāṣbayā) were formally added to Mount Lebanon in 1920. Michel Shīḥā and the French Commander General de Hartpoul called the Biqā' "notre grenier" and the "granary of the mountain" since the age of Fakhr ad-Dīn, who had been granted control over this fertile region in 1625 by the Ottomans when

chroniclers would – on the eve of the French Revolution – summarize Fakhr ad-Dīn's project thus: "*il proposait de faire une République.*"[15]

The fate of secularism in Lebanon has been inextricably tied to a broader historical quest for a shared notion – or founding myth – of Lebanese nationalism, a myth whose roots stretch further back than the nineteenth century.[16] The multiple pre–nineteenth-century sources – both local and European – cited in this chapter all underscore the prior prevalence of narratives of a tolerant amir bent on independence. Fakhr ad-Dīn's efforts were not wholly unique, but were mirrored by a host of other local potentates striving for autonomy from Istanbul, such as the beylerbey of Erzerum, Abaza M. Pasha.[17] Fakhr ad-Dīn's bid for autonomy, however, distinguished itself by his secular mode of governance as a contemporary observer of the amir's pragmatic politics underscored: "*On pourrait encore conjecturer qu'il n'avait d'autre religion que celle de sa nation.*"[18]

The historical role of Lebanon's legendary *pater patriae* has figured as the touchstone for the "great debate" on identity among Lebanese historians. The ensuing dispute pitted the partisans of Arabism and Islamism against the proponents of Lebanese nationalism, the latter often narrowly defined in terms of the Western alliances and (Maronite) Christianity.[19] Indeed, Fakhr ad-Dīn II, by dint of his entente with

his troops were amassed at the doors of Damascus. Nawfal Niʿmatallāh Ṭarābulsī, *Kashf al-Lithām* (Tarablus: Jarus Birr, 1990), 149.

15 Puget de Saint Pierre, *Histoire des Druses, Peuple du Liban* (Paris: Cailleau, 1763), 39. Bashīr II would likewise enter into a row with Darwīsh Pasha, the wāli of Damascus, who attempted to seize the Biqā' from Bashīr in 1820.

16 Yūsuf Shuwayrī states that "the myth of Fakhr ad-Dīn emerged in the nineteenth century." See Shuwayrī, *Modern Arab Historiography*, 207ff. Kamāl Ṣalībī, *The Modern History of Lebanon* (Westport, CT: Greenwood Press, 1965), 15. This would be consistent with most modern European nationalist revisionisms.

17 Another anti-Ottoman renegade was Dāhir al-ʿUmar who – aided by Russia and Egypt – extended his rule from Acre all across Palestine and Syria, causing the Ottoman Pasha to flee Damascus in 1770.

18 d'Arvieux, Mémoires, 73.

19 In effect, this contentious debate has been traced back to the Crusades, during which Louis IX, king of France, in a never fully authenticated letter declared "the nation of St. Maron" to be "a part of the French nation." Three centuries later, the infamous Medici-pope Leo X dubbed the Maronites "a rose among thorns" in 1510. For a comprehensive treatment of this debate, see, for example, Aḥmad Bayḍūn, *Al-Sirāʿ ʿalā Tārīkh Lubnān* (Beirut: Lebanese University, 1979) and Kamāl Ṣalībī, *House of Many Mansions: The History of Lebanon Reconsidered* (Berkeley: University of California Press, 1989). For the continued vibrancy of these ostensibly hackneyed dualisms, see the reactions to the antimony between Arab-Syrian-Muslim expansionism and Lebanese-Christian particularism as suggested by former Université de Saint Joseph president Fr. Salīm ʿAbdu and the no less visceral rejoinder by Raḍwān as-Sayyid in *al-Āfāq* (1998), 20. As-Sayyid reiterates the basic arguments put forward almost a century earlier by Rashīd Riḍā, who denounced the "zealots of Lebanonism" (*ghulāt al lubnānīya*) who wanted to

Florence and Rome, is often portrayed by his detractors as a lackey of the West. During his forced exile at the court of Cosimo II de Medici in Florence, the renegade prince would nourish such suspicions of collusion by advertising his emirate as an independence-seeking "Christian refuge" in a plea for help addressed to Pope Paul V.[20] The Tuscan Grand Duke – who certainly was not averse to extending and fortifying his commercial networks in the Eastern Mediterranean – was informed that "*Les Turcs lui cherchent querelle, parce qu'il a favorisé les chrétiens et donne refuge et ravitaillement aux bateaux toscans.*"[21] Another contemporary, English source corroborates Fakhr ad-Dīn's subversive agenda and lobbying efforts:

The *Grand Signior* [Fakhr ad-Dīn] doth often threaten his subuersion ... whose displeasure is not so much prouoked by his incroching, as by the reuealed intelligence which he holds with the *Florentine;* whom he suffer to harbor within his hauen of *Tyrus* to come ashore for fresh-water, buyes of him vnderhand his prizes, and furnisheth him with necessaries ... And I am verisly perswaded, that if the occasion were layd hold of, and freely pursued by the Christians, it would terribly shake if not vtterly confound the *Ottoman* Empire.[22]

Likewise, in Druze historiography – and hagiography – Fakhr ad-Dīn figures as a quasi-secular ruler who did "not discriminate between the *ṭawā'if*."[23] In fact, the amir's secular legacy was to be claimed by a prominent torchbearer of Arabism – the late Kamāl Janbulāṭ – who would explicitly invoke the Druze amir as a pathbreaker not only of Lebanese nationalism and independence, but also of secularism, albeit one in which the Druze and Muslims were preordained to rule over the Maronites.[24]

sever the umbilical cord with the Arab and Syrian umma. Needless to say, Riḍā radically opposed any notion of a secular state in Syria or Lebanon.

20 Michel Shiblī, *Fakhreddine Ii Maan* (Beirut: L'Institut de Lettres Orientales de Beyrouth, 1946), 15. Fakhr ad-Dīn was forced to flee Lebanon after the Ottomans sent sixty galleys to subdue him in 1613.

21 The Florentine Usimbardi's letter to the Tuscan grand duc as cited in Shiblī, *Fakhreddine Ii Maan*, 68.

22 Jonathan Haynes, ed., *The Humanist as Traveler: George Sandy's Relation of a Journey Begun An. Dom 1610* (London: Associated University Press, 1986), 119.

23 Abū Ṣāliḥ and Makārim cited in Bernadette Schenk, *Tendenzen und Entwicklungen in Der Modernen Drusischen Gemeinschaft Im Libanon* (Berlin: Klaus Schwarz Verlag, 2002), 221.

24 Incidentally, Fakhr ad-Dīn had granted refuge to the renegade Kurdish *wālī* of Aleppo, 'Alī Janbulad (Canpulatoğlu), although he later imprisoned the Druze shaykh when the latter became a contender in the Shūf. 'Alī Janbulad subsequently became an ally of the invading pasha of Damascus, Ḥāfiẓ when the latter pursued a "scorched earth" policy in the Shūf in 1614, but eventually was executed by the Ottomans in Belgrade in 1615. See 'Abdul Karīm Rāfiq, "The Revolt of 'Alī Pasha Janbulad in the Contemporary Arab Sources and Its Significance," in *Turk Tārīkh Kongresi: Kongreye Sunulan Bildirlir* (Ankara, 1983), 1515–1534.

To be sure, during the civil war, this positive perception came under attack, as Progressive Socialist Party troops during their conquest of the Shūf in 1982 blew up the bronze statue of Fakhr ad-Dīn in his city of birth Ba'aqlīn; at the same time, however, another portrait of Fakhr ad-Dīn at the Janbulāṭ Palace in al-Mukhtāra was left unscathed. The Christian appropriation of Fakhr ad-Dīn was thus directly contested in the first act, while his Druze and national identity continued to be affirmed in al-Mukhtāra.[25]

Kamāl Ṣalībī tried to somewhat attenuate the ostensibly "Maronite–Druze" consensus that had already been advertised in seventeenth-century sources[26] and later was revived by the likes of Maronite historians such as Jurj Ḥarūn, Asad Rustum, Fu'ād Efram al-Bustānī, the Sunni historian 'Ādil Isma'īl, Albert Ḥawrānī, Jubrān Twaynī Sr., Amīn Ma'lūf, or the late politician Raymond 'Iddih who all held that Fakhr ad-Dīn had espoused and inaugurated a coherent version of Lebanese nationalism and proto-independence. To be sure, Ṣalībī was first and foremost responding to those who championed Lebanon as an exclusively Maronite-Christian "nation,"[27] an exceptional island of freedom in a sea of proverbial "Oriental despotism."[28] Even in his revision, Ṣalībī did not contest Fakhr ad-Dīn's role as the first premodern ruler who, emboldened by his economic and military success, spearheaded the first successful revolt against the Ottoman-appointed overlord, the *wālī* of Damascus. The latter was defeated in a battle in 1623 at 'Anjar, ironically the subsequent seat of the Syrian secret service in Lebanon and the

[25] Lucia Volk, "Missing the Nation," PhD dissertation, Anthropology Department, Harvard University, 2001.

[26] Jean de la Roque, *Voyage de Syrie et Du Mont Liban* (Beirut: Dār Lahad Khatar, 1981), 181 where Fakhr ad-Dīn is "prince souverain du Liban et de la Syrie maritime forma dans ce temps-la le project de secouer tout a fait le joug de la domination Turcus."

[27] In 1687, Louis XIV instructed his ambassador in Istanbul and envoys in Syria and Lebanon to use their good offices on behalf of the "Maronite nation." Ḥittī, *Lebanon in History*, 398. The first trace of Maronite nationalism, conceived geographically as the mountain and coastland extending from the Shūf to 'Akkār, is found in Jibrīl Ibn al-Qilā'ī's poetic ode to Lebanon, *Madīḥa Kisirwān fī Jabal Lubnān*. Buṭrus Ḍaw, *Tārīkh al-Mawārina*, vol. II (Dār al-Nahār lil-Nashr, 1967), 282. Nationalisms gain greater coherence in the nineteenth century, although they are not always distinguishable from religious communalism. Monsigieur Nicolas Murād, for instance, called for an explicitly Christian, Maronite Lebanon "pour les Libanais" in 1841. Nicolas Murād, *Notice Historique Sur L'Origine de La Nation Maronite* (Paris: Libraire d'Adrien le Clere, 1844), 33. Later, Sa'īd 'Aql, a poetically gifted, if controversial standard bearer of Lebanese nationalism who at one point was affiliated with the militant Guardians of the Cedar, was branded as one of the shu'ūbī anti-Arabists, a label of treason also used to tar Salma Mūsā, Ṭāḥā Ḥusayn, Ṣādiq Jalāl al-'Aẓm, and Adūnīs. See Anwar al-Jundī, *Al-Shu'bīyat* (Tripoli: Dār al-Shamāl, 1978).

[28] See, for instance, Yūssuf al-Sawda, *Fī Sabīl Lubnān* (Alexandria: Madrasat al-Farīr, 1919), 12ff.

historic military camp, or *mu'askar*, of the 'Ummayids. When Damascus was on the brink of a major famine one year later, Fakhr ad- Dīn, now officially recognized as the *wālī* of Syria, sent 2,000 camels with provisions to ward off a catastrophe.[29]

Intercommunal alliances against foreign occupation had already occurred as early as 1441 when a joint Maronite–Druze delegation arrived in Rome to petition for help against the Mamlūks, while anti-Ottomanism in Mount Lebanon was as old as the Ottoman conquest itself, beginning in 1518 with the revolt of the Sanjakbeyi of Sidon-Beirut Nasir ad-Dīn ibn al-Ḥannāsh and continuing in 1523 and 1524 in wake of the brutally destructive campaigns of Khurrām Pasha, the beylerbey of Damascus, against seventy-four Druze villages.[30] If we add to this the periodic persecution suffered by the Shia community under Ottoman rule,[31] it becomes clear why, in 1527, the Maronite clergy would address itself to Charles V by also including the (Muslim) Arabs in its plea: "In all of Syria, not only the Christians, but also the Arabs appeal to the Emperor for his aid and succor against the Turkish oppressor."[32]

As we have adumbrated, Fakhr ad-Dīn II's father and eponymous grandfather set a biographical trajectory he himself would emulate: semi-sovereign vassal rule followed by execution at the hands of the Ottomans. Fakhr ad-Dīn II al-Ma'an I ended up being charged with sedition, despite his prior vow of allegiance to the invading Sultan Selim the Grim. His son, Qurkmāz, died battling a renewed Ottoman effort to subjugate Mount Lebanon in 1585. It was, however, Qurkmāz's son, Fakhr ad-Dīn II, who was the first governor to openly defy a *firmān* of the porte.[33] To be sure, the maverick "Amīr of Arabistān" and "Prince of Lebanon and the Galilee" would in the end plea for his life and profess his dutiful subservience to the porte, even vainly protesting that the *Sharī'a* had been applied "without mercy" during his reign, albeit, only when faced with his imminent beheading in 1635 in Istanbul, together

[29] Ṭarābulsī, *Kashf al-Lithām*, 149.

[30] The implicit sectarian justification – if not partial motivation – is evident in the fact that Khurram Pasha brought back to Damascus not only four loads of decapitated Druze, but also a large amount of (heretical) religious literature. See Abdul Raḥmān Abū Ḥusayn, "Problems in the Ottoman Administration in Syria during the 16th and 17th Centuries: The Case of the Sanjak of Sidon-Beirut," *International Journal of Middle East Studies* 24.4 (1992): 668.

[31] See the subsequent chapter for a discussion of the Shia'shuhādā.

[32] Cited in Shiblī, *Fakhreddine Ii Maan*, 16 and in *Documents Inédits pour servir à l'Histoire du Christianisme en Orient*, publiés par Antoine Rabbāth (Paris, 1905), 616.

[33] Concerning the appointment of an Orthodox patriarch (Kyrilios Dabbas), instead unilaterally appointing the local favorite (Augustus 'Aṭīyah) after presiding over an election in Ba'albak in 1626 a year after the Ottomans had bestowed on him control over the Biqā'.

with three of his sons.[34] That the announcement of Fakhr ad-Dīn's execution for apostasy and insubordination caused a sense of panic among the Maronite clergy and population – with mass emigration even being pondered as a serious option – only confirms his reputation as *"souverain sur le Liban, maître de la Syrie maritime et grand protecteur des chrétiens.*"[35]

In reaction to Fakhr ad-Dīn's bid for autonomy, the Ottomans attempted to obstruct similar, future secessionist movements by redrawing the administrative districts accordingly. The coastal stretch of Sidon–Beirut (which later was to be incorporated into the Shihāb emirate) was severed from the *wilāya/eyālat* of Damascus or Tripoli and fell under direct control of Istanbul, signaling a tightening of the Ottoman administration, which was explicitly designed to "break the arm of the Arabs."[36]

The legacy of religious tolerance, particularly as regards civil liberties extended to Mount Lebanon's Christian communities, seems to, however, have remained intact under Fakhr ad-Dīn's successors, who also lessened the onerous tax burden of *kharāj*, *'awnīya*, and *awāriz*[37] taxes, which were imposed on non-Sunni Muslims, including the (officially) heterodox Druze, Nusayri, and Shia sects.[38] Some historians have taken umbrage at the usage of epithets, such as "tolerance" and "proto-secularism," emphasizing that such vocabulary reflects a discourse of sectarianism that "was not yet present" in the premodern era.[39] While as we have ascertained in Chapter 1 that the particular concepts of "tolerance" and secularism are indeed of nineteenth-century coinage in all languages, Fakhr ad-Dīn II's and his successors' policies do in fact signal a bold, incipient move toward a mode of governance beyond the hierarchical

[34] de Saint Pierre, *Histoire des Druses*, 95.

[35] de la Roque, *Voyage de Syrie et Du Mont Liban*, 65, 183.

[36] Cited in Abū-Ḥusayn, *The View from Istanbul*, 22. The claim that "the Ottomans were not concerned with stripping Mount Lebanon of its 'independence'" seems to be belied by these precautionary measures and by contemporary travelogues such as those penned by George Sandys who noted the continued struggle against Ottoman rule. See Maqdisī, *The Culture of Sectarianism*, 199. The Jabal Druze and Kisirwān were subsumed under the authority of the newly created wilāya/eyālat of Saida, while Batrūn and Jubayl were attached to the wilāyat of Damascus in 1638. Also see Abū Ḥusayn, "Problems in the Ottoman Administration in Syria," 673.

[37] The latter were a form of ad hoc taxes, which were officially abolished in the 1535 Treaty with France. Ahmad Bayḍūn, *Identité Confessionnelle et Temps Social chez les Historiens Libanais Contemporains* (Beirut: Publications d'Université Libanais, 1984), 424.

[38] d'Arvieux, *Mémoires*, 174. Also see Duwayhī cited in Ilyā F. Ḥarīq, "Political Change in a Traditional Society," PhD dissertation, Chicago, 1964. As indicated earlier, such conciliatory steps toward religious minorities paralleled the lifting of the jizya tax for Hindus by Emperor Akbar (1542–1605) in Mughal India.

[39] Maqdisī, *The Culture of Sectarianism*, 36.

communalism of the *millet* system.[40] More to the point, the multiple testimonies of the Ma'anite emirate serving as a shelter from sectarian persecution may refute the charge of anachronistic interpolation. One visiting eyewitness underscored that "*ce qui fut la sage politique de Facardin, en admettant dans ses états la liberté de conscience.*"[41] Indigenous chronicles, such as that penned by Isṭfān Duwayhī, further bespeak a disposition that cannot but be described as one of religious tolerance. It coheres with the depiction of civic liberties recorded by a seventeenth-century French visitor to Fakhr ad-Dīn's Beirut:

> *Tous les citoyens de Beyrouth de quelque religion qu'il soient, vivent bien ensemble ... Les Chrétiens sont répandus partout. Ils ont une liberté entière de faire ouvertement tous les exercices de leur religion, de batir des églises et de porter le turban blanc.*[42]

To be sure, the premodern political environment never reached the state of full-fledged, fully enshrined secularism in which communal identities could be disregarded with impunity. While the Ma'anite amirs recognized the administrative benefits of winning the trust and support of a heterogeneous population through nondiscriminatory policies, in the larger scheme of things, they could not upend the wider, inherited confessional hierarchy and political framework entirely. Thus, in order to be recognized by the Ottoman porte, Druze amirs such as Fakhr ad-Dīn II had to not only submit their annual *mīrī* payment, but also to assiduously present themselves as Sunni Muslims in order to see their imperial investiture confirmed. After all, according to a series of *fatwās* issued from Damascus and Aleppo, the Druze were exempted from any state protection as their status was below that of the *dhimmi* Christians and Jews.[43] During his trial in Istanbul, apostasy figured as the chief accusation leading to the death verdict against the amir.[44]

The last Ma'anite amir and nephew of Fakhr ad-Dīn, Aḥmad Ma'n, would try to safeguard the legacy of Muslim–Christian coexistence and intercommunal cooperation in Mount Lebanon after he was appointed

[40] Also see Maurus Reinkowski, *Ottoman Multiculturalism?* (Beirut: Orient-Institut, 1999), 16. The earliest Arabic translation of the French tolerance is probably by Adīb Isḥāq, who identifies this practice as the "secret of European civilization." See Adīb Isḥāq, "Al-Ta'aṣṣub wa al-Tasāhul," in *Aḍwā' 'alā al-Ta'assub: Majmū'at mu'alifīn min Adīb Ishaq wa al-Afghānī* (Beirut: Dār Amwāj, 1993), 13.

[41] de Saint Pierre, *Histoire des Druses*, 26.

[42] d'Arvieux, *Mémoires*, 146, 174.

[43] The sixteenth-century historian Ibn Tulūn wrote an entire treatise entitled *Sall al-Sārim 'alā aṭibā'al-Ḥākim bi-Amr Allāh* "the extirpation of the followers of the followers of Ḥakīm." See Abū Ḥusayn, "Problems in the Ottoman Administration in Syria," 667.

[44] de Saint Pierre, *Histoire des Druses*, 95.

in 1667 over the Jurd, Gharb, Shūf, Kisirwān, and Matn.[45] The experience of the forebears of Lebanon's most celebrated poet and national symbol of *convicencia*, Jubrān Khalīl Jubrān,[46] sheds light on the confessional tolerance that marked Aḥmad Ma'n's reign.

The Amir Aḥmad Ma'n would not merely prolong Fakhr ad-Dīn's liberal domestic policies, but also emulate his grand-uncle's fatal defiance of orders ushering from the Ottoman porte. In 1687, Aḥmad Ma'n declined to serve in a holy war against the Habsburgs and instead seized the moment to stage a large rebellion in alliance with the Shia Ḥamāda's in 1697. With this pyrrhic victory, the final fate of the Ma'anite dynasty seemed sealed,[47] particularly in light of the fact that Aḥmad Ma'n died without leaving any male progeny. Both his daughter and the daughter of his father Milḥim Ma'n (d. 1658), however, married the Shihāb princes of Ḥasbayā and Rāshayā yūs, who eventually would establish themselves as the new rulers of Mount Lebanon.[48] In other words, Milhim Ma'n was the maternal grand-uncle of the first Shihāb ruler, Bashīr I (d. 1706) and the great-grandfather of the Amir Bashīr II Shihāb (1767–1850).

The lineage shared by the amirs Fakhr ad-Dīn II and Bashīr II, however, was not merely one of blood, but also of policies. Despite his revision of the classical Lebanese nationalist narrative, Ṣalībī does recognize that it was Fakhr ad-Dīn who had set the paradigm for later "*umarā*" striving for autonomy such as the amirs Aḥmad al-Ma'n and Bashīr II Shihāb. According to one European travelogue:

> [The] Emir Beshir's government resembles perfectly that of the Osmanlys in the eastern part of Syria but there is one great advantage which these people enjoy under his command – an almost complete exemption from all personal exactions

[45] Aḥmad Ma'n allied with the Shia' Ḥamāda's – who were tellingly designated as "the accursed kızılbash" by the Ottomans. Abū-Ḥusayn, *The View from Istanbul*, 61. After his death in 1697 without male offspring, the Shihāb dynasty – the family-in-laws of the Ma'an – took over until 1841.

[46] Jubrān's great-great grandfather was Jubrān Abū Rizq, a Maronite lord who was a close ally of the Amir Fakhr ad-Dīn, an alliance that stirred the suspicion and ire of the Ottomans. After being framed by a possibly trumped-up charge of embezzlement, Ḥusayn Pasha of Tripoli in 1687 forced his son Yunes Jubrān and his family to convert to Islam. Thereupon, Yunes Jubrān fled to the Ma'an emirate of where he could freely reconvert to Christianity. Yet, when he was recaptured in 1697 by Tripoli's new governor Qabalān Mohamad, he preferred to accept a humiliating and brutal public torture and execution by strangulation rather than save his skin once more by ways of a deceitful conversion. It is part of the cruel irony of history that revenues from Jubrān's English opus were used to finance various militias during the civil war of 1975. One week before the outbreak of the fighting, the grave of this most anti-sectarian author was profaned by bigots in Bisharre. Jean-Pierre Daḥdāḥ, *Khalīl Gibran* (Paris: Editions Albin Michel S. A., 2004), 34–36, 504.

[47] Abū-Ḥusayn, *The View from Istanbul*, 15.

[48] Ṣalībī, "The Secret of the House of Ma'an," 273.

and the impartiality of justice, which is dealt with in the same manner out to the Christian and the Turk.[49]

The Amir Bashīr II Shihāb and Ibrāhīm Pasha of Egypt in Barr ash-Shām in many ways resuscitated Fakhr ad-Dīn's legacy as quasi-secular rulers over a reconsolidated Lebanese emirate[50] by declining to enforce any discriminatory practices against non-Muslims[51] and enabling the Shia of Jabal 'Āmil to enjoy a brief period of economic efflorescence.[52]

They also, as we shall see, revived the Druze amir's earlier initiatives on the economic plane by launching a wide-reaching development project, expanding the infrastructure and transportation routes and planting olive and mulberry trees to promote silk production, the main source of income for Mount Lebanon's economy up until World War I. Their concomitant effort to integrate landholdings in Mount Lebanon into the regional and global economy, however, would necessitate a face-off with the feudal lords, a costly confrontation that Fakhr ad-Dīn had eschewed, having preferred cooptation.[53]

Translating the spirit of republicanism into concrete policies would, however, carry ambivalent, unintended, and often adverse consequences for the denizens of the emirate and the Barr ash-Shām. The challenge for Lebanon ever since has been how to forge a unitary nation out of a patchwork of communalisms without exacerbating the latter in the process of nation-building.

We shall now proceed to examine the features of Amir Bashīr's regime and the Egyptian interregnum (1831–1841) insofar as it may have prefigured key features of secular governance. Instead of relating the accustomed chronology of events in Lebanon, we shall pursue a bifocal

[49] Johann Ludwig Burckhardt, *Travels in Syria and the Holy Land* (London, 1877), 12.

[50] Borrowing the French terminology introduced by Napoleon in Egypt, Barr ash-Shām under Ibrāhīm was no longer divided according to eyālat, but "directorates" (mudīra). The borders in the northeast were Antep, Kilis, and under the mudīra of Aleppo, while the southern borders were marked by the mudīra of Sidon, which extended well into Palestine. Ibrāhīm personally became the ḥukumdār of Damascus after Bashīr Shihāb expressed his preference to remain the amir of the Lebanese emirate, which, besides Mount Lebanon, encompassed the Biqā' and Jabal 'Āmil. Asad Rustum, *Bashīr Bayna al-Sulṭān wa al-'Azīz: 1804–1814*, vol. I (Beirut: al- Jāmi'a al-Lubnānīya, 1966), 104.

[51] Ibrāhīm Pasha would even go so far as to reprimand the governor of Beirut, Maḥmūd Nami Bek, for uttering uncouth slurs against some Christians. Rustum, *Bashīr Bayna al-Sulṭān wa al-'Azīz*, vol. I, 97–100.

[52] Tamara Chalabi, *The Shi 'is of Jabal 'Amil and the New Lebanon: Community and Nation-State, 1918–1943* (New York: Palgrave Springer, 2006), 14.

[53] Richard van Leeuwen, "Monastic Estates and Agricultural Transformation in Mount Lebanon in the 18th Century," *International Journal of Middle East Studies* 23.4 (1991): 613.

analysis by tracing in broad if detailed sketches the respective political trajectories of Lebanon and a country sharing a roughly comparable heritage of communal diversity, size, and geographic topography: Switzerland.

In embarking upon this juxtaposition, I shall devote particular attention to the virtually synchronous subjection to Napoleonic reform, outlining the series of institutional arrangements, which were devised in wake of the parallel formation of secular and sectarian communal dynamics up until the establishment of the Republic of Lebanon and the Helvetian Confederation. In particular, this bifocal section of the book seeks to adduce multiple factors accounting for the similar initial sociohistorical parameters, and the divergent subsequent gestation of secularism and nationalism in each of the respective Swiss and Lebanese cases.

Highlighting the apparent obduracy and recurrence of confessionalism in Lebanon is not tantamount with adopting an analytical prism of primordialism pure and simple. Rather, even if *ṭā'ifīya* has been likened to a simmering volcano, then it is all the more incumbent on us to gauge the tectonic shifts – in demography and ideology – that account for periodic eruptions on the one hand, and phases of secularizing stabilization on the other, in both "Oriental" and "Occidental" history.

Origins and Formation of the Lebanese State: The Two Switzerlands: A Concise Comparison of Two Distinctly Related Consociational Models

Figure E2.2 Engraving of Beirut and environs, embraced by Mount Sannine and the Mediterranean Sea. John Carne and W. H. Barlett, Syria, London, 1838, 8.

Figure E2.3 Panorama of Zurich and Lake Zurich in the 1990s with the skyline stretching from the Säntis (on the left) to the Glarner Alps (on the right) in the horizon. Photography courtesy of Christian Heeb, Exposa Verlags GmbH.

All annals tell of what has transpired in our nations And of those who dwelled before us in Mount Lebanon	كل التواريخ بتخبرنا عن ما جرى في مواطنا والذين كانوا قبلنا سكان في جبل لبنان
There were kings among them and heroic men who protected the shores and the mountains.	كان ملوك منهم وأبطال احمو السواحل والأجبال

Jibrīl Ibn al-Qilā'ī (1450–1516)[54]

La montagne … est un obstacle, et, du même coup, un abri, un pays pour hommes libres.

Elle est le refuge des libertés, des démocraties, de républiques paysannes.[55]

Alors le Liban deviendrait une Suisse orientale.[56]

[54] Madīḥat Kisirwān fī Jabal Lubnān cited. In Ḍaw, *Tārīkh al-Mawārina*, vol. III, 282. To preserve some of the poetic rhyme of the original Arabic quatrain, I have translated *mawāṭinā* with "nations," cognizant that "abodes" or "territories" is a more accurate, less anachronistic translation.

[55] Fernand Braudel, *La Méditerranée et le Monde Méditerranéen a l'époque de Philippe II: La Part du Milieu*, vol. I (Paris: Armand Colin, 1966), 34–35.

[56] J. Yanoski and J. David, *La Syrie ancienne et moderne* (Paris: Univers Pittoresque, Asie, t. VII, 1848), 365. One should add that Switzerland is invoked here as paradigm of peace and prosperity held out for a Maronite community tortured by "tant de larmes et tant de sang." The authors entreat France to intervene to stop the Ottoman and Druze transgressions and establish a separate Maronite state, citing the Balkan precedents of Moldavia and Serbia. This call would find its echo in the discourse of the Lebanese Front, which called for a "Swiss solution" during the 1975 civil war. Federalism here, however, served as a euphemism for separatism and thus bore little resemblance to the Swiss confederation. See 'Ārif al-'Abd, *Lubnān wa al-Ṭā'if* (Beirut: Center for Arab Unity Studies, 1993), 224.

The simile likening Lebanon to Switzerland has captured the imagination of Orientalists since the early nineteenth century, both on account of political and natural topographic affinities.[57] At first glance, the famous paean to the spirit of Swiss autonomy, William Wordsworth's *Thought of a Briton on the Subjugation of Switzerland*, seems almost more fitting as a depiction of the Lebanese emirate rather than landlocked Switzerland[58]:

> Two Voices are there; one is of the sea,
> One of the mountains; each a mighty Voice:
>
> In both from age to age thou didst rejoice,
> They were thy chosen music, Liberty!
>
> There came a Tyrant, and with holy glee
> Thou fought'st against him; but hast vainly striven:
> Thou from thy Alpine holds at length art driven,
> Where not a torrent murmurs heard by thee.
> Of one deep bliss thine ear hath been bereft:
> Then cleave, O cleave to that which still is left;
> For, high-souled Maid, what sorrow would it be
> That Mountain floods should thunder as before,
> And Ocean bellow from his rocky shore,
> And neither awful Voice be heard by thee![59]

In point of fact, this poetic evocation of age-old liberties and dogged resistance to external hegemonies contains a kernel of historical truth in both the case of Lebanon, and, even more so, as regards Switzerland. One need not even engage the misty mythology surrounding the

[57] Besides David and Yanoski, the French poet Alphonse de Lamartine and the Swiss founder of the Quaker school in Brumanna, Theophilius Waldmeier, invoked this metaphor. It gained renewed popularity after the publication of Jacques Tabet, *Pour faire du Liban la Suisse du Levant: apercu sur les conditions politiques, economiques et touristiques des deux pays* (Paris: Ramlot, 1924). In which the natural beauty of the two countries is compared with a view to Lebanon's potential as a tourist destination. Fu'ād al-Khūrī and Alfred Naccache made the same case. The topos of a "mountain republic" has also been applied to the Pyrenees (Andorra) and San Marino in the Apennines. Daniel J. Elazar, "Communal Democracy and Liberal Democracy: An Outside Frien's Look at the Swiss Political Tradition," *Publius* 23.2 (1993): 3. Jackie Drucker and Khalīl Abū al-Naṣr, "A Swiss in Lebanon," *Saudi Aramco* (July/August 1975): 32–40.

[58] For a suggestive elaboration of the duality of the sea and the mountain, see Albert Ḥawrānī, "Ideologies of the Mountain and the City," in *Essays on the Crisis in Lebanon*, ed. Roger Owen (London: Ithaca Press, 1976).

[59] William Wordsworth, *Complete Poetical Works by William Wordsworth* (London: Macmillan & Co., 1888), 361. The poem was penned during Wordsworth's peregrinations through Switzerland between October 30, 1806 and February 6, 1807.

Helvetians and the Phoenicians, both of which, ironically, seem to have been refugee migrants.[60]

The joint departure point might be sought in the relative autonomy the foundational Swiss mountain cantons (Uri, Schwyz, and Unterwalden) wrested from the Habsburg Empire from 1231 onward on the one hand,[61] and the development of a feudal aristocracy based on hereditary land tenure in Mount Lebanon (Jubayl, Matn, Bisharrī, Shūf, and Kisirwān),[62] which survived even the self-same thirteenth-century period of forcible centralization under the Mamlūks on the other hand.[63] Inaccessible topography precluded direct imperial penetration and lent these constitutive cantons a considerable amount of autonomy in administrating their affairs. This held equally true for religious affairs in that the (heterodox) Druze, Shia, Maronite, and Sunni communities could circumvent or ignore ecclesiastic decrees emanating from the distant centers of religious authority.[64] We might note that, when the Maronite Bishop Nicolas Murād speaks of Jazzār's or 'Abdullāh Pasha's vain attempts to conquer "*le Liban*," he is essentially referring to these

[60] One of the oldest extant documents, *Das Weisse Buch von Sarnen*, identifies the Swiss as economic migrants from Sweden. Likewise, the Semitic origins of the Phoenicians remain an unresolved enigma of history since Herodotus. Avid Swiss and Lebanese nationalists have been wont to aver the ancient "nationhood" of their eponymous ancestors. Caesar granted the Helvetians the status of self-governship, even as the coastal cities of Tyre and Sidon were bestowed the same status in the Roman Empire. For a succinct summary of the literature dealing with the debate on the Swiss origins, see Philip Farha, "Switzerland: Coherent Incoherence," BA honors thesis, Wesleyan University, 1993.

[61] Berne and Zurich both obtained the status of autonomy in 1218. The German Emperor Friedrich II exempted the mountain-states of Uri in 1231 and Schwyz in 1240 from the jurisdiction of any counts and dukes so they would be direct ("*reichsunmittelbare*") subjects of the emperor. Along with Nidwalden, these three states are said to have participated in the foundational oath on top of the Rütli in August 1291. On October 14, 1648 the Peace of Osnabrück confirmed the full independence that the Swiss Eidgenossenschaft de facto had attained earlier.

[62] In the phase between the 'Abbasid purges and the violent Mamlūk campaign of 1305, the Kisrwān may have been predominantly Shia, whereas the Shūf only became the home of the Druze after the thirteenth-century migration of Druze from the Ḥawrān. Jabal 'Āmil occupied a similar role in Shia self-perception. Thus, the area of today's Lebanon could be conceived as not one, but several, sectarian shelters. For an early account of the Shia settlement in Kisrwān, see the vernacular history of Jurgis Zughayb (1729–1801), *'Awdat al-Naṣāra ilā Jurūd Kisirwān*, ed. Bulūs Qar'alī [1870] (Beirut: Mu'assassat Khalīfa lil-Tabā'a, 1983), 1–18.

[63] Ṣalībī, *The Modern History of Lebanon*, 5.

[64] In the views of a fifteenth-century quantrian penned by the Maronite Bishop of Cyprus and first graduate of the Maronite college in Rome, Jibrīl Ibn al-Qilā'ī (1450–1516), the Maronites would welcome those who shared their faith and sought shelter from the "promoters of heresy and sowers of innovation." Cited in Ḍaw, *Tārīkh al-Mawārina*, vol. III, 274.

Maronite mountain strongholds,[65] even as renowned Shia poets such as al-Shannāʿa al-Mariāḥī would extol the bravery of the men of Jabal ʿĀmil in fending off the oppression of the self-same despot.[66]

This is not to suggest that there was a codification of (full) civil and religious freedoms in the premodern era; that would only come after the promulgation of the constitution of 1848 in Switzerland, and after 1926 in Lebanon, even though Article 15 of the (1878) Swiss constitution would establish the full freedom of religion and proscribe coercion of any kind in a far more explicit manner than Article 9 of the Lebanese constitution.[67] In the oldest authenticated political document of 1291, the *Foedus Pactus* [68] or "federal pact" (also known as the *Bundesbrief*), the three foundational Swiss cantons reclaim their autonomy and full freedom as "*reichsunmittelbare*" cantons *vis-à-vis* the Habsburg "reeve" or "governor" (*Vogt*), a privilege of "unmediated" subordination only officially bestowed on the southern Druze ranges of the Lebanese emirate exactly three centuries later in 1591.[69] While the *Bundesbrief* contains an allusion to the observance of hierarchical ranks and rules of obedience between the social castes,[70] the overall focus is on a defense of fundamental, inviolable freedoms, rights, and obligations of the confederates/ *Eidgenossen* without any further qualifications or distinctions of rank or religion. We may rightfully doubt an exaggerated cliché of completely idyllic alpine valleys, wholly free of all feudal hierarchies and structures; still, in the 1291 pact, the radical rejection of any outside jurisdiction over the affairs of the three states is unequivocally asserted, as are the rights of

65 Murād, *Notice Historique Sur L'Origine de La Nation Maronite*, 22, 33.

66 My thanks to Shady Ḥikmat Nāṣir for lending me a copy of one of these poems.

67 The Swiss Article mentions the protection of the citizen from coerced religious education in contrast to the Lebanese constitution. The ancient prefatory phrase "In the name of God the almighty!" still adorning the 1815 *Bundesvertrag*, disappeared from the 1848 constitution, while being reintroduced in the 1874 revision. The latter still contained a confessional bias in Article 58, which proscribed any activities on Swiss territory of the Order of Jesuits. *Quellenwerk zur Entstehung der Schweizerischen Eidgenossenschaft*, three vols. (Aarau: Verlag H. R. Sauerlander & Cie. 1933), 33.

68 From the Latin *foedus*: "oath" or German: "*Eid*." The Swiss confederation derives its name from the communal, multilateral oaths that sealed cantonal alliances. French diplomatic correspondence referred to a *Corps Helvétique* (*Corpus Helveticum*), while, after 1848, the French "*Confédération Suisse*" (from the official Latin *Confoederatio Helvetica*) and the German "*Schweizerische Eidgenossenschaft*" became the official designations.

69 Like ad hoc arrangements existed under the Mamlūks. Kamāl Ṣalībī, "The Lebanese Identity," *Journal of Contemporary History* 6.1 (1971): 77.

70 The reference to a "prior pact" indicates a prior legacy of assertions of autonomy: "*Gelobt in Erneuerung des alten, eidlich bekräftigten Bundes – jedoch in der Weise, dass jeder nach seinem Stand seinem Herren geziemend dienen soll.*" *Quellenwerk zur Entstehung der Schweizerischen Eidgenossenschaft*, vol. 1, 776.

individual life and property against the "*maliciam temporis*," the "malice of time."[71]

Arguably then, the impregnable mountainous terrain did aid the rugged ranges of Switzerland and Lebanon in their premature evasion of the heavy hand of foreign overlords, and prevented their full subordination to the imperial *fiat,* even as variants of a feudalistic system remained the cornerstone of social organization. Switzerland's vital role as a safe haven for political exiles (mainly from Prussia and Germany) extended into the nineteenth and twentieth century,[72] while Lebanon filled the same role for numerous families from Tripoli, Damascus, and Aleppo during the reigns of Fakhr ad-Dīn II and Bashīr Shihāb. During the latter's reign, Lebanon became known as a "shelter which protects everyone who seeks succor."[73]

Nonetheless, the simile must take account of distinct differences. For, if (Mount) Lebanon continued to be subjected to vacillating degrees of Mamlūk and Ottoman oversight until World War I, the Habsburg yoke was thrown off rather early in the founding Swiss cantons and autonomous cities. As Rousseau would marvel during his formative travels in Switzerland, since time immemorial, the mountain cantons, unlike the urban centers, held quasi-democratic town councils in the Swiss confederation of core *Waldstädte.*[74] It was this provincial assembly of a *Dorf-, Kirch- or Landes-gemeinde,* rather than a transregional council of notables headed by a "prince," as was the case in among the various Lebanese emirates,[75] which was endowed with executive electoral powers. The Swiss *Tagsatzung*, or "Federal Diet," thus allowed for a modicum of

[71] "*Wir haben auch einhellig gelobt und festgesetzt, dass wir in den Tälern durchaus keinen Richter, der das Amt irgendwie um Geld oder Geldeswert erworben hat oder nicht unser Einwohner oder Landmann ist, annehmen sollen.*" *Quellenwerk zur Entstehung der Schweizerischen Eidgenossenschaft*, vol. 1, 778.

[72] In 1815, Metternich's angry demand for extradition of Prussian dissidents was met with dilatory disregard on the part of the Swiss authorities. See Louis Burgener, "Napoléon Bonaparte et la Suisse: Méthodes et Décisions," *The French Review* 45.1 (1971): 49.

[73] Thus runs a verse in Nicola al-Turk's Diwān cited in Rustum, *Bashīr Bayna al-Sulṭān wa al-'Azīz*, vol. I, 11. In 1804, the zu'amā of the Inkishārīya in Aleppo sought refuge with Bashīr, in 1812, the muftī of Damascus, Ḥusayn Efendi al-Murādī, did the same after entering a dispute with Sulaymān Pasha, followed in 1824 by the asylum granted to Muṣṭafā Āghā, the mutassalim of Tripoli.

[74] "There is hardly a journey undertaken by Rousseau that does not begin and end in Switzerland, hardly a work from his pen that does not model itself on the imagined virtues of its towns and villages, or defend those virtues against the ravages of a civilizing corruption." Benjamin R. Barber, "How Swiss Is Rousseau?" *Political Theory* 13.4 (November 1985): 475.

[75] Such as the Tanukhids, the Banu Sayfa, the Bani 'Assaf, and the Ma'anites inter alia. For a detailed history of the complex transmutations in the regimes over the expanse of the later Ma'anite emirate, see Makkī, *Lubnān 635–1516.*

gradually increasing centralizing integration from 1415 onward. While somewhat mirroring the council of notables in Mount Lebanon and the council of village *wakīls* sent to the *'āmmīya* convocations in Anṭilyās of 1821, 1840, and 1858, the delegates who were dispatched to the Swiss convocation – as often as twenty times a year – never wielded the sweeping powers the Lebanese amirs were endowed with.[76] Power in the formally nonhierarchical alliance of the Swiss *Eidgenossenschaft* then was always less personalized, with key prerogatives left to the communal councils, at least in the *Waldstädte* mountain cantons where political rights were at least nominally of universal application. This was not so for many of the cities, such as Bern and Fribourg, which restricted public offices to "capable ruling castes" (*regimentfähige Familien*), nor for Zurich and Basel, where oligarchic guilds and landed aristocracies held a tight grip on power prior to Napoleonic reform under the Helvetic Republic of 1798. Still, the case can be made that the authority of the Swiss notables only rarely matched that of the regional, feudal families and *mashāyikh* of Mount Lebanon.

If democratic practices were further developed in Switzerland by comparison with Mount Lebanon – and indeed compared to most of central Europe[77] – so too were the first precursors of secularism. While more an expression of territorial claims than anticlericalism, in the 1370 *Pfaffenbrief*, all clerics (*Pfaffen*) were subjected to ordinary local, worldly courts in criminal cases.[78] More to the point, by May 25, 1802 – and again in 1847 – the entire country participated in a referendum on the new Helvetic constitution, signifying a decree of official recognition of the individual citizen not attained even to this day in Lebanon.[79] Ironically,

[76] "The Emir could appoint who he wanted and dismiss as he liked, yet he could not thereby select anyone from outside [the circle of] feudal families." Rustum, *Bashīr Bayna al-Sulṭān wa al-'Azīz*, vol. I, 4.

[77] Martin Luther already singled out – half in admiration, half in desperation – the democratic intransigence of the Swiss after the Swabian Wars. Faced with the looming specter of "mobocracy" ("*Herrn Omnes*") in the peasants' revolt, Luther repeatedly railed against the potential anarchy wrought by uninhibited, frenetic masses, "*der tolle Poebel*," whose nefarious influence he associated with democracy as it was exemplified in the Swiss confederation. Joachim Ritter, ed., *Historisches Wörterbuch der Philosophie*, vol. II (Basel: Schwabe, 1971), 51; Heinrich Bornkamm, *Luther's Geistige Welt* (Gütersloh: Bertelsmann, 1953), 3.

[78] Quellenwerk zur Entstehung der Schweizerischen Eidgenossenschaft, 33–36.

[79] The full enshrinement of the national referendum as a constitutional principle came in 1874. After 1894, the possibility of constitutional amendments by popular vote ("initiatives") was adduced. Constitutional amendments require two majorities: that of the population (*Volksmehr*) and of the cantons (*Ständemehr*). Former prime minister, Salīm al-Ḥuṣṣ, has proposed introducing the referendum mechanism into the Lebanese system so as to circumvent the stranglehold of the sectarian political lords (*zu'amā'*) and imbue the Lebanese with a greater sense of citizenship. Salīm al-Ḥuṣṣ, "Prospective

the newly enfranchised electorate narrowly voted down the compromise document drafted under the aegis of Napoleon, the "*Constitution de la Malmaison.*" Thus, the reform objective of the self-avowed "son of the mountain's" plebiscite was subverted in the first referendum by the "mountain people" he claimed to know so well.[80]

Be that as it may, Napoléon Bonaparte's (1769–1821) coeval impact on the erection of the secular nation-state in both Switzerland and the Levant proved incisive. Even if the brash general may not have succeeded in his planned conquest of Syria and Palestine, in Ibrāhīm Pasha (1789–1848) and Bashīr II Shihāb (1767–1850) he would find most loyal – and no less merciless and military-minded – torchbearers of his revolutionary agenda of reforms. As we shall see, the administrative measures embarked upon under Bashīr and his patron Ibrāhīm Pasha would fall short of full-scale secularization. Nonetheless, they mark the first concerted attempt to uproot the feudal and clientelist system of Mount Lebanon, vestiges of which have survived until the present day and undergird the peculiar shape sectarianism has taken in Lebanon.

Bashīr II Shihāb was born in 1767, just after half of his family – including his father – had embraced Christianity, quite possibly for pragmatic reasons in view of the Maronite demographic majority in Mount Lebanon. Like the Maʿanite amirs, Bashīr II would extend his domain beyond Mount Lebanon upon being appointed a *multazim* (tax-farmer) over Kisirwān and the Shūf.[81] After the abdication of his cousin Yūsuf in 1788, Bashīr II was elected by the emirate's council of notables as the new amir. The governor of Damascus and Acre, Aḥmad "Jazzār"[82] Pasha (1775–1804), would later appoint Bashīr as *wāli* (governor) of Mount Lebanon, the Biqāʿ, and Jabal ʿĀmil, a territory comprising three quarters of today's Republic of Lebanon. The coastal cities of Beirut,

Change in Lebanon," in *Peace for Lebanon: From War to Reconstruction*, ed. Deidre Collins (London: Lynne Rienner, 1994).

80 Jonathan Steinberg, *Why Switzerland?* (Cambridge: Cambridge University Press, 1996), 9.

81 Michael Mishāqa bills him "the ruler of Lebanon whom all Syria obeys." *Muntakhabāt min al Jawāb ala al-Iqtirah* (Beirut, 1955), 184.

82 Jazzār's frightening sobriquet ("the butcher") is invoked in the poems of the vernacular Shia poet Al-Shannāʿa al-Maryāḥī. It appears again in the history written by Haydar al-Shihābī (1763–1835) and Napoleon's dragoman and secretary (and subsequent court poet of Bashīr II), the Lebanese Nicolas al-Turk (1763–1828), who otherwise is keen to please the views of his patrons. Bashīr's relationship with Aḥmad Jazzār vacillated between opportunistic alliances (at the outset) to full-fledged, mortal conflict (at the end). See Jurj M. Ḥaddād, "The Historical Work of Niqula El- Turk 1763–1828," *Journal of the American Oriental Society* 81.3 (1961): 247–251. Rustum cites the poem attributed by Turk to Ilyās Iddī, in which the demise of the "blood-shedder" and "butcher" of Acre is celebrated. Rustum, *Bashīr Bayna al-Sulṭān wa al-ʿAzīz*, vol. I, 3.

Sidon, and Tripoli, which had constituted part of the Ma'anite emirate, would be restored to the emirate after the conquest of Ibrāhīm Pasha in 1831.[83] No sooner had Bashīr Shihāb begun to establish his foothold, than the region was subjected to what might be seen a sudden, frontal collision with the full weight of the French Revolution. A cursory glance at developments in Central Europe will disclose a similar dynamic unleashed by the legal and economic transformations, which followed the almost concurrent, forcible introduction of the *Code Napoléon* in wake of the proclamation of the Helvetic Republic on March 14, 1798, that *annus mirabilis*.

Napoleon Bonaparte and His Arab Acolytes: Nineteenth-Century Enlightened Despotism?[84]

> These transgressions against the subjects (*ri'āyā*) are a source of our displeasure and discontent, for all Muslims and Christians are equally our subjects, and the matter of the *madhhab* (denomination) is to have no bearing on the governing of politics (*mā lahu madkhal bihukm as-siyāsa*). It is therefore imperative that everyone enjoy a state of safety to go about his Islam and his Christianity, even as nobody ought to lord over the other.
>
> Ibrāhīm Pasha[85]

When Napoleon Bonaparte first arrived on the shores of the Eastern Mediterranean on July 2, 1798, carrying the torch of the revolution and announcing the "return of the country to its citizens," tidings of the news were welcomed by many Christians in Egypt and Syria.[86] Citing this

[83] As we have seen, the coastal cities during the Ma'anite emirate largely eluded the control of the governors of Sidon, Tripoli, and Damascus, even though there was a continual tug of war with the Ottoman authorities over the coastal strip. Under the Shihābs, Ḥaydar (in 1729) and Milḥim (in 1749) succeed in reasserting control over the highly contested and lucrative port cities.

[84] References to a "very enlightened" Amir Bashīr were made by the British Counsel Edward B. Barker in Aleppo. See *Syria and Egypt under the Last Five Sultans of Turkey, Being the Experiences, during Fifty Years, of Mr. Consul-General Barker* (New York: Arno Press, 1973 [1876]), 2, 225. Subsequently, Kamāl Ṣalībī repeats this earlier designation of Bashīr Shihāb II as an "enlightened despot." Ṣalībī, "The Lebanese Identity," 76–81.

[85] Ibrāhīm Pasha upon assuming his tenure as Wālī Barr ash-Shām, in a letter addressed to the governor (mutassalim) of Latakia in 1832. Cited in Rustum, *Bashīr Bayna al-Sulṭān wa al-'Azīz*, vol. I, 99.

[86] The overall Muslim reaction to Napoleon's advent in Egypt cannot be broached here in detail. On July 24, 1798, Bonaparte issued a decree establishing the first representative body composed of local Egyptians, the *Majlis al-'ām*. All previous Mamlūk and Ottoman councils had excluded local Arabs. On October 6, 1798, however, the council – which was only given consultative, rather than full executive powers – rebuffed Napoleon's overtures and demanded a restoration of the *ancien régime*. On August 10, 1801, many of the Christian (and a smattering of Muslim) Egyptian and Syro-Lebanese advisors and soldiers departed with the French for a life in exile. Sāmī A. Ḥanna, "The Egyptian Mind

popularity of Bonaparte in Mount Lebanon, Bashīr II balked at sending troops to aid Aḥmad Jazzār Pasha in the latter's battle against Napoleon in Acre in 1799, preferring temporary exile instead. To be sure, Bashīr was equally reluctant to cast his lot with the invading troops of Bonaparte who had sent two letters asking for Bashīr's aid,[87] assuring the amir that France would defend the "Druze nation" against Ottoman oppression.[88] Only the Maronite patriarch Yūsuf al-Tayyān ordered his flock to volunteer in the French army. Only a decade later do we have a letter sent by an anonymous Maronite prelate vehemently denouncing Napoleon's heavy-handed, "disrespectful" dealings with the Catholic Church in Europe, sounding the warning bell of a like encroachment on the holdings of the Maronite Church.[89]

Context and precedent are of import in explaining the rationale for the variant positions and the confessional divide that came to the fore in reactions to the Napoleonic occupation. While the sympathies of the Christians initially lay with Napoleon, Ibrāhīm Pasha, and Bashīr II, the Muslim population tended to side with the guardians of the *status quo*, that is the Mamlūks and the Ottomans.

To those who pinned such great hopes on him, it may have been convenient to forget that Bonaparte in his first letter to the Egyptians did not conceal his primary motivation for the Egyptian invasion: to protect the (expanding) commerce and merchants of France in the region.[90] Such were the suspicions of the intruding Frank elicited among the region's majority Muslim administrators and population that a striking public relations campaign was deemed necessary to allay communal fears. Despite Bonaparte's profuse professions of his respect for Islam – culminating in his boast of being a "better Muslim" than the Mamlūks on account of his prior occupation of "the enemy of Islam," Rome – the chronicler, 'Abd al-Raḥmān al-Jabartī, notices that few

and the Idea of Democracy," *International Journal of Middle East Studies* 1.3 (1970): 238–247.

87 Ṭarābulsī, *Kashf al-Lithām*, 226–235.

88 Rabbāth, *La Formation Historique du Liban Politique et Constitutionnelle*, vol. II, 186.

89 Doc. 3 [1809] published in Kamāl al-Yāzijī, *Ruwwād al-Nahḍa al-Adabīya fī Lubnān al-Hadīth, 1800–1900* (Beirut: Maktabat Ra's Beirut, 1962), 16.

90 Stopping the "Mamlūk harassment" of the "French nation" (*fī haqq al-milla al-faransāwīya*) was the first issue raised by Napoleon right after the formulaic prefatory invocations of God. 'Abd al-Rahmān ibn Hasan al-Jabartī, *'Ajā'ib al-āthār fī al-Tarājim wa-al-Akhbār*, vol. II (Cairo: Matba'at Dār al-Kutub al-Misrīya, 1997–1998), 4. The contest with Britain over the profitable trade with India and the East can be safely inferred as the underlying mainspring for action.

Muslims were converted to his cause.[91] The account of some contemporaneous witnesses – even those critical of Muḥammad ʿAlī – confirm the jubilant reception of the Egyptian troops by the (Christian) population,[92] while, conversely, other sources indicate sporadic, mainly Sunni outbursts of open resentment toward Ibrāhīm Pasha's policies.[93] In Damascus, news of Napoleon's occupation triggered a spat of mob attacks on Christians.[94] In Cairo, the moneyed Greek Catholic mercantile elite saw more than 140 of their houses torched.

The Mashriq, Levantine Christians' welcoming of the French general, might most readily be explained with reference to the prior, rather inclement, policies minorities were subjected to under Aḥmad Jazzār in Bilād as-Shām. Unlike the Maʿanite and Shihābi amirs, Jazzār Pasha relied on Mamlūk, foreign troops united by an ethnic loyalty, including Bosnian (*Bushnāq*), Albanians (*Arnaʿūt*), and Maghribi mercenaries. Jazzār did have some Christian administrators, but virtually all of them were killed, tortured, or ended their career in exile.[95] Along with his right-hand man, the Jewish finance minister Ḥaīm Farḥī, Jazzār exercised direct control over the littoral stretch from Lattakia to Gaza and skillfully played the rival Druze factions off each other (the Yazbaq and the Qays),[96] a policy of divide and rule subsequently adopted by Bashīr II.

Indeed, the amir's unusually long tenure spanning the first half of the nineteenth century owes much to a consummate survival instinct and a character not averse to unabashed volte-face's in light of shifting strategic alliances. Bashīr II had originally cooperated with the Druze amir of the Bashīr Janbulāṭ who had granted him asylum upon his temporary deposition in 1790 and whom he in turn appointed *mudabbir*

[91] Jabartī contrasts the regrets of the infidels (*ḥasarāt al-kāfirīn*) to the elation of the Muslims (*farḥa wa bahjat al-muslimīn*) upon the withdrawal of the French in 1801. See al-Jabartī, *ʿAjāʾib al-āthār fī al-Tarājim wa-al-Akhbār*, 4–5.

[92] Pierre Hamont, "*L'Égypte sous Méhémet Alī: populations, gouvernement, institutions publiques, industrie, agriculture, principaux événements de Syrie pendant l'occupation égyptienne, Soudan de Méhémet Alī, Paris: Léautey et Lecointe*," 1843 as cited in Yitzhak Hofman, "The Administration of Syria and Palestine under Egyptian Rule (1831–1840)," in *Studies on Palestine during the Ottoman Period*, ed. M. Maoz (Jerusalem: Hebrew University, 1975), 323–333.

[93] Asad Rustum, *The Royal Archives of Egypt and the Origins of the Egyptian Expedition to Syria, 1831–1841* (Beirut: American University Beirut, 1931). As cited in Hofman, "The Administration of Syria and Palestine," 325.

[94] Moshe Ma'oz, *Ottoman Reform in Syria and Palestine, 1840–1861: The Impact of the Tanzimat on Politics and Society* (Oxford: Clarendon Press, 1968), 210.

[95] Ilyās ʿAdda fled to Mount Lebanon, Yūsuf al-Qurdāḥī to Europe, and the Sahrūj brothers were executed.

[96] The traditional arch-rival of the Qays, the Yamani faction, had been defeated by 1711 at ʿAyn Dara. Marūn Kisirwānī, "Foreign Interference and Religious Animosity in Lebanon," *Journal of Contemporary History* 15.4 (1980): 688.

("manager") of the amir's office in 1798. Relations between the two Bashīrs however soured in 1818 after the amir saw himself forced to press Shaykh Janbulāṭ for a levy to pay an onerous tribute demanded by 'Abdullāh Pasha, the *wālī* of Acre and Sidon.

At this point, the shaykh and the amir saw themselves confronted with the first large-scale popular protest, namely the "lay communes" (*'āmmīya*)[97] of Anṭilyās and Liḥfid in 1820–1821, which drafted a Lebanese magna carta of sorts against the crippling taxes levied by 'Abdullāh Pasha and his underling. This gathering of between 6,000 and 20,000 peasant leaders and notable *wukalā'*[98] marked the first recorded instance of a "civil," grassroots claim to executive power in Mount Lebanon in the name of pacts (*mawāthīq*) drafted in defense of the "general interest."[99]

To be sure, the Pact of Liḥfid's demand to have the amir nominated locally, rather than by the Ottoman *wālī* were met with the full, unremitting force of the Ottoman state authority, which, in 'Abdullāh's words, would "crush [the ungrateful rebels] like a spider's web."[100] 'Abdullāh's "child" Bashīr Shihāb would swiftly extinguish this revolt and continue to serve as a loyal mercenary of 'Abdullāh in defeating the *wālī* of Damascus, Darwīsh Pasha, becoming only the second Lebanese amir after Fakhr ad-Dīn to do so. Darwīsh complained to the porte that "the Druze, the Nusayri and the Kızılbaş (Shia)"[101] had joined in this conspiracy to oust him.[102] In 1823, Bashīr used his good offices with Mehmet 'Alī to obtain a pardon for 'Abdullāh in Istanbul, a favor which the latter would return when he executed Bashīr Janbulāṭ at the instigation of the Shihābi amir in 1825. This marked the end of Mount Lebanon's first

[97] It bears mentioning that one early, commonplace Arabic translation for "laity" is "*al-'awām*." See Badger, *An English–Arabic Lexicon*, 549. 'Ādil Ismā'īl has cast doubt on the authenticity of this document since it refers to oaths of allegiance made to the Saint (Mar) Ilyās by Muslims. See 'Ādil Ismā'īl, *al-Inqilāb 'ala al-Māḍi* (Beirut: Dār al-Nashr lil-Siyāsah wa al-Tārīkh, 2003), 70.

[98] These "delegates" were designated by each local village to attend the convocation in Antilyās.

[99] 'Iṣām Khalīfa, *Des Etapes Décisives Dans L'Histoire Du Liban* (Beirut: Publications Beyrouth, 1997), 57–59.

[100] Usāma Maqdisī, "Corrupting the Sublime Sultanate: The Revolt of Tanyus Shahin in Nineteenth-Century Ottoman Lebanon," *Comparative Studies in Society and History* 42 (2000): 190.

[101] There were, needless to say, no Anatolian Kızılbaş in Lebanon. The term, however, is found frequently in Ottoman correspondence as a derogatory tag for the (rebellious) Shia.

[102] Cited in Stefan Winter, "The Nusayris before the Tanzimat in the Eyes of Ottoman Provincial Administrators, 1804–1834," in *From the Syrian Land to the States of Syria and Lebanon*, eds. Thomas Philipp and Christoph Schumann (Beirut: Orient-Institut, Ergon Verlag, 2004), 102. Winter clarifies that while Druze and Nusayri troops were key, the Shia Ḥarfūsh Amīrs of the Biqā' had been on the side of Darwīsh all along.

full-scale Druze–Christian civil war in which each camp was mobilized by the men of religion.[103]

Bashīr's depth of gratitude for 'Abdullāh's aid against the revolting Druze chieftains, however, would prove incommensurate with his overarching concern for his career. In 1832 he would turn against 'Abdullāh Pasha at the behest of his new patrons, Ibrāhīm Pasha and Mehmet 'Alī Pasha. In fact, mutual antipathies between Bashīr and 'Abdullāh had surfaced during the latter's tenure as *wālī* of Acre in 1818, when he appointed two Muslim relatives of Bashīr II Shihāb, whereas Mehmet 'Alī ordered his son to appoint the scion of the Christian branch of the family, Bashīr II Shihāb, as the *wālī* of Sidon. Such was the Egyptian viceroy's personal predilection for Bashīr Shihāb that he publicly addressed him as his "son," much to the annoyance of the aforementioned 'Abdullāh Pasha.

It is within this context of constantly shifting webs of local intrigue among competing chieftains and vying Ottoman tax-collectors (*muḥāṣṣil*) that the advent of Ibrāhīm Pasha must be situated. The cited split in the Shihāb family between a Muslim and Christian branch[104] reflects as much a contest for power as it belies the putative secondary importance of confessional identities in premodern Lebanon.[105] After all, in 1793, 1794, and 1798, three petit civil wars had erupted over Aḥmad Jazzār's unilateral appointment of Muslim Shihābs (Ḥusayn, Sa'd ad-Dīn, and Salīm) in lieu of the elected Christian Amir Bashīr II Shihāb.[106] Thus, the notion of a premodern strata of a ruling elite within which class largely overrode confessional solidarities did not obtain.[107] On the

[103] Kais Firro, *A History of the Druzes*, vol. 1 (Leiden: Brill, 1992), 58.

[104] The two wings of the family convened in a national ceremony on December 2, 1942 to receive the remains of Bashīr II, which were returned from Istanbul to be buried in Bayt ad-Dīn. Among the seven great-grandchildren of Bashīr attending was Fu'ād Shihāb, the later president of Lebanon.

[105] Maqdisī speaks of a "non-sectarian" elite, while acknowledging that "conversion was a sin, a treachery that far surpassed secular betrayal," without duly explaining how the initial claim of nonsectarianism can stand in light of such strict endogamous strictures. Maqdisī, "Corrupting the Sublime Sultanate," 187. Khalīfa offers this summary: "C'est ainsi que le decline de la structure Iqtai ... s'est (fait) dans le sense du raffermissement des structures confessionnelles." *Des Etapes Décisives*, 58.

[106] Ṣalībī, *The Modern History of Lebanon*, 20–21.

[107] There were, to be sure, continuous intersectarian alliances between families, but even here the laws of endogamy prevented strategy from altering sociological realities. See Rustum, *Bashīr Bayna al-Sulṭān wa al-'Azīz*, vol. II, 6. Buṭrus al-Bustānī was painfully aware that the eruption of confessional strife in the nineteenth century came as a consequence of unaddressed, latent sectarian animosities that he says preceded 1860. Al-Bustānī, *Nafīr Sūrīyā*, 36–37. One could well argue that rule in premodern Lebanon (and thereafter) was held by families (the 'Assāfs, the Tanūkhids, and the Ma'anids), yet family and kinship ties almost always entailed distinct sectarian identities.

contrary, we might say that it was Ibrāhīm Pasha's push toward modernization and centralization that led to a greater intermixing of sects (on a popular level) in nineteenth-century Mount Lebanon and Syria, even if the repercussions of this development turned out to be rather double-edged. To take one prominent example, the southward migration of Christian peasants and the expulsion of the Druze counterparts from Kisirwān – which incidentally had commenced under Fakhr ad-Dīn – fueled intercommunal friction, culminating in Ibrāhīm and Bashīr's 1838 bloody crushing of the Druze rebellion in the *Ḥawrān*.

Ibrāhīm Pasha and his advisors may have striven to emulate the French republican model, yet their every policy had to be implemented in a society riven by confessional faultlines. It was due to the latter that Ibrāhīm's secularizing impulse was so readily perceived through a sectarian prism. From early on, we find ubiquitous accusations leveled at Bashīr II of having sought to exploit and even provoke Druze–Maronite prejudices. One contemporary Druze historian even laments that Druze and Maronites lived in harmony until Bashīr began "favoring the Christians."[108] Another, twentieth-century Druze historian, however, Sulaymān Abū 'Izz ad-Dīn, claims that Bashīr II, in conjunction with his patron Ibrāhīm Pasha, inaugurated a "literary renaissance" in Lebanon. Such was the Pasha's predilection for the Christians that one anticipated the announcement of Ibrāhīm's conversion.[109]

The customary interpretation has been to explain Ibrāhīm's promotion of the *Shām* Christian sects as a strategic measure directed at once against the recalcitrant, feudalist Druze, the traditional Ottoman administrative strongholds of Damascus, Acre, Sidon, and Tripoli, and the potentially hostile Europeans.[110] One might further allude to the regional

[108] Thus, the estimate of the British chronicler W. P. Hunter in 1840. Kisirwānī, "Foreign Interference and Religious Animosity in Lebanon," 691. Biṭār, a Sunni historian, confirms this image in a tirade against Bashīr.

[109] Sulaymān Abū 'Izz ad-Dīn, *Ibrāhīm Bāshā fī Sūrīyā: Huwa Tārīkh bad al-Nahḍa al-ḥadītha fī al-Sharq al-Adná wa-aḥwāl Sūrīyā fī 'ahd Muḥammad Alī wa-thawarāt al-Sūrīīn wa-Durūz Ḥawrān 'alá ḥukūmatihi* (Beirut: al-Matba' al-'Ilmīya, 1929).

[110] "The Egyptian administration lifted financial burdens from Christians and Jews visiting holy sites in Jerusalem and secured their safe passage. It cancelled the regulations restricting Jewish temples and gave permission for their repair and renovation. At the same time, however, it rejected Jewish requests to pave the area adjacent to the Aqsā Mosque and the site of the Wailing Wall on the basis that it was not religiously legal." Latīfa Muhammad Sālim, "Levantine Experiences," *Al-Ahram Weekly*, 766, November 2005. Jews may also have benefited from the greater opportunity for foreign councils to intervene on their behalf in this era; yet, in the early stage of the nineteenth century, Europe's primary concern was reserved for the Oriental Christians. Zionism was only slowly added to the diplomatic agenda of demands from the Ottomans. The latter were still given a free hand to bar Ashkenazi Jews from owning property in Palestine. See

configuration and particular balance of power, which made an alliance with the Christians in general – and Bashīr II Shihāb in particular – a more plausible option for the incoming Egyptians. While Ibrāhīm may have initially voiced some reservations, Bashīr seemed like the natural choice to his father Mehmet ʻAlī, and soon won the full admiration of Ibrāhīm.[111] After all, in 1810, the Amir Bashīr II was commissioned by Yūsuf Pasha, the *wālī* of Damascus,[112] to assemble a rare joint intercommunal assembly of 15,000 Christian, Druze, and Muslim troops to successfully fend off an impending invasion of Damascus led by ʻAbdullāh Ibn Maṣʻūd al-Wahhāb.[113] At this stage, it will be remembered, the Wahhabi puritans were conceived as a threat both by Cairo and Istanbul. As a recompense for his efforts against the Wahhabis, Muḥammad ʻAlī thrice petitioned Sultan Mahmud for an annexation of the coveted Levant; yet, after his final offer of outright purchase was promptly rejected, ʻAlī turned to forge a pact with Bashīr in preparation for the subsequent invasion of 1831.[114]

As a response to the Wahhabi encroachment on Syria, Ottoman governors attempted to enforce a stricter version of the *Sharīʻa,* triggering an emigration of a number of Christian, Druze, and Shia families to Mount Lebanon and Jabal Āmil. It was Bashīr II who opened the doors of the Shūf and Matn for these families in 1811 and – in cooperation with the lord of the Shūf, Bashīr Janbulāṭ – organized the transfer of 400 Druze families.[115]

If Bashīr was portrayed by his detractors as an enemy of Islam, the amir clearly did not invite such an image. Rather, in yet another mimicking of his Maʻanites predecessors, the amir would carefully construct a deliberately vague, hybrid religious aura for himself by building a mosque and church side by side in his palace at Bayt ad-Dīn, issuing oaths on both the Qur'ān and the Gospels and dispensing alms to Christian and Druze villagers alike.[116]

Latīfa Muhammad Sālim, *al-Hukm al-Misri Fī al-Shām (Egyptian Rule in the Levant) 1831–1841* (Cairo, 1990).

111 Rustum, *Bashīr Bayna al-Sulṭān wa al-ʻAzīz*, vol. I, 99.

112 Together with his subordinate, the *wālī* of Sidon, Sulaymān Pasha.

113 Tānnūs as-Shidyāq, *Akhbār al-ʻAyān fī Jabal Lubnān* (Beirut: Matba' Sāmīya, 1954), 914.

114 ʻAlī's chief antagonist Khasraw Pasha is said to have dissuaded the Sultan from endorsing the plans of the Egyptian viceroy. Sālim, "Levantine Experiences."

115 Ṣalībī, *The Modern History of Lebanon*, 24.

116 See Lāma Jarūdī, "The Palace of Beit ed-Dīn: Luxury and Status in a Society of Competing Notables," A. B. honors thesis, the Deparment of Architecture, Harvard College, 2000 and Maqdisī "Corrupting the Sublime Sultanate," 187.

When Bashīr's new patron Ibrāhīm arrived, such transconfessional benevolence and openness was marred by the Egyptian serasker's blithe disregard for etiquette and classification of the Druze as "heretics." To be sure, historians are inclined to interpret even this tag as ushering from an opprobrium of political recalcitrance rather than reflecting any concern with theological hetereodoxy. In fact, Muḥammad 'Alī and his son Ibrāhīm had been more willing to make concessions to Druze tradition by forbidding even isolated Druze conversions to Christianity – while, in fact, allowing a highly controversial reconversion of some Maronites who had previously embraced Islam.[117] Secular freedoms thus were embraced as long as they did not upset the public order.

Even though Bashīr may have been more attuned to confessional sensitivities of the Mountain, neither he nor Ibrāhīm showed any tolerance when it came to disturbances of civil peace, particularly if they displayed confessional contours. In fact, the case can easily be made that it was in part Bashīr's unflinching brutality and penchant for collective punishment that sowed the seeds for subsequent eruptions of sectarian strife. To cite just one emblematic example, in 1823, Shia in the northern Lebanon hamlet of Kfarhiyal harassed and injured a handful of Maronite priests, leading to the wholesale burning of two Shia villages by troops commandeered by Bashīr's son Khalīl.

In gauging Ibrāhīm Pasha's and Bashīr II's particular administration – and its ostensibly pro-Christian policies – it becomes rather difficult then to disentangle strategic from sectarian motivations for each particular policy. A comprehensive assessment would have to take several factors into account.

For one, by the onset of the nineteenth century, the Christians were demographically and economically ascendant. Even as sympathetic a writer as Volney sensed a portentous danger in the new-found confidence of some Christians. Volney feared that their "indiscreet and annoying zeal" could imperil the tenuous peace he witnessed during the reign of the Amir Yūsuf (1770–1788). Meanwhile, the Druze found themselves under increasing pressure, particularly after Bashīr II set about to brutally crush the competing Druze *muqāṭa'ajī*, such as the Abū Nakads, the Arslāns, and Imāds, a clampdown on feudalism from which eventually even Bashīr's erstwhile ally Said Janbulāṭ found no escape. As Kamāl Ṣalībī notes, while the motivation for Bashīr Shihāb's

[117] The sources speak of this rare case of officially sanctioned "Irtidād" without mentioning any repercussions. Rustum, *Bashīr Bayna al-Sulṭān wa al-'Azīz*, vol. I, 100. Ridda, as we shall see, was decriminalized in 1856 by the *Tanzimāt* Edict.

autocratic actions most probably was not sectarian in origin, the Druze community on the ground clearly saw matters differently, as became apparent when revenge was exacted for Bashīr Janbulāṭ's execution; partisans of the latter and the previously persecuted and exiled Abū Nakad's would spearhead the communal insurrections post 1839.

By launching a full-scale communal uprising, the Druze landlords did not merely avenge the diminishment of their status in the Egyptian era, but also arguably succeeded in reformulating what was in large measure a socioeconomic conflict in sectarian terms. In this venture, to be sure, they were aided by tacit and open Ottoman desires to recover a lost province and by the communal Catholic reaction in which patriarchs and bishops would summon their flock to "unfurl the standard of the cross" and plunder, burn, and murder in the name of a holy war.[118] Whipped-up sectarianism thereby served to obstruct the formation of a direct nexus between the peasants and an expanding state seeking to integrate the Mountain with Beirut's growing merchant financial capital by circumventing feudal lords.[119] At no point, however, was the degree of forcible nationalization, bureaucratization, land redistribution, and state monopolization Mehmet 'Alī pursued in Egypt duplicated by his son in the Lebanese emirate, in part due to unremitting pressure by Britain, which forced the porte in December of 1835 to issue a *firmān* formally ending the Egyptian trade monopoly in the Levant. From a strictly economic perspective, there remains a big question mark whether 'Alī may in fact have been able to ever replicate a full European-style industrialization. The sociological repercussions of the *firmān* (and the subsequent Anglo-Ottoman Treatise of 1838) however seem clear: Not only were European merchants now given the legal cover to easily subvert Ibrāhīm's mercantile economic plan for the Levant, but the accumulation of increasing, untaxed wealth among European traders (and their Lebanese, predominantly Christian, partners) would stir the envy of non-Christians, who were not profiting from consular perks. Imperialist *realpolitik* may have buoyed business and international trade but it undermined the domestic legitimacy of a (secular) state project in its infancy.

[118] The Greek Catholic bishop of Zahle cited in Colonel Charles Churchill, *The Druzes and the Maronites: Under Turkish Rule from 1840 to 1860* (London: Bernard Quaritch, 1862), 49–55. Churchill notes that the Greek Orthodox community generally sided with the Druze against the Maronites while citing the Ottoman serasker's statement that he had foreknowledge of the attack on Dayr al-Qamar fourteen days in advance.

[119] Roger Owen, *The Middle East in the World Economy, 1800–1914* (London: I. B. Tauris, 1993), 162. Very much the same dynamic was observable in Switzerland, as we shall see in the subsequent section.

This was all the more so since the Egyptian restructuring of the Lebanese emirate along secular, "*étatist*" lines was complicated from its inception by the association of modernization with Westernization. Bashīr's patron Ibrāhīm took his cue from his father and was as committed to replicating the French administrative paradigm. Most of the retinue of his advisors were the progeny of France and received their training under the French convert Colonel Joseph Sève, better known as Sulaymān Pasha (1788–1860).[120] Nominally, the coastal strip of modern Lebanon both before and after the Egyptian invasion fell under the broader administrative unit of Barr al-Shām, even though de facto the highest authority in Damascus, governor general ḥükümdar Muḥammad Sherif Pasha, was completely sidelined after November 1831 by his superiors Ibrāhīm Pasha and his chief of staff, the aforementioned Colonel Sève. The latter was instrumental in introducing universal conscription – thus anticipating a key plank of the subsequent, empire-wide injunctions of *Tanzimāt* state reform.

It is difficult to delineate with certainty where the Egyptian commander-in-chief's personal infatuation with the Western-French state model ended and where political opportunism began. Besides the aforementioned Commanding General Sève, Ibrāhīm appointed numerous local Christians as chief advisors and administrators in Lebanon, thus setting a precedent. The Armenian Catholic Ḥannā Baḥrī, for instance, headed the first *Majlis al-Shūra* in Damascus upon its first convocation in June of 1832 and became the first non-Muslim to receive the title of a "*bey*" in the Ottoman Empire. To be sure, the novelty of a Christian joining, let alone presiding over, the notable Muslim *'Ayān* and *Akābir* caused some initial resistance, but was enforced as a fait accompli under the stern paternal guidance of Ibrāhīm Pasha himself.[121]

That the prime motivation for Ibrāhīm's actions was administrative rather than sectarian in origin became clear when his jackboot began to affect Christians as much – if not more – than it did Muslims. For one, there was the blight of ever proliferating, increasingly exorbitant taxes that had to be levied to finance the ambitious development project and

[120] Hofman, "The Administration of Syria and Palestine under Egyptian Rule (1831–1840)," 326. Sulaymān Pasha's great-granddaughter Nazli Sabri would become the wife of the last Egyptian monarch, King Farouk and die in Rome after having converted to Catholicism in 1950. Sulaymān Pasha is not to be confused with his namesake, the subsequent wāli of Damascus.

[121] Rustum recounts the popular incident in which the Muslim members of the majlis refused to rise, prompting Ibrāhīm himself to visit Damscus, ordering each of the judges, notables, and the Mufti one by one in Turkish to "stand up" ("Otur!") to honor Ḥannā Baḥrī. Rustum, Bashīr Bayna al-Sulṭān wa al-'Azīz, vol. I, 99–100.

provision of an army that had swelled to 90,000 men.[122] Moreover, in 1833/1834, Ibrāhīm's introduction of compulsory military conscription led to an exodus of segments of the population of northern Syria and Lebanon to Anatolia and Cyprus (and to a concomitant, "suspiciously" rapid increase in applications to Maronite monasteries).[123] Again, sectarianism was part and parcel of Bashīr II's intractable predicament of imposing a unified, "national," intersectarian army. While the Christians claimed exemption on account of their confessional affiliation (thus, rather hypocritically, endorsing the very Islamic law they were so relieved to see ignored elsewhere), the Druze *'uqqāl* insisted on a separate, fully segregated contingent of Druze soldiers so as not to suffer contaminating habituation with Muslim and Christian soldiers. Better accustomed with the depth of local traditions, Bashīr was far more reluctant than Ibrāhīm to compel the Druze to relinquish their demand, but his warnings fell on deaf ears.

In the end, it was the Egyptian policy to attempt a heavy-handed disarmament of Druze militias while arming Maronite peasants to fight Druze rebellions – and win the Christian's allegiance[124] – which would trigger a wholesale revolt and spell the ambitious *wālī*'s own eventual demise. Only at the proverbial eleventh hour in 1839 did Ibrāhīm backtrack and, at the behest of his father, demand the Christians to disarm as well.[125] This last measure, in turn, was read as a first step toward conscription, causing Ibrāhīm to lose the backing of his last confessional constituency, the Christians[126]. Patriarch Yusuf Habaysh called the Maronites to cooperate with the Druze and Shia in expelling the Egyptians, and even went so far as to wield the ultimate clerical weapon and threatened to excommunicate any Maronite who disobeyed his order.[127] Ibrāhīm's prior campaign – coming at the heels of violent Druze–Maronite rivalry in 1822 – had already drawn the ire of subjugated Druze lords and prepared the ground for his defeat after 1840.

[122] Owen, The Middle East in the World Economy, 77. We might note in passing that the Swiss confederacy likewise complained about inordinate taxes and the obligation to provide 16,000 soldiers for Napoleon's army after the Act of Mediation of 1803.

[123] Ṭarābulsī, *Kashf al-Lithām*, 177.

[124] This is the principal reason for Muḥammad 'Alī's order to arm the Christians as it is documented in the Egyptian royal archives. See Rustum, *Bashīr Bayna al-Sulṭān wa al-'Azīz*, vol. I, 100.

[125] Rabbāth, La Formation Historique du Liban Politique et Constitutionelle, 183.

[126] Ṣalībī, *The Modern History of Lebanon*, 38.

[127] Habaysh's direct threat presaged perhaps the first such incident in the modern history of Lebanon, at least among the Christian clerics. Antwān Ḥarb Khūrī, *al-Mawārina: Tārīkh wa-Thawābit* (Beirut: al-Rābiṭah al-Mārūnīyah, 1998), 55.

To be sure, the latter was sealed only with the first landing of European troops on the shores of the Levant since the Crusades. With unequivocal words before parliament on June 28, 1839, Lord Palmerston left no doubt as to what was at stake: Britain was looking for "all means by which we could drive Mehmet out of Syria,"[128] confident that the French, mired in Algeria, could ill afford a full-scale confrontation over the Eastern Mediterranean. The integrity of the Ottoman Empire had to be persevered in order to secure and "restore Syria to the direct authority of the Sultan."[129]

With the conclusion of the "[London] Convention for the Pacification of the Levant" on July 15, 1840, the European imperial powers succeeded in their stated goal of "saving the Sultan's throne."[130] On the one hand, the conservative forces – who usually found themselves locked in fierce discord over the "Eastern Question" – were intent to thwart a perilous precedent and exorcise the specter of an anti-imperial revolution in the East just as they were expending concerted efforts to form reactionary coalitions against Bonapartism in Europe as well. On the other hand, a new balance of power was ratified in the region with Muḥammad 'Alī and his son seeing themselves forced to give up any designs of a hereditary *Pashaḷk* in Syria.

From a Levantine perspective, the premature abortion of Ibrāhīm's bid at modernization may have been instigated by a foreign Ottoman–British–Russian imperial tripartite alliance, but it was also precipitated by the rulers' alienation of virtually the entire spectrum of local sects[131] and a resultant, hitherto unprecedented, Druze–Christian–Shia–Sunni protonational united resistance inspired by the successful Greek War of Independence. In the 1840 Anṭilyās proclamation of the "sects of Lebanon," explicit reference is made to French revolutionaries who died "in the cause of freedom," reflecting a remarkably early familiarity with revolutionary discourse.[132] While such terminology percolated via the growing number of missionary schools founded under Ibrāhīm, and while the

[128] Kisirwāni, "Foreign Interference and Religious Animosity in Lebanon," 697.

[129] The (initially rejected) carrot offered to Muḥammad 'Alī was a hereditary pashalik in Egypt. See *The Middle East and North Africa in World Politics: A Documentary Record: European Expansion, 1535–1914*, ed. J. C. Hurewitz (New Haven, CT, and London: Yale University Press, 1975), 267.

[130] See doc. 84 in *The Middle East and North Africa in World Politics*, 273ff.

[131] Besides the Druze of the Ḥawran and Wadi al-Taym, the Shia of Jabal 'Āmil also staged an uprising in November of 1839.

[132] "*Ittifāq Ṭawā'if Lubnān bi-Tawḥīd al-Kalima.*" A facsimile of the June 7, 1840 treaty and its signatories is reproduced in al-Azīz Nawwār, *Wathā'iq Asāsīya*, doc. no. 83, 257; Khūrī, *Modern Arab Thought*, 21.

draping of the *tricouleur* by one of the demonstrators in Anṭilyās signaled the legacy of France, the short-lived uprising was more immediately inspired by the preceding Greek independence movement that was explicitly invoked in the pact as the "prime paradigm" (*aḥsan qudwā*). The same may be said of the pact's demands of an "attainment of independence and freedom in face of despotism," a "lowering of inordinate taxes," and the "election of a 5-member *majlis*" inter alia.[133]

In other words, even as the aftershock of the French Revolution and its central tenet of republican nationalism was prompting the imperial powers to intervene in rare unity against the looming threat of Mehmet 'Alī, the latter, along with his son, found himself combating an upswell of no less revolutionary, popular demands of equality in his domain.[134] We may thus conclude that the age of "enlightened despotism," and the revolutionary discourse of liberty, equality, and fraternity ended up fomenting, simultaneously, both eruptions of sectarian strife *and* an intercommunal proto-nationalist momentum, however feeble and short-lived this interreligious joining of ranks against a common enemy may have been. The Anṭilyās insurgents thus could petition France "to help the Lebanese who are reclaiming justice against the Egyptian oppression,"[135] even if the latter was itself but an offspring of the revolution in the Middle East.

Nor was there anything distinctly "Oriental" or "Lebanese" about this ostensibly contradictory, concurrent clash of centrifugal and centripetal dynamics unleashed by revolutionary reform. The general Muslim hostility toward France, the popularity of Napoleon, and the distrust his eventual nemesis Aḥmad Jazzār Pasha earned among Christians (and Shia[136]) of the Fertile Crescent need not necessarily be interpreted as yet another sign of a quintessentially Middle Eastern pathological affliction with sectarianism.

133 See Sawda, *Fī Sabīl Lubnān*, 85ff; Khūrī, *Modern Arab Thought*, 22. It remains disputed whether the Maronite patriarch in fact lent his support to the Antilyās rebellion. The Maronite Church, like its Catholic counterpart in Europe, was ill at ease with revolutionary rhetoric.

134 Roderic Davison points out that Sultan Mahmoud (reg. 1808–1839) had already underscored the equality of all subjects regardless of religion. See Roderic Davison, "Turkish Attitudes Concerning Christian–Muslim Equality in the Nineteenth Century," *The American Historical Review* 59.4 (1954): 845.

135 Cited in Khalīfa, *Des Etapes Décisives*, 57. The full text: al-Azīz Nawwār, *Wathā'iq Asāsīya*, 257.

136 Such was the potency of sectarian sentiment that Jazzār would brand his competitor "Abdullāh as a 'friend of the Shia'" and an accomplice of the Wahhabis. Istanbul responded by demoting 'Abdullāh and appointing Jazzār in his stead as governor of Istanbul. Winter, "The Nusayris before the Tanzimat," 101.

Rather, it behooves us to cast another cursory glance at the ramifications of the legal and economic transformations that followed the almost synchronous introduction of the Napoleonic Reform in Switzerland given that the newly established confederacy at this time passed through a remarkably similar tumultuous transformation, beginning with the forcible institution of the *Code Napoléon* on March 14, 1798. On March 5 of that self-same year, Napoleon – who during a previous trip across Switzerland had personally triggered the independence of the *République Léman*[137] – received orders from the Paris Directorate to set sail for Egypt to conquer this vital waystation to India. On the same day of March 5, 1798, Catholic France sought to secure a no less lucrative trade passage to Italy by brutally crushing the fierce resistance of the core Catholic Swiss *Ur*-Cantons,[138] even as French troops were in fact embraced by their new-found liberal, urban Protestant allies. In other words, while there is no gainsaying that denominational identity did play a salient role in the formation of opposition to Napoleonic reforms in hitherto communally defined societies – both in the Middle East as elsewhere – the particular socioeconomic status of each confession, and considerations of what each group had to gain or lose from an emboldened central state apparatus must be considered in gauging disparate responses.

After all, what was hailed as "efficiency" by the central bureaucracy was often castigated as extortion by the feudal grandees, administers of the *ancien regime*, and cantonal aristocrats. Likewise, the official promulgation of new liberties (however circumscribed) could equally be feared as a portent of permissiveness and a license for libertinism by many a conservative force, above all the Catholic Church and the Sunni clerical establishment.

Even within confessions, responses could vary according to (class) interest. Thus, while the more established, landed Nusayris would – possibly with Ottoman instigation – launch a revolt in 1834, the marginalized coastal Nusayris would welcome the Egyptian regime's investment in infrastructure and promise of equality.[139] Much the same in terms of intrasectarian divergences is observable in Switzerland, where Catholic nobles would fight the Catholic French troops to their teeth, while no-

[137] During his march across the canton of Bern and Vaud from November 17–22, 1797 he was welcomed with flowers and poems in Nyon and Lausanne. Victor Monnier, *Bonaparte et les Suisses: L'Acte de Médiation de 1803* (Geneva: Bibliothèque Publique et Universitaire, 2003), 13.

[138] The rural foundational states of Uri, Glarus, and Schwyz were the last cantons to submit to the French and accept the Helvetic Republic.

[139] Winter, "The Nusayris before the Tanzimat," 105.

less Catholic farmers would welcome the end of serfdom (*Leibeigenschaft*) even as they resented Jacobin anticlericalism.[140] Only the military dictator Napoleon, after all, broke the stranglehold of the rural feudal and urban patrician families by abolishing all feudal taxes, prerogatives, and noble titles by the stroke of a pen on November 10, 1798.[141] The Bernese peasants thus would rejoice at the unexpected, sudden relief from taxes, such as the notorious tithes (*Zehnten*) under which they had been smarting for centuries, not unlike their fellow tillers of the soil of the manorial estates of the Khāzin's and Janbulāṭ's in Mount Lebanon, who rose to demand the restriction of agricultural levies to one single, annual tithe (*mīrī*).[142] To hastily mistake either for unreserved champions of the full spectrum of enlightenment liberties however would be misleading.

As was the case in Mount Lebanon with the newly created offices of the *mutassalim* in Lebanon, so too in Switzerland the abrogation of feudal and cantonal privileges, the incipient creation of a federal bureaucracy,[143] the secularization and standardization of legal codes, taxes, and forced conscription – in conjunction with the virtual bankruptcy of the state treasury – all sparked widespread insurgencies in the nascent Helvetic Republic. The civil war of 1799 – which may equally be read as an inter-European war between Russia, Austria, and France – forced "*l'auguste médiateur*" Napoleon to compromise with his *Acte de Médiation* in February of 1803 by which the *Premier Consul* on behalf of France claimed to safeguard the unity of the "quarrelling parties" of Switzerland.[144] Swiss landlords and cantonal patricians (in Berne and Zurich) and Lebanese *'ayān* (between 1840 and 1860) thus would get a (temporary) new lease on life after the imperial armies of Russia, Austria, and Prussia invaded Switzerland once again in December of 1813 to salvage the *ancien régime* in like fashion as Britain, Austria, and the Ottomans would defeat Mehmet 'Alī in 1840. The former supreme position of the federal chairman or *Landamman* – whose function

[140] During the peasant wars of 1523–1526, Zwingli had already abolished serfdom in Zurich, even though he refused to abolish the "major tithe" (*Grosse Zehnte*) levied on the main harvest of the farmers. All other cantons brutally crushed the peasant rebellion in the 1520s and during the second major revolt of 1653.

[141] Beat Junker, *Geschichte des Kantons Bern seit 1798: Helvetik, Mediation, Restauration*, vol. I, 72–82. The Helvetic Republic was proclaimed on April 12, 1789 by 121 delegates in Aarau.

[142] The 1840 pact of Antilyās, as cited in Khalīfa, *Des Etapes Décisives*, 57.

[143] The new offices were given sweeping powers, including control over administrative supervision and intervention in minutest details of regional disputes.

[144] For the full text of the Mediation Act, see Junker, *Geschichte des Kantons Bern seit 1798*, 60. The Act favored conservative forces by limiting the right to vote to wealthy citizens (*Zensuswahlrecht*).

somewhat resembled that of Mount Lebanon's governing *mutaṣarrif* after 1861 – was replaced after the reactionary *Bundesvertrag* of 1815 by the powers of the three urban centers Zurich, Berne, and Luzern. Powers devolved once again to the peripheral cantons that had their own standing armies and were free to each entertain separate diplomatic relations with foreign powers until 1848.

The Helvetic Republic thus saw a restoration of some feudal, regional, and confessional privileges under the new *Bundesvertrag* from 1815–1848, but key components of the Napoleonic Code – and more importantly its logic of centralization – were now adopted almost *de rigeur*, even as a debate on the merits of reform raged between conservatives and liberals, an altercation which was all too reminiscent of that audible from the variant wings of *Tanzimāt* reformers in the Ottoman Empire as we shall see. Nor was Switzerland spared reform-induced sectarian strife, even if its human toll was far less severe than in Mount Lebanon. When the Canton of Zurich introduced a radically liberal constitution on March 10, 1831 enunciating a separation of powers, full freedom of belief, trade, and publication along with a secularization of schools,[145] it did not take long for a violent sectarian reaction to rise in response. The Coup of Zurich (*Züriputch*) of September 6, 1839 saw the conservative rural population descend to the streets against the city elites who stood behind secularization, riled up by the crusading battle cry: "Onwards, righteous Christian!" ("*Vorwärts, wer ein guter Christ ist!*")[146]

Within the decade in which Ibrāhīm and Bashīr began by crushing Druze recalcitrance in their pursuit of republican reform, the French-educated General (and Red Cross co-founder) Henri Dufour (1787–1875) would foist state sovereignty on the Catholic opposition of the *Sonderbund*, which resisted the secularization of Church property. It was only after the Catholic–Protestant *Soderbundskrieg* of 1848 that the liberal, largely "progressive" Protestant states – abetted by their superior wealth – would gain the upper hand in what was now a truly unified Confederation of Switzerland and succeed in imposing the

[145] These reforms would eventually lead to the founding of the University of Zurich in 1833.

[146] The ostensible casus belli was the appointment of the controversial theological David Strauss to the University of Zurich. Strauss had authored the first demytholigizing account of Jesus, *Das Leben Jesu*. While Friedrich Nietzsche allegedly confided of having lost the last remnants of his faith upon reading the book, the conservative rural militia led by the Pastor Hirzel descended on Zurich to topple the city council in a bloody battle. See Meinrad Suter, *Kleine Zürcher Verfassungsgeschichte 1218–2000*, Herausgegeben vom Staatsarchiv des Kantons Zürich (Zürich: Presse des Kantons Zurich, 2000).

unquestionable supremacy of a central, federal state authority on the refractory conservative cantons, monopolistic urban guilds, and patrician families.[147] Freedom of the press, religion, and trade were now for the first time not only promulgated (as they had been in 1789), but also enforced – nationwide.[148]

A similar rise of an urban, largely Christian and Sunni Beiruti bourgeoisie would stand behind the curtailment of landed privileges in Mount Lebanon, even if the process was subjected to greater setbacks. The Protocol of Shakib Efendi of 1845 heralded the spirit of equality by forcing the feudal lords to submit to the same single juridical council, the *Majlis istishārī* or "consultative council" all ordinary subjects were tried before.[149] The rupture seemed complete with the *Règlement Organique* of June 9, 1861, which in its sixth article contained a whiff of the French Revolution and *Tanzimāt* laïcism in promulgating equality before the law and the abolition of feudal privileges. The feudal lords thus officially lost their prerogative to set and forcibly extort arbitrary taxes. Instead, the *Règlement* charged the twelve-member administrative council with this power, paving the way for a regulation of real estate.[150] Peasant families now could accumulate property and wealth without harassment and the looming threat of expropriation. The resulting capital investments became visible in the establishment of the (silk) factories and an expanding middle class.

To be sure, all forms of feudalism were not entirely extirpated in nineteenth-century Lebanon; Article 11 of the *Règlement* still granted the notables the final say over certifying the appointment of all members of the administrative and judicial councils.[151] Nonetheless, the bonds of

[147] Liberty of conscience was asserted, but de facto arch-Protestant cantons such as Vaud would retain a Protestant state church until as late as April 14, 2003.

[148] Article 6 of the April 12, 1789 constitution reads almost verbatim like Article 9 of the 1926 (and current) Lebanese constitution: "*La liberté de conscience est illimitée; la manifestation des opinions religieuses est subordonnée aux sentiments de la concorde et de la paix. Tous les cultes sont permis s'ils ne troublent point l'ordre public et n'affectent aucune domination ou prééminence. La police les surveille et a le droit de s'enquérir des dogmes et des devoirs qu'ils enseignent.*"

[149] Caesar Faraḥ, "The Problem of the Ottoman Administration in the Lebanon: 1840–1861," PhD dissertation, University Microfilms International, Ann Arbor, MI, 1977, 453.

[150] Paul Saba, "The Creation of the Lebanese Economy: Economic Growth in the Nineteenth and Early Twentieth Century," in *Essays on the Crisis in Lebanon*, ed. Roger Owen (London: Ithaca Press, 1972), 13.

[151] The council of the Mutasarrifiya was composed of four Maronites, three Druzes, two Greek Orthodoxes, one Greek Catholic, one Sunni Muslim, and one Shia Muslim.

were loosened with the piecemeal series of reforms undertaken between 1831 and 1864 on the one hand, and with the expansion of trade and the formation of a new capitalist class on the other. As in Europe, it was this urban bourgeoisie of the nineteenth century that would come to form the mainstay of the future Republic of Lebanon in the twentieth, as we shall see. Thus, rather than viewing the introduction of reform – whether embodied in the *Code Napoléon* or the *Tanzimāt* – "teleologically," that is to say as part of a linear ascent of seemingly inexorable, steadily increasing secularization, it would be more accurate to depict the transformation as a meandering, back-and-forth contest over authority. If continental Europe was subjected to a conservative backlash during the period of the Restoration, so too during the post-*Tanzimāt* elaboration of the *mecelle* a tradition-bent young Ottoman faction won out in the debate of whether or not to derive the civil code from the Islamic Ḥanafī Corpus as opposed to the French Civil Code. The common denominator in both the larger European and Ottoman context, however, remained standardization: Judges were now forced to base verdicts on a single, centralized source and no longer could appeal to local customs. Likewise, the old privileges of the clergy, both Muslim and Christian, were gradually curtailed.

Beyond external shocks, however, the success of political reform in the direction of secularism equally rested on the prior growth of a domestic, urban intelligensia. As we shall further investigate, the new avid avatars of enlightenment ideals did not rest content with advocating a secular solidarity instead of a communal parochialism in the abstract. Rather, they attempted to live their ideal and thereby lay the groundwork for a new society in which the fraternal nation would, if not supplant, then at least supercede the fratricidal denomination.

One of the earliest explicitly secular associations in the Middle East was the Arab Society of Arts and Sciences founded by Nasīf al-Yāsijī and Buṭrus al-Bustānī with the aid of American missionaries in Beirut. By 1847, the Syrian Scientific Society was established with Muslim as well as Christian membership, including a prominent Druze notable, Muḥammad Arslān. Its curricula was the first of its kind in focusing on a study of Western history and scientific progress. Bustānī followed suit by founding the first national, expressly secular, interconfessional secondary school, the al-Madrasa al-Waṭanīya of Zuqāq al-Bilāṭ in Beirut in 1863. This school, vehemently opposed by a conservative wing of the Maronite Church, turned out to be a training ground for a host of Muslim educational reformers in Lebanon.

The first supra-sectarian civil associations in Switzerland had, arguably due to the immediate proximity to France, preceded those in Lebanon by almost a century.[152] In 1767, the first interconfessional national society was founded, the "Helvetic Society" (*Helvetische Gesellschaft*) which, analogous to the Arab Society, came as an effort to strengthen national ties, first across the Protestant–Catholic divide, and later across the cultural–linguistic cleft between a German- and French-speaking Switzerland. As had been the case in Lebanon, the members of the Swiss society became the founding fathers of a national press.[153] The first national parties would soon follow suit, even though confessional prejudice proved more difficult to erase here. Indeed, one should not exaggerate the success of these secularizing pilot projects. If egalitarianism was the credo and the commonwealth the goal of these pioneers of patriotism, elitism became their lot and the city their habitat. The scenic topographic hallmark distinguishing Lebanon and Switzerland, the dichotomy of mountain and flatlands, now revealed its shadow side in exacerbating a deeply seated biculturalism. To this day, one might easily entertain a comparison of Beirut and Zurich as cosmopolitan hubs and national economic magnets. These domineering cities, their affluence, arrogance, and corruption – may be viewed with a mix of scorn and envy not just by the conservative *Bergvolk*, but also by junior urban centers such as Geneva or Bern in Switzerland, or Sidon and Tripoli in Lebanon.[154] Nonetheless, in this instance, too, caveats are in order.

For, despite the striking similarities of two nascent states passing through the tumultuous phase of centralizing reform outlined thus far, the popular analogy drawn between the Swiss and the Lebanese polities displays significant divergences as regards the pace and scope of nationalization in the modern era. Social polarization – both in regional and ideological terms – is no longer as pronounced in Switzerland as it remains in Lebanon today.

In large measure, this difference may be explicated by the more robust – and successful – expansion of the state's sovereignty and federal institutions in Switzerland since 1848. Napoleon had already abolished

[152] The salon of Mme de Staël, the daughter of Louis XVI's finance minister Jacques Necker, embodied but one of the more (in)famous literary links to France. Georges-Paul Collet, "Some Aspects of Literary Relations between 'La Suisse Romande' and XIXth Century France," *The South Central Bulletin* 23.4 (1963): 46–50.

[153] Salomon Gessner (1730–1788), a co-founder of the Helvetic Society, established the *Zürcher Zeitung* in 1780, today known as the leading Swiss daily, the *Neue Zürcher Zeitung*. The first nongovernmental, secular newspaper in the Middle East was published by Khalīl al-Khūrī in Beirut in 1857. Its title – *al-Fakhr al-Munīr* (*the Enlightening Dawn*) – encapsulated the spirit of the day.

[154] Hawrānī, "Ideologies of the Mountain and the City."

the myriad of cantonal currencies and tariff barriers under the "single and indivisible" Helvetic Republic in 1798, introducing the Swiss Franc in their stead. National economic integration in Lebanon, by contrast, would reveal itself as a long, drawn-out process. Even the establishment of the Republic of Lebanon in 1926 and the attainment of full independence in 1946 did not always come with the usual economic perks. South Lebanon, for instance, saw its traditional trade routes to Palestine abruptly severed by Zionist colonialization and the erection of the State of Israel in 1948, while north and east Lebanon (the Biqā' and 'Akkār) suffered from the (brief) boycott imposed by Syria between 1950 and 1953, which allowed only contraband trade to percolate.

In 1956, Lebanon adopted a banking secrecy law directly modeled on Switzerland's landmark Banking Act of 1935.[155] This foundational blueprint had been drafted after a number of prominent French senators, generals, and bishops had been implicated in a spectacularly large tax-evasion scandal in 1931.[156] Both countries would reap considerable financial benefits from this overt legal loophole for money laundering, and from the capital flight that was set in motion by the instability that engulfed the surrounding countries during and after World War II.

The effect of Lebanon's adoption of the Swiss banking secrecy law was immediate and exponential. Within a mere four years after the introduction of the bank secrecy law in 1956, net bank deposits of Beirut banks more than tripled. In fact, in 1965, barely a decade after the promulgation of the secrecy law, Lebanon, at 122 percent, showed the highest rate of bank deposits as a percentage of GDP, globally. Switzerland, the country whose role as a regional banking hub it had emulated – in hindsight, perhaps too precipitously – was displaced to the second position.[157] By 1975, the service sector accounted for 75 percent of Lebanon's GDP, whereas soaring exports – spurred by the lowest tariffs in the

[155] The Bank Secrecy Law was first published on September 3, 1956 and passed by parliament on July 26 of the same year. The law was drafted by a prominent attorney and minister of parliament, the late Raymond 'Iddih who argued that Lebanese finance should not be hamstrung by legal quandaries. In June of 2002, Lebanon was removed from the list of countries judged not to be cooperating with international efforts to fight money laundering. Al-Jarīda al-Rasmīya (Official Gazette) (September 3, 1956).

[156] The scandal led to an incipient withdrawal of funds from Swiss banks by other international clients, prompting the Swiss authorities to pass the law of March 1, 1935 that penalizes the disclosure of private accounts. See Siegfried Sichtermann, *Geschichte des Bankgeheimniss* (Frankfurt, 1953).

[157] In 1965, Switzerland's ratio of banking deposits in relation to GDP stood at 78 percent, Great Britain's at 46 percent, and the United States' at 38 percent. Raymond Farḥāt, *Le Secret Bancaire: Étude de Droit Comparé (France, Suisse, Liban)* (Paris: Librarie Générale de Droit et de Jurisprudence, R.Pichon, 1970), 237, 250.

industrial world – diminished this ratio in Switzerland.[158] In sharp contrast to Lebanon, then, Switzerland managed to successfully diversify its nineteenth-century base in textile manufacturing by establishing one of the most robust industrial sectors in the world, explaining the Alpine republic's relatively speaking smaller reliance on the tertiary sector.[159] Moreover, regulatory bodies in Switzerland proved incomparably more successful in tempering and forestalling the adverse side effects of rapid, lopsided economic growth.

We thus arrive at what remains the most familiar and widespread association of Lebanon with Switzerland: the particular form of each of the two countries' political systems. Political scientists such as Arend Lijphart have grouped Lebanon and Switzerland together as "consociational democracies," a form of governance prevalent in communal societies governed by "elite cartels."[160] Lijphart for his part had borrowed the term from Johannes Althusius' (1557–1638) earlier notion of *consociatio* and Gerhard Lehmbuch's designation of Switzerland as a "proportional," "concordant democracy" (*Proporz/Konkordanzdemokratie*).[161] The underlying *raison d'être* stipulated for this form of consensual democracy is a high degree of social segmentation, whether it be along ethnic or religious lines. Clearly, Lebanon's unusual kaleidoscope of confessional diversity renders the concept as, if not more, relevant than in Switzerland, which only has known only two major denominations in its history.

In his vivid description of his *Travels through Syria and Egypt*,[162] the late eighteenth-century French author Volney leaves us with the image of multiple sectarian fiefdoms at loggerheads with one another. The confessional compartmentalization, however, is portrayed by Volney as the guarantee for peaceful coexistence, thus anticipating the argument for the "long" – if by no means frictionless – "peace" that prevailed during the *Mutaṣarrifīya* from 1864 to 1914, and the consociational (*ṭawāfuqī*)

[158] Salīm Naṣr, "Backdrop to Civil War: The Crisis of Lebanese Capitalism," *Middle East Report* 73 (1978): 6; Peter J. Katzenstein, "Capitalism in One Country? Switzerland in the International Economy," *International Organization*, 34.4 (1980): 507–540.

[159] One might add that Swiss subsidies to its farming industry far outstrip all other Organisation for Economic Co-operation and Development countries, whereas the agricultural sector in Lebanon, always neglected, has entered its death throes.

[160] Lijphart, *Democracy in Plural Societies*, 25 and "Consociational Democracy," *World Politics* 21.2 (1969): 216.

[161] Gerhard Lehmbuch, *Proporzdemokratie: Politisches System und Politische Kultur in der Schweiz und in Oestereich* (Tübingen: Mohr, 1967).

[162] Constantin François Volney, *Voyage en Egypte et en Syrie*, vol. 2 (Paris : Mouton, 1959 [1788]).

democracy as formulated by the fathers of the Lebanese 1926 constitution. It must be noted that, from the overt – and inapplicable – partition plan of 1845, to clause five of the *Règlement Organique* of 1864, which explicitly states the intent that administrative districts should be divided "as much as possible as to only include homogenous groups,"[163] the underlying, governing rationale of political settlements in (Mount) Lebanon – one which would resurface during the deliberations of the nascent republic in 1926[164] – was based on sectarian segregation. By contrast, mechanisms facilitating a state-initiated, interconfessional, national integration matured earlier in Switzerland.

The Rupture of Revolution: Did Secularizing, Republican Reform Spark Sectarianism?

> Without European colonial imagination, missionary activity, and Eastern Question diplomacy, there never would have been sectarianism. Indeed, without Ottoman reform, there never would have been sectarianism.[165]

In the previous section, we saw how the initiation of centralizing, secular reform during the period of Egyptian suzerainty could cause a communal backlash, partly instigated by overt and covert foreign intervention. This pattern of an ebb and flow of reform marked by successive outbreaks of bloody, intercommunal hostilities and increasing external embroilment was observable in the post-1840 period as well. Whether reform was pursued by the the imperial-Ottoman, the regional-Syrian, or in Mount Lebanon, it could trigger "nativist" responses asserting the primacy of feudal and family prerogatives.

There is a subtle, but important, difference that distinguishes this thesis from that holding the paradigm of nineteenth-century reform itself responsible for subsequent communalism. While we shall try to demonstrate that globalization and integration into a European-dominated

[163] Hanna Ziyāda, *Sectarianism and Intercommunal Nation-Building in Lebanon* (London: Hurst and Company, 2005), 73.

[164] Patriarch Ḥuwayyik could fathom a population transfer of Druze and Muslims analogous to what transpired in the Balkans or Silesia to safeguard the Grand Liban's razor-thin Christian majority. Decree 8837, which set forth the guidelines for naturalization in Lebanon, favored Christian rather than Muslim refugees. Thus (Christian) Armenian and Syrian refugees were specifically mentioned, while (Muslim) Kurdish refugees and Bedouins were excluded. Rania Maktabī, "The Lebanese Census of 1932 Revisited: Who Are the Lebanese?" *British Journal of Middle Eastern Studies* 26.2 (1999): 227–232.

[165] Maqdisī, *The Culture of Sectarianism*, 223.

world economy did indeed sharpen sectarian divides, the latter were largely preexistent.[166]

This book has therefore resisted the conventional, "knee-jerk" inclination to attribute the civil, confessional wars, which followed reform, to foreign powers alone. Yet, the growing impact of global forces, both economic and ideological, on the domestic development of secularism and sectarianism cannot be gainsaid.

If we were to widen our lens for a moment, we might view the period under investigation (1798–1864) as one of increasing capitalist integration of the region into the world economy. Following our discussion regarding the concurrent premodern mercantilism in Chapter 2, such economic commercialization and linkeage with European trade networks may have acted as a catalyst for secularism in the eighteenth century as well. Timur Kuran has contended that the increasing demands of European merchants for accountable laws – after 1535 – initiated a progressive "de-Islamization" – and thus secularization – of the Ottoman economy and legal framework for trade.[167] Ibrāhīm Pasha's revivification of Fakhr ad-Dīn's mercantile "free trade policy" can thus be analyzed within the wider geopolitical milieu, which may be described as an early phase of "globalization."[168]

It is instructive to briefly revisit the contradictory and at times adverse repercussions of this integration as a function of the interplay of a triad of local (Levantine), regional (Ottoman) and global (European) interest groups. While administrative proto-secularism seems to have figured as a natural corollary of the *force majeure* of capitalism and sound "civil" administration both in the seventeenth and nineteenth-century Lebanese emirates, there have been alternative explanations, which have identified the upsurge of inter-confessional strife in the nineteenth century as a symptom of the contradictions engendered by capitalist development.

In a perspicacious article, Paul Saba has noticed that the Egyptian occupation put upward pressure on prices for basic foodstuffs due to the provisions made for the large corps of soldiers.[169] Moreover, we have

[166] Curiously, the impetus to romanticize the pre–nineteenth-century past is not found in contemporaneous sources of the nineteenth century itself, one of which states point-blank that "before Muḥammad ʿAlī, Syria was a theater of wars and inter-sectarian dissension." Cited in Ṭarābulsī, *Kashf al-Lithām*, 117.

[167] Timur Kuran, *The Beginnings of Economic Modernization in the Middle East*, chapter 10 (2005), 34 (unpublished manuscript). Ibrāhīm Warda is among those scholars who has contested the premise of Kuran's thesis. See *Islamic Finance in the Global Economy* (Edinburgh: Edinburgh University Press, 2000), 44–45 and personal correspondence with Ibrāhīm Warda.

[168] Owen, "Using Present Day Notions of Imperialism."

[169] Saba, "The Creation of the Lebanese Economy," 13ff.

seen how an integration of Mount Lebanon into the global economy via Beirut could no longer afford costly feudal intermediaries. Bashīr II thus set about to deprive the feudal shaykhs – with the notable exception of himself and his family[170] – of retaining collected agrarian taxes at their discretion. By the end of the nineteenth century, the feudal aristocracy fell on hard times and former lords, such as the Khāzins and the Janbulāṭs, found themselves increasingly indebted, while a "*nouveaux riche*" class of bankers and merchants was flourishing in Beirut. The latter's success was in turn linked to Lebanon's incorporation into the global economy, for Ibrāhīm Pasha's reign coincided with a growing inflow of British and French imports, a development that was facilitated by the successive trade conventions the Ottomans saw themselves forced to sign with the British and French between 1838 and 1841. The principal objective of these successive treatises was not so much a secularization and standardization of law – even though these were implicit – but rather to break the local monopolies and provide for the establishment of mixed commercial tribunals devoid of judges with a religious background. It was here that the jurisdiction of the '*ulamā*' was particularly curtailed and where the constant intervention of European powers on the behalf of businessmen caused resentment of the reforms.[171] Despite his chagrin over the foiling of his mercantilist economic plans, in the legal realm, Ibrāhīm had in fact anticipated secularization with his confinement of the jurisdiction of the religious court system (*al-maḥākim al-shar'īya*) to cases of personal status laws in addition to his placement of the *awqāf* under direct government supervision, thereby further infringing on a traditional source of (tax-exempt) revenue and power of the clergy.[172]

This bold set of centralizing and secularizing reforms undertaken in the emirate between 1831 and 1840 had prefigured the curbs on clerical power that would characterize the reform movements in the Ottoman Empire during and after the *Tanzimāt*. One might even go so far as to say that starting with 1839 Edict of Gülhane, which ushered in an air of

170 Bashīr, for instance, entrusted his son Khalīl Shihāb with the vast holdings of the Janbulāṭs in the Shūf.

171 'Abdul Laṭīf Tibāwī, *A Modern History of Syria* (New York: St. Martin's Press, 1969), 140.

172 Philip Khūrī, *Urban Notables and Arab Nationalism: The Politics of Damascus: 1860–1920* (Cambridge: Cambridge University Press, 1983), 16. Once a milk property was converted to a *waqf*, the property was legally proscribed from being sold, pawned, or leased. The conversion of mīrī lands into *waqfs* in the course of the sixteenth century stripped the government of crucial revenue.

freedom and introduced a discourse of egalitarian constitutionalism,[173] the imperial *Tanzimāt* reforms themselves were not merely hastened by extraneous, European pressures as Reşid Pasha himself lamented, but also additionally spurred by the looming threat gathering in Mount Lebanon under Ibrāhīm Pasha, particularly after the latter's stunning defeat of the imperial Ottoman army on December 31, 1831 in Konia. Clearly, the edict was also intended as a goodwill gesture toward European powers who were anxious to ward off the looming danger of Muḥammad 'Alī.[174]

Formally, the *Tanzimāt* were the first edicts not to officially win the imprimatur of the *Şeyhülislām* who no longer was presiding over the *nizamīya* court system that was to be erected across the empire and in which the testimony of non-Muslims for the first time was to be granted equal weight. Even at this last stage, however, the *Şeyhülislām* remained the ultimate legal authority, if only by dint of his appointing the judicial inspectors (*müfettişler*) to the mixed appeals courts (*Divan-Û Temyiz*).[175] Even if the degree of their (non)application remains a matter of intense debate,[176] the *Tanzimāt* edicts heralded a sea change insofar as they triggered the momentum to break the judicial monopoly of *Sharī'a* courts, particularly after the judicial reform law of 1864, which officially established – beyond the *Sharī'a* courts – *maḥkeme,* councils (*mecliser*) and provincial appeals court.

It is important to bear in mind that the 1856 imperial decree to secularize the courts and to allow for lay participation in formerly religious councils stirred the resentment of segments of the increasingly besieged '*ulamā'* and the Orthodox bishops. Maronite bishops likewise

[173] The 1838 Edict explicitly states that it applies to "all our subjects, whatever religion or sect they may belong to." The 1856 Edict expands and specifies this principle of equality to the domains of taxation, military service, education, and public administration, even though the Turkish version differs its formulation equality from the French one. Nawāf Salām points out that the subject was still defined as a subject of an (unelected) sultan and that interconfessional segregation was cemented by the *Tanzimāt.* Nawāf Salām, *La Condition Libanaise* (Beirut: Dār an-Nahār, 1993), 113ff.

[174] Davison further highlights the fact that the 1856 Edict was issued in wake of the crisis of the Crimean War. Davison, "Turkish Attitudes Concerning Christian–Muslim Equality in the Nineteenth Century," 850.

[175] Avi Rubin, "Ottoman Modernity: The Nizamiye Courts in the Late Nineteenth Century," unpublished dissertation, Harvard University, 2006, 17.

[176] Avi Rubin has shown that the secularization of the courts and the introduction of the mecele that was elaborated between 1868 and 1876 itself cannot be taken to be a secularization as a new division of labor in the juridical bureaucracy. Rubin cautions that the heavy borrowing from the French legal system should not be confounded with wholesale imitation. Rather, by amalgamating provisions from European and Ottoman-Islamic legal systems, the Ottoman criminal code of 1840 stood on its own. Rubin, "Ottoman Modernity," 6ff.

expressed their opposition to the *Tanzimāt* insofar as they jeopardized their traditional privileges.[177]

With the 1858 new Land Code, the *'ulamā'* suffered a severe blow as it lost its privilege to inherit and bequeath land. Meanwhile the population was no longer subject to the state's right of land confiscation (*muṣādara*), a practice that de facto had rarely been implemented in the Mount Lebanon and other parts of Greater Syria, where a tradition of inheritable, private property (*mulk*) prevailed, quite possibly since Mamlūk times.[178] The latter has been held to serve as a precondition for the formation of capitalist enterprises on the one hand,[179] and as one of several factors explaining the longevity of the quasi-feudal dynasties of Lebanon on the other, as we shall see. By the nineteenth century, however, once dominant feudal families such as the Khāzins[180] were being sidelined by the rising power of the Maronite Church. The church rose to become the major economic player due to the monasteries assuming the lead in silk, fruit, and wine production.[181] The rise of the church was initiated by the formal end of the *muqāṭa'ajī* feudal dominance, which in turn was occasioned by the *Tanzimāt* and reinforced and confirmed by *Règlement Organique* of 1861 and 1864, as we have seen. After the 1736 "Lebanese Council" (*al-majma'al-lubnānī*), lay founders of endowments and monastic estates were proscribed from deriving any revenue from their gifts. With the shift in the balance of power, the church may have obtained some of the formerly Khāzin lands during the second half of the nineteenth century. Be that as it may, it is clear that

177 Faraḥ, "The Problem of the Ottoman Administration in the Lebanon," 456.

178 The Druze historian Salih Bin Yayha provides the earliest source attesting to a premodern hereditary system of land tenure. As a member of the ruling Druze Buḥturid clan his account may be somewhat biased. Four centuries later, Volney notes the presence of private, rather than sultanic, property in Lebanon. Engin Akarlı qualifies this characterization; the lands of the Maronite and later Greek Catholic Churches in Mount Lebanon "could be conceived as the private estates of the *muqāṭa'aji* who sponsored these settlements. The right of ownership of a private estate was inheritable and entitled its holder to a rent, but it did not represent an absolute proprietorship in the modern sense of the term." Engin Akarlı, *The Long Peace: 1861–1920* (Berkeley: University of California Press, 1993), 29. Akarlı omits mention that, unlike other regions of the Ottoman Empire, the Lebanese *iqṭa* only rarely was treated as a military fief mandating military service on its owner. See Yaḥyā, *Tārīkh Bayrūt* and Havemann, *Geschichte Und Geschichtsschreibung Im Libanon.*

179 Timur Kuran has argued that Islamic inheritance laws, by fragmenting family holdings, tended to prevent the accumulation of capital facilitated by some European inheritance laws. *The Beginnings of Economic Modernization in the Middle East*, chapter 10, 34 (unpublished manuscript of author).

180 By 1633, the Khāzin's obtained veto power from the Vatican in elections of Maronite patriarchs and, in 1657, Louis XIV appointed Abū Naufal al Khāzin as the Consul de France.

181 Sa'āda, *Social Structure of Lebanon*, 50.

the Louaize Synod ratified the autonomy of the Maronite clergy from the feudal lords, eventually leading to the ascension of the first patriarch of peasant stock, Bulūs Mas'ad in 1854.[182]

When the Maronite peasantry – influenced by revolutionary rhetoric and encouraged by the *Tanzimāt* promise of equality and the avid aficionado of Rousseau and Voltaire, Ilyās Ḥabalīn[183] – rebelled against the feudal lords under Tannyūs Shahīn in the uprising of 1858, demanding full equality in all matters, the Church and the Lebanese order[184] for the first time did not side with the landed nobility, perhaps thereby tacitly acquiescing in a further curtailment of the Khāzins in Kisirwān, who ironically had been instrumental in the expansion of church *awqāf* throughout the eighteenth century. This 1858 peasants rebellion against the exploitation of the landlords marks an insubordination that is often taken to have been informed by the global diffusion of (French) revolutionary ideals on the one hand, and a new consciousness of political representation and ethos of equality as enunciated in the *Tanzimāt* on the other.[185] Indeed, the Arabic vocabulary of "republican government" ("*al-Ḥukūma al-jumhūriya*") first appears as a contemporary description of Shāhīn's revolt against the Khāzin lords.[186] Significantly, the rebellion – from beginning to end – was an almost entirely intra-Christian affair. It was another Christian warlord, Yūsuf Karam (1823–1889) of Iḥdin, who, after having won the trust of Fu'ād Pasha for his moderation and willingness to subdue Shāhīn, was appointed as the Christian military governor (*qā'im maqām*) in the northern districts in 1862.

The Karam–Shahīn nineteenth-century rivalry is reminiscent of the intra-Maronite clashes between General Michel 'Awn and the head of

[182] Prior patriarchs hailed from *muqāṭa'ajī* families. Ḥarīq, Political Change in a Traditional Society, 35ff.

[183] Ḥabalīn's fierce anticlericalism is documented in Khalīfa, *Des Etapes Décisives*, 55–56. 'Āṭif Pasha, the Foreign Minister under Selim III, identified Rousseau "and other well-known heretics" as the source of the dangerous demands of equality and the abolition of the feudal system. Khūrī, *Modern Arab Thought*, 23.

[184] Founded around 1700, and benefiting from wide-ranging tax exemptions granted by Yūsuf Shihāb in 1767, the Lebanese order came to take over lands of Maronite landlords in financial difficulties, which were exacerbated after 1806 by the Amir Shihāb's bid to levy new taxes in Kisirwān and cut the notables to size.

[185] See Article 5 of the Kisirwān Rebel Charter as cited in 'Iṣām Khalīfa, "Lubnan lam yufsal 'an Suriya," *An-Nahār*, December 1, 2004, 12. Shahīn eventually submitted to the *fait accompli* of the *Mutaṣarrifīya* and was sent into exile and paid an Ottoman pension, which was only cut in 1877 "because his writings make clear that he still nourishes certain hopes and is not remorseful." Akarlı, *The Long Peace*, 37.

[186] Khūrī, *Modern Arab Thought*, 22. In Ottoman, like vocabulary was first found in Thomas Xavier Bianchi, *Dictionnaire Francais–Turc*, vol. I (Paris: Typ. De Mme Ve Dondey-Dupré, 1843–1846), 465 who translates democrat as "*ḥukūmati jumhūr nāsi taba'*," or "following the popular government of the people."

the Lebanese forces, Samīr Ja'ja' a century later. Both Karam and 'Awn rejected the externally imposed political compromise of the Statute of the *Mutaṣarrifīya* and the Ṭā'if Accord, respectively.[187] Both ambitious leaders laid claim to serve as national, native rulers (*Ḥākim-ra'īs*), and both trumpeted a transcommunal patriotism, even as their political power rested on a largely Maronite-base constituency.[188]

Ironically, Karam would fall out of favor with the Ottomans and die a somewhat ignominious death while leading a bitter polemic in penning invective pamphlets against the regime in Mount Lebanon from his exile in Naples from 1867 to 1889. While Shāhīn's revolt carried the signature of a Maronite peasant rebellion, Karam entertained alliances with the Shia Ḥarfūsh and – in cooperation with 'Abdul Qādir al-Jazā'irī – may have envisaged a secular, Syrian nationalism predicated on the Napoleonic Code, possibly within the wider context of a highly decentralized, federal Ottoman state.[189] As such, he constituted a threat of a different order to the governor Dawūd Pasha and the Ottomans. The Maronite Church would later demand the restitution of the Khāzin lord's property, at a time when the church itself was establishing itself as the major owner of real estate in Lebanon during the late nineteenth century. While the vast territorial holdings of the church endowed it with a power, which to this day mirrors that of the Catholic Church in premodern Europe,[190] the Muslim (Sunni)[191] religious institutions faced greater marginalization throughout the nineteenth and early twentieth century.

[187] Karam, who had initially refused an offer by Daūd Pasha to serve as the head of the security forces under the Ottomans, eventually hoped to gain an appointment as governor of the Christian district.

[188] For Karam's patriotic speeches, see Khāzin, Yūsuf Bayk Karam, 246; Ziyāda, *Sectarianism and the Intercommunal Nation-Building in Lebanon*, 78.

[189] The degree to which 'Abdul Qādir in fact was aware of or espoused such a vision remains unclear.

[190] Richard Van Leeuwen, *Notables and Clergy in Mount Lebanon: The Khāzin Sheikhs and the Maronite Church, 1736–1840*, vol. 2 (Leiden: Brill, 1994). The usage of Maronite *awqāf* for support of the clergy were theoretically prohibited according to Islamic law, yet in the eighteenth century this law was disregarded in Lebanon in light of the hegemony of the Khāzin lords. At present, the Maronite Church alone is, according to some estimates, said to own approximately 15–30 percent of real estate in Lebanon via its endowments (*awqāf*). When Buṭrus Labaki, the former vice president of the Council for Development and Reconstruction and right-hand of Premier Ḥarīrī, suggested putting the *waqfs* of the church to public use he met with the opposition of the church hierarchy. The Shia *awqāf* are usually managed by founding families or '*ulamā*', while the Sunni *awqāf* are supervised by the Supreme Council.

[191] Under the Ottomans, Shia' *waqfs* were virtually inexistent so that the demise of Ottoman power in the nineteenth century was of no consequence. The real marginalization of Shia' institutions came roughly a century later due to the expansion of the state. This also held true for the principal Shia' city of learning in Iraq, Najaf, where between 1918 and 1957 the number of students dropped precipitously from 6,000 to

In the end, the nineteenth-century reforms, which aimed at fostering interconfessional equality in the empire backfired as Tibawi has noted.[192] This was so even if the actual implementation of the *Tanzimāt* was highly contingent on the ability of the fledgling state to win local administrators who were willing to act as effective stewards and enforcers of the reform agenda. Ironically, the reform efforts pursued by the porte (and Ibrāhīm) were obviated by the very European powers who demanded the execution of the *Tanzimāt* centralizing reform and yet simultaneously weakened the government by dismantling state monopolies and lending support to nascent nationalisms in an ethno-religiously heterogeneous empire. Thus, the *Tanzimāt*, while conceived and executed as a measure to shore up an ailing empire's central authority, also ended up empowering local intermediaries, whether it be the *Çorbacı* Christian nobility in the Balkans or their counterparts in Lebanon.[193] In fact, this inherent paradox was even more pronounced in the latter case as in the Balkans, high-rank administrative positions were still reserved for Sunni Muslims, while the Lebanese Druze and Christian notables could claim a greater provincial role, as we have seen. In both cases – indeed across the globe – communal sentiments were on the rise.

The *Tanzimāt* were of import even though, by dint of its special, semi-sovereign status, (Mount) Lebanon – during the emirate (1831–1841), the *Qā'imaqāmayn* (1842–1860), and the *Mutaṣarrifīya* (1861–1914) alike – never directly fell under the jurisdiction of the *Tanzimāt* injunctions. Legally speaking, however, Mount Lebanon was still subject to the Ottoman *Sharī'a* for all legislation not relating to personal status matters, and certain civil matters, such as the granting of *awqāf*, which were continued to be issued by the Maronite Church in adherence to Ḥanafīte injunctions.[194] Moreover, the coastal cities of Beirut, Sidon, and Tripoli, in addition to the Syrian hinterland, were formally subjected to the *Tanzimāt* so that the repercussions of the reforms would be felt in neighboring Mount Lebanon as well, presaging as they did a larger process of political deconfesssionalization.

Aiming to level the distinctions between Muslim and non-Muslim, the *Tanzimāt* – to the chagrin of the conservative-minded father of the

less than 2,000. Rodger Shanahan, *Shi'a of Lebanon: Clans, Parties and Clerics* (London: I. B. Tauris, 2005), 141.

[192] Tibāwī, *A Modern History of Syria*, 90ff.

[193] Yonca Köksal, "The Application of the Tanzimat Reforms in Bulgaria: State Building in the Ottoman Empire (1839–1878)," electronic publication of Kokkalis Program, Harvard University, 1999, www.ksg.harvard.edu/kokkalis/GSW1/GSW1/11%20Koksal.

[194] Faraḥ, "The Problem of the Ottoman Administration in the Lebanon," 34.

mecelle, Ahmet Cevdet Pasha[195] – abolished the *jizīya* in 1855,[196] followed by the abrogation of the *ḥudūd* laws one by one, from the stoning of the fornicator to the cutting of hands of burglars to, in 1858, the abolition of the death penalty for apostasy (*ridda*) and religious defamation.[197] The resultant freedoms for Christians (and Jews) to showcase their religion – and hoist foreign flags – did result in sporadic flare-ups of violence, most notably in Nablus immediately after the promulgation of the *Islahāt Fermanı* ("Reform Edit") of February 1856.[198] The President of the Arab Academy identified the 1856 Decree – and the diminished status *vis-à-vis* minorities it implied for Sunni Muslims – as the root cause for the violence in Damascus in 1860. Even the sultan himself could not eschew the backlash of the bold reform he had lent his approval to. The foiled "*Kuleli*" assassination attempt of Sultan ʿAbdul-Mecid in 1859 was, according to the testimony of its leader Shaykh Ahmad, motivated by a desire to protest the 1856 Edict's flagrant contravention of Islamic Law, particularly with its elevation of the civil rights of non-Muslims.[199]

If the upshot of the *Tanzimāt* has been accordingly summarized as amounting to a "leveling up for the minority, and a leveling down for the majority,"[200] such a macro-synopsis fails to take into account why the other significant religious minority, the Jews, were spared in the communal recriminations that ensued.[201] As is almost always the case,

[195] Aḥmad Cevdet Pasha's (1822–1895) reaction to the abolition of the *jizīya* expressed a communal concern: "Today we have lost our sacred national rights which our ancestors gained with their blood; while the nation used to be the ruling nation it is now bereft of this sacred right. This is a day of tears and mourning for the Muslim brethren." Cited in: Moshe Ma'oz, "Changing Relations between Jews, Muslims and Christians," in *Jews, Turks, Ottomans*, ed. Avignor Levy (Syracuse, NY: Syracuse University Press, 2002), 113.

[196] Under the Mamlūks and Ottomans, a form of the *jizīya* was also levied on "heterodox" Muslims such as the Druze and the Nusayris. Abū Ḥusayn, "Problems in the Ottoman Administration in Syria," 666.

[197] Only after the Young Turk rebellion of 1908 and the political rise of such freethinkers such as Aḥmet Riza and ʿAbdullāh Cevdet was a clause (Article 55) added, which mandated one to three years of prison for "defamation of prophets." This article in fact survived the Kemalist Revolution in the form of Article 132 and Article 175 of the Turkish penal code, which prohibits public "defamation of religion." The article led to a tragicomic scene when Nuri Ceman, a die-hard Kemalist, faced a trial for publishing what was considered a perilously reverential paean of praise to Atatürk in the 1950s. Gotthard Jäschke, "Ehrenschutz Gottes und der Propheten in der Türkei," *Oriens* 15.1 (1962): 296–303.

[198] See Ma'oz, *Ottoman Reform in Syria and Palestine*, 209. Tibāwī, *A Modern History of Syria*.

[199] Davison, "Turkish Attitudes Concerning Christian–Muslim Equality in the Nineteenth Century," 861.

[200] Tibāwī, *A Modern History of Syria*, 128, 133.

[201] Ma'oz, *Ottoman Reform in Syria and Palestine*, 209.

socioeconomic discontent undergirded most, though not all, acts of sectarian violence.[202] Thus, it is not fortuitous that the relatively small Syrian Jewish community (not numbering more than 25,000) was virtually left unscathed during the riots in Nablus and Aleppo in 1850 or Damascus in 1860, whereas the Christian community, which numbered almost a quarter of a million, was perceived as a distinct threat, particularly in light of its affiliation with the growing presence of Western schools, consulates, and enterprises. Moshe Ma'oz notes that some Jews joined the Muslim mobs in the anti-Christian vendettas due to a mix of economic, political, and religious animosities.[203] During Ibrāhīm Pasha's occupation, Christian merchant families had increasingly crowded out Jewish competitors, often peddling vicious anti-Jewish blood-libel charges, thus adding (religious/ethnic) insult to (socioeconomic) injury. When the Egyptian authorities were replaced in Damascus by the Ottomans in 1841, the first Muslim–Jewish retaliation ensued against Christians before matters came to a head in 1860.

Ibrāhīm Pasha's prior opening to Western commercial and educational enterprises after 1831 paved the way for the subsequent Christian economic paramountcy and a communal polarization, which was only exacerbated by the European powers deliberate boycott of Muslim agents. While, in 1826, six out of thirty-four merchants trading with Europe were Muslim, by 1848, only three remained.[204] As Owen notes, the main artery of trade stretched from the financial and industrial center in France (Lyon) via the mercantile waystation of Beirut to the mulberry trees in Mount Lebanon. The concomitant expansion of an often "usurious"[205] commercial sector after 1860 further upended the *status quo* by sharpening regional and confessional rivalries and animosities.

[202] Khalīl Sa'āda, who had in 1879 rapped the internal Lebanese discord in Beirut, would subsequently bewail the eruption of riots between Muslim and Christian factions on the streets of Buenos Aires in 1915. "Al-Ta'assub al-Dīnī fī al-Mashriq wa al-Sharqīīn," in *Aḍwā' 'alā al-Ta'assub: Majmū'at mu'alifīn min Adīb Ishāq wa al-Afghānī* (Beirut: Dār Amwāj, 1993), 122.

[203] See Ma'oz, "Changing Relations between Jews, Muslims and Christians." This sorry tale of bigotry begetting bigotry continued right up until the Armenian massacres, although the Jewish millet was shielded and may even have benefited from the purges as Greek and Armenian competitors were eliminated. Significantly, the Committee for Union and Progress government did not contain a single Christian but a number of Jews. Mehmed Cavid was minister of finance in this critical period. Emmanuel Karasu (Carasso Effendi) was a confident of Talat Pasha and CUP member who amassed a fortune after he was put in charge of food distribution during World War I. See Feroz Ahmad, "The Special Relationship: The Committee of Union and Progress and the Ottoman Jewish Political Elite, 1908–1918," in *Jews, Turks, Ottomans*, ed. Avigor Levy (Syracuse, NY: Syracuse University Press, 2002), 216.

[204] Owen, *The Middle East in the World Economy*, 99.

[205] Saba, "The Creation of the Lebanese Economy," 13.

As European manufactured goods flooded the market in the second half of the nineteenth century, many Muslim artisans lost their jobs at the moment the local textile industry was suffering its worst crisis yet. At the same time, a *comprador* class of largely Christian agents and middlemen continued to flourish. These wrenching socioeconomic dislocations eventually precipitated the riots of 1860.[206] As Faruk Tabak put it:

> Restlessness and anti-Christian sentiment in Mosul starting in the 1840's and leading to the events of 1854, the Aleppo revolt of 1850 [full of animosity towards the Europeans] and the massacres in Damascus in 1860 can be seen as assaults launched to prevent erosion of the Muslim [and Jewish] mercantile community's share in the expanding networks of commerce – notwithstanding the contact and cooperation between parties of different faith or ethnic origin throughout the region.[207]

These flare-ups of communal confrontations between 1840 and 1860 have cast a long shadow. Paradoxically, the trauma of civil, confessional war has also served as the crucible for the modern Lebanese state, while external powers have acted as the godfathers of every political compromise concluded in Lebanon since 1840.

Aḥmad Bayḍūn has pointed out how some historians tend to slight the psychological effect on the Christian and Maronite population of what is somewhat euphemistically referred to as the "movements" (*ḥarakāt*) of 1860.[208] He notes how one prominent Lebanese historian is insistent on claiming that the French colonialists "lured" the Maronites into an alliance instead of noting that, in fact, the explicitly Sunni Ottoman system and Druze intimidation may equally have "pushed" them toward France, even as local Maronite warlords such as Ṭānyūs Shahīn galvanized the population to pursue what turned out to be a reckless revolt against feudal privileges.[209]

[206] See Khūrī, *Urban Notables*, 23.

[207] Faruk Tabak, "Local Merchants in Peripheral Areas of the Empire: The Fertile Crescent during the Long Nineteenth Century," *Review (Fernand Braudel Center)* 11.2 (1988): 204. Tabak draws a fascinating comparison between the Levant and similar social explosions involving the Bahais in Qajar Persia and the Taiping rebellion in late Ch'ing China.

[208] Within the span of three months, some 20,000 Maronites were killed in Mount Lebanon and up to 10,000 Christians slaughtered in Damascus according to Ḥittī, *Lebanon in History*, 438.

[209] Bayḍūn is writing in response to Wajīh Kawtharānī. By absolving the Ottoman administration of all responsibility for the mayhem in Lebanon, the latter stands accused of "fomenting an anti-Lebanese, Islamist" discourse, see Bayḍūn *Identité Confessionnelle Et Temps Social Chez Les Historiens Libanais Contemporains*, 386. Incidentally, both Bayḍūn and Kawtharānī, a student of Asad Rustum, were raised in Jabal 'Āmil. Kawtharānī relates his exposure to Rustum's Arabism and his "dispassionately neutral," objective school of history at the Lebanese University in Wajīh Kawtharānī, *al-Thākirat*

To be sure, far from seeing a consensus on the matter of apportioning responsibility, the debate on European (non)involvement in the civil war raging in Mount Lebanon and Syria divided European parliaments in the nineteenth century. With the governmental cabinet reluctant to commit troops, the French delegate de Malville gave an emotional speech in front of the French parliament in 1846 in which he admonished his colleagues not to let the "Switzerland of the East" descend to a state resembling "Poland."[210] In London, Karl Marx warned his readers "not to be carried away by the sentimental declamation of the Decembrist press, the feelings of horror at the atrocious outrages of wild tribes and the natural sympathy felt for the sufferers."[211] In an (almost) disparaging tone, Marx dismissed the mayhem of 1860 as a mere play, a "thrilling crusade" put on by "the conspirators of Petersburg and Paris" who were, in his view, more than happy to first foment sectarianism in the Ottoman Empire in order to subsequently pursue an ostensibly humanitarian cause abroad while deflecting from brewing discontent at home. Reports of the 1860 massacres elicited Marx's cynicism rather than anger; the latter was reserved for French, British, and Russian efforts to impose a "quasi-independence" on Mount Lebanon in 1846, which Marx lamented was thereby stripped of the prior Turkish imperial sway that had "curbed the wild tribes of the Lebanon."[212] Marx singles out Lord Palemerston's decision to furnish the Druze with weapons in 1841 as part of the recipe for the subsequent "harvest of blood." Faced with these ubiquitous allegations, the British Colonel-General Hugh Rose retorted defensively that Britain was left with "no choice" but to support the Druze after France had sent 200,000 piasters to the Maronites.[213]

European public opinion was swayed by the British press and the reports of massacres recorded in the "Blue book"[214] toward the coreligionist Christians. Meanwhile, the British Lord Dufferin, who initially

wa al-Tārīkh (Beirut: Dār al-Talī'a, 2000), 15ff. For Shahīn's role in the revolt, see Maqdisī "Corrupting the Sublime Sultanate," 180–208. Maqdisī writes of "the anxieties and memories [of 1860], whose veracity is completely beside the point."

210 Sawda, *Fī Sabīl Lubnān*, 226. See the following section for a more thorough study of this theme.

211 Karl Marx "Events in Syria," London, July 28, 1860 as published in *K. Marx and F. Engels Collected Works*, vol. 17 (Moscow: Progress Publishers, 1980), 429.

212 *K. Marx and F. Engels Collected Works*, 431.

213 Colonel Rose cited in Faraḥ, "The Problem of the Ottoman Administration in the Lebanon," 119.

214 *Despatches from Her Majesty's Consuls in the Levant, Respecting Past or Apprehended Disturbances in Syria: 1858 to 1860, Further Papers Relating to the Disturbances in Syria. June 1860* (London: Harrison and Sons, 1860).

had arrived in Beirut voicing outrage at the suspected Druze and Muslim culprits would soon find himself castigating the Maronite leadership and Bishop Ṭubīyā 'Awn as the principal instigators and provocateurs.[215]

Dufferin's diatribe would be echoed a century later by none other than Kamāl Janbulāṭ, the grandson of Said Janbulāṭ who stood accused of having planned and numerous instances of ethnic cleansing, such as in Sakbīn in 1841 and in Jazzīn in 1860.[216] Otherwise considered an icon of the secular left, Kamāl Janbulāṭ viewed 1860 as the humiliating end of Druze predominance in Mount Lebanon. The necessary "corrective" to this beginning of a "Maronite usurpation" would only come in the civil war of 1975. It is difficult to distinguish Kamāl Janbulāṭ's ostensibly "secular" disdain for the Maronites from the nineteenth-century Druze shaikh Khattar al-'Imād's tirade against the "wretched Maronite villagers ... our abject subjects" in the name of the "sword of Islam."[217] After all, Janbulāṭ took great pride in his descent from a "warrior aristocracy," and insisted on "a multi-confessional Lebanon, dominated politically by the Druze and the Muslims," all the while only thinly disguising his paternalistic, typological loathing for the Maronites *sui generis*:

> The Maronites may take excellent care of their own affairs, but they are poor managers for a Republic. They are too closely bound by their sectarianism, and by a sense of their own interest ... [By contrast] it is not surprising that there are so many people in liberal inclination amongst the Druses ... They are famous throughout history for their ... lack of chauvinism.[218]

Janbulāṭ's lament of innate Maronite ineptitude was prefigured almost verbatim in the verdict rendered by the British Commissioner Lord Frederick Dufferin that "the Maronites are savages incapable of self-government."[219] Part of the motivation for Dufferin's sweeping caricature of the Maronites – which was matched by like derogatory French

215 Layla Fawwāz, *An Occasion for War: Civil Conflict in Lebanon and Damascus in 1860* (London: I. B. Tauris, 1994), 210. Despite Dufferin's suspicions, evidence of Bishop Ṭubīya actually stirring up Maronites in the Shūf remains flimsy at best according to Fawwāz.

216 Colonel Churchill speaks of 210 casualties in the 1841 raid on Sagbeen and describes Janbulāṭ as "the most wayward, overbearing and unscrupulous of these feudal marauders (whose) grasping and unprincipled covetousness extended even to the direct and open confiscation of landed property, overtaking at times both Druze and Christians alike." Churchill, *The Druzes and the Maronites*, 58, 99.

217 Cited in Maqdisī, *The Culture of Sectarianism*, 75–76. The Imāds had been subjugated and expelled under Bashīr, but staged a comeback after the amirs exile.

218 Cited in Kamāl Janbulāṭ, *I Speak for Lebanon* (London: Zed Press, 1982), 29ff.

219 Cited in Cesar Faraḥ, "The Problem of the Ottoman Administration in the Lebanon, 1840–1861," 378.

caricatures of the "insolent" Druze[220] and "blood-thirsty" Muslims – stemmed from the intense British–French rivalry for control of the "buffer-zone" of Mount Lebanon in which the Druze would become the natural – and invariable – ally of the British, if only by dint of the preexisting Maronite–French axis and the British preoccupation to contain Muḥammad 'Alī.[221] In the end, Dufferin obtained the removal of the French military occupation and succeeded in isolating Mount Lebanon from both Damascus and the former adjacent provinces of the emirate in the negotiations over the borders of the *Mutaṣarrifīya* in 1861. Backed by Britain, Istanbul could thus ignore the 1867 petitions of the provinces of the eastern Biqā', Rāshayā, and Ḥāṣbayā asking to be attached to the *Mutaṣarrifīya*. By contrast, a previous request by Beiruti merchants to establish the central commercial and civil tribunal for the entire *Mutaṣarrifīya* in Beirut was met.[222] The imperial fiat also prevailed over the aspirations of the first *Mutaṣarrif*, Dāūd Pasha, who continuously lobbied for a formal incorporation of Beirut into the *Mutaṣarrifīya*, claiming with unbound optimism that with unification, "all the sectarian differences would disappear."[223] In the end, Dāūd only won the concession to administer Western Biqā' after 1865 and would have to contend himself with the customs duties, which the *Mutaṣarrifīya* received from Beirut until 1867.

The British–French rivalry over hegemony over the Middle East cannot be expounded in full. Suffice it to say that the legendary British Counsel Richard Wood, shortly upon his installation in Damascus on a mission to drive a wedge between France and the Maronites, boasted that "all governors and public positions are owed" to him.[224] By 1858, however, he had to concede that the French had become the virtual

220 See, for instance, Murād, *Notice Historique Sur L'Origine de La Nation Maronite*, 22. Yanoski and David, *La Syrie ancienne et moderne*, 365.

221 Cited in Faraḥ, "The Problem of the Ottoman Administration in the Lebanon," 378. Dufferin's aversion toward Maronites led to the appointment of a non-Maronite Christian governor. Kamāl Janbulāṭ would later echo this sentiment in declaring the Maronites unfit to rule, while claiming that the "Druses have never needed [foreign] protection." Janbulāṭ, *I Speak for Lebanon*, 30.

222 After 1861, this court would arbitrate all commercial and civil cases in the *Mutaṣarrifīya*. See Owen, *The Middle East in the World Economy*, 165.

223 John P. Spagnolo, "Mount Lebanon, France and Daud Pasha: A Study of Some Aspects of Political Habituation," *International Journal of Middle East Studies* 2.2 (1971): 161. Beirut was formally annexed to Damascus by the imperial *firmān* of May 1, 1865, meaning that the city lost its status as the provincial seat of the government of Sidon. In 1888, a separation was ordered by 'Abdul Ḥamīd, who relented after being pressured by Beiruti merchants and notables. See Jens Hanssen, *Fin de Siècle Beirut: The Making of an Ottoman Provincial Capital* (Oxford: Clarendon Press, 2005), 47ff.

224 Ma'oz, *Ottoman Reform in Syria and Palestine*, 212. Wood's main mission was to woe Bashīr II away from Muḥammad 'Alī and France.

rulers of the Levant. In 1914, French investment in the Ottoman Empire exceeded the cumulative sum of all British, German, Italian, American, and Russian investments.[225] It is little wonder then that the search for the roots of the confessional predicament has centered on the role ascribed to foreign powers in fomenting local fissures.

In addition to Lebanon's variant exposure to foreign powers, any juxtaposition of the political anatomy of each of the Swiss and Lebanese consociational systems must account for the divergent chronologies and contexts. After all, full independence and national consolidation under the aegis of a modern state was attained in Switzerland in 1848 almost exactly one century prior to Lebanese independence and final liberation from the tutelage of the French mandate in 1946. It was the latter that warded over the institutionalization of the consociational democracy (*al-dimuqrāṭīya al-ṭawāfuqīya*) within the framework of a republican regime from 1920 onward. Ever since, the formula was to be denounced by opponents who identified it as the chief obstacle to national unity and secular integration, even as the same covenantal arrangement has been hailed by its proponents as the most preferred solution for a society marked by a mosaic of demographic diversity.

The framers of the Lebanese constitution in 1926 were quite conscious that it was Switzerland, with its coalition governments and mutual communal vetoes, which resembled the Lebanese analog far more than England or France, despite Lebanon's constitutional debt to the latter.[226] The chief architect of Lebanon's 1926 constitution, Michel Shīḥā, repeatedly pinpointed and touted Switzerland as an exemplary prototype "of prudence and moderation" for Lebanon.[227] Shīḥā drew an analogy between the federal sovereignty of the cantons in Switzerland and the confessional groups in Lebanon, without, however, ignoring the difference between the (largely) territorial basis of the former and the communal identity of the latter.[228] The Chamber of Deputies is identified as the pivotal meeting point, the official manifestation of "*vouloir vivre en commun*," expressing the shared desire of the confessions to coexist and come to a political consensus in a multicommunal society. In this sense, the Swiss Federal Council can indeed be likened to the Lebanese Council of Ministers as a form of coalition government on the

[225] Joseph G. Shāmī, *Le Mémorial du Liban*, vol. I (Beirut: Chemaly & Chemaly, 2002), 51.
[226] Thus opined the president of the constitutional commission, Shiblī Dammūs, during its deliberations. *al-Ṭā'ifīya fī Lubnān Min Khilāl Munāqashāt Majlis al-Nuwwāb 1923–1987*, 15–16.
[227] Michel Shīḥā, "Sur la Révision de la Constitution," *Le Jour*, April 13, 1948; "L'Exemple Suisse," *Le Jour*, July 30, 1947 in *Politique Intérieure*, 134–135, 316.
[228] Shīḥā, *Politique Intérieure*, 316.

basis of representative allocations, which are distributed in the Swiss case primarily according to ethno-linguistic and political – rather than strict sectarian – affiliations.

The inclusive spirit of the Swiss "magic formula" or *Zauberformel*[229] then closely resembles that animating the rationale for the Lebanese practice of power sharing (*muḥāṣaṣa*/*mushāraka*),[230] which, since the Ṭā'if Accord of October 22, 1989, has become an even fifty-fifty Muslim–Christian split or "*munāṣafa*." The governing formula of confessional parity (*konfessionelle Parität*) in both cases goes back to a common origin, for it had first been instituted in wake of the 1648 Peace of Westphalia in select cities such as Augsburg and indeed across Switzerland, which had largely escaped the ravages of the Catholic–Protestant Thirty Years' War, in part due to its prior adoption of confessional segregation. In fact, the Swiss "*Gemeindeprinzip*" of 1529 antedated the "*cuius regio eius religio*," which first had been enunciated in the Peace of Augsburg in 1555. Vestiges of this administrative principal are visible until today in so far as the relationship between state and religion is delegated to the individual cantons in the Swiss Confederacy.[231] With the exception of the bifurcation of the Canton of Appenzell into a Catholic, mountainous, agrarian *Innerrhoden* and a Protestant, industrial *Ausserrhoden*, however, the principle of "Westphalian" confessional allocations has largely faded in Switzerland, whereas in Lebanon it has been accentuated by civil wars fomented by confessions vying for primacy.

[229] The "magic formula" or *Zauberformel* regulating the party affiliation and tacitly also providing for the French or German identity of the seven federal counselors was instituted in 1959 and lasted until December 10, 2003 when a marginal adjustment was made as a seat of the Catholic conservatives, the Christliche Volkspartei, was given to the Schweizerische Volks Partei (Swiss Populist Party; SVP) due to the latter's success in the national election. By contrast, in Lebanon the Council of Ministers has mushroomed from seven members in 1926 to twenty-four at present. Before 1891, the Swiss Federal Council lacked a Catholic representative. Today, the confessional representation is less salient an issue than the divide between left and right, which almost overlaps with the chasm between the Swiss- and French-speaking cantons, the proverbial *Röschtigraben* "*Röschti-rift*." Indeed, federal elections as late as 2004 revealed a re-opened chasm between the Romande French-speaking and left-leaning cantons and the more conservative, nationalist SVP wave, which is dominant in the German-speaking states. Language here may play a similar role religion does for many marginalized Shia in Lebanon.

[230] Ziyāda differentiates between the two, the former denoting the "allocation of shares," while the latter is translated as "equal participation in administration and government." In political fact, the two terms appear interchangeable. Ziyāda, *Sectarianism and Intercommunal Nation-Building in Lebanon*, 107.

[231] Article 72 of the Swiss Constitution in Paragraph 2 also charges the cantons with the preservation of peace between the different religious communities. A 1980 initiative proposing a complete separation of church and state was overwhelmingly rejected by the Swiss electorate.

Considering the rather similar premodern departing point, the question arises: Why could Switzerland afford to largely dispense with confessional parity whereas this principle was to become enshrined with increasing meticulousness in Lebanon? A comparative history of the evolution of the two power-sharing models reveals as many striking parallels as it does illuminating distinctions, particularly as concerns the gradual diminution of communal competitiveness in the Swiss case, and its persistence – and resurgence – in the Lebanese one.

Both the Swiss confederate and Lebanese republican political systems were initially engineered – and dominated – by an urban, at times cosmopolitan, bourgeoisie eagerly embracing economic liberalism. In Switzerland such liberalism was embodied by the "Free Democratic Party" (FDP), which represented the Protestant cantons and from 1848 until 1891 enjoyed a virtual monopoly of seats in the Federal Council. In Lebanon, a similar if less complete political monopoly was exerted by the Maronite *classe politique* from 1920 to 1943. Even after 1959 the Protestant FDP continued to command a disproportionately high number of seats in the Federal Council, thus resembling the continued primacy of the Maronites in Lebanon by dint of their control of the presidency, the army, internal security services, foreign service, and the central bank after 1943. The respective Protestant and Maronite mercantile elites in both systems thus only belatedly and incrementally gave up their hegemony for a more equitable representation of the initially marginalized groups: the Sunni and the Shia in Lebanon, and the Catholics and Social Democrats (SP) in Switzerland.

The main point of divergence between the two systems, however, is salient in the respective locus of ultimate executive and legislative power in each country. As we shall further elaborate in the subsequent chapter, far more executive power has been vested in the Lebanese Council of Ministers after the 1990 Ṭā'if amendments to the constitution. Even prior to this major revision, however, the locus of political power was elsewhere than in Switzerland.

Lebanon's first constitution of 1926 – drafted in the shadow of the French mandate and described as a mere calque (*décalquage*) of the constitution of the Third Republic by High Commissioner de Jouvenel – invested the president of the new republic with sweeping powers. These included the right to dissolve parliament and dismiss the cabinet, powers totally unbeknownst to the largely ceremonial position of the president of the Swiss Confederacy. To placate growing Sunni discontent, the premiership was earmarked for the Sunnis (by convention rather than law) in Lebanon in 1936, while the Shia were accorded the position of the speaker of parliament only after independence. Due to Lebanon's oscillating demographic balance, changing majoritarian claims could unsettle and unhinge what should be a consensus-driven concordant democracy based on a proportional electoral system. No such vacillations in the interethnic composition and no comparable external shocks buffeted Switzerland, which could thus afford a more static conservatism in which the German–Swiss hegemony[232] would be countervailed by a strong tradition of federal protection extended to the countries minorities.

From 1814 onward, Switzerland would successfully insulate itself from foreign intervention and continental conflict by adopting an official national policy of neutrality.[233] Meanwhile, Lebanon in the same era would increasingly become a magnet for repeated, direct intervention and a theater for wars carrying regional and even global dimensions. As we have seen, such meddling exacerbated domestic divides and thereby further encumbered the road to secular nation-building. Thus, while rates of mass emigration from Switzerland declined in the course of the nineteenth century, in Lebanon they continued to steadily rise and peaked in World War I as the Levant was ravaged by civil wars, famine and a grave economic crisis.[234]

Most germane to the development of secularism perhaps is the fact that the Swiss system proved far more conducive to spawning an individualist notion of citizenship, one which in time would sideline confessional and ethnolinguistic identities By contrast, political formation in Lebanon was – and remains – clustered around the confessional bloc. Besides Switzerland's adoption of a transconfessional, civil personal status code, this key difference may be attributed to the fact that Lebanon

[232] The case can be made that the secret of Swiss political stability lay in the fact that the demographic majority also enjoyed economic supremacy. In Lebanon and such cases as the late Ottoman Empire, by contrast, the disproportionate concentration of wealth among demographic minorities proved to serve as a cause for contestation and intercommunal conflict. I thank Professor Heinrich Feichtinger of the ETH Zurich for this valuable insight.

[233] Neutrality and nonintervention had been the de facto politic of the Swiss confederacy after the battle of Marignano in 1515 in which Swiss mercenaries had fought each other.

[234] The first major emigration from Lebanon after the famine of 1816/1817 coincided roughly with the exodus of Lebanese to Muḥammad ʿAlī's Egypt. The last wave in Switzerland occurred between 1880 and 1885. Subsequently, Switzerland would itself serve as a safe haven in war-torn Europe. If one wanted to invoke yet another metaphor, Switzerland would become the sedate, calm eye of the storm during World War II and the Cold War, while Lebanon found itself periodically tossed and turned – and shred to pieces by regional perturbations. See Albert Ḥawrānī and Nadīm Shahādī, eds., *Lebanon and the World: A Century of Emigration* (London: Centre for Lebanese Studies and I. B. Tauris, 1992).

has adopted a parliamentary system with fixed quotas, whereas Switzerland is the world's only direct democracy in which the simple popular majority has the final say in national referenda and initiatives, two mechanisms would constitute the heart and soul of a participatory *Res Publica.*

The sovereign in Switzerland are the people, that is the individual citizen or *Bürger*: "*Der Souverän ist das Volk*" is the very first lesson Swiss schoolchildren memorize by rote when learning about their political system.[235] In Lebanon, by contrast, ultimate power lay with the heads of the confessional parties who mediate the individual voice and who usually exert direct, quasi-dictatorial control over their sectarian blocs in the highest executive body, the Council of Ministers. In other words, politically, the citizen in Lebanon only exists as part of the larger community he or she is born into.

Consequently, the "politics of the notables," that is the rule of a thin elite of feudal-sectarian "leaders" or "*zu'amā*," is virtually unknown to post-1848 Switzerland where the highly circumscribed authority of the Federal Council (*Bundesrat*) is of an entirely different order than the powers accorded to the Lebanese Council of Ministers (*Majlis al-Wuzarā*).[236] This is not to claim that parliamentary pork-barreling and "sweetheart deals," the proverbial "*Vetterliwirtschaft*," are foreign to Bern; a suspiciously high percentage of members of parliament serve simultaneously on the board of major Swiss firms. Unlike in Lebanon, however, all extra-parliamentary income is carefully registered as required by a special parliamentary law. The penchant for nepotism and opportunity for graft is ultimately checked in Switzerland in that final decisions cannot be imposed and laws not tailored by the political class or Lijphart's "elite consensus."[237] Nor can a regional or political hegemonies be easily foisted on the entire country given that constitutional changes require a "double majority," both of the states and of the popular vote. Thus, clear systemic safeguards – rather than "cultural

[235] The Lebanese constitution does contain a like phrase that the "people are the source of sovereignty" in section d of its preamble. Unlike in Switzerland, this statement, however, is largely rhetorical.

[236] The Swiss president – who serves on an annual term as the head of the Federal Council of Ministers – wields largely representative powers hardly exceeding those of the queen of England. The Lebanese president – elected by parliament to a six-year term – has seen his authority curtailed, but still remains the formal head of state whose signature (along with those of the prime minister and the speaker of parliament) is required for any law or decree *marsūm* to be passed. The post-Ṭā'if powers of the Lebanese head of the Council of Ministers, however, may exceed those of the French premier, particularly if the former enjoys an absolute parliamentary majority.

[237] Lebanon can be deemed a more orthodox embodiment of Lijphart's definition of consociational democracies than contemporary Switzerland. Lijphart, *Democracy in Plural Societies*, 25.

specificities" – explain why Swiss political corruption could never reach quite the proportions oligarchic clientelism (*zubūnīya*) has in Lebanon. Nor did the centripetal forces of the quarreling "*Kantönligeist*" ever set canton against canton in the same way confessionalism did in Lebanon. The Catholic–Protestant war of 1848 marked the last time that Swiss parties would seek foreign aid to assert themselves against each other, whereas seeking succor from external patrons to embolden each sect's domestic standing ("*al-istiqwā bil-khārij*") has become a recurring symptom of Lebanese political life until today.[238]

Inherited Sin or Inescapable, Saving Grace? Tracing the Lineage of the Lebanese Confessional System

> In view of the continued division of the people of Mount Lebanon into numerous *ṭawā'if*, all of which ought to enjoy the beneficence of the esteemed Sultanate, the members of the council are to elect from among the notables the most capable of each sect. Each sect is to elect a member – besides the judges elected by these sects – who shall attend the sessions of the council with the members of the other sects. Specifically, they are mandated to look into and settle the cases of the children of their denomination (*abnā' madhhabihim*) according to their religious belief (*wifqān li-'aqīdatihim ad-dīnīya*).[239]
>
> Shakib Efendi's *nizām* of 1845, establishing the partition of Mount Lebanon

Unfortunately, the preferred ways to cope with the nagging legacy of intercommunal clashes in Lebanon have been deliberate evasion, deflection of blame on external culprits, and a suppression of historical memory. The same predisposition also informed the drafters of the first "consociational" compromises that were formulated in response to the civil wars of the nineteenth century.

After the 1840 Maronite–Druze hostilities in "Mount Lebanon" (*Cebel-i Lübnan*),[240] the Ottoman authorities represented by Shakib Efendi – voicing bewilderment at the "rudeness of character" displayed

[238] Significantly, Article 6 of the April 12, 1789 French constitution, which prohibits such reliance on foreign powers, was one of the articles not added to the Lebanese constitution: "Les rapports d'une secte avec une autorité étrangère ne doivent influer ni sur les affaires politiques, ni sur la prospérité et les lumières du peuple."

[239] See al-Azīz Nawwār, *Wathā'iq Asāsīya*, doc. no. 106, 395.

[240] Formerly known as (*Cebel-i Düruz*). Maqdisī tells us that, while the designation of *Cebel-i Lübnan* first appears in 1845, the Ottomans did not refer to it in this period. From 1911 onward, however, Istanbul ceased to refer to Lebanon as the *Mutaṣarrifīya*, instead preferring the designation *Jabal Lubnān*. The Young Turks also replaced the last Ottoman Christian *Mutaṣarrif* with a Muslim one in further violation of the *Reglement*. On June 5, 1915 the last Christian governor, Ohannes Pasha saw his term prematurely

by the Lebanese – were resolved to "terminate this question of Lebanon once and for all."[241] Accordingly, the imposed peace protocol invoked the slogan "*maḍā mā maḍā*" ("let bygones be bygones"), a formula that prefigured the later refrain of *lā ghālib wa lā maghlūb* ("no victor and no vanquished"), a euphemism akin to that used to describe – or suppress – the memory of the massacres of 1860 and which continues to be recited in the aftermath of the 1975 civil war "events" (*aḥdāth*).[242]

The objective of these mantras was tantamount to imposing a collective amnesia. In each instance, they have forestalled a frank coming to terms with the bloody historical past as was the case in post-apartheid South Africa or postwar Germany. Ultimately, this deliberate oblivion has proven powerless to exorcise the ghosts of *ṭaifīya*, which has come to haunt Lebanon time and again. The sanitized remembering and redactions – or papering-over – of Lebanon's scarlet, sectarian history have a bearing on the present as they directly shape decisions on national policies, the 1991 General Amnesty Law serving as the most recent testimony to this antihistorical rationale.

A sizable segment of post-civil war Lebanese historians, politicians, and school textbooks continue to display a marked proclivity to diagnose sectarian sentiments and strife as a concoction of the nineteenth century, that is to say a direct result of a deliberate policy of divide and rule of France and Britain. This historical narrative tends to ascribe sectarianism as an imported imperial legacy, extraneous to the Lebanese national character and a feudal social structure in which rank rather than religion was the all-decisive marker of identity.[243]

terminated by the porte and in August of the same year Cemal Pasha replaced the Armenian with a Turk, Munif Bey, and officially abolished Lebanon's semiautonomous status and elected representative bodies. From 1917 to 1918, a Shia pasha was appointed (Ismāʿīl Ḥaqqī Bey), followed by a Sunnite Turk, Mumtaz Bey. Ṣalībī, *The Modern History of Lebanon*, 115.

241 "Ottoman Circular on Changes in the Administration of Lebanon of July 28, 1845," doc. 96, The Middle East and North Africa in World Politics, 296.

242 Fawwāz, *An Occasion for War*, 182.

243 While Maqdisī in *The Culture of Sectarianism*, 35, qualifies his bold stance on the absence of sectarian sentiments prior to the turmoil of 1839, his central assertion of the relative of sectarian identities remains salient and is reiterated again as the conclusion. "European and Ottoman … decisive effort to rebuild a sectarian orthodoxy where none had previously existed" (78). Thus, Maqdisī maintains that Islamic metaphors were deployed not to impose a sectarian supremacy over persecuted minorities, but rather to reinforce an already inviolable social hierarchy in which religion had not been salient (46). Sectarianism to Maqdisī then is an "imagined" discursive tool wielded by the ruling power to legitimize subordination, not a preexistent identity ready to be exploited. "Their heresy had been their rebellion" (56). As shall be restated in the conclusion, this book maintains that sectarian

Religious communalism and sectarianism are bracketed as decidedly modern "inventions," rather than resurfacing primordial identities. In fact, casting blame for the allegedly nineteenth-century concoction of sectarianism on outside, Western meddling has become the near-dominant narrative, promoted by journalists, historians, and politicians alike:

> The sectarian strife of the year 1840 was the result of civil relations in which sectarianism played no palpable role whatsoever. As for what is related about 'historical persecutions' between Maronites and Druze and between Christians and Muslims before the aforementioned year, such claims fall under the category of historical 'sectarian jingoisms' and falsifications of historical truths for political ends not the least of which is the capture of foreign sympathy and help.[244]

Sectarianism in this nationalist historiography of amnesia becomes an alien disease, one which even manages to "derail the [1975 Civil] war from its natural course"[245] – although we are left in the dark as to what this Spencerian selection may have entailed. This discourse – which was also endorsed by the leading theoretician of the Phalange party, Amīn Nājīj[246] – bears a certain affinity to the apologetic notion of a "war of the others," a mantra conjured by Ghassān Tuwaynī in order to deflect responsibility for the nightmarish killings from the Lebanese and their allegedly "inexistent" sectarian inclinations to the fabricated animosities hatched by foreign machination. The late Pierre Jummayil would even go so far as to blithely deny – on the eve of the civil war of 1975 no less – the very existence of confessionalism (*ṭāifīya*) in Lebanon.[247]

The implication of such a reading is that an original, supra-sectarian identity is putatively buried in the feudal order that prevailed *in illo tempore* before the (foreign) imperial intrusion of Ibrāhīm Pasha in 1831. The patent fallacy of such historical reductionism notwithstanding,[248] it was indeed Ibrāhīm who, mimicking Napoleon's precedent in

identities do in fact often exhibit primordial, ideological premises that can and should, however, be critically reconceptualzed in a secular state of law.

[244] Khalil Arzūnī, "Masa'lat al-ṭā'ifīya fī Lubnān," *as-Safīr*, December 18, 2003. Kamāl Janbulāṭ was keen to identify "French intervention to protect the militarily defeated Maronites" after 1864 as the source of all sectarianism in Lebanon.

[245] "ḥarrafu al-ḥarb min masārihi al-ṭabīa'ī." Arzūnī, "Masa'lat al-ṭā'ifīya fī Lubnān."

[246] The distinguishing nuance of the Phalange discourse is that the Ottomans – rather than the French – become the chief culprit for the imp lantation of sectarianism in Lebanon. See Amīn Najī, al-Katā'ib wa al-'Almānīya as cited in 'Isām Khalīfa, "A la Récherce d'une Politique Ou d'un Concept de Secularisation dans le Liban Multiconfessionnel (1858–1975)," doctoral thesis, Paris-Sorbonne University, 1980, 132.

[247] an-Nahār, March 2, 1972 cited in Khalīfa, "A la Récherce d'une Politique Ou d'un Concept de Secularisation dans le Liban Multiconfessionnel (1858–1975)," 134.

[248] One need only peer back less than a decade to see the Druze–Maronite civil war of 1821–1825. For a good panoramic survey of earlier, premodern intersectarian strife, see Muḥammad 'Alī al-Makkī, *Lubnān 635–1516: Min al-Fatḥ al-'Arabī ilá al-Fatḥ al-'Uthmānī* (Beirut: Dār an-Nahar, 1979). To see how overt sectarian biases shaded the

Egypt, established the formal, institutional moorings of the Lebanese consociational system. In June 1832 the first *shūra* council was setup in Damascus followed on January 24, 1834 by a municipal council (*diwān*) in Beirut whose membership – prefiguring the post-1990 parliament – was evenly divided between six Muslims and six Christians delegates respectively.[249]

The same logic of an even confessional division informed the creation of the "dual district" (*Qā'im Maqāmayn*) (1842–1860), an arrangement which was originally devised by the Austrian chancellor Prince Metternich and elaborated under the auspices of the Ottoman foreign minister Shekib Efendi in 1845. A staunch champion of the *ancien régime*, Metternich arrived at a compromise solution midway between the demand of the French and the Lebanese Christians for a restoration of the Shihābite emirate on the hand and the British–Ottoman–Russian insistence on integration and rejection of any return to Lebanese autonomy.[250] Once again stripped of the coastal cities, Mount Lebanon was divided along the rather arbitrary line of the Beirut–Damascus road into a northern, Christian-governed district ("*nasara kaymakamlıgı*") and a Druze, southern equivalent ("*druzi kaymakamlıgı*").[251] The two governing councils were composed of one Sunni, Maronite, Druze, Orthodox, and Melkite member. The Shites were notably being left out. In Shakib Efendi's revised *Nizām* of 1845, however, the *Matāwila* (Shia) were allowed to nominate one *qāḍī* as their representative on the council. The councils were nominally subservient to the Ottoman *wālī* of Sidon, thus losing the autonomy that they had enjoyed prior to 1840 and which they would regain after 1861 as an autonomous province (*Mutaṣarrifīya*). As would be the case for virtually all subsequent political accords in Lebanon's history, the regime of 1842 was imposed on Mount Lebanon after the

historiography of the era, see Yaḥyā, *Tārīkh Bayrūt*, 7ff. in which the conversion of Crusader churches into mosques is related in celebratory prose and poetry.

249 In later decades this proportion was occasionally subject to shift. Jens Hanssen has sifted through the Ottoman salnames and carefully tabulated the composition of the popularly elected council members between 1868 and 1909 and found that the Muslim–Christian parity, formally required by the Ottoman Law, was not the rule. The Druze, many of whom had been expropriated, were entirely excluded. See Hanssen, *Fin de Siècle Beirut*. After the withdrawal of Ibrāhīm, the Majālis in Sidon and Beirut were staffed with more Christians than that in Damascus (where there were none) or Aleppo (where there were two).

250 Ṣalībī, *The Modern History of Lebanon*, 62.

251 "Ottoman Circular on Changes in the Administration of Lebanon of July 28, 1845," doc. 96, in *The Middle East and North Africa in World Politics*, 271. Lords Clarendon and Holland appended their dissent. Maqdisī, *The Culture of Sectarianism*, 79.

landing of international (in this case British and Ottoman) troops on September 10, 1840.[252]

After the renewed and even more violent outbreak of Christian–Muslim conflict on July 6, 1860, representatives of the clashing Maronite and Druze parties were forced by the Ottoman governor of Sidon Hürşid Pasha to sign a peace accord in which each side agreed to bury the hatchet without discussing, let alone resolving, the source of the conflict. It was, however, only after the eruption of the ferocious anti-Christian riots in Damascus only three days later on July 9 that the Ottomans were constrained to convene a conference of the five great powers. A French-dominated European naval force was also sent on August 16, 1860 to restore order and protect the civilian population.[253] While peace returned to the Levant, the political solution entailed only limited accountability.

In reaction to the renewed resurgence of violence, the sublime porte dispatched its foreign minister Fu'ād Pasha. After meting out severe punishments against the perpetrators of the massacres in Damascus – including the secret, summary execution of the erstwhile Governor Aḥmad Pasha[254] – Fu'ād Pasha returned to Beirut where he let the main culprit of the massacres, Khurshid and his retainer off scot-free, while the Druze chieftain Said Janbulāṭ saw his sentence commuted.[255] No reparations were exacted from the Druze, nor from the Shia and Sunni villagers and farmers who abetted them in some of the carnage during the razing of Christian villages in the Biqā'.[256]

Contrary to the prevalent belief that European intervention redounded to the benefit of the Maronites, the apportionment of seats in the administrative council at this point did not reflect the full demographic preponderance of the Maronites who got four seats (while comprising three quarters of the population) whereas the Druze received three, the Orthodox two and the Catholics, (Sunni) Muslims, and Shia each one seat.[257]

[252] The Treaty of London of 1840 demanded that Muḥammad 'Alī withdraw from the Syrian provinces. When he refused, the British–Ottoman alliance forced its will. Amir Bashīr was deposed and sent into exile in Malta.

[253] 'Abdul Qādir reprimanded Fu'ād Pasha for the Ottoman role in instigating the Damascus riots. See Churchill, *The Druzes and the Maronites*, 275.

[254] The omission of a regular trial facilitated the subsequent veneration of Aḥmad Pasha as a shahīd in Syrian history books. Tibāwī, *A Modern History of Syria*, 130.

[255] Said and his sister Naiyfa were suspected by the Christians of Ḥāṣbayā of having commanded some of the massacres. Ṣalībī, *The Modern History of Lebanon*, 100. Fu'ād Pasha ordered the release of 500 Druze prisoners and thirty Shia implicated in the massacres, leading Churchill to describe the proceedings as a mockery of justice. Churchill, *The Druzes and the Maronites*, 243.

[256] Ṣalībī, *The Modern History of Lebanon*, 101.

[257] For a full reprint of the *Règlement*, see appendix C in Ziyāda, *Sectarianism and Intercommunal Nation-Building in Lebanon*, 224–228.

The (Armenian) Christian Ottoman *Mutaṣarrif* Dāūd Pasha was quickly challenged by grassroots Christian revolts in Kisirwān led by Yūsuf Karam. To be sure, this conflict may in part be read in purely statist center-periphery dynamic rather than in sectarian terms, for the 1861 *Règlement* revealed a marked change in the ultimate source of authority; no longer were the village commissions and *vekīl* (ombudsman) entrusted with mediating interreligious disputes, this went to the central state or the administrative council of the *Mutaṣarrifīya* (autonomous province). Moreover, the tax-levying privileges that still had been bestowed on the feudal grandees (*Aṣḥāb al-Iqṭā'āt*) in the 1845 statute were now revoked in their entirety.

By establishing a unified "federal" authority, the *Mutaṣarrifīya* thus redressed the most significant shortcoming attendant on the bicommunal *qā'imaqāmayn* and discarded its logic of pure and complete communal segregation. Administration of mixed districts in a strictly confessional manner had proven a nightmare for all parties involved. A neat and simple division had been precluded by the heterogeneity and interwoven demographics of Lebanon. These lessons, as we shall see, would retain their relevance in the subsequent constitutional history of Lebanon. In particular, the recognition of the ineluctably shared destinies of Muslim and Christian *ṭawā'if*, which after 1943 came to be known under the premise of "conviviality" (*'aysh al-mushtarak*).

To cite and criticize the multiple shortcomings of the regimes of 1845 and 1861 – as some scholars have been wont to do – begs the question of what exactly the more salutary alternative might have been. Would Lord Dufferin's suggestion of turning Lebanon into an Ottoman *pashalık* really have constituted a viable solution rather than a recipe for prolonged conflict?[258] Would the imposition of a full-fledged laic, Jacobin state have been a realistic option – or even a remote possibility – at this blood-stained stage and against the backdrop of fresh, lingering mutual resentments spawned during the preceding intercommunal hostilities?

After all, each Lebanese "fraternal" political compromise invariably followed a prior period of "fratricidal" conflict, which, while jolting the *status quo ante* and animating a constitutional revision, severely reduced the viability of a secular, noncommunal nationalism. Nor were the foreigners alone in their estimate of the necessity of external mediation. Staunch secularists and most committed patriots such as Buṭrus al-Bustānī and Yūsuf Karam likewise reached the sobering conclusion that

[258] Fawwāz, *An Occasion for War*, 210.

a people so given to sectarian conflict "deserved" the yoke of foreign patronage as a quasi "divine retribution" for "domestic sins."[259]

Lastly, we might equally recall that the external imposition of political compromises was by no means unique to Lebanon, nor, *ipso facto*, inhibitory to subsequent democratic progress. As previously alluded to, the quarrelling Swiss cantons saw the first two federal constitutions dictated to them by France (on April 12, 1798 and the *Act Fédérale de l'An 1803*, respectively). In the Swiss case, foreign intervention to facilitate political settlements arguably contributed to dampen interconfessional animosities. Intercantonal instances of civil strife only sporadically resurfaced after the Swiss confederation was placed under "European guarantee" by the imperial powers at the Congress of Paris in 1814.[260] Even the last Swiss civil war of 1847–1848, while unfolding along squarely confessional, Protestant–Catholic fronts, pales in comparison to the heavy toll exacted in the Druze/Muslim versus Maronite/Christian Lebanese civil wars of the same period.

To simply shift the bulk of the blame for eruptions of confessionalism to the machinations of foreign powers appears both ethically insincere and historically inaccurate. This, at any rate, was the conclusion drawn by Buṭrus al-Bustānī as early as 1860.[261] The same may be said about the resultant political compromises. No doubt external players had a major say in determining specific outcome, and, yet, whatever the balance of power or particular aspirations may have been, variations of the same "consociational" model seems to have almost inevitably imposed themselves as the solution to periodic flare-ups of confessional strife in 1840, 1860, 1926, and 1989. It is well to remember that even the most progressive, multiconfessional nativist movements, such as the communal councils of the *'ammīyāt,* clamored for set confessional quotas to govern the seats of a prospective non-Ottoman locally elected, interconfessional governing council. The declaration of 1840 also listed the demand for a

[259] Yūsuf Karam cited in Fawwāz Ṭarābulsī, "al-Istiqlālān:'Asi'la ilā al-Tārīkh," *As-Safīr*, November 25, 2006. Bustānī echoed this sentiment: "We thus believe that the [foreign] intervention was injurious due to the disparate religious and civil interests of the intruders, even if there were some temporary benefits for individuals. Nonetheless, we assert that the intervention this time [1860] was beneficial to all groups and necessary to stop the spread of the hysteria and devastation which, like the diseases of a pandemic, spread from place to place with rapidity. Would that this intervention had begun and created its effect before the spread of the destruction and the deterioration of matters. The hands of Syria remain indebted to these hands which helped the sincere … and reigned in the nefarious perpetrators of a rebellion against God." Bustānī, *Nafīr Sūrīyā*, 52.

[260] Gordon E. Sherman, "The Neutrality of Switzerland," *The American Journal of International Law* 12.4 (1918): 787.

[261] Bustānī, *Nafīr Sūrīyā*, 52.

bifurcation of judicial authorities for Druze *qāḍī* in the Shūf, Matn, Gharb, and Jurd and a separate Christian judge for the Christians of *Kisirwān.*[262]

To be sure, there is no denying the exploitation and even fomenting of local fissures by foreign powers. As the mission of Colonel Wood showed, *dividia et impera*, that is the sowing of dissension, particularly in Maronite ranks, was very much part of British policy in the region. Nonetheless, far from merely being the brainchild of any such devious "divide and rule" strategy, Lebanon's successive constitutional compromises evidently developed as documents designed to quell *prior,* inter-Lebanese conflict by assuring the representation of all major confessions that had been at loggerheads. However flawed the result, to ignore the latter backdrop for confessionalism seems at minimum disingenuous and at most a mode of analysis suffering from wanton neglect. Evidently, consciousness of a common notion of citizenship – with all the implicit political rights and duties – was simply too frail to assert itself and prevail over the dominant logic of communalism. Given the right amount of social, political, and economic pressure, this "logic" could all too quickly morph into a most irrational and incendiary mass hysteria.

Birth of the Vaṭan

> In Europe, indeed, zeal for country has taken the place of zeal for religion, but this arose after the decline of their feudal age. But among us, if we were to adopt the term *vatan* now, all that would come to the minds of our soldiers is their village quarters...In a tight spot, would Private Hasan obey the order of Captain Christo?
>
> Ahmet Cevdet Pasha[263]

The still feeble appeal of a nonsectarian, patriotic allegiance was not a sociological characteristic exclusive to nineteenth-century Lebanon, but also, we might add, observable in the Ottoman Empire where the communal attraction of a secular *vaṭan* was widely perceived as inferior to a religious, communal identity.[264] The quote of the architect of the *mecelle,*

[262] Khalīfa, *Des Etapes Décisives*, 58. Al-Azīz Nawwār, *Wathā'iq Asāsīya*, 257.

[263] Cited in Bernard Lewis, "Watan," *Journal of Contemporary History* 26.3/4 (1991): 526.

[264] The word Turk (Chinese: *Tu-Kü*, *Tukoi*; Greek: *Turkoi*) is cited as a synonym for "vigor" in the oldest Turkish document, the seventh-century Orchon inscriptions. Like the analog of national adjectives in Europe, it was initially not infused with a positive sense of national pride until the publication of the poem of Mehmet Emin in 1897. By the time Mustafa Kemal founded his *Vatan ve Hürriyet Cemeyeti* in 1905 in Damascus, the term *vaṭan* had obtained a greater revolutionary currency. Gotthard Jäschke, "Vom Osmanischen Reich zur Türkischen Republik: Zur Geschichte eines Namenswechsels," *Die Welt des Islams* 21 (1939): 87–89.

Ahmet Cevdet Pasha, expressed a low estimate of the rallying potential of secular nationalism, one that was not necessarily merely a reflection of Cevdet Pasha's conservative disposition. In the November 3, 1839 Edict, the term *vaṭan* received only a generic, passing mention in an appeal to the "defense of the fatherland."[265] Likewise, the 1843 edition of Bianchi's *Dictionnaire Francais–Turc* lists "*vaṭanī seven*" (lover of the nation) for patriot, but does not contain any reference to "citizen." The *Kulturnation,* then, preceded the *Rėpublique.*[266]

It is interesting in this context to note that Shakib Efendi used the term *vaṭan karadeşi* (brother of the nation) as early as 1845 in order to exhort the Lebanese to patriotism, albeit one subservient to the imperial, patriarchal fiat; the "inhabitants of Lebanon" were thus reprimanded – with "high paternal solicitude" – to conform to the "duties of obedience and their status as subjects."[267] Despite the unmistakable air of the *ancien régime*, this may well have been one of the earliest official usages of the term *vaṭan* prior to its popularization by the Ottoman poet and playwright Namik Kemal (1840–1888) in a play of the same title.[268] While Kemal saw his plays banned due to the (now feared) subversive implications of the term *vaṭan* in a multicommunal empire, one might bear in mind that the playwright and poet remained – along with ʿAlī Suavi and the majority of *New Ottomans* – a fierce opponent of the *Tanzimāt* reforms. The reforms were seen as excessive concessions by a besieged empire to the encroaching foreign powers, and thus denounced as heralds of increasing inequality rather than equality.

The 1856 "Reform Edict"(*Islahāt Fermanı*) in turn contains an apparently new coinage in Turkish when it introduces a clause vowing to strengthen the "cordial ties of citizenship" ("*revabıtı kalbiyeyi vatandaşī*").[269] The *-daş* suffix seems to be used here for the first time in the Turkish language.[270] Analogous to the almost coeval Arabic neologism of *muwāṭin,* it signifies a relation of reciprocity, while succinctly

[265] Kağıt Kaynaklar, *Düstur, Birinci Tertip*, vol. 1, s.-7, *Türk Anayasa Metinleri*, eds. Suna Kili and A. Şeref Gözübüyük (Ankara: Türkiye İş Bankası Yayınları, 1985), 11–13.

[266] Bianchi, *Dictionnaire Francais–Turc*, vol. II, 597. I thank Aziz al-Aẓmeh for this insightful exegesis.

[267] "The inhabitants of Lebanon will come to understand that the more they conform to the duties of obedience and of their status as subjects, the more they will obtain tokens of goodwill and of graciousness from His Highness." Maurus Reinkowski, "Beyond the Mountain Refuge," in *From the Syrian Land to the States of Syria and Lebanon*, 233.

[268] Nermin Menemencioğlu, "The Ottoman Theatre 1839–1923," *Bulletin (British Society for Middle Eastern Studies)* 10.1 (1983): 48–58.

[269] Doc. 104 in *The Middle East and North Africa in World Politics*, 315.

[270] Bianchi cited in Davison, "Turkish Attitudes Concerning Christian–Muslim Equality," 852.

and elegantly underscoring the shared notion of civic identity on an equal footing.[271]

In his 1860 report on the events in Mount Lebanon and Syria, Fu'ād Pasha likewise entreated the conflicting Christian and Muslim parties to treat each other as *vaṭandaşlar,* even though his point of reference for nationhood (*vaṭandaşlık*) was clearly pan-Ottoman rather than Syrian or Lebanese. Standing at the cusp of a new age, Fu'ād was a cosmopolitan, suave Ottoman statesman who sought to introduce just the right dose of republican reform to strengthen – rather than subvert – the empire. It may thus be a mark of an anachronistic judgementalism to charge these administrators for not having rid themselves of what appears to us today as paternalistic, imperial terminology such as *ra'āyā* (the subject "flock") in their correspondence.[272] We have previously cited Ibrāhīm Pasha employing the same vocabulary in order to affirm the fundamental equality of Muslims and Christians,[273] as would other secular-minded Ottoman administrators. While the reformers' intentions may have been progressive, Maqdisī astutely points out that Fu'ād's campaign for "egalitarian citizenship" (*hemişirilik*) and "patriotism" (*ḥubb al-waṭan*) was predicated on a demand of unqualified obedience to the sultanic "father figure" and thus implied a strengthening of paternalistic, imperial hierarchies.[274]

Be that as it may, the evolution of Ottoman political terminology in conjunction with its assimilation to the secular-republican spirit of the age would be mirrored in like transformations in the Arabic political lexicon. Indeed, the pace of the assimilation and forging of republican terms in Arabic may have, if anything, lagged slightly behind.

Indicatively, Article 21 of the 1926 Lebanese constitution – which in all likelihood was first drafted in French – contained a curious translation error: where the French text speaks of the "*citoyen libanais*," the Arabic rendition reads "*waṭanī lubnānī*," which would correspond to "Lebanese patriot." Rather than fault the ostensibly poor translation skills of Muḥammad al-Jisr and Yūsuf al-Khāzin as the renowned constitutional scholar Edmond Rabbāth has,[275] one might conjecture that the very

[271] I would like to express my gratitude to Himmet Taşkomür and 'Alī Yagicoğlu for kindly aiding me in translating the relevant Ottoman passages.

[272] See Reinkowski, "Beyond the Mountain Refuge," 233. After all, the terms "subjects" could carry the same connotations elsewhere as well.

[273] Rustum, *Bashīr Bayna al-Sulṭān wa al-'Azīz*, vol. I, 99.

[274] Usāma Maqdisī, "After 1860: Debating Religion: Reform and Nationalism in the Ottoman Empire," *International Journal of Middle East Studies* 34.4 (2002): 606. Even more portentous fusions of paternalism and patriotism are found in European analogs.

[275] Edmond Rabbāth, *La Constitution Libanaise: Origines, Textes et Commentaires* (Beirut: Université Libanaise, Distribution, Librairie Orientale, 1982), 38.

ceonceptual term of "*muwāṭin*" had still not been firmly established as part of the Arabic political lexicon.

In Buqṭur's Arabic–French dictionary of 1828 we still find the highly generic "*ibn al-balad*" ("son of the land," "*Landmann*") as the translation for *citoyen.*[276] During the emirate, the inhabitants of what was called Barr ash-Shām were simply referred to as *as-shawām* or the even more frequent and generic "*al-Ahālī*," sometimes qualified as "*Ahālī al-Ṭā'a*" ("subjects of obedience")[277] Bustānī's seminal reference work in 1864 expounds the (popular) dichotomy of urban civilization (*tamaddun*) *versus* "state of nature" barbarism (*barbarīya/tawaḥush*) in conjunction with the binary attributes of uncouthness (*khushūna*) *versus* ignorance (*jahl*). However, we find no separate entry for "citizen" save the accustomed *ibn al-balad*, even though Bustānī lists almost the entire roster of verbal and nominal derivations of the trilateral root *wāw/ṭā/nūn*, including the Qur'ānic and apolitical plural from the singular *mawṭin* ("territory"), *mawāṭan.*[278]

Barely half a century later, the vocabulary becomes slightly more differentiated, but the category of a citizen/*muwāṭin* has still not been coined. One can see the efforts expended at this stage to find the proper Arabic renditions of a terminology commensurate with a still indistinct notion of nationalism. Khalīl Sa'āda in the first modern English–Arabic dictionary of 1911 translates "patriot" with the familiar "lover of nation" (*muḥibb lil waṭan*) in one instance, while citizen is rendered in circumscribed form either as "*mustawṭin al-madīna*"[279] ("city occupier") or as "*rajul thū ḥūqūq madanīya*" ("a man bearing civic rights"), a phrase no doubt inspired by the *Tanzimāt* discourse while finding renewed expression in Article 7 of the Lebanese constitution of 1926.[280] At this point, however, the mere mention of "*waṭan*" sufficed to launch an Ottoman prosecution of the editor of the Beirut journal *al-Munīr* in 1914 on suspicion of sedition.[281]

[276] Ellious Bocthor, *Dictionnaire Français-Arabe par Ellious Bocthor; Revu et augmenté par A. Caussin de Perceval* (Paris: Chez F. Didot père et fils, 1828–1829), 158. The term *Landmann*, however, is more clearly defined in the Swiss *Bundesbrief* of 1291.

[277] Ironically, this designation appears in the 1840 Pact.

[278] Buṭrus al-Bustānī Muhīt al-Muhīt, *Ay Qāmūs Muṭawwal lil-lugha al-'Arabīya* (Beirut, 1867), vol. 2, 60–64.

[279] See David Samuel Margoliouth, ed., *Sa'āda's Dictionary*, vol. 2 (Beirut: Librairie du Liban, 1974), 323.

[280] "All Lebanese are equal under the law and they are to equally enjoy political and civil rights" (*ḥūqūq madanīya*). See *Al-Dustūr Al-Lubnānī*, ed. Shafīq Juḥā (Beirut: Dār al-'Ālam, 1991), 38.

[281] Sylvia G. Haim, "Islam and the Theory of Arab Nationalism," *Die Welt des Islams* 4.2/3 (1955): 142.

It is Anṭūn Ilyās who in the first edition of his 1923 English–Arabic dictionary printed in Cairo adds perhaps the earliest entry for "compatriot" as "*mawāṭin al-insān*,"[282] even though an appeal to "*al-mawāṭīn*" surfaces two decades earlier in Būlus Mas'ad's monograph on Lebanon and Ottoman constitutionalism of 1909.[283] Given the novelty and apparent absence of the term in more standard Arabic reference works, however, the framers of the 1926 Lebanese constitution can hardly be held accountable for not availing themselves of this vocabulary. After all, the ebullient exchange of views between parliamentarians during the discussion of the 1926 constitution amply confirm an eloquent engagement – and deep familiarity – with the whole gamut of issues related to secularism and sectarianism as we shall see. Before the discussion on secularism could reach that maturity at the dawn of the twentieth century, however, it would have to pass through numerous trials and tribulations.

This book has thus far proposed that, up until the mid-nineteenth century, the introduction of social and secular reform proceeded *grosso modo* in lockstep in Europe and the Middle East. Proto-secular and -national structures of governance did develop organically, as we saw in our treatment of the regimes of Fakhr ad-Dīn II, Bashīr II, and the *'ammiyāt* insurgencies, even if these secular reform movements were often tied to foreign, European, and Egyptian sponsors or inspiring paradigms. By the end of the nineteenth century, however, a noticeable divergence seems to emerge, less in the pace, but certainly in the comprehensive scope of a final transition to fully enshrined secularism.

The subsequent chapter shall examine some possible explanations for this discrepancy. I shall devote particular focus on the respective role assumed by the *secular intelligentsia*, which, invariably, would come to constitute the backbone of secularism and provide the intellectual cement for nation-building. One need not be a disciple of Carlyle's "History of Great Men" to acknowledge the direct indebtedness the French Revolution owed to the likes of Rousseau and Voltaire, Condorcet and Danton, or the American Revolution to the republic's founding fathers. It is not that there were no Arab and Syro-Lebanese counterparts to these avatars, men who could and would persuasively argue for a society – and modern state – freed of the shackles of communal discrimination. Rather, the

[282] Antoon Elias, *Elias' Modern Dictionary, English–Arabic* (Cairo: Elias' Modern Press, 1943), 673. Any conclusions regarding this still understudied topic are necessarily preliminary and inconclusive.

[283] Bulus Masad, *Lubnan wal-Dustur al-Uthmani* (Lebanon and the Ottoman Constitution) (Egypt: al-Ma'arif Press, 1909), 8. In which Mas'ad, writing in 1908, pleads for Lebanese unity and a return to the 1860 Accord, while retaining cordial relations with the Ottomans.

predicament faced by the advocates of an Arab Enlightenment was that they saw themselves constrained to formulate their bold ideas within different historical, sociological, and political variables.

As in Europe, the call for secularism dovetailed with the germination of nationalism, that solvent that was fraying the fabric of the multicommunal imperial patchwork. The (Catholic) Habsburg and (Orthodox) Romanov empires entered their final days almost concurrently with the (Sunni) Ottoman Empire, and, yet, in the European cases, the struggle – with notable exceptions – unfolded as primarily an internal, "internecine" battle, whereas extraneous imperialist intrusion loomed large in any political debate in much of the Middle East and particularly the Levant.[284] Thus, ideological stigmatization of secularism, which by no means was foreign to continental Europe, was exacerbated in Muslim and Christian "nativist" discourse by a combustible mix of anticolonialism and a bevy of "Occidentalist" stereotypes, which had to be debunked before political secularism could be proposed with greater openness, intellectual coherence, and political success.

Occidentalist Defamation of Secularism: Missionaries, Masons, and the *Mutanawwirūn*

We mortals are composed of two great schools
Enlightened knaves or religious fools.

al-Maʿarrī (973–1957) ʿAbbasid poet[285]

The Moslems were divided rather sharply into the intelligentsia and the Arabs. The first were those who had thrown of Arab things, and bared themselves to the semi-Levantine, semi-European fashions of the renegade Moslem – the Moslem who had lost his traditional faith – and with it the belief in all faith.

T. E. Lawrence, *War Diaries*[286]

Secularists are the sick and the agents of Foreign Powers.

Zuhair Sulaymān[287]

[284] It is interesting to note that Ibrāhīm Müteferrika, the Masonic Hungarian convert from Calvinism to Islam who founded the first Turkish printing press in the Ottoman Empire in 1727, pointed to the reforms of Peter the Great in Russia as an example of the successful strengthening of a non-Western culture with Western techniques. See Nizayi Berkes, "Historical Background of Turkish Secularism," in *Islam and the West,* ed. Richard Frye (The Hague: Mouton, 1957), 51.

[285] Cited in Phillip Ḥittī, *History of Syria: Including Lebanon and Palestine* (New York: St. Martins Press, 1957), 583.

[286] "Syrian Cross Currents," February 1, 1918, cit. in Malcolm Brown, ed., *TE Lawrence in War and Peace: An Anthology of the Military Writings of Lawrence of Arabia* (Barnsley: Frontline Books, 2005), 162.

[287] Cited in Raghid al-Solh, "Religious Identity and Citizenship," in *Peace for Lebanon?* ed. Deidre Collings (London: Lynn Rinner, 1994), 237.

The roots of modern apostasy lay in scientific atheism, dialectical materialism, rationalism, illuminism, laïcism, and freemasonry – which is the mother of them all. Pope Pius XII, May 23, 1958[288]

In Lebanon there is no such thing as individual faith as there is in France … You cannot import French secularism because it simply is part of a history which is not ours. Archbishop Jurj Khidr[289]

There is no gainsaying that secularism traveled a difficult, serpentine path in the Arab world. The mere European provenance of secularism exposed it to the violent eddies of populist polemics and cynical power-politics and tainted it by its association with Western imperialist designs of domination, which themselves were often at odds with a progressive, secular agenda.[290] Unfortunately, the politically charged atmosphere in the Arab world throughout the nineteenth and twentieth centuries further distracted from an objective analysis of the historical moorings, characteristics, and purport of European secularism. Rarely do we find attestation to the fact that the separation of church and state was first and foremost a pragmatic solution to a bloody affair: the drawn-out inter-sectarian strife that rent Europe from the papal schisms and Inquisitions to the Reformation and down to the Wars of Religion. It was this basic political challenge posed by governance in confessionally heterogeneous societies to which secularism primarily responded to,[291] far more than any alleged epistemological incompatibility of religion and science or the waning of religion *per se*. As such, the specter of intercommunal bloodshed in the Middle East and such pluralistic societies as Lebanon has motivated and continues to motivate marginalised Arab secularists to espouse the same solution to the same basic predicament[292] posed by "deadly [communal] identities."[293] Yet, these proponents of secularism have had to confront a deep-seated and widespread suspicion of overt political platforms calling for a secular state. The reasons for the predicament of secularism, however, go beyond scholarly debates on proper

[288] Address to the Seventh Week Pastoral Adaptation Conference, Italy.

[289] Jurj Khidr, "Huwwīyāt al-Lubnānīyīn," *an-Nahār*, July 27, 2003.

[290] Nawāf Salām notes that the progressive, democratic institutions introduced by the imperial powers contradicted the mandatory authorities' preference for distinct families and confessions, "manipulated elections" and "suspended constitutions." See Nawāf Salām, "The Emergence of Citizenship in Islamdom," *Arab Law Quarterly* 12.2 (1997): 147.

[291] William of Orange (1650–1702) was the first European monarch to fully institute full freedom of religious toleration. See Wolfart Pannenberg, "How to Think about Secularism," *First Things* 64 (1996): 28.

[292] Bernard Lewis has made this point repeatedly. See Bernard Lewis, *Islam and the West* (Oxford: Oxford University Press, 1993), 186.

[293] Amīn Ma'lūf, *Les Identités Meurtrières* (Paris: LGF, 2001).

etymological derivations of secular political vocabulary, even though the latter are not an entirely arcane matter, as we have seen.

Three principal handicaps have received the attention of scholars as regards the difficulties faced by secularism in the Middle East[294]:

1. Its association with (Western) colonialism, Christianity, and aloof urban elites and secret societies from the nineteenth century to the present day.[295]
2. Its sponsorship and besmirchment by repressive regimes post-independence.[296]
3. The attempts by states to establish hegemony over religion and to exploit religious discourse and institutions rather than properly separate secular and religious spheres.[297]

While the focus in this section shall rest on the first of the three factors, one might recall that the deficiencies besetting secularism are decidedly not exclusive to the Middle East.[298] Indeed, whether it be Ivan the Terrible raising himself above the church as the sole *Imperator Dei*, Peter the Great (r. 1682–1725) abolishing the Russian patriarchate, Catherine the Great (r. 1762–1796), or Napoleon setting about to confiscate church lands, secularism in Europe was almost uniformly a top–down affair. Large swaths of the rural population remained staunchly committed to the "medieval" notion of a Christian commonwealth long after

294 See Vali Naṣr, "Lessons from the Muslim World," *Daedalus* 132.3 (2003): 67–72.

295 It is worth noting that squarely secular leaders continue to be associated with foreign intervention, thus enhancing the appeal of advocates of a religious state. The twist in Iraq between the American-backed Iyad ʻAlawī and the United Iraqi Alliance – with the latter platform of a *Sharīʻa* state gaining the upper hand – is one of many examples.

296 Secular policies pursued in post-independent Kemalist Turkey, Algeria, Syria, Egypt, and Tunisia were tainted by oppressive dictatorships. See, for instance, John L. Esposito, *The Islamic Threat: Myth or Reality?* (New York: Oxford University Press, 1999), 161; Nilüfer Göle, "Authoritarian Secularism and Islamist Politics: The Case of Turkey," in *Civil Society in the Middle East: Social, Economic and Political Studies of the Middle East*, ed. Augustus Richard Norton (Leiden and New York: Brill, 1995), 18.

297 Examples include – to varying degrees – Ba'athist Syria, Iraq, Nasserist Egypt, and Kemalist Turkey. The contradictory marketing of Israel as a Jewish state adhering to standards of Western European states has likewise further sullied the image of Western democracy and secularism.

298 Talāl Asad, an ostensibly anti-Orientalist anthropologist, has fallen prey to this notion of exceptionalism, endorsing the arbitrary epistemological division between a "Judean–Christian" and "Islamic" worldview without explaining the underlying rationale on which this dichotomy is based. Talāl Asad, *Formations of the Secular: Christianity, Islam, Modernity* (Palo Alto, CA: Stanford University Press, 2003), 221. Asad subsequently disavows fixed cultural tags by recalling the Hellenic heritage of Islam and the Muslim–Christian–Jewish cultural cross-fertilization in Andalusia.

"enlightened despots" such as Fredrick the Great and Robespierre had charted their course toward order and progress.[299] Case in point is the furies of the French Revolution during the famous uprising of the peasants of Vendée who – along with a number of refractory clergy – refused to take the new oath of allegiance to the new state due to the omission therein of any reference to God.[300]

Nonetheless, the respective trajectories of secularism in much of Western Europe and the Levant do exhibit profound divergences. After all, the Middle Eastern transmission belt for secularism – along with the roster of European liberalism, anarchism, Darwinism, social-Darwinism, Positivism, and democracy – was the colonial powers of the nineteenth century that were ready to split the spoils bequeathed by the Ottoman "Sick man of Europe" even as national movements were unraveling the Catholic monarchies of the Austro-Hungarian Empire.

Given its non-Muslim majority, situated on the periphery of a Sunni empire, the *Mutaṣarrifīya* of Mount Lebanon was perhaps the most conspicuous candidate for anti-Ottomanism, proto-nationalism, and secularism, even though the three strands did not always arise in tandem. It is not coincidental that Lebanon's early secularists – many of them Christians – have been associated with Lebanon's historic proximity to the European powers. Stereotypical and reductionist depictions of an ostensibly "Western," "Christian" exceptionalism stem from this era and abound to this very day, particularly as regards the depiction of secularism as an import forever alien to the Middle East.[301] Western colonial efforts at domination and subjugation of the "Orient" have on occasion given rise to a defensive discourse of counter-dominance and a no less

299 *Volksfrömmigkeit*, or "popular piety," has entered modern languages as a standard, if not undisputed, idiom. Hobsbawm has underscored this intrasocietal lag of secularization in Europe. Much the same phenomenon may be observed in the Middle East and the urban–rural divide in the United States. Eric Hobsbawm, *Age of Extremes: The Short Twentieth Century 1914–1991* (London: Abacus, 1995); *The Age of Revolution: Europe 1789–1848* (London: Weidenfeld and Nicolson, 1962), 159, 164ff.

300 The death toll of the Vendée massacres has been estimated at well over 100,000, that is almost one-fifth of the population. See Reynald Secher and George Holoch, *A French Genocide: The Vendée* (Notre Dame, IN: University of Notre Dame Press, 2003). The relation of the Vendée farmers to local Church administrators according to some accounts was strained, so that an ideological explanation of the uprising seems to be more plausible in this case, rather than a socioeconomic one.

301 The late Muḥammad Shams ad-Dīn has depicted secularism as "an exclusively European phenomenon." See Muhammad Mahdī Shams ad-Dīn, *al-'Almānīya: Tahlīl wa naqd lil 'Almānīya Muhtāwan wa Tārīkhīyan* (Beirut: al-Munsharāt al-Dawla, 1980), 160. We will examine this proposition in greater detail in the subsequent section on the Lebanese discourse.

essentialist counter-orientalism.[302] Nor did such "Occidentalism" wane with flag independence and the formal end of colonialsm. Thus, Ḥassan Ḥanafī has been one of the most prominent late–twentieth-century Egyptian intellectuals to openly embrace Occidentalism (*al-istighrāb*) as a "corrective" response to the distortions and damage inflicted by Western Orientalism.[303] In its virulent strain, Occidentalist discourse could brand Muslim secularists from Salama Mūsā to Ṭāhā Ḥusayn to Adūnīs as traitorous heirs to the early "*shu'ubī*" heretics in Islam or closet Christians.[304] Averting this pitfall of Occidentalism necessitates a frank confrontation with global and local power dynamics and societal developments, which alone can clarify our understanding of the formation of cultural and religious discourse over history.

To be sure, an elite – and by no means the majority – of Lebanon's Christians did in fact come to form a small if salient beachhead of secular thought in the Arab world. This is due to this small vanguard's high level of education and their close ties with Europe, particularly after the extension of capitulatory trade agreements in the nineteenth century. These observations pertain to a particular, narrow segment of Lebanese Christian intellectuals rather than the Christian community as a whole. 'Abdul Laṭīf Tibāwī[305] and Yūsuf Shuwayrī have disputed the thesis that Christian Arabs initiated or monopolized the discourse on secularism or patriotism in the Ottoman Empire, averring that they "merely restated, as loyal subjects, the principles and beliefs of Ottoman officials."[306] While there was certainly no shortage of Christian journalists and public administrators who were at pains to showcase their loyalty to the Sultan,[307]

302 Ṣādiq al-'Aẓm has argued in his rejoinder to Edward Sa'īd that Occidentalism is but the mirror image of Orientalism and shares the latter's symptomatic defects. Sadek al-'Aẓm, "Orientalism and Orientalism in Reverse," *Khamsin* 8 (1981): 5–26. See Carter Vaughn Findley, "An Ottoman Occidentalist in Europe: Aḥmad Midhat Meets Madame Gülnar, 1889," *American Historical Review* 103 (1998): 15–49 and Usāma Maqdisī, "Ottoman Occidentalism," *American Historical Review* 107 (2002): 768–797.

303 Ḥassan Ḥanafī, *Muqaddima fī 'ilm al-Istighrāb* (Cairo: al-Dār al-Fannīya, 1991).

304 The *shu'ubīya* refers to an early ethnic-religious resistance movement in the Abbasid Empire that opposed Arab dominance. See Jundī, *Al-Shu'bīyāt*.

305 Tibāwī is more interested in debunking the myth of a Christian, Western-induced "Arab renaissance," rather than secularism proper. See Tibāwī, *A Modern History of Syria*, 140.

306 See Shuwayrī, *Modern Arab Historiography*, 208.

307 Faraḥ Antūn and Salīm Bustanī, the latter an advocate of Turkish as a national language. Sheer opportunism cannot be discounted as a motif for rapidly shifting stances. Thus, the Maronite poet Shiblī Mallāṭ could write effusive laudations to the Young Turks during World War I, only to *ex post facto* justify this slip of the pen as a survival tactic, claiming that he was forced to "eulogize" ("*madaḥa mukrahan*"). See *al-Mashriq*, August 1920, 636. Mallāṭ, to be sure, had a double motivation to remain on good terms with Istanbul as the founder of a journal in 1906 (*al-Waṭan*) and as an

there is a long list of strongly anti-Ottoman, Maronite-Christian (proto-) nationalists from the sixteenth century onward. As we have seen, certainly by the onset of sectarian strife in the nineteenth century, trust in the Ottoman authorities – who were often implicated in abetting the killings – was far from rock-solid among large segments of the Christian community, causing even erstwhile stalwart supporters of Ottomanism to qualify their stance. The Palestinian sociologist Hishām Sharābī consequently adopts almost the diametrically opposite interpretation, drawing a sharp distinction between the sociological, psychological, and historical experiences of Muslim and Christian intellectuals, thereby seeking to explain what he deems a bolder and somewhat earlier embrace of secularism and nationalism of the latter.[308] Following Sharābī's lead, we might identify historical and economic factors that shed light on the quantitative and qualitative difference in the overall articulation of secular and liberal stances among different communities, taking due account of the proverbial exceptions, which prove the rule.

In reaction to France's patronage of the Maronite Church – which had enjoyed close ties with France stretching back to their formal union with Rome since at least 1180[309] – other Christian communities would gradually wrest outside protective powers and privileges from Istanbul. In the case of the joining of some urban Orthodox with the Uniate Catholic

occupant of numerous posts in the Ottoman administration of Mount Lebanon. Likewise, Shakīb Arslān could move from an ardent Ottomanist to a self-promoting Francophile candidate for the governship of Lebanon. Journals such as *al-Mashriq* and *al-Jinān* would preface their first editions with showering grandiloquent praise to the "Sultan of Sultans" and the "Government of the Sunna." See opening editorial, *al-Mashriq*, first Edition, 1898, 2. Defying the orders of Istanbul could spell the end of a publication, as Aḥmad Fāris al-Shidiyāq discovered when his pathbreaking *al-Jawā'ib* was forced to shut down in 1879 after it declined to publish an Ottoman statement against the Egyptian *khedeve*. See Azīz al-'Aẓma and F. Ṭarābulsī, "Aḥmad Fāris al-Shidiyāq: Su'lūk al-Nahḍa," *al-Nāqid*, 79, January 1995, 26.

308 "Intellectual rebellion for the Muslim secular intellectual was strictly a political experience, whereas for the Christian it represented a total existential experience." Hishām Sharābī, *Arab Intellectuals and the West* (Baltimore: Johns Hopkins University Press, 1970), 89, 53. Sharābī defines Christian intellectualism as a sociological rather than a denominational outlook.

309 The seventeenth-century historian Isṭfān Duwayhī and the fifteenth-century chronicler Ibn al-Qil'ā'ī contest that the formal union with Rome predates 1180. Charlemagne was granted rights of protection over Oriental Christians in a treaty with the 'Abbasid Caliph Harūn-al-Rashīd in the early ninth century. There is historical documentation for Pope Innocent III's recognition of the Maronite patriarch as the "Patriarch of Antioch and all the Levant" in 1215 and Louis IX of France's vow of protection to the "Maronite nation" during the Crusades in 1250 as well as the 1535 Treaty of Suleyman and King Francis reaffirming France as the Maronite ally. Ḥittī, *Lebanon in History*, 257. Kamāl Ṣalībī, *Maronite Historians of Medieval Lebanon* (Beirut: Ams Pr Inc., 1959), 142. Ristelhuber, Traditions Francaises au Liban, 40ff.

Church, this was achieved by a strategic, pragmatic conversion.[310] By the nineteenth century, the head start in education in combination with privileged trade ties led to an economic efflorescence of Christian minorities in the Ottoman Empire. Data on actual capital investments in the Ottoman Empire in 1914 reveal the domination of minorities, led by the Ottoman Greeks who controlled approximately 50 percent of such investment followed by the Armenians (20 percent), Ottoman Turks (15 percent), foreign nationals (10 percent), and finally the Jewish community (5 percent).[311] What was true for the empire as a whole also obtained under Ibrāhīm Pasha and in the *Mutaṣarrifīya* after 1861. By the end of the nineteenth century, trade with European markets, above all France, was largely dominated by a disproportionate number of Christian families who capitalized on the special status granted to them as counsels and agents for Western enterprises.[312] Such privileges – and the wealth that could accrue with them – could quickly become a source of resentment, prompting the founder of American pragmatism, John Dewey, to remark laconically: "Happy the minority which had no Christian nation to protect it."[313]

The overwhelming Christian and Levantine provenance of the generations of Arab secularist writers, such as Aḥmad Fāris as-Shidyāq, Adīb Isḥāq, Francis Marrāsh, Buṭrus Karāma, and Faraḥ Anṭūn, to name a

310 The Uniate Melchite Church of Syria was recognized by the Ottomans in 1847 in wake of French diplomatic pressure. In the course of the eighteenth century, the Orthodox of Sidon embraced the Melkite Unitiate denomination as well. Many of these Greek Catholic families were originally from Aleppo, Homs, or Damascus, but had sought refuge in the coastal cities of Beirut, Sidon, and Tripoli to escape persecution as "unitiates" with the Catholic Church. Robert M. Haddad, "On the Melkite Passage to the Unia: The Case of Patriarch Cyril of al-Za'Im, 1672–1720," in *Christians and Jews in the Ottoman Empire*, eds. Benjamin Braude and Bernard Lewis (New York: Holmes and Meier, 1982), 67–90; Thomas Philipp, "Image and Self-Image of the Syrians in Egypt," in *Christians and Jews in the Ottoman Empire*, 167–184.

311 Alexēs Alexandrēs, *The Greek Minority of Istanbul and Greek–Turkish Relations, 1918–1974* (Athens: Center for Asia Minor Studies, 1983), 32, where this skewed economic prosperity is also related to inter-ethnic and -communal tensions.

312 Fawwāz Ṭarābulsī cites twenty-six Christian families versus only three Muslim families who monopolized trade with European capital. See Fawwāz N. Ṭarābulsī, "Identités et Solidarités Croisées dans les Conflicts du Liban Contemporain," PhD dissertation, Université de Paris VII, 1993, 223. Ma'oz cites consular reports relating that the ostentatious displays of wealth of the Christian merchants and clergymen in the Sham stirred the envy of the Muslim population in Aleppo, Damascus, and Beirut before the riots of 1850 and 1860. Ma'oz, "Changing Relations between Jews, Muslims and Christians," 113.

313 Cited in Walter Weiker, *Ottomans: Turks and the Jewish Polity* (Boston: University Press of America, 1992), 242. Also see Tabak, "Local Merchants in Peripheral Areas of the Empire."

few, need not be related as much to cultural identity, let alone theological dogma, as to social class and educational background.[314]

Acknowledging this historical constellation of an alliance of Arab Christians with European commercial, educational, and religious institutions, however, can and should not lead us to dismiss secularism as a distinctly and exclusively European concoction.[315] Unfortunately, as we have seen in the preceding section, even ostensibly liberal-minded polemicists – both Muslim and Christian – have tried to do just that by branding and dismissing secularism as an illegitimate child of the Christian West , an extraneous implant eternally alien to Islam and the "religious East." This stigma was only compounded by the foreign institutions with which secularism was associated.

The very advent of the first articulations of secular political ideologies coincided with the "Arab Renaissance" or *naḥda*,[316] which, in turn, was in no small measure instigated and propelled by Protestant and Catholic missionary schools in the region. The latter were, in the estimate of Faraḥ Anṭūn (1874–1922), the prime handmaidens for the age of the *naḥda.* Although by no means oblivious of the blight of imperialism, Anṭūn does not fall prey to Occidentalist jingoism and instead offers a nuanced evaluation of the legacy of the Catholic and Protestant missionaries:

> The East must not forget that the very missionaries who could do harm in one instance benefited us from another. There would have been no return to life and no call for civilization without the mediation of these missionaries. Syria alone bears clear testimony to the veracity of this proposition, for its age of a modern *naḥda* is the age of the entry of the American missionaries and French Jesuits.[317]

As has been elaborated elsewhere,[318] by the end of the nineteenth century, Lebanon had become the regional frontrunner of the Ottoman Empire in terms of the general level of education. Access to primary and secondary schooling, however, still remained confined to a thin segment

314 For an anthology see: Yāzijī, *Ruwwād al-Nahḍa al-Adabīya fī Lubnān al-Hadīth, 1800–1900.*

315 See for instance: Lehmann, *Säkularisierung.* Azīz al-'Aẓma has disclaimed any "direct or indirect link between Arab secularism and Arab nationalism allegedly spearheaded by a Christian vanguard." See 'Aẓma, *al-'Ilmānīya min Manzūr Mukhtalif,* 129.

316 The word *al-nahḍa* first appeared in an 1888 edition of the journal *al-Muqaṭṭaf* with reference to medical developments see Thomas Philipp, *Jurgi Zaydan: His Life and Thought* (Beirut: F. Steiner, 1979). It appears as a somewhat inaccurate translation of the European notion of Renaissance. Rebirth in Arabic would be better connoted by *inbi'āth* or, indeed, the more familiar *ba'th.*

317 Farah Anṭūn, *Ibn Rushd Wa Falsafatuhu* (Beirut: Dār al-Talīa lil-Ṭibā'a wa al-Nashr, 1983), 273.

318 Farha, "Historical Legacy and Political Implications of State and Sectarian Schools in Lebanon," 64–85.

of the population; an urban, largely Christian (and Beiruti Sunni) elite. Nonetheless, rising literacy rates hastened the publication of a bevy of journals and newspapers so that, by the turn of the century, twenty-five newspapers were published in Lebanon, establishing it as a hub for printing houses together with Cairo and Alexandria, cities in which the newspapers were largely founded and run by Syrian and Lebanese émigrés. To be sure, the earliest publications – as in Europe under Gutenberg – bore an unmistakable religious, devotional stamp.[319] It was only later that a more secular outlook percolated to a wider audience. The first secular printing press was established by Khalīl al-Khūrī, beginning with the publication in 1857 of the first private Arabic newspaper whose title encapsulated the spirit of the day: *al-Fajr al-Munīr* (the Enlightening Dawn).[320] Renamed the *Ḥadīqat al-Akhbār* (Garden of News), this paper was to serve as a trailblazer. In 1870, Bustānī founded *al-Jinān,* a cultural-political journal the famous motto of which was emblazoned on the cover of every issue: "*Ḥubb al-Waṭan min al-Imān*" ("Love of the nation is the better part of faith"), a slogan Bustānī had already ceaselessly intoned in wake of the 1860 massacres.

In 1875, the first explicitly Arab-Syrian nationalist secret society was founded at the Syrian Protestant College (SPC) by the Francophile Maronite Ilyās Habbalin, the erstwhile iconoclast leader of the 1840 Anṭilyās rebellion. The group was disbanded a decade later due to its inability to attract Muslim support and to find a common stance on the Ottoman-Turkish presence.[321] Nonetheless, this "Secret Society of Beirut" ("*Jam'īyat Bayrūt al-Sirrīya*") is often hailed as the first organized political party in the Middle East.

Upon passing through the SPC or the patriarchal schools, the graduates often found that intellectual *fora* and Masonic lodges allowed them to continue to explore political secularism and build personal and professional networks outside traditional church and mosque affiliations.[322]

[319] The earliest Arabic printed book in Lebanon was a translation of J. S. Nieremberg's *De la Diferencia Entre lo Temporal y Eterno*, translated and printed by 'Abdullāh Ẓāhir (1690–1748) in al-Shwayr in 1773 as *Mizān al-Zamān*. In it, an almost total dichotomy is posited between mundane, transient, and eternal spheres of life, reflecting the quietist character of these early publications. This held true up until the early nineteenth century, when Thomas a Kempis' *Imitatio Christi*, translated as *al-Iqtidā bil-Masīḥ*, became the bestseller.

[320] The first daily was founded in Leipzig, Germany in 1650, in Britain in 1702 followed by France in 1777 and Switzerland in 1780.

[321] Antonius, *The Arab Awakening*, 79.

[322] The first, albeit largely Christian, secular-national forum was the "Society of Refinement" ("*Jamī'at al-tahghīb*") founded by Bustānī and Yāsijī with the aid of the Protestant missionaries in 1847 in Beirut.

Translating some of the grand notions of reform – including the political aspirations of secularism – into reality, however, proved exceedingly difficult in so stratified a society.

Indeed, there is little doubt that confinement of the vast majority of secular-minded intellectuals in the Middle East to small circles of academic round tables and secret societies compounded the elite–popular divide to a degree not seen in Europe. There, the tapestry of Masonic networks and secret revolutionary societies that had formed in wake of the French Revolution and Congress of Vienna in 1815 gradually could integrate into mainstream political parties and disseminate their ideas to a broader public. Moreover, many anticlerical and humanistic ideals from the onset were part and parcel of nineteenth- and early twentieth-century reformist Catholic and Protestant thought, which was gradually imbued with a spirit of self-criticism and historical literal criticism to a degree not seen in the Middle East even in the present day. Indeed, even mildly critical studies of the Qur'ān and the Bible remain a red line rarely crossed.[323] Along with the French 1789 Declaration of Human Rights, Faraḥ Anṭūn did translate Ernest Renan's groundbreaking *Vie de Jesus* into Arabic over century ago, and, yet, with precious few exceptions, Renan would probably find himself having a similarly barren debate with his Muslim – and many Christian – counterparts in the region today regarding the (in)compatibility of religious and scientific modes of inquiry and reasoning.[324]

It is significant to point out that the role of Masonic lodges, social clubs, and progressive enlightenment ideals was viewed domestically with some apprehension by Europe's conservative regimes; yet they were equally seen as useful pawns, which could be moved together with religious reactionaries on the chessboard of the Middle East.[325] Elisabeth Thomson has pointed out the contradictory, double-edged domestic and

323 Some recent examples in the West include a scholar of Lebanese descent who has published only under the pseudonym "Christoph Luxenberg" and Sayyid al-Qimnī, an Egyptian writer forced to recant upon receiving death threats. Muṣṭafā Juḥā, another outspoken critic of religion, was killed in Lebanon in 1992.

324 It is often mistakingly asserted that Renan confined his notion of an inherent compatibility of the two to Islam when in fact he included Christianity and all religions in his argument. Ernest Renan, *Histoire des Origines du Christianisme* (Paris, 1863–1883).

325 The popular committees with young volunteers founded by Fatāt such as the ḥizb-al-istiqlāl al-'Arabī in 1919, the an-Nadi al-'Arabī, and al-Ḥizb al-Watani created new venues for popular political participation in Syria. Some of these societies enjoyed financial backing from the British and Faysal and were originally propaganda extensions of the state. Thus, the British financed the Arab Club and Literary Society and newspapers like *al-Kawkab* to foster anti-Turkish movements. Money, however, could also attract a number of turncoat opportunists – such as Muḥammad Fawzī

foreign policies of the French as regards secularism.[326] Even though the secularist Freemasonic networks were sponsored in the colonies, Masonry interestingly found greater difficulty in riding piggyback on the French and British imperialist project as one might surmise, for the Catholic and Protestant missionaries would countervail Masonic activity in the collapsing Ottoman Empire. Moreover, Catholic orders abroad were exempted from all anticlerical laws and never ceased to receive French government subsidies as part of the latter's multipronged efforts to stem the rise of any "nativist" Islamist movement.[327]

Far from joining forces in a secret cabal, as some undifferentiating Occidentalists would have imagined it, Masonry and the Catholic Church in Europe were facing each other on opposing sides of the trenches. Whereas the Church aligned itself with the *ancien régime* and Catholic royal houses, Masonry casted its lot with the rising nation states in France, Italy, and Germany. Even before the nineteenth century, Mahmoud I (1730–1754) was asked by Pope Clement XII in Rome to act against "seditious societies" in Salonika.[328] The Church reacted with even more vehemence when faced with the burgeoning Italian nationalism of the *Risiergomento*. The besieged Vatican responded by convening the First Council of 1871 during which it desperately tried to assert its temporal power by issuing a sharp denunciation of the secular nation-state and proclaiming the infallibility of a pope who had all but lost the last remnant of his secular power. What is often forgotten is that the Eastern Orthodox Churches, in the 1871 synod at Constantinople, came out with a very similar castigation of all parochial national and ethnic identities.[329] Freemasonry had been branded as the enemy of the Church and formally prohibited since 1738[330] and inveighed against in Lebanon by the likes of the Jesuit scholar Louis Cheikho.[331] At the beginning of the twentieth century, the Maronite Church denounced secularization as a Masonic doctrine, which denies the existence of the soul and leads to

al-ʿAẓm and ʿAbdul Raḥmān Yūsuf – who would find no difficulty in adopting reactionary stances. Khūrī, *Modern Arab Thought*, 68.

326 Thompson, *Colonial Citizens*.

327 Cited in Nikki Keddie, "Secularism and Its Discontents," *Daedalus* 132.3 (2003): 19.

328 Thierry Zarcone, "La Franc-Maconnerie dans l'Empire Ottoman et dans la Turquie Contemporaine," *Les Cahiers d'Orient* 69 (2003): 75–86.

329 Khidr, "Huwwīyāt al-Lubnānīyīn."

330 April 28, 1738, Pope Clement XII in his Pontifical Constitution "In Eminenti" condemned and forebade Masonic societies on both temporal and spiritual grounds.

331 See, for instance, Louis Cheikho, Al-Sirr al-Masūnī fī Shia' al-Farsūn. Beirut, 1910.

atheism. A Church program was spelled out to combat secular forces in the press, schools, and society at large.[332]

It was only most recently, in 1983, under John Paul II, that membership in masonry was no longer decreed a crime punishable by excommunication.[333] A century earlier, in 1884, Pope Leon XIII had still openly upheld the Church's resolute opposition to freedom of religion[334] and renewed this prohibition. This led to the prosecution of the Lebanese Adīb Isḥāq, the founder of the secular journal *taqaddum* in the self-same year. Isḥāq eventually refused the last vows at his death bed, leading to a tiff between the Church and his family over the last sacraments. Isḥaq may have drawn a last inspiration – and consolation – from the impudent Voltaire who famously was denied the privilege of dying as a Christian.

Arab masons were well aware that, in the West, Freemasonry was associated with the majority of the *illuminati* fathers of secularism: Herder and Goethe in Germany, Lafayette and Franklin in the United States, Condorcet and Auguste Comte in France, and Garibaldi in Italy. The latter, as a friend of Ahmet Riza, established one of the many links between European and Ottoman Masonry, the roots of which stretch back to the mid eighteenth century.[335] It was, however, only after the mid nineteenth century that Masonic lodges associated with the Grand Orient of France were opened in Cairo (1845), Istanbul (1858), Palestine (1861), Salonika (1864), and Beirut in 1866 by Rashīd Pasha, the

[332] See *Risāla ar-Ri'ā'iya (al-Dīn wa al-'ilmānīya)* (Beirut: Imprimerie Catholique, 1911), 22–34.

[333] Pope John Paul II promulgated the 1983 Code of Canon Law on January 25, 1983, which, in contrast to the previous code of 1917 (Canon 2335), does not mention Masonry let alone stipulate any sanction in cases of Masonic membership. Upon intense questioning, the Vatican issued an ambiguous defense, writing that the omission of the condemnation of Masonry did not imply a reversal of the Church's prohibition. It was rather due "to an editorial criterion which was followed also in the case of other [secret] associations likewise unmentioned inasmuch as they are contained in wider categories." "Sacred Congregation for the Doctrine of the Faith-Declaration on Masonic Associations," *L'Osservatore Romano* (English Edition), December 5, 1983. Many leading Lebanese politicians – including Michel 'Awn and Rafīq al-Ḥarīrī – openly claim the support of Lebanon's Masonic lodges, as was seen in election posters sponsored by lodges. On the other hand, the Phalange Party of America explicitly denounces masonry.

[334] Pope Leon XIII's tirade against freedom of religion in his *Libertas Praestantissimum* rests on a creedal absolutism bearing affinities to late twentieth-century Islamic reactionaries. His fear of freedom of faith opening the door to the corruption of the "holiest of hollies" is but one example of this discourse.

[335] Paul Dumont, "Le Franc-Maconnerie Ottomane et les idées françaises à l'époque des Tanzimat," *Revue des mondes musulmans et de la Méditerranée* 52.1 (1989): 150. Masonry's impact on the Turkish reform movement is attested. Ibrāhīm Müteferrika, Namik Kemal, Midhat, Enver, and Talaat Pasha were all noted Masons.

wālī of Damascus.[336] Earlier lodges affiliated with the British councillor Alexander Dramond were present in Aleppo beginning in 1764, although this Scottish lodge catered exclusively to the British expatriate community. The first branches of the Scottish Rite with an indigenous membership were founded by Halim Pasha, a son of Muḥammad ʻAlī in Turkey in 1861 and in Cairo in 1866.

It is indicative that the total membership of all lodges strewn across the major cities of the Middle East never exceeded 1,500, many of whom were in fact French nationals.[337] Despite their scarcity and isolation from the populace, Masons did prevail in the political arena. Hardly a reform-minded nineteenth-century Levantine writer and politician of note, Christian or Muslim, was not tied to Masonry. Muḥammad ʻAbduh, Rashīd Riḍā, Afghānī, Ṣa'd Zaghlūl, Mustafā Kāmil and Buṭrus Ghālī in Egypt, and ʻAbdul Raḥmān al-Shahbandar[338] and Fāris al-Khūrī in Syria were members of lodges. The same holds true for most of the Lebanese émigrés to Egypt who played such a pivotal role in establishing the first publishing houses.[339] This guard of the new intelligentsia would also contribute to the cause of Ottoman reform – and fall under suspicion due to its affiliation with secret societies. One of the co-authors of the 1876 Ottoman constitution, the Maronite journalist and Beiruti lawyer Khalīl Ghānim eventually fell out of grace with the Ḥamīdian government, coming under suspicion of being a member of the Phoenicia Lodge.[340]

The role of missionary schools, Masonic networks, and enlightenment ideals encapsulated in the biography of such *fin-de-siècle* Arab secularists deserve greater consideration as they all too often served as the handmaiden of secularism in the Middle East. Khalīl Saʻāda in more than one way personifies this prototype of this generation of Arab secularists. Unlike his son, Anṭūn, Khalīl would remain a committed Mason all of his life, which allowed him to forge close ties with Egypt's nationalist

[336] Fāris Nimr (1854–1951) is often identified as the (co)founder of the Beirut lodge, but only after 1875.

[337] Dumont, "Le Franc-Maconnerie Ottomane," 151.

[338] Shahbandar's murder on July 6, 1940 has never been solved, although suspicions of French involvement persist. Shahbander's Masonic indifference to Islam, however, made him a heretic in the eyes of the clerics, many of which sanctioned his assassination. Sāmī Mubayyid, *The Politics of Damascus 1920–1946* (Damascus: Tlass House, 1999), 150.

[339] The most famous are Jurgi Zaydān's *Dār al-Hillāl* and Bishāra al-Naqla's *al-Ahrām* papers.

[340] For a longer list of Arab Masons, see Karim Wissa, "Freemasonry in Egypt 1798–1921: A Study in Cultural and Political Encounters," *British Journal of Middle Eastern Studies* 16.2 (1989): 143–161.

leadership such as 'Urabī Pasha, Muṣṭaphā Kāmil, and Sa'd Zaghlūl. Sa'āda was also a graduate of the SPC and thus had gained exposure to the missionaries' education. Lastly, Sa'āda remained an agitator against imperialism all his life, fleeing from 'Abdul-Ḥamīd's despotism to Egypt, only to subsequently suffer exile by the Khedeve during the British protectorate. Arriving in his native Lebanon, Sa'āda did not hold back in his criticism of the French protectorate, once again finding himself forced by the authorities to pack his bags and leave his home in 1920 for his final refuge in Brazil. He died in 1934, a year after Jubrān Tuwaynī Sr. would found the *al-Aḥrār* (subsequently *an-Nahār*) newspaper as a citadel of secular liberalism in 1933.[341]

Despite the prominence and ubiquity of Masonic secularists, it would be anachronistic to attribute secular tendencies to Masonry. The early generation of *al-nahda* intellectuals hailing from the missionary schools, such as Buṭrus al-Bustānī (1819–1883), preceded the spread of Masonry.[342] To be sure, in later decades, Lebanese Masons were as omnipresent as their counterparts in Egypt in the upper echelons of government and commerce. This political and financial clout, however, did not necessarily advance the progress of secularism. For one, we may bear in mind that the Masons, while espousing the lofty slogans of the French Revolution and positivism, were not necessarily a revolutionary lot.[343] The anti-imperialism and secular agenda of Masonry was always

[341] 'Alī Ḥāmi, "Khalīl Sa'āda: L'Homme et L'Oeuvre 1857–1934," PhD dissertation, Paris-Sorbonne University, 1986.

[342] Like Asad and Ṭannūs al-Shidyāq, Bustānī was educated at the seminary of 'Ayn Waraqa, a monastic seminary founded in 1789 by Asad Ghandūr. Bustānī later converted to Protestantism after working with the Presbyterian missionaries on a translation of the Bible. Besides Bustānī and Naṣīf al-Yāzijī (1800–1871), the Azhar-educated Sunni jurist Yūsuf al-'Aṣīr (1815–1889) cooperated in this historic venture, see Ḥittī, *History of Syria*, 461–467. The so-called Lebanon schools initiated by Greek Orthodox families (Ṣalībī, Sulaiman, and Ilyās) and funded from contributions from England and Scotland constituted another project aiming at transconfessional education between 1853 and 1873. In 1879, the Sunni scholar Ḥusayn al-Jisr (1845–1909) founded another *madrasa waṭanīya* in Tripoli. Unlike Bustānī's prototype, the Islamic pendant did not advertise itself as a transconfessional school and did not have any non-Muslim graduates. Jisr later together with Muḥammad 'Abdū was a champion of educational reform in the Sunni community in which Arabic rather than Turkish was propagated as the language of instruction. During World War I, the Young Turks closed one of these schools, the kulliyāt al-'uthmānīya al-islāmīya. See Martin Strohmeier, "Muslim Education in the Vilayet of Beirut 1880–1918," in *Decision Making and Change in the Ottoman Empire*, ed. Caesar Farah (Kirksville, MO: Thomas Jefferson University Press, 1993), 215–241 and Havemann, *Geschichte Und Geschichtsschreibung Im Libanon*, 83–86.

[343] Thus, most of the ruling Khedeve family in Egypt were members of lodges, while Levantine lodges would sport a portrait of the Ottoman sultan. Such pandering,

tamed by the decidedly bourgeois origins and *status quo* driven career interests of its constituents.

Thus elitism, both social and intellectual, remained the principal Achilles heel of secularism and would reinforce a social caste division that – as the case of Lebanon illustrates– often overlaps with or reinforces religious divides.[344] For Levantine society at the onset of the twentieth century remained highly bifurcated. The inability and unwillingness of the self-styled "enlightened" *mutanawwirūn* nationalist elite to bridge the gap with the (rural) masses "relinquished the nationalist field to others," who in turn were not willing to turn Syrians into "slaves in the name of [Comtean] progress."[345] Moreover, bourgeois Masonry's preoccupation with unshackled individual freedoms and financial success could vitiate a strong national state and potentially lend itself to a ringing endorsement of comprador capitalism.[346] This occasional right-wing *laissez-faire* bent of some Arab apostles of secularism would impair its chances of success on the national plane to this very day.[347]

Case in point is Jurjī Zaydān who was heavily influenced by the prevalent Victorian wealth gospels embodied in such role models as "Disraeli, Rothschild and other men of action and hard work who

however, did not prevent the latter from ordering their closure in 1891. Karīm Wissa cited in 'Aẓma, *al-'Ilmānī ya min Manẓūr Mukhtalif*, 96.

344 See the discussion Chapter 1 and Saffīya Sa'āda's elaboration on a Lebanese "caste system."

345 See James Gelvin, "Secularism and Religion in the Arab Middle East," in *The Invention of Religion*, ed. Donald Peterson (New Brunswick, NJ: Rutgers, 2002), 128. While Gelvin has recanted the "sterile dialectic of [religious] popular and [secular] elite cultures," he postits a dichotomy between modernizers mimicking the West (*mutafarnujūn*) and pious conservatives (*mutadayīnūn*). Gelvin has vehemently refuted the "return to Islam" paradigm and with it the medieval roots traced in Islamic fundamentalism by "Middle East naïfs."

346 See Albert Ḥawrānī, *Arabic Thought in the Liberal Age: 1798–1939* (Cambridge: Cambridge Unviersity Press, 1983), 256ff.

347 Ilhām Khūrī-Maqdisī acknowledges that the owners of the *muqaṭṭaf* journal were champions of free enterprise and competition, both economic and social. Ya'qūb Ṣarrūf (1852–1927) and Fāris Nimr (1857–1951) made the headlines upon their dismissal from the SPC by President Penrose on account of their membership in "dangerous politics" and "secret Arab societies." While Ṣarrūf and Nimr later went on to found both the *muqaṭṭaf* journal in Beirut and later the *al-Muqattam* in Cairo, they were primarily heavily influenced by positivist and Spencerian Darwinist notions, which dominated the *laissez-faire* liberalism of the Victorian age. Thus, Darwin and Adam Smith figured prominently. Maqdisī nonetheless seeks to dispel the image that socialism made no inroads during the *nahḍa*. She bases her revisionist history on the great number of articles and books published on these topics before World War I, which dealt the death knell to the first phase of liberalism. See Ilhām Khūrī-Maqdisī, "Levantine Trajectories: The Formulation and Dissemination of Radical Ideas in and between Beirut, Cairo, and Alexandria, 1860–1914," PhD, Harvard University, 2003, chapter 1.

achieved wealth through their efforts." Zaydān called for an increased publishing of their biographies, which he hoped would be emulated as he endeavored to dispel the "popular fantasies that wealth is not to be attained in a legitimate, *ḥalāl* manner; that the true believer lives in poverty and dies a needy man; so that only liars, cunning people and sly men get rich is the excuse of those who fail in their efforts."[348] The emphasis on the role of the entrepreneur as the maker of his destiny mirrors the advent of the Renaissance man in the city states of the sixteenth and seventeenth centuries. The "Calvinist" disdain, which shines through in Zaydān's depiction of the more fatalist religious ethos and quietist tradition, is unmistakable. In the end, Zaydān's own career would run up against insurmountable communal barriers.[349] Arguably, Zaydān's haughtiness *vis-à-vis* the general populace – more perhaps than his Christian parentage – did not aid his cause. Zaydān's repeated denigration of the "pious poor" and converse extolling of the self-made capitalist shark finds its analogy in a similarly dichotomous, albeit intellectual, elitism of another widely cited Lebanese secularist, Faraḥ Anṭūn (1874–1922).

Socially, Anṭūn, along with Shiblī Shumayyil – would shed libertarian indifference for the poor for a socialist call for a welfare state. Here he was inspired by his stay in the United States after 1904.[350] Intellectually, however, Anṭūn remained inspiried by the supercilious spirit of the medieval "philosopher-kings" al-Farābī and Ibn Rushd in flatly proclaiming that philosophy was reviled by the populace (*sha'b*), since "in all places they despise distinction, whether it be of money or knowledge."[351] Having come to Egypt to work as a teacher in an Orthodox secondary school, Anṭūn in 1899 founded the journal *al-Jāmā'at al-'Uthmānīya*, mainly in order to introduce some of the leading nineteenth-century European thinkers to the Arab world such as Marx Mueller, Tolstoy, Auguste Comte, Ernest Renan, Shakespeare, and Victor Hugo. Sensing the suspicions he was bound to stir among the *Salafi* scholars and *'ulamā'* as a Christian calling for secularism in a Muslim land under British occupation, Anṭūn sought to couch his bold agenda in the rhetoric of

[348] Cited in Philipp, *Jurgi Zaydan*, 15.

[349] Jurjī Zaydān was dismissed from his appointed position at the newly founded Egyptian University "in consideration of the sentiments of the nation" after fierce Muslim opposition arose in conservative circles (led by Rashīd Riḍā) against a Christian teaching Islamic History. Zaydān left a lasting mark in Egypt with his Dār al-Hilāl printing house, which in its heyday was to become the mainspring of a vast body of secular literature and modern Arabic novels. See Philipp, *Jurgi Zaydan*, 66ff.

[350] See Sharābī, *Arab Intellectuals and the West*, 84.

[351] See Anṭūn, *Ibn Rushd Wa Falsafatuhu*, 42. See Sharābī, *Arab Intellectuals and the West*, 84.

Ibn Rushd. He therefore hoped to prove that the secular values he advocated were anything but a Western import, but rather revealed roots springing from one of the lodestars of the Arab heritage and an Islamic luminary of the bygone Golden Age of medieval Andalusia.[352] Essentially, Anṭūn reformulated Ibn Rushd's rationalism in the vocabulary of the scientific age. The mystery of the universe and knowledge of God was best unveiled not by philosophy, but with scientific inquiry. Anṭūn also reasserted the (Catholic and Muslim) heresy of Averroism by proclaiming humanity itself as eternal, echoing Comte's divinization of humanity.[353] As if this assertion was not enough, Anṭūn crossed a red line and inflamed *Salafi* Muslim passions with his bold plea for a separation of religion and state as well as his conclusion that Christianity was more amenable than Islam to endorsing religious tolerance (*at-tasāhul ad-dīnī*).[354] The latter statement by the editor of the leading liberal-secularist journal in Egypt infuriated the editor-in-chief of the leading Islamist journal, Rashīd Riḍā. At the *Manār* journal, Riḍā lobbied his mentor and the Mufti of Egypt Muḥammad ʻAbduh to write an immediate response to Anṭūn's contentious claims "in defense of the Islamic faith and the Imāms of the Muslims."[355] Despite all the precautions initially taken to avert public exposure, Anṭūn had sparked an unusually frank debate with another Lebanese, Tripoli-born icon of the *naḥda*, Riḍā, and the Mufti. The debate was revelatory in that it unveiled ʻAbduh's skin-deep liberalism and fundamental aversion to secularism.[356] While Anṭūn in his defensive rejoinder denied that his was a religious treatise as his detractors charged, he had, in fact – whether by design or by force of argument – attacked the very foundations of the prevalent religious discourse. Whatever his protestations to the contrary, there was no doubt that his was a political cause to boot:

[352] Such was the anticlerical force surmised in Ibn Rushd's works that Friedrich of Hohenstaufen (1215–1250) commissioned their translation in a bid to fight the Church's claims of divine authority.

[353] Cited Sharābī, *Arab Intellectuals and the West*, 75.

[354] Anṭūn, *Ibn Rushd Wa Falsafatuhu*, 9. Anṭūn arrives at this verdict after having briefly exposed the checkered history of both religions. He also adds the caveat that the term "tolerance" was coined in modern Arabic in the nineteenth century. His own definition of religious tolerance pivots on the full freedom of (un)belief of each individual citizen, which, in turn, is predicated on a separation of religious and secular powers. Anṭūn later denied that his was seeking any confrontation by engaging in this disquisition. See Anṭūn, *Ibn Rushd Wa Falsafatuhu*, 243–245.

[355] Anṭūn, *Ibn Rushd Wa Falsafatuhu*, 10; Wahbah, "Al-Iltibās Al-Mītāphysīqī Fī ʻAsr an-Nahḍa," 38.

[356] ʻAbduh reverted to classical Islamist apologetics in his book *al-Islām wa al-Naṣrānīya*, in which he asserted that there was no way to separate religion and state in Islam.

The goal of the two powers, temporal and spiritual, do not only differ but stand in outright contradiction to one another. For religion holds fast to belief and tends, unfortunately, when in power, toward persecution of those who differ with it in opinion, particularly the intellectuals. Whereas the purpose of governance is to safeguard human freedom within the confines of the constitution. *Therefore secular governments do not persecute individuals on account of their faith.* As for social equality, no society will enjoy its fruits unless religious differences are overcome by ways of a separation of these two powers.[357]

Such was the bold, if perhaps somewhat naive, and idealistic invocation of an "ideal type" secularism by Faraḥ Anṭūn. This high-brow intellectual and knight-errant of Comtean positivism, however, stood for a whole class of an urban, (Western-)educated guard that had risen to the forefront in wake of the reforms that had been underway across the Ottoman Empire since the *Tanzimāt.*

In addition to its association with Western missionaries and Masonic networks, the relative scarcity of Muslim secularists in the early phase of the *nahḍa* has lent further ammunition for the diatribes of the Occidentalists.[358] In this context, and in order to refute the aforementioned truism, 'Abd al-Raḥmān Kawākibī (1854–1902) has frequently been singled out as the first articulate "Muslim" secularist. While Kawākabī's discourse was not devoid of a measure of eclecticism,[359] secularism in a full political sense was not one of his concerns. Upon closer examination, we find that Kawākibī, most notably in his *Umm al-Qura*, espoused a disparate set of notions, mixing and melding slogans of the greatness of the Islamic *umma* with Arab nationalism. The fact that the ideal society envisaged by Kawākbī was Muslim and based in Mecca casts a shadow on the putative secularism and situates him closer to a moderate strain of *Salafism,*[360] the tenets of which would trickle down to later Lebanese

[357] Anṭūn, *Ibn Rushd Wa Falsafatuhu*, 151. [358] See Jundī, *Al-Shu'bīyat.*

[359] I would like to thank Ryuichi Funatsu for drawing my attention to the writings of Jan Daya, Sa'd Zaghlūl, Kawākbī, Nazīḥ Kubbār, and Samīr Abū Ḥamrān on Kawākbī's thesis from the 1970s onward, which try to paint Kawākbī as a Salafi Islamist and *avant-garde* secularist of the nineteenth century. 'Abdu al-Mun'im al-Ḥāshimī, *Silsila Alam al-'Ulama'* (Beirut/Damascus: al-Awā'il, 1996), 21–44; Aḥmad al-Rahbī, *al-Afkār al-Siyāsīya wa al-Ijtimā'īya'and al-Kawākibī* (Damascus: al-Ahālī, 2001), 5–8, 35–43, 59–70.

[360] Sāṭi'al-Ḥuṣrī noted this very point. See Khaldun Sati Husry, *Three Reformers: A Study in Modern Arab Political Thought* (Beirut: Khayats, 1966). Likewise, Kawākibī's stance on women appears "illiberal" when he touted the Chinese practice of female foot deformation as a means of preventing women from corrupting the earth. See 'Aẓma, *al-'Ilmānīya min Manzūr Mukhtalif*, 108. The prefiguration and pedigree of thought of Rashīd Riḍā, Muḥammad 'Abduh, and Kawākibī in the writings of Ibn Taymīya have been traced in: Nazih Kubbār, *'Abd al-Raḥmān al-Kawākibī: Ḥayātuhu wa 'Aṣruhu*

reformers.[361] On the one hand, Kawākibī had not managed to rid himself of a communalist, Islamic reading of politics and history; on the other hand, he did seek to integrate non-Muslim Arabs into his political vision and anti-despotism. In the absence of full-fledged secularism, and despite his conception of communal identity being rooted in Islam, Kawākibī's efforts to personalize religious belief and dogma, and his rejection of any discrimination against non-Muslim Arabs, do reveal an inclination of secular Arabism and progressive Islamic modernism, which survives until this day.[362] Kawākibī's political orientation is probably best described neither as one of matured secularism nor of *Salafism*, but as a somewhat inchoate form of (anti-despotic) Arabism, which still drew heavily from Islamic precepts of governance. A similar ambiguity marked the discourse of another much-cited ostensible secularist, Kurd 'Alī (1876–1953).[363]

It remains difficult to substantiate the precise number of advocates of secularism within clandestine groups of the nineteenth century. The ostensible dearth of Muslim Arab secularists in the public limelight – particularly in the Ḥamīdian age – can conceivably be attributed to variant historical alliances and political interests rather than ideological factors or cultural constraints.[364] After all, Ḥamīdian Ottomanism (*Osmanlık*) was embraced – sometimes with glib disregard for its autocracy and its implicit Turkism – as much for its "enlightened," modernizing bent (and the associated career opportunities) than for any Islamic slogan by many an aspiring bureaucrat in Damascus and Beirut. Regional factors and the variant socioeconomic roles of individual cities also played a role.

(Tripoli: Gross Press, 1994), 108–109. Nāzik Saba Yārid, *Secularism in the Arab World* (London: Saqi Books, 2002), 157.

[361] Ṣubḥī Ṣaliḥ, for instance, frankly acknowledged that Islamic institutions were to serve as the building-blocks for Arab modernization. See Subhi Salih, *al-Islām wa Mustaqbal al-Ḥadātha* (Damascus: Dar al Qatiba, 1989), 291.

[362] A statement espousing Kawākibī's vision was adopted by forty Middle Eastern and North African civil society groups that met in Beirut on September 5, 2004, *The Daily Star (Beirut)*, September 25, 2004.

[363] Kurd 'Alī did display an infatuation with European secularism: "The West has taught us the meaning of fatherland and patriotism, love of nation and of language ... that religion alone cannot save [us] from our plight." Despite being one of the early Arab recruits of the CUP, 'Alī would severely criticize the Kemalist secularizing reforms while still patronizing Christians and Jews as *ahl al-dhimma*. Kurd 'Alī, cited in Yārid, *Secularism in the Arab World*, 25, 134.

[364] Hishām Sharābī has listed a roster of sociological reasons for the variant Muslim stance on secularism. Even twentieth-century popular movements in Lebanon such as *Harakat al-Wa'ī* have, in spite of their nonsectarian attitude, been constrained in their appeal and activities by a largely Christian majority of members. See Yāzijī, *Ruwwād al-Nahḍa al-Adabīya fī Lubnān al-Hadīth*.

In fact, Sultan ʿAbdul-Ḥamīd's Pan-Islamism – on the administrative and social (rather than the political) plane in particular – was not devoid of elements of secularization. The modernization, centralization, and partial secularization of the *nizamiye* court system initially caused disaffection among some provincial *ʿulamāʾ*, even though some notable families with clerical members may have benefited from leveraging their past connections to win civil administrative positions.[365] Meanwhile, the army and the gates of the Istanbul Law School often served as the conduit through which passed a new Turko-Arab bureaucratic elite bent on reform.

ʿAbdul Ḥamīd's modernist Islamist rhetoric and his discourse of selective, instrumental modernization eventually co-opted and silenced the reactionary opposition. We are thus called to consider the specific consequences ʿAbdul Ḥamīd's policies carried for each particular profession, confession, region, and respective vested interest of those on the receiving end of the Ḥamīdian state-building project. Often enough, pragmatic interests could prove to have a greater impact on the formation of religious and political identities than *vice versa*.[366] Of greater consequence yet were seismic shocks such as world wars, as the following chapter shall demonstrate.

From Anti-imperial Dissent to National Consent: World War I and the Formation of a Trans-Sectarian National Consciousness in Lebanon

> There now is no Muslim, Christian, Druze and Jew amongst us. For the scaffolds were erected for all alike. And the famine claimed the lives of all equally. And the locusts descended on everybody. This war has melded us all together in its boiling pot [*saharatnā fī bawtiqatihā*], so that we now are Syrians, Lebanese and Palestinians without distinction of religion or denomination.[367]
>
> Khalīl Saʿāda taking stock in 1917

[365] See Stephan Winter, "The Ashraf and the Ashraf al-Niqabat in Egypt," *Asian and African Studies* 19 (1985): 17–41. The career path of the Ottoman foreign minister Fu'ād Pasha illustrates how a scion of a family of clerics could rise through the ranks – and overseas posts – to a bearer of the scepter of republican reform.

[366] Rafīq al-ʿAẓm, the president of the Ottoman Decentralization Party, encapsulates the pragmatic and ambivalent attitude toward fixed identities shared by so many of his contemporaries: "Syria is Ottoman as long as the Ottoman state is capable of defending it. If, God forbids, the Ottoman state collapses ... then Syria is an Arab country indivisible from Arab territory (al-Jism al-'Arabī)." Cited in Maḥmūd Ḥaddād, "The Rise of Arab Nationalism Reconsidered," *International Journal of Middle East Studies* 26.2 (1994): 216.

[367] Khalīl Saʿāda, *Silsilat al-'Aʿmāl al-Majhūla, ʿKitāb Maftūh ʿilā as-Sūrīīn wa al-Lubnānīīn wa al-Filistīnīīn'* (Beirut: Dar al Rayes, 1987), 140.

As is indicated in this quote by Khalil Sa'ada (1857–1934), a trans-sectarian spirit of solidarity emanated out of the cauldron of World War I. Not only did the crippling famine of 1915 claim both Christian and Muslim lives, periodic repression and press censorship had already alienated authors, editors, and activists of all confessions during Hamidian and Young Turk rule. This is not to paint a picture of an idyllic trans-sectarian harmony or homogeneity. For the political orientation of the various dissident groups in the period 1876–1920 was fluid, and communal faultlines were evident in the ownership and political orientation of the major newspapers in Beirut and Damascus. Yet, in the shadow of the horrific dislocation wrought by World War I, and the lethal contagion of emerging national and religious chauvinisms, disillusionment had set in, as ethno-nationalistic separatisms won the day in the Balkans, Anatolia, and Palestine. With Ottomanism discarded, and Turkism resented by Muslim and Christian Arab intellectuals alike, interconfessional polarizations softened; a still inchoate mix of Arabism and Syrian and Lebanese nationalism emerged as the default solution. To be sure, a communal rationale may still have colored the conception and embrace of a new political identity and entity (*kiyān*). This was particularly the case for Maronite Christians who – unlike the geographically more spread and urbanized Orthodox – feared the prospect of being subordinated to a larger, pan-Arab, or Syrian state dominated by a Muslim majority. But, as Khalil Saadeh indicates, the shared suffering spawned a new consciousness that was reflected in symbolic and concrete acts of unity spanning the sectarian divide. This chapter reviews this crystallization of Muslim–Christian cooperation and political secularism that the cataclysm of World War I helped to spawn.

Reflecting the political turmoil and rapid transformations of this era, the political orientation of the proliferating dissident groups in the period 1876–1920 was neither monolithic nor etched in stone.[368] At the dawn of the twentieth century, a whole plethora of Syrian and Lebanese opposition groups began raising the pitch of open agitation against the repressive policies that marked Hamīdian autocracy, Young Turk military rule after 1909, and, subsequently, the French mandate after 1920. Vestiges from this traumatic, intrigue-laden period in late Ottoman history are still apparent in the contemporary Lebanese political system, such as the law governing the formation of political organizations and parties, which

[368] Slogans for a full Arab "*istiqlāl*" appeared in local papers as early as 1858. Consul Skene reported from Aleppo that "the Muslim population of Northern Syria hoped for a separation from the Ottoman Empire and the formation of a new Arabian state under the Sharif of Mecca." Ma'oz, *Ottoman Reform in Syria and Palestine*, 246.

was drafted in 1909 and remains in force until the current day.[369] Dubbed the "Law of Midhat Pasha," this important piece of legislation explicitly prohibited the formation of secret organizations, betraying the importance of the latter at this historical juncture.

Indeed, the (clandestine) opposition movements that emerged in defiance of the Hamīdian regime often functioned as a forum for interethnic and transreligious cooperation in pursuit of a common goal of independence; plethoric as their number was, they were not all of the same political stripe. There were CUP cells in Beirut, Damascus, and Istanbul that continued to support a quasi-secular Ottoman state in the form of a constitutional, parliamentary monarchy. Other factions were veering toward a Lebanese national agenda such as was the case with the Lebanese Union of 1909, founded by Antoine Jummayil, Dawūd Barakāt, and Adīb Yūsuf, the Association of the Cedar of Lebanon, founded in 1910 under the leadership of (subsequent president) Bishāra al-Khūrī, ʻĀdil Arslān, and Habīb Pasha Saʻd, or *Nahda Lubnān*, founded by Nawm Mukarzil and Ibrāhīm Najjār. The secularism of some of these opposition groups, such as that of the Central Party of Syrian Unity was still not of a comprehensive kind. The fourth article of the party (headed by Abd al Rahmān Shahbandir, Fāris Nimr, Yakub Sarruf, Rashīd Ridā, and Mukhtar al-Sulh) called for civil laws and decentralization in Syria "with the exception of personal status laws which are to remain as they are."[370] The same incomplete endorsement of secularism was apparent in the leading liberal journals of the time such as *al-ʻAhd* and *al-Jadīd*. The *Sharīʻa* courts were never put in question in this time, although leading liberal voices of the Sunni elite such as Salīm ʻAlī Salīm, Riyād al-Sulh, and ʻAbdullāh al-Mashnūq were calling for a separation of Islam and Arabism on the one hand and religion and state on the other.[371] Another case in point is the *Jam'īyat al-ʻArabīya al-Fatāt*, which was founded in Paris in 1911 in opposition to the Young Turk's oppressive push at centralization. Its stated goal was to "detach itself from the worm-eaten Ottoman trunk."[372] Although self-avowedly secular in its

[369] The ministerial decision no. 60/93 in fact added an additional clause requiring all political parties to obtain the permission of the cabinet before registering with the ministry of the interior. On August 8, 2005 this law was abrogated. Today there still is no specific law regulating the establishment of parties proper in Lebanon, as the Ottoman Law of 1909 is a generic law for all nongovernmental "associations."

[370] Khalīfa, "A la Récherce d'une Politique Ou d'un Concept de Secularisation dans le Liban Multiconfessionnel (1858–1975)," 56.

[371] *See Saʻb, The Arab Federalists in the Ottoman Empire, 207.*

[372] Membership did not exceed seventy from 1911 to 1918. It was only after 1918 when *al-Fatāt* became the chief beneficiary of its previous alliance with the Hashemites that tried to join, leading the *al-Fatāt* vanguard to found the Arab Independence Party to absorb

political orientation, *al-Fatāt* would support the campaign of Sharīf Husyan and endorse numerous calls to *jihād* for pragmatic reasons. Most importantly, like most dissident groups, *al-Fatāt* was confined to a small membership and failed to make significant inroads.

It was Jamīl Ma'lūf's "*Sūrīyā al-Fatāt*" that spelled out perhaps the clearest platform of Muslim–Christian unity and political secularism at this time, calling for a total separation of religious and civil powers and a national unification of education across Syria. In his Cairene exile, Ma'lūf issued a plea for human rights across the Ottoman Empire in *La Turquie Novelle et Les Droits de L'Homme*. Confessing his continued fear of Hamīdian censorship, Ma'lūf obliquely mentions the "painful crisis" in Lebanon, but preferred to defer a more detailed discussion of Lebanon's predicament "to a later, more opportune date."[373] Yet another opposition group espousing a (pan-)Syrian agenda was the Syrian–Palestinian Congress.[374] Founded by Rashīd Ridā along with a host of other Syrian Sunni notables, such as Shakib Arslān, Mūsā al-Husaynī, and Ihsān al-Jabrī, it suffered from a lack of sectarian diversity,[375] in the same way the Christian-dominated counterpart organizations lacked significant Muslim participation.[376] However, after its schism in 1927, one branch of the party – the faction of Michel Lutfallāh and 'Abd al-Rahmān Shahbandar – renounced the Islamic revivalism that marked the discourse of Rashīd Ridā and Shakīb Arslān and even veered toward embracing a Greater Lebanon as it had become a *fait accompli* against the objection of (largely Muslim) Lebanese unionists after 1920.[377] Thus, the Party of Arab Independence – which counted such noted figures as 'Ādil Arslān, Riyād Sulh, and Rashīd Ridā among its members – reiterated its plan to constitute an Arab, Damascus-based emirate.

With nationalism in the air, we find that the discourse of Phoenicianism[378] took on more strident tones just as Islamist ideologies became

the new recruits after 1918. James Gelvin, *Divided Loyalities: Nationalism and Mass Politics in Syria at the Close of Empire* (Berkeley: University of California Press, 1998), 65.

373 Jamīl Ma'lūf, *La Turquie Novelle et Les Droits de L'Homme* (Cairo: Dar al Hilal, 1906), 25.

374 Stephen Longrigg, *Syria and Lebanon under French Mandate* (London: Oxford University Press, 1958), 143.

375 The notable Maronite exception was the co-president and financier of the congress, the wealthy businessman Michel Lutfallāh.

376 Kaufman, *Reviving Phoenicia*, 198.

377 Kaufman, *Reviving Phoenicia*, 240.

378 The first writer to speak of Phoenician Lebanon was possibly Tannūs al-Shidyāq (1784–1861), although his was a pluralistic, religiously heterogeneous feudal confederacy, as opposed to the ethnocentric Phoenicia propagated by some right-wing Christian factions during the 1975 civil war. Subsequently, Phoenicianism figured prominently in the writings of Charles Qurm, Ferdinand Tayyān's *La Nationalité*

more pronounced in the wake of World War I. Antonius notes that it is only after the advent of Young Turk despotism in 1909 that Arab nationalism got a decidedly Islamist imprint in such organizations as *al-Qahtānīya* of Amīn Quzma or *al-Hizb al-Lāmarkazīya al-Idārīya al-'Uthmānīya* founded by the Lebanese exile Iskandar 'Ammūn.[379] Secular notions of equality and national unity came to imbue the discourse of Islamism and Phoenicianism alike, particularly in light of the 1909 failure. Thus, the *Alliance Libanaise* was founded in Cairo in 1909 by Yūsuf al-Sawda, who would subsequently assume a leading role as the head of the *Hizb al-Ittihād al-Lubnānī* – the first party to explicitly embrace the idea of an expanded *Grand Liban*[380] – and as one of the drafters and main sponsor of the precursor to the National Pact of 1943. Sawda's role in formulating the fundamental premises of an independent, intercommunal, geographically expanded Lebanese state proved pivotal. While Sawda described both Arabs and Turks as invading *ghuzāt,* and while he promoted Lebanon as the haven of the Christians (*mau'il al-masīhīīn*), his brand of Lebanese nationalism was explicit in its insistence on the inclusion of Muslims as fellow Lebanese citizens.[381]

For most Muslims and a number of Christians, however, it was the Ottoman State and the (dashed) promise it held out of secular egalitarianism and common citizenry as propagated in 1908 that was to remain the political umbrella under which protection was sought from an encroaching West, at least up until the Young Turk July Revolution. In fact, Midhat Pasha, the erstwhile Ottoman governor of Syria, had still equated "the Lebanese" with the "Maronite Christians," reflecting the common linguistic conflation of "Lebanese" and "Christian" at the turn of the century:

> As France was supporting the Lebanese, England found herself to support the Druze ... all these influences produced the very worst effect on the country, for one party of the Christians cherish a dream of union with Lebanon, whilst ... the Mussulmans can only marvel at the disorder.[382]

Maronite and Paul Jouplain's *La Question du Liban* (Paris: A. Rousseau, 1908). See Iliya F. Harik, *Politics and Change in a Traditional Society: Lebanon, 1711–1845* (Princeton, NJ: Princeton University Press, 1968), 146.

379 Antonius, *The Arab Awakening*, 109.

380 Presided by Antūn al-Jummayil, a petition was sent to Istanbul in 1910 asking for direct, popular elections, the restitution of previously enjoyed privileges (*imtīyāzāt*), and the return of the *Biqā'a*s Bishāra al-Khūrī notes in his memoires. Bishāra al-Khūrī, *Hāqāiq Lubnānīya*, three vols. (Beirut: Manshūrāt al-Harf, 1961), 81.

381 Sawda, *Fī Sabīl Lubnān*, 10.

382 Midhat Pasha in a letter to the Grand Vizier, Sa'īd Pasha, March 29, 1879. 'Alī 'Midhat Bey, *The Life of Midhat Bey* (London: J. Murray, 1903), 181.

Half a century later, after Midhat's elimination, 'Abdul Ḥamīd's toppling in 1909, and, in particular, after the pro-Turkish, anti-Arab policies imposed by the new interior minister Talat Pasha after 1910, Christian and Muslim reformers alike began to harbor increasing resentment of what were considered discriminatory, acrimonious Young Turk policies at odds with the previously advertised slogans of liberty, egality, justice, unity, and fraternity.[383] Whereas Sultan 'Abdul Ḥamīd had actively recruited (largely Sunni) Arab administrators, many an Arab graduate of Western and Ottoman law schools now saw his career hopes dashed by Turkish bias in appointment policies. This discrimination against Arabs first became apparent in the central administration, as al-'Asaylī lamented as early as 1908.[384] After 1911, the ethnic and linguistic bias extended to the provincial administration as well as when Talat Bey discharged most *qā'imaqāms and mutaṣarrifs* of Arab descent. Turkification thus continued to block the career paths of an ascending Arab middle class. On the one hand, the post-*Tanzimāt* era enabled a segment of the local Arab elites to study in Istanbul's modern military schools (*ḥarbīya mektebi*) and other prestigious institutions, yet, on the other hand, this new Arab administrative and military elite could scarcely find adequate employment in both the central and provincial administration, particularly after 1911, so that both (Arab) *'ulamā'* and former CUP members in Beirut and Damascus were "lost" to nascent Arab, Syrian, and Lebanese nationalisms, which often, although not invariably, displayed a secular orientation.[385] Even a *bona fide* pan-Islamist like Rashīd Riḍā would be forced to condemn "Young Turks who discriminated against and undermined the Arabs and Syrians at a time when they are in dire need of cohesion and unity."[386] Abdel-Ghani Arayssi's *al-Mufid* newspaper went even further in labeling the Turkification policies as

[383] Kawākibī articulated what some deem the contours of an anti-Turkish Arab nationalism. 'Abd al-Raḥmān al-Kawākibi, *Tabā'i'u al-Istibdād wa Masārī'u al-Isti'bād*, ed. Muhammad Jamāl Taḥḥān (Damascus: al-Awā'il, 2003).

[384] Ḥaddād, "The Rise of Arab Nationalism Reconsidered," 208.

[385] Nonetheless, Syrian Christians like Zaydan and Anṭūn were afraid of the ramifications of a potential Young Turk failure and thus remained firm advocates of Ottoman unity. When Atatürk finally established the secular Turkish republic, Kurd 'Alī (1876–1953) severely criticised the latter's reforms. See Yārid, *Secularism in the Arab World*, 34, 159.

[386] Riḍā adds that "it is important not to vent our hostilities on the Turks in general so as not to weaken the Caliphate. Rather, we should focus our efforts on uniting the Arabs so as to create a new and powerful force that is equipped to defend themselves, to press for their independence if the Ottoman state is defeated and to safeguard their rights if the Ottoman state emerges victorious, as is the wish of every Muslim." Yunān Labīb Rizq, "Looking Towards the Levant," *Al-Ahram Weekly*, September 20, 1999.

downright "anti-Islamic."[387] Like many of his colleagues, Arayssi would be led to the gallows on May 6, 1916. His parting words manifest an ideological transformation from pan-Islamism to the embrace of a nascent Lebanese-Arab nationalism: "The glory of the Arabs is coming. States are not formed save through the suffering of their heroes. And ours form the basis for Lebanese independence."[388]

The public execution of Muslim and Christian dissidents was just the culmination of a number of policies imposed from 1914 to 1919 by the Young Turk triumvirate, which fed a growing alienation. All schools instructing in French were ordered to be closed in Beirut, with the notable exception of the *Alliance Israelite* school.[389] Regional identities were further fomented by the Young Turks' enforcement of Turkish *in lieu* of Arabic in state courts and schools in 1909, a policy initially pursued by 'Abdul Hamīd II, but one which until then had hitherto never been implemented in the Levant.[390] While initially nominally committed to Ottoman pluralism, the Young Turks drive at Turkification is better conceived as a partial inheritance from 'Abdul Hamīd, who – while increasing the number of Arabs in the central administration – first decreed Ottoman Turkish the official language of all state institutions at all levels.[391]

The resultant anti-CUP sentiments could forge alliances between (Arab) Muslims and Christians in pursuit of a common cause (while conversely collaborators with the "Turkish tyranny" were equally found

[387] Elieyer Tauber, "The Press and the Journalist as a Vehicle in Spreading National Ideas in Syria and the Late Ottoman Period," *Die Welt des Islams* 30 (1990): 172.

[388] Shāmī, Le Mémorial du Liban, vol. I, 59.

[389] Mas'ūd Dāhir, *Tārīkh Lubnān Al-Ijtimā'ī: 1914–1926* (Beirut: Dar an Nahar, 1974), 177. The CUP's ties to the nascent Zionist movement were a topic of controversy even within Young Turkish circles. See the accusation leveled by Serif Pasha against CUP members who were Freemasons and Zionists. Şükrü Hanioğlu, "Turkish Nationalism and the Young Turks: 1889–1908," in *Social Constructions of Nationalism in the Middle East*, ed. Fatma Müge Göçek (New York: State University of New York Press, 2002), 19ff. It should be noted, however, that an irascible Cemal Pasha at the end of his reign cast all caution to the wind once his defeat was sealed and expelled 7,000 Jews from Jaffa, causing an embarrassing rift in the otherwise solid and amicable Turkish–Zionist alliance. See Ahmad, "The Special Relationship."

[390] Kemal Karpat, *Studies on Ottoman Social and Political History* (Leiden: Brill, 2002), 13.

[391] Hamīd's *firmāns* never affected Syria since Midhat and Aḥmad Ḥamdī Pasha (1879–1885) had bowed to the demands of Syrian notables and reformers to retain Arabic as the language of administration. While Arab delegates and students gained access to the *Mulkiye* and *Yildiz* under 'Abdul Ḥamīd, the latter also Turkified higher positions of local bureaucracies, again prefiguring the later CUP policies. Şükrü Hanioğlu has perceptively pointed out that "although the [Ḥamīdian] state endeavored to Ottomanise its subjects, the symbols used to evoke a supranational culture were Turkish." Hanioğlu, "Turkish Nationalism and the Young Turks," 86. Ḥaddād, "The Historical Work of Niqula El- Turk 1763–1828," 216.

among opportunistic Christian war profiteers)[392]. In Beirut, opposition to the Young Turks culminated in 1913 with the formation of a short-lived Committee of Reform, composed of eighty-six members of all denominations who demanded a form of home rule for the *sanjak* of Mount Lebanon.[393] These hopes were deflated with the execution in Beirut of fourteen dissident Christian and Muslim activists in what came to be known as Martyrs' Square on May 6, 1916. The "martyrs" had appealed to the French consul in Beirut – none other than later foreign minister Georges Picot – for support in gaining independence. The incriminating letters were obtained by Cemal Pasha, putatively thanks to a tip from Philip Zalzal, a former dragoman translator for Georges Picot who had kept the files hidden in the Beirut French consulate. On May 6, 1916, fourteen dissidents were hanged in Beirut and seven in Damascus. These were, however, not the only executions based on the Georges Picot files. On June 6, two Christians (the Khazin brothers) and two Muslims (the Mahmasani brothers) were sent to the gallows in Beirut. This sectarian equilibrium set a precedent until the present day in Lebanon, whereby it is all but impossible to sentence to death a member of one major sect without a counterpart from another sect.

The 1915 famine probably was the single most incisive tragedy to beset Lebanon. Inhabitants of southern Lebanon and northern Palestine suffered and perished from swarms of locusts, rampant inflation, and

[392] Famous examples include the Sursocks and Bayhums who cornered the market in the grain trade. Opportunism was also evident in the Maronite poet Shiblī Mallāt's effusive laudations to the Young Turks during World War I. He would ex post facto justify this slip of the pen as a survival tactic, claiming that he was forced to "eulogise" ("*madaha mukrahan*"). See *al-Mashriq*, August 1920, 636. Mallāt, to be sure, had a double motivation to remain on good terms with Istanbul as the founder of a journal in 1906 (*al-Watan*) and as an occupant of numerous posts in the Ottoman administration of Mount Lebanon. Likewise, Shakīb Arslān could move from an ardent Ottomanist to a self-promoting Francophile under the mandate. Journals such as *al-Mashriq* and *al-Jinān* would preface their first editions with showering grandiloquent praise to the "Sultan of Sultan's" and the "Government of the Sunna." See opening editorial, *al-Mashriq*, First Edition, 1898, 2. Defying the orders of Istanbul could spell the end of a publication as Ahmad Fāris al-Shidiyāq discovered when his *pathbreaking al-Jawā'ib* was forced to shutdown in 1879 after it declined to publish an Ottoman statement against the Egyptian Khedeve. See 'Aẓma and Ṭarābulsī, "Aḥmad Fāris al-Shidiyāq: Su'lūk al-Nahḍa," 26.

[393] Nicholas Z. Ajay, "Political Intrigue and Suppression in Lebanon during World War I," *International Journal of Middle East Studies* 5 (1974): 143. British and French intelligence gathering was at its height upon the eruption of WWI. The demarcation line of respective spheres of influence seems to have been Sidon, with the French controlling the northern coastline and the British the southern one. Under the aegis of Cemal Pasha, the commander of the fourth army, the Young Turks abrogated the Reglement of 1861 and eliminated the nascent Lebanese independence cells. Cemal Pasha would later act as a liaison between Mustafa Kemal and the Bolsheviks in Russia.

the war-induced disruption of trade routes. Elisabeth Thompson has estimated that Mount Lebanon – suffocated by a punitive siege imposed by Cemal Pasha and a recalcitrant decision by Beirut's governor Azmi Bey to stop vital US Aid administered through the Red Cross[394] – may have lost approximately 18 percent of its population to conscription and famine in World War I, an unusually high decimation that far outstripped the human toll of 5 percent in France and Germany in the war. Indicatively, the Turkish word for conscription ("*serferbelik*") came to be synonymous with "famine" in Levantine Arabic.[395] The victims of the massive famine between 1914 and 1917 were geographically centered in northern Mount Lebanon and thus overwhelmingly Christians, yet, beyond Turkish bias, the Allied blockade that was designed to produce "shortages in supply" and thus stir the Arabs to revolt, exacerbated matters. Only in November 1919 did the Allies effectively put an end to the calamity by importing tons of grain, rice, and vegetables.[396]

Even if the largely (Maronite) Christian areas of northern Lebanon were hit hardest, the World War I famine also claimed several victims among the Sunni population of Beirut and the Shia population of Jabal 'Āmil.[397] In his history of Jabal 'Āmil during the war, Sulaymān Ḍāhir recounts that vital grain supplies from the Hawrān were being siphoned off to Beirut, with war profiteering running rampant, so that inhabitants of southern Lebanon and northern Palestine suffered famine as well. The economic blockade imposed by the Allies – and the manifold disruptions of trade – in 1915 also served to strain intercommunal relations between the erstwhile trading partners of the Shia of Jabal 'Amil and the Druze of the Ḥawrān.[398]

Despite its gravity, the famine never received any official recognition, in contrast to the execution of opposition figures on May 6, 1916, which

394 Umar Abu Nasr, *Al-Harb al-Uthma, 1914–1917*, vol. 17 (Beirut: al-Majmū'ah al-Tārīkhīyah al-Muṣawwarah, 1938), 20.

395 See Thompson, *Colonial Citizens*, 38.

396 Shāmī, *Le Mémorial du Liban*, vol. I, 45. According to one contemporary witness, "the discrimination program of the Turks was not based on religion but on politics. But then again, most of Mount Lebanon was Christian. Many Muslims fled to Syria." Ḥalīm Ashqar cit. in Ajay, "Political Intrigue and Suppression in Lebanon during World War I," 152.

397 For an earlier study of the famine and its regional political parameters, particularly the role of the Allied blockade of the Syrian coast, see Linda Schatkowski, "The Famine of 1915–18 in Greater Syria," in *Essays in Honor of Albert Hawrānī*, ed. J. Spagnolo (Reading: Ithaca Press, 1992), 229–258.

398 Chalabi, *The Shi'is of Jabal 'Amil and the New Lebanon Community and Nation State, 1918–1943*, 14. By contrast, a local Arab dispatch mentions that the Turkish authorities prevented Western aid shipments. *Al-Muqattam*, March 30–April 1, 1916 as cited in Arnold Toynbee, *Turkey: A Past and a Future* (New York: D. H. Doran, 1917), 33.

was commemorated as Martyrs' Day.[399] Indicatively, the memory of the Beiruti martyrs was itself subject to the political dichotomy of the day: until 1937, two martyrs' days were celebrated: one unionist, Syro-Lebanese commemoration on March 6, and another, mandate-sponsored official commemoration on September 2. In 2007, the Lebanese government under then-prime minister Siniora took the decision to abolish this holiday, erasing the memoralization of one of the rare instances of transconfessional solidarity in Lebanon's contentious history.

A final verdict on this calamity must still be withheld. Even Lebanese history books diverge along confessional lines in their interpretation of the famine.[400] Still, its crucial role in eroding the legitimacy of the Ottoman state and fomenting local identities seems indisputable. Suffice it to say that fresh memories of the horrors of World War I left an indelible mark on the subsequent Christian and Muslim founding fathers of the Lebanese republic, including Bishāra al-Khūrī and Riyād al-Sulh, members of the leading Shia families Zayn, Khalil, and Ussayran (all of whom were arrested by the Turkish authorities), as well as the founder of the staunchly secular Syrian Nationalist Party, Anṭūn Sa'āda. A young and brash Sa'āda – still smarting under the death of his mother during World War I – staunchly refused to carry the Ottoman flag during a reception held in Broumanna for Cemal Pasha and tore the Ottoman flag to shreds in intrepid defiance of the presence of the feared commander of the fourth army.[401]

The Levantine legacy of the Young Turks – and the brutal reign of Cemal Pasha in particular – remains fraught with controversy.[402] Even in the estimate of the German general Liman von Sanders – a key ally of

[399] Mu'awwad attributes this official neglect to the large number of Christian victims, which does not lend the famine to serve as an intercommunal connector. Yūsuf Mu'awwad, "Jamal Pasha en Une Version Libanaise : L'Usage Positif d'Une Légende Noire," in *The First World War as Remembered in the Countries of the Eastern Mediterranean*, eds. Olaf Farschid, Manfred Kropp, and Stephane Daehne (Beirut: Orient-Institut, Ergon Verlag, 2006), 440.

[400] Reflecting the sectarian lens of history textbooks in Lebanese schools, some textbooks (such as the Evangelical Pine secondary school) still adopt the official Ottoman narrative of á British embargo as the sole reason for the famine, while others (such as the Shia Yew school), hold a deliberate Ottoman policy culpable. Kamāl Abū Shadīd, "The State of History Teaching in Private-Run Confessional Schools in Lebanon," *Mediterranean Journal of Educational Studies* 5.2 (2000).

[401] See Bishāra, *Lebanon: Politics of Frustration*, 41.

[402] See, for instance, Muḥammad Jamāl Ṭaḥḥān's fierce critique of Azīz al-'Aẓma's attempt to de-link secularism from Arab nationalism and the later from Cemal Pasha's repressive policies in Lebanon and Syria. *Al-Ijtihād*, vol. 54, Spring 2002, 306. Ṭaḥḥān – who ironically espouses an antisecularist Islamist position – accuses 'Aẓma of attempting to "whitewash" the bloody episode of Young Turkish quasi-secularism in Lebanon and of using secularism to "combat Islam." Şükrü Hanioğlu has provided us

the Young Turks – it was Cemal Pasha's brutal crackdown that dealt the final death blow to any Turkish–Levantine alliance and managed to alienate Muslims and Christians alike, precipitating the formation of joint, nationalist *fora* and a plethora of opposition movements of variegated communal identities. As Melanie Schulze Tanielian has underscored, World War I was a "political event that was both destructive *and* formative in the civilian realm."[403]

One salient instance of Muslim–Christian solidarity was evident in the press when the editors of the Sunni-owned *Al-Ittihad al-Uthmani* published an editorial in the Christian-led paper *Lisan ul-Hal* conjointly with the Christian-run paper *al-Thabet*, which published its editorial in *al-Ittihad al Uthmani.*[404] When the Reform Society of Beirut was dissolved by the Turkish authorities in 1913, Lebanese papers of all stripes joined in another coordinated symbolic protest by framing their front pages with a black border. The spirit of solidarity even stretched to the highest clerical levels. Cemal Pasha, upon asking the Maronite Patriarch Huwayyik why the latter lobbied for the release of Druze (rather than merely Maronite) exiles as well, was astounded to hear the prelate respond that his was not just a Maronite, but a Lebanese cause.[405]

While the prior dichotomy of predominantly Christian, Lebanese nationalist-separatists and the largely Muslim Arab unionists still obtained, it would be a mistake to conclude that the two poles shared no cause in common, or that individuals could and would not shift their allegiances in this time of flux.[406] After all, Syrian-Lebanese nationalisms were still in their infancy and anything but coherent political ideologies with fixed boundaries as seen in Jubrān Khalīl Jubrān's embrace of hybridity in 1916:

> I am a Lebanese and proud of it. I am not an Ottoman and proud of that. I shall remain an Easterner – Easterner in my conduct. Syrian in my desires, Lebanese in my feelings. Regardless of how much I admire Western progress.[407]

with the most nuanced account of this controversial, blood-stained period. Şükrü Hanioğlu, *The Young Turks in Opposition* (New York: Oxford University Press, 1995).

403 Melanie Schulze Tanielian, "Feeding the City: The Beirut Municipality and Politics of Food during World War I," *International Journal of Middle East Studies* 46.4 (2014): 740.

404 Tauber, "The Press and the Journalist as a Vehicle in Spreading National Ideas in Syria and the Late Ottoman Period," 170.

405 Mu'awwad, "Jamal Pasha en Une Version Libanaise," 435.

406 Ṣalībī, *The Modern History of Lebanon*, 159.

407 Jubrān Khalīl Jubrān, *al-Majmū'a al-Kāmila li-Mu'alifāt Jubrān Khalīl Jubrān*, vol. IV (Beirut: Dār Sādir, 1997), 208.

Jubrān's colleague, the novelist Amīn al-Riḥānī (1876–1940) confirmed that the categories of Syrian and Lebanese still were not cut and dried and that a secular Syrian identity for some superseded any Lebanese patriotism, which Riḥānī feared would carry confessional connotations:

> I am Syrian first, Lebanese second, and Maronite third. I am Syrian born in Lebanon, and respect the source of my Arabic language. I am a Syrian-Lebanese who believes in the separation of religion from politics, because I realize that the main obstacle to national unity is religious partisanship. The Lebanese idea, i.e., the national sectarian idea, is an old and impotent idea. If we go by it, it will be a devastating blow to us. It was the cause of our defeat and misery in the past, and will be, if it prevails, the reason for our misery in the future. What a narrow conception of Lebanon.[408]

Riḥānī's steadfast secularism, however, was not always congruent with all strands of Syrian (or Arab) anticolonialism. As late as 1920, the Turkish troops who came to aid the Syrian rebels in their *jihād* against France would carry a flag, Turkish on one side, and Arab on the other with the words "believers are brothers" emblazoned on it.[409] Five years later, Sultān al-Aṭrash, the legendary leader of the Druze insurgency in the *Ḥūrān*, grandly vowed to "make no distinction in religion or sects, as our only aim is to obtain our legal rights which belong equally to the sons of Syria."[410] The rebellion he led, however, bore a heavy confessional-Islamist tint, as is seen in the charged "holy-war" vocabulary that Aṭrash himself would invoke at its onset, even as he cited the French revolutionary ideals of liberty, egality, and fraternity.[411] Sectarianism was, in other words, at once deployed and deplored, instrumentalized, and inveighed against by both parties to the conflict. The French cited the raids of armed bands (*'iṣābāt*) against Christians in such regions as Idlib and Tripoli as a pretext for intervention, even as individual Christian clans participated in the fight against the French, while a full third of Faysal's advisory cabinet (*Majlis al-shūrā*) after October 6, 1918 was staffed by Christians. Two out of nine ministers of his second cabinet formed on March 3, 1920, also were Christian. Even as Faysal and his modernist cabinet repeatedly emphasized their intent not to discriminate in governance according to religious identity, there was no consistency in the secularism of the Sharifian regime, which, after all, based much of its legitimacy on the claim of the "Sultan of the Arabs and Caliph of the

408 Amīn Riḥānī, *Qalbu Lubnān* (Beirut: Dar al-Jil, 1971), 56.
409 'Abdul Karīm Rāfiq, "Gesellschaft: Wirtschaft und Politische Macht in Syrien: 1918–1925," in *Der Nahe Osten In Der Zwischenkriegszeit* (Stuttgart: Franz Steiner, 1989), 479.
410 Rāfiq, "Gesellschaft," 426, 469.
411 Rabbāth, *La Formation Historique du Liban Politique et Constitutionnelle*, 363.

Muslims" to prophetic descent.[412] Moreover, as the French threat grew along with shipments of French armaments to minorities in Syria, the references to Islamic rhetoric proliferated along with sporadic sectarian attacks in northern Syria. Incidentally, aside from the onset of the French occupation, it was the ascendancy of Turkish secular nationalism and Mustafa Kemal's final abandonment of pan-Islamist goals that would seal the Syrian revolt's fate. With the conclusion of the French–Turkish pact in London on March 11, 1921, the rebellion was stripped of vital Turkish support before it was launched.

Lebanese nationalism developed out of this crucible of the First World, even if its contours – and geographic borders – still lacked clarity.[413] After all, secular strands had pervaded Ottomanism, Syrian, and Arab nationalism alike, so that Lebanism, even if it could hark back to a long legacy of quasi-secularism and proto-nationalism in the emirate and Mount Lebanon, was not a foregone conclusion. Kais Firro notes that after 1920 a merging of (predominantly Muslim) Syrianist and (largely Christian) Lebanese nationalisms occurred, with the latter often borrowing arguments for a secular nationalism from the former.[414] Sometimes the two identities were fused in a single person. A perfect example is Shukri Ghānim who was at once member of Sawda's *Alliance Libanaise* in 1909, and the founder of the *Comité Central de la Syrie* in 1917 and the *Comité Libanais de Paris,* which had been established in 1912 (the Egyptian branch was tellingly called *Comité Libano-Syrien*). Clearly, Ghānim's foremost preoccupation was to resist the unification of Damascus and Arabia, which he deemed a "violation of history."[415] By 1919, Ghānim – along with the French – had begun to yield to the logic of communal division and edged toward the embrace of a Lebanese nationalism to counter the threat of greater Syrian-Islamic unity, which he surmised was propelling the Arab Revolt and the Amir Faysal.[416]

[412] Fred Lawson, "The Northern Syrian Revolts of 1919–1921 and the Sharifian Regime: Congruence or Conflict of Interests and Ideologies," in *From the Syrian Land to the States of Syria and Lebanon*, 270.

[413] Ibrāhīm Bek, *al-Aswad Dalīl Lubnān* (Baabda: al-Maktaba al-Uthmaniyya, 1906), 139 in which the borders of the 1926 republic are prefigured.

[414] The Jesuit professors at St. Joseph Pierre Martin and Henri Lammens played an important role in propagating the lore of a Syrian homeland. See Kais Firro, "Lebanese Nationalism versus Arabism: From Būlus Nujaym to Michel Shīḥā," *Middle Eastern Studies* 40.5 (2004), 3.

[415] Firro, "Lebanese Nationalism versus Arabism," 3.

[416] Aziz al-Azmeh has stated that the Arab Revolt "does not belong to the register of Arab nationalism ... It was Arab only in the narrow, ethnological, pre-nationalist sense. It was an Islamist rebellion, undertaken not in the name of the Arabs, but of a Meccan Caliphate." Aziz al-Azmeh, "Nationalism and the Arabs," in *Arab Nation, Arab Nationalism*, ed. Derek Hopwood (New York: St. Martin's Press, 2000), 69.

Ghānim was part of one of two Lebanese delegations in Versailles in 1919 lobbying for full independence. Commissioned by Decree number 80 of the administrative council of Mount Lebanon, an interconfessional delegation led by Dāūd ʻAmmūn called for an expansion of Mount Lebanon and a return to the natural borders of the emirate, a popularly elected parliament, and French assistance to hasten independence.[417] Since the great powers were still holding parallel negotiations with Faysal, they did not commit themselves to the proposed state as yet so that, after a second promulagation of the administrative council on May 20, 1919, a second delegation headed by Patriarch Huwwayek was dispatched, returning to Lebanon with a written commitment to Lebanese independence signed by President Poincaré and Prime Minister Clémenceau.

ʻAmmūn had himself gone through a very similar transformation as Ghānim. Both had set out as ardent supporters of the 1908 revolution that had revitalized pro-Ottoman secular liberals, as Carole Ḥakīm has shown in a cogent *exposé* of the fluid political identities of this era.[418] A liberal, pluralistic Ottomanism, it was thought, might allow Mount Lebanon to escape the clutches of a parochial, "clergy-ridden" system. Even the suspended December 23, 1876 constitution, however, in Article 11, still identified Islam as the religion of state. Just as had been the case in 1876, the administrative council of the *Mutaṣarrifīya* refused to send any delegates to the Ottoman parliament in 1908, fearing that Lebanese privileges might be curtailed. For a brief moment, ʻAmmūn even joined the CUP, accepting Faysal's invitation to serve as ambassador in Washington. In 1920 he was elected to the head of the administrative council in which he defended Lebanese claims to autonomy by establishing a court of cessations independent of Damascus and by opposing the Zionist land claims in the south.[419] In effect, the unilateral proclamation of a "United Syrian Kingdom" took the Lebanese Maronites aback. After learning of fifteen Muslim delegates who had joined the Syrian congress on behalf of Lebanon, another delegation was dispatched to Paris in protest against Syrian claims to Lebanon, leading to a

[417] The members were Maḥmūd Janbulāṭ, ʻAbdullāh al-Khūrī, Ibrāhīm Abū Khāṭīr, Tāmir Ḥamāda, ʻAbdul Ḥalīm Hajjār, and Emile Iddih. Jisr, *Mithāq 1943*, 45–47.

[418] Carole Ḥakīm, "Shifting Identities and Representations of the Nation amongst the Maronite Secular Elite," in *From the Syrian Land to the States of Syria and Lebanon*.

[419] Fawwāz Ṭarābulsī, *Ṣilāt bi-lā Waṣl: Mīshāl Shīḥā wa al-Idyūlūjīya al-Lubnānīya* (Beirut: Riyād al-Rayyes, 1999), 20.

French reaffirmation of Clémenceau's pledge one year earlier to prefer Lebanese national autonomy.[420]

Eventually, Ottomanism had made way for pan-Syrianism and finally for Lebanism. This trajectory is reflected in Ghānim's involvement in the *Ligue Ottoman*, followed by his founding of the *Comité Central Syrien* in 1917 and, finally, upon the dissolution of the latter at the dawn of independence, the *Comité de Defense des Droits du Grand Liban* in 1920. In the shadow of the horrific dislocation of World War I and the global contagion of national and religious chauvinisms, disillusionment had set in, with corporate, ethno-nationalistic separatisms winning the day. That having been said, contrary to pervasive thought, the nineteenth-century champions of an independent Lebanon were not – in the main – advocates of a communal Christian country. One of the first advocates of the *Grand Liban*, Yūsuf as-Sawda, explicitly included the Lebanese Muslims and rejected both French and Syrian tutelage.[421] While the administrative council in its declaration of March 12, 1920 explicitly rejected the Syrian congress proposal of a federal Syria with Lebanon, this did not mean that the threat of (French) colonialism was completely ignored. Rather, for the first time a policy of nonalignment was proclaimed: Lebanon was to enjoy complete autonomy and neither "be the subject nor object of any war'" ("*lā yuhārib wa lā yuhārab*"),[422] a mantra which was to be reformulated as the central plank of the National Pact of 1943.[423]

Still, the question remained: what mode of secular modernity was within the margins of the possible for as unusually pluralistic a society as Lebanon? And where ought the borders of the prospective state to be drawn? By the end of the Young Turk occupation in 1918, a general consensus had settled among a class of urban, largely Christian politicians on the "natural" boundaries of the republic (which were predicated on those of the Ma'anite and Shihabite emirate).[424] It is often forgotten that these borders were first drawn in December 1918 by the

420 Zayn N. Zayn, *The Struggle for Arab Independence* (Delmar, NY: Caravan, 1960), 133 and appendix H.

421 Sawda, *Fī Sabīl Lubnān*, 10ff. Sawda was not part of the six Christian exiles who on March 12, 1913 had petitioned the French counsel in Beirut to occupy Syria in order to save the Christians of the Near East.

422 Decree of July 10, 1920 cited in al-Azīz Nawwār, *Wathā'iq Asāsīya*, 457–458. The eight signatories of this resolution included the brother of the patriarch, S'adallah al-Ḥ uwwayyik, who was arrested by the French before he could reach Damascus to mediate with the Syrian leadership. Zayn, *The Struggle for Arab Independence*, 150.

423 Jisr, *Mithāq 1943*, 84, 114.

424 Būlus Jouplain (in *La Question du Liban*) had already suggested the enlargement of the "Lebanese nation" within Syria in precisely this manner, even though Jabal 'Āmil was conspicuously left out.

Administrative Council under Ḥabīb Pasha Saʿd. Under the subsequent French mandate, Article 1 of Decree 318 of August 1920 formally codified the geographic borders of the *Grand Liban*, composed of the Cazas of Baʿalbak, the Biqā', Rāshayā, and Ḥāṣbayā, and the Sanjaks of Beirut, Sidon, and Tripoli. As the sole state in the region, the May 23, 1926 constitution cannot be reduced to a "gift" to the Maronites, as its detractors are wont to claim. The very boundaries of the new state (by adding Tripoli, Beirut, Sidon, and the Biqā') – ironically supported by Patriarch Huwayyak, yet opposed by most Maronites – was bound to dilute Christian demographic dominance, which had prevailed in the *Petit Liban* from 1860 to 1914. The overwhelming majority of war-scarred Christians had expressed their support for an independent Lebanese state during the King-Crane questionnaire in 1919, but the borders remained a contested issue as a small Lebanon was not deemed viable economically, and given that the Orthodox preferred a different set of boundaries which would have granted them, as opposed to the Maronites, the status of the largest Christian demography.[425]

In the end, Lebanon's constitution introduced a novelty: confirming prior decrees passed by the High Commission, the 1926 constitution is the only one to explicitly delineate a nation's borders in Article 1. This innovation came as a *fait accompli* retort to the Muslim (and occasional Christian) opposition to the new state. At the same time, the creation of the enlarged republic in 1920 also signaled Lebanon's fuller – if still incomplete – adoption of French secularism.[426] In the decades to come, the political identity of the new state, however, would have to pass through a more arduous process of debate, argumentation, and constant renegotiation of the terms of any prospective social contract.

In navigating the course from this tempestuous sea of virulent nineteenth-century communalisms and identities in flux to a more stable shore of nationhood, intellectuals and politicians oriented themselves according to past domestic and foreign lodestars. To the likes of Jamīl Maʿlūf, Yūsuf al-Sawda, Makram Zakour, Khalil Saadeh (and his son Antun), or Buṭrus al-Bustānī's son Salīm al-Bustānī national sovereignty

[425] The 1919 King–Crane commission revealed that all Lebanese Christians wanted independence (with or without a French mandate). The Orthodox were the only Lebanese Christian community favoring a union with parts of Syria, given the high number of Orthodox in the "Wadi Nasaara" region. Thākirat al-Kanīsa, ed., *Jūrj Mughāmis* (Beirut: Manshūrāt Jāmiʿat Sayyidat al-Luwayza, Notre Dame University, 2000), 128.

[426] See Mark Farha, "Secularism in a Sectarian Society? The Divisive Drafting of the Lebanese Constitution of 1926," in *Constitution Writing, Religion and Democracy*, eds. A. Ü. Bâli and H. Lerner (Cambridge: Cambridge University Press, 2016).

Figure E2.4 "The Holy Union." *Al-Ma'rad (Beirut)*, March/April 1922, 11

and secularism, it seemed, were the hallmarks of progress and the ineluctable destiny of the age. This conviction was further strengthened by a large Lebanese exile community in France, the Americas, and Egypt who acted as vocal ambassadors of republicanism. Khalil Saadeh's odyssey, leading him to flee Ottoman and French persecution from Beirut to Cairo to Argentina and Brazil, is a case in point. For the two journals he founded in exile, *al Majalla* and *al Jaridah*, became sounding boards for the same ideas of emancipation and antisectarianism Beiruti papers such as Michel Zakour's *al-Ma'arad* promulgated simultaneously.[427] Case in point is Al-Ma'arad's publication of a picture of a Muslim and Christian member of the American University student union shaking hands in front of a flag emblazoned with a juxtaposed crescent and cross and the words "holy union" (Figure E2.4). On the occasion of the prophet's birthday, Christian students presented the gift of a copy of the Qur'ān to their Muslim colleagues.[428] Lebanon had come a long way since the communal fires and jihads of World War I.

[427] Khalīl Sa'āda, *Suriya min al Harb wa al Maja' ila Mu'tammar al Sulh*, ed. Badr el Hage (Beirut: Saadeh Cultural Foundation, 2014).
[428] *Al Ma'arad (Beirut)*, March/April 1922, 11

Figure E2.5 The original "Martyr's Statue" sculpted by Yūsuf Huwayyik.
(author's photo)

Even as the opposition to secular nationalisms began to recede in wake of the trauma inflicted by World War I, societal confessionalism – and the real and perceived threat of communal hegemonies – still was perceived as a stumbling block to any full political secularization. But the latter was increasingly advertised as the aspired goal in political discourse. World War I had spawned a transconfessional solidarity that had grown on the seedbed of shared sorrow.

Politically, even a sentimentalist like Jibran Khalil Jibran admitted to being shaken out of his stupor by the horrific tragedies and uncharacteristally assumed an active role as secretary of the Syria–Mount Lebanon Relief Committee and, subsequently, the League of Liberation, which called for emancipation from "Turkish rule" in a government based on full intersectarian equality.[429]

Artistically, there was no more vivid expression of this spirit of unity born from searing experience than the original "Martyrs' sculpture" crafted by Yusuf Huwayyik, see Figure E2.5. This commemoration of

[429] Adel Bishara, "A Syrian Rebel: Gibran Khalil Gibran," in *The Origins of Syrian Nationhood: Histories, Pioneers and Identity* (New York: Routledge, 2011), 148. Gibran's seminal poem "Dead Are My People" is one of his best, eloquently expressing the poet's anguish in exile, and the inadequacy of words to lessen the pain of his people.

Muslim and Christian women poised in dignified, unifying mourning over the victims of World War I was defaced by vandal journalist Salīm Slīm in 1948, perhaps an omen of the subsequent intercommunal strife. The sublimely simple, limestone masterpiece was ultimately replaced on May 6, 1960 when President Camille Sham'ūn unveiled the melodramatic "Martyrs' Statue" cast in black bronze by the Italian sculptor Mazzucati. Tellingly, Huwayyik's solemn original was left isolated and abandoned in the garden of the Sursuq Museum, while the foreign ode to patriotic pathos has since occupied Martyrs' Square, riddled with the bullets of the 1975 civil war.[430]

[430] Upon being released from prison after a bare week of internment, Slīm said he had been irritated for a long time by the "tears and resignation" of the "ugly" statue, and proudly recounted how he eagerly chipped off the noses and eyes of the two ladies before being stopped and detained by the police. See Shāmī, *Le Mémorial du Liban*, vol. II, 257; *Lisān al-Ḥāl*, September 9, 1948. For the artist's own recollection, see Yūssuf Huwayyik, *Yaqzat al-Hajar, A'māl Nahtīya* (Beirut: Dār al-Nahār, 2004), 47.

3 Way Stations of the Lebanese Republic

Confessionalism as a Colonial Legacy or Domestic Necessity?

There has been a widespread penchant in historiography on Lebanon to pin the responsibility for the confessional articles in the 1926 constitution on the French mandate authorities. Hardly ever, however, is evidence adduced to substantiate this claim that is simply taken for granted, and often used in a polemical way to question the validity of the constitution itself. A review of memoires and minutes from the drafting process of the constitution yields a more ambiguous picture. The constitution emerged as a drawn-out negotiation between three principal stakeholders: the French Mandate High Commission, an urbane, mercantile Christian elite, and an initially reluctant Muslim bourgeoisie that, committed to unity with Syria, still had to be won over to the very legitimacy of a Lebanese republic.[1] Confessional provisions were inserted during the French mandate (1920–1943), yet not necessarily at the latter's behest. Rather, confessional guarantees were made, often indirectly, to recognize local identities. Far from being an invention to create division, confessional concessions were a strategy to stave off communal strife.[2] After all, the civil wars of 1840 and 1860 – which were concluded with similar arrangements of power sharing – were still fresh in the memory of all parties. The 1926 constitution then emerged as an amalgam of impulses, a cross of imported French egalitarian republicanism and inherited

[1] To be sure, each of these "blocs" was divided internally: The French between left and right, secular and more conservative Catholic dispositions, the Christians mainly between Maronites and Orthodox, and the Muslims between Sunni and Shia constituents.

[2] To Maqdisī ("Corrupting the Sublime Sultanate," 53) sectarianism is an "imagined" discursive tool wielded by the ruling power to legitimize subordination, not a preexistent identity ready to be exploited. The present author suggests that sectarian identities do in fact often exhibit primordial, ideological premises.

Ottoman segmented confessionalism, fused together in a document designed to bestow legitimacy on a newly fashioned state.

Faced with the demand to remove the confessional clauses of the constitution and allow for a full-fledged secularism, the president of the Constitutional Committee of 1926, Shiblī Dammūs, would aver categorically that the Lebanese case was incomparable to any other, including that of England and France. After all, were these states not devoid of Lebanon's communal diversity? Dammūs' historical comparison sparked a most fascinating, sophisticated parliamentary debate that transcended "Occidentalist" polemics. It is cited here in full as it elucidates the variant, well-grounded interpretations of the European experience, which was no longer merely vilified, but analyzed with a pressing desire to derive the most useful lessons for the Lebanese predicament:

- "Let us not adopt a [confessional] system no nation on earth does." (Ibrāhīm al Manthar)
- "The honorable gentleman Dammūs has said that our situation is without comparison in Europe. I beg to differ. Europe has paid dearly in blood and money to rid itself of this malady [of *Ṭā'ifīya*/confessionalism]." (Jurj Zawīn)
- "The honorable gentlemen claims that Europe has advanced due to its extrication of confessionalism. That is incorrect. Rather, they progressed because they distributed justice … We have adopted [political] confessionalism in order to implement justice, so as not to deprive one against the another."[3] (Jamīl Talḥūq).

At the end of these prolonged deliberations, the deputies conceded to a compromise solution between the secular, republican ideal most espoused emotively and the disheartening communal reality they were confronted with on the ground. The political covenant that emerged from this quandary was to become known as a "consociational democracy" ("*al-dimuqrātīya al-tawāfuqīya*"), a blend of Mount Lebanon's previous consensual covenants of 1832, 1840, 1842, and 1864 and the constitution of the Third French Republic.

The First Republic of 1926: Constitutional Contradictions and Lacunae

Mais si nous sommes les descendants des Croisés, nous sommes les fils de la Révolution, épris de liberté et de progrès, respectueux de toutes les religions et fermement résolus à assurer une justice égale aux adeptes de chacune.

[3] Cited in *al-Ṭā'ifīya fī Lubnān Min Khilāl Munāqashāt Majlis al-Nuwwāb*, 15–16.

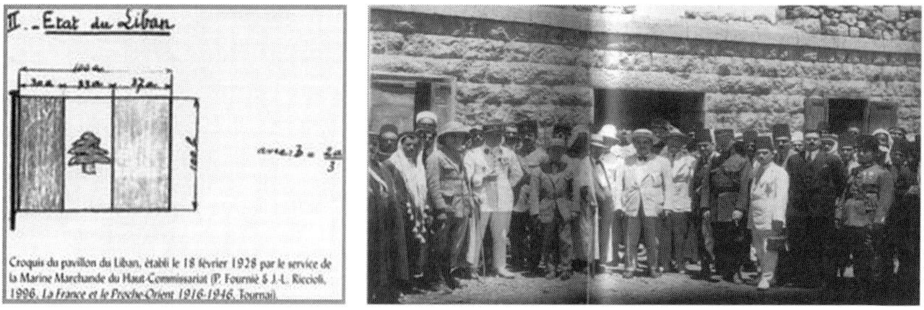

Croquis du pavillon du Liban, établi le 18 février 1928 par le service de la Marine Marchande du Haut-Commissariat (P. Fournié & J.-L. Riccioli, 1996, *La France et le Proche-Orient 1916-1946*, Tournai).

Figure E3.1 Members of the Constitutional Commission during one of their visits to the villages of Lebanon. Doumet-Serhal, Michel Shīḥā 1891–1954, 82–83; *Lisān ul Hāl* No. 365/8015 March 23, 1920, 2.

> Even as we might be the descendents of the Crusaders, we are also the children of the revolution, loving freedom and progress, and respectful of all regions while firmly resolved to guarantee equal justice to the followers of each.
>
> General Gouraud, November 22, 1919 at the reception of Lebanon's *corps constitutes*[4]

The tricolor adorned with the Lebanese cedar, first raised atop the B'abda Serail on March 22, 1920, provides a graphic illustration of the identity crisis that beset the newly founded Republic of Lebanon: Most compromising to the legitimacy of the Lebanese constitution was the fact that it was drafted under the French mandate, which remained the ultimate executive decision-maker until 1943. The question raised by Gouraud's declaration was whether the "heirs to the Crusaders" could in fact pose as credible godfathers of a secular *Republic à la libanaise.* Gouraud's solemn commitment to universal tolerance and impartiality, reiterated two weeks later in Beirut's Mosque of 'Umar, and again at the end of his tenure in 1925, may well have been sincere on a personal level. Yet, even as the Quai d'Orsay proudly presented itself as the standard-bearer of progressive laicisme, when it came to Lebanon, France only thinly concealed its historical guardianship over the "Maronite-Franc" Christians, which had prompted it to intervene in the past.[5]

[4] Cited in Philippe Gouraud, *Le General Henri Gouraud au Liban et en Syrie* (Paris: L'Harmattan, 1993), 39.

[5] Nicolas Murād notes with polemical pride that the alliance between Maronites and France was of such proximity that the (Ottoman) Turks would address the Maronites in letters as "*la nation maronite-franque.*" Murād, *Notice Historique Sur L'Origine de La Nation Maronite*, 32. Almost four centuries earlier, another militant Maronite chronicler

In the event, French interests in Lebanon were not merely born from the long-standing historical ties with the Maronite community or humanitarian compassion for the fate of fellow Catholics, but were equally informed by sheer pecuniary interest. For one, France did not hesitate to unilaterally extend the 1883 tobacco monopoly given to it – and protected – by the Ottomans by dint of the *Régis Du Tabak* for another twenty-five years in 1935.[6] Such blatant "economic imperialism" could cool even those hearts that usually overflowed with yearning for the proverbial "solicitude of mother France." In a stunning speech that earned him multiple laurels and honorific epithets in the Syrian press, Patriarch ʿArīda would react to the unilateral French decision, proclaiming that:

> Lebanon and Syria are linked by language, habits, traditions and economic interests ... one cannot demand *ad infitinum* for the members of a single house, of a single country, to live in discord.[7]

This rare patriarchal proclamation in favor of unionism – exuberantly celebrated in Damascus – was to remain a singular departure from the accustomed role of the Maronite patriarchate as a stalwart lobbyist for French guardianship and Lebanese nationalism. Ironically, the appeal to the French tradition was to prove a double-edged sword for the clergy due to the strong strand of secularism in French republicanism.

After all, the promulgation of the May 23, 1926 constitution was not merely a gift to the Maronites as its detractors are wont to claim,[8] but also signaled Lebanon's fuller – if still not complete – adoption of French secularism. The newly created *Grand Liban* is defined as a republic modeled on the (1875 and 1905) constitution of the French Third Republic and includes the latter's stipulation of (full) freedom of belief and the separation of religion and state. As such, Lebanon appeared legally "predisposed" to secularism in the estimate of Shaykh ʿAbdallāh al-ʿAlāylī.[9] However, the self-same constitution also essentially

claims that the Crusaders did not distinguish between Maronites and Franks. Jibrīl Ibn al-Qilāʿī cited in Ḍaw, *Tārīkh al-Mawārina*, vol. III, 365.

6 The French strove to limit Lebanese tobacco exports in cooperation with the Ottoman authorities.

7 Shāmī, *Le Mémorial Du Liban*, vol. I, 149.

8 The communist intellectual Mahdī ʿĀmil has taken umbrage at the historian Mas'ūd Ḍāhir's contention that "the sectarian problem in Lebanon is in essence a political problem confined to the Maronites." See Mahdi ʿĀmil, *Fī Dawlat al-Tāʾifīya* (Beirut: Dār al-Farabī, 1984), 187. ʿĀmil attempts to root sectarianism in the material, present setting rather than its constructed, putative past.

9 "Considering the Lebanese case, everything seems predisposed for secularism, be it from a legal or constitutional perspective – both of which are secular if we disregard the few

pigeonholed Lebanese citizens as subjects of the religious denomination they were born into. In a conspicuous departure from the French blueprint that enshrined the state's right to surveil religious dogmas in Article 6, the Lebanese constitution in Article 10 grants the sects virtual autonomy from any state interference.[10] While many Lebanese would like to pin the blame for the confessional articles on the French mandate authorities, the actual drafting of the constitution betrays a more ambiguous picture of competing Lebanese communalisms, which almost inexorably asserted themselves to wrest confessional concessions from the new constitution.

In March 1922, the mandatory authority established by Decree 1307 a thirty-member representative council consisting of sixteen Christians and thirteen Muslims plus one minority.[11] Next, the category of Lebanese citizenship was legally established on August 30, 1924 with Resolution 2825, replacing the prior Ottoman Citizenship Law of 1869 that had been abrogated with the Treaty of Lausanne.

After the heavy civilian toll claimed by the French bombing of Damascus on October 18, 1925, Henri de Jouvenel was moved to expedite the process of importing "Occidental democracy" to Syria and Lebanon; by bestowing a constitution, the French sought to meet the requirement of the first Article of the mandate charter on the one hand and to placate local opposition on the other.[12] In 1925, the French high commissioner appointed Shiblī Dammūs and Mūsa Nammūr to cochair a smaller, thirteen-member commission entrusted with consulting 240 confessional representatives and regional representatives in order to draft the "*Statut Organique*." This document would become the blueprint for the 1926 constitution.

While the consultation suggests a democratic process, it suffered from one major handicap: 104 of the prospective interviewees, Sunni Muslims in the main, declined to participate in the survey, citing their categorical

paragraphs with a confessional character … there is no way then to save this sinking ship other than to discard the relics and tribal ideas in order to usher in a better life built on true citizenship." See al-'Alāylī, "Kalimat 'Almana," 2. Antūn 'Azzār has argued that the Belgium constitution of 1831 and the Egyptian one of 1923 left a greater trace on the Lebanese one than the French blueprint. See Ṭarābulsī, *Ṣilāt bi-lā Wasl*, 205.

10 April 12, 1789, "*Tous les cultes sont permis s'ils ne troublent point l'ordre public et n'affectent aucune domination ou prééminence. La police les surveille et a le droit de s'enquérir des dogmes et des devoirs qu'ils enseignent.* " See *Al-Dustūr Al-Lubnānī*, 5.

11 Usually this "neutral" seat was given to a Protestant. Regionally speaking, communal representation was not unusual and is found in the Persian constitution of 1909 (for Zoroastrians and Armenians) and the Jordanian electoral law of 1928 and 1947. Neither case matches the Lebanese insofar as no single community holds a comparable confessional hegemony similar to the Shia in Iran or the Sunnis in Jordan.

12 At this point, Iraq was the only mandate state to have a constitution.

refusal to recognize an autonomous Lebanon separate from Syria under a French mandatory authority whose "temporary" duration was nowhere fixed. Of the remainder, 121 of the 132 notables questioned expressed their preference for a republic (as opposed to a constitutional monarchy) and the "provisional" setting of confessional quotas for parliament, public offices, and ministerial portfolios,[13] a demand that found entry in Article 12 of the subsequent constitution. The draft of the commission was presented on May 19 and swiftly accepted four days later by the mandate authorities without going through any major revision.[14]

It was the Beiruti deputy and commission member Michel Shīḥā (1891–1954)[15] who would prove to wield the greatest influence behind the scenes, both by leveraging his friendship with the French General Gouraud and by dint of his financial clout and ramified family connections.[16] Shīḥā was the brother-in-law of President Bishāra al-Khūrī – whose campaign for a renewed presidency he vehemently opposed. He was also the cousin, brother-in-law, and business partner of the richest man in Lebanon, Henri Fir'awn, with whom he joined the Constitutional Bloc, which would form the cornerstone of the 1943 independence government. Not given to grandstanding, Shīḥā kept a low profile about his personal role in drafting the constitution; only on rare occasions would he – *ex post facto* – disclose his pivotal contribution.[17]

A Chaldean banker by vocation, Shīḥā adopted a mercantilist notion of nationhood, which nonetheless was suffused with a romantic notion of Lebanon's destiny. With his compromise vision of "consociationalism" and his shrewd dealings behind the scenes, Shīḥā managed to attract the support of the Maronite and Sunni merchant elites who outflanked the

[13] Shāmī, *Le Mémorial Du Liban*, vol. I, 102. Also see Bishāra al-Khūrī's handwritten responses published in Claude Doumet-Serhal, ed., *Michel Shīḥā 1891–1954* (Beirut: Foundation Michel Shīhā, 2001), 86.

[14] According to the minutes of the May 19 meeting (which amounted to nothing more than a verbal discussion), Shīḥā was absent due to illness, leading some to suspect (without evidence) that Paul Souchier, de Jouvenel's assistant, may have designed the constitution.

[15] Besides Shīḥā, Mūssa Nammūr (president), and Shiblī Dammūs, the commission included 'Umar Da'ūk, Fu'ād Arslān, Yūsuf Sālim, Jurj Zuwayn, Petro Trād, Rūkūs Abī-Nādir, Sūbhī Haidar, Abū 'Abdul Rāziq, Jurj Tābit, and Yūsuf al-Zayn. Ṭarābulsī cited in Michelle Hartman and Alessandro Olsaretti, "The First Boat and the First Oar: Inventions of Lebanon in the Writings of Michel Shīḥā," *Radical History Review* 86.1 (2003): 40.

[16] See Hartman and Olsaretti, "The First Boat and the First Oar," 37–65.

[17] "*Nous étions depute de Beyrouth alors, et nous avons rédigé nous-même cette Constitution.*" Michel Shīḥā cited in "Pour faire réflechier," June 16, 1950 in *Politique Intérieure* (Beirut: Editions du Trident, 1964), 201. There have been doubts cast on the actual role accorded to Shīḥā that I shall address in what follows. See Roger Owen, *State, Power, and Politics in the Making of the Modern Middle East* (London: Routledge, 2000), 235.

more reform-minded figures such as Yūsuf as-Sawda and Yūsuf Ibrāhīm Yazbak. Propelled by a renaissance spirit, and endowed with vast material means, Shīḥā extended his interests (and influence) beyond finance and politics to the press by acquiring the leading daily *Le Jour* in 1937 and facilitating the establishment of the *Cénacle Libanais* with Michel Asmar in 1946.

His contribution in coauthoring the constitution, however, would turn out to be Michel Shīḥā's most lasting legacy. His was a fluid identity of Lebanon, a country destined to flourish as a polyglot and diverse crossroads of civilizations. Once applied to the economic plane and fiscal policy, however, such a romanticized discourse of untrammeled freedoms could act as an impediment to the étatist centralization efforts commenced by the French administration. In the event, the running of an efficient central bureaucracy was to be subverted by the venality and parochial interests of the Lebanese elites who found themselves entangled in several corruption scandals in the 1930s.[18]

Edmond Rabbāth has cast doubt on the towering role scribed to Shīḥā and has downplayed the personal testimony of numerous committee members such as Khālid Shihāb, Yūsuf Sālim, or Khayr ad-Dīn al-ʿAdra, who all attested that it was Shīḥā who revised and edited the texts.[19] Even if we were to accept Rabbāth's assumptions – and they remain such in light of the absence of the complete original minutes and draft editions of the constitution – Shīḥā's role in adducing and formulating key articles can be documented from his personal notes. Rabbāth himself thus recognizes that Articles 6, 7, and 8 of the constitution – which proscribe state infractions on full freedom of belief – carry the signature of Shīḥā.[20] For the purposes of this book, then, Shīḥā's pivotal involvement in promoting and legislating secular freedoms is beyond dispute.

Ironically, it seems that Shīḥā's early opposition to confessional quotas was overruled by the majority of the commission.[21] Initially, the

18 Owen, *State, Power, and Politics in the Making of the Modern Middle East*, 235.

19 Rabbāth, *La Constitution Libanaise*, 25ff.

20 Rabbāth, *La Constitution Libanaise*, 40.

21 According to Yūsuf al-Sālam, Shīḥā contested the majority's endorsement of Article 95, which mandated quotas. Fawwāz Trabulsi conjectured that that these reservations stemmed from Shīḥā's belief that a mere meritocracy would in fact work in favor of the Christians, who were better educated and qualified at this point. Ṭarābulsī further pegs Shīḥā as a "monarchist" rather than a republican, yet it was Shīḥā who insisted both on prerogatives and firm term limits for the president and who opposed the attempt of his brother-in-law Bishāra al-Khūrī to extend his presidential term. See Shīḥā, "Sur la révision de la Constitution," *Le Jour* (April 13, 1948); Ṭarābulsī, *Ṣilāt bi-lā Wasl*, 33, 200–202. Lastly, Ṭarābulsī reads a putative prohibition of free speech into a statement by Shīḥā. In fact, the latter neither intimates nor advocates any restriction of the press. What remains clear is that in later years Shīḥā amended his position to view religion as an integral part not only of Lebanon's identity, but also of its polity.

members voiced their unanimous condemnation of confessional criteria for parliamentary seats. In the end, however, they yielded to the argument that "inveterate traditions" could not be extirpated overnight. Confessionalism, being part of the "*physiognomie du pays*,"[22] could not be uprooted in one fell stroke without causing a severe shock to the nascent country. Bishāra al-Khūrī spoke for the majority of Christians at the time when he argued that parliamentary representation had to be "confessional so as to preserve the rights of the minorities."[23] Deconfessionalization and a full emulation of the French 1875 constitution, however, remained an overruled, minority position. The constitution ended up enshrining the principle of confessional quotas.

Article 9 was to provide the cornerstone for the sectarian system, "guaranteeing to the people, regardless of their denomination, respect for the system of personal status laws and the religious interests." Additionally, Article 10 enshrines the rights of the sects – represented by their religious institutions[24] – to establish confessional schools and prohibits any state interference. Most significantly, Article 95 prescribes a "just representation" of the sects as a temporary measure, "*à titre transitoire/bi sūratin mu'waqatin*"[25] in all political positions. Tellingly, the records we have of the constitutional deliberations eschew mention of "sects" and instead confine themselves to a diplomatic reference to the country's "constituent bodies" or "*corps constitutés*."[26]

Thus, during the parliamentary debate prior to the ratification of the constitution in 1926 confessional quotas were ratified. While closely associated with providing Maronite safeguards, Article 95 was also defended by Sunni politicians such as 'Umar al-Da'ūq. Only one delegate, Subhī Haydar, suggested the removal of this particular, vaguely formulated clause, objecting that there was no way of telling whether it implied that confessionalism was to remain "one year or a century."[27]

22 Cited in Rabbāth, *La Constitution Libanaise*, 25.

23 In reponse to the commission question: "Should the parliamentary representation be confessional or not and why?" cited in Doumet-Serhal, *Michel Shīḥā 1891–1954*, 36.

24 In 1955 and 1967, respectively, the Sunni and Shia sects were given full control over their *waqf* networks that fell under the auspices of the Higher Islamic Shia Council and the Sunni Mufti of the republic, respectively.

25 The article's verbal form – but not its content – was rephrased once again in the 1989 amendment to read: "*fī marḥala intiqālīya*"("in a transitory stage"). See *Al-Dustūr Al-Lubnānī*.

26 Rabbāth, *La Constitution Libanaise*, 17.

27 Cited in *al-Ṭā'ifīya fī Lubnān*, 17. Ḥayḍar also found himself isolated in his petition for unity with Syria.

The speaker of parliament thereupon pointedly summoned all deputies who supported Haydar's objection to stand up. Only Haydar rose from his seat.

Respective Rates of Confessional Accommodation to the New State

The search for the roots of confessionalism – and the culpable party for its existence – which dominated political discourse in the nineteenth century, very much was at the center of the elaboration of the constitution in 1926 and directly impinged upon its content. Deputy Ḥamīd Franjīya put the matter bluntly:

> No two disagree that sectarianism is a heritage from the past which must be extirpated. I for one however do not accuse the Mandate for being responsible for this legacy for it germinated and was enracinated prior to the Mandate.[28]

Franjīya's candid moment of self-critical introspection notwithstanding, the formation of a joint Muslim–Christian opposition to the regime of the French mandate must be considered a positive phenomenon just on account of the rare national consensus it resulted in. Indeed, the instances of genuinely transconfessional, truly national alliances across Lebanese history are few and far between. As regards the historical span covered thus far in this book, we can identify three such instances, all of them transpiring as a reaction to a foreign threat: the rallying around Fakhr ad-Dīn II, the emirate-wide, anti-Egyptian, anti-Bashīr II communal uprising of 1840, and the 1943 united front against the last-ditch French attempt to scuttle the declaration of independence of the Lebanese government after the arrests of Bishāra al-Khūrī, Riyāḍ al-Ṣulḥ, ʻAbd al-Ḥalīm Karāmī, and three other deputies on November 11, 1943.

This last display of national unity and the rallying of the vast majority of Lebanese parties around a common cause was by no means a foregone conclusion in light of the intra-Lebanese divisions left in wake of the French occupation. As we saw earlier, some Christian Lebanese and French officials were predisposed to view Lebanon as a "Christian foyer" or a "solitary Christian island in a Muslim sea," a metaphor to be evoked by the late President Emile ʻIddih and Patriarch Ḥuwayyik in the latter's letter to the French prime minister Briand on the eve of the promulgation of the First Republic.

Nor were the French alone in exhibiting a distinctly sectarian bias in their foreign policy in the Levant. While one of the first presidents of

[28] Cited in *al-Ṭāʼifīya fī Lubnān*, 7.

Harvard, Increase Mather (1639–1723), dreamt aloud of destroying the Ottoman Empire to make way for Israel,[29] Pliny Fisk and Levi Parsons set shore in Lebanon in 1821 with the explicit aim of preparing the way for the return of the Jews to the Holy Land.[30] As early as 1891, the American-sponsored Blackstone Memorial signaled the first official US governmental endorsement for the erection of a Jewish state side-by-side "Christian Lebanon," heralding the inauguration of what would be a century-long US sponsorship of a settler ethnocracy in the region.[31]

If only due to their historic ties to Western powers, the Maronites were most susceptible to entering alliances with the Zionist state project as is illustrated by Cardinal 'Arīdī's 1936 meeting with President 'Iddih and Chaim Weizman to unite ranks against "the danger of Islam." Another secret agreement between the Jewish Agency and the Maronite Church was signed on May 30, 1946, shedding light on why Bishop Ignatius Mubārak would lend his support to the creation of a Jewish state during the deliberations on Palestine at the UN in 1947.[32]

Such overt and covert sponsorship of ethno-religious nationalisms may explain a lurking sectarian legacy left by the French. On the one hand, High Commissioner Henry de Jouvenel did seek to aid the establishment of a Jewish state in Palestine and a Maronite-dominated counterpart in Lebanon.[33] On the other hand, the same de Jouvenel published a decree

[29] Cited in Michael Oren, *Power, Faith and Fantasy* (New York: W. W. Norton, 2007), 89.

[30] Sermon preached in Park Street, Boston, October 31, 1819, just before the departure of the Palestine mission, Levi Parsons, *A. M. Missionary to Palestine* (Boston: Samuel T. Armstrong, 1819), 7.

[31] Addressed to President Harrison and signed by Supreme Court justices, key senators, and the captains of industry (including John D. Rockefeller and J. P. Morgan), the Blackstone Memorial was informed by an evangelical fervor and called for the United States to exert political and financial pressure on the Ottomans and Russia to hasten the establishment of a Jewish state in Palestine. The full text can be accessed online at: www.amfi.org/blackmem.htm, last accessed on March 3, 2007.

[32] Kristin E. Schulze, "Israeli and Maronite Nationalisms: Is a Minority Alliance 'Natural?'" in *Nationalisms, Minorities and Diasporas* (London: I. B. Tauris, 1996), 19–22, 158.

[33] The only wish de Jouvenel saw dashed (by Henri Ponsot) was the establishment of a monarchy in Syria. During his meeting with Chaim Weizman in Beirut in 1926, de Jouvenel adamantly opposed any Jewish settlements in southern Lebanon and instead suggested an expansion into Syria, an idea that found little resonance in Zionist circles, whose priority remained the colonization of Palestine. The Zionists' long-standing design to incorporate the Litani River in the future state of Israel thus came to naught, even though David Ben Gurion would continue to reiterate Israel's need to seize the Litani water resources as its northern border. See Laura Eisenberg, *My Enemies Enemy: Lebanon in the Early Zionist Imagination, 1900–1948* (Detroit, MI: Wayne State University Press, 1994), 20ff. Incidentally, the grand Lebanese Litani dam projects have not made any headway since the creation of the National Litani Office in 1954. Naṣr, "Backdrop to Civil War," 5.

on April 28, 1926 (Arrêté no. 266) that called on judges to reduce the competence of communitarian courts and foresaw the institution of civil marriage.[34] De Jouvenel was also partly responsible for a distinct measure of republican laicism, which was to leave its imprint on the Lebanese constitution, even though republicanism here can and should neither be confounded with democratic populism nor equated with Swiss standards of direct democracy.

In the event, the 1926 constitution promulgated under the auspices of the French high commissioner initially suffered from a boycott by the Muslim leadership, which, insistent on unification with Syria,[35] turned down the invitation to participate in the (interreligious) constitutional committee. The Muslim Congresses of 1927, 1933, and 1936, repeatedly demanded full unification with Syria, culminating, in 1936, with Tripoli's unilateral – albeit ephemeral – proclamation of unity.

The landmark "conference of the coast" ("*mu'tamar al-sāḥil*"), which was held at the mansion of Salīm 'Alī Salām in October 1936, reaffirmed in its first article the desire of full independence within the context of Syrian unity, the return of the amputated *qadās* (*aqdīya*) and a demand for a more equitable distribution of governmental positions. Both these demands were not met by the Franco–Lebanese accord of the same year. Against this overall political backdrop, the proposal of secularization figured as a most incendiary issue. De Martel's decision to codify the personal status laws of the Christians, Jews, and Muslims would push the country to the brink of civil war. What exactly did the French proposal contain to kindle such opposition, which eventually forced the French to rescind their bold initiative?

Arrêté no. 60 of 1936 – which was renewed and amended in 1938 by Arrêté no. 148 – was designed to codify the civil status of the country's confessional communities on an equal footing, allow for the creation of a "secular sect" ("*une communauté de droit commun*") in Article 14, and permit and regulate the passing from one confession to another. Both decrees provoked the immediate, fervid opposition of the *'ulama* of Damascus, Beirut, and Tripoli, forcing the French authorities to publish Arrêté no. 53 L. R. on March 30, 1939, which specified that the afore-cited Arrêtés 60 and 148 "*sont et demeurent sans application a l'égard des musulmans.*"[36] In short, the French venture to prolong the process of

[34] Massara, *La Gouvernance D'un Système Consensuel*, 233.

[35] Four Muslim members of the constitutional council protested the boundaries of the *Grand Liban* and demanded a union with Syria. These members were 'Umar ad-Da'ūq, 'Umar Bayhūm, Khayr ad-Dīn 'Adra, and Khalīl Shihāb. Abū Khalīl, "The Politics of Sectarian Ethnicity," 43.

[36] Cited in Massara, *La Gouvernance D'un Système Consensuel*, 233.

juridical secularization and fashion a neutral, deconfessionalized public sphere only met minor success.[37]

Even as secularization suffered this significant setback at the hands of an opposition led by the Sunni clerical establishment, Lebanese nationalism was steadily gaining new adherents among segments of this confession. Harbingers of this trend may be traced all the way back to 1927. In this year, the Party of Arab Independence, which counted such notable figures as ʿĀdil Arslān, Riyāḍ al-Ṣulḥ, and Rashīd Rida among its members, reiterated its plan to constitute an Arab empire under Syrian aegis. Yet, only one year later Riyāḍ al-Ṣulḥ declared – for the first time in public – his preference to "live free in an independent Lebanon rather than colonized in a vast Arab empire."[38] Al-Ṣulḥ was articulating a distinct minority position at the time.[39] Gradually, he came to accept the independence of Lebanon in wake of Syria's preceding accord with France in 1936, which comprised an implicit renunciation of all past Syrian claims to territories annexed to the *Grand Liban*.

Ulterior motives have been ascribed to al-Ṣulḥ's sudden endorsement of the newly fashioned republic. At the time, his incipient "Lebanism" could have been intended as a temporary subterfuge of what would only in retrospect reveal itself as the ultimate utopia of pan-Arab unity. Considering that as late as 1935 – after the signing of the French–Lebanese treaty[40] – al-Ṣulḥ could still vent a visceral anger at the Christian collusion with France and threaten the expulsion of all Christians from Lebanon, suspicion of al-Ṣulḥ's conversion do not seem baseless.[41] It seems plausible that sheer political opportunism lay behind al-Ṣulḥ's shifting stances, which evolved over time away from a classical notion of pan-Arab unity to an embrace of a more loose federation of independent Arab states such as came to be embodied by the Arab League. By 1945, al-Ṣulḥ began to defend an "Arab, independent Lebanon within its

[37] We shall further discuss the concrete repercussions for this reform effort as regards marriage laws in contemporary Lebanon in the subsequent chapter. See Ḥasan Amīn Al-Baynī, *ʿĀdāt Al-Zawāj Fī Lubnān* (Beirut: Baysān lil nashr wa al-Tawzīʿa, 1998), 28.

[38] See *al ʿAhd al-Jadīd*, January 26, 1928 and Nayla ʿAtīya, "The Attitude of the Lebanese Sunnis towards the State of Lebanon," PhD dissertation, University of London, 1973, 130.

[39] The very word "Lebanese" had been so closely associated with "Christians" that the identity papers of Muslims in Beirut were marked as "Beruti" until the French mandate.

[40] Al-Ṣulḥ ironically was residing in Paris in an attempt to leverage his own close contacts and personal friendships to gain a better bargaining position upon his return.

[41] "From now on, I will think and act as a Muslim … As a Muslim, I cannot have any faith or hope in the Christians … I have decided to pursue a distinctly Islamic policy, disregarding your existence as Christians in the East … You will have no peace in Lebanon, neither the Christians nor the French." Meir Zamir, *Lebanon's Quest* (London: I. B. Tauris, 1997), 209.

present borders," openly rejecting any talk of pan-Syrian unity as anachronistic by 1946.[42]

Conversely, we may add, the allegedly dyed-in-the-wool anti-Muslim chauvinist 'Iddih could in fact in 1934 support the candidacy of a Muslim friend, Khayr ad-Dīn al-Ahdab, for the premiership – while the putatively pro-Muslim Bishāra al-Khūrī and the patriarch questioned the loyalties of a Sunni to Lebanon.[43] 'Iddih's proposal won the support of High Commissioner de Martel and thus Ahdab became Lebanon's first – if short-tenured – Sunni premier. Ahdab, a Sorbonne-educated scion of a prominent Tripoli family, had in fact collaborated with Riyāḍ al-Ṣulḥ, both in supporting the Syrian rebels in 1926 and in founding an Arab nationalist newspaper, *al-'Ahd al-Jadīd.* But after joining parliament in 1934 and finding employment with the *Sûreté Générale*, he was finally won over to the cause of Sunni integration in Lebanon, at the expense of an open divorce with Damascus.

In light of the shifting stances of single individuals such as Riyāḍ al-Ṣulḥ or Khayr ad-Dīn al-Ahdab, we should consider the broader currents that may have impelled a rapprochement with the nascent Lebanese republics. In fact, Riyāḍ's cousin Kāẓim al-Ṣulḥ (1909–1976) had inched toward an embrace of Lebanese nationalism in his declaration of dissent published in the aftermath of the Conference of the Coast in 1936. The title bespoke an effort to bridge the chasm between Lebanism and Arabism: "Between Unionism and Separatism" ("*bayna al-ittisāl wa al-infsāl*").[44]

There is little doubt that Khayr ad-Dīn al-Ahdab's nomination as the first Sunni premier of the Lebanese republic buoyed a Lebanese nationalist strand among the Sunni elite, which was openly "flattered."[45] Beyond emotional pride, Ahdab's premiership reaped concrete dividends for the Sunnis, who saw more funds allocated to their regions and censorship of Muslim papers lifted. Still, the process by which Lebanese nationalism would gain broader currency among Lebanese Sunnis was a gradual one, with resistance lingering on. Ahdab would subsequently fall out of favor with the Sunni notables of Beirut who were irked by the unilateral imposition of a unity government by de Martel. The precedent Ahdab set, however, was soon to become a prized prerogative, particularly for the urban Sunni aristocracy of Beirut and

42 Al-Ṣulḥ cited in al-Jisr, *Mithāq 1943*, 178. 43 Zamir, *Lebanon's Quest*, 214.

44 Kāzim al-Ṣulḥ was the only member of the 1936 conference to object to a Syrian–Arab unity based on Islam. See Riyāḍ al-Ra'īs, *Tārīkh Lubnān Maskūt 'Anhu* (Beirut: Riyād al-Rayyes, 2001), 40. The full speech of Kāzim al-Ṣulḥ can be read in al-Jisr, *Mithāq 1943*, 466–478.

45 Zamir, *Lebanon's Quest*, 219.

Tripoli. Meanwhile, the French actively sought to co-opt the small circle of elite candidates that came to dominate the premiership.[46]

The greater propensity to accept the premises of an independent, sovereign Lebanon among the upper echelons of the Sunni bourgeoisie did not come by chance. After all, beyond any ideological attachment to pan-Arab unity and longing for past Islamic grandeur, the Muslim complaints of *Grand Liban* were predicated on a more palpable sense of economic marginalization after the demise of the Ottoman patron state on the one hand, and the subsequent French predilection for (Maronite) Christians in public administration on the other. Moreover, to both Sunnis and a number of Christian families from northeast Lebanon, the borders of the republic were seen to pose a threat to the Lebanese economy's historic trade-dependency on the Syrian hinterland.[47] It was the joint struggle for independence from the French mandate that in fact would solidify the Christian–Muslim entente and later would permit Riyāḍ al-Ṣulḥ to openly turn down the appeal for Syrian–Lebanese unity made by the Syrian premier on January 20, 1951.[48] His stance, while still highly contested at the time,[49] was facilitated by a concurrent Maronite reconciliation with the Arab identity of Lebanon, spearheaded most famously by presidents Bishāra al-Khūrī and Camille Sham'ūn.

As for the Lebanese Shia leadership, it generally shared many of their Sunni coreligionists misgivings of a Christian-dominated *Grand Liban*,[50] albeit exhibiting less of a wistful nostalgia for the bygone Sunni-dominated Ottoman order that, after all, had failed to grant the Shia any official religious or institutional recognition.[51]

This changed in 1922 when the Ja'afarī school of law – the legal reference for scholars of Jabal 'Āmil and Iraq since the ninth century – was

[46] The short list of Lebanese premier's since independence illustrates the thinness of this political elite. Since 1934 a Sunni Muslim has been assigned the position of prime minister, who, until the advent of Rafīq al-Ḥarīrī, has almost always been an al-Ṣulḥ, Karāmī, or a Salām. The Tripoli notable Muḥammad al-Jisr – who served as a deputy in parliament from 1926 to 1932 – was another early convert to Lebanese nationalism.

[47] This latter concern was – and is – of course shared by many Christians as well, particularly the families from the Biqā' and northern Lebanon whose trade relations with Syria have always been close.

[48] Khalīfa, "A La Récherce D'une Politique Ou D'un Concept De Secularisation," 128.

[49] We might bear in mind that the motley crew of Arab nationalist parties remained banned up until 1970 given their refusal to recognize the independence of Lebanon, and their espousal of the inclusion of Lebanon into a larger Arab entity. See Raghīd al-Ṣulḥ, *Lebanon and Arabism: National Identity and State Formation* (London: Center for Lebanese Studies and I. B. Tauris, 2004), 325.

[50] The Shia leadership of Jabal 'Āmil in general supported the Syrian revolt of 1925 and union with Syria, as evidenced in the odes published by Muḥammad Ḥumāmī in his literary journal *al-'Urūba*.

[51] As late as 1918, the Ottoman authorities proscribed all public 'Ashūra processions.

officially recognized and granted separate jurisdiction for the first time.[52] This step was partly intended to win over the Shia of Jabal ʿĀmil and dissuade them from siding with the Druze rebellion of 1925 against the French mandate.

Indeed, the French archives contain numerous (Shia) petitions from the *qadas* of Marjʿayūn, Tyre, and Sidon demanding a "return to Mount Lebanon of which we were a part."[53] Likewise, the King–Crane commission received a request in September 1919 from the head of the Ismāʿīlī community for an annexation to Greater Lebanon on account of the attacks and killings the Ismāʿīlī had suffered at the hands of Faysal's troops.[54]

Among the Shia *beys*, a debate ensued on whether or not to lend support to the new *Grand Liban*. Muhammad Tāmir and Rashīd ʿUsayrān, for instance, lobbied for a joining of Lebanon preserving the economic and political ties to Syria. Tamara Chalabi contrasts this urbane accommodation with the insurrections of the rural *ʿisābāt* or "gangs." These were tied to outside patrons, the Maronite militias receiving support from the French while the Shia counterparts were being supplied with weapons by Faysal and Abdullāh of Jordan. Intersectarian clashes erupted prior to the conference of Wādī Hujayr in Tyre after members of the local Maronite community had apparently defamed the prophet Muhammad. This triggered the pillaging and burning of a village by the *ʿusba* of Muhammad Bazzī after Sayyid ʿAbdul Ḥusayn Sharaf ad-Dīn had incited the populace in *ʿAyn Ibl*. The High Commissioner General Gouraud subsequently sent in 3,600 troops to exact a severe tribute, further exacerbating the preexistent economic disparities. Chalabi's sober conclusion of this chapter is that Jabal ʿĀmil entered Mount Lebanon dejected, impoverished, and "paralyzed," even seeing its name erased from the early maps of the *Grand Liban*.[55]

This does not imply that the Shia secular and religious elite – which in the Hujayr convention of April 24, 1920 had still declared its intention to fight for unification with (Greater) Syria and that had participated from

[52] Rūlā Abi Ṣaʿb, "Shi'ite Beginnings and Scholastic Tradition in Jabal ʿĀmil in Lebanon," *The Muslim World* 89.1 (1999): 9.

[53] Cited in Chalabi, *The Shiʿis of Jabal ʿAmil and the New Lebanon Community and Nation State, 1918–1943*, 109.

[54] Letter of the Ismāʿīlī notables to the American commission dated September 6, 1919, as cited in Anne-Lucie Chaigne-Oudin, *Le France et les Rivalites Occidentales au Levant, Syrie-Liban 1918–1939* (Paris: L'Harmattan, 2006), 71.

[55] Chalabi, *The Shiʿis of Jabal ʿAmil and the New Lebanon Community and Nation State, 1918–1943*, 139.

the beginning in Arab nationalist movements[56] – was wholly won over to the nascent Lebanese state, nor necessarily at ease with its geographical confines.[57] On the contrary, even after the fait accompli of 1926, Sulaymān Ḍāhir pronounced in 1930 that it was force, and force only, which "Lebanized" Jabal 'Āmil without due consultation of the population.[58] The editors of the leading Shia journal at the time, Ahmad 'Ārif al-Zayn's *al-'Irfān* of 1909, squarely placed Jabal 'Āmil within the orbit of Syria and utterly rejected the coerced amputation of Jabal 'Āmil from Syria and annexation to Lebanon. Congruent with the Shia communities' historic ties, the journal defined its mission to serve as a bridge of mutual knowledge between the scholars of Jabal 'Āmil and Iraq.

In the final analysis, the Shia reconciliation with the *Grand Liban* must – as with the Sunnis – be related to the gradual appearance of a secular Shia bourgeoisie in tandem with an expansion of state institutions under the mandate to peripheral, hitherto neglected regions.[59] Starting in the 1930s, members of the Zayns, 'Usayrāns, Baydūns, As'ads, and Hamāda's began to embrace a Lebanese nationalism and – like the Maronite and Sunni *zu'amā'* before them – converted (Ottoman) administrative positions and landed wealth into political power,[60] However, as we shall see in the following section, this did not lead to proper political parties,[61] nor was it without controversy, as the fierce debate between Sayyid Sharaf ad-Dīn and Muhsin al-Amīn showed.[62] Upon entering the "politics of the notables" in the Byzantine Beiruti parliament, Shia political discourse could gradually distance itself from the larger Muslim boycott of "Lebanese" identity and begin to refer back to a reservoir of

[56] Muhammad Rustum Ḥaydar, Ba'albak notable and graduate of the Ottoman imperial college and the Sorbonne, for instance, was one of the cofounders of *al-Fatāat* in Paris. Sayyid 'Abdul Husayn Sharaf ad-Dīn led a Shia delegation to Damascus to lobby for Greater Syria.

[57] The incorporation of the Biqā' in particular ran against the historic economic ties of this region with the Syrian hinterland, and, religiously speaking, with Iraq.

[58] Bayḍūn, *Identité Confessionelle et Temps Social chez les Historiens Libanais Contemporains*, 43.

[59] Over 80 percent of the new state schools opened during the French mandate were constructed in the traditionally marginalized, Muslim regions.

[60] This conversion had already taken place in the Ottoman era with the As'ad family, for instance, which served in the Ottoman bureaucracy.

[61] This ailment is of course by no means exclusive to the Shia *zu'āmā'*, but one that afflicted all notables who tried to use parties to leverage the power of charisma. Thus, Baydūn's Ḥizb al-Tala't and Ahmad al-As'ad's Ḥizb al-Nahḍa of 1949 vanished as soon as their leaders died or joined other political movements.

[62] Sharaf ad-Dīn was accused of being an agent for foreign powers by Amīn after the former expressed his support of al-Ṣulḥ's endorsement of Lebanon in 1936. Sa'ūd al-Mawlā, "Al-Shī'a wa Lubnān," *al-Hayāt*, March 25, 2005.

"indigenous," 'Āmili[63] premodern narratives of Lebanese proto-nationalism, which now was resuscitated and elaborated by the likes of historians such as 'Alī al-Zayn.

Waḍḍaḥ Sharāra is but one prominent scholar who claims that Lebanon – which he defines à la al-Shīḥā as a "federation of minorities" – has a centuries-old unique presence in Shia identity and lore, as evidenced by an eighteenth-century colloquial poet who wrote a heroic ode extolling the resistance in Jabal 'Āmil against the Ottomans.[64] There were also earlier anti-Ottoman martyrs such as the renowned scholar Zayn ad-Dīn Ibn 'Alī, more commonly known as "*al-Shahīd al-Thānī*," who was executed in Istanbul in 1559 for his unorthodox, charismatic preaching – and, more likely, for his rumored conversion of a number of Sunnis.[65] His sobriquet as the "second martyr" indicates that he was venerated together with an earlier anti-Mamlūk martyr as a symbol of Shia suffering at the hands of Sunni rulers, Muhammad Shams ad-Dīn Ibn al-Makkī al-Jazzīnī (1333–1384).[66] This process of a construction of a Lebanese Shia identity also kindled a renewed interest in the history of the 158 'Āmilī scholars who traveled to Safavid Iran and served as advisors to Shah Ismā'īl and subsequent Shahs, thus introducing "orthodox" twelver Shiism to Iran. Not Iran, but Jabal 'Āmil in this historiography figures as hub of Shiism, an inversion of the perceived hierarchy thought to govern today's Iranian–Lebanese relations.[67]

63 Jabal 'Āmil is commonly ascribed to the lineage of the tribe of Āmil a ibn Saba', which in turn is traced back all the way to Qahtani origins. See Darwish, *Jabal 'Āmil Bayna 1516–1697*, 19–26 who also speaks of the lore of hospitality associated with the Qahtānī tribes who fled Yemen three centuries before Christ. The Shia of Jabal 'Āmil claim to have been converted with the advent of Abū Dhurr al-Ghufār after the death of Abū Bakr in 634, thus refuting Kamāl Ṣalībī's claim that the *tashīa'* took place only in the eleventh century. The term *mutawila* does not appear before the thirteenth century and refers to the allegiance or "love" ("*muwāla*" for the Ahl al-Bayt) or possibly as a reference to a war reference of dying in loyalty to 'Alī (walīyan lī 'Ālī). The term *rawāfiḍa* was the other synonym used by Muḥibbī.

64 Namely, al-Shannā'a al-Maryahī. My thanks to Shady Hikmat Nāṣir for lending me a copy of one of these poems. Also see Carole Dāghir, *Bring Down the Walls* (New York: St. Martin's Press, 2000), 45.

65 I thank Himmet Taskomur for alerting me to the Istanbul court records of the execution verdict. Rūlā Jurdī Abī-Ṣa'b, "History and Self-Image: The 'Āmili 'ulamā' in Syria and Iran," in *Distant Relations*, ed., Houchang Shihābi (London: I. B. Tauris, 2006), 65.

66 Albert Ḥawrānī conjectures that until as late as the fifteenth century, the variety of Shia denominations (Imāmis, Rāfidis, Zaydīs, Isma'īlis, and Nusayrīs) constituted the majority of the Muslim population of Bilād ash-Shām. Albert Ḥawrānī, "From Jabal 'Āmil to Persia," in *Distant Relations*.

67 Chehabi and Mneimeh point out that, in part, Muruwwa and Muhājjir may be trying to turn the tables on the traditional narrative and re-establish the historical importance of Jabal 'Āmil, and, with it, lend a lost agency to the Shia of Lebanon. See Chehabi and Mneimeh, "Five Centuries of Lebanese-Iranian Relations," 7; 'Alī Murūwwa,

The peripheral status of the Shia community endured until the community was gradually integrated into the Lebanese state with the development of its own legal and administrative structures in the post-1946 period, together with the remainder of Lebanon's sects.[68] From independence into the 1940s, the Shia cause was vociferously presented in parliament by the likes of Yūsuf al-Zayn and Rashīd Baydūn who underscored the oblivion and "belittlement" (*istikhfāf*) of the south in general and the Shia sect in particular.[69] On occasion, non-Shia members of parliament from the south – such as Khālid as-Shihāb or Mount Lebanon's delegate Jurj Zuwayn – would express solidarity and lament the inadequate Shia representation in government.[70] As a rule, this litany of complaints were glibly ignored, for there was no Shia interlocutor who perforce had to be consulted in the plans of the top powerbrokers. The 1943 National Pact had come as a "*partage de pouvoir*" or "sharing of the spoils" between Maronite Christian and Sunni Muslim notables, represented by Bishāra al-Khūrī and Riyāḍ al-Sulh.[71] Even the Maronite and Sunni base constituency was not consulted and may well have opposed the terms of the compromise. The Shia, the poorest and politically weakest of the *tawā'if*, were not included at all until 1947. Only henceforth was the seat of the speaker of parliament informally reserved for a Shia, routinely a scion of less than half a dozen feudal families.

Such was the distrust of the Shia in some extremist circles that the thought was entertained to deliberately exclude them. As late as 1941, Eliahu Sasson, director of the Arab Bureau in the Jewish Agency's Political Department[72] and Muhammad Hājj 'Abdullāh met in Beirut

al-Tashayyu' Bayna Jabal 'Āmil wa Irān (London: Riyād al-Rayyes, 1987); 'Ālī Ibrāhīm Darwīsh, *Jabal 'Āmil Bayna 1516–1697* (Beirut: Dār al-Hādi, 1993).

68 The French mandate established the 'Alawite (1922), Ja'afirite (1926), and Druze (1929) courts.

69 For the intervention of Rashīd Baydūn see *al-Tā'ifīya fī Lubnān*, 53. For the major Shia grievances mentioned in Zayn's 1927 speech, see Darwīsh, *Jabal 'Āmil Bayna 1516–1697*, 20ff.

70 See the minutes of the January 18, 1928 session published in *al-Tā'ifīya fī Lubnān*, 25–26.

71 It should be noted that some members of the Maronite elite opposed the pact, among them Yūsuf al-Sawda, MP Yūsuf Karam, and Bishop Mubārak, the latter calling for a petit Lebanon with a decisive Christian majority. See Bāsim al-Jisr, *As-Sirā'āt al-Lubnānīya* (Beirut: Dār al-Nahār, 1981), 91. From Ibrāhīm Yazbak, a confidante of Riyāḍ al-Ṣulḥ, we learn that the terms of the National Pact with Bishāra al Khūrī did not remain secret, but were disclosed by al-Ṣulḥ to Lebanese notables and to Shukrī al-Quwattlī and Jamīl Mardam Bey. See Sa'āda, *Social Structure of Lebanon*, 60.

72 Sasson proposed that the Zionist movement consider devoting resources to bringing about the partition of Lebanon between Muslims and Christians, preventing the expansion of the League of Arab States, and helping Iraq's Shi'i community against that country's strongly anti-Zionist Sunni rulers. Sasson is also said to have persuaded

to consider transferring the entire population of Shia in Jabal ʻĀmil to Iraq. Sasson even suggested to Bishāra al-Khūrī to supplant the Shia Muslims with overseas Maronites. While this drastic measure of ethnic cleansing was never acted upon, suspicions of Shia loyalty to the state linger on even today, as we shall in subsequent chapters.

This legacy of Shia political marginalization – particularly in the neglected hubs of the south and the Biqā' – has never been fully overcome, in part due to the weakness of a state in which confessional pork-barreling remained the name of the game. The fact that so many Shia flocked to the Communist (and Syrian Social) Party has also been attributed to this disaffection and alienation from state organs.

A number of scholars have identified Mūsā Sadr as the most critical single figure in formulating and promoting a coherent Lebanese-Shia nationalism. His return in 1959 to Lebanon, the 1967 recognition of the Islamic Shia Supreme Council by the Lebanese parliament, followed by the founding in 1974 of the *harakat al-mahrumīn* (and the subsequent formation of Afwaj al-Muqawama al-Lubnaniyya [AMAL]), are commonly cited as key landmarks in this process of Shia political self-assertion. This was accompanied by an increasingly audible "discourse of demands" or "*matlabīya*" within the context of the now-recognized framework of the Lebanese state.[73] Sadr, too, raised the banner of deconfessionalization, thus raising fears among Christian and Sunni circles of a jeopardization of communal privileges.

In reviewing the post-independence period, then, one must conclude that the pledge for a secular, nonconfessional Lebanon made by Riyāḍ al-Ṣulḥ during his 1946 inauguration speech thus would ring hollow as yet another lofty rhetorical flourish. Even with the end of the French mandate, Lebanon still lacked a social contract – rather than a "*safqa*," a backroom deal such as constituted the National Pact. The latter never quite reflected a full consensus on Lebanon's national identity, but rather

the head of the Arab league, ʻAbdul Rahmān ʻAzzām, as well as his former colleagues in the National Bloc Shukrī Quwatlī and Jamīl Mardam Bey to consign to a Jewish state in 1946. The Iraqi foreign minister at this time was Ishak Sasson. See Lockman, *Comrades and Enemies*. Also see Reuven Erlich, *Bi-Sevakh ha Lebanon [The Lebanon Tangle] 1918–1958* (Tel Aviv: Tsahal, Hotsa[illegible]at "Maʻarakhot": Miśrad ha-biṭaḥon, 2000), 4. Central Zionist Archives (CZA), S25/3016, November 20, 1946 Sasson to Joseph, 20 December 1939 (CZA S25/3140(1)).

[73] See Chalabi, *The Shiʻis of Jabal ʻAmil and the New Lebanon Community and Nation State, 1918–1943*, 33. With the Iranian Revolution and the Israeli occupation of southern Lebanon, this Shia momentum of self-assertion took a more strident, radical turn, culminating in the birth of Ḥizballāh. The latter found its first sympathizers among those uprooted and disenfranchised segments, which had failed to reap the fruits of Lebanon's liberal experiment.

a division of the spoils of the state.[74] Even before coming under assault in the civil war, the National Pact faced a series of crises. The inordinate powers accorded to a Christian president espousing the Baghdad Pact and the Christian-Maronite confessional stranglehold over the higher echelons of the public administration led to the 1958 "mini-civil war,"[75] in which largely Nasserist pan-Arabists rallied against President Sham'ūn's pro-American agenda (and ambitions to extend his own term). The chairman of the pan-Islamist Najjāda Party, Adnān al-Hakīm, issued a call for a new system based on a presidency rotating between the Muslim and Christians. He even presented himself to the Chamber of Deputies in 1970 as a Muslim candidate for the highest office – which constitutionally is not restricted to any one denomination – to no avail.[76]

In short, neither the commission entrusted with the drafting of the constitution in 1926, nor the closed circle of politicians concluding the National Pact of 1943, nor indeed the overwhelming majority of delegates assembled in the Saudi Arabian city of Ṭā'if in 1989 ever seriously considered relinquishing the confessional system *in toto*. Whatever statements were made in this regard could be regarded as *pro forma* expressions of goodwill, amounting to no more than mere "ink on paper."

To be sure, the foundational blueprint of the National Pact, which was drafted in 1938[77] under the aegis of Yūsuf al-Sawda, entailed several

[74] This shortcoming was famously captured by Jurj Naqqāsh's quip: "Two negotiations do not make a nation!" and his description of the state as coveted booty: "*Ce qu'on appelle l'état n'est plus que cette immonde foire ouverte aux plus insolents enterprises des aventuriers qui ont mis au pillage les biens de la nation.*" "Deux Négotations ne font pas une Nation!" *L'Orient*, March 10, 1943.

[75] The terminology is borrowed from As'ad Abū Khalīl, "The Longevity of the Lebanese Civil War," in *Prolonged Wars: A Post-Nuclear Challenge*, ed. Magyar Danopolous (Montgomery, AL: Mawell Air Force Base, 1994), 41–67. Abū Khalīl contends that both 1958 and the Syrian intervention of 1976 prevented a decisive resolution of the Lebanese conflict in favor of the Muslim–left alliance, which had been emboldened by the Syrian–Egyptian unity. Bāsim al-Jisr describes the fronts in 1958 as falling along a pro-Western Christian alliance contra a pro-Nāṣirite Muslim one. These confessional fronts coincided in 1958 with the Cold War US–Soviet rivalry. No Muslim politician, however, publicly raised the demand for Lebanon to join the United Arab Emirates, according to al-Jisr. See al-Jisr, *Mithāq 1943*, 185, 192.

[76] There was a precedent in 1932, when Muḥammad al-Jisr, a Sunni notable from Tripoli, ran for president in protest against the French mandate, which subsequently shutdown parliament on May 9, 1932 to prevent a non-Maronite president. Ironically, the Francophile Emile 'Iddih backed Jisr in order to provoke the crisis, as did a number of Christian MPs such as Michel Zakūr, Yūsuf al-Khāzin, and Sāmī Kan'ān.

[77] These articles of the National Pact were first spelled out and recorded on March 3, 1939 at a meeting at Yūsuf al-Sawda's apartment. The twenty-eight signatories included 'Ādil 'Usayrān, Naṣrī Ma'lūf, Taqī ad-Dīn al-Ṣulḥ, Salīm Idrīs, and Najīb al-Sā'igh. al-Jisr, *Mithāq 1943*, 84, 114. While this document for all intents and purposes was Lebanese in origin, the subsequent National Pact received British sponsorship.

articles foreseeing secularization in various domains, most notably in Article 4, which insisted on the creation of a free, uniform, and national primary education, and in Articles 3 and 7, which enunciated inalienable equality before the law irrespective of confessional identity. This constitutive precursor to the 1943 pact, however, was stillborn, and its secular momentum broken by the unilateral French suspension of the constitution from 1939 to 1943. Nonetheless, the select provisions aimed at secularization, which had found entry in the 1926 Lebanese constitution were reconfirmed in the 1947 amendment.[78] They underwent a further revision in wake of the 1989 Ṭā'if Accord, to which we now turn.

The "Ṭayf" ("Ghost") of Ṭā'if

In a conscious play on his own famous quote describing the Civil War as "the war of the others," Ghassān Tuwaynī has called the 1989 Accord signed at Ṭā'if the "peace of the others" in light of its sponsorship by the Tripartite Alliance.[79] If outside patronage made peace possible, it also would subject its terms to the respective interests and shifting influence each of the godfather's of Ṭā'if could bring to bear.

In effect, American nonchalance about details meant that Syria could fill the void and impose its writ, only challenged by Saudi financial might, which, in turn, was personified by Rafīq al-Ḥarīrī.[80] It was al-Ḥarīrī who was suspected by a senior diplomat as having been the author of the Ṭā'if blueprint, even though it remains difficult to view the final accord as the product of any single hand.[81]

The primary goal and overarching concern of the Ṭā'if conference was to end the protracted civil war and to reestablish state sovereignty. The second objective was to readjust the political system in order to reflect the new political and demographic balance of power. Thus, upon ratification of the accord and the new, amended constitution on September 21, 1990, the prerogatives of the Sunni premier were enlarged at the expense of those previously held by the Maronite president, while the prior Christian–Muslim ratio in the Council of Ministers and parliament

[78] Khalīfa, "A La Récherce D'une Politique Ou D'un Concept De Secularisation," 99.

[79] In Ḥanān 'Āad, "Hādirat bi-Da'wa Min Markaz Al-Tawthīq Wa Al-Abhāth," *an-Nahār*, March 6, 2004.

[80] This latent conflict would brew on silently only to erupt in full during the presidential re-election campaign of Syrian-sponsored Emile Lahḥūd in 2004, which was adamantly opposed by Rafīq al-Ḥarīrī.

[81] Al-Akhdar al-Ibrāhīmi cited in al-'Abd, *Lubnān wa al-Ṭā'if*, 188.

altered from 6:5 to 1:1.[82] Articles 17 and 52 were amended so that the collective of the Council of Ministers headed by the Sunni premier was endowed with ultimate executive powers instead of the (Maronite) president, as had hitherto been the case. While the 1943 Pact had remained a verbal agreement instituting a (senior) Maronite – (junior) Sunni diarchy, the internationally brokered 1989 Ṭā'if Accord paved the way for the Sunni–Shia–Maronite troika operative ever since.[83] It thereby merely restated the terms of the June 13, 1987 "Declarations of Principles," which was drafted under Syrian auspices to solve the Lebanese Crisis.

Paragraph G of the Ṭā'if Accord was added as paragraph H to the preamble to the 1990 constitution and announces the ending of political sectarianism ("*Ilghā' at-Ta'ifīya As-Siyāsīya*") as a "fundamental national goal to be realized in accordance with an [unspecified] plan in stages."[84] The objective of deconfessionalization thus was amplified in the 1990 constitution to a greater degree than in the 1926 constitution, but as an appendix and with the customary caveats. While there are no minutes of the secret deliberations at Ṭā'if, we can safely surmise that, once again, secularizing reform took the form of window-dressing.

This becomes even more apparent if one probes another small, seldom noticed, but highly indicative alteration made to the first, original draft of the National Accord in the second paragraph B, which concerns the identity of Lebanon. For while the original text defines Lebanon as a "parliamentary democratic republic" which is predicated on the respect for public and "*private (individual)* freedoms," the final version conspicuously omits the reference to personal freedoms and only guarantees "public freedoms," ("*hurīyāt 'āma*").[85] Considering the central importance to secularism of an individual – rather than communal – conception of citizenship, this ostensibly subtle substitution must be taken as a significant setback to the stated aspirations. For, if the ultimate goal of the Ṭā'if Accord was to pave the way for what Theodor Hanf has called a

[82] This ratio was established based on a controversial 1932 census in which 67,403 exile Lebanese mughtaribīn, 82 percent of whom were Christian, were included in order to tip the demographic balance in favor of the Christians. Article 34 of the Lausanne Treaty permitted emigrants to obtain citizen status up until 1939. Muslim–Christian parity had long been on the agenda of reform.

[83] One fine, but significant, shift signaled by the Ṭā'if Accord was the change in the preamble of the constitution from asserting the "Arab face" of Lebanon to its "Arab identity and belonging." Both expressions were used conjointly in a speech by Jubrān Tuwaynī Sr. at Westhall Palace on March 15, 1936.

[84] This clause is commonly thought to have been added at the insistence of Speaker Ḥusayn al-Ḥusaynī.

[85] al-'Abd, *Lubnān wa al-Tā'if*, 370.

"syncretic nationalism," which may lessen the claims of the individual *Tā'ifa*, the subsequent obstruction of this path to national integration can be related to a number of internal and extraneous reasons. In the event, three members of the 1989 Ṭā'if conference refused to sign the final accord in protest against the opacity enveloping the critical clause on the elimination of confessionalism.[86] The validity of their concerns was subsequently confirmed as the Ṭā'if agreement has not been implemented with respect to three interrelated issues, all of which directly pertain to the envisaged establishment of a secular state:

- Establishing a unitary electoral district for the entire country instead of the current *muhāfadha* – districts that safeguard confessional parity.
- Deconfessionalising the election requirements for parliament (*majlis al-nuwwāb*) while setting up – or rather reviving[87] – a "*majlis lil-Shuyūkh*," a "House of Lords," akin to an upper-house of parliament reflective of the sectarian balance (Article 22).
- Setting out a roadmap to eliminate sectarianism "in stages" by ways of a commission (*haī'a*) of experts to be entrusted with this task (Article 95).

It quickly became apparent that the politicians in place were neither capable nor willing to enforce the above stipulations of the Ṭā'if Accord aiming at a gradual secularization. The available margin for political reform simply did not encompass these articles. At best, secularization was wielded as a strategic weapon by politicians such as Walīd Janbulāṭ in political campaigns, at worst, deconfessionalization was feared to signal a threat to Lebanon's sectarian diversity.[88] The result of this impasse is that the Lebanese constitution, even after the amendments of the Ṭā'if Accord, still suffers from multiple internal ambiguities as regards the identity of the state and its treatment of citizens. The afore cited Article 22 stipulating a semi-deconfessionalized, bicameral system is contradicted by Article 24, calling for a single parliament based on Muslim–Christian sectarian parity.

On the one hand, Article 7 of the constitution clearly states that "all Lebanese … without distinction are equal before the law" and

[86] They were Zāhir al-Khatīb, Tawfīq 'Assāf, and Ḥasan al-Rifa'ī. See al-'Abd, *Lubnān wa al-Tā'if*, 224. Three other parliamentarians boycotted the Ṭā'if conference from the start: Raymond 'Iddih, Albert Mukhaybir, and Emile Saqr. MP Pierre Dakkāsh and Michel 'Awn also expressed their opposition.

[87] The original constitution of 1926 had initially outlined a bicameral system, but the senate was formally abolished by a congressional vote on October 17, 1927.

[88] Interview with Amīn Jummayil, cited in Muriel al-Ma'lūf, "*Ilghā' At-Ta'ifīya* (Beirut: Sharika al-Khalīj, 2005), 107.

Article 12 holds that "all Lebanese are equally admissible to all public positions of employment without any other cause for preference except their merit and competence."[89] On the other hand, numerous key paragraphs also defined Lebanese citizens as subjects of one of their religious sects, as "*milal*," a wording that appears in Article 9, which obligates the Lebanese state to respect intrinsically hierarchical confessional personal status laws discriminating between Lebanese citizens according to confessional identity.[90] Article 12 is further contradicted by Article 95 and the previous codification of sectarian distribution in government offices according to "quotas," which still are observed today.[91]

Such remain the glaring internal contradictions besetting the Lebanese "consociational" constitution, as Lebanon's leading scholars of constitutional law have pointed out time and again.[92] In theory, the amended, post-1990 version of Article 95 could – if implemented – offer an avenue for a resolution of these contradictions: The Lebanese Chamber of Deputies is entrusted with the task to "adopt the necessary measures to abolish political sectarianism according to an established timeline and the formation of a national council headed by the President of the Republic and the Speaker of Parliament as well as political, social and intellectual leaders." This committee then should present a plan for the abolition of quotas in all government positions except for "grade one" positions in which "Muslim and Christian communities shall be equally represented without the designation of any position to a particular confession."[93]

If historical precedent and past political practice offer any guidance, they suggest that all significant, incisive reforms of the Lebanese constitution consistently followed severe crises. Article 95's post-Ṭā'if legislation of confessional parity (*munāṣafa*) on all levels of the polity had already been introduced under Fu'ād Shihāb, who had issued Decree 112 to mandate Muslim–Christian parity in all administrative positions as a provisional measure "for the sake of justice."[94] This reform, taken as a precautionary measure in the shadow of the 1958 eruption of civil

[89] Nawāf Salām, "Individu et citoyen au Liban," in *Le Liban Aujourd-hui*, ed. Fādī Kiwān (Beirut: CERMOC, 1994), 146.
[90] *Al-Dustūr Al-Lubnānī.*
[91] Decree no. 112, June 6, 1929 and no. 4800, dated July 25, 1970 see Mughayzil, *Kitābāt* Joseph Mughayzil, vol. I, 350.
[92] Joseph Mayla, Edmond Rabbāth, Joseph Mughayzil, and Riyāḍ as-Samad among others. See Riyād as-Samad, *Mu'assasāt al-Dawla al-Hadītha al-Ijtimāīya wa-al-Siyāsīya: al-Numūdhaj al-Lubnānī 'alā Daw Ahdāth al-Tashrīyāt* (Beirut, 1995).
[93] *Al-Dustūr Al-Lubnānī*, 96.
[94] Article 96 of this decree refers back to Article 95 of the constitution. See al-Jisr, *Mithāq 1943*, 239.

unrest, already prefigured the Ṭā'if clause. In both cases, constitutional reform was designed to provide for a more equitable confessional allocation and thereby diffuse the prime cause for violent interconfessional political contestation in 1958 and 1975–1990.

In historical hindsight, a cursory glance cast on the salient moments of political reform in modern Lebanon discloses what seems to be a recurrent pattern: the periodic recalibrations of the terms of Lebanese consociationalism were contingent on the respective pressure each political group could bring to bear on the system. Even if one duly concedes that confessional demographics were never the sole factor leading to an upending of the system,[95] the underlying dynamic accounting for the sporadic series of civil strife (1840, 1860, 1958, and 1975) might be interpreted as readjustments to a preceding dissonance between demographic and political representation of the confessions. Clausewitz's famous dictum of "war being the prolongation of politics by other means" thus seems tragically applicable to Lebanon's history. Communal prerogatives were asserted with peaceful suasion, veiled threats, and, ultimately, the final resort to violence. The overriding objective to enforce a more equitable, just, and proportional representation and (re) distributive allocation was blocked by the recalcitrance of an *ancien régime* holding fast to outdated quotas and vested interests. Thus, while elements of (proactive) secularization did inform periodic constitutional reform, the primary incubator for and benchmark of (reactive) change were communal demands.

One of the critical amendments to the constitution at Ṭā'if in fact bestowed more, rather than less, power on the sectarian heads. Article 19, which hitherto had been confined to a rather generic clause describing the prerogatives of parliament, adduced a paragraph on the formation of a constitutional council charged with supervising the constitution. The "recognized heads of the sects" are explicitly invested with the power to challenge the verdicts of the constitutional council in all matters touching religion and religious education. Thus, the clerical establishment was given yet more constitutional grounds to appeal any legislation deemed injurious to their sect. While these clauses can be justified and defended for safeguarding the "free exercise of religion," they actually instantiate

[95] The disruptive changes to Mount Lebanon's economic base have been well documented. Moreover, a purely communal interpretative prism could ill explain why a number of Druze and Christian politicians, for instance, came out in support of majoritarian democracy and lent their support to a deconfessionalized, majoritarian reform of the system in 1975.

clerical prerogatives, while depriving individual citizens of commensurate freedoms. Article 19 must then be read as a legal regression by which the state was further voiding Article 16, which vests all legislative power in parliament.

De facto, as the veteran statesman and former foreign minister Fu'ād Buṭrus has lamented, since the 1989 Ṭā'if Accord, Lebanon's legislative branch has functioned as a mere extension of the executive branch, rendering parliament a rubber-stamping ally of a government unrestrained by any checks and balances.[96] Clientistic networks thus face little restraint in exploiting the state politically, further aided (then and now) by an electoral law unbridled by any campaign spending limits and prone to gerrymandering.[97]

The Proposed Reform of the Electoral Districts and Demographic Dilemmas

The case has been made that from the political regime under the Ma'nite Druze emirate to the Shihābist Christian emirate clientelist system of the nineteenth century *muqāta'jīs,* to the interconfessional advisory councils of *qa'imaqāmīya* (1845–1860), to the no less clannish elite of the Representative Council established under the French mandate in 1922 to the Council of Ministers in the twentieth century, Lebanon moved through different communal hegemonies predicated on the demographic numbers and political clout each respective sect and interest group could marshal.[98]

Despite the patent bias for the (Maronite) Christians displayed in the national census and elaboration of the constitution, a single, mixed electoral college meant that in post-1926 elections, in five out of six voting constituencies, Christian candidates could be vetoed by Muslim ones.[99] The expanded territorial confines of the new republic of the *Grand Liban* resulted in a sudden dilution of the erstwhile overwhelming Christian majority in the *Mutaṣarrifīya* and "*petit Liban*," raising periodic

[96] See interview with Fu'ād Buṭrus, *an-Nahār*, June 16, 2003.

[97] A commission led by Fu'ād Buṭrus drafted a new electoral law on June 1, 2006, which included campaign spending limits and a proportional voting system. The proposal, however, was stillborn.

[98] Ziyāda, *Sectarianism and Intercommunal Nation-Building in Lebanon*, 97ff.

[99] Pierre Rondot, "Lebanese Institutions and Arab Nationalism," *Journal of Contemporary History* 3.3 (1968): 44. This feature of the Lebanese electoral system is observable today where the Sunni vote is decisive in electing the Christian deputies of Beirut, while non-Shia deputies of the south cannot win without the backing of Ḥizballāh and AMAL, whereas Shia representatives in the north need Sunni and Christian support. See Ziyāda, *Sectarianism and Intercommunal Nation-Building in Lebanon*, 143.

calls from rightist Christian quarters, such as the Lebanese forces, for a return to this hardly viable mountain enclave.

Considering their status as a steadily dwindling demographic minority, it is not surprising that much of the balking at a full implementation of the Ṭā'if clauses aimed at deconfessionalization emanated from Christian quarters. Tellingly, the postwar Christian leadership – such as Qurnat Shahwān – tended to ignore the stipulations in the accord calling for an elimination to confessionalism and instead focused all attention on the ending of the Syrian occupation. Conversely, Muslim politicians such as Nabīh Birrī or Rafīq al-Ḥarīrī, Ḥizballāh, Janbulāṭ's Progressive Socialist Party, and Syria-friendly Christian leaders, such as Michel Murr, Sulaymān Franjīya, and President Lahhūd, were no less inclined to pass over in silence the thorny issue of the Syrian suzerainty to which they owed much of their political existence. Apart from the traditionally secular parties such as the Syrian Socialist National Party, the Communists, the Ba'th and the Progressive Socialist Party (PSP), AMAL and Ḥizballāh have proven the most favorably disposed to an elimination of political confessionalism that could end the disenfranchisement of the largest single sect in Lebanon.

This postwar splitting of pro- and anti-confessional camps along the lines of Syrian loyalists and opponents was anything but fortuitous. The Christian opposition's long-standing battle cry for a Syrian troop withdrawal – predicated as it was on the Ṭā'if Accord – was long disregarded with cool aplomb by Syria's erstwhile power behind the throne, Vice President Khaddām, who shrewdly conditioned such a move on the "abolition of the confessional formula, the most important of all reforms in our estimate."[100] The fact that the self-same Khaddām – echoing President Asad – openly harbored pan-Syrian ambitions during the civil war by proclaiming that "Lebanon actually is a part of Syria" did little to instill trust in Lebanese Christians.[101] The 1991 "Treaty of Brotherhood and Cooperation" between the two countries only mentions a possible redeployment, not outright withdrawal, as outlined in the Ṭā'if Accord. That is not to say that Mr. Khaddām, the late Ghāzī Kana'ān, and the

[100] President Sarkis officially petitioned a Syrian withdrawal at the Arab Summit held in Fez, Morocco, in 1982. A year later his successor President Jummayyil demanded the "withdrawal of all foreign troops" at the same venue. Otto Schnittger, *Der Libanon im Kreuzfeuer* (Berlin: Arno Spitz, 1993), 82, 258.

[101] In his landmark speech on July 20, 1976 aired on Damascus Radio, Asad spoke of Lebanon and Syria as "one country and one people." Asad further maintained that "Syria had not consulted anyone when it entered Lebanon, nor would it consult anyone when it decides to withdraw from Lebanon … Lebanon is an Arab land belonging to [Syria]." Quoted in Antūn Khuwayrī, *Al-Harb fī Lubnān 1976* (Jounieh: AI-Bulūya, 1977), 154.

Syrian secret services showed particular compunction in removing Muslim opponents to their veiled protectorate.[102]

As regards Lebanon's political infrastructure, the heavy Syrian hand was perhaps most palpable in the drafting of the countries electoral laws. Electoral laws in Lebanon since 1946 were designed to encourage inter-confessional alliances by preserving significant minorities in each of the seven districts. Over time, however, migration led to the steady evaporation of these minorities, rendering the imperative for such cross-sectarian alliances increasingly obsolete so that electoral steamrollers (*mahādil*) could dictate electoral lists. Moreover, voting laws still impose a grid of confessionalism on the entire country. Since Lebanese are obliged to vote in their district of birth, the election laws have been held responsible for reinforcing the very parochial identities that may have otherwise have been offset by urbanization and the prospect of a national, civic education.[103] After 1990, the countries sectarian communities

[102] PSP leader Kamāl Janbulāṭ's tragic fate in 1977 is well known. According to a confidential source, Abdul Halīm Khaddām personally issued an explicit threat to have Janbulāṭ killed two weeks before his assassination "if he does not shut up". Whether or not Syria was behind the assassination of Riyāḍ Tāhā, the head of the Union of Newspaper Editor's on July 22, 1980, is a subject of debate. Minister Nāẓim al-Kadirī was eliminated in 1989 after he spoke out against Syrian hegemony; Muḥammad Shuqayr suffered the same fate after he tried to mediate between Muslim and Christian parties two months later. Syria's agents stand accused of murdering Shaykh Subḥī Sāliḥ, who was shot in broad daylight on October 7, 1986, four years after the assassination of Shaykh Ahmad 'Assāf on April 27, 1982. The perpetrators of the assassination of Rene Mu'awwad on November 22, 1989 in Syrian-controlled West Beirut have never taken responsibility, yet a number of fingers point in the direction of Syria. On the other hand, Mu'awwad shortly before his death declared that "there is no solution to the Lebanese ordeal without the active help of Syria, to which Lebanon is bound geographically, historically and nationally." Cited in "Lebanon's 9th President," United Press International November 6, 1989, www.upi.com/Archives/1989/11/06/Personality-Spotlight-Rene-Moawad-Lebanons-ninth-president/7924626331600/, last accessed February 5, 2019. General 'Awn had bitterly opposed the election of Mua'wwad, whom he considered a puppet of Syria, but subsequently called Mu'awwad's killing "an ugly crime" and urged an official inquiry. Iraq, which backed 'Awn, suggested that Syria and Iran were behind the bombing. The Iranian-backed Ḥizballāh had opposed Mu'awwad's election as vehemently as 'Awn. Walīd Janbulāṭ charged General 'Awn with having committed the crime. A shroud of mystery also still surrounds the death of former premier Rashīd Karāmī in a bomb blast aboard an army helicopter that was flying him from Syrian-controlled northern Lebanon to Beirut on June 1, 1987. 'Umar Karāmī has pointed the finger at Samīr Ja'ja', who has failed to issue an unequivocal disavowal. Whether or not elements in Syria can be held responsible for the assassination of Rafīq al-Ḥarīrī is unresolved. That Ḥarīrī's ties to Syria suffered from a gradual deterioration, however, is clear, as is the unprecedented tilting of many Sunni Lebanese against Syria after his assassination.

[103] Volker Perthes, *Der Libanon Nach Dem Buergerkrieg: Von Tā'if Zum Gesellschaftlichen Konsensus?* (Baden-Baden: Nomos Verlag, 1994), 130. There is a measure of apologetic wishful thinking in this argument linking urbanization to secularization. For a

engaged in a competitive gerrymandering during each election (1992, 1996, 2000, and 2005). In fact, in each of these elections, the former head of the Syrian secret services in Lebanon, Ghāzī Kana'ān, would single-handedly draw up districts, not to ensure the election of any particular sect, but rather to secure trustworthy allies of Damascus. Such was secularism "*à la Syrienne*," as some Lebanese would reflect in retrospect, with an undertone of wistfulness considering the post-Syrian fragmentation and political deadlock.

While a constitutional council was nominally established as mandated by Article 19 of the Ṭā'if Accord in order to combat electoral malpractice, it was widely seen to be impotent, and, until 2005, in the firm grip of Syria.[104] The council was powerless to prevent the parliament and cabinet from resorting to overt gerrymandering in the election of 1996, although it did manage to decree new elections in four flagrant cases.[105]

When the late President Harāwī ventured to implement Article 22 of the Ṭā'if Accord by suggesting a national electoral district ("*dā'ira muwaḥḥada*"), his proposal to stage a two-tiered national election was met with the usual charge from Christian quarters who ascribed it to another "Syrian ploy" hatched by the "proconsul" in Anjar, Ghāzī Kana'ān, and Vice President Khaddām in Damascus. Nobody, it was reasoned, save for the Syrians, could cobble together a 128-member national list.[106] By contrast, advocates of a single district reason that national lists might actually force parties to transcend their provincial constituency and seek coalitions across sectarian faultlines based on common, issue-driven political platforms. According to the 1996 (and 2005) election laws, all parliamentary constituencies were made to coincide with the boundaries of larger governorates (*muhāfadha*), as mandated by Ṭā'if. However, the Council of Ministers decided not to enlarge Walīd Janbulāṭ's Druze stronghold in Mount Lebanon, thereby insulating the *qadā'* of Shūf and Alay against Christian and Shia demographic pressures in the region. The same gerrymandering tainted the 2005 elections and subsequent proposal drafted by the commission headed by

civic-minded citizen should theoretically be able to transcend rural strictures, while, conversely, confessionalism has not evaporated in urban settings.

104 The council ceased its activities completely after the Syrian withdrawal and has fallen into desuetude due to the Future Movement's efforts to stall an inquiry by Michel 'Awn's Tayyār al-Watanī into the bribes and irregularities, which marred the 2005 parliamentary elections, particularly in the contested areas of north Lebanon. The highest institution of judicial oversight in the country has since been disbanded in 2006.

105 In 2000, the council rubber-stamped the political annulment of opposition leader Gabriel Murr's victory in the Matn against his Syria-sponsored opponent and relative.

106 See Michael Young, "The Electoral System: A Modest Proposal," *The Lebanon Report* 1 (1996).

Fu'ād Buṭrus. The law proposed by this commission was based on a majority of small electoral districts (*qaḍā*) with a majoritarian electoral law, and a minority of large governorates with a proportional system. A limit on campaign spending and the partial adoption of the proportional electoral system constituted the most encouraging reforms. However, the major political parties, including the Future Movement, vowed to prevent a ratification of this law.

For its part, the Christian opposition under the aegis of the patriarch and the alliance of Qurnat Shahwān expressed its dismay at the unification of Shia-majority governorates in south Lebanon, which hitherto had comprised of two *muhāfadha*, but which were united into a single super-governorate at the behest of Nabīh Birrī. Already outnumbered in the south, in Beirut, and in the Biqā', the apprehensions of Christian constituencies were aggravated by the Ṭā'if proposal for a single, national electoral constituency. Former President Amīn Jummayil articulated the fears militating against further reform: "It is as if we are saying to the Christians: 'Get into the bus with Hezbollah, AMAL or the *Ahbāsh*, where you will be safe and sound, otherwise, bye-bye.'"[107]

The counter-argument made for a unification of electoral districts is that it would foster cross-sectarian cooperation and transregional alliances based on national political programs rather than clientelist affiliations. In fact, mixed electoral districts with lists reflective of sectarian quotas have already mandated interconfessional cooperation since 1926. The problem has been that lists have been dominated by regional steamrollers (*maḥādil*). To remedy this defect, a proportional system (*nisbīya*) in combination with a "single transferable vote" (STV), which weighs votes for multiple, ranked candidates was suggested to ensure an adequate representation of minorities and popular independent candidates running without the backing of a confessional lord.[108] To the layman, however, it remains difficult to comprehend how even the most creative electoral engineering could fully solve the inherited conundrum posed by the National Pact and the cold arithmetics of the demographic disequilibrium. As long as parliament and the Council of Ministers are to remain equally divided, the election of Christian deputies by Muslims

[107] Cited in *Monday Morning*, no. 1555, Oct. 14, 2002.

[108] The most succinct study is Rudy Jaafar, "Democratic System Reform in Lebanon: An Electoral Approach," in *Breaking the cycle: Civil Wars in Lebanon*, ed., Youssef Choueiri (London: Stacey International, 2007), 285–305. 'Abdū Sa'd, a Lebanese pollster, first suggested a "preferential vote" (*Ṣawt tafḍīlī*). "Wāqa'i Mu'tamar bi-'Anwān Nahwa 'Itimād an-Nisbīya fī al-Intikhābāt," in *Abḥāth fī al-Qānūn al'Am*, vol. 1 (Beirut: Markaz Beirut lil Ma'lumaat, 2005), 24–37, which was then integrated into the last election.

Table E3.1 *Demographic development from the* Mutaṣarrifīya *to the present*

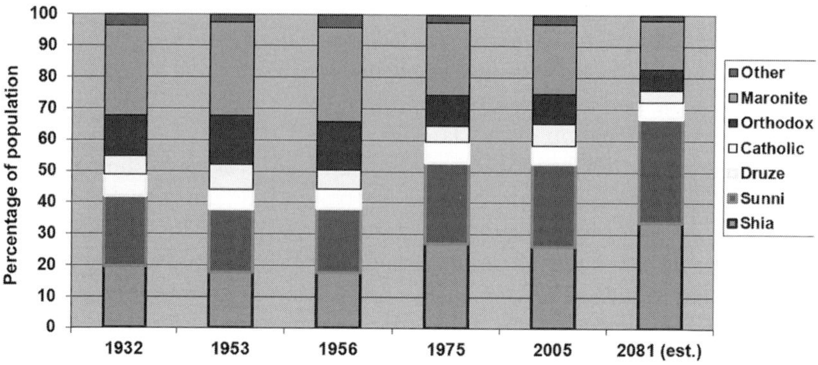

Sources: Ḥittī, *Lebanon in History*, 439; Ewald Wagner, "Untersuchungen zur Sozialgeographie christlicher Minderheiten im Vorderen Orient (Beihefte zum Tübinger Atlas des Vorderen Orients. R. B: Geisteswissenschaften. Nr. 43) by Klaus-Peter Hartmann;" *Zeitschrift der Deutschen Morgenländischen Gesellschaft* 132.2 (1982): 438; 'Abdallāh al-Mallāh, Mutaṣarrifīya Jabal *Lubnān fī 'ahd Muzaffar Bāsha:* 1902–1907 (Beirut: 'Abdallāh al-Mallāh, 1985), 105, 256; list of eligible voters as published by the interior ministry in *al-Hayāt*, August 16, 1958 and *An-Nahār*, February 11, 2005. The cited census of 1932 is only one of three made in that year. The first census, including only Lebanese residents and temporary absentees, was vetoed by the Christian leadership and arrived at a near parity of 396,748 Christian and 386,499 Muslim Lebanese. The second census was refused by both Muslims and Christians and contained the exile Lebanese still in possession of Lebanese citizenship. Upon the intervention of General Spears in 1943, the third census would serve the basis for the 6 to 5 ratio. It included those expatriates who had lost their citizenship but intended to regain it and was accepted by the Christians while rejected by the Muslims. al-Jisr, *As-Sirā'āt al-Lubnānīya*, 30; Maktabī, "The Lebanese Census of 1932 Revisited," 230.

cannot be avoided entirely, particularly in larger voting districts that are mandated by the Ṭā'if Accord. The precipitous demographic changes over the past century underscore the anachronism of confessional parity as an electoral principal.

Despite the dearth of official statistics, one can safely infer from Table E3.1 that the cumulative Christian presence has dwindled from 80 percent of the residents of the *Mutaṣarrifīya* until World War I, to around 50 percent after the establishment of the *Grand Liban* and the appendage of the Biqā', Beirut, and Tripoli in 1920, to about 30–40 percent today. In other words, the republic since its establishment has passed through an interlude of Muslim–Christian parity until the late 1950s, to a phase of Muslim, and more particular Shia preponderance due to the steady exodus of Christians and their lower birth rates.[109] During the post-independence decades, the Shia showed the highest fertility rate at 3.8 percent followed by the Sunnis (2.8 percent), the Catholics (2 percent), the Druze (1.8 percent), and the non-Catholic Christians (1.7 percent).[110] By 1988 the number of Shia's had almost doubled to 32 percent, while the number of Maronites has dwindled to 17 percent.[111] The fact that fertility rates tend to be inverse to levels of income has further compounded the sectarian and demographic divisions, with further social stratification in Lebanon.[112] It should be noted, however, that the high Shia and Sunni birth rates decreased slightly in the 1990s and that poor, rural Christian families tend to have more children.

Overall, the linear demographic trends plotted in Table 3.1 are only punctuated markedly by the official numbers of the Lebanese electoral lists published in 2005 in which the number of Shia in particular appears deflated. There are several conceivable reasons for this disparity. For one, the highly controversial, almost surreptitious naturalization of at least 160,000,[113] largely Sunni Syrians and Palestinians in 1994 has arguably diminished the Sunni–Shia disparity. Second, voting lists only include adults above the ages of twenty-one and thus do not take account of the disproportionately large number of Shiite youth. Lastly, in addition to outright identity forgeries, voting lists may include a number of

109 Buṭrus Labakī has estimated that around 827,000 people were displaced during the war, ca. 670,000 Christians and 157,500 Muslims. See Buṭrus Labakī and Abū Rjayī, *Khalil, Bilan des Guerres de Liban* (Paris: L'Harmattan, 1998), 256.

110 Joseph Shāmī, *Religion and Fertility* (New York: Cambridge University Press, 1981), 85.

111 Ḥalāwī, *A Lebanon Defined*, 50. Ḥalawī estimates the number of Shia at 1,325,499 out of a population of 4,044,784 in 1988.

112 Such was the observation of Joseph Shāmī, who currently serves as the head demographer at the UN. See Joseph Shāmī, "The Lebanese Civil War: An Investigation into the Causes," *World Affairs* 139.3 (1976): 171.

113 The numbers cited are those given by interior minister 'Ilyās Murr who stated that 110,000 Muslims and 50,000 Christians were granted Lebanese citizenship by virtue of the government Decree 5247, which was published in its full length of 1,279 pages in the *Official Gazette*, no. 26, supplement 2 on June 30, 1994. Some Christian parliamentarians put the number at 300,000 and upward, but another scholar in a detailed study of the government decree comes up with a more reasonable estimate of 222,730 based on an average family size of six members. A total of 62 percent of the naturalized citizens were foreigners – mainly Syrian (Bedouins) from the Wadi Khālid in 'Akkār on the Syrian border and Palestinians – living in Lebanon, while 15 percent hailed from the so-called seven villages. The seven villages is a border region ceded to (northern) Palestine by the French after they concluded the Paulet–Newcombe agreement with the British on February 3, 1922. Most of these refugees after 1948, however, were Shia. For an in-depth analysis, see Tony Jurj 'Atāllāh, "al-Mujannisūn fī Lubnān Mā B'ad al-Ḥarb," *Al-Abhath* 45 (1997): 100–102.

Lebanese living abroad and even some of the long deceased. Nonetheless, the massive discrepancy between official lists and unofficial estimates cannot easily be explained away, even if the aforementioned irregularities are factored in.

Confusion over precise demographic statistics seems to have beset even the US Central Intelligence Agency (CIA). The World Factbook in 1998 reported that the Muslim population of Lebanon was 2,414,704 (70 percent) while the number of Christians was given as 1,034,873 (30 percent). After the intensified American–Israeli preoccupation with Lebanon in 2004, these numbers curiously were adjusted to reflect a – well-nigh impossible – precipitous 11 percent-decrease in the Muslim population to 59.7 percent.[114] Doctored numbers, however, will have little effect on changing the demographic dilemmas facing Lebanon. Patriarch Sfyar lamented that Christians, in contradistinction to other religious groups in Lebanon, are unable to elect their representatives. In the 1992 election, voters from other sects elected 35.93 percent of Christian deputies, whereas Shia, Sunni, and Druze deputies were elected by their own group,[115] prompting the Maronite patriarch *inter alios* to call for the ostensible nostrum of smaller voting districts.

In the end, this quandary – and its proposed remedy – begs the question: Why should the sectarian identity of the voter matter as long as a secular social contract is adhered to? After all, the self-same patriarch himself emphasized that political leaders must not be representatives of their particular confessions, but rather act as servants of the nation at large.[116] The very threat of a forcibly imposed sectarian state seems remote in a nation in which no single sect holds a decisive numerical majority. On the other hand, the palpable regional radicalization of the political sphere during recent decades has been viewed with some trepidation, not only by Christian Lebanese, but by Muslim secularists as well. We should recall that the "depression" (*al-ihbāt al-masīhī*) often attributed to the Christians in light of their demographic besiegement is matched by a similar "minority-complex" among the Druze. Similarly, many Shia and Sunni secularists feel a sense of exclusion and unjust (*mazlum*) marginalization. As we have seen and will further elaborate, the absence of intercommunal trust is intimately related to the sociological

[114] See www.cia.gov/library/publications/the-world-factbook/geos/le.html, last accessed February 2, 2019.
[115] Farīd Khāzin, *Lebanon's First Postwar Parliamentary Election* (Oxford: Center for Lebanese Studies, 1998), 44ff.
[116] See, for instance, the interview with Patriarch Ṣfayr in *an-Nahār*, April 15, 2006.

roots of political sectarianism in Lebanon on the one hand, and to the weakness of state institutions on the other.

Thus, we conclude our quest for the historical roots of the secular paradigm in Lebanese political thought and practice. The preliminary conclusion we may draw is that neither premodern proto-nationalism, Ottomanism, Arabism, nor the attainment of Lebanese independence in the form of the First and Second republics managed to fully supplant religious identity as a locus of sociopolitical identity in Lebanon. Confessionalism would remain a central plank in the edifice of economics, education, and politics.

Nor would Lebanon's incorporation into a European-dominated world economy lessen the hold of communal ties. On the contrary, some of the new cosmopolitan elites would actually stoke sectarian animosities to deflect from economic inequalities and secure their positions. Their comportment in this regard differed little from that of previous feudal notables who had endeavored to redirect peasant discontent by pursuing the same strategy. This mutually reinforcing interplay of creed and class has led one leftist historian to characterize the Lebanese state as a "confessional class-state" ("*dawla ṭā'ifīya ṭabaqīya*").[117] As shown in Chapter 2, elitism was a double-edged sword: It could facilitate a free debate in closed circles, while simultaneously limiting the wider dissemination of secular ideas.

With the jolting of the social structure and increasing levels of Levantine trade toward mid-nineteenth century, an urban bourgeoisie and *Bildungsbürgertum* did develop some iconoclastic sentiments first among Christian and Sunni,[118] and by the 1930s also among Shia segments. Yet, despite the periodic sealing of cross-sectarian alliances based on common class identity and shared interests, these relatively thin echelons of urban, Western-educated elites – many of them graduates of the American University Beirut (AUB) and political power brokers – could not fully break out of the cocoon of their respective *ṭā'ifa*, let alone dismantle its political and societal pillars. Certainly it is true that among segments of the Beiruti *haute bourgeoisie* interconfessional marriages were not uncommon, and friendships a daily staple. But then again, so too the reigning premodern dynasties such the Ma'n and Shihāb could afford to pay scant regard to confessional divides. To truly gauge the larger

[117] Leftist historians have tried to back up their Marxist interpretation of Lebanese sectarianism by claiming that intra-religious class strife was far more violent than interreligious conflict. See Ḍāhir, *al-Judhūr al-Tārīkhīya lil-mas'ala al-Zirā'īya al-Lubnānīya*. Interview with Mas'ūd Ḍāhir in Beirut, August 20, 2005.

[118] Nadā Shahnāwī, *L'Occidentalisation de la vie Quotidienne à Beyrouth, 1860–1914* (Beirut: Éditions Dar an-Nahar, 2002).

significance of these phenomena on the national plane, the general rule ought to be distinguished from the elite exception.

Even after the passing of the Ottoman order and down to the past century of rapid urbanization, feudal fiefdoms survived in the mountains and neglected peripheral regions. Meanwhile the urban capital – despite all the trappings of cosmopolitan modernity – *de facto* remain largely divided according to independent, self-contained districts (*ḥāra*) reserved for each confessionally largely endogamous *ṭā'ifa*.[119] Such lamentable segregation – at once geographic, political and ideological – was severely exacerbated by the civil war of 1975–1990, leading to the sobering *status quo* of today: a *de facto* demographic cantonization of the country. In such districts as Kisirwān or the northern Matn, for instance, the number of Christian electors is almost 100 percent. The inverse is true in Sidon or Nabatīya, where the number of Muslim electors ranges between 85 and 95 percent.[120]

This book will not revisit the civil war of 1975, which has been covered from multiple vantage points in a wide body of literature.[121] Suffice it to say that the dislocation wrought by the civil war constituted an immense strain on intercommunal relations and contributed to the spatial *tatyīf* or "confessionalization" of Lebanese society. The sundry psychological, political, and legal consequences of this inauspicious development would also affect the course charted by Lebanon's political parties.

[119] Himself a resident of intercommunal Beirut during his productive period, the renowned Syrian poet Adūnīs held a much-discussed speech in 2003 in which he eloquently warns of the tribal sentiments lingering under the outer façade of development in Beirut. See the conclusion in *an-Nahār*, November 19, 2003.

[120] See *an-Nahār*, Monday, June 5, 2006. These particular numbers take into account a prospective lowering of the voting age to eighteen proposed by the Electoral Reform Commission headed by Fu'ād Buṭrus.

[121] The first spark for the civil war could also be conceivably traced back to the December 1968 obliteration of thirteen airplanes in the Beirut airport by Israel or April 10, 1973, when Israeli commandos, headed by Ehud Barak, infiltrated Beirut in a daring raid and attacked Palestinian command centers in the heart of the capital, killing three prominent Palestine Liberation Organization (PLO) leaders: Kamāl Nāṣir, poet and the PLO's official spokesman; Muḥammad al-Najjār, head of the Higher Political Committee for Palestinian Affairs in Lebanon, member of the PLO Executive Committee and Fateh Central Committee; and Kamāl 'Udwān, also a member of the Fateh Central Committee. Barak subsequently would defend the shooting of the latter's wife and daughter. The assassination of Ma'arūf Sa'd in Sidon in 1975 is another date commonly referred to. For more on the civil war, see Theodor Hanf, *Coexistence in Wartime Lebanon* (London: Center for Lebanese Studies, 1993). James R. Stocker, *Spheres of Intervention: US Foreign Policy and the Collapse of Lebanon, 1967–1976* (New York: Cornell University Press, 2016). Fawwaz Traboulsi, *A History of Modern Lebanon* (London: Pluto Press, 2018).

Given the historical context surveyed thus far, it may not seem surprising that neutral, nonconfessional party allegiances had a difficult time to assert themselves over ingrained societal cleavages predicated on a patchwork of confessional chauvinisms. Still, in the course of the twentieth century, secularism did make inroads, at least as a rhetorical element in the discourse of but a handful of Lebanese parties.

Twentieth-Century Lebanese Parties and Secularism: A Brief Outline of the Debate (1926–2006)

> The Lebanese people have still not learned to put patriotic above confessional solidarity ... The communities of Lebanon take the place of political parties.
>
> Shiblī Dammūs, head of the council entrusted with framing the 1926 constitution[122]

Nominally speaking, the issue of secularism has been on the political agenda in twentieth-century Lebanon since the founding of two multi-sectarian, yet initially illegal political parties: The Lebanese–Syrian Communist Party (LCP) of 1925 and Anṭūn Sa‘āda's SSNP.[123]

The LCP's precursor, the Lebanese People's Party (*Hizb al-Sha‘ab al-Lubnānī*), was founded on October 24, 1924 at the suggestion of a number of mainly non-Lebanese activists: The Palestinian Jewish communist Joseph Berger, the Christian Yūssuf Yazbak, the head of the Armenian Spartak, Artine Madoyan, and the Odessa Jew, Eliahu Teper. The intellectual pedigree of the party can be traced to Fu'ād Shimālī who had imbibed the enlightenment socialism of Shiblī Shummayal, Farah Anṭūn, and Niqūla Haddād, alluded to in Chapter 2. Both the Communist Party and the Syrian Socialists faced the constant, stiff resistance of the mandate authorities, seeing their paper *Humanity* (*al-insānīya)* fold after only five editions.

The LCP did not adhere to orthodox Marxism or Leninism, but sprang from a somewhat romantic egalitarianism that had struck its social roots among the communist tobacco workers of Bikfayya. According to

122 Offering a sobering summary at the end of deliberations in 1925. Rondot, "Lebanese Institutions and Arab Nationalism," 43.

123 The Communist Party was initially outlawed by the French mandate authorities but this ban was relaxed in 1943, only to be reimposed in 1948. In 1970, interior minister Kamāl Janbulāṭ lifted the ban on the party. The party participated in the Syrian Revolt of 1925 and was officially called the "Syrian Communist Party" in the 1930s. In 1930, the Ḥizb al-Sha‘b al-Lubnānī fused with the Syrian Communist Party and the Armenian Spartak League until a renewed split occurred in 1944.

his own account, Yazbak was stirred to found the party after encountering a starving mother with her two children bewailing her fate in front of a church in the aftermath of the World War I famine.[124]

At its May 1, 1925 convention the party announced its political program, which carried the unmistakable, if modified, imprint of the anticlericalism of the October Revolution. Besides insisting on the development of industry and agriculture, it contained three articles directly pertaining to secularism, even if the express term itself was not employed. The first concerned an interdiction of the clergy to project its influence in the political sphere, the second demanded a support of public education and a trimming of private schools, while the last foresaw a nationalization of all religious endowments (*waqf*).[125] Even at this stage, however, the party leadership, while it did include three Armenian émigrés, did not list any Muslim members. This glaring lacuna may have less to do with mere confessionalism than with the infant stage – and nature – of Lebanese capitalism. Given an economy almost wholly reliant on services and agriculture, Lebanon at independence was not predestined to see the formation of (intersectarian) unions.[126] It is only by the 1940s that we find increasing numbers of Muslim day laborers, factory workers, déraciné urban migrants, and farmers flock to secular parties such as the SSNP and the communists.

The SSNP was founded at the AUB in 1932, although it became a public party only on November 16, 1935 when its leader Sa'āda was arrested for founding a clandestine party. On March 17, 1936, the party was outlawed and its paper, *al-Nahda,* subsequently banned.[127] It was the SSNP's secularism rather than its pan-Syrianism that provoked the ferocious crackdown ordered by the Christian and Muslim notables in the government, for other groups advocating a unification with Syria were spared persecution.[128] As a matter of fact, the program of the SSNP was perhaps the most explicitly secularist in the history of Lebanese parties, comparable only with that of the Lebanese Communist Party.

It bears mention that both these parties at their inception were not reconciled with Lebanese nationalism and were subjected to suspicions

[124] The mother apparently asked plaintively: "Why is there no equality on earth as there is in heaven," perhaps signifying the impotence of the church in alleviating, let alone warding off, the famine, and expressing the widely perceived need for a new political body. See Alexander Flores, "Die Anfange des Kommunismus im Nahen Osten," in *Der Nahe Osten In Der Zwischenkriegszeit* (Mainz: Franz Steiner, 1989), 426; Thompson, *Colonial Citizens*, 29.

[125] Interview with Maurice Nahra, LCP Headquarters, Beirut, June 2005.

[126] Owen, *State, Power, and Politics in the Making of the Modern Middle East*, 235.

[127] Bishāra, *Lebanon*, 32.

[128] Such as the Lebanese–Syrian Unionists. Bishāra, *Lebanon*, 34.

of harboring divided loyalties. No less than the SSNP's founding father, the "*Za'īm*," Anṭūn Sa'āda, himself, openly accused the Communist Party of "being steered by foreign interests," while fiercely fending off the self-same accusation leveled at the SSNP by the Katā'ib and the Maronite patriarch.[129] Even after its bifurcation into national branches in 1944, both the Syrian and the Lebanese Communist parties would continue to suffer from their association with the internationale after Stalin's recognition of the State of Israel in 1948. As for the SSNP, its leader, Sa'āda, would have to seek exile in Brazil due to his denial of the legitimacy of the Lebanese state. Pressurized by the Lebanese authorities to recant in exchange for permission to return to his homeland, Sa'āda would only concede a recognition of the historic, Phoenician geographical unity as a "*Kiyān*," but not as a proper nation ("*laysat ummatan*").[130]

Despite their uneasy relationship with the Lebanese republic, their variant socioeconomic perspectives and their divergent trajectories since their foundation, both the LCP and the SSNP to this day continue to share a common goal in their stated quest for full secularism. In 2004, they joined forces in forming a broad coalition named the "National Council for the Abolition of Sectarianism."[131] Nonetheless, as regards political rhetoric, the LCP and the SNNP were by no means the only parties to espouse this cause.

In reviewing the Lebanese landscape, we may conclude that – extremist exceptions aside[132] – all prominent Lebanese parties and politicians after 1926 have at one point or another nominally called for the deconfessionalization of the political system. Even though wholly Sunni in

[129] See Anṭūn Sa'āda, *Al-'A'māl al-Kāmila*, vol. III (Beirut: Dār as-Sa'āda lil-Nashr, 2001), 94. It is one of the bitter ironies of history that both Sa'āda and the most salient leader of the LCP, Farjallāh Ḥilū, would become victims of the Syrian regime, Ḥilū being tortured to death in 1959 in Damascus, while Sa'āda saw himself betrayed by Syrian president Husnī al-Za'īm and summarily shot in Beirut a decade earlier.

[130] "It is not a matter of impugning the Lebanese entity." ("*Laysa al-mawḍū' naqḍ al-kiyān al-lubnānī*.") Anṭūn Sa'āda, "al-Mawārina Siryān Sūrīyūn," *al-Zawabi'a* 1 (1948), http://antoun-saadeh.com/works/book/book8/1264, last accessed February 6, 2019.

[131] The council calls for a secularization of personal status laws and the political system. Despite its name, the council is not the Tāi'f-mandated government body commissioned with abolishing sectarianism. Interview with Tawfīq Muḥanna, secretary general of SSNP, Beirut, August 18, 2005 and with Maurice Nahrā, LCP headquarters. The communists have not enjoyed the political clout – or even a single parliamentary seat – to advance their secular agenda, while the SSNP has since the civil war increasingly become affiliated with the Syrian security service, thus tarnishing its secular agenda.

[132] Among the parties explicitly espousing a theocratic form of governance are al-Jam'īya al-Islāmīya, Harakat al-Tawhīd, and al-Mashārī' al-Khayrīya al-Islāmīya (al-Ahbāsh) as well as Ḥizballāh, even if the latter has also endorsed political deconfessionalization as a party objective.

membership and outlook, the Najjāda Party, for instance, professed its openness to all sects when it was faced with a ban on November 10, 1936.[133] Upon the announcement of the unanimous ratification of the Lebanese–French Treaty of 1936 by the Lebanese parliament, members of the Najjāda descended on the streets to burn Lebanese flags, venting their rage against the Christian and Muslim parliamentarians who had all voted in favor of the treaty. The most prominent party to be founded in the cauldron of this crisis was the Katā'ib Party. Since most of the parties of the day were confessional in their constituent membership, the ensuing clashes on the streets of Beirut, Tripoli, and Sidon led to victims falling along the sectarian trenches, prompting the government to impose martial law from November 15 to 23, 1936, and to ban all "confessional parties" until 1943. A debate flared up in the Lebanese papers on the pros and cons of this drastic decision, which may well have forestalled an impending full-scale civil, and potentially regional war, albeit at the expense of Lebanon's democratic development.

The national opposition to the French mandate during World War II effectively relegated the sectarian makeup of Lebanese parties to a salutary, secondary importance. This lull was not to last long beyond independence. On July 20, 1949, a now sovereign Lebanese government saw itself constrained to (re-)issue another decree prohibiting "all paramilitary confessional parties" after clashes between the Sunni Najjāda and Futuwwa al-Lubnānīya on the one side, and the Maronite Katā'ib and al-Ghasāsina on the other, once again resulted in casualities.[134]

In hindsight, we might conclude that, as unpalatable and undemocratic these summary government bans may have been, they did put a (temporary) lid on civil hostilities. Cynics and critics may retort that such prohibitions only served to suppress the underlying tensions that erupted in 1958. To be sure, there also was a somewhat more positive fallout of this period; the specter of civil war, which had raised its head in 1936 and 1949 would equally fuel the political debate on secularism.

Still reeling from the ban of his party, the Katā'ib founder Pierre Jummayil, Sa'āda's chief antagonist, went so far as to echo the call of the SSNP *za'īm* and demand the erasure of the confessional identity written on Lebanese identities in 1942. In 1949 and again in 1953, the party publicly advocated complete deconfessionalization, a plank that

[133] Its leadership included 'Imād al-Ṣulḥ and Muhī ad-Dīn Nusūlī.
[134] The interior minister, Gabriel al-Murr, resigned in protest, claiming to have been bypassed by President Khūrī. Shāmī, *Le Mémorial Du Liban*; vol. II, *Le Mandat Béchara el Khūrī, 1943–1952*, 299.

had been implicit in the Katā'ib's earlier constitution.[135] Just prior to officially adopting the Arabic synonym of "*al-Katā'ib*" on May 20, 1952, the Phalange also lent its support to the general strike for civil marriage in Lebanon organized by the Lawyers' Syndicate on April 2, 1951. Camille Sham'ūn's National Liberal Party by contrast would help to bring the self-same legislation to fall in parliament. The word "secularism" *per se*, however, was not uttered directly in this early phase. Moreover, the Phalange, owing to its party slogan of "God, Fatherland, and Family," could never endorse a full epistemological separation of religion and politics. In November 1954, the Phalange's Pierre Jummayyil and Patriarch 'Arīda vetoed a law designed to ban public manifestations of religion tabled by the Lebanese parliament. Of the major political leaders, only Kamāl Janbulāṭ came out in support of the proposed law, averring that the "street must remain laic."

In short, although the Katā'ib did periodically call for the creation of a "*laïque*" state, the latter was qualified in the words of Pierre Gemayyel as a "faithful, not atheist Laicism," "*le Liban de la laïcité croyante et non celui du confessionalisme atheé.*"[136] Here the guarded, conditional vision of a "believing" secularism of the Katā'ib coalesced with that of the major Islamic parties who have endorsed the abolition of confessionalism, albeit not without adding the perpetual *proviso* of the retention of *Sharī'a* legislation.[137] Prime ministers Ṣā'ib Salām and 'Abdullāh al-Yāfī thus would second Jummayyil, the latter by stating:

> There is no place for atheism in a Muslim society; the prescriptions of religious law must be respected at any price, for the Muslims refuse to act in opposition to this law. This is why they resist the secularization of the state.[138]

During the thirteenth party congress of the Phalange, a program for a comprehensive secularization of the state was elaborated in the context of the party's "categorical rejection of a state religion for Lebanon" as one of the "essential guarantees for national unity."[139] Secularism in the Phalange conception is perhaps best summarized as state equidistance and neutrality toward religion. As such, its primary focus rested on administrative changes. It did not – in sharp contradistinction to the SSNP and

135 "*Notre objectif est de replacer les vieux idéaux confessionnels par un idéal national moderne.*" Cited in Khalīfa, "A La Récherce D'une Politique Ou D'un Concept De Secularisation," 100, 140.
136 Khalīfa, "A La Récherce D'une Politique Ou D'un Concept De Secularisation," 142.
137 This stance has remained unchanged in the discourse of the Najjāda, National Movement, and Ḥizballāh.
138 As cited in Khalīfa, "A La Récherce D'une Politique Ou D'un Concept De Secularisation," 171.
139 Khalīfa, "A La Récherce D'une Politique Ou D'un Concept De Secularisation," 136.

the communists – go so far as to infringe on the spiritual powers' right to retain control over their institutions, most notably in the educational field. This latter prerogative was, as we have seen, retained in the Lebanese constitution, both before and after the Tāi'f Accord. Moreover, a most glaring lacuna emerges in that the party never forwarded its bold proposals in written form to the parliament, leaving doubts regarding the extent of the leadership's actual commitment to tackle sectarianism. In the event, with tensions running high in 1974, a Phalange party declaration explicitly excluded the possibility of a "numerical democracy" in Lebanon, citing the angst of a return to an Ottoman-Islamic order in which Christians would be deprived of their rights.[140] In the foreboding atmosphere prior to 1975, Christian politicians would soon close ranks. When some top-level administrative posts were conceded to Muslims in a reform bid under then Premier Ṫaqī ad-Dīn al-Ṣulḥ, Camille Sham'ūn immediately sounded the clarion call of an impending "liquidation" of the Christians in Lebanon.[141] Finally, with the onset of the war in 1975 and its participation in the ensuing tit-for-tat acts of ethnic cleansing, the Katā'ib lost much of the goodwill it had won in some non-Christian quarters, further undermining the party's self-avowed mission as a trans-sectarian and national party rather than a confessional, Christian (militia) movement.[142]

If the Phalange secularization program lacked a firm will, the other major Christian party to espouse secularism, Raymond 'Iddih's Constitutional Bloc, lacked the constituency and wherewithal, as was made apparent in his botched attempts to advance a civil marriage bill in the 1950s. 'Iddih's subsequent exile in Paris further marginalized an exponent of secularism in Lebanon. In all, there was only a handful of Lebanese statesmen who ran on an explicitly secular platform in Lebanese politics.

Subsequent to Anṭūn Sa'āda, it was another feudal leader, PSP head Kamāl Janbulāṭ, who took on the mantle of secularism proper. Janbulāṭ had in fact turned down an offer to head Sa'āda's SSNP in 1949, thus

[140] Cited in Salām, *La Condition Libanais*, 75.
[141] Raymond Anderson, "Religious Balance in Lebanon Upset," *New York Times*, February 23, 1974.
[142] One thinks, for instance, of the expulsion of the Muslim, largely Shi'a, residents of al-Naba' (including Muhhamad Ḥusayn Fadalllah) in August of 1976, or the emergence of the Lebanese forces. Maurice Jummayil's more moderate stances may have tempered the excesses of radicalization, but his premature death in 1970 silenced this alternative voice.

forfeiting a unique opportunity to build a large, potent trans-sectarian alliance.[143] Instead, Janbulāṭ preferred the greater degree of patriarchal control he enjoyed over his National Socialist Front (NSF), which he had established in 1947. On May 21, 1951 its members (which then included Ghassān Tuwaynī, Pierre ʻIddih, Anwār al-Khatīb, and Camille Sham'ūn) announced their initiative to abolish confessionalism. The NSF, however, was short-lived and Janbulāṭ would soon thereafter turn against Camille Sham'ūn, discarding his prior ardent espousal of Phoenicianism and critique of Arab nationalism for an alliance with Palestinian Arabism.[144] Unlike Sa'āda, who did not emphasize a doctrine of armed revolution until the end, Janbulāṭ's infatuation with cathartic, "historical violence" as the primary means to advance secularism lead him to extol the civil strife of 1958 as an indication of the birth pangs preceding the creation of a secular and socialist regime in Lebanon.[145] In congruence with a Marxist-inspired ideological lens, Janbulāṭ, filled with scorn for the Beiruti bourgeoisie, castigated liberal capitalism, which he claimed "lies hidden in the shadow of this "pretended secularism."[146]

It soon became apparent that Kamāl Janbulāṭ's presidential ambitions would force him to tailor his secular agenda to accommodate the reservations of his political allies. Thus, in May of 1976, after having rejected the Syrian-sponsored constitutional reform document introduced by President Franjīya on February 14,[147] Janbulāṭ limited secularization to political deconfessionalization only after having been induced by Palestinian and Sunni leaders to backtrack on the program of comprehensive secularization he had elaborated a year earlier.[148] Within the span of less than two years, Janbulāṭ shed his and his party's prior avant-garde secularism,[149] suddenly inveighing against civil marriage as a means to

143 *An-Nahār*, July 9, 1949.

144 "Lebanon has a role to assume in liberating the Arab mind." Cited in Farīd al-Khāzin, "Kamal Janbulatt, Uncrowned Druze Prince of the Left," *Middle Eastern Studies* 4.2 (1988): 180ff.

145 Khalīfa, "A La Récherce D'une Politique Ou D'un Concept De Secularisation," 203

146 *al-Anba'*, October 19, 1974. Janbulāṭ's embrace of socialism was never free of contradictions. Bragging about the vast holdings of "feudal warrior aristocracy" he descended from, the "probably biggest landowner in Mukhtāra" nonetheless called for "land reform in Lebanon which will do away with the big estates." Janbulāṭ, *I Speak for Lebanon*, 31–33.

147 Janbulāṭ charged that "the [Syrian] minoritarian military dictatorship made them hostile to any democracy." Itamar Rabinovitch, *The War for Lebanon* (Ithaca, NY: Cornell University Press, 1984), 77.

148 Havemann, *Geschichte Und Geschichtsschreibung Im Libanon Des 19. Und 20. Jahrhunderts*, 78.

149 Janbulāṭ retained his earlier support of a secular marriage law right up to the outbreak of the civil war see *al-Anba'*, August 25, 1972. His volte-face was not necessarily reflective of the position of all PSP members such as the constitutional lawyer Edmond Na'īm.

integrate the Lebanese. Janbulāṭ now questioned the utility of secular civil status laws, claiming that few Protestants and Catholics had ever profited from this liberty in France,[150] a fact flatly contradicted by all sociological studies and statistics, which point to the centrality of secular legislation for national integration.[151] Janbulāṭ would move even closer to the camp of the religious reactionaries by showcasing his revulsion of a "spiritless occidental secularism," paradoxically reflecting the same reservations previously highlighted in the discourse of Pierre Jummayyil and Ṣā'ib Salām who expressed his dislike for "what is called Western secularism since in practice it leads to immorality and the death of spiritualism."[152] The late Imām Mūsā Sadr, politically speaking an antagonist of Salām and Jummayyil, echoed this polemical sentiment:

> Those who call for complete secularism simply wish the destruction of religious values … there is no difference between those who are atheists and those who are Israelis.[153]

Conveniently forgotten in this diatribe is the fact that the confession-based personal status laws in Israel are virtually identical with Lebanon's. Instead, we once again encounter an almost archetypical Occidentalist mischaratarization and demonization of secularism, propounded by such self-avowed secularists as Kamāl Janbulāṭ and by ostensibly liberal-minded men of religion such as the Imām Sadr and Ḥasan Khālid. During his tenure as mufti of the republic, the latter went so far as to declare a fully secularist system worse than a confessional system.[154]

The self-same powerful Occidentalist trope would serve to deflect the blame for both secularism *and* for Lebanese sectarianism on external, imperialist machinations rather than indigenous identities. Thus, the religious right and the Communist Party's discourse shared a rather simplified attribution of the scourge of sectarianism to "foreign interests."[155] Likewise, leaders of the left such as Faraj'Allāh Ḥilū[156] and Kamāl Janbulāṭ – who incidentally received his education at French missionary schools and the Sorbonne[157] – held the French mandate wholly responsible for imposing a confessional system to serve the Christian majority in Lebanon.[158] As we have seen, this majority was put in

[150] *al-Anba'*, February 1, 1974.
[151] Intermarriages have continuously risen since the adoption of the Napoleonic Code, not just in France, but also in Germany and Switzerland, both countries evenly divided between Catholics and Protestants.
[152] *al-Anba'*, October 19, 1974. [153] *L'Orient Le Jour*, May 24, 1976, 4.
[154] Ḥasan Khālid, *Al-Muslimūn fī Lubnān* (Beirut: Dār al-Kindī, 1978), 209.
[155] Mahdi 'Amil, "al-Ist'imar wa al-takhalluf," *al-Tariq* 6 (1969), 48.
[156] Faraj Allāh Ḥilū, *Kitābāt Mukhtāra* (Beirut: Dār al Farābī, 1974).
[157] The Lazarus Fathers Institute in 'Ayn at-Tūra and the Jesuit St. Joseph University.
[158] Speech of Kamāl Janbulāṭ, *al-Anba*, August 23, 1974, no. 1152, 6.

question since the first and only census under the French mandate in 1932. It had dissipated by the 1950s, at which point the PSP advocated an opening of the system together with the National Movement. All the while, the PSP's discourse tied the edification of society and the necessity of secularism in the Arab world to the protection of minority groups.

Similar incongruities survive until the present day in the form of the daily about-faces of Kamāl's son and heir Walīd Janbulāṭ. The latter has periodically demanded full secularization in some instances and insisted on the preservation of the confessional system in others, depending on the shifting dictates of political expediency and the feudal chieftain's personal mood.

Political tectonics also compromised some of the secularism of other, pan-Arab parties sometimes hastily identified as standard-bearers of secularism. Post-World War II Arab nationalism – in both its Ba'thist and Nasserist guises – is often (mis)portrayed as a progenitor of secularism, which was dealt a lethal blow by the defeat at the hands of Israel in 1967. Indeed, in Lebanon, the disavowal of the Najjāda Party seems unambiguous in its abandonment of a "political Muslim unity" and espousal of secular Arab nationalism – and yet the self-same Najjāda, formed as a Muslim boy scout movement – would also espouse a nostalgic return to Islamic governance.[159]

In his jeremiad on the regression of secularism in the Arab world Kamāl Dīb notes that Nāṣir's Arab nationalist line "did not see any need for religious belief or principles in order to see his nationalism accepted by the electrified Egyptian masses."[160] Such an analysis would contradict Hishām Sharābī's estimate that there has been no successful mass political movement in the Arab world, which has not utilized religious symbols and discourse. In fact, Jamāl 'Abd Nāṣir's communalist pretensions do shine through in his *Philosophy of the Revolution*.[161] Sana Ḥasan casts further doubt on the secular track record of Nasserism by recalling that

[159] Khalīfa, "A La Récherce D'une Politique Ou D'un Concept De Secularisation," 163

[160] Kamāl Dīb, "Fashl al-Quwwāt al-'Ilmāniya," *as-Safīr*, February 6, 2004.

[161] "I stood before the Ka'aba ... I said to myself ... Our regard of the Ḥajj must change. Our pilgrimage to the Ka'aba must not become a means of remembrance to enter paradise, or an innocent effort to purchase forgiveness after a life full (with sins). The Ḥajj must rather become a great political force, alerting the global press to cover those who pursue it, not as quaint traditions which make cute pictures for the readers of papers, but rather as a regular political conference in which all the leaders of the Islamic countries, and all scientists and merchants and industrialists meet. As I ponder these hundreds of millions of Muslims, all welded into a homogenous whole by the same faith, I come out increasingly conscious of the potential achievements cooperation among all these millions can accomplish – cooperation naturally not going beyond their loyalty to their original countries, but which will ensure for them and their Brethren-in-belief unlimited power." 'Abd al-Nāṣir, *Falsafat al-Thawra*, 110–111 as cited in Lewis, *Islam and the West*, 66–67.

the Free Officers were exclusively Muslim. Christians were completely sidelined from administrative positions under Nāṣir as opposed to the prior reign of the *Wafd* during which several Copts served in key ministerial positions. It is often forgotten that it was under Nāṣir's one-party rule that an Islamization of the textbooks of Arabic, history and civics commenced and the Azhar establishment buttressed.[162]

The ambiguous secular legacy of Nāṣir was summarized by Ṣādiq al-'Azm. After the 1956 victory, Nāṣir was handed a golden opportunity to invest his unparalleled popularity in pursuit of a progressive secular agenda, but the opportunity was missed and instead a single party hegemony bearing features of a religious authoritarianism was erected.[163]

In Lebanon, the communal tint of Nasserism became unmistakable in 1958. Far from publicly endorsing a coherent form of secularism, Nāṣir explicitly marketed a Muslim solidarity as the religious cement of the short-lived Arab republic, the constitution of which identified Islam as the religion of state in Article 5.[164]

It is no wonder then that Nasserism was viewed with deep suspicion even by *bona fides* secular Lebanese parties. Their shared aversion to the Islamic communalism undergirding the discourse of Arabism explains why even erstwhile archenemies such as the SSNP and the Katā'ib could join a rare alliance in support of Sham'ūn against Nāṣir. Ideologically speaking, both Pierre Jummayyil and Anṭūn Sa'āda shared rejected the discourse of Arabism, which Sa'āda emphatically dismissed as Islamic chauvinism in disguise, refuting the "simplistic" and "deceptive" talk of those trying to convince non-Muslims otherwise.[165]

The contours of a deadlock in the debate on secularism were then visible early on, even as they became increasingly apparent as the country steered toward a political crisis. Polarization on the question of secularism opened up fault lines both between and within each confession. On

[162] S. N. Ḥasan, *Christians versus Muslims in Egypt* (Oxford: Oxford University Press, 2006), 172, 179; al-'Aẓma, *al-'Ilmānīya min Manzūr Mukhtalif*, 286ff.

[163] See Ṣādiq Jalāl Al-'Azm, *al-'Almānīya wa al-Mujatma' al-Madanī* (Cairo: Markaz al-Dirāsāt wa al- Ma'lūmāt al-Qānūnīya li-Huqūq al-Insān, 1998), 18ff.

[164] "The UAR [the brief union between Egypt and Syria under Nāṣir] represents the largest Arab force in the Arab world. In it live around 28 million people that make up a people homogenous in its make-up, which speaks Arabic, believes in Arabism, and has Islam for religion." Jamāl 'Abd al-Nāṣir, *Official Yearly Book of the United Arab Republic* (Cairo: Ministry of Information, 1959).

[165] Sa'āda, *Al-'A'māl al-Kāmila*, vol. III, 176–177. When the leader of the [Syrian] National Bloc, Fakhrī al-Barūdī, was asked about whether he recognized the SSNP, his answer was clear: "God forbid. The National Bloc recognizes in Syria only Arab nationalism." Cited in 'Ādil Bishāra, *Syrian Nationalism: An Inquiry into the Policial Philosophy of Antun Sa'adeh* (Beirut: Bissan, 1995), 63.

the eve of the 1975 civil war, for example, three major discourses on secularism were discernible among the Sunni communal leadership:

One, spearheaded by Ḥusayn al-Quwwātli, director general of Dār ul-'Iftā, entailed a categorical, *a priori* rejection of all aspects of secularism. In response, the Islamic Foundation of the Maqāṣid issued an unprecedented statement on November 21 calling for full "equality among all Lebanese in rights and duties so that the rights of the Lebanese citizen will be complete without any deficiency."[166] The Maqāṣid thus endorsed Kamāl Janbulāṭ and the 'Imām Mūsā Ṣadr's basic call for an abolition of political confessionalism in accordance with Articles 12 and 95 of the constitution. These bold stances in turn called forth a condemnation by the Sunni council of *'Ulamā'*, lamenting that the Maqāṣid had fallen prey to the propaganda of secularization, which was portrayed as a deviation. In 1975, the Sunni Council of *'Ulamā'* issued a statement in which it denounced secularism as an unfortunate result of a struggle with an oppressive Catholic Church, culminating in the historical materialism of Feuerbach and Lenin.[167] Unlike Quwwātlī, the *'Ulamā'*, however, did not advocate for a totalistic application of Islamic law, once again exempting personal status laws from the discussion. They thereby took a middle position, one which differed from that of the Maqāṣid more in tone than in substance.

In a rare joint public declaration in 1983, the mufti of the republic, Ḥasan Khālid and the Lebanese patriarch Mar Antonius Khuraysh would sanction electoral and political deconfessionalization as not merely acceptable, but salutary to religion as it freed faith from the strictures of politics.[168] The omission of any reference to legal secularization, however, foreclosed any political conversion of this auspicious statement. A previous initiative in 1974 under Premier Taqī ad-Dīn al-Sulḥ had been met with Camille Sham'ūn's rebuttal:

> If one wants to eradicate confessionalism, this must be done in all spheres, including marriage. It is necessary to accept that a Muslim woman can marry a Christian man as much as a Christian woman may marry a Muslim man. Only then can confessionalism disappear, not by trying to dissimulate the essential problems with banalities of this sort.[169]

[166] David Grafton, *The Christians of Lebanon* (Lebanon: I. B. Tauris, 2003), 64.
[167] *An-Anwār*, March 25, 1975, 3.
[168] Cited in Bassām Hāshim, *Ilghā' At-Ta'ifīya As-Siyāsīya* (Beirut: Al-Dār al-Lubnānī lil Nashr, 2000), 117.
[169] Khalīfa, "A La Récherce D'une Politique Ou D'un Concept De Secularisation," 160.

Thus, the onus of secularizing reform was put on the Muslim community leaders and conditioned on a comprehensive secularization generally presumed to be incompatible with accustomed interpretations of Islamic law.

Other Christian voices shed all pretense of secularism and thereby unwittingly approximate the conservative Islamic discourse. Voicing a similar complaint, as we have seen earlier in Islamist circles, the Christian historian Fu'ād Afram al-Bustānī discarded laïcism and democracy as concepts that – unlike in the "Occidental West" – do not carry the same (positive) meaning in the Lebanese context.[170] In the shadow of the freshly erupted civil war of 1975, Bustānī suggested a "federal" solution putatively modeled on the Swiss cantonal paradigm, even though the latter can hardly be equated to the degree of regional autonomy envisaged.[171] Outright partition into federal sectarian statelets had been entertained as early as 1948. Needless to say, the appeal of this solution – which is tantamount to a death verdict of the 1926 republic – is proportional to the depth of ailment besetting the Lebanese state. It has been reinvoked ever since in times of crisis chiefly by parties on the Christian right and the radical Islamic fringe until the present day.[172]

To summarize, twentieth-century Lebanese political discourse remained stuck in a barren "dialogue of the deaf."[173] While Christian leaders stood accused of feigning interest in a secular system merely in order to provoke the precalculated negative response of the Muslim leaders, particularly in light of the latter's (assumed) opposition to the laïcization of personal status laws, Muslim parties intermittently raised the banner of political secularization in anticipation of Christian angst of the specter of an Islamic state imposed by dint of a (*Shia*) demographic hegemony.

In such an environment, political parties had a difficult stance to win cross-sectarian, genuinely national constituencies and advance secular agendas. The LCP and SSNP excepted, contemporary Lebanese parties that nominally have espoused a secular agenda – such as General 'Awn's[174] Tayyār al-Watanī – has seen their progressive reform agenda

[170] See Fu'ād Afrām al-Bustānī, *Le Problème du Liban* (Kaslik: C. R., 1976).

[171] It should be noted that, while Swiss federalism accords a similar if not superior degree of prerogatives to cantonal and municipal authorities as is available in current-day Lebanon, the outright segregation proposed by some far-right Christian or Islamist groups finds no equivalent in Switzerland.

[172] Khalīfa, "A La Récherce D'une Politique Ou D'un Concept De Secularisation," 94.

[173] "Ḥiwār "at-tarshān" or "al-turush" is the oft-cited Lebanese designation for this stalemate.

[174] Up until mid 2006, General Michel 'Awn was the most popular contender for the presidency, both among Christians and among Lebanese as a whole. See survey published in *Ṣadā al-Balad*, April 26, 2006 in which 70 percent list 'Awn as the

belied by a largely monochrome constituency.[175] Former prime minister, Salīm al-Ḥuṣṣ, has, along with a host of other politicians, called for an amendment to the constitution prohibiting sectarian parties, yet his suggestion has fallen on deaf ears.[176] Instead, the ostensibly liberal, pro-American then-interior minister, Ahmad Fatfat, in 2006 granted a license to Ḥizb al-Taḥrīr, a stridently fundamentalist, antidemocratic party of global reach. The party is banned in Syria and Jordan due to its intention to re-establish a Sunni caliphal state and persecute dissenters.[177]

As for those small secular parties with an intercommunal membership, which did emerge in the post-independence era, many of these would come to suffer from the same deficiency of elitist alienation, which beset the campaign for secularism espoused by the nineteenth-century Arab illuminati. Case in point are the valiant, yet ultimately limited, efforts of the late Joseph Mughayzil and Bāsim al-Jisr.[178] In the 1970s and 1980s this association of prominent Muslim and Christian lawyers and intellectuals formed various semi-official civil *fora* such as the Democratic Secular Party (founded in 1963) in which a number of men of letters and independent professionals could find refuge. One of its members, the attorney ʻAbdullāh Lahhūd, put a series of proposals aimed at a secularization of personal status laws on the table between 1974 and 1976. Another independent member of parliament at that time in support of this project was 'Ilyās Harāwī, who, as president of the republic, would subsequently kindle a national controversy in 1997 after forwarding an almost identical bill of secularization. The Democratic Party, however, bore greater resemblance to a closed lodge rather than a proper party. With most of its meetings held in secret, the party lacked any grassroots network and its activities petered out by the late 1990s.[179]

preferred candidate. Surveys one year later, however, showed a steep 30 percent drop in the support for ʻAwn due to the latter's alliance with Ḥizbullah. Subsequenty, Awn's Tayyar Party entered the parliament in 2008 and by 2009 made up one third of the government. ʻAwn's 2016 bid for the presidency was blocked by Saudi Arabia's allies, but met unsuspected success after being supported by the Lebanese forces.

175 The Free Patriotic Movement reform programme of May 2005 advances an almost paradigmatic list of reforms aimed at greater accountability, transparency, and secularization (including the introduction of an optional civil marriage bill).

176 Charles Jabbūr, "Interview with Salīm Al-Huss," *al-Masīra*, March 22, 2004, 12.

177 The Ḥizb ul-Taḥrīr unequivocally denounces freedom of belief and democracy and even after its recognition called for "the return of Lebanon to what was before 1920, i.e. as an inextricable part of the Muslim countries." See *al-Balad*, May 29, 2006 and *an-Nahār*, October 9, 2006.

178 Joseph Mughayzil, *Al-ʻUrūba wa al-ʻAlmānīya* (Beirut: Dār an-Nahār, 1980).

179 One exception was the "permanent conference for a secular movement" of 1983, which came out with a declaration affirming secularism and yet denouncing its iconoclastic

Jisr and Mughayzil had envisioned the establishment of an "Arabic Center for the Study of Secularism," which, however, never came into being. Nonetheless, a "front for a unified Lebanon for change" ("*jabha lubnān al-wāhid lil-taghrīr*") with Ḥasan Ṣa'b, and, after 1986, Munīr Shamma' and Ḥasan Maṣrafī was formed, as were cooperative links with the harakat ul-wa'ī and the tayyār ud-dimūqrātī together with the renegade Bishop Gregoire Haddād.

Haddād's "Civic Society Movement" ("*Tayyār al-Madanī*"), a grassroots nongovernmental organization at the forefront of the struggle for secularism in Lebanon, would face very much the same obstacles, even in its heyday. Haddād's movement was launched by a man of the clergy and distinguished itself by a hands-on approach, which crossed all sectarian borders. It thus, by and large, avoided the entanglement in the politics of the *zu'amā'*, in the process, however, essentially forfeiting any direct entry into the political arena and patronage-driven party politics.

Perhaps the ultimate testimony to the centrality of the cult of personality in Lebanon is provided by another telling fact: the sole party to elude the hegemony of a towering *za'īm*, the Lebanese Communist Party, would also be the only major party to never win a single seat in parliament. Since political mobilization appears so governed by the patronage paradigm under the rule of the *zu'amā'*, this enduring feature of Lebanese political life warrants examination as it affected secular reform in post- Tā'if Lebanon.

The Old and New *Zu'amā'* Emerging from the Civil War

Where civil blood makes civil hands unclean

Shakespeare, *Romeo and Juliet*

In the *locus classicus* of the patronage discussion on Lebanese neofeudalism, Arnold Hottinger has astutely summarized the dynamics of economic favors, political fealty, and family kinship that govern this relationship of party patrons (*za'īm*/ pl. *zu'amā'*) and followers in Lebanon.[180] If we look at the list of family names of Lebanese parliamentarians over the decades, it quickly becomes apparent that the circle of

Turkish and French variants. It did, however, spell out a familiar program announced by its secretary general Bāsim al-Jisr with the familiar planks of a deconfessionalization of the political system and personal status laws.

180 Hottinger, "Zu'ama in Historical Perspective," 85–105. A more recent study on the historic and sociological origins of patronage in Lebanon is Nizār A. Ḥamza, "Clientalism, Lebanon: Roots and Trends," *Middle Eastern Studies* 37.3 (2001): 167–178. As well as Johnson, *All Honorable Men*.

families that control parliament has only marginally changed.[181] Instead, there has been both a recycling and a reincarnation of notables and elites. We may roughly sketch three generations of *za'īms* in Lebanon. A first generation of traditional *zu'amā'*, the landed notables whose feudal roots go back to the nineteenth century, and, in some cases, extend to the premodern feudal age. A second generation of *zu'amā'*, who were co-opted politically and economically under the French mandate after 1920, and a last generation of upstart businessmen who rode on the crest of the successive petroleum booms in the Gulf States.

Most of these first generation of traditional *zu'amā'* hailed from families such as the Khāzins, the Janbulāṭ's, the Bayhūms, Arslāns, Sulhs, Asa'ds, Salāms, Jummayils, and Franjīya, who could parley some of their landed wealth into political power. There also were the prominent Orthodox urban families like the Tuwaynīs, the Sursuqs, the de Frayj, the 'Asaylīs, or Trāds who benefited from the "Long Peace" after 1860 as (silk)traders, merchants, and (absentee) landlords.[182] On the one hand, this period marked the onset of continual waves of emigration from Lebanon right up until World War I.[183] On the other, the calamity of war – and the regional transformations that came in its train – also provided the opportunity for the accumulation of many a family fortune. Besides isolated incidences of hoarding of foodstuffs during wartime inflation and shortages, a significant part of the Beirut aristocracies wealth stemmed from the sale of large estates in the Jizrīl Valley in Palestine to the Jewish Agency in the first decades of the twentieth century.[184] The weakness of the Ottoman state allowed some families like the Sursuqs and 'Iddih's to appropriate estates in the Biqā' with the

[181] Farīd al-Khāzin, *Lebanon's First Postwar Parliamentary Election* (London: Center for Lebanese Studies, February 1998), 44ff.

[182] Ṭarābulsī notes that at one point in the late nineteenth century almost half of the labor force was employed in the silk industry. Ṭarābulsī, "Identités et Solidarités Croisées dans les Conflicts du Liban Contemporain," 208. With over 40 percent of Lebanon covered by mulberry trees, domestically oriented agriculture suffered, contributing to the massive waves of (Maronite) emigration between 1860 and 1900. Brigitte Rieger, *Rentiers, Patrone Und Gemeinschaft: Soziale Sicherung Im Libanon. Europaeische Hochschulschriften*, European PhD dissertations (Frankfurt: Peter Lang, 2002), 35.

[183] Due to the demise of the silk industry, which had come to constitute over 60 percent of the entire Levantine GDP, 10,000 textile workers lost their livelihoods in 1833. Owen, *The Middle East in the World Economy*, 105ff.

[184] See Kenneth Stein, *The Land Question in Palestine 1917–1939* (Chapel Hill: University of North Carolina, 1984), 38, 56. Land sales to the Jewish colonialists were not confined to Beiruti families but included the Baydūns in Acre as well as the Sabbāhs and Habbībs.

aid of Ottoman troops, or to buy up large swaths of Palestinian real estate from an empire strapped for cash.[185]

The "politics of the notables" or rule of the *z'uāmā'* then withstood the test of time through the upheavals of Ottoman rule, the French mandate, independence and civil strife. While it is true that during the last civil war (1975–1990) the militias could supplant kin groups, they usually submerged the latter into a supra-kin sectarian identity in which family ties formed a constituent element. In other words, kin-based mobilization on the microlevel clearly has facilitated sect-based forms of no less patriarchal political organization on the macrolevel. Su'ād Joseph notes that:

> The kin contract has been grounded in material realities in which kin relationships have been, for the Lebanese, the core of social identity, economic stability, political security, and religious affiliation … It has been the kin who care and against whom one has irreconcilable rights and toward whom one has had religious mandated (at times legally prescribed) moral responsibilities.[186]

Such overlap of personal and political responsibilities was amply illustrated in parliamentary elections, in as much as families would exert pressure on their members to elect the dominant politicians of their own confessional community. Even in the select instances in which large numbers of voters transcended this pattern and voted outside of their "confessional box," they often did so in obedience to coalition strategies dictated by sectarian authorities.[187]

While the social infrastructure of *ṭā'ifīya* outlined in the previous chapters has proven resilient to change, the identity of the particular spokesmen of each caste has been subjected to much greater historical flux and altered according to political constellations. To take one example, while Cardinal Ṣfayr has virtually monopolized the Maronite "pulpit" in the absence of a competing secular political leadership from 1989 to 2011,[188] up unto the early nineteenth century it was the Maronite

[185] In 1872, the Ottoman government sold the Yajur village lands to the Sursuq brothers and Salīm al-Khūrī of Beirut. Such land was later sold for handsome profits to the Jewish Agency in Palestine in the interwar period. Stein, *The Land Question in Palestine 1917–1939*, 38, 56; Owen, *The Middle East in the World Economy*, 166; chapter 5 of Zachary Lockman, *Comrades and Enemies: Arab and Jewish Workers in Palestine, 1906–1948* (Berkeley: University of California Press, 1996).

[186] Suād Joseph, *Gender and Citizenship in the Middle East* (Syracuse, NY: Syracuse University Press, 2000), 117.

[187] One should add the caveat that voter participation ran as low as 28 percent in Beirut, besides bespeaking a general nausea and lack of trust in the electoral system, these numbers may also potentially indicate a larger (if silent) secular body of voters.

[188] Ṣfayr's stature was such that Sa'ad al-Ḥarīrī and Shiblī Mallāt even nominated the patriarch to serve as the president after the aspired toppeling of Emile Lahhūd. Ṣfayr declined the offer. Earlier, in 1989, General 'Awn's militia supporters stormed the

patriarch who sought the *imprimatur* of the powerful Khāzin lords, the muqāta'ajīs of Kisirwān. Later, in the post-independence period, Maronite presidents such as Camille Sham'ūn (reg. 1952–1958), or party leaders such as the Katā'ib's Jummayils, were identified as the representative figure for the Maronites. After the civil war, the influence of the lay Maronite leadership waned due to factional infighting of competing militia leaders beholden to variant foreign sponsors.

With the partial exception of the outspoken Beirut bishop Elias Audi, ecclesiastical sway over the political arena declined among the Orthodox where such family clans as the Murr loomed large.[189] Much the same may be said about the authority of the Druze *'uqqāl,* which has all but disappeared as a force to be reckoned within the Druze community. Instead, the most authentic archetype of a feudal *za'īm,* Walīd Janbulāṭ, established himself as the sole spokesman of what arguably is the most tightly knit Lebanese confessional caste. This was illustrated when Walīd Janbulāṭ faced the opprobrium of the Druze religious leadership (the mashāyikh and 'uqqāl) after he decided to marry a non-Druze in 1982. The elders saw themselves constrained to eventually visit Janbulāṭ's Mukhtāra Palace to humbly apologize to the *za'īm* for their impertinence, signaling the demise of the Druze clerical establishment and new balance of power in the Druze community, which remains in place today with the dominant Janbulāṭ dynasty.[190]

Lastly, the mantle of Shia leadership passed through its own set of different stages in modern Lebanon. From 1943 to 1984, a mere three feudal families monopolized the supreme Shia political office, the seat of the speaker of parliament. Politically speaking, many of the feudal lords were affiliated with various streams of Arab nationalism, even if parochial interests seem to have prevailed in many cases.

The last of these feudal giants to occupy the most prestigious Shia office had been Kāmil al-As'ad. The latter's lack of popularity among disenfranchised Shia came to the fore in Ba'lbak on March 14, 1974 when the 'Imām Mūsā Sadr was cheered on by a riled-up crowd casting

Maronite patriarch's chanting blasphemous slogans such as "*'Awnak jayī min Allāh*" ["Your help – i.e. "*Awn'* – comes from God"] and forced the patriarch to kiss 'Awn's picture in humiliation.

189 This particular family itself was long split between a pro-Syrian faction headed by the patriarch and (former) interior ministers Michel and Ilyās Murr versus former MTV-owner Gabriel Murr. A *pro forma* reconciliation of the two branches occurred after the near assassination of Ilyās al-Murr in 2005.

190 Abū Khalīl, "The Politics of Sectarian Ethnicity," 103.

aspersions at the erstwhile feudal lord.[191] It has (justly) been argued that Kāmil al-As'ad signed his final political death sentence when he added his signature to Amīn al-Jummayyil's in the US-brokered Armistice Accord with Israel of May 17, 1983.[192]

Subsequently, from approximately 1984 onward, we may speak of the eclipse of the erstwhile feudal aristocracy and the rise of a somewhat[193] secular AMAL interregnum under Ḥusayn al-Ḥusaynī and Nabīh Birrī.[194] This was then followed by the coming hegemony of "Islamic AMAL,"[195] aka Ḥizballāh, whose parliamentary block has already tripled in size since 1992. Forgotten in all this is the largely silent, marginalized, yet sizable, secular Shia minority.[196]

What sets AMAL and Ḥizballāh apart from the traditional *zu'āmā'*, is that the new Shia parties (thus far) do not seem to have established a hereditary, patrilineal bequeathment of authority. For this reason, AMAL and Ḥizballāh have been heralded as marking communal political movements in which kinship ties have been sidelined. We may maintain that, in fact, a distinct variant of this paternalistic *za'īm-zilm* political hierarchy and patronage extends even to such religious parties as Ḥizballāh, which, beyond rendering a myriad of material and social services, also exerts an ideological allure that ensures party loyalty on a

191 See Mājid Ḥalawī, *A Lebanon Defined: Mūsā Al-Sadr and the Shi'a Community* (Boulder, CO: Westview Press, 1992), 184.

192 Kāmil al-Asad would maintain until the present day that the agreement was not tantamount to treason as claimed by its detractors, but rather provided a pragmatic disengagement from Israel.

193 The charter of the AMAL Movement, for all its socialist impetus and antisectarian rhetoric, is unambiguous about the tenet that "faith in God requires that family laws should follow the revealed law of God as must be the case with other social, political and economic matters." Cited in Augustus Richard Norton, *AMAL and the Shia* (Austin: University of Texas Press, 1987), 152. Party leader Birrī would pay homage to Khomeini. AMAL incidentally derives its legitimacy from the late 'Imām Mūsā Sadr, while Ḥizballāh emerged out of the Islamic branch of AMAL in 1985.

194 According to a poll conducted in 2000, Nabīh Birrī was identified as the main Shia leader, well ahead of Naṣrallāh. "Post-Parliamentary Election Poll 2000," *Ii International*, September 23–October 5, 2000, 46. However, after the aggravation of the political climate in 2005, Birrī lost this pole-position to Naṣrallāh.

195 After Nabīh Birrī joined the National Salvation Committee in 1982, a whole cadre of subsequent commanding Ḥizballāh members left AMAL in protest. Among them were Ḥasan Naṣrallāh, Na'īm al-Qāsim, and Ḥusayn al-Mussawī, the founder of Ḥizballāh. Amal Sa'd Ghurayyib, "Factors Conducive to the Politization of the Lebanese Shia and the Emergence of Ḥizballāh," *Journal of Islamic Studies* 14 (2003): 278.

196 One may note that, as of 2005, only approximately 40 percent of Shia are officially registered as party members of AMAL and Ḥizballāh. This is not to say that these parties also received additional votes from nonmembers, yet, if the 2005 participation rate in the south is any indication (slightly over 70 percent), then one might reasonably deduce the presence of a sizable nonpoliticized, secular-leaning Shia contingent.

grassroots level as Nizār Hamzah has trenchantly observed.[197] Despite Ḥizballāh's immersion in Shia symbolism and its direct beholdness to Iran, Naṣrallāh has been at pains to claim exception to being typecast as yet another sectarian *za'īm*, stating: "Perhaps I am a *za'īm* in Lebanon, but I am not a *za'īm* within the party."[198] Such disavowals notwithstanding, the leadership style of the Party of God's general secretary betrays all the characteristics of that of a communal lord. If one were to differentiate Ḥizballāh from the traditional Lebanese party model, one could point out that the party's internal hierarchy is not feudal-hereditary but religious-hierarchical in nature. As such, this theocratic party is arguably the only party in Lebanon – apart from the secular communists and the SSNP– which has come close to overcoming the fundamental social dichotomy between the notables (*wūjāhā/a'yān/söz sahibileri*) and common folk (*al-ahālī/al-'awām/halk*), the major hallmark of the nineteenth-century social structure that survived into the twentieth century in a modified form.[199]

As we have observed in our review of the nineteenth century, it was this ingrained social bifurcation that provided the fertile ground for clientelism and continued to stymie a wider dissemination of secularism. Whatever positive results may have come from the shared, quasi-secular life of Muslim and Christian elites, these alliances were effectively futile against outbreaks of sectarian strife. This was because the ruling class would desperately avail themselves of the potent symbols of sectarianism as the preferred means to combat their alienation from popular concerns and establish a new rapport with their confessional base constituency. This was as true in 1860 as it was in 1958 when "the revolt of the have-nots"[200] was quickly exploited by the "revolt of the [surrogate] Pashas,"[201] who endeavored to convert mass discontent into personal political capital. In the last instance of 1975, the increasingly shrill discourse pitting the partisans of Arab nationalism against those of Lebanese independence in wake of the mounting Palestinian crisis overshadowed any public debate on secularism and instead constituted the prelude to civil strife.[202]

[197] Ḥamza, "Clientalism in Lebanon: Roots and Trends," 167–178.

[198] Cited in *as-Safīr*, April 27, 2006.

[199] See Maqdisī, *The Culture of Sectarianism*, 77. The hierarchy separating laity from clergy is still apparent in pubic spaces of encounter among all denominations. To this day, for instance, commoners are often debarred from kissing the hand of religious dignitaries.

[200] Helena Cobban, *The Making of Modern Lebanon* (New York: Hutchinson, 1985), 95.

[201] Tabitha Petran, *The Struggle Over Lebanon* (New York: Monthly Review Press, 1987), 51.

[202] Maqdisī, *The Culture of Sectarianism*, 43.

This reading differs slightly from those who have characterized the sectarian strife that gripped Lebanon after 1975 as a product of a "revolt of the masses" against the high-handed establishment governing the Lebanese state.[203] Despite the upsurge of popular pressure amid an economic and political crisis, a firm dichotomy between the allegedly cosmopolitan quasi-secular elite and the retrograde sectarian masses is not necessarily borne out by the actual alliances and policiea observable during the war. The Janbulāṭs, Franjīyas, Sham'ūns and Jummayils, the Salāms, and Karāmīs were all at some point or another sponsoring certain militia. As Roger Owen put it, during the civil war urban families such as the Salāms of Beirut or the Karāmīs of Tripoli found themselves performing a "balancing act" by sharply critizing the Lebanese government and whipping up Arab nationalist sentiments from one end, without, however, alienating themselves to the degree of losing access to the benefits that accrued to them from the very Lebanese state that was the object of their rhetorical scorn on the other.[204] Even Kamāl Janbulāt, despite his progressive rhetoric, reverted to the old ways of a *za'īm* and struck a confessional alliance with his old rivals, the Arslāns, in the 1972 parliamentary elections, casting his all-decisive vote for the feudal lord Franjīya in the presidential election of 1975. Conversely, elites were exposed to groundswell pressures from the lower (middle) class clamouring for sectarian self-defense.

The slogans of Islamic and Christian communalisms and Palestinian and Maronite jingoisms may thus be likened to ideologies affording vicarious satisfaction in the midst of dashed economic hopes, identity crises, rural decline, and urban angst and alienation. Arguably "vertical," socioeconomic chasms put a severe strain on Lebanon's social structure and would prove as pernicious as the "horizontal"-sectarian ones, particularly before the civil war of 1975 when the opposition would meet in the *Sāhat il-Najma* railing against the "twelve thieves and ninety-nine crooks."[205]

[203] "Whereas the elites compromised in the hope of containing sectarian conflicts, many of the citizens used sectarianism to express their discontent with the product of elitist compromises." Usāma Maqdisī, "The Modernity of Sectarianism," *Middle East Report* 26 (1996): 26. Also see Kamāl Suleiman Ṣalībī, *Crossroads to Civil War: Lebanon 1958–1976* (Ithaca, NY: Ithaca Press, 1976), 54ff who contends that the Muslim bourgeoisie was "caged in" by popular pressure to support the Palestinian commandos by 1970. Conversely, the three major Christian parties, Shamoun's Partie National Libéral, Raymond 'Iddih's National Bloc and the Katā'ib formed the Triple Alliance (*al-ḥilf al-thulāthī*) in opposition to the threat posed by the Palestinian commandos.

[204] Roger Owen, "The Political Economy of Grand Liban: 1920–70," in *Essays on the Crisis in Lebanon*, ed., Roger Owen (London: Ithaca, 1976), 26.

[205] See Abū Khalīl, "The Politics of Sectarian Ethnicity," 217

Hence, 1975 remains as a traumatic illustration of an at once political-sectarian and a socioeconomic implosion.[206] To the prescient,[207] it was clear that the top-heavy, hierarchical system as embodied by the sectarian giants could not achieve the "revolution from above" in time to stave off the "revolution from below" that was in the offing.[208] On the contrary, rigged elections and gerrymandering only increased pent-up frustrations and eventually led to a violent backlash. Indeed, a whole roster of failed candidates in the 1972 elections subsequently reappeared as the lords of various militias during the war.[209] Such were the steep costs of sectarian nepotism and an unresponsive, corrupted political system.[210]

After the guns fell silent in 1990, a new, postwar elite of *nouveaux riche* businessmen and politicians appeared alongside the war elite of neo-*zu'amā'*. In many cases these were merchants and middlemen returning from the Gulf, Saudi Arabia, or West Africa armored with enough (oil rent) resources to muscle themselves into the patronage system and invest in real estate. Among those were entrepreneurs such as 'Alī Jamāl, Jamīl Ibrāhīm, and Georges Frem, politicians such as Prime Minister Najīb Miqātī[211], Muhammad al-Ṣafadī, former vice premier 'Iṣām Fāris, and, above all, the new "super"-*za'īm*, the late premier Rafīq al-Ḥarīrī (1944–2005) who had laid the groundwork for his future role in Beirut during the war itself. At this juncture, hopes arose that the new flush of investment might wash away the remaining feudal structures. While a *quid pro quo* business ethos did spur Muslim–Christian cooperation in select ventures, its positive effect on healing the wounds of war and nourishing secularism was less apparent. This was in part due to the postwar *Zu'ama*'s use of communal symbols and policies in their quest for power as well as the fact that the rent-seeking *modus operandi* of monopolistic and nepotistic capitalism was ill-suited to act as a catalyst

[206] In 1956, 14 percent who were in finance and commerce reaped 46 percent of the GNP, by 1976, some 50 percent of the GNP was controlled by 5 percent of the population. Joseph Shāmī, "Religious Groups in Lebanon: A Descriptive Investigation," *International Journal of Middle East Studies* 11.2 (1980).

[207] In a book written almost one decade before the war, Michael Hudson argued that political liberalization in Lebanon has not kept abreast with economic development. Hudson, *The Precarious Republic*, 12ff.

[208] Ṣā'ib Salām had spoken of the necessity of a revolution that would break the commercial monopolies.

[209] See Abū Khalīl, "The Politics of Sectarian Ethnicity," 220–225.

[210] In light of the disaffection caused by the Syrian orchestrated elections after the end of the civil war, and the prolongation of the gerrymandered "Ghāzī Kana'ān" election law that marred the 2005 parliamentary elections, a similar tension was in the air.

[211] Miqātī would later serve as the prime minister two times; the first was for a short period of two months in 2005, and later again in 2011. He submitted his resignation in early 2013.

for a nonparochial notion of nationhood. Instead, the new, affluent capitalist barons would tend to ally with the preexisting confessional and family networks rather than risk mounting a challenge to them.

The Sunni scepter of leadership, which never really was in clerical or party hands, passed from an urban aristocracy, which dominated much of the twentieth century, to the Saudi billionaire Rafīq al-Ḥarīrī. Finally taking hold of the reigns of the supreme Sunni political office in 1993, Ḥarīrī only partly overcame the handicap of past Sunni (and Shia) oligarchs who suffered from an inability to organize viable political parties. Likewise, Sunni leaders traditionally did not control significant rural constituencies comparable to those beholden to the Shiite, Druze, and Maronite lords.[212]

To his critics, the vast sums of money Ḥarīrī attracted to Lebanon – or allowed the state to borrow from domestic banks, including his own – were not so much expression of benevolent philanthropy, or of a national project in the proper sense, but rather an extension of profit-seeking tentacles of a Gulf-based rentier economy bent on transforming Lebanon into a neoliberal nirvana,[213] thus deepening the countries inherited structures of caste, class, and confession.

To his admirers, after his assassination on February 14, 2005, Ḥarīrī, however, became a larger-than-life national symbol for a Sunni–Christian–Druze entente and a symbol of Lebanese independence. His patriotic martyrdom led one commentator to rebaptize the late premier as "Fakhr ad-Dīn Ḥarīrī."[214] Indeed, there is, the obvious historical hiatus aside,[215] much to recommend a comparison between the strategies pursued by the two cosmopolitan builders of the nation. Both Ḥarīrī and Fakhr ad-Dīn began their careers as vassals whose increasingly independent policies and consolidation of local power proved worrisome to Istanbul and Damascus. Both Fakhr ad-Dīn and Ḥarīrī had tied their fates to

212 "No Sunnite (nor, for that matter Shia) oligarch ever succeeded in organizing a political party in any viable sense of the term, not even one confined to his sect (such as Pierre Jummayil's Phalanges). These closely interrelated failures are probably to be attributed to a fundamentally proprietary state of mind which regards leadership as a matter of ascription rather than achievement." Walīd Khālidī, *Conflict and Violence in Lebanon* (Cambridge, MA: Harvard's Center for International Affairs, 1979), 97.

213 See Guilain Denoeux and Robert Springborg, "Harīrī's Lebanon: Singapore of the Middle East or Sanaa of the Levant?" *Middle East Policy* 6.2 (1998): 158–173; and Hannes Baumann, *Citizen Hariri: Lebanon's Neoliberal Reconstruction* (London: Hurst, 2016).

214 "Fakhr ad-Dīn al-Harīrī," *an-Nahār*, March 21, 2005.

215 Fakhr ad-Dīn II was appointed *sanjakbey* of Sidon-Beirut in 1593 while Ḥarīrī began his first premiership almost exactly 400 years later in 1993.

their Western sponsors (Ferdinand I/Cosmo II, Jacques Chirac)[216] with whom they enjoyed personal friendships and engaged in business contracts. Both were cosmopolitan Muslim leaders in constant contact with the *Consul de France* in Lebanon who had successfully tried to win the favors of the respective grand vizir (Murād) and vice president (Khaddām). Both were constrained to pay "protection money" to the more threatening overlords in Damascus and Istanbul with generous presents while monopolizing political and economic power.[217] Most importantly, the ambitions of both for personal power and an autonomous Lebanon were brutally cut to size in the end. Both rulers were put in harm's way once they lost their supporting patrons when the Ottoman grand vizier and Syrian vice president, respectively, were removed from power. The competing trade networks of Damascus also played a role in the demise in both cases, even though the perpetrators of the Ḥarīrī assassination remain unknown, with no hard, ironclad evidence implicating the Syrian regime or Ḥizbullah to date despite conflicting allegations.

The analogies to the Ottoman past were drawn by those skeptical of Syrian suzerainty, which was referred to in critical editorials as the new Sublime Porte or *bāb al-'ālī.*[218] Pictures of the pilgrimages of the Lebanese classe politique as supplicants to Damascus or 'Anjar reinforced this perception. The order of old may be said to have been replicated in the post-Tā'if troika as Rafīq al-Ḥarīrī took over the role of the Sunni *wālī* of Sidon, residing as prime minister in Beirut while the other two major communal heads, the Shia speaker, and Maronite president, were granted relative autonomy over their own particular fiefdoms.

Yet no single individual has left a greater stamp on the socioeconomic policies and character of the postwar Lebanese state than Rafīq al-Ḥarīrī. Taken as a euphemism for globalization and (rentier) capitalism bearing

[216] Just as Ḥarīrī relied on Chirac's good offices, "*l'emir considérait le voisinage du Grand-Duc comme une garantie pour lui-meme.*" Shiblī, *Fakhreddine Ii Maan*, 33. In the postwar era, the historic legacy of French bidding for Lebanese contracts and concessions, mainly for construction ventures continued. One example was OGERO (Organisme de Gestion et d'Exploitation de l'ex-société Radio-Orient), a joint venture half-owned by the government, and the rest by France Telecom (40 percent) and Telecom Italia (10 percent).

[217] Formally, Sidon-Beirut was still subordinated to the eyalet of Tripoli ruled by the antagonistic Yūsuf Sayfa when Fakhr ad-Dīn II was appointed sanjakbey.

[218] Jubrān Tuwaynī, the author of this phrase and an outspoken critic of Syrian influence, was assassinated on December 12, 2005, months after his colleague at Nahār, Samīr Qaṣṣīr, fell victim to another car bomb. Thus, the two most vocal critics of Syrian hegemony were silenced. In his last recorded statements before his fatal return to Beirut, Tuwaynī told his wife that a "foreign secret service" explicitly assured him that it was safe for him to return to Lebanon. Sihām Tuwaynī cited by Rīm Ghazāl in *Daily Star*, December 13, 2005.

a distinct Saudi imprint, the repercussions of the Ḥarīrī era, and its effect on a secular, democratic state must be viewed with a jaundiced eye. After taking hold of the reigns of the supreme Sunni political office in 1993, Ḥarīrī was able to expand the sway and clout of the Sunni premiership to a degree hitherto unknown. His unprecedented political stature and seemingly boundless financial reserves, along with his Beirut-centric reconstruction plans, however, never enabled him to fully integrate the countries confessions, nor its marginalized areas. The legacy of this postwar period, particularly with respect to its ramifications for the secular state in discourse and practice, shall be assessed in the following chapter.

4 Socioeconomic Globalization and Secularism 1990–2005

The Merchant Prince: The Impact of the Postwar Ḥarīrī Era

If the rulers of a state are involved in commerce, both the government and commerce are ruined. Ibn Khaldūn as cited by the late Pierre Hilū

Are you going to argue that the Prime Minister should be a poor man?
Mr. Miracle[1]

Money has no value, it does not mean anything to me … I am not intent on holding power.[2]

Our family has been rich for four generations. One of our grandfathers was Lebanon's first prime minister. Fifteen years ago, this Ḥarīrī was nothing.[3] Mahmūd Shatīla

I am a simple Lebanese guy who made a fortune in Saudi Arabia. The more my wealth grew, the more I helped my country.[4] Rafīq al-Ḥarīrī

Woe to the nation that sees the victor's pomp as the perfection of virtue.
Woe to the nation whose politics is subtlety, whose statesman is a fox, whose philosophy is jugglery, whose industry is patching.
Jubrān Khalīl Jubrān[5]

I stretch out my hand to the moderate Christian who is closer to me than the extremist Sunni.
Rafīq al-Ḥarīrī shortly prior to his assassination, February 14, 2005[6]

1 Rafīq al-Ḥarīrī cited in *Time Magazine*, Febuary 3, 1993.
2 Rafīq al-Ḥarīrī in an interview with Ghassān Shirbil, *al-Hayāt*, February 13, 2006.
3 Cited in Peter Waldman, "Stepping Forward: Lebanese Premier Uses Own Resources to Spur Rebuilding of Beirut," *The Wall Street Journal*, March 29, 1994.
4 Waldman, "Stepping Forward."
5 Kahlil Gibran, *The Kahlil Gibran Reader: Inspirational Writings* (New York: Citadel Press, 2005), 33–34.
6 As cited by his son, PM Saad al-Ḥarīrī in Al Diyar, "Ana min madrasat al shahid Rafiq al Hariri", Beirut, November 3, 2018, 1.

It was in March 1984 during his first major appearance on the parquet of international diplomacy during the Lausanne Peace Conference that Rafīq al-Ḥarīrī uttered a remarkable repudiation of any future political ambitions:

> It is natural that some might conclude from what I have done and am doing in Sidon and Beirut that I have my eyes set on the Prime Ministry. Rest assured however that I will prove the opposite and will turn these rumors on their head. I shall work with a spirit of sincerity and service to Lebanon in order to contribute to the realization of the initiative of his Highness King Fahd who loves Lebanon and is intent to restore its complete sovereignty and rebuild the symbols of its civilization. When I have finished this work I shall be like one who contributed his share to a higher purpose not because I am Rafīq al-Harīrī who refuses to serve Lebanon or is shy about being Prime Minister, but for the simple reason that it is construction which is my vocation and not the practice of politics in Lebanon.[7]

In retrospect, this public disavowal made at the height of the civil war appears as an illustration of a measure of dissemblance that would not disappear during Ḥarīrī's subsequent tenure as Lebanon's prime minister. Today, the erstwhile Boulevard Ramlat al-Bayda has been rebaptized "Boulevard Rafīq Harīrī."[8] The latter served, intermittently, over a decade as Lebanon's premier, thus becoming the longest serving prime minister in Lebanon's history. In a country in which politics is personalized to a high degree, Rafīq al-Ḥarīrī's impact on the political character and future of the country looms large.

Rafīq al-Ḥarīrī was born in 1944 in Sidon as the son of a petty trader and landholder. After a fierce storm devastated a season's entire agricultural production, Ḥarīrī's father fell into bankruptcy and saw himself forced to sell all his lands and seek work as a laborer on the manorial estate of the notable Za'tarī family.[9] This harrowing, humiliating experience, Ḥarīrī later recounted, instilled in him a sense of the total absence of governmental aid and the necessity of radical self-reliance in a mercilessly Darwinian world.[10]

[7] Cited in Jurj Bashīr, *Umar' al-Tawā'if, min Junif ila Luzān* (Beirut: Wakālat al-Anbā' al-Markazāya, 1984), 248.

[8] A Boulevard Emile Lahhūd was opened with fanfare on September 1, 2002 by President Lahhūd himself.

[9] Emmanuel Bonne, *Vie Publique: Patronage et Clientèle* (Beirut: CERMOC, 1995), 48. I thank the Za'tarī family for corroborating this.

[10] Interview with Ghassān Shirbil, *al-Hayāt*, February 13, 2006. Ḥarīrī recounts first discovering (Mount) Lebanon during the summer while picking apples in farms in Kisirwān, Bisharrī, and Ihdin.

Having attained his baccalaureate certificate in Cairo, Ḥarīrī returned to Beirut to enroll in the Arab University, then a hotbed of Nasserist and leftist ideologies. While the adolescent Ḥarīrī's relationship to the communist movements on campus remains somewhat nebulous,[11] his role in distributing leftist and Arab nationalist leaflets during demonstrations, and even chanting slogans from the shoulders of his confidante, Fu'ād Siniora, to some was indicative of an aptitude to change political colors.[12]

Indeed, the initial streak of fervent Arab nationalism was to quickly dissipate in Saudi Arabia, a habitat less hospitable to blossoming Nasserist aspirations, which had suffered a sobering blow in 1967. Reflecting back on this period, Ḥarīrī contrasts the Nasserist bravado and anti-Saudi agitation to the low-key, more efficient development drive he experienced first hand in Saudi Arabia.[13] Sensing the impending sea change, Ḥarīrī terminated his studies at the Arab University and departed to the new Mecca of business opportunities. He first sought employment in the kingdom as a math teacher and accountant. Upon founding the Sidonist Contracting Company in 1971, Ḥarīrī became a subcontractor for Oger France and began his saga as a contractor of grand hotels, plush palaces, airports, and military installations in the kingdom.

Due to the exceptionally quick completion of the Messara Hotel in Tā'if in 1977 for an impending Islamic conference and his intimate personal contacts with then Crown Prince Fahd, Ḥarīrī was granted Saudi citizenship in 1979, a rare privilege. In 1983 he bought the Banque de la Méditerranée from French bankers, which became the second largest bank in Lebanon. Its chairman and general manager from 1983 to 1992, Fu'ād Siniora, would become Ḥarīrī's finance minister from 1992 onward and served as premier from 2005 to 2008. By 1992, Ḥarīrī's personal fortune was estimated at US$4–5 billion. These assets would swell further during the construction and real-estate tycoon's subsequent tenure as Lebanon's premier. In 2003, Ḥarīrī's Saudi Oger

11 Ḥarīrī has denied joining any parties, communist or other, but confirmed his joint activism with Muhsin Ibrāhīm and his participation in demonstrations protesting the split of Syria and Egypt on the Arab University campus. Interview with Ghassān Shirbil, *al-Hayāt*, February 13, 2006.

12 Sa'd Mihyū (Saad Mehio), "Ḥarīrī: A Globetrotter Who Wants to Live History," *Daily Star*, December 12, 2002. Some of Ḥarīrī's advisors have underwent conversion from (atheistic) communism to (Saudi-sponsored) capitalism.

13 Interview with Ghassān Shirbil, *al-Hayāt*, February 13, 2006.

purchased 11 percent of the largest Arab financial institution, the Arab Bank, thereby circumventing Jordanian laws that limit ownership of any single person to 5 percent.[14]

The blurry lines between business, politics, and philanthropy have intersected and overlapped throughout Mr. Ḥarīrī's career. Social and political concerns motivated the establishment of the Islamic Foundation for Culture and Education in Sidon in 1979, whose declared goal was to put an end to the "deprivation Southern Lebanon has suffered."[15] During the Israeli invasion of 1982 approximately 40 percent of Sidon was completely destroyed, at which point Ḥarīrī – who by 1984 was acting in his capacity as the semiofficial Saudi representative to Lebanon[16] – generously financed, with undisclosed Saudi backing, the reconstruction of basic infrastructure of about 3,500 houses. To this end, a special branch of Oger Liban was founded and commissioned by the Ḥarırı Foundation to clear the debris and rebuild part of the devastated sections of Sidon and Beirut.[17] At this initial stage in 1983, even one of his fiercest subsequent opponents, Salīm al-Huss, touted Ḥarīrī's philanthropy as "manna in the desert," thus expressing the popular aura the upstart billionaire benefactor had gained as the aspired savior of a Lebanon ravaged by a heinous war. In fact, Ḥarīrī had tried to insert himself as a player in the civil war early on, financing the militia on different sides, whether it be the Lebanese forces, Ussāma Sa'd, or Janbulāt's PSP.[18] Given the need to establish an independent Sunni base, it is not

14 "Harīrī Buys 11 Percent Stake in Arab Bank," *an-Nahār*, December 3, 2003. Forbes in 2006 estimated the combined wealth of Ḥarīrī's second wife and six out of seven children at US$15.7 billion. A controversy was stirred in Lebanon due to the special exemption of this fortune from the usual Lebanese inheritance tax of 10 percent, depriving the state of US$2 billion.

15 Renamed as the Rafīq Baha ad-Dīn al-Ḥarīrī Foundation, it was built on a million-square-meter plot of land in Kfar-Falus, a small town in the vicinity of Saida, Ḥarīrī invested US$300 million to build a medical, educational complex, which was devastated by an Israeli raid in 1985. Ḥarīrī's Oger was the company charged with the costly reconstruction of Beirut after 1982. Bonne, *Vie Publique*, 49.

16 After the April 1984 Iranian assault on the Saudi Embassy in Beirut, the Saudis decided to recall their ambassador and in his stead commissioned Ḥarīrī as the chief Saudi liaison to Lebanon. See al-'Abd, *Lubnān wa al-Tā'if*, 181–182. Ḥarīrī brushed off claims of dual loyalty. "King Fahd doesn't need a man in Lebanon. Saudi Arabia doesn't have a policy of expansion or of trying to be influential in Lebanon. He is my friend. But I'm not here on a Saudi mission." "Mr. Miracle," *Time Magazine*, February 3, 1993. Ḥarīrī's first diplomatic venture on behalf of Saudi Arabia was to facilitate the (short-lived) trilateral agreement between Hobeika, Birrī, and Janbulāt, which was received with some resentment by Sunnis.

17 Rieger, *Rentiers*, 303.

18 Jurj Ḥāwī repeated the allegations that Ḥarīrī has never denied: "It is known that Ḥarīrī provided aid to both sides ... and he was generous to both sides. He paid the Lebanese

surprising that the administrative staff and beneficiaries of the Ḥarīrī Foundation were largely members of the premier's confession. Moreover, funding was markedly Beirut-centric (over 90 percent) and not invariably need-based, further feeding suspicions of ulterior, political, and electoral motives.[19]

In principle, a man of vast means would appear to be the ideal candidate to cast off the shackles of the inherited system of confessional patronage. Arguably extensive philanthropic assistance, the distribution of which was to be devoid of confessional criteria, was predisposed to function as a fulcrum for national integration. In practice, the policies pursued and public gestures made by Ḥarīrī and his Foundation to win support from his Sunni constituency base in Sidon and Beirut and please his patrons in Saudi Arabia, unfortunately often followed the old sinews of confessionalism and clientelism.[20]

The Ḥarīrī Foundation quickly established itself as the leading educational philanthropy in the country in the near anarchic period after 1983. Before the cut-back of the university scholarship program in 1990 and its termination upon the inauguration of Ḥarīrī as prime minister in 1993, the Ḥarīrī Foundation provided approximately 44 percent of all university scholarships in Lebanon.[21] Despite the evident effort to win

Forces and the Progressive Socialist Party." Jurj Hāwī, *Yatathakar* (Beirut: Dār al-Nahār, 2005), 118. Allegations of Ḥarīrī's financing of Christian and Muslim Lebanese militias were made by former business patner Roger Tamraz in 1997 and by Najāh Wakīm, *al-'Ayād al-Sawdā* (Beirut: Dār al-Adab, 1998), 64 and Bonne, *Vie Publique*, 25. MTV was prevented from airing an interview with Johnny 'Abdu, the Paris-based former head of the Lebanese secret service and confidante of Ḥarīrī. Katrin Nesemann, *Medienpolitik Im Libanon* (Hamburg: Deutsches Orient Institut, 2001), 91. Likewise, Robert Hātim's *From Israel to Damascus* was banned in Lebanon as much on account of its explosive political revelations as due to its listings of sexual escapades of the Lebanese elite.

19 A total of 52 percent of those surveyed by Hilāl Khashshān stated that their parents would have been able to cover their college expenses with relative ease. Of those polled in the same study, 89 percent held that the foundation's primary motivation was political, not academic, while 94 percent see Mr. Ḥarīrī simply acting as a coordinator for foreign financial interests, most likely an oblique reference to Saudi Arabia, which hired Ḥarīrī as its emissary in Lebanon in 1979. Hilāl Khashshān, "How Grantees Relate to Grantor: A Study on a Lebanese College Scholarship Foundation," *Research in Higher Education* 33.2 (1992): 268.

20 See S. N. Eisenstadt and L. Roniger, eds., *Patrons: Clients and Friends: Interpersonal Relations of Trust in Society* (Cambridge: Cambridge University Press, 1984). Ernest Gellner and John Waterbury, *Patrons and Clients in Mediterranean Societies* (London: Duckworth, 1977).

21 After the foundation folded its scholarship program, it concentrated its remaining activities on securing international aid. In 1999 Ḥarīrī erected another network of philanthropy, the "Alliance for Social Development" and the Ḥarīrī Center. Most of the scholarships were not grants but interest-free student loans, the repayment of which is used to finance the activities of the Ḥarīrī foundation today. The foundation

the support and loyalty of his core confessional constituency, the Sunni recipients of Ḥarīrī loans expressed the greatest dissatisfaction with the foundation, while the smaller number of Druze and Orthodox recipients displayed greater degrees of gratitude. With a view to the foundation's potential to advance national integration, an in-depth study by Khashshān finds that the majority of students admit to have received aid solely due to the aid and mediation of militia leaders and politicians.[22] Nonetheless, the Ḥarīrī Foundation did in fact break part of the old mold of the patron–client relationship by establishing English-speaking schools and supporting individual students enrolled at heterogeneous universities, such as the AUB, rather than traditional, strictly Sunni educational institutions. The oldest of the latter in Lebanon was the century-old Maqāsid Foundation, of which Ḥarīrī himself had been a beneficiary in his youth in Sidon. The Maqāsid was most emblematic of the old nexus of patronage, prestige, and piety that Ḥarīrī sought to emulate and remold, albeit within a more modern, more personalized, and more American-oriented philanthropic network of his own.[23] The erosion of the Salām family's control over the oldest Sunni educational philanthropy organization in Lebanon after Ḥarīrī's gradual buyout heralded this sea change and the passing of the torch to the new (super) *Zaʿīm*.[24]

Having thus launched his career as a benefactor politician in the provincial, impoverished, and deeply conservative town of Sidon, Ḥarīrī achieved an unusual feat in twentieth-century Lebanon. With no prior notable pedigree (*nasab*) and concomitant base constituency to rely on, he quickly assumed, and held on to, the position of the paramount Sunni *zaʿīm* in Lebanon.

To better understand the nature of the sudden, comet-like ascent of Ḥarīrī we must take a step back and place it within a larger (time-)frame

encouraged its former beneficiaries – the number of which is put at 32,000 – to repay the loans "as a matter of courtesy and obligation."

22 Khashshān, "How Grantees Relate to Grantor," 272. The majority (64.5 percent) stated they would not want to support the Foundation in the future.

23 English has replaced Arabic as the language of instruction in the sciences in the Maqāsid high schools, which were established by disciples of the Egyptian reformer Muhammad ʿAbdūh in 1885.

24 The Maqāsid was teetering on the brink of bankruptcy and was taken over by Premier Rafīq al-Ḥarīrī, after briefly seeing itself forced to close its doors due to insolvency in June of 2003. Ḥarīrī had been a long-time contributor to the Maqāsid, having donated the land for the Husām ad-Dīn Ḥarīrī High School. By 2003, he was the society's main financier and preeminent patron. For the history of the Maqāsid and the role of the Salām family, see Michael Johnson, *Class and Client in Beirut: The Sunni Muslim Community and the Lebanese State 1840–1985*, vol. 28 (New York: Ithaca Press, 1986); "Factional Politics in Lebanon: The case of the 'Islamic Society of Benevolent Intentions' (Al-Maqāsid) in Beirut," *Middle Eastern Studies* 14 (1978): 56–75.

and regional context. The starting point for Ḥarīrī's career can most properly be placed in the aftermath of the assassination of King Faysal in 1975 and the subsequent rise of the Fahd faction of the Saudi royal family. It was this party, headed by then Crown Prince Fahd, which took Ḥarīrī under its wings in lieu of the previous Saudi representatives to Lebanon, Khālid Khidr Āghā and General ʻAlī Shāʻir, who were subsequently sidelined. Shāʻir briefly served as Saudi ambassador in Beirut but was recalled to serve as minister of information immediately after the mysterious assassination in Beirut of the leading Saudi leftist dissident Nāsir al-Said in 1979.[25] As the Saudi envoy in Lebanon, Ḥarīrī facilitated the (short-lived) trilateral agreement in 1984 between Hubayqa, Birrī, and Janbulāt, a mediation that was received with some resentment by the Sunni parties.

Prior to Ḥarīrī, the first major business agent of the Saudi royal family to ascend to the (Sunni) summit of Lebanese politics and serve as prime minister in 1951 and 1964–1965 had been Hājj Husayn ʻUwaynī.[26] Like Ḥarīrī, ʻUwaynī was known to have continued his business activities while serving as finance minister and prime minister, a position which has had its prerogatives significantly expanded by the 1990 Tāi'f Accord. Incidentally, Ḥarīrī's business background initially was generally viewed as an asset rather than a handicap by the majority of Lebanese who pinned their hopes on Rafīq al-Ḥarīrī's record of entrepreneurship upon his inauguration in 1992. The arrival of the successful construction tycoon was to bring a fresh breeze of economic activity that might sweep away the war-hardened sediments of sectarianism of the *ancien régime*. Yet, Ḥarīrī's focus on eye-catching reconstruction and economic development left the confessional infrastructure in place, reinforced by his political ambition and strategic alliance with Wahabi Saudi Arabia.[27] Networks of patronage and elite nepotism proliferated once again, often enough among the premier's own associates.[28] The implications of the

[25] René Naba, *Rafīq Harīrī: Un homme d'Affaires Premier Ministre* (Paris : L'Harmattan, 1999), 18. Also see the interview with Khālid Khidr āghā, *Al Jazeera: Ziyārat Khāssa*," December, 2004. It should be noted that Ḥarīrī's – as well as Walīd Ibn Talāl's – ties with the Amīr Sultān in particular remained strained.

[26] See Mihyū, "Harīrī." Ḥarīrī would blur the private/public distinction even more by appointing a coterie of former private associates. Similar practices were not without precedent, as President Sarkis appointed Farīd Rufa'il as minister of finance without forcing the latter to abdicate his private banking position.

[27] Najīb Hawrānī questioned whether the changes in property relations wrought by reconstruction in fact created the "rational economic sphere" predicted by market. See Najīb B. Hawrānī, "Capitalists in conflict: A Political Economy of the Life, Death and Rebirth of Beirut," PhD dissertation, New York University, 2005, 4.

[28] Such as former ministers Hubayka, Demarjian, Barsomian, and Seniora. Most of the court cases raised against the aforementioned ministers during the Huss regime

importation of the Saudi political template – and its grafting onto the Lebanese system – is further discussed toward the end of this chapter. At this point we should merely note that the propulsion of Ḥarīrī and a whole coterie of other prominent Lebanese politicians to the upper echelons of financial and political power is directly traceable to the vast oil-rentier revenues generated in Saudi Arabia and the Gulf States from the 1970s onward.[29] These new economic fortunes were parleyed into political positions that, in turn, were leveraged overtly and covertly to multiply wealth.[30] Ḥarīrī's own Saudi Oger cooperation – subsequently run by his son Sa'd, who would later accede the post of premier – is but a further illustration of these persistent patterns of nepotism at the nexus of financial and political capital.[31] It is also well worth recalling that these kinship loyalties and patriarchal family nuclei have been singled out by some sociologists as the structural obstacles to secularization and the formation of a civil society in the Arab world.[32] There can be little doubt that in the case of Lebanon, the paramount dominance of family-based politico-economic interests, which, with rare exceptions,[33] usually carry a distinct confessional identity, have stymied the growth of a rational, "Weberian" bureaucracy, business culture, and civil society. The numbers speak for themselves: In 1975, only 10 percent of industrial

(1998–2000) were dismissed after Ḥarīrī regained power in October 2000. One of the most notorious protégés of Ḥarīrī is the runaway former governor of Mount Lebanon, Suhayl Yamūt, who was indicted on charges of embezzlement, kickbacks, and dereliction of duty during the 1999 anti-corruption campaign and again in 2004. Yamūt sought exile in Brazil as a manager of Ḥarīrī's South America portfolio. "Ex-Mount Lebanon Governor Indicted as Embezzler," *an-Nahār,* February 5, 2004. Another employee accused of mass graft in the finance ministry in 1996, Rif'at Sulaymān, was shot and killed together with his associate by a security patrol in an unauthorized raid. Sulaymān, was an associate of then defense minister, Muhsin Dallūl – a business ally and relative of Ḥarīrī. The inquiry into the forgery and stealing of funds in the finance ministry was closed after the elimination of the prime suspect.

29 Among the prominent Lebanese politicians who made their money in Saudi Arabia we find entrepreneurs such as Deputy Premier 'Isām Fāris, Ḥarīrī contender, Fu'ād Makhzūmī, and the late presidential candidate, Nasīb Lahhūd, who terminated his business activities upon entering Lebanese politics.

30 Candidates who want to enter prospective electoral coalitions sponsored by the political lords are known to pay at least several hundred thousand dollars in "entry fees."

31 Saudi Oger was forced to declare bankruptcy in July 2017.

32 See Hishām Sharābī, *Neopatriarchy: Theory of Distorted Change in Arab Society* (New York: Oxford University Press, 1988) and his former Georgetown colleague Halīm Barakāt, *The Arab World: Society, Culture* (Berkeley: University of California Press, 1993).

33 Minister Marwān Hamāda is often cited as an individual whose identity is, by dint of his Druze father, Christian mother, and Muslim and Jewish grandparent, eminently trans-sectarian. Despite his remarkably heterogeneous pedigree and personal aversion to sectarianisms, Hamāda's political loyalty has never veered from the constantly shifting dictates of his patron at the PSP, Druze strongman, Walīd Janbulāt.

firms were intersectarian in ownership.[34] Today, the overwhelming majority, that is to say over 90 percent of all enterprises in Lebanon, continue to remain family owned or controlled.[35]

Family Farms and the Patronization of Privatization after 1990

Shaykh Butrus is infringing on Lebanon's free-wheeling economic system.

Are investors prohibited from making profits in Lebanon?

Prime Minister Harīrī in Parliament responding to allegations of graft in wake of the debate on the cellular scandal, which ended on Febuary 24, 2004 due to a lack of quorum.

If the shepherd is a wolf, who will protect the sheep?

Former Speaker of Parliament Husaynī
citing the Imām 'Alī in response[36]

Rafīq al-Ḥarīrī has usually been compared to his most prominent predecessor, Riyād al-Sulh. On occasion, he has also been likened to the late President Fu'ād Shihāb as a paternalistic leader and builder of a new "state project" in Lebanon.[37]

Yet, General Shihāb's militarist étatism, reluctance to hold on to power and indefatigable, albeit ultimately quixotic, fight against the scourge of monopolization[38] share little in common with the Berlusconi-like comportment of a billionaire businessman *cum* premier who has overseen the extension of local and foreign monopolies over vast sectors of the economy. Indeed, Henri Fir'awn's or Michel Shīḥā's (guarded) confidence in the *laissez-faire, laissez-passer* economic liberalism of a "*république marchande*" seems to resemble Ḥarīrī's disposition and political philosophy more closely.[39] Upon closer scrutiny, Shīḥā's economic liberalism was tempered by his predeliction for a productive, rather than a mere rentier,

[34] See Hāshim, *Ilghā al-Tā'fī ya al-Sīyāsīya,* 97.

[35] According to one study, Lebanese family-owned businesses on average show a far greater rate of success. Interview with Marwān 'Assaf, chairman of the advisory board of the Institute of Family and Entrepreneurial Business at Lebanese American University's School of Business. Published in *Daily Star,* April 23, 2004.

[36] "Jalsa Majlis al Nuwwab," An-Nahar (Beirut), February 25, 2004, 2.

[37] See, for instance, Radwān as-Sayyid, "Mashrū'a Dawla," *Al-Mustaqbal,* February 13, 2007.

[38] See Fuad Shihāb, "Bayyān 'Uzūf Fu'ād Shihāb," *an-Nahār,* reprinted on March 11, 2004.

[39] "*Toute la politique économique de ce pays doit être orientée vers la liberté car s'il y a un lieu au monde où la formule des physiocrates s'impose encore, c'est bien ici.*" Shīḥā, *Politique Intérieure,* 64.

economy and by his keen alertness to the potential social dangers a completely unregulated free market economy might invite.[40] Shīḥā warned that man's insatiable pecuniary greed might "buy silences"[41] and corrupt what he viewed as an essentially "spiritual" social contract. For Shīḥā, the health of the economy was in fact secondary to the nation's moral probity. The latter was indispensable for Lebanon to become a "*corps compact*," free of all personal favoritisms.

If this lofty ideal was rarely reflected by political reality in Shīḥā's own day, the post-1990 era rendered what remained of the strong Chehabist state a shell, shifting power to visible and invisible private hands. This shift followed a pattern of oligarchic "privatization," or rather patronization, not unlike the one set by the Sham'ūn regime (1952–1958).[42] Indeed, instances of family favoritism under previous regimes in Lebanon's post-independence history are legion; the reigns of presidents Bishāra al-Khūrī, Camille Sham'ūn, and Sulaymān Franjīya are often highlighted as periods particularly stained by corruption and cronyism. Even Shihāb stood accused of having appeased the old *zu'amā'*, who he had initially vowed to dethrone, by striking alliances with the likes of Kamāl Janbulāt and Pierre Jummayil.[43] What distinguished the 1990s then was less a change in practice of the politics of the (neo)*zu'āma* than its continuation, and possible aggravation, under the promulgation of a novel discourse, namely that of privatization.

Privatization was first announced as an official Lebanese government policy designed to attract foreign direct investment under the short-lived premiership of 'Umar Karāmī on November 2, 1992.[44] After Karāmī was forced to tender his resignation in wake of a grave financial and currency crisis,[45] then President 'Ilyās Harāwī appointed Ḥarīrī as the new prime

[40] "*Tirons de notre sol tous ce qu'il peut donner avant de recourir a l'étranger. Devenous des producteurs au lieu d'être des intermediares.*" Michel Shīḥā, "Des Résolutions! Des Actes!" *Le Reveil,* September 1, 1921.

[41] Michel Shīḥā's, "Le Règne de l'Argent" cited in *Politique Intérieure*, 187.

[42] The degree to which Lebanon may be said to constitute a *laissez-faire* economy is very much in the eye of the beholder. The movement of labor and capital has been relatively unrestricted in Lebanon since the 1948 official decree authorizing a free foreign exchange market. Gates, however, points out that the Beirut elite's slogans of *laissez-faire* in Lebanon never advanced competition in the internal markets. Such hypocrisy is of course common to oligopolies around the Middle East and indeed the globe. Gates, *The Merchant Republic*, 96 and Gaspard, *A Political Economy of Lebanon*, 143.

[43] Bishāra, *Lebanon*, 166.

[44] 'Umar Karāmī was briefly reappointed as prime minister on September 20, 2004 and resigned on April 19, 2005 following the protests triggered by the Ḥarīrī assassination.

[45] According to Mustafā Zaryān, a Ḥarīrī employee for sixteen years and director of one of his banks, Ḥarīrī made the decision to sell massive amounts of dollars for three months to overcome a wave of currency speculation. Waldman, "Stepping Forward."

minister in 1993.[46] The Ḥarīrī government quickly jumped on the privatization bandwagon, committing the country to the usual *quid pro quo* arrangements with international lenders and embarking on socially painful structural adjustment programs, which entailed a freezing of government wages, a lowering of private and corporate income taxes from a maximum of 50 percent to a flat 10 percent, and a commitment to privatize key national services and sell off government lands.[47]

Ideally, so the theory went, privatization, a blanket term that in Lebanon, as elsewhere, encompassed a wide gamut of different arrangements,[48] was to ensure that key government assets would not longer be "farmland" (*mazrʿā*) to be distributed among supporters, or as rewards for personal loyalty and support in elections. As such, privatization, besides reducing costs for vital utilities by increasing competition and encouraging allocative efficiency in the economy, was to dismantle the Lebanese patronage system and encourage not only a more transparent, but also a more secular system of governance, in so far that a "rational" business ethos was to supplant the confessional pork barreling.

What transpired in actual fact, and in violation of the stated laws,[49] was that a clique of businessmen, their affiliated companies, and (former) militiamen, all swearing fealty to Damascus, gained control of the state apparatus and key distributive networks.[50] This proliferation of patronage

[46] Harāwī assumed the presidency after the assassination of Rene Mu'awwad with whom Ḥarīrī had but lukewarm relations. After Muʿawwad's death, Ḥarīrī bestowed a villa to Harāwī in lieu of the presidential palace at Baʿbada, which was occupied by General ʿAwn. Harāwī's term was extended in 1996 upon the lobbying of Ḥarīrī to amend the constitution, despite the fierce opposition of the Maronite patriarch, Nasīb Lahhūd, ʿUmar Karāmī, and others. President Lahhūd was nonetheless elected as president on October 15, 1998 after the parliament bowed to Syrian pressure to amend Article 49 of the constitution, which hitherto had barred members of the army from running for the highest office.

[47] The Huss government and then minister of finance Jurj Qurm increased the maximum individual and corporate tax rates. Parliament also approved a new pay scale for public employees. Ilyās Abū Rizq, the outspoken head of the General Labour Confederation found himself at loggerheads with the Huss government after his election to the presidency of the NSSF (National Social Fund for Retirement) was vetoed by major business leaders. Sāmī Barūdī, "Continuity in Economic Policy in Postwar Lebanon: The Record of the Harīrī and Huss Government Examined 1992–2000," *Arab Studies Quarterly* 24, 1 (2002); 8.

[48] On May 31, 2000 Prime Minister Huss and President Lahhūd passed the Privitization Law 228, which ratified the procedures for privatization and charged the Higher Privatization Council as the principal coordinating agency.

[49] The Privatization Law of May 31, 2000 signed by presidents Huss and Lahhūd contained numerous provisions to prevent monopolies and provide for independent monitoring mechanisms.

[50] Such as the Ḥarīrī-controlled Higher Council for Privatization, which was created on May 30, 2000 (in accordance with Law 228 signed by Huss and Lahhūd) to oversee the sale of monopolized electricity, water, and communications networks.

networks contributed to a bloated bureaucracy that expanded together with the ballooning national debt. Meanwhile, the state as a provider of public goods and services shrank, unable to pay even the pensions of its own employees or sustain the provision of electricity, while seeing itself forced to levy new regressive consumer (VAT) taxes (in the continued absence of any capital gains taxes).[51]

Thus, along with the ever-widening networks surrounding the Lebanese political lords, the number of state employees soared from 75,000 in 1975 to 175,000 in 2000.[52] This nominal expansion of the bureaucracy provides scarce indication of a fortified state, but rather came as the result of the exigencies and competing demands of patronage as administered by the reigning troika.[53] To take one example, the continuous nominal rise of school teachers says nothing about a *qualitative* improvement of state education, let alone about the deconfessionalization and (secular) integration of the hodgepodge of current curricula, as the appointments of teachers and administrators are habitually made along strict confessional lines. A similar *quid pro quo* pattern of appointments could be observed in the ministries of the interior (the fiefdom of Michel and ʻIlyās Murr from 1992), finance (Ḥarīrī and Seniora), the displaced (Janbulāt), and electricity (Hubayka and Birrī).

The immediate economic upshot was that the same Lebanon that suffers from a crippling debt also has more billionaires in the highest executive rank of its government than most countries. Throughout much of the 1990s, at least three members of the highest governing body, the Council of Ministers, were also members of the elite club of billionaires; a portion of their fortune made on home turf and while in office. Affiliates of the regime, ministers, and their kin as well have lined their pockets and become ostentatious multimillionaires.

[51] One of many symptoms is the bankruptcy of the NSSF, which announced its inability to subsidize medical care and maternity costs due to the government's failure to pay its debts of LL270 billion. *Daily Star*, July 16, 2003. Electricité du Liban has distributed concessions in Jubayl, Alay, and Zahla and has drained at least US$300 million per annum.

[52] Government-sector employment rose from 13.6 percent in 1997 to 15.3 percent in 2001. See Salīm Naṣr, "The New Social Map," in *Lebanon in Limbo*, eds., Theodor Hanf and Nawāf Salām (Beirut: Nomos Verlag, 2003), 153. It should be pointed out that official government policy, as formulated in the "reform paper" of 1997, was designed to implement a strict hiring freeze. See Barūdī, "Continuity in Economic Policy in Postwar Lebanon," 3. From 2001 to 2005, Lebanon was continually ranked first on the Fraser Institute's "Index of Economic Freedoms in the Arab World," see page 12 of www.fraserinstitute.org/sites/default/files/economic-freedom-of-the-arab-world-2018.pdf, last accessed on February 4, 2018.

[53] Premiers Ḥarīrī and Huss, speaker of parliament Birrī, and presidents Harāwī and Lahhūd.

The ritualistic professions of allegiance to the Washington Consensus notwithstanding, and despite the declared commitment to accountability (*muhāsaba*) and transparency (*shaffāfīya*), "privatization" (*khasskhassa*) in Lebanon so far has seemed more like an euphemism for a Lebanese reenactment of post-Soviet "Red Capitalism" under Boris Yeltsin, or, perhaps more accurately, a mimicry of entrenched habits of oligarchic Saudi clientelism (*zabūnīya/zabā'inīya*).

To be sure, the World Bank and International Monetary Fund (IMF) have repeatedly bewailed the absence of real privatization in Lebanon, a complaint that rings true inasmuch as the government has been dragging its feet and has stalled at auctioning off vital sectors such as electricity, telecommunications, or the national airline, MEA. On the other hand, the current system of monopolistic clientelism itself may be characterized as a form of privatization of state revenue. One astute commentator was thus led to remark that "government donations through the Ministry of Social Affairs can also be considered 'privatized' since they are restricted to confessional and politically linked NGOs [and their lords] which receive more than $50 million annually."[54] Far larger public funds are indirectly channeled to private institutions by ways of payments and subsidies administered by the ministry of social affairs, the powerful Sûreté Génerale, and the army.[55]

Further examples abound as contractual terms of tenders involving public, private, and semiprivate utilities were tailored so as to end up in the possession of affiliates or relatives of the political lords. Case in point was the distribution of state licenses to waste-management companies and two highly profitable cellular companies, one of which was owned by the son-in-law of Premier Ḥarīrī, the other by his close ally, Tripoli minister Najīb Miqātī, who would later serve as premier, and high-ranking Syrian officials, including Jamāl Khaddām and former chief-of-staff, Hikmat Shihābī.[56]

54 Jawād al-'Adra, "Neither Privatization nor Liquidation," *Ii-Monthly*, February 8, 2003.

55 See Kamāl Ḥamdān, "Le Social dans la Reconstruction du Liban," *Maghreb-Machrek* 169 (2000): 70–79.

56 Najīb Miqātī is rumored to have commenced his career – together with his brother Tāhā and their company Investcom – as an internationally active business front for the Assads, while Khaddām, Kana'ān, and Shihābī were Ḥarīrī's support base in Syria. See *Daily Star*, October 12, 2003. In 2001, the Ḥarīrī government cancelled the contract with the firms, making the Lebanese state liable to a US$266 million penalty to be paid to Dallūl and the Miqātī family's Libancell and Cellis after a 2003 verdict. After a tainted first tender (again won by the same duopoly), the government retrieved the management of the sector from the companies and since garnered over US$70 million per month after signing another buy, operate, transfer contract with a Kuwaiti and a German firm. The cumulative profits of the duopoly are estimated at over US$10 billion. Currently, the cellular revenues of US$1.3 billion go directly to the government.

Yet, crony capitalism and "patronized privatization" was by no means confined to the affiliates of the Sunni premier. Licenses for Lebanon's stone quarries were granted to Orthodox interior ministers Michel and Ilyās al-Murr (the son-in-law of President Lahhūd), exclusive contracts for the import of petroleum were awarded to Maronite president Harāwī's sons, those for the registration of car licenses were given to the son of his successor President Lahhūd, while the coveted rights to build the coastal highway to the south were surrendered to Geneco, owned by the prime minister's brothers Walīd and Shafiq Ḥarīrī, a Syrian company partly owned by the Khaddām family, and a company owned by Randa Birrī, the wife of the speaker of parliament.[57] The latter was given full control over the Council of the South (*Majlis al-Janūb*).[58] Former militia leaders Walīd Janbulāt and Elie Hobeika were assigned ministerial portfolios for the displaced and electricity, respectively. In his capacity as the minister of the displaced, Janbulāt established himself as a figure of Christian–Druze reconciliation in the war-torn Shūf. He is also, however, alleged to have diverted some of the funds earmarked for the ca. 600,000 displaced in the civil war to pay off the Shia families who had occupied the squatters in the Beirut central district and to cover part of the expenses for Beirut's costly new Camille Sham'ūn sports stadium, thus coming to the aid of Solidere, a private company.[59]

President Lahhūd may well have assumed the presidency in 1998 on an "anti-corruption" platform, yet, as *The Economist* quipped, "if he stuck to his pledge [to sever the arms of graft] … no civil servant or politician would be able to applaud his diligence."[60] Tellingly, no senior Lebanese politician had to renounce his position on account of corruption since the creation of the *Grand Liban,* and only one head of state, Amīn Jummayil, was ever charged by parliament with wrongdoing, although this decision was inconsequential as it came long after his tenure and was never enacted. Law no. 13, which theoretically permits the impeachment and trial of presidents and ministers thus remains a perfunctory gesture of

[57] See Economist Intelligence Unit, "Country Report: Lebanon – 3rd Quarter," 1996, 19. The southern highway was allegedly overpriced by over US$100 million.

[58] Also referred to in jest by some Lebanese as *Majlis al-Juyūb*, or the "Council of the Pockets."

[59] The Ḥarīrī camp wanted to name the stadium after Rafīq al-Ḥarīrī but failed to win broader support. For the Shia and Sunni establishment's reaction to this misappropriation see Perthes, *Der Libanon Nach Dem Buergerkrieg,* 50ff, 87ff. The stadium – al-Madīna al-Riyādīya – was renamed on April 10, 2007 after Camille Sham'ūn.

[60] "Silent clapping, an investigation into political corruption may not be all it seems to be," *The Economist* 352, August 12, 1999, 37, www.economist.com/international/1999/08/12/silent-clapping, last accessed February 6, 2019.

window dressing.[61] In addition, the Lebanese parliament even went so far as to pass a theoretically even more sweeping law (no. 154) against illegitimate enrichment (*Qānun al-Ithrā' ghayr al-mashrū'*) on December 27, 1999.[62] Again, these high principles remained ink on paper, as not a single case has been prosecuted, in spite of the fact that expenditures of state funds by political lords have reached historic highs together with the number of cabinet ministers, which , in wake of the Tā'if Accord, was raised to an unprecedented number of thirty ministers.

The ubiquity of cronyism and corruption in the postwar era has not dissuaded opposition politicians, such as former Premier Salīm al-Huss and former minister of finance Jurj Qurm, from laying the principal blame for Lebanon's crippling debt at the doorsteps of Premier Ḥarīrī. A closer examination, however, reveals that the premier's portfolios, while no doubt substantial, cannot solely be held responsible for the entire debt crisis; the latter rather must be attributed the larger structure underlying Lebanon's postwar evolution.

To be sure, Ḥarīrī undoubtedly was the chief architect of Lebanon's postwar economic and reconstruction policy, as evidenced most conspicuously by the premier's direct control over the prime real estate of central Beirut via the Council for Development and Reconstruction (CDR). Ironically, it was then Prime Minister Huss who presided over the CDR's creation in 1977 under Decree Law no. 5, which stipulated that the CDR was to be held accountable solely to the prime minister. The underlying premise of these prerogatives was that the government would give credits and infrastructure for private enterprises directly and rapidly, bypassing the notorious red tape that usually stymies the bureaucratic process in Lebanon, as elsewhere.[63]

After the guns fell silent, Ḥarīrī thus was able to adroitly take advantage of the legal framework of the CDR to fund the infrastructure needed for the private holding established for the Beirut central district, Solidere,[64] which in turn was exempted from paying property taxes to

[61] Muhammad Farīd Matar, "Hawl al-Fasād wa Subul Mukāfahatiha," in *Khayarāt Lilubnān* (Beirut: an-Nahār, 2004). Law no. 666 of 1995 extended a general amnesty for war crimes committed between 1975 and 1990 and pardoned all crimes related to drugs.

[62] The NGO Nahwa al-muwātinīya launched a campaign to remove the legal loopholes within the law impeding prosecution.

[63] Cited in Tom Najm, *The Collapse and Reconstruction of Lebanon* (Durham: Center for Middle Eastern and Islamic Studies, 1998), 40.

[64] The name denotes the French acronym for the "Lebanese Company for the Development and Reconstruction of Beirut Central District." See www.solidere.com, last accessed on March 16, 2007.

the state.[65] The ambitious plan for the reconstruction and economic salvation of Lebanon, as outlined in the CDR Horizon 2000 program, embraced what could be seen as mutually contradictory targets. Drafted and published in cooperation with the US construction behemouth Bechtel and the Lebanese counterpart Dār al-Handasa in 1991,[66] the plan, on the one hand, advertised reconstruction to serve private interest and profits. On the other hand, the same plan was to be a catalyst for the recovery of essential public services, "supporting an economic and social environment in which the private sector, and all Lebanese, may grasp recovery and development opportunities."[67] The implicit hazy line between private and public spheres fades even more when the same report cautions that, while Horizon 2000 gives "a well defined public recovery program, it allows the private sector to evolve at will."[68]

The originally envisaged role assigned to the CDR as a supervising agency for the implementation of individual reconstruction projects was to be subsumed under the growth of a more robust and lean public sector. In fact, the CDR subverted the latter by serving to attract a whole coterie of international consultants and construction companies, which, due to the unique legal prerogatives assigned to the premier, in fact managed to circumvent state control.[69] They illuminate the political ambiguities and economic costs of the parallel business enterprise and murky patronage networks that Ḥarīrī established within the state proper. When a 157-page government report was published in April 1999 under the Huss regime, it corroborated the amount embezzled by the CDR at US$600 million.[70] A UN commissioned report released in January 2001 revealed that only a meager 2.4 percent of the US$6 billion worth of projects contracted by the CDR were offered in free competition on the open market. The bulk of the contracts were closed in backroom deals tainted by bribes and kickbacks.[71]

65 "The company [Solidere] shall be reimbursed by the state for all infrastructure costs incurred, in one or a combination of the following ways: in cash, in state-owned land within the BCD, in land within the reclaimed zone" *Solidere Information Booklet*, 1995.

66 Ḥarīrī himself had presented earlier, hitherto unrevealed reconstruction plans in the 1980s.

67 See *Horizon 2000 for Reconstruction and Development: Main Report*, Beirut, CDR, 1993. Virtually all the projections of "progress reports" of the Horizon Plan fell short of reality. The original ten-year program envisaged an expenditure of US$11.7 billion, while the debt stock was supposed to peak at 84 percent of GDP in 1995. Since 2001, the debt has stood at approximately 180 percent of GDP.

68 Samīr Maqdisī, *The Lessons of Lebanon* (London: I. B. Tauris, 2004), 34, 123.

69 Denoeux and Springborg, "Harīrī's Lebanon," 158–173.

70 See Naba, *Rafīq Harīrī,* 50 and *Liberation,* Paris, April 3, 1999.

71 Denoeux and Springborg, "Harīrī's Lebanon;" Gary Gambill, "Dossier, Rafīq Harīrī," *Middle East Intelligence Bulletin* 2 (2001), www.meforum.org/meib/articles/0107_ld1.htm, last accessed February 6, 2019.

This checkered record notwithstanding, it is hard to gainsay the fact that the ambitious reconstruction projects have shown impressive results, which have allowed at least parts of Beirut to regain – and even surpass – their former elegance and glistening splendour, while "only" consuming approximately US$ 5 billion over the past ten years. By comparison, approximately US$11 billion, that is to say a full ara of the entire postwar national debt, was spent on the electricity sector, which was moved to Speaker Birrī's (Shia) AMAL portfolio, although Ḥarīrī had earlier, under Syrian duress, appointed one of the key culprits for graft in this sector, former warlord Elie Hobayka, as minister of electricity in 1994, thus ousting the previous minister, George Fraym, a widely respected businessman.

Part of the *quid pro quo* arrangement of the postwar era entailed that each politician was given a portfolio to warm over and in return was granted full immunity from political scrutiny in cases of alleged financial impropriety. The numerous files of embezzlement and allegations of graft in the postwar era in turn could be linked by malevolent politicians to confessional favoritism. Corruption thus could fan the flames of sectarianism. The latter were only extinguished by ways of a standard operating procedure adopted by the postwar nomenclature: no sooner a particular financial scandal would erupt than members of the main power brokers would burry past grudges and scurry to cover for each other as they set about to safeguard the *status quo* and the divvying-up of the spoils. In this process, however, sectarian affiliations, patronage networks, and identities are once again underscored as each political leader generally felt constrained, with precious few exceptions, to justify his action by pandering to his base constituency, which almost invariably is of a monochrome confessional color. We may then conclude that economic competition over state distributive networks has heightened confessional identities.

Social Stratification, Status, and Intersectarian Relations in Postwar Lebanon

From a macroeconomic perspective, the Achilles heel of the Lebanese postwar economy consisted not so much in the absence of economic growth[72] and development, but in its tendency of reconstruction to accentuate rather than attenuate socioeconomic – and, as we shall see, geographic, cultural, and sectarian – chasms. According to Buṭrus Labakī, a former Ḥarīrī aide and vice chairman of the CDR, the

[72] The rapid (expected) postwar GDP expansion petered out by 1995 and turned negative by 2000.

proportion of low-income families soared from 20.4 percent in 1974 to 54 percent in 1997 to 62 percent in 1999.[73] Conversely, the percentage of medium-income families fell from 60 percent in 1974 to 40 percent in 1992 to 29 percent in 1999. The Gini coefficient indicating capital concentration in Lebanon rose accordingly, defying the regional trend since 1966, which has seen a constant decline of income inequalities in Arab countries. Overall, the Gini coefficient decreased from 43.67 in 1966 to 38.17 in 1990 in Arab states.[74] The Ḥarīrī era thus was marked by lopsided development and a greater concentration of wealth in fewer hands than ever before, a development exacerbated by the lowest tax rate in Lebanese history, a measure taken to boost investment. In 1992, 2.4 percent of depositors owned 40 percent of total deposits, by the end of 2002 the share of total bank deposits of the same thin oligarchy had risen to 60 percent.[75] By 2014, Lebanon wealth concentration had reached such staggering degrees that 0.1 percent of the population, or about 3,000 citizens, obtained the same national income as 50 percent, or 1.5 million compatriots.[76]

This top-heavy socioeconomic pyramid may be related to the most conspicuous feature of Lebanon's postwar economy: the staggering national debt. It rose from US$1.5 billion[77] in 1992 to US$38 billion in 2003, further doubling to over US$79 billion by 2017, surpassing a

[73] Buṭrus Labakī, "al-Faqr wa al-Batāla wa al-Tanmīya fī Lubnān," *an-Nahār*, August 24, 2003. According to a 1994 UNDP report, 32.1 percent of households or 35.2 percent of the population live below the satisfaction threshold. Last accessed June 4, 2015 at: www.undp.org.lb/programme/pro-poor/poverty/povertyinlebanon/index.html

[74] Klaus Deininger and Pedro Olinto, *Asset Distribution, Inequality and Growth* (Washington, DC: The World Bank, 1999); One study of 1998 calculates a pre-tax Gini cooefficient in Lebanon of 0.71 and an after-tax coefficient of 0.69. 'Abdullāh Dah, Ghassān Dibah, and Wassīm Shāhīn, *The Distributional Impact of Taxes in Lebanon: Analysis and Policy Implications* (Beirut: Lebanese Center for Policy Studies, 1999). However, other sources show an improving income Gini coefficient from 0.61 in 1951 to 0.51 in 1966 and 0.41 in 1997. See Gaspard, *A Political Economy of Lebanon*, 74. It stands to reason that a significant amount of income is underreported.

[75] Maqdisī, *The Lessons of Lebanon*, 150.

[76] See Lydia Assouad, "Rethinking the Lebanese Economic Miracle: The Extreme Concentration of Income and Wealth in Lebanon 2005–2014," WID.world Working Paper 2017/13, 10.

[77] In the election booklet *Government and Responsibility*, the pre-1992 debt is put at US$3 billion. However, this computation neglects the pound stabilized at around 1,500 LP to 1 US$ only after Ḥarīrī assumed power late in 1992. Before that, the going rate of 3,000 LP to 1 US$ would indicate a cumulative debt of ca. US$1.5 billion before the arrival of Ḥarīrī. A similar "numbers game" was played when it came to assessing the costs of Horizon 2000, which were originally put at US$11.672 billion, but in current prices actually amounted to US$18.4 billion. Najm, *The Collapse and Reconstruction of Lebanon*, 29, 39.

ratio of 150 percent of GDP.[78] Not everybody was hurt by the debt, however. Two separate recent studies estimate that approximately half of mountain of the (then) US$33 billion debt can be attributed to graft and astronomic, untaxed interest rates of up to 40 percent on government treasury bills granted to the local Lebanese, which have seen their profits soar exponentially.[79]

While the banks enjoyed a veritable bonanza in the postwar era – some of which was paid to depositors – unemployment in 1997 stood at over 20 percent and one third of Lebanese families were living on or below the subsistence level of US$600 a month.[80] Moreover, high interest rates benefited those financiers who had extra cash disposable and "crowded out" those seeking loans for investment in Lebanon.

Even the former head of the CDR came to concede the perilous link between growing indebtedness and the hollowing out of the state.[81] Paradoxically, the acuteness of the economic crisis may have in fact mitigated some of the most grievous of its consequences, as the massive postwar emigration of up to 900,000 Lebanese and the uninterrupted brain drain have arguably reduced the rate of unemployment, while increasing remittances. The exodus thus ended up providing additional safety valves for accumulating social tensions and could soften the economic blow for individual families. Lebanon had the highest mean rate of remittances per capita in the world and the third highest as a percentage of GDP between 1999 and 2004.[82] In the absence of reliable statistics,

[78] Dona Abu-Nasr, Dana Khraiche, and Onur Ant, "It Could be Crunch Time for World's Third Most Indebted Country," *Bloomberg,* March 5, 2018, www.bloomberg.com/news/articles/2018-03-05/it-could-be-crunch-time-for-world-s-third-most-indebted-country, last accessed January 23, 2019.

[79] Through 2002, at least half of the 18 percent on Lebanese lira treasury bills (i.e., US$8.5 billion) was paid in excess of "what the cost would have been in a normally operating market." See Maqdisī, *The Lessons of Lebanon*, 204ff. The inordinately high domestic interest rates made it lucrative for banks to borrow in the foreign market to buy up government bonds (rather than invest domestically).

[80] Gaspard, *A Political Economy of Lebanon*, 75.

[81] The head of the CDR, al-Fadl Shalaq began to critique the practice of privatization in Lebanon, stating that "the steady rise of the national debt is viewed by the large financial interests as an opportunity to deliver the *coup de grace* to state holdings by ways of privatization. It is the latter which in turn has become a cause for the debt spiral rather than a cure to it" *as-Safīr*, June 6, 2003.

[82] Dr. Nāsir Ghubrīl estimates remittances have increased from US$1.4 billion to US$2.7 billion in 2003 (chiefly from the Gulf Cooperation Council), although these remittances do not include *hawala* and other informal cash transactions, which possibly might even double official estimates. Salīm Zīnī, for instance, president of the American Lebanese Chamber of Commerce, claims that between US$5 billion and US$8 billion are sent to Lebanon each year from Lebanese abroad. Speech of Dr. Nāsir Ghubrīl, April 21, 2004 at the Notre Dame University Lebanese Emigration Research Center.

we may further surmise that remittances from overseas have considerably grown according to estimates provided by the IMF.[83]

The overall negative fallout of this social stratification and a continuously shrinking middle class for the prospects of secularism in Lebanon cannot be overestimated. The growing impoverishment of parts of the citizenry coupled with a constant curtailment of social services and cutting of state salaries is bound to erode vital trust in national institutions and to precipitate a search for alternative, family or religiously based networks of support. This observation coheres with the findings of global study that has identified greater social insecurity as the chief factor accounting for higher degrees of religiousity in the United States.[84]

Lebanon's history has shown time and again that gross class disparities tend to foment religious radicalism and parochialism. Even if the divide of rich and poor did – and does – not invariably neatly overlap with the myriad particular sectarian fault lines, as some Lebanese Marxist historians have been wont to argue,[85] there is no gainsaying that the postwar policies have amplified growing "vertical" class chasms that render the "horizontal" sectarian segmentation in Lebanon a potential tinderbox. The "Revolt of the Hungry," mobilized by the renegade Shia cleric Ṣubḥī Tuffaylī in Ba'albak and the Biqā' in 1998, the riots in the Southern Shia suburbs of *Hay al-Sulm* in 1997[86] and 2004, or indeed the proliferation of hitherto unknown Sunni fundamentalist groups such as the *Hizb ul-Tahrīr, Jund as-Sham,*[87]

[83] *World Economic Outlook: Globalization and External Imbalances* (Washington, DC: IMF, April 2005), 72.

[84] The thesis of a significant – almost direct – correlation between economic income, social security, and secular outlook in Lebanon – as elsewhere – has resisted refutation. See Norris and Inglehart, *Sacred and the Secular,* 109.

[85] The late Hasan Hamdān alias Mahdī 'Āmil was one of the most prominent exponents of this conflation of sectarian and social identities, as was Jurj Hāwī, the former head of the Communist Party in Lebanon, who coined the alliteration "*Tabqa/Tā'ifa*" which was also referred to by the historian Mas'ūd Dāhir. See Mahdī 'Āmil, *Madkhal li Naqd al-Fikr al-Tā'ifī: al-qadāya al-Filastīnīya fī al-idyulujīyāt al-burjuwāzīya al-Lubnānīya* (Beirut: Dār al-Farabī, 1985); *Fī Dawla al-Tā'ifīya,* 177–180, 221 where 'Āmil lays out his critique of Dāhir.

[86] The riots in Hay al-Sulm on June 26, 1997 were sparked after the authorities took punitive measures and cutoff water supply to the suburb after the inhabitants prevented waste from reaching the incinerator in their midst.

[87] The *Jund al-Shām* (not to be confused with the *Jund Allāh,* which merged with the *Harakat al-Tawhīd* in 1982) is an extremist Islamist group that emerged in the past decade among the seas of destitution and despair of the largest of the Palestinian refugee camps in Lebanon near Sidon, 'Ayn al-Hilwa. It was surmised that renegade members and outcasts of other extremist fundamentist groups such as the '*Usbat al-Ansār* (which was outlawed in Lebanon after an uprising in Dinnīya in northern Lebanon) found shelter in the camps, periodically resulting in violent clashes the Fatah partisans therein (*al-Hayāt al-Wasat,* September 24, 2004). '*Usbat*'s head Abū Mihjin was rumored to be

Fathī Yakan's[88] *Jamāʻat al-Islamīya*, and the repeated intrusion of isolated al-Qā'ida cells have demonstrated as much.[89] Temporary electoral alliances by prominent Sunni politicians such as Ḥarīrī,[90] Najīb Miqātī,[91] or 'Umar Karāmī with Islamist groups did little to alleviate the lot of the destitute peripheral areas in Lebanon that have become the chief recruiting grounds for fundamentalism.

To be sure, regional tensions engendered by the mayhem in Palestine and the bloody Iraqi quagmire, as well as an increasingly acrimonious struggle with the Syrian security apparatus over its hotly contested role in Lebanon provided further ideological fodder for such outgrowths of religious polemics and zealotry. This explosive mix of deprivation and dogmatism exploded in the February 2006 anti-cartoon riots during which largely Lebanese Salafists and extremists descended from Tripoli's, Sidon's, and 'Akkār's shantytowns to wreak havoc in the posh Christian city-quarter of Ashrafīya. The government was quick to identify Syria as the instigator of the riots, only to find itself acknowledging in the aftermath that over 80 percent of the rioters were Lebanese.[92] Minister Ahmad Fatfat saw himself forced to retract his prior accusation that "radical Shiite elements" and "Christian troublemakers allied with the Syrian regime" were behind the destruction wrought after it was revealed

conducting operations in Iraq. See Nizār A. Ḥamza, "Islamism In Lebanon: A Guide to the Groups," *Middle East Quarterly* 4.3 (1997): 47–54.

88 Yakan was head of the Lebanese branch of the Muslim Brotherhood after it split from the larger Syrian branch in 1971 until 2009. Under the spell of Hasan al-Bannā, Mustafā as-Sabā 'ī, and Sa'īd Qutb, Yakan railed against "the crusaders, Jews and communists" and called for a "holy war" (*jihād muqaddas*) against the West, likening the coming Islamic revolution to the French and Russian revolutions. With Syrian tutelage and support, Yakan became a member of parliament and established his own Islamic university (*al-Jinān*). He moderated his tone slightly and enjoyed close personal ties with Erbakan, Erdogan, and Gul in Turkey. At one point, Rafīq Ḥarīrī lauded Yakan for exerting a moderate influence on northern Lebanon, even though Yakan after 2005 became a Sunni representative of the Hizballāh-led opposition. Asad Harmush succeeded the ailing Yakan as the head of the Jamā'a. For a comprehensive monograph on Fathi Yakan and the history of the Muslim Brotherhood's activities in Syria and Lebanon, see Sebastian Elsaesser, "Die Theorie des Islamischen Aktivismus Bei Fathi Yakan," dissertation, Zentrum Moderner Orient, Berlin, 2005.

89 Seven Syrian and three Lebanese al-Qā'ida members were arrested on January 1, 2006.

90 The militant Sunni mufti of the Biqā', Khalīl al-Mays, became a supporter of the Future Movement.

91 Najīb Miqātī lobbied successfully in 2000 for the release of Hashim Minqarah who belonged to Harakat al Tawhīd and was detained by the Syrians in 1985.

92 Whatever Syrian role may be imputed, almost all those arrested as members of Hizb ul-Tawhīd, Ahbāsh, and the Jamā'at Islamīya were Lebanese citizens.

that the militant rioters included members of the notorious Dinnīya group.[93] The Dinnīya group consisted of Sunni Islamists who in January 2000 launched a failed attempt to establish an Islamic "mini-state" in north Lebanon. The insurgents, many of whom were non-Lebanese Arabs and had trained in al-Qā'ida camps in Afghānīstan, were evicted from dozens of villages they captured in the Dinnīya district east of Tripoli after several days of clashes with Lebanese troops and forty casualties. The leaders of this terror cell were imprisoned until 2005 when Sa'd al-Ḥarīrī paid US$48,000 in bail for their release.[94]

If deprivation has nourished irredentist communal terrorism, in a curiously positive twist of fate, the sheer magnitude of the nation's economic woes and political dissatisfaction have also, conversely, lead to the formation of cross-sectarian alliances across the political spectrum. On the one hand, we find the coalition of former communists (Movement of the Democratic Left), rightist Christians (Qurnat Shahwān), and independents, which would later coalesce into so-called Bristol gathering, the backbone of the subsequent anti-Syrian March 14 movement. In response, another alliance based on an anticorruption platform between 'Awn's Free Patriotic Movement and Hizballāh was formed.

Some opposition parties have nominally adopted a secular discourse, a discourse whose depth still must pass the test of time and further turmoil. An optimist might have viewed the closing of the ranks among the multifaceted opposition to Syria as a harbinger of political secularization dictated by political and economic exigency. Such political alliances, however, were liable to be notoriously ephemeral and based on temporary strategic calculations that do little to affect underlying structural and economical dividing lines riddling the mosaic of religiously defined communities. For this reason, a deeper examination of the socioeconomic fault lines, both within and between communities, is in order.

[93] *Nouvel Observateur*, February 8, 2006, http://enacademic.com/dic.nsf/enwiki/2867494, last accessed February 6, 2019.

[94] Ḥarīrī described this as "a humanitarian action," in conjunction with the concurrent amnesty of Samīr Ja'ja', the Lebanese forces leader sentenced to life imprisonment in connection with political assassinations, most notably the murder of former Prime Minister Rashīd Karāmī in 1987. Ja'ja' was the only prominent warlord to be sent to jail. After the elections, Ḥarīrī used his parliamentary majority to secure amnesty for twenty-two of the Islamists as well as seven militants detained in September 2004 on suspicion of plotting to bomb the Italian and Ukrainian embassies in Beirut Crisis Group interview, Beirut, 27 October 2005. See *Al-Mustaqbal*, *An-Nahār*, and *The Daily Star*, 10 June 2005.

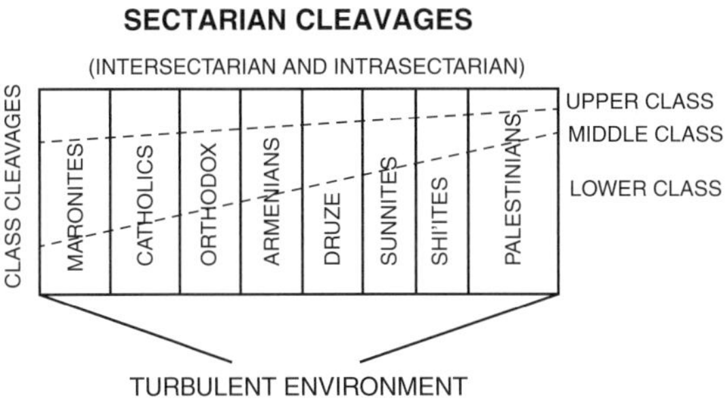

Figure E4.1 Topography of *Tā'fiya*: Class and Confession in Lebanon
Source: Richard Hrair Dekmejian, "Consociational Democracy in Crisis: The Case of Lebanon," *Comparative Politics* 10.2 (1978): figure 1, 259.

> The Carthaginian constitution deviates from aristocracy and inclines to oligarchy, chiefly on a point where popular opinion is on their side. For men in general think that magistrates should be chosen not only for their merit, but for their wealth: a man, they say, who is poor cannot rule well ... The government of the Carthaginians is oligarchical, but they successfully escape the evils of oligarchy by enriching one portion of the people after another by sending them to their colonies. This is their panacea and the means by which they give stability to the state.[95]

Ever since the end of the Chehabist *étatism* in 1970, and throughout the war and postwar period, we have seen a decided shift in the economic makeup and confessional balance of Lebanese society. This includes the Shia demographic explosion (see Table 3.1) and the much-cited Christian exodus, but this is only part of the story. Ghassān Salāma has traced the gradual transition over the century from a land to a capital-based economy, with a new class of businessmen and lawyers, the classical compradors, replacing the landed notables.[96] Seminal studies by Joseph Shāmī[97] and Yūsuf Sā'igh[98] confirmed a Christian predominance in the upper echelons of the Lebanese economy before 1977. However, this

[95] *The Politics of Aristotle*, II: 1272, 50–51.

[96] Ghassān Salāma, *al-Mujtama' wa al-Dawlat fī al-Mashriq al-'arabī* (Beirut: Center for Arab Unity Studies, 1987), 202.

[97] Shāmī, "Religious Groups in Lebanon," 175–187.

[98] Yūsuf Sā'igh, *Entrepreneurs of Lebanon* (Cambridge, MA: Harvard University Press, 1964). Theodor Hanf has sought to deny these well-documented findings while citing scant statistical data to refute them: "From the mid-1970s onward, a number of authors more or less equated social class and community in Lebanon, and interpreted conflicts between these communities as class struggles. Of course, this thesis was an effective mobilizer. It also satisfied the desire of some media for simple explanations of complex

does not exclude the simultaneous presence of a large body of lower-class Christians.[99] According to another study conducted just before the war by Shmeil, 47 percent of Orthodox had an income below 6,000 LL in 1974, compared to 47.6 percent of the Greek Catholic, 52.4 percent of the Maronites, 59.1 percent of the Druze, 60 percent of the Sunnis, and 70.7 percent of the Shia.[100] Since (and during) the civil war, the centers of wealth have tended to further shift from a Christian (Orthodox, Maronite, and Greek Catholic) to a (Sunni and Shia) Muslim elite and from an indigenous landed to an internationally based financial aristocracy.[101] This is not to deny the continued importance of real estate nor the ongoing presence of a Christian upper class, but merely to draw attention to broader trends that can be deduced from multiple demographic and economic statistics. According to one sample of the early 1960s, for instance, only one sixth of Lebanon's 207 leading businessmen were Muslim, and Christians owned eleven of fourteen financial enterprises, in effect dominating all spheres of the economy in the prewar era.[102]

In part, prominent Christian merchants and agents often benefited from monopolies they inherited from the prewar era. Most notably and controversially, the so-called *Wikālat al-Hassrīya* (pursuant to Decree 34 of 1967) has frozen almost 75 percent of exclusive distributing licenses and agencies in the hands of Christian, and often (Greek) Catholic families. When Premier Ḥarīrī attempted to change this highly controversial legislation in 2002 that protects the sectarian monopolies, the reform project was put on ice.[103] The legislation also favors the

situations. The cliché of 'rich Christians' and 'poor Muslims', has had a brilliant journalistic career – and it may not be over yet." Hanf, *Coexistence in Wartime Lebanon*, 138. Hanf does not acknowlegdge the cited data nor Buṭrus Labakī's findings that two thirds of the industrial and trade firms of Lebanon were controlled by Christians.

99 Shāmī concludes that "whatever reasonable criteria one chooses to utilize, the [socioeconomic hierarchy] is unmistakably clear: non-Catholic Christians and Christians at the top, Druze around the middle, Sunnis near the bottom, and Shi's at the very bottom." Shāmī, "The Lebanese Civil War," 171. The same findings were confirmed by Salīm Naṣr.

100 Y. Shmeil, "La Sociologie du Systeme Politique Libanais," PhD thesis, University de Grenoble, 1975, 118.

101 In 1976, 3 percent of the population owned 40 percent of the land. Shāmī, "Religious Groups in Lebanon," 175–187.

102 See Sā'igh, *Entrepreneurs of Lebanon*, 24.

103 In his eulogy commemorating the passing of Premier Ḥarīrī, Speaker Birrī obliquely alluded to this incident in a double entendre: "You [Ḥarīrī] rejected all *Wikālāt al-Hasrīya,*" *An-Nahār*, February 13, 2007, 1.

survival of established monopolies, as it prohibits foreign companies from replacing local agents without the latter's consent.[104]

Geographically speaking, the Beirut-centric development policy came at the expense of Lebanon's periphery. The northern, largely Sunni and Maronite regions of 'Akkār, the Shia south, and the Biqā' constituted the most deprived of Lebanese regions in the 1990s. Child labor,[105] unemployment, and the rate of poverty in 'Akkār, Nabatīya, and the Biqā' tends to be almost double that of Beirut. As of 1997, 32.5 percent of all Lebanese lived in Greater Beirut, 37.6 percent in Mount Lebanon, 20.1 percent in north Lebanon, 13.6 percent in the Biqā', and 11.8 percent in southern Lebanon.[106] Although the aforementioned areas are not mono-confessional, and while a Sunni fundamentalist opposition to Ḥarīrī has taken root in destitute Sunni areas, the strong focus on Beirut in the allocation policy of the Ḥarīrī government came to be interpreted through a sectarian lens, particularly by politicians representing the somewhat neglected Maronite and Shia periphery.

In a 1998 memorandum directly addressed to Premier Ḥarīrī, the Maronite patriarch flagrantly denounced a list of specific policies such as: rampant graft, a spreading culture of materialism, and the marginalization of the "Christians in general and the Maronites in particular." To the chagrin of Ḥarīrī, the patriarch demanded a restoration of the prerogatives to the (Maronite) presidency.[107] Matters came to a head in the summer of 2003 when Lahhūd and Ḥarīrī clashed over the distribution of funds for about 250 new public schools, most of which, according to the Ḥarīrī plan, were to be erected in Sunni areas of west Beirut, whereas President Lahhūd and Patriarch Sfayr made the case for a more dispersed, nationwide distribution.[108] To the Ḥarīrī government, Beirut seemed to deserve primary attention, both due to the disproportionate destruction the capital suffered during the war and due to its salient role as the port of Lebanon to the world.

104 Naṣr, "Backdrop to Civil War," 5.

105 Over 50 percent of all child labor in Lebanon is concentrated in the suburbs of Beirut, Tripoli, and 'Akkār. See Adīb Na'mī, "Shughl al atfaal," *an-Nahār,* December 5, 2005.

106 See the revealing MSA-UNDP Tableau in Raoul 'Assāf, ed., *Atlas Du Liban* (Beirut: Saint Joseph University, 2003), 74.

107 *Bkerke Memorandum to Premier Rafīq al-Harīrī,* March 6, 1998. For Ḥarīrī's reaction see Antoine Sa'd, *as-Sādis wa as-Saba'ūn: Mar Naṣr Allāh Butrus Sfayr. al-Jāmi'a al-Lubnānīya lil Thaqāfa,* vol. 2, 190ff.

108 Sfayr also lamented that Ḥarīrī had bought Catholic schools and prohibited the teaching of religion. Cited in Sa'd, as-Sādis wa as-Saba'ūn, vol. 2, 74, 191. Another aspect of the dispute was (ostensibly) economic: Lahhūd argued that real estate outside of west Beirut would be less costly.

The 2006 political pact between General 'Awn and Hizballāh revolved around a strategic calculation and an anticorruption agenda, but was quickly also perceived in sectarian terms, as conjectures were made of a Maronite–Shia alignment, possibly facing a Sunni–Druze axis.[109] While any past generalizations must be taken with a grain of salt in light of Lebanon's constantly shifting political seas, historically speaking, the Shia–Sunni rift in Lebanon has arguably run as deep or deeper than the Sunni–Maronite one. The virtual absence of any villages inhabited solely by Sunnis and Shia in Lebanon provides one illustration of this point. Intermarriages between the two sects, however, have become far more common over the past two decades. In Syria, intermarriage of the Alawite upper class (including Bashār al-Assad and his Sunni wife Asma) led one scholar to – prematurely perhaps – announce the disappearance of an Alawite sectarian identity on the elite level.[110]

The power shift to the Sunni premiership effected by Ḥarīrī was interpreted by some as coming at the expense of the Shia, particularly when Ḥarīrī decided to appoint a Sunni (rather than a Shia) as the minister of finance,[111] together with a virtually uniform Sunni staff, against Shiite protestations. This bold move carried broader ramifications in light of the fact that the first Ḥarīrī budgets rapidly increased the allocations for the finance ministry and prime minister at the expense of the ministries of education, health, and agriculture.[112] Solidere and the CDR were placed under another Sunni Ḥarīrī aide, al-Fadl Shalaq (1991–1995)[113] and another former Sunni partner of Saudi Oger,[114] Nabīl Jisr, and dominated by local and foreign Sunni investors, many of them from the Gulf. Previously, during the height of Saudi–Iranian

[109] Interviews with Dr. Albīr Farhāt in Yarzī and Prof. Theodor Hanf in Byblos, June 6, 2003. Druze leader Walīd Janbulāt's political positions are predisposed to change according to long- and short-term interests. Throughout the postwar era, Janbulāt, however, generally cast his lot with Premier Ḥarīrī.

[110] Yahya Sadowski cited in "The Evolution of Political Identity in Syria," in *Identity and Foreign Policy in the Middle East* (Ithaca, NY: Cornell University Press, 2002), 146.

[111] First himself, then the former chairman and CFO of his Mediteranee Banking Group, Fu'ād Siniora.

[112] The share of the budget, which went to the prime minister for instance, increased from 6.2 percent in 1992 to 14.4 percent in 1993. The ministry of health has suffered from an over US$200 million debt owed to private hospitals in 2000. 'Assaf, *Atlas Du Liban*, 101. Perthes, *Der Libanon Nach Dem Buergerkrieg*, 83.

[113] al-Shalaq meanwhile has turned into one of the fiercest critics of his former patron and launched a vehement critique of the postwar economic program. He was subsequently reappointed to head the CDR.

[114] Tom Najm cites one senior consultant who draws attention to the intimate links between the "superministry" CDR and Ḥarīrī's own construction behemoth: "We think of Oger as part of the CDR." Cited in Najm, *The Collapse and Reconstruction of Lebanon*, 43.

tensions in the wake of the Iranian Revolution, and due to his annoyance with AMAL's blackmailing, Ḥarīrī proceeded to bar Shiites from employment in his enterprises, in particular his construction giant Oger.[115]

Moreover, the mainly Shia *lumpenproletariat* was forcibly removed from the city center as the Solidere facelift was embarked upon after 1993. The precise amount and source of the exorbitant compensations have remained a subject of controversy until this day. Sayyid Fadlallāh's *fatwā*[116] against Solidere one year later was indicative of the depth of the Sunni–Shia split at this juncture, as was Ḥarīrī's later boast to Patriarch Sfayr that he had dispensed with the (Shia) resistance. The premier's relations with the Shia community could best be described as strained and limited to temporary strategic accords and *ad hoc* gentlemen's covenants with Speaker Nabīh Birrī. As to the other major Shia actor, Hizballāh, Premier Ḥarīrī evinced himself as its greatest counterweight. However, he was cautious not to step on the party's home turf in the 2000 parliamentary elections and came out in favor of Hizballāh's positive role as a resistance force to Israel in the south.[117] This nominal support was balanced by Ḥarīrī's occasional anxieties over Hizballāh's perilous brinksmanship with Israel, which increased after the formal Israeli withdrawal, fears that were echoed by Janbulāt's lament that Lebanon cannot be the Middle East's Hong Kong and Hanoi simultaneously. After an Israeli soldier fell to a Hizballāh attack on April 14, 2001, Ḥarīrī's *al-Mustaqbal* openly questioned whether Lebanon could "bear the consequences of such an operation and its political, economic and social impacts."[118] So outraged was Syrian President Bashār Assad by the editorial that he canceled a scheduled meeting with the Lebanese premier in Damascus, shutting the doors of Damascus to Ḥarīrī for over a month.

115 Cited in Bonne, *Vie Publique*, 52.

116 See Fadlallāh as cited in *an-Nahār*, January 15, 1994.

117 Ḥarīrī was careful in the 2000 elections not to challenge Hizballāh's territory and left the Shia candidate open on his Beirut list. See Hilāl Khashshān and Simon Ḥaddād, "Lebanon's Dramatic 200 Parliamentary Elections: The Swooping Return of Rafīq Harīrī," *Journal of South Asian and Middle Eastern Studies* 26.3 (2003): 1–22. Ḥarīrī's willingness to compromise was met by an attack on his Future Television station. Ansar Allāh issued a statement that said the attack was designed to prevent "anyone, even if they are powerful and influential," from firing "poison arrows at the heart of the resistance." Ḥarīrī had earlier stated publicly that "to solve the problem and to be practical and pragmatic, we should sit together and solve the problems between Arabs and Israelis. We believe in dialogue, we believe in trusting the US, we are not looking for a confrontation for sure." Cited in Michael Young, "Targeting Harīrī," *Daily Star*, June 18, 2003.

118 Cited in: Gary Gambill and Ziad K. Abdelnour, "Hezbollah: Between Tehran and Damascus," *Middle East Intelligence Bulletin*, 4.2 (2002), www.meforum.org/meib/articles/0202_l1.htm.

Meanwhile, Christian antipathy to the Ḥarīrī project was stirred primarily by the buying up of vast swaths of real estate by investors from the Gulf and Saudi Arabia. This trend gained unprecedented momentum particularly after September 11 and was interpreted as coming at the expense of the (often Christian) sellers.[119] While resorts such as Bhamdoun were known to attract Gulf Arabs long before the civil war, Ḥarīrī was credited as the godfather of the renewal and intensification of this liberal policy as he was instrumental in loosening Lebanon's hitherto restrictive property rights for foreigners,[120] and, according to Cardinal Sfayr, buying up real estate for himself.[121] Moreover, the establishment of a potent new patronage system around Ḥarīrī earned him the resentment of the bourgeoisie left out of the new network. The exclusion of Maronites from ministerial positions by Ḥarīrī constituted a further bone of contention that impaired his oft-declared bid for national integration.[122]

This is not to gainsay the fact that the Premier astutely cultivated ties with an array of Christian (business) allies, most notably Bank of Lebanon President and former Ḥarīrī portfolio manager Riyād Salāma. In fact, during his $100 million campaign during the 1998 elections, Ḥarīrī spent more money on Christian dignitaries ($3.7 million) than on Muslim ones ($2.7million).[123] Some of Ḥarīrī's closest business partners and political allies were Christian: Johnny ʿAbdu, Hagop Demarjian, Robert Dabbās, Ghattās Khūrī, Michel Firʿawn, Michel al-Murr and Jacques Chirac.[124] Conversely, some of the Premier's most implacable

[119] In the wake of September 11, 2001 and after the significant withdrawal of Arab funds from the United States, Lebanon reemerged as a premier destination for windfall Arab capital and tourists.

[120] The new law made it possible for foreigners to buy up to 3,000 m^2 of land without a ministerial permission, and more upon obtaining the latter. Tourism has steadily increased since 1992 and skyrocketed since September 11. A total of 1,123 million tourists entered Lebanon by the end of October 2004 compared with 891,384 during the same period in 2003.

[121] "Cardinal Sfayr: 'There is a matter which is cause for distress amongst the Christians. It is said you are buying lands of Christians.' PM Ḥarīrī: 'This is incorrect. Pray tell me were I am said to have made a purchase?' Sfayr: 'In the vicinity of Balamand.' Ḥarīrī: 'If I were not to buy this land, then someone else from the Shia would. The rich are selling their lands. I was returning in a plane with someone from the Suma family, and it was he who asked me to purchase the real estate as he wanted to marry his son.'" Cited in Saʿd, *as-Sādis wa as-Sabaʿūn*, vol. 2, 74.

[122] Khashshān, "Lebanon's Dramatic 200 Parliamentary Elections."

[123] See Naba, *Rafīq Ḥarīrī*, 140.

[124] President Chirac's close ties to Ḥarīrī were confirmed when the French president fired the head of the French intelligence, Jean-Claude Cousseran, and the head of the internal state security department, Jean-Jacques Pascal, who stood accused of having "ordered or tolerated" investigations into payments made to Chirac by Ḥarīrī and the

foes were fellow Sunnis. Among those were competitors for the post of Prime Minister such as Salīm al-Huss and ʿUmar Karāmī, or indeed the Sunni fundamentalist movements such as the *Jamā'a al-Islāmīya* and *Ansār al-Islām*, which stood accused of bombing Ḥarīrī's Future TV on June 15, 2003, or *al-Tawhīd* whose TV and Radio stations the Ḥarīrī government forcibly shut in 1997.[125]

Tellingly, one potential contender to the prime minister's throne was not only a Sunni, but in fact a Saudi, billionaire like Ḥarīrī, albeit of "noble" ancestry: Prince Walīd Ibn Talāl, son of the "red" Saudi prince Talāl Ibn ʿAbdul ʿAzīz and grandson of the late Lebanese premier Riyād as-Sulh. Like the Sunni *Zaʿīm* before them, the Saudi–Lebanese billionaires Walīd Ibn Talāl and Ḥarīrī cultivated their contacts with Damascus; both augmented their investments in Syria in wake of the change of guards in Damascus after the death of Hāfiz al-Assad.[126]

The new petro-*Zuʿamā's* clientelism, however, has been distinguished from the traditional patriarchal patronage system of the old notables. Talāl and Ḥarīrī's primary clients/*zilms* are not the lower, but the upper, classes of key Lebanese power brokers. Their contact to the population at large is reduced to the indirect and impersonal means of financial donations and public relations campaigns before elections; the billionaire benefactors have thus dispensed with some of the cumbersome etiquette of old. This ostensibly more efficient commodification of social relations has marked a profound change in nature of social capital between the leadership and the base of the Sunni community. The patron–client relationship still remains highly contingent on the proper distribution of charitable funds. However, traditional communal occasions have assumed a commercial size unbeknownst to the Lebanon of old.[127]

Japanese financier Shoichi Osada. Chirac is suspected of having paid the ransom for the French hostages in Lebanon during his tenure (1986–1988) via Ḥarīrī who was a major donor to Chirac's presidential campaign. The socialist interior minister Daniel Vaillant asked the Parisian state prosecutor on January 19, 2001 to reopen the hostage file to verify the payment of kickbacks. Chirac's presidential immunity and Lebanon's closely guarded bank secrecy laws, however, have obstructed any investigation into the manifold claims of bribery. "Chirac to Sack Spy Chiefs for Probing Him," *Dawn*, March 11, 2012, www.dawn.com/news/44309/chirac-to-sack-spy-chiefs-for-probing-him, last accessed February 5, 2019.

125 There was some speculation that one of these renegade Sunni groups may have assassinated Ḥariri. Al-Jazeera aired a tape claiming credit for the assassination from a group called "al Nusra wa al Jihad fi Bilad al Sham" immediately after the assassination on February 14, 2005.

126 Ḥarīrī has likewise not tarried in cultivating his ties with Bashār al-Assad, promising massive investments in Syria during the 2000 elections "Whispers," *The Economist*, August 31, 2000, www.economist.com/international/2000/08/31/whispers.

127 Rieger, *Rentiers*, 305, All Lebanese confessions engage in such public charity, even if displays of wealth of other, "rival" sects are not always viewed with favor. Patriarch Sfayr

Moreover, after 1996, the mufti of the republic no longer was elected by the *'ulāmā'*, but nominated by the government (and confirmed by the president and premier).[128] Ḥarīrī saw to it that a more pliable mufti would not pose a challenge to his claim of leadership of the Sunni community.[129]

Nonetheless, Ḥarīrī's Sunni grassroots power base was less secure than his financial wherewithal. While the elections after 1992 all saw sweeping wins for Ḥarīrī-sponsored lists, most conspicuously in the 2000 municipal elections, the limits of financial prowess as an agent of political success in Lebanon were revealed in Ḥarīrī's failure to garner votes on his very own home turf in Sidon in the municipal elections of 2004. The particular political alliances accounted for part of the debacle, but more intangible matters such as the premier's popular image also played a role.

His past generous philanthropic activities notwithstanding, Ḥarīrī could never quite manage to bridge the cultural cleft that had emerged between the jet-setting, Western-oriented billionaire and the conservative climate that characterized his native Sidon. It is thus symbolic that the Ḥarīrī mansion occupied by MP Bahia al-Ḥarīrī lives in an enclave of luxury at a distance from the somewhat estranged, impoverished population of Sidon. By the same token, Ḥarīrī's home in west Beirut would sport Christmas trees and serve alcohol, practices alien to many constituents. To be sure, Ḥarīrī subsequently tried to recoup the popularity with his conservative Sunni base by banning alcohol from the Grand Serail in Beirut, an unprecedented public gesture for a Lebanese premier.

A yet more conspicuous showcasing of Sunni communal identity was the erection of the gargantuan Muhammad Muḥsin al-Amīn mosque adjacent to Martyr's Square in the heart of Beirut, which the premier stepped in to finance with a contribution estimated to top US$25 million after his arch-competitor Walīd Ibn Talāl had offered a US$2 million

has expressed his opposition to the pretentious display of sumptuous *Iftār* dinners. Sa'd, *as-Sādis wa as-Saba'ūn*, vol. 2, 191.

128 Legislative Decree 18 of 1955 regulates the position of the mufti of the republic as the "chief Islamic authority and position," with the tacit assumption of Shia–Sunni legal concord. Official recognition of Shia jurisdiction only followed in 1967 with Decree 18 and and the Supreme Shia Council (Law 72) of 1969. The precise relation between the civil power of the premier and the religious power of the mufti have not been regulated, although Article 5 of the aforementioned legislation does stipulate his subservience to "public powers" illustrated by the mufti's formal confirmation by the Sunni premier and Maronite president. *De facto,* the Sunni premier oversees the state payments to the *Dār al-Fatwā*. Rabbāth, *La Formation Historique du Liban* Politique et Constitutionnelle, 111–115.

129 Namely, the current mufti of the republic, Muhammad Qabbānī. By contrast, Patriarch Sfayr is arguably the single most significant leader of the Maronite community. His political sway and broad appeal is only contested by General Michel 'Awn.

donation to the bankrupt foundation. The shadow cast by the mammoth mosque, both architecturally on its immediate environment,[130] and figuratively on the future climate of intercommunal relations in Beirut and Lebanon as a whole, has yet to be gauged.[131] Needless to say, all confessions in Lebanon are susceptible to use architecture and public venues to showcase confessional prowess, so that this last instance should be seen as a culmination of a long-standing rivalry over the confessional identity of the public space.

Incidentally, since independence there have been several attempts in modern Lebanon to ban public displays of religion, most of which never saw the light of day.[132] The historical concurrence of increased public sectarian markings and the privatization of formally state-owned services and institutions in the postwar Lebanese state need not be conceived as mutually contradictory developments. The high pace of globalization and the opening of economic markets has dovetailed with the rise of religious identities and ideologies around the globe, and it stands to reason that Lebanon, on account of its equally competitive economy and religious pluralism, should be susceptible to the same dynamic in which "*Jihād*" and "*McWorld*" (un)happily coexist.

Ḥarīrī for his part entered the postwar fray showing he was capable of turning in almost any direction, donning the clothes of the Sunni *Za'īm* here, displaying sanguine disregard for confessional and other barriers elsewhere, even courting communists if need be.[133] In short, Ḥarīrī rose rapidly to fill the role of Lebanon's paramount patron and consummate "cosmo-politician" all in one, evincing an ability "to combine naked self-interest pursued with concern for the local community" and the nation at large.[134]

This exceedingly pragmatic instinct has (mis)led some to lend credence to the belief that the businessman premier who invested heavily in US realty and presidential campaigns might be amenable to a long-standing

[130] Approximately 1,000 m^2 of Phoenician, Roman, and Islamic ruins were destroyed, prompting a public outcry that in turn led Oger Liban president Nabīl Ḥarīrī and the mufti of the republic to issue a statement on June 2, 2003 promising to preserve whatever archeological artifacts construction should reveal.

[131] See Ward Vloeberghs, "A Building of Might and Faith: Rafiq Hariri and the Muhammad Al-Amin Mosque: On the Political Dimensions of Religious Architecture in Contemporary Beirut," Universite Catholique De Louvain, 2010.

[132] For the various initiatives launched under the French mandate to secularize personal status laws, as well as interior minister Salāh Salmān's attempt to get rid of confessional identification cards in 1977.

[133] In 1996, to take but one example, the arch-capitalist Ḥarīrī stunned the Armenian community by entering an alliance with an Armenian communist.

[134] Johnson, *All Honorable Men,* 54.

United States–Israeli plan to settle Palestinian refugees in exchange for a massive debt forgiveness.[135] President Lahhūd repeatedly confirmed the existence of such offers – the amount of debt to be forgiven standing at US$20 billion – only to reject them out of hand.[136] One should note that, of all of the contentious issues in Lebanon, none is quite as divisive as the naturalization of Palestinian refugees residing in Lebanon, a measure first suggested by US secretary of state John Foster Dulles during the 1950s and explicitly proscribed by the Lebanese constitution. Survey's confirm most Lebanese are opposed to naturalization.[137] Nonetheless, Druze leader Walīd Janbulāt suggested that several thousand Palestinians driven out of east Beirut during the civil war be resettled in a deserted village on the southern margin of the Shūf, Quray, arguing that the "implantation of Palestinians in Lebanon was inevitable."[138] Janbulāt received backing from Ḥarīrī, who shared his opinion about the impracticality of expelling Palestinians from the country and had concluded massive real-estate purchases in the designated region. Shortly thereafter, during the parliamentary session of June 21, 1994, Prime Minister Ḥarīrī stunned the assembly when he announced a naturalization decree.[139] An official number of at minimum 160,000 applicants were granted Lebanese citizenship. Ḥarīrī and interior minister Murr stood accused of having used the naturalized Palestinians and Syrians to shore up their (Sunni) electoral base in the 1996 elections; approximately 80 percent of the naturalized were Sunni Muslims. Such suspicions were not laid to

[135] Sa'd Ḥarīrī made a US$1 million contribution to Neil Bush's financially strapped Ignite software company. Mimi Swartz, "Cast Away," *Texas Monthly*, 32, 5, May 2004, www.texasmonthly.com/politics/cast-away/, last accessed February 6, 2019.

[136] The Maronite Church periodically reiterated its apprehensions of efforts to foist a naturalization or settlement on Lebanon. Shāmī, *Le Mémorial Du Liban*, vol. II, 158.

[137] Of the population, 86 percent of Maronites, 83.3 percent of Orthodox, 73.3 percent of Catholics, 72 percent of Sunnis, 62.9 percent of Shiite, and 93.8 percent of Druze are opposed to naturalization. Cited in Jawād Al-'Adra, "Naturalization: In Defense and Opposition," *Ii-Monthly*, September 2, 2002. An earlier survey comes to the opposite conclusion, citing 81.2 percent of Sunni, 71.4 percent of Armenian, and 61.1 percent of Druze students in favor of a naturalization (compared to only a paltry 0.9 percent of Maronites and 3.3 percent of Catholics). Hilāl Khashshān, *Inside the Lebanese Confessional Mind* (Lanham, MD: University Press of America, 1992), 94. It is difficult to reconcile the diametrically opposed results of the two surveys; it does stand to reason that, given the fact the refugees are mostly Sunni, a naturalization would be seen as bolstering the communal clout of the Sunnis as a sect.

[138] Walīd Janbulāt cited in Carole Dāghir, *Ces Hommes qui font la Paix* (Paris: Editions FMA, 1994), 331.

[139] Simon Ḥaddād and Attitudes Towards Integrated Education, "Palestinians in Lebanon: Towards Integration or Conflict?" *Journal of International Migration and Integration* 14 (2000), http://prrn.mcgill.ca/research/papers/hadda_000514.htm, last accessed February 4, 2019. Majdoline Hatūm, "Ḥarīrī's comments on citizenship issue provoke criticism," *Daily Star*, March 23, 2004.

rest by Rafīq al-Ḥarīrī when he bared his soul in a private audience with Cardinal Sfayr, averring point-blank that "this decree was useful as it bestowed the citizenship on Sunnis more so than it did on Shia."[140]

The *fait accompli* of this massive naturalization can be seen as a result of a convergence of interests of Syria and Ḥarīrī.[141] This entente prevailed over the protestations of the Maronite patriarch, who had complained of a "loss of Lebanese identity" and the (electoral) exclusion of the (overwhelmingly Christian) Lebanese abroad.[142] Rumors persisted that Ḥarīrī was ultimately acting on behalf of US–Israeli designs aimed at a settlement of (Palestinian) refugees in Lebanon. On the record, however, Ḥarīrī remained steadfast in his public defense of Palestinian rights, including the right of return enshrined in UN Resolution 191 and his opposition to Israeli occupation of southern Lebanon and the (still contested) Šibʿā farms.[143] It was only after his assassination that US ambassador Jeffrey Feltman tabled another offer of debt cancellation in return for the naturalization of 100,000 Palestinian refugees during a dinner hosting Lebanon's major politicians.[144]

In the end, Ḥarīrī's geopolitical attitude is perhaps best summarized by his own words that at once bespeak a dogged pragmatism and, as some would argue, a measure of wishful utopianism: "we should forget Israel and develop our country."[145] To be sure, a number of Lebanese besides

140 Cited in Sa'd, *as-Sādis wa as-Saba'ūn*, vol. 2, 161. The issue was put to rest until it flared up again in wake of Emile Lahhūd's presidential extension campaign in 2004 when the Maronite League won its case before the highest constitutional supervisory body, the Majlis al-Shurā, to revoke 4,000 of the previously bestowed naturalizations. Ḥarīrī was in no mood to hurry the implementation of this decree. Hasan Rifāʿī, a leading constitutional expert in Lebanon, argued that Ḥarīrī's measure violated the constitution. Lebanese forces lawyer Edmond Naʿīm justified it.

141 The pro-Syrian President Emile Lahhūd promised several times to lift the aforecited decree.

142 Walīd Janbulāt immediately responded with caustic sarcasm charging Bkirki with racism: "Indeed, how could they not be aware that there is a danger to the Lebanese race? … [After all] these fellows can't even use forks and knives. They don't speak Lebanese and don't have authentic Lebanese blood in their veins." Cited in Sa'd, *as-Sādis wa as-Saba'ūn*, vol. 2, 161.

143 "The Lebanese government is fully convinced that the Šibʿā Farms area is a Lebanese territory and must be liberated by all means available … One way to regain Shaba Farms is through diplomatic contacts, while another way is through armed resistnce. Only circumstances determine which course we should follow." Saad al-Ḥarīrī as cited in Arieh O'Sullivan, "Hariri: Hizbullah has right to attack Israel," *Jerusalem Post*, March 21, 2001, 5.

144 An enraged Michel ʿAwn apparently left the dinner in response. "Tāriq Tarshīshī," *Al-Balad*, June 23, 2005.

145 Interview in Nevine Khalil, "Seeking Stability," *al-Ahram Weekly*, 540, June 28, 2001, http://weekly.ahram.org.eg/Archive/2001/540/re5.htm, last accessed February 6, 2019. Ḥarīrī also intervened on the behest of the United States and Israeli government to

Ḥarīrī have come to espouse this axiom, many of which coalesced in the March 14 alliance.

Ḥarīrī himself finally became a larger-than-life political actor whose Delphic threats of imminent retirement from politics (1994, 1996, 1998, 2003, and 2004) were intermittently issued, or indeed acted upon, in order to gain greater bargaining power upon each subsequent return. One of several popular explanations for Ḥarīrī's assassination in February 2005 is that it was a meant to cut short precisely yet another *déjà vu* comeback.

Ḥarīrī's business interests, development agenda, and attraction of foreign capital may indeed have come at the expense of less affluent, ordinary Lebanese who faced rising rents and spiraling real-estate prices in an increasingly tight market.[146] Likewise, the old entrenched Christian bourgeoisie did not always look with favor toward the towering Sunni *über-Zaʿīm,* and certain satirical journals of the Christian right did not hold back from sectarian parodies of Ḥarīrī's Saudi provenance.[147] Yet, arguably, the Syrian stifling of the so-called Christian opposition, such as the 2001 closing of the MTV TV station, was ordered by Syria and the Maronite president Emile Lahhūd while Ḥarīrī was out of the country. Ḥarīrī's principal enemies were socialists, syndicates, and unions on the left, as well as the Islamic fundamentalists on the right, not necessarily the Christians as a religious group. In the municipal elections in Beirut of 1998, as in 2004, Ḥarīrī was insistent on piecing together a broad coalition of Christian and Muslim candidates, resulting in a list combining such unlikely partners as Hizballāh, the Jamāʿat al-Islāmīya, the Katā'ib, AMAL, and the Lebanese forces.[148] Nonetheless, these intersectarian

cancel an international conference sponsored by the Holocaust-denying Institute for Historical Review, entitled "Revisionism and Zionism," which was scheduled to take place in Beirut in late February. Ḥarīrī's intervention was justified in purely pragmatic terms: "Lebanon has more important things to do than holding conferences that hurt its international standing and smear its name."

146 In 1996, the oldest steel factory in Lebanon in Amshīt, owned by Michael Abū Zayd, was forced to reduce its staff of 1,500 to 250 employees due to the sudden competition of cheaper steel imports from the Ukraine by Ḥarīrī's finance minister Fu'ad Siniora and his business partner Hagop Demerdjian. Prime Minister Ḥarīrī, of course, ended up supporting his closest ally, presumably not out of any anti-Maronite sentiments, but simply in light of business rationale that dictated importing less expensive Ukranian steel. Naba, *Rafīq Ḥarīrī,* 102–103.

147 See the satirical weekly published by the Lebanese forces, www.facebook.com/Addabbour.lebanon/, last accessed February 5, 2019 .

148 Ḥarīrī sought to come to an accord with the Greek Orthodox, who traditionally have been given the governorship of Beirut while the Sunnis retained the position of mayor. The Shias, who arguably constitute the largest denomination in greater Beirut, felt left out of the power-sharing formula.

"marriages of convenience" among political elites cannot, properly speaking, be deemed as harbingers of secularism in practice. Rather, they were squarely entangled in the premier's personal patronage network that partly cooperated with, and partly supplanted, that of the traditional *zu'amā'*.[149]

The broader political agenda pursued could in fact be pernicious to the fragile state–citizen relationship. The government's concerted crackdown on the General Labor Confederation (GDL), one of the precious few trans-sectarian unions in Lebanon, was a salient example of the perils an extreme neoliberal agenda could bring.[150] These organizations were reliant on a government supportive of a social vision above and beyond narrow and short-term calculations of nominal profit.

If, to paraphrase Marx, "capital knows no religion," sectarian strongholds conversely have shown a remarkable resilience to withstand the forces of incorporation and monopolization: One case in point was the fierce row between Hizballāh and Ḥarīrī over the latter's plans of expansion in the southern suburbs;[151] another was the intransigence displayed by certain Christian institutions such as the Catholic Church, which barred the tycoon from taking over the University of the Holy Spirit of Kaslik in Jounieh.[152] Finally, when Mr. Ḥarīrī wanted to expand the tentacles of his media empire, à la Silvio Berlusconi, and sought to acquire a majority stake in the prestigious daily *an-Nahār,* he was prevented from doing so by dint of the veto of the Orthodox archdiocese of Beirut. The traditional flagship of Lebanese papers, and one priding itself

[149] Ḥarīrī appointed his confidants to head a number of key positions such as the Bank of Lebanon (Riyād Salāma, his former stockbroker), the ministry of finance (Siniora, his former account and portfolio manger), and ministry of justice (Bahīj Tabāra, his former attorney).

[150] The GDL was a conglomerate of various originally sectarian unions that banded together due to shared interests. On May 30, 1997 the Ḥarīrī government arrested its elected leader, 'Ilyās Abū Rizq, who had vowed to keep the union free from government control. His efforts had been undermined by the former head of the GDL, Antoine Bishāra, who, seeking to cover-up an embezzlement involving his presidency of the sea port, sided with the Ḥarīrī government against Abū Rizq, thus sealing the fate of the union.

[151] Much of the dispute has centered around the government's construction project "Elissar" in Beirut's southern suburbs of Awzā'ī. The government has failed to implement its 1995 cabinet decree blaming Hizballāh's thirst for kickbacks, local residents intransigence, and insufficient funds for the failure to start the revival plan. Nonetheless, construction has begun on a bridge that would circumvent traffic from Awzā'ī. Future MP Walīd 'Īdū did not endear himself with the Hizballāh deputies in parliament when he referred to the squatters in Awzā'ī as "multiplying algae." see Nayla 'Assāf, "Ouzai row draws fire onto handling of public funds," *Daily Star,* June 25, 2002, www.dailystar.com.lb/ArticlePrint.aspx?id=39377&mode=print, last accessed February 3, 2019. 'Īdū was assassinated on June 13, 2007.

[152] Naba, *Rafīq Harīrī*, 101.

on a secular outlook, *an-Nahār* has had a shifting relationship with Ḥarīrī. Banque de la Méditerranée had salvaged *an-Nahār* from the brink of bankruptcy several times during the war. After Ḥarīrī took over the bank in 1983 from Lebanese financier Joseph Khūrī,[153] he gained leverage over the crown jewel of the Lebanese press, asking for "fair coverage,"[154] while subsequently denying having ever interfered in any way in the papers publishing policy. Likewise, the traditionally left-oriented daily *as-Safir* received a financial injection from Ḥarīrī in 1997, whereupon a number of critics of the premier left the paper.[155] In 2004, the outspoken general manager of *an-Nahār,* Jubrān Tuwaynī, finally decided to buy back the Ḥarīrī shares. Ḥarīrī announced that his decision to sell his stake of 34 percent of *an-Nahār* shares sprang from "personal reasons" and that he sold the stock at a "low price."[156] He thereby contradicted editor-in-chief Jubrān Tuwaynī's testimony that confirmed that the shares were bought back from Ḥarīrī to "safeguard the independence of the paper from outside pressure for a very high price."[157] Even later-day fierce critics of Ḥarīrī, such as Charles Ayyūb, the editor-in-chief of *al-Diyyār,* have acknowledged receiving hefty bribes in exchange for positive coverage from Ḥarīrī.[158] The Saudi-Lebanese premier found little difficulty in outspending the competing offers extended by (Syrian-controlled) Lebanese secret service head Jamīl as-Sayyid to journalists.[159]

153 Khūrī had taken over the Eastern Commercial Bank in 1969 and founded the Bank Mediterranée with the aid of the Kuwaiti Princess Badīra as-Sabāh and Saudi investors. Antoine Sfayr, *L'Argent Des Arabes* (Paris: Herme, 1992), 209.

154 Nesemann, *Medienpolitik Im Libanon,* 64.

155 This trend continued after the Ḥarīrī assassination with the resignation of Ibrāhīm al-Amīn and editor-in-chief Joseph Samāha himself. Both journalists were critical of the March 14 pro-Ḥarīrī alliance.

156 *As-Safīr,* December 10, 2003.

157 "He did good business. But I think politically it was good for *An-Nahār.* A long time ago, I asked him to sell me back the shares, but he didn't want to at the time. Now I think he feels that the policy of *An-Nahār* for the time being is very independent and maybe he thought that he cannot exert pressure to change that policy. Maybe he thought that it was too much for him to support." Interview with Jubrān Tuwaynī, *an-Nahār,* May 24, 2004. As irony would have it, Jubrān Tuwaynī would burry his hatchet with Ḥarīrī and run on the 2005 Ḥarīrī-sponsored electoral list as east Beirut's (i.e., Ashrafīya's) representative to the Lebanese parliament.

158 Charles Ayyūb claimed to have received US$100,000 a month from Ḥarīrī. This amount may be inflated due to Ayyūb's falling out with the Future movement. Dubai TV, September 25, 2005. Less disputed are the inordinately high wages paid by Ḥarīrī to his employees at the Future TV and newspapers.

159 Sayyid confirmed that he was "rendering services" to influence journalists through the Office of General Relations, but added with uncharacteristic understatement that the entire budget of all security agencies was limited to US$400,000. Ghassān Sharbil

Embattled Freedom and Secular Sphere of the Media 1977–2004

The waning of effective state power and authority, as opposed to the expansion of the highly personalized patronage state with its sectarian domains, is reflected in the postwar metamorphoses of the Lebanese media landscape. As Fawwāz Ṭarābulsī has shown, the origins of this trend can be traced to the civil war during the course of which government institutions were in effect hollowed out by the various militias who established a patchwork of informal economies as large as US$15 billion within their largely confessionally defined ministates.[160] Some of the public properties seized during the war in fact remain in the hands of those who seized them.[161]

Following the analysis of Elisabeth Piccard, we may trace the evolution of the Lebanese economy from an initial stage of prewar clientelism. This later evoloved to the initially haphazard looting, blackmail, and predation at the onset of the war, to the formal consolidation of the militia into orderly, wage-paying, and service-rendering statelets (and profitable enterprises) in the 1980s, to the return back to a more centralized, officially regulated clientelism, which marked the post-Tā'if period. In fact, the postwar era saw a formal incorporation of the militias in parliament and government even as the Tā'if Accord foresaw a disbandment of all militias.[162]

The continuum between pre- and post-war economies can be traced further yet, for the war era was marked by an unregulated privatization, and hence "confessionalization," of the media, a process that was to be ratified *de jure* under the Ḥarīrī tenure. Amid the cantonization that ensued during the war, a bevy of confessional and militia-affiliated stations proliferated. Over sixty television stations and up to 150 radio stations mushroomed as anarchy held sway and the state's historic monopoly over the media was broken.

interview with Jamīl as-Sayyid, "Muqabal ma' Jamīl as-Sayyid," *al-Hayāt*, July 13, 2005, 1.

[160] Fawwāz Ṭarābulsī, "The Role of War in State and Society Transformation: The Lebanese Case," SSRC Paris, November 2–4, 1994, 7 and Michel Murqus, "Muqabal ma' Jamil Al-Sayyid," *An-Nahār*, October 15, 1990.

[161] Jawād al-'Adra estimates that the seizure of coastal properties alone signifies that the state is bereft of US$50–70 million a year plus $US0.5 billion in compensation. Jawād 'Adra, "Corruption: The Lebanese Syndrome: Maintaining the System, Depleting the Resources," *Ii-Monthly*, October 25, 2005, 21.

[162] Elisabeth Piccard, "The Political Economy of Civil War in Lebanon," in *War, Institutions and Social Change in the Middle East*, ed., Steven Heydemann (Berkeley: University of California Press, 2000).

In 1994, the landmark Law 382 was passed to dismantle the state monopoly, which had been granted until 2012 to the country's only nonconfessional station, Télé Liban. Just months before this decision revoking the exclusive broadcasting rights of this station, Rafīq al-Ḥarīrī sold his majority shares of Télé Liban back to the government for US$12 million.

Meanwhile, an "oligarchic" arrangement was sealed among the leading cast of former militiamen and businessmen, each of whom was granted ownership of individual television stations in contravention to Lebanese law, which explicitly proscribes sectarian affiliation and ownership beyond a 10 percent ceiling. The nation's media spoils were divided up among Rafīq al-Ḥarīrī (Future, al-Mustaqbal, and al-Liwā' newspapers), AMAL's Nabīh Birrī (NBN),[163] the deputy premier 'Isām Fāris and Pierre Dāghir of the Lebanese forces (Lebanese Broadcasting Corporation [LBC]),[164] NTV[165] (Tahsīn Khayyāt) as well as Hizballāh (al-Manār). The government decided to grant licenses to an-Nur Radio and al-Manār while forcing the three Catholic channels Voix de la Charite, Radio Alleluia, and Télé Lumière to suspend their broadcasting service.

Like the aforementioned Catholic stations, Hizballāh originally failed to obtain a license for its TV channel al-Manār, unlike the five officially recognized channels. When President Harāwī attempted to enforce the prohibition of political broadcasting (for religious channels) on al-Manār, it was Premier Ḥarīrī, who, strong-armed by Syrian President Assad, retracted the initial ban so that the government granted a license to the Hizballāh channel on October 2, 1996. By contrast, the Sawt al-Haqq radio station of the militant Sunni Harakat al-Tawhīd in Tripoli

[163] Nabīh Birrī and Michel Murr have both denied any direct, personal investment in the channels; indeed, only their kin appear as shareholders in the published lists, see *Official Gazette*, no. 47, September 16, 1996, 3315–3319.

[164] LBC was the first privately owned national television in Lebanon. Apparently Fāris sold the shares he acquired in 1995, although his son and brother also held shares in Ḥarīrī's Future TV. Nesemann, *Medienpolitik Im Libanon*, 77. Syrian investors are also said to hold shares of LBC. Walīd Ibn Talāl was the largest single shareholder of LBC Satellite, which has since split from the LBC group.

[165] Despite repeated attempts by Ḥarīrī to shut it down, the NTV channel managed to obtain a license under the Huss government. After a recent closure of the station by Ḥarīrī due to the planned airing of a program critical of Saudi Arabia, the station was salvaged by dint of owner Tahsīn Khayyat's backing from President Lahhūd after the investigative report on Saudi Arabia was cancelled. See Human Rights Watch Middle East, *Lebanon, Restrictions on Broadcasting: In Whose Interest?* (New York: Human Rights Watch, 1997), 10.

was stormed,[166] while Henri Sfayr's Nidā al-Watan TV station was closed down in June 1994 along with the *Nidā al-Watan* daily newspaper after it aired concerns by Christians over the prime minister's land purchases in traditionally Christian areas. The official reason given for the closure, however, was the airing of "tapes, news, and images that undermine national unity and security by instigating confessional passions and conflicts among various sects of the nation."[167]

Likewise, in September 1997, MTV was prevented from airing an interview with Johnny ʻAbdu, the Paris-based former head of the Lebanese secret service, co-architect of the 1982 Israeli invasion, and former confidante of Ḥarīrī. When in November 1997 an interview with the former business partner of Ḥarīrī and convicted US felon, Roger Tamraz, was to be broadcast on LBC, a barrage of threats was triggered by the Lebanese government.[168] Lastly, after opposition maverick Najāh Wakīm appeared in January 1998 on LBC sharply discrediting the regime, Decree no. 11657 was issued that withdrew licenses from all private channels to air political programs. Thus, the press was temporarily tamed. More portentously, virulent attacks launched against Wakīm to the extent of branding the *bona fide* agnostic Arabist an "anti-Islamic Christian polemicist" dealt a severe blow to one of Lebanon's most popular icons of secularism.[169]

166 Three members of Shaykh Shaʻbān's Harakat al-Tawhīd were killed during the government raid. Harakat al-Tawhīd, along with other fundamentalist Sunni groups such as al-Jamāʻa al-Islāmīya, seek to establish a religious state, a goal still (in)directly espoused by Hizballāh.

167 Mark Dennis, "If You Can't Beat'em, Buy'em," *Columbia Journalism Review* 33 (1994): 1.

168 Born in 1940 in Cairo, Roger Tamraz is a Lebanese–American businessman who began his career in the CIA working as an admissions officer at Harvard University. Upon obtaining his Harvard MBA, Tamraz was involved in investment banking and international energy projects and was convicted in 1996 by a US congressional hearing. In Lebanon he stands accused together with Ahmad Chalabi of having diverted funds of Gulf investors in the Intra Bank. Tamraz had to leave Lebanon in 1989 after being charged with embezzling US$200 million. The head of the Bank al-Machrek escaped Lebanon allegedly with the help of Walīd Janbulāt, "Article I," *The Washington Report on Middle East Affairs*, XVI, December 1997, 4. Committee on Governmental Affairs, *Investigation of Illegal or Improper Activities in Connection with 1996 Federal Election Campaigns, vol. 6.6, chapter 30 "The Sage of Roger Tamraz"* (Washington, DC: Congress Press, March 10, 1998), 2095 ff. In June 1997, a Lebanese military court sentenced Tamraz in absentia to fifteen years of hard labor for "contacts with the Israeli enemy" as a result of his dealing with David Kimche, a former Israeli official who was trying to aid the late newspaper magnate Robert Maxwell. *Wall Street Journal*, September 12, 1997, 24. Tamraz had gained a reputation for his loose tongue after he boasted in front of a US congressional commission about his ties to the CIA and Israeli intelligence.

169 Wakīm served as the youngest ever Lebanese MP from 1970 to2000. A popular politician in Lebanon, particularly among university students of both sects, he

Ḥarīrī also attempted, in defiance of a decision reached by the highest constitutional court, the Shūrā Council, to censor channels infringing on "relations with friendly Arab countries." Walīd al-Husaynī and Tālib 'Abdallāh, owners and editor-in-chief of the popular left-leaning weekly *Kifah al-'Arabī,* were arrested in accordance with paragraph 23 of the press law and sentenced to two months imprisonment and a US$33,000 fine for insulting the Saudi king.[170] After opposition leader Gabriel Murr's MTV channel was forcibly shutdown in 2001, Tahsīn Khayyāt, the owner of one of the remaining vocally antigovernment channels, NTV, was arrested on December 6, 2003 for trumped-up charges of spying for Israel.[171] Khayyāt's NTV station was forced to drop an investigative report on Saudi Arabia, and on December 18, 2003 was temporarily suspended for forty-eight hours due to "threatening ties with a friendly country," an oblique reference to the station's intent to air a program on the largest bank fraud in postwar Lebanese history, the Medina Bank scandal.[172]

The official justification for the ban imposed on critical coverage of Saudi Arabia rested on the concern over potential reprisals against over 50,000 Lebanese expatriates working in Saudi Arabia. After the November 9, 2003 suicide attack on the al-Muhaya residential compound in Riyadh claimed a dozen of these very ex-pats, the question arose whether the legislation mandating censorship of all critical investigations of "sisterly Arab states" is in fact to the (long-term) benefit and security of Lebanese, Saudis, and Arabs in general, or whether such state-enforced silencing actually is compounding social tensions by averting a frank, public discussion on the underlying causes and symptoms of the scourge of fundamentalism. Its vaunted reputation as the "lighthouse" of the Arab press notwithstanding, when it comes to free debate on religion, Lebanon unfortunately does not enjoy a fundamental advantage over other Arab states.

For one, the nation's delicate diversity renders discourse on religions a potential minefield. Second, a heightened sensitivity toward certain topics can be attributed to the fact that large swaths of the Lebanese

boasted an over 50 percent approval rating among both Christians and Muslims. Information International, "University Students Survey (II)", *An-Nahar*, January 14, 1997, 10.

170 Nesemann, *Medienpolitik Im Libanon*, 92.

171 Ḥarīrī on May 5, 2004 filed another law suit against NTV and its owner Tahsīn Khayyāt, charging the station with defamation and slander.

172 The owner of the bank remained at large in Saudi Arabia despite the Lebanese government's issuance of an arrest warrant and a request to extradite him to Lebanon in order to testify on the disappearance of approximately US$1 billion.

press are financed by outside sources from the Gulf that tend to display a preoccupation either with commercialism or conservative values (or both). This domination became particularly apparent after the oil gush of the 1950s, prompting a prominent Lebanese journalist to quip that his colleagues had grown accustomed to "writing with oil, not ink."[173] It is more than coincidental that the 1992 Saudi press law almost verbatim resembles the Lebanese counterpart, the postwar audio-media law (382/1994).[174] To be sure, the latter chiefly was based on Lebanese precedents, namely, laws 386 and 385 of the penal code likewise prohibit libel and slander (*qadh wa damm*) of the countries' leading politicians as well as the 1962 and 1977 press laws that already roundly prohibited the "instigation of sectarian strife" and the defamation of Arab leaders.[175] The earlier, foundational press law of August 24, 1948, incidentally, did not contain such a specific restrictive clause, although Lebanon's record of press freedoms was not without blemishes even after independence.[176] The extreme measures taken during the French mandate were, to be sure, *passé*.[177] But independence in 1946 did not reduce the authorities penchant to wield censorship as a weapon of control. Arrests of journalists and closures of papers accused of inciting sectarian strife marred the record of public freedoms. As early as March 19, 1946 the famous daily *L'Orient* was suspended for six months as a punishment for Jurj Naqqāsh's memorable editorial: "Two negotiations do not make a nation!"[178] On January 3, 1947, the uncle and namesake of the current

173 Saʿīd Abūrīsh, *The Rise, Corruption, and Coming Fall of the House of Saud* (New York: St. Martins, 1995).

174 Decree 104/77 cited in Naomi Saqr, *Satellite Realms: Transnational Television, Globalization and the Middle East* (London: I. B. Tauris, 2001), 30.

175 To be sure, in contrast to Lebanese media in the 1990s, Lebanese papers in the 1960s rarely suffered from censorship and were usually banned in other Arab countries rather than in Lebanon proper, if and when "transgressions" occurred. Marwān Kraydī, "State Control of Television News in 1990s Lebanon," *Journalism and Mass Communication Quarterly* 76.3 (1999), 489.

176 Article 31 of the 1948 Law did define an array of sanctions against newspaper articles of a polemically sectarian character jeopardizing the "public order" without, however, mentioning foreign heads of state. On February 16, 1950, Muhammad Shukayr, director of the daily *Nidā'*, was convicted by a press tribunal to serve twenty days in prison for defamation of King Saʿūd, despite the defense of the political giants Camille Shamʿūn, Hamīd Franjīya, Muhammad Baʿalbakī, and Habīb Sā'igh. On the same day, Ghassān Tuwaynī and seventeen other members of the SSNP were arrested. Shāmī, *Le Mėmorial Du Liban*, vol. II, 329.

177 *An-Nahār* was suspended in 1936 for six months and in 1943. Lebanon still is subjected to the Decree no. 115 issued by the French high comissioner Jean Helleux on August 12, 1932, which regulates all transgressions pertaining to "general security" in Lebanon. Decree no. 74 (issued April 13, 1953) restricts the "granting of any new licenses for daily or periodical printed publications."

178 "Deux Négotations ne font pas une Nation!" *L'Orient*, March 10, 1943.

president, the deputy Emile Lahhūd, demanded the erection of a press censoring committee in parliament.[179]

More often that not, however, these efforts to control Lebanon's "Fourth Power" backfired. When President Bishāra al-Khūrī tried to silence the press' criticism of his corruption and desire to extend his term with a restrictive decree, a vast press strike contributed to the election of Camille Sham'ūn in 1952 instead. The latter proceeded to abolish the previous decrees, one year after the Jordanian king Talāl lifted all press censorship, including the prohibition of government criticism in October 1951.[180] Lebanon's reputation as a beachhead for freedom of expression in the Arab world would take on its somewhat legendary aura in the 1950s and 1960s, the heyday for the publication of a vast number of decidedly secular literary and political journals such as *al-Adab, as-Shi'r,* and *al-Mawāqif.*

This is not to say that Lebanon's press freedoms enjoyed a sheltered existence in "splendid isolation" apart from the trials and tribulations the rest of the society was subjected to. Prior to the outbreak of the civil war in 1958, the political escalation was reflected in an increasingly sweeping crackdown on the press. On November 8, 1956 the Council of Ministers led by 'Abdullāh al-Yāfī ordered the arrest of Ghassān Tuwaynī for defamation of its dignity in an acerbic article. Tuwaynī escaped the sentence of three months prison due to his parliamentary immunity and backing by Sā'ib Salām and multimillionaire Robert Abéla. On February 17, 1958 the Council of Ministers promulgated by decree an amendment to the Press Law 41 allowing for preventive detentions of journalists, causing an immediate strike of the press syndicates and a refusal of parliament to ratify the law. On May 8, 1958 Nasīb al-Matnī, owner of the opposition *Télegraphe,* was assassinated. On September 19 of the same year, Fu'ād Haddād, who had often penned his fiercely anti-Nassirite views under the pseudonym of 'Abd ul-Hanīn al-Amal, fell victim to another assassination plot.[181]

President Shihāb's Press Law of 1962 delineated the taboo topics that remain off limits until today: national security and unity, national borders, and instigation of religious or confessional sentiments.[182] The notorious Press Law of 1977 – which President Sarkīs passed due to pressure from neighboring Arab countries and which remains in

[179] Shāmī, *Le Mémorial Du Liban,* vol. II, 189.
[180] See Sāmī Mubayyid, "Talāl: The Sad Story of the King of Jordan," *al-Mashriq* 4.15 (2005): 55–68.
[181] Shāmī, *Le Mémorial Du Liban,* vol. III, 302, 330.
[182] Nesemann, *Medienpolitik Im Libanon,* 44.

effect – is even more restrictive in prohibiting any insult of a Lebanese president or foreign leader. An even more direct and conspicuous interference with press freedoms came with the arrival of Syrian troops in the capital beginning on December 15, 1976, when seven Beirut dailies were briefly closed down including *al-Muharrir, al-Dustūr, as-Safīr, L'Orient le Jour*, and *an–Nahār.*[183]

In the postwar era, censorship was exercised by dint of the 1994 law, which also provided for the establishment of a "National Council" for audio-media, which was empowered to shutdown stations in violation of the aforementioned law.[184] Implementation was haphazard and governed by political interests of the security apparatus (Sécurité Général), Syrian intelligence, and the personal interests of the governing troika. The main legal pretext used to implement censorship was alleged affiliation with Israel and insult or slander of any (Arab) head of state. The third most commonly invoked justification for censorship was the charge of instigating sectarian discord. This clause was cited in the famous cases against Sādiq al-'Azm in 1969 and the popular Lebanese singer Marcel Khalīfa in 1999, the latter having cited an innocuous Quranic verse in one of his songs.[185] While in 1969 'Azm himself denied the charge of having intended a direct critique of religious texts in his court interrogation, a number of intellectuals rushed to assert his right to do, among them a cleric (Bishop Jurj Khidr), who wrote a "defense of atheism" under a pen name ("Wā'il ar-Rāwī"). Khalīfa's case two decades later, by contrast, even those clerics who came to his defense, such as Fadlallāh and Muhammad Hasan al-Amīn, did not do so by affirming the right of freedom of speech *a priori*, but by arguing that Khalīfa's Quranic citation was not defamatory to religion.[186] The legal prohibition of blasphemy in Lebanese criminal law was never put to question.

The audio-media law was ratified in the same year the Ḥarīrī government banned all public demonstrations. This latter decree was lifted by

183 Petran, *The Struggle over Lebanon*, 220.

184 Paragraph 47 of the law states that "by request of the Ministry of Information, the National Council of Audio Visual Media practices censorship over TV and radio stations." Cited in Nesemann, *Medienpolitik Im Libanon*, 69.

185 The Sunni mufti's *Dār al-Fatwā'* had filed a suit against 'Azm for religious defamation in his book on religious criticism. After the intercession of Kamāl Janbulāt and a coterie of prominent lawyers, 'Azm was eventually exonerated. The court proceedings can be found in the annex to 'Azm's book. See Sādiq Jalāl Al-'Azm, *Fī Naqd al-Fikr al-Dīnī, Dār al-Talīa lil-Ṭibā'a wa al-Nashr* (Beirut, 1969), 246ff.

186 Kim Ghattas, "Read the Koran, Never Sing it," *International Press Service*, November 3, 1999, www.ipsnews.net/1999/11/rights-lebanon-read-the-koran-never-sing-it/, last accessed February 5, 2019.

the Huss government in 1999, only to be reimposed by interior minister Michel Murr in October 2002.[187] Overt political and police crackdowns on the press largely subsided after the MTV closure of 2001, the brief NTV harassment of 2003, and the Syrian exit. Nonetheless, confessionally dictated forms of (self-)censorship remain as solid as elsewhere across the Arab media world, although far more leeway has been given to the printed press. The absolute prohibition of any direct or indirect criticism of religion is codified in constitutional and criminal clauses.[188] L ebanon's clerical authorities have made use of this allotted prerogative by mandating the annual censorship of about half a dozen books in Lebanon due to their (allegedly) controversial religious content. Religiously informed censorship has also affected the film industry, as was seen in the selective censorship of scenes of Randa Sabbagh's *Civilisé* and other movies.[189] Even as innocuous a matter as a letter supplicating divine intervention against the, highly unpopular, impending US attack on Iraq led to a law suit from the mufti of Tripoli against the *an-Nahār* newspaper.[190] Publications deemed offensive to both Islam and Christianity are still banned on a regular basis by the security forces, including Western bestsellers such as Rushdie's *Satanic Verses* and Dan Brown's *Da Vinci Code*, but also scholars such as Theodor Nöldeke and lesser known, obscure Shia–Sunni polemical tracts.

By brandishing this (legal) sword of Damocles above the heads of publishing houses and TV stations in Lebanon, the margins for a free debate, so necessary for the flourishing of a secular public sphere, are

[187] Freedom of expression is safeguarded by the constitution. Since, however, no explicit reference is made to demonstrations various regimes have sought to justify their suppression of public gatherings. As a member of the UN, Lebanon, however, is subject to Article 19 of the 1966 International Pact of Civil and Political Rights, which refers to the right of peaceful demonstration.

[188] See Articles 9 and 10 in *Al-Dustūr Al-Lubnānī*. Germany – in Paragraph 166 of its penal code – also prohibits the defamation of religions and religious symbols of acts disturbing the "civil peace" or "*öffentlichen Frieden*" on penalty of up to three years of prison. The Christian Democrats have proposed to tighten the aforementioned law.

[189] See: www.censorshiplebanon.org/know-your-rights/, last accessed February 2, 2018.

[190] Provoked by the title of the article ("Letter to God") rather than its anti-American content, Mufti Sabunjī denounced the article as blasphemous and "more evil than Satanism" and demanded that the public prosecutor and the information and interior ministries take action. Muslim dignitaries met at Sunni headquarters at *Dār al-Fatwā* on March 11 and appealed to the government to ban the paper in Tripoli. *An-Nahār* owner, Jubrān Tuwaynī, and media and journalists' associations protested at once against these demands as attacks on press freedom and the paper sent a written protest to state prosecutor 'Addūm concerning the threats. The controversy died down eventually after the author of the article, 'Aql al-Awīt, apologized and Prime Minister Rafq Ḥarīrī, as well as clerics such as Fadlallāh and Muhammad Hasan al-Amīn, came to his defense.

severely constrained. Particularly with respect to religious topics, the Lebanese press was never entirely immune to censorship, supervised as it was by Egyptian, Saudi, Libyan, and US paymasters, as well as the Syrian security apparatus until 2005. Such dependency on financial injections by outside patrons would compromise the integrity and autonomy of Beirut's press. This trend became palpable once again after the war as Gulf and Saudi investments came to *de facto* constitute the economic backbone of the Lebanese economy in general, and media in particular.

Enter Saudi prince Walīd Ibn Talāl who, alongside Ḥarīrī, ascended as largest press baron and largest single benefactor in Beirut and the Arab world.[191] As the grandson of late Lebanese premier Riyād al-Sulh, he allied himself with President Lahhūd against Ḥarīrī after 1998, marking a new constellation in the Saudi–Syrian struggle for hegemony over Lebanon.[192]

As a leading business competitor and Saudi counterweight to Rafīq al-Ḥarīrī, Prince Walīd Ibn Talāl made headlines, not only with his freely and widely dispensed philanthropic contributions, but also with his Rotana entertainment channel, which is squarely modeled on the American genre of music television. This was a telling new phenomenon as it heralded a new wave of cultural liberalism, ignoring the prohibitions of smoking, dancing, alcohol, and gambling. Hizballāh's al-Manār and the Maronite Church's Télé Lumière channels were the exceptionally conservative counter-examples to this trend. Al-Manār claims to turn down up to 90 percent of potential advertising clients on religious grounds, preferring to draw most of its footage from in-house production sources. It is, of course, not surprising that the diffusion of "pagan" hedonism should be condemned in unison by Christian and Islamic conservatives in Lebanon. What seems more startling is that this commercialized brand of television is being beamed to Lebanon from unsuspected Saudi quarters. In this respect we may say that, far from leading to a dissemination of any puritan Wahabi ideology in Lebanese culture, Saudi-owned channels such as Rotana have, on the contrary, avidly emulated the "light" entertainment celebrated on Lebanese channels such as LBC Satellite

[191] Walīd Ibn Talāl, whose maternal grandfather was Riyād al-Sulh, has extensive holdings, including 30 percent of ART (Arabic Radio and Television). Talāl unsuccessfully sought to acquire a 50 percent stake of *Dār Assayad* after the Civil Appeals Court ruled that his mother Mona al-Sulh 's name "was only assumed as a façade" for Al-Walīd. Gary Gambill, "With Syrian Backing: Saudi Prince Challenges Ḥarīrī," *Middle East Intelligence Bulletin* 4.9 (2002).

[192] Claims of Talāl's ambitions of Lebanese premiership remain a matter of speculation and insinuation.

and Future, both of which in turn were owned by Talāl and Ḥarīrī. In fact, confessional ownership of media may not constitute as severe a threat as its propensity for shallow commercialism. Over half of the programs on Lebanese TV can be classified as belonging to the insipid "entertainment" category.[193] Whether this kind of marketing can and will engender a more substantially secular and self-critical political culture is by no means self-assured. As adumbrated earlier, the prevalent regional media parameters – as formulated in the censorship guidelines of official Saudi TV and Shaykh Sālih Kāmil's ART in 1980 – explicitly outlawed criticism of religion and political leaders.[194] The taboo has, by and large, not been broken, even as Kāmil and Talāl have launched the immensily popular Quranic channels 'Iqrā' in 1998 and Risāla in 2005. Even the vanguard of ostensibly liberal satellite channels such as Qatar's al-Jazeera or al-'Arabīya have – with rare exceptions[195] – treaded carefully and preferred to pander to populist Islamism rather than embark on any critical investigation of the role of religion[196] in politics.[197] In the end, the steady barrage of incendiary pictures of Israeli atrocities, music videos, and scantily clad women may allure viewers and augment profits, but will scarcely instigate a deeper, depolemicized engagement with secularism, nor suffice to instill a more robust national identity and civic responsibility across confessional divides. On the contrary, excessive indulgence in these diversions may nourish stereotypes of a decadent West and revive the familiar summary Occidentalist rejectionism of all things "Western" and "secular."

[193] Nabīl Dajānī, "The Changing Scene of Lebanese Television," in *The Mission: Journalism, Ethics, and the World,* ed., Joe Atkins (Ames: Iowa State University Press, 2002).

[194] Saqr, *Satellite Realms*, 34.

[195] I.e., Sādiq al-'Azm's almost legendary face-off with Shaykh Yūsuf al-Qaraḍāwī in 1996 or the intrepid Jordanian MP Tujān Faysal's encounter with an Egyptian Islamist Safināz Kāzim on al-Ittijāh al-Mu'ākis.

[196] Al-Jazeera channel has been a trendsetter in promoting a culture of relatively free debate. On the other hand, while the occasional secularist may be invited to its talk shows, al-Jazeera itself, bears a clear Islamist imprint (evident in the sanctimonious citation of traditional religious formulae). The initial inroads made toward an open discussion of state and religion have given way to sectarian polemics and firebrands such as the Egyptian preacher Youssef al-Qaradawi. Mohamed Zayani, "Al Jazeera's Complex Legacy: Thresholds for an Unconventional Media Player from the Global South," *International Journal of Communication* 10 (2016): 3554–3569.

[197] When red lines were crossed, Lebanon reacted with greater tolerance and a more mature culture of debate than other Arab states. While al-Jazeera aired controversial series on all protagonists of the Lebanese war, such criticism did not lead to the explusion of al-Jazeera staff, as had been the case in Jordan (1998), Kuwait (1999), and Egypt.

Promise and Peril of (Rentier) Capitalism Serving As a Catalyst of Secularization

If the postwar Ḥarīrī era in Lebanon can be associated with any single political or social paradigm, then the economic hegemony and socio-political imprint of "petro-Islam" would probably have to be singled out as its dominant hallmark.[198] Fu'ād Zakarīya encapsulates the traits of this culture of plenty that has also held sway over Lebanon.[199] Despite its emblems of glamorous modernity and bland slogans of peace and moderation, "petro-Islamism" remained ill suited to challenge or countervail the more strident battle cries of fundamentalism that foster in precisely the environment of social deprivation and political alienation that clientelism, unchecked privatization, and social stratification may spawn. Aziz al-Azmeh has formulated the perhaps most trenchant summary of the social mechanics of this "tributizing" polity retaining power by ways of extortion and *panis et circences* ("bread and circus").[200] In effect, the economic development social relations paradigms advanced by the two most prominent representatives of Saudi Arabia in postwar Lebanon, Walīd Ibn Talāl and Rafīq al-Ḥarīrī, were for all intents and purposes replicas of this model. The Lebanese journalist, and former director of Future TV, Sa'd Mihyū, together with the economist Shirbil Nahhās and Elie Yachoui have voiced their concern over this exclusive emphasis placed on tourism, services, and consumerism and the near complete neglect of technology, research and development, agriculture, and import substitution industrialization as a means of economic revival or indeed national integration.[201] The service-based economy, according to this view hampers the growth of indigenous, trans-sectarian associations and instead consolidates confessionalism since the system is predicated on an elite group of individual families administering and recycling capital inflows from abroad rather than on domestically based firms and associations of value-adding production.[202]

198 The phenomenon of "petro-Islam" in this discourse refers to Sunni Islam financed by states and individuals resident in the Gulf and Saudi Arabia. Nonetheless, AMAL in its rivalry with Hizballāh has not shunned from labeling the latter as a "petro-party" due to its Iranian lifeline in the 1980s and 1990s. See Hanf, *Coexistence in Wartime Lebanon*, 316–317.

199 Fu'ād Zakarīya cited in Ibrāhīm Abū Rabīa', *Contemporary Arab Thought* (London: Pluto Press, 2004), 118.

200 'Azīz al-'Azma, *Islam and Modernities* (London/New York: Verso Press, 1993), 112.

201 Sa'd Mihyū, "Prime Minister Alwaleed bin Talāl?" *The Daily Star*, July 9, 2002. Al-Walīd has tabled ambitious five- and ten-year plans to rescue the Lebanese economy.

202 Ilī Yashuy, *Iqtisād Lubnān: Mawqif wa-Tawlīl* (Beirut: Maktabat Lubnān, 2002).

If Fu'ād Shihāb's civic vision for Lebanon suffered from a general's fixation with security in a turbulent environment, Ḥarīrī's wager on rapid reconstruction along with his almost exclusive focus on the tertiary sector, privatization, and physical reconstruction likewise was unable to trump *tā'ifīya,* in part due to the personal nature of the development plan. As far its contribution to national integration goes, the CDR functioned as the very antithesis to, say, Singapore's Housing Development Board.

In Lee's Singapore, which Ḥarīrī ostensibly sought to emulate,[203] the provision of affordable, state-owned, mixed housing for 90 percent of the population effectively countervailed sectarian animosities and, although somewhat less so, social stratification. In Beirut, the obverse pertained, with Solidere remaining a privately owned jewel for the (foreign) few. Moreover, macroeconomic policies differed significantly. Singapore's tax structures were, and are, significantly more progressive than Lebanon's.[204] The decentralized patchwork of sectarian fiefdoms that characterizes Lebanon, and even the greater Beirut metropolitan area, is distinct from the dirigiste paternalism of the central state in Singapore. Its government-enforced savings and pay increases are virtually unheard of in Lebanon. On the contrary, wages for public offices have been frozen since 1994, although Premier Ḥarīrī did briefly push for an increase of the minimum wage in the private sector up until 1996.[205] By contrast, government-mandated pay increases in Singapore meant that workers reaped the fruits of their labor and production increases. Another study concludes that in Singapore (as opposed to Lebanon):

> government policies ... were designed to use the market, both domestically and externally, as an instrument to suit and achieve specific development objectives. The market was an instrument, not a master.[206]

Hence, Singapore successfully channeled its foreign direct investment to foster its industrialization and high tech, while the opportunity to industrialize was lost on Lebanon in the 1950s and 1960s, i.e., at a time when huge Arab markets were beckoning in the same way Southeast Asian

203 Denoeux and Springborg, "Harīrī's Lebanon," 158.
204 In 2002, taxes on income and profits constituted 7 percent of Singapore's GDP, while only 2.9 percent of Lebanon's. Jonathan Haughton, "An Assessment of the Tax System of Lebanon," Suffolk University, 2004, 34–36. It should be noted that Lebanon's GNP far exceeds its GDP due to remittances, prompting Haughton to suggest a tax on expenditure (rather than income) as a possible nostrum to Lebanon's chronic deficit. The current VAT indirect taxation places a higher burden on the poor but constitutes the single largest source of government revenue.
205 Barūdī, "Continuity in Economic Policy in Postwar Lebanon," 8.
206 Gaspard, *A Political Economy of Lebanon,* 139.

markets formed the initial target of Singaporian exports. Instead, Lebanon focused almost exclusively on the tertiary sector, a legacy that would prove hard to surmount.

The excessive expansion of the service sector is sometimes cited as one of the inauspicious portents of the civil war of 1975. From 1950 to 1970, the share of the tertiary sector of the total economy surged from 62 percent in 1952 to 72 percent in 1970. It has remained at this level.[207] There are, of course, subtle differences. While Western financial institutions constituted 75 percent of foreign enterprises in Lebanon in 1970, today Arab companies hold the predominant position.[208]

This balance sheet may strike one as excessively negative. (Oil) rentier revenue may not only please the banks, but also directly and indirectly spur domestic production and local firms, however artificially. Moreover, Talāl's and Ḥarīrī's foundations can be credited for substantial investments in the crisis-ridden agricultural sectors and (private) educational institutions, and generous donations to rebuild destroyed infrastructure. With the exception of the latter, however, private NGOs, rather than the state, were strengthened. We have seen earlier that political ambitions did taint the vaunted trans-confessional premise and promise of many a philanthropic activity of the Ḥarīrī Foundation, which, by and large, sought to buy the support of preexistent confessional cells rather than fund non-confessional institutions.

The Escalating Saudi–Syrian Rivalry for Lebanon and Its Fallout for Secularism

The Ḥarīrī-led buyout of Lebanese real estate, banks, and political blocs, and the vast sums of Gulf oil money purchasing real estate, even in such traditionally Christian and Druze strongholds as the Matn, the Shūf, and Kisirwān, fed fears that Lebanon may be turning into a Saudi fiefdom, an impression increased by the sight of a central Beirut teeming with tourists – and investors – from the Gulf.[209] Mr. Ḥarīrī's own real-estate

[207] 73.8 percent in 2002. The ratio of bank deposits to national income was 122 percent in 1970, a world record. Naṣr, "Backdrop to Civil War," 3. Economist Intelligence Unit, "Country Report: Lebanon," 2006.

[208] Less of a change is perceptible in imports, 75 percent of which in 1970 originate from Western countries. Naṣr, "Backdrop to Civil War," 4ff.

[209] The same Walīd Janublāt who initially mocked the patriarch's concern over naturalization as racism could also display the same existential angst of the "foreigner": "We're going to become strangers and displaced from our fatherland. They're altering the identity of the country." Dāghir, *Bring Down the Walls*, 4. Janbulāt, due to his dependence on Ḥarīrī, later adopted an inverse stance.

holdings at one point dwarfed even those amassed by the legendary Henri Fir'awn,[210] while money extended his political influence and allies.[211]

During Ḥarīrī's almost twelve-year reign, it became clear that, for all the air of cosmopolitanism, the billionaire's business ties and approach were ill designed as an effective catalyst for a full deconfessionalization and secularization of the Lebanese public space. Too closely were the political allegiances interwoven with even equivocal elements in the Kingdom of Saudi Arabia to allow for a true national integration to progress unencumbered.[212] Moreover, the growing enfeeblement and financial indebtedness of the Lebanese state made it all the more susceptible to the vacillating whims and dictates of surrounding states, be it Syria, Iran, or the Gulf States who helped defray the exhorbitant costs of debt servicing.[213]

This influx of Gulf money, and the no less palpable inflow of funds from Shia expatriot networks stretching from Iran to West Africa, heightened fears in some Christian quarters after Tā'if of a more general, undifferentiated "Islamic" threat. The increasingly salient Sunni–Shia rift and the escalating Saudi–Iranian regional rivalry, however, led to Christian and Druze minorities splitting into opposing camps. By 2005, the scales were tipping in favor of the Saudi and Gulf axis at the expense of Iran and Syria, which, as the only Arab neighbor and largest trade partner of Lebanon, was losing its status as the imminent, ultimate power broker in Lebanon.

210 It is an open secret that his vast networks of companies, such as IRAD, Fradim, Saudi Oger, and over 100 shell companies ensure him a 19 percent stake at minimum. Waldman,"Stepping Forward."

211 "*D'autant qu'il semble montrer un malin plaisir à afficher son arrogance et à mépriser la contestation, tout étant pour lui matière à acquisition, les silences comme les consciences.*" Samīr Qassīr, *Histoire de Beyrouth* (Paris: Fayard, Libraire Artheme, 2003), 631.

212 The manifold links between Ḥarīrī and the Saudi Bin Lādin Group have been a subject of discussion. Rafīq Ḥarīrī's Group Méditerranée – which also comprises the Saudi–Lebanese Bank, Allied Bank and a majority of MEDGULF – has merged with Banque Indosuez (Banque Francaise pour l'Orient), which, in turn, had salvaged the Bin Laden's Banque al Saoudi in 1989. The board of directors of the bank included Shaykh Sālim Bin Lādin and leading Saudi arms traders such as Prince Muhammad Bin Fahd, Shaykh Bogshan, and Khālid Bin Mahfuz. Banque al Saoudi and Indosuez' connections in the Middle East were instrumental in financing a portion of the weapons contracts of the 1970s and 1980s. The Paris-based Saudi Arab Finance Corporation owned 75 percent of Banque al Saoudi. Richard W. Carlson, "Mr. Ḥarīrī Goes to Washington. The Prime Ministers Real Estate," *Weekly Standard*, May 12, 2003; Sara Leibovich-Dār, "Taking Care of Family Business," *Haaretz*, April 17, 2004.

213 According to the Investment Development Authority of Lebanon. See www.idal.com.lb, last accessed January 23, 2019.

While Syria was forced to withdraw its troops, it was not until 2008 that Damascus reluctantly agreed to demarcate its borders and exchange ambassadors with Lebanon. The Syrian constitution of 1950 – modified in 1953 – did not specify Syria's boundaries.[214] Intermittant border closures and harassments plagued the relationship each time tensions ran high. In the 1950s, Damascus in vain attempted to (re)establish a full economic and monetary union with Lebanon, which had lasted until a unilateral Lebanese exit from the common currency in 1948.[215] In 1958, slogans were raised in demonstrations for an incorporation of Lebanon in to the United Arab Republic (UAR). On May 22, 1958, Charles Mālik had famously lodged his complaint at the UN against UAR intervention in the affairs of Lebanon. In a memorandum to Dag Hammarskjold, secretary general of the UN, the SSNP complained that the head of the Syrian secret service, Captain Burhān Adham, was orchestrating the armament of 3,500 militants in Lebanon. After the Tā'if Accord, economic and political cooperation was once again tightened and codified in a seperate "Treaty of Brotherhood."

In this context, the towering presence of Rafīq al-Ḥarīrī was seen by some to offer a certain Saudi counterweight to Syrian predominance, much to the concern of the traditional Sunni notables, the Ba'ath Party, and Maronite presidents Harāwī and Lahhūd, as well as the Shia axis of AMAL and Hizballāh, all of which are almost unreservedly loyal to Damascus and Tehran. Indeed, in 2001 Ḥarīrī upset the Syrian overlords repeatedly by taking bold stances without prior consultation, such as supporting a cease-fire in the south and the return of the exiled General 'Awn on state-run television.[216] As alliances continued to shift, it seems ironic that a former arch-enemy of Syria such as Maronite patriarch Sfayr, who once welcomed Ḥarīrī as a "beacon of hope for Lebanon" in 1992, would on occasion seem closer to Damascus than the Lebanese philanthropist politician who donated so much in order to win the favors of the Syrian power brokers. Most of Ḥarīrī's lobbying in Syria had occurred long before the end of the civil war, when Saudi Oger, acting on behalf of King Fahd, sponsored and undertook the construction of the

[214] For the first and only official Syrian recognition of the sovereignty of Lebanon one must go back all the way to the founding of the Arab League on March 13, 1945. Jamīl Mardam Bey apparently promised Bishāra al-Khūrī that, if Lebanon comitted itself to Arabism, Syria was willing to not only surrender the four governorates taken from it in wake of the creation of the *Grand Liban*, but to actually give Lebanon "more lands." al-Jisr, *Mithāq 1943*, 170–173.

[215] Of the major politicians, only Rashīd Karāmī supported this measure at that time.

[216] Ḥarīrī was immediately rebuked for flouting official Syrian policy by 'Adnān Addum and Samīr Jisr. See Gambill, "Dossier, Rafīq Harīrī."

US$500 million presidential palace of then President Hāfiz al-Assad. In this period too Ḥarīrī managed to ingratiate himself with Hikmat al-Shihābī and Abdul Halīm Khaddām, the notorious Syrian vice president and former secret service proconsul of Lebanon.[217] Khaddām's son Jamāl would become a key partner of the lucrative Liban Cell company. Ḥarīrī did secure Syrian support for his own premiership but failed to win the Syrian *imprimatur* for former secret service chief and Israeli confidante Johnny 'Abdū as president.[218] Instead, in 1989, upon the conclusion of the Tā'if Accord, Rene Mu'awwad was elected, an unassuming, equanimious man. The latter's refusal to send the army to oust General 'Awn was promptly followed by his assassination on November 22, paving the way for the more pliable Harāwī and, after 1998, General Emile Lahhūd.[219] Lahhūd's close ties to Damascus forced Ḥarīrī to seek a second tranche of his strategic investment in Syria. On the eve of Bashār al-Assad's election to the presidency, a Saudi consortium including Oger and the Bin Laden Group invested US$100 million in Syria, just three days before the inauguration of Bashār al-Assad as president.[220]

The Syrian "veiled protectorate" directly impinged on the fate of political sectarianism and secularism in Lebanon. In principal, many members of the Ba'th elite indeed appeared nonchalant about religion and favorably disposed toward secularization. Hāfiz al-Assad always prided himself of maintaining an equidistance to all religious communities in Lebanon.[221] In 1988 *eminence grise* and Ḥarīrī business partner, Vice President Khaddām, echoing Hāfiz al-Assad's paternalism, announced that Syria was intent on ridding Lebanon of confessionalism lest it plague Lebanon for another century.

Some analysts have accordingly been inclined to identify Ba'thist Syria as a secular bulwark against the Gulf's petro-Islam. Such a rivalry did come to the fore as early as 1975, when the Syrians sought to bring the Saudi-sponsored Karāmī government to fall.[222] Insofar as Syria had been at loggerheads with Rafīq al-Ḥarīrī's expansionist policies, a clash of

[217] According to Elie Sālim, Ḥarīrī spent more time in Damascus than in Riyād during the mid-1980s. See Elie Sālim, *Violence and Diplomacy in Lebanon* (London: I. B. Tauris, 1995), 179.

[218] 'Abdū was head of the Lebanese secret service during Israel's 1982 "Peace of Galilee" operation led by Ariel Sharon. Ḥarīrī's alleged ties to Israel have been used by his detractors to impugn his patriotism.

[219] General 'Awn, to be sure, had been ill disposed toward Mu'awwad and obliquely warned that he "could not protect [Mu'awwad] from subversive elements." J. F. O. McCallister, "Lebanon: A Bomb Aimed at Peace," *Time Magazine,* December 4, 1989.

[220] Gary Gambill, "Dossier: Wafic Said," *Middle East Intelligence Bulletin* 5.2 (2003): 9–13.

[221] See the address by Al Assad from April 13, 1976 as cited in Rabinovitch, *The War for Lebanon*, 192–199.

[222] See Janbulāṭ, *I Speak for Lebanon,* 95.

interests might seem evident. Damascus, or rather 'Anjar,[223] did periodically intervene to prevent Ḥarīrī – who was dubbed in popular talk as a "bulldozer" (*jarrāfa/mahdala*) – from steamrolling all the opposition, seeking to limit his quota to 50 percent of seats in the municipal elections of 2000, in vain.

On the other hand, as evidenced by Ḥarīrī's substantial investments in Syria (Lebanon's biggest export market) and his profuse praise for the Syrian security apparatus until the eleventh hour,[224] a simple dichotomy fails to take account of the strategic and financial interests that could bind ostensibly "secular-oriented" Syria and "religious-minded" Saudi Arabia.[225] Moreover, the secularism of the Ba'th Party was always adulterated by pan-Islamist and pan-Arabist mantras. After all, founding father Michel 'Aflaq maintained that, whereas in Europe religion was an external importation to the continent, Islam could not but remain an integral part of Arab consciousness.[226] Even the staunchly secular neo-Ba'thist regime saw itself forced to publicly reprimand an army officer who had derided God as a "mummy of history" in 1967.[227] From Michel 'Aflaq onward, Ba'athism always remained couched in a discourse in which Islam was invoked as the ultimate premise and promise of Arabism,[228] or, in the case of Assad's Syria, upheld as a discursive shield to

[223] In the parliamentary elections of 1992, 1996, and 2000 Syrian strongman General Ghāzī Kana'an was critical in giving or withholding his imprimatur for any prospective candidate. His successor in Anjar, General Rustum Ghazali, did not loosen the reigns of the Lebanese puppet theater until Syria's withdrawal from Lebanon in April 2005 in the aftermath of the Ḥarīrī assassination.

[224] "You [Ghāzī Kana'ān] have clean hands [*ayād bayḍā'*] as regards this country... You have bestowed on us the greatest of presents, brother Rustum Ghazāla." Prime Minister Ḥarīrī during a ceremony in the Grand Serail at which a golden key to Beirut was handed to the outgoing chief of Syrian security forces in Lebanon, Ghāzī Kana'an, in appreciation for his work in Lebanon. Cited in *Al-Afkār,* no. 1052, October 14, 2002, 9. One might note that, apart from certain Christian politicians in exile (such as Raymond 'Iddih and Michel 'Awn) and public personae (such as the former president of the University of St. Joseph Salīm Abū and *an-Nahār* editor Jibran Tueni), the political class was united in expressing support of the Syrian presence until 2004.

[225] One source claims that Assad was barred by Saudi Arabia from performing the pilgrimage. See Mordechai Kedar, "In Search of Legitimacy: Asad's Islamic Image in the Syrian Official Press," in *Modern Syria: From Ottoman Rule to Pivotal Role in the Middle East*, eds., Ma'oz Moshe, Joseph Ginat, and Onn Winkler (Portland: Sussex Academic Press, 1999), 23. This piece of information may not in fact be correct as other sources do report of Assad's pilgrimage.

[226] Michel 'Aflaq, *Fī Sabīl al-Ba'ath* (Beirut: Dār al-Talīa lil-Ṭibā' a wa al-Nashr, 1975), 91ff.

[227] I.e., Ibrāhīm al-Khallās, an Alevite officer who ascribed Arab retardation (in part) to religion.

[228] In the 1934 Communist Congress attended by 'Aflaq, the Arab fatherland – which in its geographical confines virtually overlapped with the Ummayad Empire at its greatest expanse – was affirmed as the geographic boundary of the prospective state. See al-Shuwayrī, *Modern Arab Historiography,* 156.

deflect suspicions of a "treasonous" Alawite betrayal of Sunni Islam on the other.[229] In fact, Hāfiz al-Assad did not spare efforts to display his credentials as a *bona fide* (Sunni) Muslim, commissioning the construction of up to 80,000 mosques and hundreds of Sunni seminaries during his tenure, despite the absence of like institutions for Alawis, and despite the pursuit of other, drastically Jacobin measures, such as forbidding the headscarf.[230]

If the Syrian dictator refrained from invoking the *bismillah* before his addresses, he just as assiduously eschewed the term "secularism" in his speeches. This was not necessarily a merely semantic matter. Rather, the Ba'thist regime pursued a janus-faced policy, pandering to popular religious sensitivies here, while cracking down on fundamentalist challenges to its power elsewhere. While the Syrian leader commissioned his brother Rif'at to ruthlessly quash the political challenge of the Muslim Brotherhood (making membership in this organization a capital crime), he also proudly mentioned his support for the Palestinian *sā'iqa* brigade which engaged in numerous sectarian attacks on churches in Lebanon before 1975. President Assad's repeated trumpeting of Damascus as the "proud citadel flying high the flag of Islam"[231] may in fact be read as rhetoric designed to defuse any suspicion of a hidden agenda of full secularization that the president by many accounts harbored in private.

As for Lebanon, the secular potential of Ba'thism was compromised by its authoritarianism that would brook no dissent, even – or particularly – when the latter carried a trans-confessional potential, as was the case with Antūn Sa'āda's SSNP[232] or Kamāl Janbulāt's PSP.[233] Both eventually

[229] The Alawite minority status of many of the leading Ba'th Party members is often interpreted to be a key reason for the predisposition to secularism, as former French ambassador Alain Choet has pointed out.

[230] Eyal Zisser, "Syria, the Ba'th Regime and the Islamic Movement," *The Muslim World* 95 (2005): 43.

[231] Assad's speech of July 20, 1976 on Damascus Radio cited in Patrick Seale, *Asad of Syn'a: The Struggle for the Middle East* (Berkeley: University of California Press, 1989), 328. Assad's famous speech was not devoid of contradictions, which maybe bespoke his dispassionate concern for a balance of power. On the one hand, Assad acknowledges that Syria entered to "save the resistance" against the Phalange, asking Kamāl Janbulāt to remember the arms he gave him for this purpose. On the other hand, the threat of a total Christian defeat is cited as justification for renewed intervention." Rabinovitch, *The War for Lebanon*, 192–199.

[232] In Sa'āda's case, the Syrian premier Muhsin al-Barazī and his brother-in-law, the Lebanese premier Riyād al-Sulh, coordinated the arrest and execution of Sa'āda together with the head of the Lebanese security forces. Bishāra, *Lebanon*, 181.

[233] On April 4, 1976, Kamāl Janbulāt objected to Syrian forces deployed in Lebanon "without justification." Janbulāt was scolded by an angry Hāfiz al-Assad on March 27, 1976 who asked Janbulāt why he still refused the constitutional document of February 14, 1976. Janbulāt replied that he wanted to eliminate the Christians "who have been on

fell out with Syria and paid with their lives, despite the ideological compatibility of many of their secular axioms with those of Syrian nationalism. In the end, the preservation of power and stability won out over any revolutionary dreams.[234]

Indeed, the ambiguity of the official Syrian stance on secularism became particularly apparent in Syria's handling of the "Lebanon file."[235] Thus, the general secretary of the Lebanese branch of the Ba'th Party, 'Āsim Qānsūh, would vigorously defend secularism in one instance, only to, when faced with a (then) mounting challenge to Syrian military hegemony over Lebanon, revert to visceral castigations of all "enemies of Islam" and theatrical threats of "crucifixion" of Western puppets in another.[236] In a 2004 interview, Syrian foreign minister Walīd Mu'allim underscored the indissolubility and interchangeabilty of Islam and Arabism while claiming to want to preserve secularism as a program (*nahj*).[237]

Equivocations such as this have evoked concerns, particularly among some Lebanese Christians who were prone to view the Syrian role with an apprehensive eye. When the civil war was nearing its bloody final act, the Syrian procurator of Lebanon, Abdul Halīm Khaddām sought to weaken the Maronite presidency to such a degree that US former under-secretary of state for Near Eastern affairs, Richard Murphy, quipped that Khaddām wanted a robot, not a president. Khaddām's wishes were fulfilled, perhaps beyond his expectations, with the unquestioning obeisance displayed by presidents Harāwī and Lahhūd, who could, for their part, count on the support of a significant segment of the Lebanese beholden to Hizballāh and other pro-Syrian parties.[238] By 2004, and

top of us for 140 years." Alternative theories claim that Janbulāt's last minute overtures to his arch-enemy Christian opponents prompted his assassination on March 16, 1977. Rabinovitch, *The War for Lebanon*, 192ff.

234 Assad would have none of Kamāl Janbulāt's Jacobism, while siding with Pierre Jummayil in pinning the blame for the failure of secularism on "the Muslims." Rabinovitch, *The War for Lebanon*, 77.

235 Elie Sālim, *Violence and Diplomacy in Lebanon*, 255.

236 Qānsūh threatened to "crucify [the agitating Walīd Janbulāt] on the garbage dump of history" on February 3, 2005, twelve days before the assassination of Ḥarīrī. Qānsūh later retracted this statement and testified to the Arab nationalist credentials of Janbulāt who had in turn (briefly) regained the support of Damascus. See Bilāl Khubayz, *Elaph*, March 18, 2005. After the Syrian pullout, Qānsūh also extended a "warm welcome" to Syria's former arch-enemy, General 'Awn, inviting him to return from exile in Paris.

237 Interview with Ahmad Mansūr on "Bilā Hudūd," *Al-Jazeera*, April 19, 2004.

238 Khaddām stated that Lebanon should follow the Syrian paradigm: "Past events confirm that Lebanon must follow a new mentality, one which does not endanger stability. The successful Syrian experience has confirmed that political stability leads to the continuity of the regime, just as continuity engenders stability as well. As guardians over the Lebanese government of the National Accord it is our hope that you follow this

after the changing of the guard in Damascus that removed Ḥarīrī's erstwhile Syrian patrons,[239] Lahhūd had won the almost complete favor of Damascus. In 2005, the latter ensured him another three-year extension of his mandate in violation of the Lebanese constitution, thereby amending Article 49 of the constitution once again after May 22, 1947, when it was done for Bishāra Khūrī, and 1995, when then-President 'Ilyās Harāwī was granted yet another "exceptional" extension.[240] In that last particular instance, Rafīq al-Ḥarīrī had been the first to lobby for the constitutional amendment and congratulate the new old president, even as 89 percent of Lebanese were set against the extension of the mandate.[241] The sympathizers of General 'Awn, Nasīb Lahhūd, and presidential hopeful and constitutional lawyer Michael Dāhir, had then protested against this flagrant violation of the constitution, but saw themselves overruled by Speaker Birrī and the majority of Syria-appointed allies in parliament who had been exposed to a thinly disguised threat issued by the feared Syrian proconsul of Lebanon, Ghāzī Kana'ān.[242]

Matters were different with President Lahhūd. Ḥarīrī, who had vowed to "cut ofh" his hand[243] before signing another constitutional amendment to extend the term of his arch-foe, instead saw his own arm twisted, leading him to sign the fated document in the cabinet session of Saturday, August 28, 2004. Far from making good on his earlier promise of categorical opposition to any extension, a week later Ḥarīrī himself issued

model which took the form of stability and continuity" Salīm Nassār, "Al-Tamdīd Li-Lahhūd wa Al-Tajdīd Lil-Harīrī," *An-Nahār*, July 3, 2004.

239 Besides Hāfiz al-Assad, these included 'Abdul Halīm Khaddām, Ghāzī Kana'ān, and Hikmat Shihābī.

240 With the exception of presidents Shihāb and Sarkīs, all Lebanese presidents have pushed the country to a crisis due to their ambitions to amend the constitution. When Camille Sham'ūn made a bid to extend the constitution for himself, a civil war broke out in 1958. Earlier, in September 1952, President Khūrī was forced to resign after having rigged the elections in his favor. Bishāra, *Lebanon*, 177.

241 Lebanese parliamentarians and speaker Birri initially blocked the requisite constitutional amendment until Syrian president Assad asserted that "there is, in Lebanon, a national consensus over the extension of the president's mandate." Carole Dagher, "With Lebanese President's Second Term, Democracy Suffers Severe Blow," *Washington Report on Middle Eastern Affairs*, December, 1995, 35.

242 The account of a dinner hosted by 'Umar Karāmī was published in *al-Hayat* on October 1995 and reveal the *modus operandi*: "Kanaan then raised his hand, saying that the vote would take place by a raising of hands and would not be secret … Everyone looked as if they had just taken a cold shower … The party broke up early. Presidential hopefuls departed with their wives, one complaining of tiredness, another saying he had a headache." Robert Fisk, "Syria's Ally Stays in Beirut," *The Independent*, October 20, 1995.

243 Arnoud de Borchgrave, "Syria Ignores Criticism as It Opts to Extend Lahhūd's Term," *UPI*, August 29, 2004.

orders to members of his parliamentary bloc to sign the extension bill for President Lahhūd or face expulsion.[244] It was not the first time Ḥarīrī was forced to swallow his own words of disagreement with Syria. During a trip to Saudi Arabia in 2004, Ḥarīrī surprised everyone by openly boasting that "the Lebanese Premier does not receive orders from anybody, including Syria," only to backtrack shortly thereafter by meekly declaring his readiness to step down immediately if Damascus so desired given that he was in his position "due to the will of Syria."[245] Some speculate that this ambiguity and maneuvering of Ḥarīrī, in addition to his proximity to France and the United States, was quite possibly a triggering cause for a suspected Syrian decision to eliminate him barely five months later, when the prime minister's entire motorcade was pulverized by a massive bomb on February 14, 2005. Opponents of this theory, however, point to the Sunni premier's critical role in mediating with Hizballāh, and his averral to maintain ties to Syria:

> Now there are some who would like to have Lebanon as an island. I believe that sort of talk is far from reality. Look at what surrounds Lebanon: Israel, the sea and Syria. So if we were to close ourselves off from Syria, where do we want to go? To the sea?...[246]

In sum, from 1990 to 2005, with the balance of power insured by Syrian suzerainty and a rising inflow of Gulf and Saudi revenue, and with political discourse held hostage by the unresolved Gordian knots stemming from the Israeli–Palestinian conflict, imperative institutional changes to the confessional system were shelved until further notice. As the twentieth century drew to a close, the challenge to balance Lebanon's Arab identity with national interests became further complicated by the vortex of clashing Saudi–Iranian proxy wars and the foreign-fueled civil wars in Iraq and Syria. Strategic dissimulation and incantation of hackneyed patriotic rhetoric masked the pursuit of narrow personal and communal agendas.

In the final analysis, it is clear that neither Mr. Ḥarīrī's and Saudi Arabia's financial prowess nor Syria's military might could break the ice of sectarianism since both still relied, willy-nilly, on the same *modus operandi* in leveraging inherited patronage systems in which political services and philanthropy are bartered for an "*omerta*" of unquestioned

[244] Only one Future MP, the Maronite doctor and businessman Ghattās Khūrī, dared to defy these orders.

[245] Antoine Ja'ja', "Al-Harīrī Fī Qalb Al-Hisār," *al-Massīra*, March 2004. Also see Matar, "Hawl al-Fasād wa Subul Mukāfihatihi," 203.

[246] Rafiq al-Ḥariri, January 5, 2005. Interview with Future TV, www.youtube.com/watch?v=9-uyYsUuQuc, last accessed on March 3, 2018.

fealty. As soon as one yields to the terms of this role-playing, one is bound to become the prisoner of the confessional rhetoric and solidarity any *zaʿīm* is forced to resort to if only to secure his power base.

Both partisans siding with Syria and Saudi Arabia were instrumental in the marginalization of secular institutions and parties. This is best illustrated in the Ḥarīrī-led campaign against the multisectarian GDL, Syria's containment of the Communist Party – both in Lebanon and in Syria[247] – or Hizballāh's refusal to rend homage to secular communist and SSNP "martyrs" who had fallen in the guerilla war against the Israeli occupation of southern Lebanon.[248] Moreover, the enfeeblement of the state and indebtedness of the treasury, in addition to the freezing of public sector wages since 1996, effected the segmentation of society into a prospering elite of rentier brokers and bankers and a population smarting under rising (regressive) taxes, low wages, and rampant unemployment.

On the whole, the web of an (intersectarian) *Gemeinschaft* and civil society was weakened by the Syria–Ḥarīrī hegemony between 1990 and 2005. The "gemeine *Gesellschaft*" of clan, confession, and class continued to foster and, often, fester in the shadow of derelict state institutions and a judiciary suffering from a lack of credibility. A series of (protest) resignations of prominent state lawyers in 1997 and the deliberate suspension of the countries highest juridical oversight body were omens of the state of the dismal rule of law in Lebanon. The judiciary was unable to challenge or avert the usurpation of the nation-state by the patronage alibi, sectarian cells, and the (Syrian) security apparatus. The secular state in this environment had too few, and too narrow, legs to stand on. The returns on an investment in it simply did not appear as secure and promising as the *status quo* alternative.

While the late Rafīq al-Ḥarīrī spearheaded the country's economic reconstruction drive under the agenda of privatization and structural adjustment, and while he was able to expand the sway and clout of the Sunni premiership to a degree hitherto unknown, his unprecedented political stature and his seemingly boundless financial reserves did not allow him to entirely escape the matrix of the confessional triumvirate.

247 The repeated imprisonment of the former secretary general of the Syrian Communist Party, Riyād al-Turk, provided an indication of the regime's fear of secular opposition. Both Assad and Bashār al-Assad arrested leftist and secular dissidents such as activists Michel Kīlū, Ahmad al-Bunnī, Mamūn Murei, Riyād as-Sayf, and Nidāl Darwīsh (many of which are signatories to the 2005 "Damascus Declaration").

248 The Lebanese Communist Party was often at odds with Syrian foreign policy during the civil war – particularly after the Tripartite Agreement of the Lebanese forces, AMAL, and Janbulāt in 1985 and its aftermath. The Movement for a Democratic Left published its list of complaints against Syrian hegemony on February 4, 2004. One of its key members, Jurj Hāwī, was killed one year later.

Nor was he, anymore than Hizballāh,[249] able to elude the watchful eye of the Syrian security suzerainty. While Damascus and its allies proved particularly resilient to a downsizing of state institutions and a slashing of government wages in the post-Tā'if state, Syria, too, lacked both wherewithal and will to act as a successful agent of secularization. Damascus could realign and recalibrate the balance of power between the different Lebanese players to its own advantage. It could – or would – not reform, let alone uproot, the sectarian system itself. When Hāfiz al-Assad sponsored President Harāwī's 1997 bill to introduce an optional, secular, "civil marriage," the seminal venture ended in an acrimonious "political divorce" filed for by Ḥarīrī and the recalcitrant religious establishment of all denominations.[250] The secularization of marriage laws was seen as the first step in fulfilling deconfessionalization as stipulated in the Ṭā'if Accord. The storm of debate it unleashed unmasked the prevalent camouflaging of sectarian stances in Lebanon. Thus, the ostensible beacons of liberal Shiism, Shaykh Muhammad Mahdī Shams ad-Dīn and Sayyid Muhammad Ḥusayn Faḍlallāh, both feigned a cautious approval of the bill at first, claiming that "Muslim marriage is no different from civil marriage,"[251] only to subsequently reverse their stances and pronounce any Muslim who contracts a civil marriage an apostate guilty of adultery, an offense Faḍlallāh himself has decreed punishable by death.[252] A familiar set of vituperative, "Occidentalist" stereotypes secularism (re)surfaced with a vengeance amid the allergic reactions to Harāwī's proposal. The self-same "holy alliance" that had foiled the government's attempt to establish a unified, deconfessionalized curriculum for history would mount a demagogic defense of its vested interests, wielding the scepters of medieval dogmatism. Echoing the Shia shaykhs Shams ad-Dīn and Sayyid Faḍlallāh's threats of "excommunication," Cardinal Ṣfayr warned that any "children of civil marriages would be considered bastards by the Church" and that the Church would effectively excommunicate those who contracted a civil marriage by withholding

[249] Robert Fisk has related the brutality with which Ghāzī Kana'ān cracked down on Hizballāh in 1987, killing two dozen cadres in cold blood and parading their bodies in the suburbs. Robert Fisk, "The Ghāzī Kana'ān I Knew Was Not the Sort of Man Who Would Commit Suicide," *The Independent*, October 13, 2005.

[250] Cited in Harāwī, *'Awdat al-Jumhūrīya*. The blocs of Nabīh Birrī and Walīd Janbulāt both supported the bill.

[251] Cited in Ahmad Bayḍūn, *Tis'at 'Ashara Firqa Nājīya: al-Lubnānīyūn fī M'arakat al-Zawāj al-Madanī* (Beirut: an-Nahār, 1999), 46.

[252] Besides adultery, Faḍlallāh also singled out murder, highway robbery, and homosexuality as capital offenses. Muḥammad Mahdī Shams ad-Dīn, in turn, rhetorically asked why thieves' hands are not cut, murderers not killed. Ilyās Harāwī, *'Awdat al-Jumhūrīya*, ed., Camille Munsa (Beirut: Dār an-Nahār, 1999).

their last sacrament.[253] The highest Catholic prelate made the curious, casuistic case that civil marriage was not only at variance with the teachings of the Church, but was also an infringement on "equality before the law;" hence, a stance of solidarity with "our Muslim brothers" in a united opposition to secular reform was deemed incumbent.[254] Echoing his Catholic and Shia peers, the highest Sunni authority, Grand Mufti Shaykh Muhammad Rashīd Qabbānī, branded anyone who considered the introduction of (voluntary) civil personal status laws licit a *murtadd* or apostate, summoning the Lebanese to mount a *jihād* against the proposal.[255] The acerbic words of the mufti of the republic constituted a heavy blow to the hopes invested in an open, secular society in Lebanon and the Arab world in general:

> We shall never allow him [Harāwī] to sow the microbe ... germ (*jurthūma*) of secularism in Lebanon, nor shall we ever allow Lebanon to be its port of export to the wider Arab world which neither applies secularism nor civil marriage. We will overturn this civil marriage even if we are forced to lay down our lives to this end ... It violates the *Sharī'a* of God and the *Sharī'a* of Muhammad. Hence, it is no exertion for us to pay the ultimate price and lay down our lives in order to make this project come to naught.[256]

In his tirade, the mufti revealed many of the recurring symptoms of a latent complex besetting the hard-line polemical defamation of secularism, one that immediately associates freedom of belief with Zionism, which "sowed secularism in Europe to strip people from their beliefs. Civil marriage was but one episode within the drama of secularism. Those that do not read history do not understand how secularism was born in Europe."[257] As outlined in Chapter 2, again we are confronted with the dubious, tendentious "Occidentalist" historiography informed by a heavily distorted and rather illogical depiction of a nefarious Zionist–secularist–Christian–atheist alliance. The head of the Sunni Sharī'a courts Nāsir al-Sāliḥ raised this very canard, alleging that the plan to introduce civil personal status laws in Lebanon was conceived by Zionism in general, and the Masonic society in particular.[258]

253 Ṣaffīya Sa'āda, "Basic Issues Concerning the Personal Status Law in Lebanon," in *Religion: Violence and Reconciliation*, ed., Thomas Scheffler (Beirut: Ergon Verlag, 2002), 454.

254 Also 'Harāwī, '*Awdat al-Jumhūrīya*, 587.

255 See interview with Mufti Qabbānī cited in Bayḍūn *Tis'a 'Ashara Firqa Nājīya*, 44. It should be noted that these accusations border on an incitement to murder as apostasy is punishable by death according to all major schools of Islamic jurisprudence.

256 Cited in Jarīda ul-Bayān (UAE), February 10, 1998.

257 Jarīda ul-Bayān (UAE), February 10, 1998.

258 Cited in Dalāl al-Birzī, "Al-Sulta Wa Al-Mujtama'," in *Al-Muwātnīya Fī Lubnān* (Beirut, 2000), 174.

In the end, the proposed secular civil status bill was defeated by sheer intimidation and the specter of a return to a civil war. The real tragedy of this episode was that the controversial bill had in fact won the approval of the highest executive body in Lebanon on March 19, 1998 by an overwhelming margin of 21 to 6.[259] Its success had been sealed due to the alliance of President Harāwī, Walīd Janbulāṭ, and Speaker Nabīh Birrī. The latter came around to support the draft after an amendment was made mandating the abolition of political sectarianism, a long-standing platform of AMAL. The rest of the political and, with precious few exceptions,[260] the entire religious establishment deemed deconfessionalization "inappropriate" and an overly sensitive issue. Still, the legislation could well have been pushed through had Prime Minister Ḥarīrī not lent all of his weight to block the proposal. A visibly angered President Harāwī neither attended Easter Mass nor sent *'Īd al-'Aḍhā* greetings in this fateful year, which saw the return of the most unsavory of petty, but perilous, parochialisms.

Conclusion: The Secular State between Political and Social Reform

Perhaps in partial reflection of its historical backdrop and its heterogeneous social composition, Lebanon's constitution is riddled with internal contradictions. To a large degree, a separation of religion and state prevails insofar as the constitution affords a maximum amount of jurisdiction to the sects over personal status laws and education. This relative autonomy and freedom in turn, however, may threaten to spur confessional subnationalities encased within their own schools, mosques, and churches. The question remains whether the Lebanese state, by extending prerogatives to corporate communal identities, is thereby depriving individual citizens from a direct, unmediated relationship of rights and obligations toward the state.

[259] With two absentions. The opposing block formed around Prime Minister Ḥarīrī, Fu'ād Siniora, Bāsim al-Saba', 'Umar Misqāwī, Bahīj Tabbāra, and Bishāra Mirhij. Ironically, the latter two ministers concluded civil marriages themselves in spite of their opposition to the bill. Harāwī, *'Awdat al-Jumhūrīya*, 575

[260] Besides Gregoire Haddād, the religious dignitaries who have publicly expressed their full support for the civil marriage proposal included the Druze shaykh Salmān al-Maṣrī – who thereby went against the verdict of his superior *'uqqāls* – Shaykh Sulaymān Ghānim, and Ismā'īl Shaykh as well as the attorney Khidr al-Hamāwī. The only head of Lebanon's seventeen religious denominations to openly support civil marriage was tellingly Deacon Habīb Badr of the Evangelical Church in Lebanon. Gregoire Haddād, *Al-'Almānīya Al-Shāmila* (Beirut: 'Anāsir al-Hiwār, 1999).

To validate a voluntary status of secular citizenship against the forcible subservience to a confessional identity, Lebanon's interior minister Ziyad Baroud issued a remarkable, if unlikely, circular on February 11, 2009, approving the voluntary removal of religious affiliation in the civil registry records (*Ikhraj al-qayd*).[261] As it turns out, this bold measure opened more issues than it solved and is undermined by the sectarian quotas, which define the political system. As long as no citizen in Lebanon can vote or run for office without declaring his confessional identity, removing the latter from the registry ironically amounts to an effective disenfranchisement of the self-declared secular citizen rather than his or her liberation.

It remains to be seen whether the rush of globalization and the spread of a consumer culture can subvert the sectarian subcultures, or, whether, on the contrary, an enfeebled state and the perceived threat to the nuclear family wrought by an untrammeled individualism will provoke a backlash and retrenchment into the safety afforded by confessional cocoons.[262]

Skeptics have maintained that, in a society in which primary allegiance is owed to one's family and sect, secularism in the form of a coercive laicization of personal status law would constitute a perilous utopia. This, they argue, would merely ratify, and exacerbate, the deeply rooted confessional fragmentation of a country in which a "privatized" reconceptualization of religion has been stalled by instincts of communal survival.

Thus, the imposition of political secularism (*'almaniyya*) from above has been (pre)conditioned on the prior dissemination of a nonsectarian, civic solidarity and advanced social secularization (*'almana*) from below. In this context, the Arabic catchphrase "*an-nufus qabl an-nusus*" ("spirits before texts") has been invoked, suggesting that a secularization of "souls," must precede the secularization of legislative "texts" and institutions.

Polls confirm that support for an agenda of political secularization has fluctuated up and down according to the severity of political crises afflicting Lebanon. Within the space of a particularly violent month, i.e., January and February 1987, overall support for a secular state and society could tumble from 74 percent to 56 percent.[263] A 2006 survey further confirmed that the percentage of Lebanese citizens who consider their confessional identity paramount over their Lebanese identity surged

[261] "Removal of Confession from Civil Registry Records," *The Monthly*, April 2009, 81.
[262] Benjamin Barber, *Consumed* (New York: W. W. Norton, 2007).
[263] Hanf, *Coexistence in Wartime Lebanon*, 546.

when posed in a context of conflict.[264] Thus, the broader political climate – the "fear factor," as it were – must be considered as a crucial additional determinant of stances toward secularism.

Whatever their continued vigor, to presume (sectarian) attitudes as perpetually frozen bespeaks not only a fatalistic anthropology, but also rests on an empirically fallacious assumption. For individual political positions and convictions remain an additional, astonishingly autonomous agent that can, and must, not invariably be explicated by dint of materialistic determinism, political circumstance or reference to religious dogma. Indeed, one of the syndromes of *ṭa'fīya* haunting Lebanon is the hegemonic imposition of a pat tribal prism as the omnipotent, omnipresent, all-interpretative grid.[265]

One of the arguments of this book has been that it is not so much "culture" (or "religion") as a fixed primordial determinant that "matters" as a facilitator or inhibitor of secularism.[266] Rather, what is required is the full, official protection by state and law of vibrant, unrestricted, free realms of debate within which ideas and ideals of secularism as a historical arrangement of statecraft in pluralistic societies may be debated and exposed. If such space is provided, along with a state that retains the trust of its citizenry, unshackled by clientelist corruption and able and willing to meet the elemental needs of sustenance and security, the way is paved for a civic allegiance to take precedence. One need look no further than to the extraordinary entrepreneurial success shown by Lebanese outside of Lebanon in a variety of professions, including Arab media, even as Lebanon itself has its economy and media suffer, with four major newspapers, including *al-Safir, al-Anwar*, and *al Hayat* closing. The former premier Salīm al-Ḥuṣṣ is but one of countless observers who have bewailed the disparity between the successful, active, and inventive Lebanese emigrant abroad and the ossified political and communal straightjacket suffocating accomplishment at home.[267]

[264] The poll revealed that 34 percent stated they belonged to Lebanon first while 37.3 percent affirmed their confession as their primary identity. This latter number surged to 48.8 percent in a hypothetical context of conflict, underscoring the precarious fragility of national identity in Lebanon. Cited in 'Jawād Al-Adra, "Crisis of Identity and the Role of the Zu'ama," *Il-Monthly*, May 2006, 19.

[265] On the distortive danger of self-fulfilling confessionalist and even ethnic historiographies of Lebanon, see Qurm, *Le Liban Contemporain*, 63ff. We might also refer to Anthony Giddens' proposed balance between individual agency and social structure elaborated in his Salīm al-Ḥuṣṣ, *The Constitution of Society: Outline of the Theory of Structuration* (Berkeley: University of California Press, 1984).

[266] See Lawrence Harrison and Samuel Huntington, eds., *Culture Matters: How Values Shape Human Progress* (New York: Basic Books, 2000).

[267] "Lebanon is beautiful, but the Lebanese …" [Arabic], *as-Safir*, April 22, 2006.

Conclusion

Secularism and Lebanon in the Eye of the Sectarian Storm

> And Arab society will retain its resemblance to a tottering cart attached to the train of Western hegemony, lost between the haphazard imitation which steals its self, and the equally random clinging to the traditional values of the past which rob it of its innovative power and deprive it of its place in the living present.
> Adūnīs[1]

> From Israel's perspective … establishing a single multinational country is a tenuous path that does not bode well for peace but, rather, enforces the conflict's perpetuation. Lebanon, ravaged by bloodshed and instability, represents only one of many examples of an undesirable quagmire of this nature.
> Former Israeli president Shimon Peres[2]

The book commenced by positing a triad of spheres: religious ideology, state institutions, and socioeconomic interests, which, in their cumulative interaction, determine the station, form, and fate of secularism in a given society.[3] I have further argued that the success of secularism hinges on a depolemicized intellectual understanding of the concept, a fair and equitable economy, judiciary and political system, and, ultimately, the development and dissemination of a shared national consciousness across individuals, confessional communities, and political parties.[4] We thus turn to a review of the trajectory of the secular state in our recapitulation.

Secular Signposts in the Evolution of the Polity

As adumbrated in Chapter 1, Lebanon has averted a whole-scale secularizing cultural revolution à la China or Turkey, while the consociational

1 Adūnīs, *Ash-Shi'rīya wa al-'Arabīya* (Beirut: Dār al-Adab, 1985), 9.
2 Shimon Peres, "One Region, Two States," *Washington Post,* February 2009.
3 See Figures I.1 and I.2.
4 For the role of parties as agents of national integration see Daniele Caramani, *The Nationalization of Politics: The Formation of National Electorates and Party Systems in Western Europe* (Cambridge: Cambridge University Press, 2004), 32.

republic has, at least formally, overcome the costly partitions that divided India or Palestine in 1947, and rent Lebanon itself during the civil war from 1975 to 1990.[5] Yet Lebanon has not managed to cultivate the same degree of syncretic nationalism and communal consensus of a "nation of wills" or "*Willensnation*," which matured over time in other multiconfessional, multiethnic republics such as Switzerland or the United States.

In summarizing the development of the Lebanese state, we may conclude that, while elements of secularism have been enshrined in the Lebanese constitution, Lebanon remains an "incomplete nation."[6] In adopting the perspective of the *longue durée,* this book intended to trace the sequential transitions toward secularism observable on the historical, ideological, socioeconomic, and, finally, political plane. Overall, we might delineate four main phases through which Lebanon has passed as the country was exposed to successive waves of globalization from the sixteenth to the twentieth centuries:

1) Premodern proto-secularism in the seventeenth-century Ma'anite emirate during which state practices of sectarian prejudice were lifted or attenuated, albeit within a feudal and authoritarian context under the aegis of an open-minded Emir Fakhr ad-Dīn II.
2) The more formal pursuit and announcement of a nondiscriminatory administrative policy under the aegis of Ibrāhīm Pasha and Bashīr Shihāb in the nineteenth century, which, while establishing intercommunal bodies of power sharing, still left the confessional set of civil status laws untouched.
3) The first formal constitutional enshrinement of full civic freedoms in Articles 10 of the constitution of 1926 drafted under the French mandate. This pilot program of full secularization was brought to a standstill by domestic resistance and by an overarching colonial concern to prioritize the preservation of law and order over reform.
4) A post-independence stage marked by isolated and intermittent efforts to advance a full deconfessionalization of the political sphere, the roadmap to which was spelled out for the first time in the 1990 Tā'if Accord. The Civil Marriage Bill of 1997 heralds the first time this issue has been advanced by a sovereign Lebanese government. Campaigns for a full, comprehensive secularization of both the

[5] Farha, "Global Gradations of Secularism."
[6] Thus, the German title of Michael Kuderna's *Christliche Gruppen im Libanon: Kampf um Ideologie und Herrschaft einer Unfertigen Nation* (Wiesbaden: Franz Steiner, 1983).

political and civil system have since been largely confined to Lebanese NGOs, with some success.[7]

We thus may record a process of growth and expansion of national institutions and laws beginning in the Ottoman and French mandate era, accelerating with independence, to reach its historical zenith under Fu'ād Shihāb's presidential tenure from 1958 to 1964. To date, even in the heat of the fiercest polemics, the major institutions of state have remained beyond contestation in the Middle East's oldest democracy, despite their origins under imperial (Ottoman and French) patrons.

Still, this gradual maturation and widening recognition of civic state *institutions* does not tell us whether or not Lebanon still suffers from an absence of a common national *identity*.[8] In other words, how has the Lebanese state fared with respect to the decidedly global challenge of engendering a civic, national consciousness within a multidenominational society? If, as one school of thought claims, most modern nationalisms are tied to a corresponding confessional background,[9] and if the evidence suggesting an almost linear correlation of attachments to religious and national identities is indeed valid,[10] then Lebanon, given the absence of an overarching shared religious identity, might be consigned to remain an atavistic patchwork of religious subnationalities competing for the resources of the state.[11] Put differently, from this perspective, a

[7] For a critical reading, see Elias Muhanna, "Lebanon's Confused Secularism," *The Guardian*, April 23, 2010. Elinor Flora Bray-Collins, "Sectarianism from Below: Youth Politics in Post-war Lebanon," PhD dissertation, University of Toronto, 2016.

[8] The suggested recognition of state institutions is not obviated by the patent lack of trust – even by the Lebanese government itself – in the actual operation of the self-same state institutions. This came to the fore after the assassination of Prime Minister Ḥarīrī and the resultant controversy over an international tribunal under the auspices of the UN. While the lack of confidence in the Lebanese judicial system is by no means misplaced, given the latter's dismal failure to uncover any of the country's record number of political assassinations, there is scant precedent for a country soliciting international arbitration for a domestic murder.

[9] The Lebanese anthropologist Fu'ād Khūrī draws a cogent comparison of nationalisms in history, which have been shaded by a particular sectarian identity. See the conclusion of Fu'ād Khūrī, *From Village to Suburb: Order and Change in Greater Beirut* (Chicago: Chicago University Press, 1975) and Peter van der Veer and Hartmut Lehmand, eds., *Nation and Religion: Perspectives on Europe and Asia* (Princeton: Princeton University Press, 1999).

[10] Samuel Huntington, *Chosen People*, unpublished draft reviewed at Harvard University in joint graduate seminar in November 2005.

[11] Roschanack Shaery-Eisenlohr, "Constructing Shi'ite Nationalism," PhD dissertation, 2004, 52. This book does not share the author's "premise that sectarianism as a practice is eminently compatible with [secular] nationalism." Shaery-Eisenlohr, "Constructing Shi'ite Nationalism," 99. For a similary positive validation of communalism, see Melani Cammett, *Compassionate Communalism: Welfare and Sectarianism in Lebanon* (New York: Cornell University Press, 2014).

consolidation of a cohesive national identity necessarily and inevitably is all but contingent on antecedent societal waning, or constitutional relegation, of centrifugal communal identities.[12]

The largest national demonstration Beirut witnessed on March 14, 2005 might defy both these alternate hypotheses held by culturalist priomordialists and by positivist constructivists, respectively. In defense of a common cause in defense of national sovereignity, religious pluralism and a shared political patriotism could coexist. After all, Lebanese flags were hoisted next to crucifixes and Qu'rāns. The collective assembly of one third of the nation's entire population stunned even the most die-hard doubters. What was scarcely recognized in face of this unprecedented moment of mass mobilization fusing secular and religious symbols, and what was easily lost in the ensuing euphoria, however, was that this demonstration still could be read as coming about as an alliance of sects, most of which still fell under the aegis of quasi feudal families. From the onset, the absence of large segments of the Shia community, most of whom had participated in the preceding, March 8 demonstration, was all too salient.[13] Significantly, in this latter, pro-Syrian demonstration, Ḥizballāh had displayed equal intent to pledge its national allegiance by waving only Lebanese flags, for the first time in its history. The yellow-green Kalashnikov-adorned Ḥizballāh flag soon returned. The finality of the Lebanese state of 1920 still remained contested. Ḥasan Naṣrallāh's outburst in 2006 was indicative of this latent, unresolved tension:

> [They want us to] speak about Lebanon the country, Lebanon the people, Lebanon the entity, Lebanon the nation, Lebanon the history, Lebanon the geography, and if this continues, two or three years from now we will arrive at Lebanon the god.[14]

Naṣrallāh drastically tempered his tenor in a subsequent interview, squarely professing Ḥizballāh's "primary allegiance" to Lebanon.[15] Yet, his prior lament of a "deification" of Lebanon was reminiscent of Kamāl

[12] See Benedict Anderson, *Imagined Communities: Reflections on the Origins and Spread of Nationalism* (New York: Verso, 1991).

[13] Reinhold Leenders argues that, from a strictly economic perspective, it is by no means apparent why the Shia as a whole should have been so opposed to the Syrian withdrawal. In fact, there was a prior resentment voiced at Syrian laborers who had monopolized unskilled menial jobs. Reinoud Leenders, "How the Rebel Regained His Cause: Ḥizballāh & the Sixth Arab–Israeli War," *MIT Electronic Journal of Middle East Studies* 6.2 (2006): 38–56. However, the pullout of Syrian troops did disrupt trade in some of the border areas such as the Biqā'. Since these areas are heavily populated by Shiites, the economic fallout carried negative ramifications for the community.

[14] Ḥasan Naṣrallāh, March 30, 2006, al-Manār Television.

[15] "Muqabala," *as-Safīr*, April 27, 2006.

Janbulāṭ's almost verbatim complaint of the "isolationists" who "divinize the Lebanese entity."[16] Despite his accommodationist inclinations, political flexibility, and professed readiness for dialogue, Naṣrallāh had once outlined Ḥizballāh's mission in Lebanon as entailing the "Islamisation of the Muslim individual and community, its values and way of life."[17] From its "Open Letter" of 1985 to the present, Ḥizballāh never terminally relinquished its ultimate goal of an Islamic state, although from the onset the official party line has repeatedly rejected any forcible imposition of theocracy and instead focused on political reform.[18] Whether or not an actual blueprint for the constitution of a Lebanese state modeled on clerical rule was ever drafted in Tehran, as some sources suggest, is in this sense secondary.[19]

Paradoxially, political deconfessionalization also formed part of the agenda of Ḥizballāh, while the pro-Western opposition camp of March 14, which was mainly composed of minority sects, generally speaking was less favorably inclined toward the abolition of political sectarianism than a party that stood to benefit from its growing demographic base. Thus, Walīd Janbulāṭ publicly abandoned his father's legacy of striving to abolish the current confessional system. Likewise, the Druze chieftain's erstwhile demands to revive a deconfessionalized senate, which he once aspired to chair, have fallen silent. Instead, the Druze lord counseled US vice president Cheney in 2007 to arm the Muslim Brotherhood in an effort to pressure Bashār al-Assad.

As Saffīya Sa'āda has bluntly put it, ultimately, the advancement of secularism in Lebanon is contingent on the cosolidation of a class

16 Cited in al-Jisr, *Mithāq 1943*, 386. Jisr interprets Janbulāṭ's jibe at "al-infisālīūn" as a code for Christians. Ironically, during his opening address on November 18, 1946 at the Cénacle Libanais, Kamāl Janbulāṭ had wallowed in Phoenicianism and extolled the "civilizing mission" of Lebanon.

17 Eqbal Ahmad , "Encounter with a Fighter," *Al-Ahram Weekly*, no. 388, July 30–August 5, 1998.

18 "We confirm our convictions in Islam as a tenet and a system, both intellectual and legislative, calling on all to learn of it and abide by its code. And we summon the people to adopt it and commit to its instructions, at the individual, political and social levels. Hence we call for the implementation of the Islamic system based on a direct and free choice of the people, and not through forceful imposition as may be assumed by some." "Open Letter to the Oppressed." Cited in Na'īm Qāsim, *Ḥizballāh: The Story from Within* (London: Saqi Books, 2005), 31. Shiblī Mallāt has trenchantly summarized the deliberate ambiguity of this discourse. Shiblī Mallāt, "Aspects of Shia' Thought from the South of Lebanon," Papers on Lebanon, 7, Centre for Lebanese Studies, Oxford.

19 See Stephan Rosiny, *Der Islamismus Bei Den Schiiten Im Libanon* (Berlin: Das Arabische Buch, 1996), 216–217 and Houchang Chehabi and Ḥassan Mneimeh, "Iran and Lebanon in the Revolutionary Decade," in *Distant Relations*, ed., Houchang Chehabi (London: I. B. Tauris, 2006), 227.

capable, and desirous, of championing and implementing it.[20] Even the seismic shockwaves sent by the "earthquake" assassination of the late Premier Rafīq al-Ḥarīrī, followed by a string of further assassinations, while resulting in a Sunni–Maronite–Druze realignment, did not dislodge the sectarian islands. Although democracy, freedom, and resistance to outside interference are on everybody's tongue, none of the parties is seriously willing to risk a push for a secular state. The familiar remedies – spelled out by academics and reformers – are destined to remain ink on paper, for now.

Politically, the opportunity to advance a secularization of the political system was forfeited at several key junctures. In the absence of any structural political reform, and due to the neglect of the relevant articles aimed at political secularization in the Tā'if Accord, the ambitious reconstruction of the country perforce had to operate within the inherited confessional system. The latter was tailored to satisfy mafiaesque civilian and military networks benefiting from state largesse. The (non-) implementation of the reform agenda of the Tā'if Accord of 1990 ended up ratifying a political order whereby "hard" financial power was centered in the hands of former militia heads and governmental elites or "cheese-nibbling" *fromagistes.*[21] Meanwhile, soft power, that is to say political legitimacy, either evaporated into a vacuum of political apathy or devolved to the radicalized sectarian periphery.

Economically, Lebanon today is arguably more closely integrated into the global economy than ever before in its history, albeit on less favorable terms ever since Dubai replaced Beirut as a regional hub of finance and trade after the 1975 civil war. Gone are the days when close to one third of the global gold traffic passed through Beirut.[22] That is not to say that a merchant mentality is not still alive and well, with banking thriving as the last successful sector in the domestic Lebanese economy. Whether globalization (*al-'awlama*) can serve as an efficient (and sufficient) sponsor of secularism (*al-'almānīya*) and engender liberal, democratic states in the region is, however, a different, highly debatable proposition. As we have seen in Chapter 4, *Homo economicus* may indeed transcend *Homo religious*

[20] Sa'āda, *The Social Structure of Lebanon*, 123.

[21] Roughly translated: "The ones who share the pie (lit. 'cheese')." "*Fromagistes*" was President Shihāb's scornful epithet reserved for his competitors among the political and financial elite of Lebanon in the 1950s. There was a double-standard in the Shihābist campaign against the "parastical cheese-nibblers" in so far as Shihāb allowed his own security apparatus to succumb to corruption and turned a blind eye to its wanton exercise of power. Kamāl Janbulāṭ for his part likened the *zu'amā'* to "nattering old women."

[22] Samīr Khalaf, *Heart of Beirut: Reclaiming the Bourj* (London: Saqi Books, 2006), 233.

in many a business transaction or investment joint-venture, and even seal the occasional political pact across confessional lines. Yet, political stability – and indeed secularism – has been ill served by an emasculated, socially irresponsible, and corrupted state riddled with nepotism. The postwar era witnessed an unprecedented indebtedness of the state treasury, record debt insurance costs, along with a steady demographic exodus and brain drain.[23] This was accompanied by widening social disparities, which have in turn exacerbated the dependence of the country's confessional communities on foreign sponsors, chiefly Saudi Arabia, Iran, the United States, and France. Streams of revenue from the Gulf States in particular, whether it be in the form of tourism, aid or loans, dried up, exacerbating Lebanon's debt and debt servicing costs to record levels at the expense of public infrastructure, health care, and education. Instead, in the wake of the Arab Spring tens of billions of petrodollars were squandered to fund pro-jihadist militia – and propagandistic, partisan media – wreaking havoc in Iraq, Libya, and Syria, the latter having a particularly negative fallout for Lebanon.[24]

While "partition" along sectarian lines may have been averted *de jure,* yet *de facto*, demographic segregation and political polarization has been increasing since the civil war of 1975, only to be further fed by US-led regime changes across the Middle East and the wildfire of sectarian strife lit in Iraq and Syria. While the worst-case scenario of a new civil war has been averted thusfar, the embrace of secular principles of citizenship is undermined by the continued spread of communitarian social formations and (sub)states arising from the ashes of the anarchical Arab Spring and its attendant proxy wars.[25]

This book has not absolved the Lebanese, neither individually nor collectively, from responsibility for the trials and tribulations of the secular state. But in adopting a broad, comparative lens, the book argues that one would be remiss not to equally recognize how the broader milieu, both (geo)political and ideological, has impinged on the travails of the secular state. In essence, secularism in Lebanon and the Middle

[23] The economic crisis has had a leveling effect among the sects insofar as a rough estimate of up to 700,000 Lebanese have emigrated over the past years in search of jobs abroad since 1990. See Guita Hourani, "Lebanese Diaspora and Homeland Relations," Center for Migration and Refugee Studies' First Meeting on Migration and Refugee Movements in the Middle East and North Africa, The American University, Cairo, 2007.

[24] Mark Farha, "Searching for Sectarianism in the Arab Spring: Colonial Conspiracy or Indigenous Instinct?" *The Muslim World* 106, 1 (2016): 8–61.

[25] Imad Salamey has documented this trend of "communitarian" forms of (sub)states emerging from the debris of the Arab Spring. See Imad Salamey, *The Decline of Nation-States after the Arab Spring: The Rise of Communitocracy* (Baton Rouge, FL: Taylor & Francis, 2016), 111.

East might be summarized as being haunted by a devilish dialectic of sectarian specters and dreams of domination embodied in the Jewish and Islamic state projects, respectively. The United States and North Atlantic Treaty Organization have consistently coddled the former and occasionally colluded with the other latter since the end of World War II. In both cases, such instrumentalization of politicized religion has been justified under the pretext of supporting "democracy," whether it took the form of stirring (and arming) Islamist communal fervor during the "Arab street,"[26] or underwriting (and arming) the "democracy" self-righteously purported by the "Jewish" state. And, despite their outwardly antagonism, Zionists and Islamists have cooperated, often under the pretext of overthrowing maligned autocrats such as Bashār al-Assad, with Lebanese proxy powers siding with one side or the other. The resultant conflict in turn has served as the fertile breeding ground for sectarian militia filling the void of authority left by collapsed states, confirming the familiar dynamic outlined in Table 3.1.

While the last two decades have witnessed an increasingly skewed and wanton system of international (dis)order being imposed on the region, as an entirely predictable collateral effect, sowed chaos and fueled intercommunal animosities. At the same time, Lebanon is also witnessing a flurry of civil society activism, partly sparked in reaction to these crises, and partly evolving from its own history.

In one sense, then, Lebanon has come a long way since Buṭrus al-Bustānī issued his *crie de coeur* bewailing the absence of a national identity in 1860 in his pamphlet "Clarion of Syria" (*Nafīr Sūrīyā*).[27] Despite the periodic setbacks suffered to a (positive) secularization of the political system, a growing (negative) consciousness of the prohibitive costs of *Ṭā'ifīya* for Lebanon seems firmly instilled in virtually all protagonists in Lebanon today. As surveys bear out, despite all the obstacles, and despite the searing experience of the civil war, identification with a national, civic

[26] Arguably, the roots of this strategy to leverage Islamists stretch back to the 1950s, when the likes of Robert Dreher and President Eisenhower himself sought to harness the Muslim Brotherhood's networks in their fight against communism. CIA director Miles Copeland famously noted the "penetration" of the upper echelons of the Muslim Brotherhood by Western and Soviet intelligence services. Miles Copeland, *The Game of Nations: The Amorality of Power Politics* (New York: Simon & Schuster, 1970). Also see I. Johnson, *A Mosque in Munich, Nazis, the CIA and the Rise of the Muslim Brotherhood in the West* (Boston: Houghton Mifflin Harcourt, 2010).

[27] For all his passionate exhortations to the love of nationalism (*waṭanīya*), Bustānī could not fully define what nation he had in mind. He was even in two minds about the necessity of foreign intervention to secure peace in the Levant, both resenting and crediting it. See Stephen Paul Sheehi, "Inscribing the Arab Self: Buṭrus al-Bustānī and Paradigms of Subjective Reform," *British Journal of Middle Eastern Studies* 27.1 (2000), 23.

identity remains stronger in contemporary Lebanon than in any other Arab country.[28] Even if the historical record has only been rarely subjected to any accounting, few are those who would underestimate the peril of a confessional war, which would quickly turn into an uncontrollable wildfire as the Iraqi and Syrian precedents have amply shown. Indeed, a security accord concluded between otherwise antagonistic Sunni and Shia powerbrokers in Lebanon can be credited for preventing terror groups from Syria wreaking havoc in Beirut after a series of suicide bombings portended a spillover in 2012. The question then remains why this acute awareness of the perils of sectarianism has not been met with a corresponding to promote a properly national, transconfessional identity where it matters most: In the spheres of education, personal status laws, and, ultimately, politics and the public sphere where the paralyzing influence of wider ideological reservations toward secularism still holds sway. Espousing a secularist stance in the open does not come without a price. It is a sad testimony to the state of intellectual freedom in the Middle East that so large a number of liberal thinkers from all countries saw themselves impelled to choose a life in exile for large segments of their adult life: ‘Abdul Raḥman Munif, Ahmad ‘Abdul Mu‘ti al-Hijazi, Nizar Qabbani, Muhammad Arkun, Raymond Eddé, Amin Ma‘luf, Adūnīs, Hisham Sharabi, Aziz al-Azmeh, Jurj Ṭarabishi, and Nasr Ḥamid Abu Zayd, just to name a select few. Others, such as Faraj Fudah in Egypt, Maḥmoud Muḥammad Ṭaha in the Sudan, or Mustafa Juḥa and Ḥusayn Muruwwa in Lebanon, were assassinated. Most recently, outspokenly secular leaders of the Arab Spring, most notably Muhammad Brahimi and Shukri Beleid in Tunisia, were assassinated, while the pro-secular blogger Raif Badawi remains incarcerated in Saudi Arabia, arguably as much for political as for ideological reasons. Beirut, especially before, but also during and after the eruption of the civil war in 1975, continued to serve as a haven of freedom, in part due to the weakness of the government, a mixed blessing in the larger scheme of things as we have seen. But the vibrant intellectual epidermis of the Arab world also would become the

[28] A Zogby poll has revealed that 77 percent of Lebanese view themselves as citizens of their own country rather than "Arab," Muslim," or "Citizen of the World." The strongest adherence to religion as a principal form of nationality identity is found in Saudi Arabia. A subsequent survey conducted by the Pew Research Center revealed that 81 percent of British, 69 percent of Spanish, 66 percent of German, and 46 percent of French Muslims consider themselves as Muslim first (rather than a citizen of their country), while only a (world) record low 30 percent of Lebanese Muslims did. A total of 42 percent of US Christians and only 14 of French and Spanish Christians think of themselves as Christians (rather than citizens) first. See Pew study as cited in Rampe, "Muslims and Europe," 4. Six Arab Nation Survey Report, Zogby International, WEF, Davos, November 2005.

sepulchral scene for a series of assassinations of liberal journalists from Fuad Haddad, Salim al-Lawzi, Kamil Muruwwa, Riyad Taha, Samir Qassir, and Jubran Tuwayni, to writers such as the Palestinian poet Ghassan Kanafani to men of religion such as Shaykh Ahmad 'Assaf, Philippe Slayman, Subhi Salih, and Hassan Khalid, to name but the most prominent. Censorship and assassinations aside, the question remains why the secular theoreticians have not made greater strides in advancing secularism in the latter half of the twentieth century. Why, in other words, were progressive ideas not translated into more effective, political parties?

For one thing, in contrast to Kemalist Turkey, secular intellectuals in most Arab countries, and in Lebanon in particular, found themselves, by and large, at arm's length from political power.[29] In Chapter 2, I examined the legacy of the nineteenth-century *nahḍa* trailblazers and concluded that the "enlightened elite's" effort to advance a secularization "from the salon," so as to speak, only made limited inroads. Thus, the fundamental predicament remains largely unresolved: how can secularism in the Arab world be "liberated" from its confinement to high-brow academic conferences and idle debates among bourgeois intellectuals? Prominent Arab champions of the secular state have seen themselves forced to wistfully acknowledge the broad popular base of communalism.[30] Those self-avowed Arab neoconservatives who euphorically antipated secularism as an organic corollary of externally imposed democracy in Iraq found themselves confronted with a popular consensus opposed to a secular state.[31] Perhaps the once most influential Lebanese pundit in America, the late Fu'ād 'Ajamī, exhibited a measure of positivist credulousness in his rejoinder to (and dismissal of) Huntington's thesis after prematurely auguring the imminent "secularization of [Arab]-politics."[32] The liberal dream of an efflorescence of Arab democracy

[29] The secular Ba'thist al-Husrī (1880–1967) drafted a curriculum for Syria's secondary schools that was of ephemeral duration. In Lebanon, the secularist Ghassān Tuwaynī assumed several ministerial posts.

[30] "Islamism is no longer represented by a peripheral group but constitutes mass grassroots movement, while secularism still consists of an internally diverse, largely avant-garde movement of critical intellectuals, writers, professionals, scholars, and students." Sharābī, *Neopatriarchy*, 11. Interview with Hishām Sharābī in Beirut, Rawsha, July 12, 2002.

[31] Kanan Makīya, "Secularism and Democracy are the Pillars of a New Iraq," *Wall Street Journal*, February 9, 2005. Contrary to the premature and misplaced talk of secularism in Iraq, two years after Desert Storm only 2 percent of Iraqis believed that religion should play no role in lawmaking, while 74 percent indicated Islam should be the sole or main source of legislation. "Three Out of Four Iraqis Say Islam Should be Source of Law," *Agence France-Presse*, May 6, 2005.

[32] Fu'ād Ajamī, "The Summoning: A Reply to Huntington's 'The Clash of Civilizations?'" *Foreign Affairs* 72, 4 (1993): 4.

stood in contrast with the subsequent reality of duly elected populist theocrats in Iraq, Palestine, and Egypt.[33]

On the level of discourse too, secularism still suffers stigmatization. Well over a century after the Arab Enlightenment, an open rapport permitting an autonomous critique of religious and secular use and abuse of power remains sorely absent from Lebanon and the Arab world as a whole as Jurj Khidr and Adūnīs have remarked.[34] Yet, the very fact that a Lebanese-Christian cleric and a Syrian-Muslim poet could frame the predicament in such bold words bespeaks the evolution of secular discourse. In a 2003 public address at American University Beirut, Adūnīs offered perhaps the most scathing, synthetic analysis of the far-reaching consequences for politics and society alike of the still pervasive culture of censorship.

Just as it is anathema – and legally proscribed[35] – to critique all things religious and sacrosanct, so too the image of the sect has become a sacred, untouchable icon. Just as the prophets and sultans of yore enjoy a stature beyond critical inquiry, so too the king and strongman of today are not to be questioned.[36] Much to its dislike, Adūnīs pointed out that even the so-called liberal intelligentsia of Beirut may exhibit its own form of exaggerated deference to the "image of the nation," quite apart from the reactionary men of religion. Even self-proclaimed secular parties in the Arab world may unwittingly mimic an intolerant, all but religious dogmatism brooking no dissent.[37] Quoting the Shāfiʿī jurist al-Mawardī (972–1058), Adūnīs concludes that truth, whether religious or secular, becomes a function of power and authority. Where the later wanes, the claims of the former are undermined. In a society governed by the communal clout of the *Ṭāʾifa*, truth does not exist outside of the power of the herd, the consanguineous *gens.*[38]

[33] Mark Tessler's attempt to disprove an incompatibility of Islam and democracy begs inquiry of the more germane relationship between Islam and secularism. Mark Tessler, "Arab and Muslim Political Attitudes: Stereotypes and Evidence from Survey Research," *International Studies Perspectives* 4.2 (2003): 175–181.

[34] Adūnīs, "Risala Maftuha ila ar-Rais Bashar al Assad," *as-Safir*, June 14, 2006; Jurj Khidr, "*al Almaniyya*," *an-Nahār*, December 12, 1992, 1.

[35] See the restrictive Penal Laws 386 and 385 and the restrictive Lebanese Press Law, which, as in most Arab constitutions, condition freeom of expression on the arbitrary clause of "preserving the dignity of the heads of state," opening the door for state censorship of "defamatory" criticism, both political and religious.

[36] To be sure, prosecution of libel and slander cases, as in the United States, for instance, remains difficult in Lebanon, save for criticisms of religion for which there is a near zero-tolerance policy. For a complete list of censorship laws in Lebanon, see www.censorship lebanon.org/, last accessed February 6, 2018.

[37] Cited in Adūnīs, "Beirut Madina bila Madaniyyat," *as-Safir*, November 1, 2003.

[38] Adūnīs, *Ash-Shʿirīya wa al-ʿArabīya*, 90.

That secularism or the "secular" continues to be misunderstood as a terms of opprobrium has thus as much to do with the animus of the religious reactionaries as with the intelectual cowardice of career-minded, calculating reformists who eshew mention of the word. Whether secularism is glibly dismissed as an "anachronism," brand marked as a heresy, or vilified as a tool of autocratic oppression, such slights of hands effectively eschew a deeper discussion of a concept whose very meaning and relevance is in continuous need of rearticulation to meet the shifting exigencies of time and context.[39] Instead, as we have seen in our discussion of Occidentalism, the "secular state" has time and again figured as a foil on which to project many a fear and fault.

There remain, to be sure, a guard of vocal proponents of a radical break between religion and state, not just in Lebanon, but across the Arab world. Incidentally, a disproportionate number of secularists in Lebanon tended to hail from neighboring Arab countries (chiefly Syria and Palestine, both of which are now drowning in communalism). Moreover, some of the most dauntless champions of secularism, and most incisive social analysts, in the Arab world happen to be poets, including Adūnīs, the late Unsi al Hādj, Aḥmad ʻAbdul Muʻṭī al-Ḥijāzī, or Turki al-Hamad. Over the past decades, they have had to contend with an accusation this book may be liable to encounter as well. Namely, the charge of having adopted an excessively Eurocentric approach toward secularism. The endeavor to bridge continents and to compare contexts, the quest to synthesize kindred experiences of states and societies struggling to forge unity within diversity, emanates not from a desire of denigration or distinction, but from empathy for universally shared challenges of statecraft. If an eye has been cast on the evolution of secularism in Europe in this book, then the aim of adopting such a broad, comparative lens has not been to juxtapose a savagely tribalistic Orient to an ever-enlightened Occident. Quite the contrary. If secularism first evolved into a mature political principle in the West, as Arab intellectuals since al-Tahtāwī have attested,[40] then this was so precisely as a result of the prior "barbaric" confessional wars, prejudices, and competing bids for hegemony that brought the continent to the brink of self-annihilation. There is no reason why the genie of communalism (*Ṭā'ifīya*), which has haunted Lebanon and is tearing at the fabric of the region, should be viewed any differently. Indeed, while Lebanon has not been inoculated against the

[39] Raḍwān as-Sayyid, for instance, has dismissed secularism as a passé, "no longer relevant anachronism." Interview with Raḍwān as-Sayyid, Beirut, ministry of finance, July 17, 2001.

[40] See Khūrī, *Modern Arab Thought*, 13.

latest regional eddies of sectarianism, its own searing experience of civil war may be precisely the reason for why Lebanon still records the largest segment of nonsectarian citizens in the Arab world, followed another war-ravaged state, Iraq.[41]

As indicated, along with many other structural factors outlined in this book, popular support for secularism may be born from sheer fatigue with sectarian strife. With cross-sectarian consensus a rarity in today's Lebanon, one precious exception that stands out is the 80 percent of Lebanese who concur that "tyrannical egoisms" (*al-anānīyāt al-tāghīya*) constitute a greater danger than sectarianism proper.[42] In point of fact, sectarianism can be interpreted as but a euphemism for communal egoism. Secularism then may gain more adherents as a result of nausea and sheer exasperation from confessional wars of extinction and pecuniary greed hiding behind the guise of identity politics and religious populism. As Tacitus put it, "*Pietas obtenditur, aurum quaeritur.*" Religion may be the pretext, but it is gold that is the goal, quite literally, as plentiful instances of the Lebanese, and more recently the Syrian, civil war amply illustrated with opposing sides trading and looting for profit.[43]

Geopolitically, a reduction of sectarian tension in the Middle East would be contingent on the United States and Russia terminating their utterly gratuitous proxy war that has exacerbated the Sunni–Shia, Saudi–Iranian antagonisms. Unfortunately, despite the Iraqi quagmire and the serial fiascoes of the Arab Spring, despite the ever-festering, open wound in Palestine, and despite the trail of blood left by CIA-sponsored Jihadists from Libya to Syria and Iraq, the Washington establishment shows no inclination to abandon the nation's one-sided partisanship for a Middle East policy consistent with the most basic, cardinal principles of all but secular equality enshrined in America's own Declaration of Independence. At least this is the conclusion reached by the coauthors of a study who nevertheless felt constrained to qualify their academic worldview as

41 72 percent of Lebanese and 34 percent of Iraqis affirmed that "religious practices are private and must be separated from political and social life." 11 percent and 34 percent of Iraqis "somewhat agreed" with this proposition, making both nations the most pro-secular one's in the Arab world, followed by Tunisia and Egypt. *Arab Opinion Index 2012* (Doha: Arab Center for Research and Policy, 2012), 63.

42 Ghassān Yaqūb, "Istibiyan'", *As-Safīr*, January 28, 2005. Another, more generic questionnaire revealed that 76 percent of Lebanese oppose the current political system (leaving open the question of the preferred alternative).

43 Tellingly, the single successful intervention of the still unified Muslim–Christian Lebanese army at the beginning of the 1975 war was its effort to keep Beirut's gold *sūq* unscathed from destruction and looting. Fawwāz Ṭarābulsī recounts how warring militias would call temporary cease-fires to engage in joint plunder. Ṭarābulsī, "Identités et Solidarités Croisées dans les Conflicts du Liban Contemporain," 574.

that of "philo-Semites."[44] Secularism, one feels compelled to respond in light of such brazen avowals of tribal partisanship, is by definition indiscriminately *philanthropic*, that is to say, predicated on the respect for an innate and inalienable humanity that can, by definition, never be determined by an individual's nominal denomination or ethnic identity. As such, secularism fulfills at once all of the requirements of citizenship and the deeper meaning of *religio*, the bonding of men and women in solidarity. Crucially, the political framework of a secular state must neither be seen as a threat to any given identity, nor to morally edifying expressions of religious faith, nor to cultural authenticity and social integrity of the individual or the confession. Rather, a secular state is to provide a constitutional check on desires for discrimination and supremacy, which are themselves products of arrogance and human hubris.[45]

Lebanon's consociational system of intersectarian quotas and power sharing has been hailed as a nostrum and check on supremacist inclinations by some scholars.[46] Others have identified consociationalism as the chief culprit for confessional conflict.[47] The late Shimon Peres has repudiated the Lebanese multicommunal paradigm as a "quagmire" and direct danger to the ethnocratic antithesis represented by Israel.[48] Certainly, the monopolization of power by a single ethno-religious community would spell disaster for Lebanon's pluralistic mosaic.[49] To be sure,

[44] Cited in Julian Borger, "US Professors Accused of Being Liars and Bigots over Essay on Pro-Israeli Lobby," *The Guardian*, March 31, 2006; Stephen Walt and John Mersheimer, "The Israeli Lobby and US Foreign Policy," *London Review of Books* 28.6 (2006): 3–12. Another Harvard professor confessing to having become a "thorough philo-Semite" is Niall Ferguson cited in Janet Tassel, "The Global Empire of Niall Ferguson," *Harvard Magazine*, May–June 2007, 91.

[45] "The existential aspect of religion … must be distinguished from its more nefarious political functions." Nur Yalman, "On Secularism and Its Critics: Notes on Turkey, India and Iran," *Contributions to Indian Sociology* 25.2 (1991): 250.

[46] See Imad Salamey, "The Double Movement & Post-Arab Spring Consociationalism," *The Muslim World* 105.3 (2016): 187–203. Imad Salamey, Mohammed Abu-Nimer, and Elie Abouaoun, "Comparative Post-Conflict Power Sharing Models for Syria," in *Post-Conflict Power-Sharing Agreements: Options for Syria*, eds., Imad Salamey, Mohammed Abu-Nimer, and Elie Abouaoun (London: Palgrave Macmillan, 2018) as well as Stephan Rosiny, "Power Sharing in Syria: Lessons from Lebanon's Taif Experience," *Middle East Policy* 20.3 (2013), 41–55; M. Young, *The Ghosts of Martyrs Square: An Eyewitness Account of Lebanon's Life Struggle* (New York: Simon & Schuster, 2010).

[47] Tobias Mathiessen, *Sectarian Gulf* (Palo Alto, CA: Stanford University Press, 2013), 15. Francisco Salvador Barroso Corta and A. Joseph, "Lebanon Confronts Partition Fears: Has Consociationalism Benefitted Minorities?" *Contemporary Review of the Middle East* 5, 1 (2018): 5–29.

[48] Peres, "One Region, Two States."

[49] The phrasing is that of Joshua Landis who has described a enthno-religious "great sorting out" across the region since World War I. Elias Muhanna, "The Great Sorting Out: Ethnicity & the Future of the Levant," December 18, 2003, https://qifanabki.com/2013/12/18/landis-ethnicity/, last accessed on June 13, 2018.

there are those Lebanese kindred souls of Peres who have harbored no less chauvinistic aspirations of erecting a Maronite, Shia, or Sunni state, with the predictably lamentable results. The fact remains that the thrust of the Lebanese constitution is one aiming toward the *inclusion* of multiple identities, much in contradistinction to the implicit and explicit premises of communal supremacism and exclusion inherent in the paradigms of political Islamism and Zionism that are ascendant in the region. Ultimately, as discussed, the lofty goal of the Lebanese constitution is not just to merely accommodate constituent communities, but to imbue a spirit and forge a national identity transcending parochialisms. Whatever stability the fractious Lebanese political system has evinced against all odds over the past two centuries must be attributed to an underlying recognition of the shared destiny and interdependence of Lebanon's protagonists (*al aish al mushtarak*).

In this idealistic sense, secularism has remained a mirage and we might conclude with the skeptics that the rise of the secular state in Lebanon (as elsewhere in the region) has not been merely resisted, but aborted once and for all. Such a verdict, however, would not reflect the fluid *status quo*, but a gloomy prediction of things to come. Not just the Lebanese state, but secularism as a whole, remains subject to decisions taken on the international and the regional plane.

Cognizant that the student of history is not carelessly to overstep his proper bounds of diagnosis and venture into the ethereal vagaries of prognosis, a word on the future is nonetheless apposite. For if it is not the historian's *métier* to foretell or speculate, it is his duty to forewarn, not in order to strike panic and alarm, but to heighten individual and collective consciousness in the silent hope of a reappraisal of the course struck. In this spirit, and against the backdrop of the bleak parameters delineated in the course of this book, we may conclude that secularism and the voice of reason in the Arab world are not destined to flourish as long as the administration of the premier power continues to squander its resources and reputation on unaccountable interest groups upholding sectarian agendas and neocolonial delusions of war, control, and conquest. What would be sorely needed for secularism to gain a greater foothold in the region is for US "national interest" to be redefined in a way consistent with the prudent noninterventionism embraced by the founding fathers and the nonpartisanship enshrined in the US constitution in lieu of the brute right of might in defense of parochial interests and monied lobbies in Washington.[50] The tired refrain, eagerly repeated by a cynical chorus

[50] "But at its best, the U.N. has been, and still can be, a useful amplifier of American power, helping us to accomplish important global tasks that we deem to be in our own

of court intellectuals and armchair warriors, postulating power's putatively "inevitable" creation of envy and enmity, is belied by history itself. For power deployed prudently by the strong has evinced itself as a potential source of respect, while, conversely, the blind rage and vengefulness of the impotent, righteous victim may despoil even the most hallowed and just of causes. Students, policymakers, and protagonists of the modern Middle East alike thus may ponder the significance of the fact that major avenues in Istanbul and Beirut were named in honor of a great American president, who, unlike his successors, was unusually attuned to the prohibitive costs of a Middle East arms race, narrow partisanship, and Machiavellian greed hijacking the cause of justice.[51] John F. Kennedy's clarion call for global comity, interdependence, and cooperation with the Soviet Union were echoed by President Trump who came to office campaiging to bury the Cold War hatchet and repudidate the regime change playbook.[52] Yet, the president's campaign promise of rapprochement with Russia and vowed withdrawal from meddling in the Middle East faced immense pressure by spoilers in the intelligence establishment and the media, as well as the recycled neoconservatives appointed to his own administration. On the topic of Israel, President Trump did not muster the courage JFK laid bare placing American interests above the dictat of the Israel lobby, when, in August of 1963, the young president compelled David Ben Gurion to resign after demanding a halt to Israel's nuclear program. By contrast, after calling for "neutrality" toward the Arab–Israeli dispute during the campaign to the chagrin of both Democrats and Republicans, President Trump backtracked and surrendered to maximalist Israeli demands on Jerusalem and settlements, thus isolating the United States diplomatically. Trump's initial rhetorical revocation of neoconservatism and regime change delusions was soon undermined, not only by his obeiscence to the whims of lobbies, but also by Washington's state and intelligence apparatus, which

interest. In short, I don't much care how the U.N. works as a bureaucracy; I care about how often it can be enlisted to support, endorse and amplify U.S. power. That is what serves our national interest." Thomas Friedman cited in the "The Best Man for the U.N.," *New York Times*, April 27, 2005. Friedman's callous instrumentalism omits a definition of US national interest. It stands to reason that Friedman would serve as one of the most vocal agitators for American adventures and the costly regime change efforts in Iraq, Iran, Libya, and Syria.

51 "The men who create power make an indispensable contribution to the nation's greatness, but the men who question power make a contribution just as indispensable, especially when that questioning is disinterested, for they determine whether we use power, or power uses us." President John F. Kennedy, Amherst College, Octover 26, 1963.

52 Mike Whitney, "The Donald Trump Speech Nobody Heard," *CounterPunch*, January 19, 2017.

has shown no compuncture to contrive an enmity with Russia while colluding with Islamists and neofascist nationalists in an effort to reshape the Middle East and undermine Russia in the Ukraine, respectively. Some opportunistic Lebanese leaders have sought to align themselves with this rather cynical policy of leveraging fundamentalists. We may recall that Druze leader Walid Jumblatt had called for ISIS to be included in a post-Assad framework in Syria, while rejecting any terrorist designation for Jabhat al-Nusra.[53] He thus echoed former CIA director David Petraeus, who recklessly advocated arming the al-Qaida-affiliated al-Nusra Front in order to combat ISIS.[54] Influential pundit Thomas Friedman, reiterating a logic embraced by Barack Obama,[55] went even further by suggesting tacit support for ISIS, reasoning that "if we defeat territorial ISIS in Syria now, we will only reduce the pressure on Assad, Iran, Russia and Hezbollah."[56]

From a Lebanese perspective, the question emerges whether a liaison with sectarian ideologies and agendas is not a recipe for summoning the countries own lingering myriad confessionalisms. After all, minorities around the globe will bear the brunt of a continued spread of such supremacist ideologies and policies, whether it be the Christians in the Middle East, the Shia in majority Sunni nations and *vice versa*, the Muslims and Jews in the West, non-Jews in Israel, or, indeed, virtually all of Lebanon's interdependent mosaic of communities.

As this book has attempted to show, the betrayal of secularism has taken on many forms: a polemic vilification and (un)witting distortion of the concept by intellectuals and ideologues, reckless exploitation of communal fervor by populist politicians, and equally cynical geopolitical calculations to arm sectarian state and nonstate actors in the region in past and present.

[53] "Jumblatt: Nusra Front Are not Terrorists," *Daily Star*, October 15, 2015, www.dailystar.com.lb/News/Lebanon-News/2014/Oct-15/274141-jumblatt-nusra-front-are-not-terrorists.ashx, last accessed February 3, 2018.

H. Illeik, "Jumblatt: I am with Al Nusra Front Against Assad," *Al Akhbar* March 3, 2013, http://english.al-akhbar.com/node/15162, last accessed November 3, 2015.

[54] T. Timn, "David Petraeus' Bright Idea: Give Terrorists Weapons to Beat Terrorists," *The Guardian*, September 2, 2015, www.theguardian.com/commentisfree/2015/sep/02/david-petraeus-bright-idea-give-terrorists-weapons-to-beat-isis, last accessed June 3, 2018.

[55] "The reason that we did not just start taking a bunch of airstrikes all across Iraq as soon as ISIL came in was because that would have taken the pressure off of al-Maliki. That would only have encouraged other Shiites to think: 'We do not have to make compromises.'" Barack Obama cited in Thomas Friedman, "Obama on the World," *New York Times*, August 8, 2014.

[56] Thomas Friedman, "Why is Trump fighting ISIS in Syria," *New York Times*, April 12, 2017.

Kamāl Ṣalībī has likened Lebanon to a fish piloting the (Arab) whale below the (Middle Eastern) sea. This may be an exaggeration and indeed one might feel prompted to invert the metaphor: Lebanon more often than not has been the hostage to outside powers, the staging ground for the "wars of the others." Today, the secular state in Lebanon is once again in the crosshairs of competing communalisms and an utterly gratuitous new cold war. In spite of the gloomy present and scarlet past, we may retain the liberty to end on a forward-looking note from the pen of a solitary secularist Arab poet, "There is no such thing as a golden age. And if it exists, it lies ahead of us and not behind us."[57]

[57] Adūnīs, "al-Khatf."

Bibliography

Primary Sources

al-Azīz Nawwār, ʻAbd, ed., *Silsila al-Wathā'iq Asāsīya min Tārīkh Lubnān al-Ḥadīth, 1517–1920* (Beirut: Arab University of Beirut, 1974).

Documents Inédits pour servir à l'Histoire du Christianisme en Orient, publiés par Antoine Rabbath (Paris, 1905).

Doumet-Serhal, Claude, ed., *Michel Shīhā 1891–1954* (Beirut: Foundation Michel Shīhā, 2001).

Al-Dustūr Al-Lubnānī (the Lebanese Constitution), ed. Shafīq Juḥā (Beirut: Dār al-ʻĀlam, 1991).

Abū-Ḥusayn, Abū Raḥmān, ed., *The View from Istanbul: Lebanon and the Druze Emirate in the Ottoman Chancery Documents: 1546–1711* (London: I. B. Tauris, 2004).

al-Jabartī, ʻAbd al-Rahmān ibn Hasan, *ʻAjā'ib al-āthār fī al-Tarājim wa-al-Akhbār*, vol. II (Cairo: Matba'at Dār al-Kutub al-Misrīya, 1997–1998).

Kaynaklar, Kağıt, *Düstur, Birinci Tertip*, vol. 1, Türk Anayasa Metinleri, eds., Suna Kili and A. Şeref Gözübüyük (Ankara: Türkiye İş Bankası Yayınları, 1985), 7.

Quellenwerk zur Entstehung der Schweizerischen Eidgenossenschaft, three vols. (Aarau: Verlag H. R. Sauerlander & Cie., 1933).

Risāla ar-Ri'ā'iya (al-Dīn wa al-ʻilmānīya) (Beirut: Imprimerie Catholique, 1911).

Saʻāda, Antūn, *Al-'Aʻmāl al-Kāmila*, vols. I–X (Beirut: Dār as-Saʻāda lil-Nashr, 2001).

Saʻd, Antoine, *as-Sādis wa as-Saba'ūn: Mar Naṣr Allāh Butrus Sfayr. al-Jāmiʻa al-Lubnānīya lil Thaqāfa*, vols. 1 & 2, 2005.

al-Ṭā'ifīya fī Lubnān Min Khilāl Munāqashāt Majlis al-Nuwwāb, 1923–1987, Tahqīq Yūsuf Qazmā Khūrī (Beirut: Dār al-Ḥamrā, 1989).

The Middle East and North Africa in World Politics: A Documentary Record: European Expansion, 1535–1914, vol. I, second edition, ed. J. C. Hurewitz (New Haven, CT, and London: Yale University Press, 1975).

Zughayb, Jurgis (1729–1801), *ʻAwdat al-Nasāra ilā Jurūd Kisirwān*, ed. Bulūs Qarʻalī [1870] (Beirut: Muʻassassat Khalīfa lil-Tabāʻa, 1983).

Travelogues

d'Arvieux, Laurent, *Memoires*, ed. Antoine Abdelnour (Beirut: Editions Dar Lahad Khater, [1653] 1982).

Burckhardt, Johann Ludwig, *Travels in Syria and the Holy Land* (London, 1877).
Haynes, Jonathan, ed., *The Humanist as Traveler: George Sandy's Relation of a Journey Begun An. Dom 1610* (London: Associated University Press, 1986).
Mariti, Giovanni, *Des Herrn Mariti Geschichte Fakkardin's wie auch der Uebrigen Gross-Emire bis auf das Jahre 1773* (Gotha: Ettinger, 1790).
Niebuhr, Carsten, *Reisebeschreibung Nach Arabien* (Zurich: Manesse Verlag, [1772] 1992).
de la Roque, Jean, *Voyage de Syrie et Du Mont Liban* (Beirut: Dār Lahad Khatar, [1680] 1981).
de Saint Pierre, Puget, *Histoire des Druses: Peuple du Liban* (Paris: Cailleau, 1763).
Sandys, George, *A Relation of a Journey* (London: Printed for Andrew Crooke, 1637).

(Historical) Dictionaries

Badger, G. W., *An English–Arabic Lexicon, in Which the Equivalents for English Words and Idiomatic Sentences Are Rendered into Literary and Colloquial Arabic* (Beirut: Reprinted by Librairie du Liban, [1881] 1967).
Bianchi, Thomas Xavier, *Dictionnaire Francais–Turc*, vol. I (Paris: Typ. de Mme Ve Dondey-Dupré, 1843–1846).
Bocthor, Ellious [Buqtur, Ilyās] (1784–1821), *Dictionnaire Français–Arab par Ellious Bocthor; Revu et augmenté par A. Caussin de Perceval* (Paris: Chez F. Didot père et fils, 1828–1829).
Elias, Antoon, *Elias' Modern Dictionary, English–Arabic* (Cairo: Elias' Modern Press, 1943).
Margoliouth, David Samuel, ed., *Sa'āda's Dictionary* (Beirut: Librairie du Liban, [1911] 1974).
Muhīt al-Muhīt, Buṭrus al-Bustānī, *Ay Qāmūs Mutawwal lil-lugha al-'Arabīya* (Beirut, 1867).
Ritter, Joachim, ed., *Historisches Wörterbuch der Philosophie*, vols. I–XII (Basel: Schwabe, 1971).

Books in Arabic

al-'Abd, 'Ārif, *Lubnān wa al-Tā'if* (Beirut: Center for Arab Unity Studies, 1993).
Abū 'Izz ad-Dīn, Sulaymān, *Ibrāhīm Bāshā fī Sūrīyā: Huwwa Tārīkh ba'd al-Nahdah al-hadītha fī al-Sharq al-Adnā wa-ahwāl Sūrīyā fī 'ahd Muhammad Alī wa-thawarāt al-Sūrīīn wa-Durūz hawrān 'alā hukūmatihi* (Beirut: al-Matba' al-'Ilmīya, 1929).
Adūnīs, *Ash-Shi'rīya wa al-'Arabīya* (Beirut: Dār al-Adab, 1985).
'Aflaq, Michel, *Fī Sabīl al-Ba'ath* (Beirut: Dār al-Talīa lil-Ṭibā' a wa al-Nashr, 1975).
'Āmil, Mahdī (Hamdān, Hasan), *Madkhal lī Naqd al-Fikr al-Ṭā'ifī: al-qadāyā al-Filastīnīya fī al-idyulujīyāt al-burjuwāzīya al-Lubnānīya* (Beirut: Dār al-Farabī, 1985).
Fī Dawlat il-Ṭā'ifīya (Beirut: Dār al-Farabī, 1984).

Anṭūn, Farah, *Ibn Rushd Wa Falsafatuhu* (Beirut: Dār al-Talīa lil-Ṭibā'a wa al-Nashr, 1983).

Arzūnī, Khalīl, *Ilghā al-tā'ifīya fī Lubnān wa-fasl al-tawā'if 'an al-Dawla: Dirāsa fī al-Tārīkh al-Ijtimā'ī* (Beirut: Khalīl Arzūnī, 1997).

Al-'Azm, Ṣādiq Jalāl, *Fī Naqd al-Fikr al-Dīnī, Dār al-Talīa lil-Ṭibā'a wa al-Nashr* (Beirut, 1969).

al-'Almānīya wa al-Mujatma' al-Madanī (Cairo: Markaz al-Dirāsāt wa al- Ma'l-ūmāt al-Qānūnīya li-Huqūq al-Insān, 1998).

al-'Aẓma, 'Azīz (al-Azmeh, Aziz), *al-'Ilmānīya min Manzūr Mukhtalif* (Beirut: CAU, 1993).

Qunstanṭīn Zurayk: 'Arabī lil-Qarn al 'Ashrīn (Beirut: Mu'assasat lil-Dirāsāt, 2003).

Bashīr, Jurj, *Umar' al-Tawā'if, min Junif ila Luzān* (Beirut: Wakālat al-Anbā' al-Markazāya, 1984).

Bayḍūn, Aḥmad (Beydoun, Ahmad), *Al-Sirā' 'alā Tārīkh Lubnān* (Beirut: Lebanese University, 1989).

Tis'at 'Ashara Firqa Nājīya: al-Lubnānīyūn fī M'arakat al-Zawāj al-Madanī (Beirut: an-Nahār, 1999).

Al-Baynī, Ḥasan Amīn, *'Ādāt Al-Zawāj Fī Lubnān* (Beirut: Baysān lil nashr wa al-Tawzī'a, 1998).

Bek, Ibrāhīm, *al-Aswad Dalīl Lubnān* (Baabda: al-Maktaba al-Uthmaniyya, 1906).

al-Bustānī, Buṭrus, *Nafīr Sūrīyā* (Beirut: Dawāfir lil-Abhāth, 1990).

Cheikho, Louis, *Al-Sirr al-Masūnī fī Shia' al-Farsūn* (Beirut, 1910).

Ḍāhir, Mas'ūd, *al-Judhūr al-Tārīkhīya lil-Mas'ala al-Zirā'īya al-Lubnānīya, 1900–1950* (Beirut, 1984).

Tārīkh Lubnān Al-Ijtimā'ī: 1914–1926 (Beirut: Dar an Nahar, 1974).

Darwīsh, 'Alī Ibrāhīm, *Jabal 'Āmil Bayna 1516–1697* (Beirut: Dār al-Hādi, 1993).

Ḍaw, Buṭrus, *Tārīkh al-Mawārina* (Beirut: Dār al-Nahār lil-Nashr, 1967).

Duwayhī, Isṭfān, *Tārīkh al-Azmina: 1095 M–1699 M 425* (Beirut: al-Matb'a al-Kāthūlīkīya, 1951).

Faḥṣ, Hānī, *as-Sh'īa wa-al-Dawla fī Lubnān: Malāmih fī al-Ru'ya Wa al-Dhākira* (Beirut: Dār al-Andalus, 1996).

Haddād, Gregoire, *Al-'Almānīya Al-Shāmila* (Beirut: 'Anāsir al-Hiwār, 1999).

Ḥanafī, Ḥassan, *Muqaddima fī 'ilm al-Istighrāb* (Cairo: al-Dār al-Fannīya, 1991).

Harāwī, 'Ilyās, *'Awdat al-Jumhūrīya*, ed. Camille Munsa (Beirut: Dār an-Nahār, 1999).

Hāshim, Bassām, *Ilghā' At-Ta'ifīya As-Siyāsīya* (Beirut: Al-Dār al-Lubnānī lil Nashr, 2000).

al-Ḥāshimī, 'Abdu al-Mun'im, *Silsila Alam al-'Ulama'* (Beirut/Damascus: al-Awā'il, 1996).

Hāwī, Jurj, *Yatathakar* (Beirut: Dār al-Nahār, 2005).

Ḥilū, Faraj Allāh, *Kitābāt Mukhtāra* (Beirut: Dār al Farabī, 1974).

Huwayyik, Yūssuf, *Yaqzat al-Hajar: A'māl Nahtīya* (Beirut: Dār al-Nahār, 2004).

Ibn Yaḥyā, Ṣāliḥ, *Tārīkh Bayrūt, wa-huwa akhbār al-salaf min dhurriyat BuḤtur ibn 'Alī Amīr al-Gharb bi-Bayrūt*, ed. Kamāl Salībī (Beirut: Dār al-Mashrik, 1969).

Ismā'īl, 'Ādil, *al-Inqilāb 'ala al-Mādi* (Beirut: Dār al-Nashr lil-Siyāsah wa al-Tārīkh, 2003).
al-Jisr, Bāsim, *Mithāq 1943* (Beirut: Dār an-Nahār, 1978).
As-Sirā'āt al-Lubnānīya (Beirut: Dār al-Nahār, 1981).
Jubrān, Jubrān Khalīl, *al-Majmū'a al-Kāmila li-Mu'alifāt Jubrān Khalīl Jubrān* (Beirut: Dār Sādir, 1997).
al-Jundī, Anwar, *Al-Shu'bīyat* (Tripoli: Dār al-Shamāl, 1978).
al-Kawākibi, 'Abd al-Raḥmān, *Tabā'i'u al-Istibdād wa Masārī'u al-Istibād*, ed. Muhammad Jamāl Taḥḥān (Damascus: al-Awā'il, 2003).
Kawtharānī, Wajīh, *al-Thākirat wa al-Tārīkh* (Beirut: Dār al-Talī'a, 2000).
Khālid, Ḥasan, *Al-Muslimūn fī Lubnān* (Beirut: Dār al-Kindī, 1978).
Khūrī, Antwān Ḥarb, *al-Mawārina: Tārīkh wa-Thawābit* (Beirut: al-Rābiṭah al-Mārūnīyah, 1998).
al-Khūrī, Bishāra, *Hāqāiq Lubnānīya*, three vols. (Beirut: Manshūrāt al-Harf, 1961).
Khuwayrī, Antūn, *Al-Harb fī Lubnān 1976* (Jounieh: AI-Bulūya, 1977).
Kubbār, Nazih, *'Abd al-Raḥmān al-Kawākibī: Ḥayātuhu wa 'Aṣruhu* (Tripoli: Gross Press, 1994).
al-Makkī, Muḥammad 'Alī, *Lubnān 635–1516: Min al-Fath al-'Arabī ilá al-Fatḥ al-'Uthmānī* (Beirut: Dār an-Nahar, 1979).
al-Mallāh, 'Abdallāh, *Mutasarrifīya Jabal Lubnān fī 'ahd Muzaffar Bāsha: 1902–1907* (Beirut: 'Abdallāh al-Mallāh, 1985).
al-Ma'lūf, Muriel, *"Ilghā' At-Ta'ifīya* (Beirut: Sharika al-Khalīj, 2005).
Masad, Bulus, *Lubnan wal-Dustur al-Uthmani* (Lebanon and the Ottoman Constitution) (Egypt: al-Ma'arif Press, 1909).
al-Masīrī, 'Abdul Wahāb, *al-'Almānīya al-Shāmila wa al-'Almānīya al-Juzīya*, vols. I & II (Cairo: Dār al-Shurūq, 2002).
Mishāqa, Michael, *Muntakhabāt min al Jawāb ala al-Iqtirah* (Beirut, 1955).
Mughayzil, Joseph, *Kitābāt Joseph Mughayzil*, vols. I & II (Beirut: Mua'ssasat Mughayzil wa Dār an-Nahār, 1997).
al-'Urūba wa al-'Almānīya (Beirut: Dār an-Nahār, 1980).
Murūwwa, 'Alī, *al-Tashayyu' bayna Jabal 'Āmil wa Irān* (London: Riyād al-Rayyes, 1987).
Nasr, Umar Abu, *Al-Harb al-Uthma, 1914–1917*, vol. 17 (Beirut: al-Majmū'ah al-Tārīkhīyah al-Muṣawwarah, 1938).
Naṣṣār, Nāṣīf, *Naḥwa Mujtama' Jadīd* (Beirut: Dār al-Talī'a, 1970).
an-Nuṣūlī, Anīs, *Rasā'il al-Amīr Fakhr al-Dīn min al-Tūskānā* (Beirut: Manshurāt, 1946).
al-Ra'īs, Riyāḍ, *Tārīkh Lubnān Maskūt 'Anhu* (Beirut: Riyād al-Rayyes, 2001).
Riḥānī, Amīn, *Qalbu Lubnān* (Beirut: Dar al-Jil, 1971).
Rustum, Asad, *Bashīr Bayna al-Sulṭān wa al-'Azīz: 1804–1814*, vols. I–III (Beirut: al-Jāmi'a al-Lubnānīya, 1966).
Sa'āda, Khalil, *Silsilat al-'A'māl al-Majhūla, 'Kitāb Maftūh 'ilā as-Sūrīīn wa al-Lubnānīīn wa al-Filistīnīīn'* (Beirut: Dar al Rayes, 1987).
Suriya min al Harb wa al Maja' ila Mu'tammar al Sulh, ed. Badr el Hage (Beirut: Saadeh Cultural Foundation, 2014).
Salāma, Ghassān, *al-Mujtama' wa al-Dawlat fī al-Mashriq al-'arabī* (Beirut: Center for Arab Unity Studies, 1987).

Salih, Subhi, *al-Islām wa Mustaqbal al-Ḥadātha* (Damascus: Dar al Qatiba, 1989).
Salīm, Latīfa Muhammad, *al-Hukm al-Misri Fī al-Shām (Egyptian Rule in the Levant) 1831–1841* (Cairo, 1990).
as-Samad, Riyād, *Mu'assasāt al-Dawla al-Hadītha al-Ijtimāīya wa-al-Siyāsīya: al-Numūdhaj al-Lubnānī 'alā Daw Ahdāth al-Tashrīyāt* (Beirut, 1995).
al-Sawda, Yūssuf, *Fī Sabīl Lubnān* (Alexandria: Madrasat al-Farīr, 1919).
Shams ad-Dīn, Muhammad Mahdī, *al-'Almānīya: Tahlīl wa naqd lil 'Almānīya Muhtāwan wa Tārīkhīyan* (Beirut: al-Munsharāt al-Dawla, 1980).
Sharāra, Waḍḍāh, *Al-Umma Al-Qaliqa Al-'Āmilīyūn wa al-'Asabīya Al-'Āmilīya* (Beirut: Riyāḍ al-Rayyis lil-Kutub wa-al-Nashr, 1996).
as-Shidyāq, Tānnūs, *Akhbār al-'Ayān fī Jabal Lubnān* (Beirut: Matba' Sāmīya, 1954).
Shumayyil, Shiblī, *Magmu'at, vol. I, Falsafat an-nushu' wa-l-'irtiqa'* (Cairo: Matb'a, al-Muqtataf, 1910).
Ṭarābulsī, Fawwāz, *Ṣilāt bi-lā Waṣl: Mīshāl Shīḥā wa al-Idyūlūjīya al-Lubnānīya* (Beirut: Riyād al-Rayyes, 1999).
Ṭarābulsī, Nawfal Ni'matallāh, *Kashf al-Lithām* (Tarablus: Jarus Birr, 1990).
Thākirat Al-Kanīsat, ed. *Jūrj Mughāmis* (Beirut: Manshūrāt Jāmi'at Sayyidat al-Luwayza, Notre Dame University, 2000).
Wakīm, Najāh, *al-'Ayād al-Sawdā* (Beirut: Dār al-Adab, 1998).
Yashuy, Ilī, *Iqtisād Lubnān: Mawqif wa-Tawlīl* (Beirut: Maktabat Lubnān, 2002).
al-Yāzijī, Kamāl, *Ruwwād al-Nahḍa al-Adabīya fī Lubnān al-Hadīth, 1800–1900* (Beirut: Maktabat Ra's Beirut, 1962).

Books in English

'Abd al-Nāṣir, Jamāl, *Official Yearly Book of the United Arab Republic* (Cairo: Ministry of Information, 1959).
Abū Rabīa', Ibrāhīm, *Contemporary Arab Thought* (London: Pluto Press, 2004).
Abūrīsh, Sa'īd, *The Rise, Corruption, and Coming Fall of the House of Saud* (New York: St. Martins, 1995).
Alexandrēs, Alexēs, *The Greek Minority of Istanbul and Greek–Turkish Relations, 1918–1974* (Athens: Center for Asia Minor Studies, 1983).
Akarlı, Engin, *The Long Peace: 1861–1920* (Berkeley: University of California Press, 1993).
Anderson, Benedict, *Imagined Communities: Reflections on the Origins and Spread of Nationalism* (New York: Verso, 1991).
Antonius, Jurj, *The Arab Awakening* (London: H. Hamilton, 1938).
Aristotle, *The Politics of Aristotle*, trans. Benjamin Jowett (London: Colonial Press, 1900).
Asad, Talāl, *Formations of the Secular: Christianity, Islam, Modernity* (Palo Alto, CA: Stanford University Press, 2003).
al-'Azma, 'Azīz (al-Azmeh, Aziz), *Muslim Kingship: Power and the Sacred in Muslim, Christian and Pagan Polities* (London: I. B. Tauris, distributed by St. Martin's Press, 1997).
Islams and Modernities (London/New York: Verso Press, 1993).

Barakāt, Halīm, *The Arab World: Society, Culture* (Berkeley: University of California Press, 1993).

Barber, Benjamin, *Consumed* (New York: W.W. Norton, 2007).

Barker, Edward B., *Syria and Egypt under the Last Five Sultans of Turkey, Being the Experiences, during Fifty Years, of Mr. Consul-General Barker* (New York: Arno Press, 1973 [1876]).

Başkan, Birol, *From Religious Empires to Secular States: State Secularization in Turkey, Iran and Russia* (Abingdon: Routledge, 2014).

Baumann, Hannes, *Citizen Hariri: Lebanon's Neoliberal Reconstruction* (London: Hurst, 2016).

Bishāra, 'Ādil (Beshara, Adel), *Lebanon: Politics of Frustration – the Failed Coup of 1961* (London: Routledge, 2005).

Syrian Nationalism: An Inquiry into the Political Philosphy of Antun Sa'adeh (Beirut: Bissan, 1995).

Brown, Malcolm, ed. *TE Lawrence in War and Peace: An Anthology of the Military Writings of Lawrence of Arabia* (Barnsley: Frontline Books, 2005).

Cammett, Melani, *Compassionate Communalism: Welfare and Sectarianism in Lebanon* (New York: Cornell University Press, 2014).

Caramani, Daniele, *The Nationalization of Politics: The Formation of National Electorates and Party Systems in Western Europe* (Cambridge: Cambridge University Press, 2004).

Chaaban, Jad, Ghattas, Hala, Habib, Rima, et al. *Socio-economic Survey of Palestinian Refugees in Lebanon* (Beirut: American University of Beirut, 2010).

Chalabi, Tamara, *The Shi'is of Jabal 'Amil and the New Lebanon Community and Nation State, 1918–1943* (New York: Palgrave Macmillan, 2006).

Churchill, Charles, *The Druzes and the Maronites: Under the Turkish Rule from 1840 to 1860* (London: Bernard Quaritch, 1862).

Cobban, Helena, *The Making of Modern Lebanon* (New York: Hutchinson, 1985).

Committee on Governmental Affairs, *Investigation of Illegal or Improper Activities in Connection with 1996 Federal Election Campaigns, vol. 6.6, chapter 30 "The Sage of Roger Tamraz"* (Washington, DC: Congress Press, March 10, 1998).

Copeland, Miles, *The Game of Nations: The Amorality of Power Politics* (New York: Simon & Schuster, 1970).

Dāghir, Carole (Dagher, Carole), *Bring Down the Walls* (New York: St. Martin's Press, 2000).

Dah, 'Abdullāh, Dibah, Ghassān, and Shāhīn, Wassīm, *The Distributional Impact of Taxes in Lebanon: Analysis and Policy Implications* (Beirut: Lebanese Center for Policy Studies, 1999).

Deininger, Klaus, and Olinto, Pedro, *Asset Distribution, Inequality and Growth* (Washington, DC: The World Bank, 1999).

Despatches from Her Majesty's Consuls in the Levant, Respecting Past or Apprehended Disturbances in Syria: 1858 to 1860, Further Papers Relating to the Disturbances in Syria. June 1860 (London: Harrison and Sons, 1860).

Eisenberg, Laura, *My Enemies Enemy: Lebanon in the Early Zionist Imagination: 1900–1948* (Detroit, MI: Wayne State University Press, 1994).

Eisenstadt, S. N and Roniger, L., eds., *Patrons: Clients and Friends: Interpersonal Relations of Trust in Society* (Cambridge: Cambridge University Press, 1984).

Erlich, Reuven, *Bi-Sevakh ha Lebanon [The Lebanon Tangle] 1918–1958* (Tel Aviv: Tsahal, Hotsa⊠at "Ma'arakhot": Miśrad ha-biṭaḥon, 2000).

Esposito, John L., *The Islamic Threat: Myth or Reality?* (New York: Oxford University Press, 1999).

Fawwāz, Layla (Fawaz, Leila), *An Occasion for War: Civil Conflict in Lebanon and Damascus in 1860* (London: I. B. Tauris, 1994).

Firro, Kais, *A History of the Druzes*, vol. 1 (Leiden: Brill, 1992).

Fox, Jonathan, *A World Survey of Religion and the State* (Cambridge: Cambridge University Press, 2008), 219.

Gaspard, Tawfīq, *A Political Economy of Lebanon* (Leiden: Brill, 2004).

y Gasset, José Ortega, *The Revolt of the Masses* (New York, W. W. Norton & co., 1994).

Gates, Carolyn, *The Merchant Republic* (London: Centre for Lebanese Studies in Association with I. B. Tauris, 1998).

Gellner, Ernest, *Postmodernism: Reason and Religion* (London: Routledge, 1992).

Gellner, Ernest, and Waterbury, John, *Patrons and Clients in Mediterranean Societies* (London: Duckworth, 1977).

Gelvin, James, *Divided Loyalities: Nationalism and Mass Politics in Syria at the Close of Empire* (Berkeley: University of California Press, 1998).

Gibran, Kahlil, *The Kahlil Gibran Reader: Inspirational Writings* (New York: Citadel Press, 2005),

Giddens, Anthony, *The Constitution of Society: Outline of the Theory of Structuration* (Berkeley: University of California Press, 1984).

Grafton, David, *The Christians of Lebanon* (London: I. B. Tauris, 2003).

Halawī, Mājid (Halawi, Majed), *A Lebanon Defined: Mūsā Al-Sadr and the Shi'a Community* (Boulder, CO: Westview Press, 1992).

Hanf, Theodor, *Coexistence in Wartime Lebanon* (London: The Center for Lebanese Studies, 1993).

Hanioğlu, Şükrü, *The Young Turks in Opposition* (New York: Oxford University Press, 1995).

Hanssen, Jens, *Fin de Siècle Beirut: The Making of an Ottoman Provincial Capital* (Oxford: Clarendon Press, 2005).

Harik, Iliya F., *Politics and Change in a Traditional Society: Lebanon, 1711–1845* (Princeton, NJ: Princeton University Press, 1968).

Harrison, Lawrence, and Huntington, Samuel, eds., *Culture Matters: How Values Shape Human Progress* (New York: Basic Books, 2000).

Ḥasan, S. N., *Christians versus Muslims in Egypt* (Oxford: Oxford University Press, 2006).

Ḥawrānī, Albert (Hourani, Albert), *Arabic Thought in the Liberal Age: 1798–1939* (Cambridge: Cambridge University Press, 1983).

Ḥawrānī, Albert, and Shahādī, Nadīm, eds., *Lebanon and the World: A Century of Emigration* (London: Centre for Lebanese Studies and I. B. Tauris, 1992).

Ḥittī, Phillip, *History of Syria: Including Lebanon and Palestine* (New York: St. Martins Press, 1957).

Lebanon in History (London: Macmillan Press, 1957).

Hobsbawm, Eric, *Age of Extremes: The Short Twentieth Century 1914–1991* (London: Abacus, 1995).

The Age of Revolution: Europe 1789–1848 (London: Weidenfeld and Nicolson, 1962).
Hourani, Albert, *A History of the Arab Peoples* (New York: Faber & Faber, 2013).
Hudson, Michael, *The Precarious Republic* (New York: Random House, 1968).
Human Rights Watch Middle East, *Lebanon, Restrictions on Broadcasting: In Whose Interest?* (New York: Human Rights Watch, 1997).
Husry, Khaldun Sati, *Three Reformers: A Study in Modern Arab Political Thought* (Beirut: Khayats, 1966).
al-Ḥuṣṣ, Salīm, *The Constitution of Society: Outline of the Theory of Structuration* (Berkeley: University of California Press, 1984).
Inglehardt, Ronald, and Welzel, Christian, *Modernization, Cultural Change and Democracy* (Cambridge: Cambridge University Press, 2005).
Janbulāṭ, Kamāl, *I Speak for Lebanon* (London: Zed Press, 1982).
Johnson, I., *A Mosque in Munich: Nazis, the CIA, and the Rise of the Muslim Brotherhood in the West* (Boston: Houghton Mifflin Harcourt, 2010).
Johnson, Michael, *All Honorable Men: The Social Origins of the War in Lebanon* (London: I. B. Tauris, 2001).
Class & Client in Beirut: The Sunni Muslim Community and the Lebanese State, 1840–1985, vol. 28. (New York: Ithaca Press, 1986).
Joseph, Suād, *Gender and Citizenship in the Middle East* (Syracuse, NY: Syracuse University Press, 2000).
K. Marx and F. Engels Collected Works, vol. 17 (Moscow: Progress Publishers, 1980).
Karpat, Kemal, *Studies on Ottoman Social and Political History* (Leiden: Brill, 2002).
Kaufman, Asher, *Reviving Phoenicia* (London: I. B. Tauris, 2004).
Khalaf, Samīr, *Heart of Beirut: Reclaiming the Bourj* (London: Saqi Books, 2006).
Khālidī, Walīd, *Conflict and Violence in Lebanon* (Cambridge, MA: Harvard's Center for International Affairs, 1979).
Khashshān, Hilāl, *Inside the Lebanese Confessional Mind* (Lanham, MD: University Press of America, 1992).
al-Khāzin, Farīd (al-Khazen, Farid), *Lebanon's First Postwar Parliamentary Election* (London: Center for Lebanese Studies, February 1998).
Khūrī, Fu'ād (Khuri, Fuad I.), *From Village to Suburb: Order and Change in Greater Beirut* (Chicago: Chicago University Press, 1975).
Khūrī, Philip (Khoury, Philip S.), *Urban Notables and Arab Nationalism: The Politics of Damascus: 1860–1920* (Cambridge: Cambridge University Press, 1983).
Khūrī, Ra'īf (Khoury, Raif), *Modern Arab Thought: Channels of the French Revolution to the Arab East*, ed., Charles Issavi, trans. Ihsān 'Abbās (Princeton: The Kingston Press, 1983).
Künkler, Mirjam, Madeley, John, and Shankar, Shylashri, eds., *A Secular Age Beyond the West* (Cambridge: Cambridge University Press, 2018).
Lerner, David, *The Passing of Traditional Society* (Glencoe: The Free Press, 1958).
Lewis, Bernard, *Islam and the West* (Oxford: Oxford University Press, 1993).
Lijphart, Arendt, *Democracy in Plural Societies: A Comparative Exploration* (New Haven, CT: Yale University Press, 1977).

Lilienthal, A., *At What Price Israel?* (Chicago: Henry Regnery Co., 1953).
Lockman, Zachary, *Comrades and Enemies: Arab and Jewish Workers in Palestine, 1906–1948* (Berkeley: University of California Press, 1996).
Longrigg, Stephen, *Syria and Lebanon under French Mandate* (London: Oxford University Press, 1958).
Madan, T. N., *Modern Myths: Locked Minds: Secularism and Fundamentalism in India* (New York: Oxford University Press, 1987).
Ma'oz, Moshe, *Ottoman Reform in Syria and Palestine: 1840–1861: The Impact of the Tanzimat on Politics and Society* (Oxford: Clarendon Press, 1968).
Maqdisī, Samīr, *The Lessons of Lebanon* (London: I. B. Tauris, 2004).
Maqdisī, Usāma, *The Culture of Sectarianism* (Berkeley: University of California Press, 2000).
Mathiessen, Tobias, *Sectarian Gulf* (Palo Alto, CA: Stanford University Press, 2013).
'Midhat Bey, 'Alī, *The Life of Midhat Bey* (London: J. Murray, 1903).
Mubayyid, Sāmī, *The Politics of Damascus 1920–1946* (Damascus: Tlass House, 1999).
Najm, Tom, *The Collapse and Reconstruction of Lebanon* (Durham: Center for Middle Eastern and Islamic Studies, 1998).
Norris, Pippa, and Inglehart, Ronald, *Sacred and the Secular: Religion and Politics Worldwide* (Cambridge: Cambridge University Press, 2004).
Norton, Augustus Richard, *AMAL and the Shia* (Austin: University of Texas Press, 1987).
Obermann, Heiko, *The Reformation: Roots and Ramifications* (Edinburgh: T & T Clark, 1994).
Oren, Michael, *Power, Faith and Fantasy* (New York: W. W. Norton, 2007).
Owen, Roger, *The Middle East in the World Economy: 1800–1914* (London: I. B. Tauris, 1993).
State, Power, and Politics in the Making of the Modern Middle East (London: Routledge, 2000).
Parsons, Levi, *A. M. Missionary to Palestine* (Boston: Samuel T. Armstrong, 1819).
Petran, Tabitha, *The Struggle Over Lebanon* (New York: Monthly Review Press, 1987).
Philipp, Thomas, *Jurgi Zaydan: His Life and Thought* (Beirut: F. Steiner, 1979).
Porath, Yehoshua, *The Emergence of the Palestinian-Arab National Movement, 1918–1929* (London: Frank Cass, 1974).
Qāsim, Na'īm (Qassem, Naim), *Ḥizballāh: The Story from Within* (London: Saqi Books, 2005).
Rabinovitch, Itamar, *The War for Lebanon* (Ithaca, NY: Cornell University Press, 1984).
al-Rahbī, Ahmad, *al-Afkār al-Siyāsī ya wa al-Ijtimā'īya 'anda al-Kawākibī* (Damascus: al-Ahālī, 2001).
Rawls, John, *Political Liberalism* (New York: Columbia University Press, 1993).
Reinkowski, Maurus, *Ottoman Multiculturalism?* (Beirut: Orient-Institut, 1999).
Sa'āda, Ṣaffīya (Saadeh, Sophia), *Social Structure of Lebanon* (Beirut: Dār an-Nahār, 1993).

Sa'īd, Edward (Said, Edward), *Orientalism* (New York: Random House, 1978).
Salamey, Imad, *The Decline of Nation-States after the Arab Spring: The Rise of Communitocracy* (Baton Rouge, FL: Taylor & Francis, 2016).
Ṣalībī, Kamāl, *Maronite Historians of Medieval Lebanon* (Beirut: Ams Pr Inc., 1959).
The Modern History of Lebanon (Westport, CT: Greenwood Press, 1965).
House of Many Mansions: The History of Lebanon Reconsidered (Berkeley: University of California Press, 1989).
Ṣalībī, Kamāl Suleiman, *Crossroads to Civil War: Lebanon 1958–1976* (Ithaca, NY: Ithaca Press, 1976).
Sālim, Elie, *Violence and Diplomacy in Lebanon* (London: I. B. Tauris, 1995).
Sā'igh, Yūsuf (Sayigh, Yussuf), *Entreprenuers of Lebanon* (Cambridge, MA: Harvard University Press, 1964).
Saqr, Naomi, *Satellite Realms: Transnational Television, Globalization and the Middle East* (London: I. B. Tauris, 2001).
Seale, Patrick, *Asad of Syn'a: The Struggle for the Middle East* (Berkeley: University of California Press, 1989).
Secher, Reynald, and George Holoch, *A French Genocide: The Vendée* (Notre Dame, IN: University of Notre Dame Press, 2003).
Shāmī, Joseph (Chamie, Joseph), *Religion and Fertility* (New York: Cambridge University Press, 1981).
Shanahan, Rodger, *Shi'a of Lebanon: Clans, Parties and Clerics* (London: I. B. Tauris, 2005).
Sharābī, Hishām, *Neopatriarchy: A Theory of Distorted Change in Arab Society* (New York: Oxford University Press, 1988).
Arab Intellectuals and the West (Baltimore: Johns Hopkins University Press, 1970).
al-Shuwayrī, Yūssuf (Choueiri, Youssef), *Modern Arab Historiography* (London: Routledge, 2003).
Smith, Eugene, *India As a Secular State* (Princeton, NJ: Princeton University Press, 1963).
Stein, Kenneth, *The Land Question in Palestine 1917–1939* (Chapel Hill: University of North Carolina, 1984).
Steinberg, Jonathan, *Why Switzerland?* (Cambridge: Cambridge University Press, 1996).
Stocker, James R., *Spheres of Intervention: US Foreign Policy and the Collapse of Lebanon, 1967–1976* (New York: Cornell University Press, 2016).
al-Ṣulḥ, Raghīd (al-Solh, Raghid), *Lebanon and Arabism: National Identity and State Formation* (London: Center for Lebanese Studies and I. B. Tauris, 2004).
Suster, Gerald, *Hitler and the Age of Horus* (London: Sphere, 1981).
Tabbāra, Riyād, *The Educational System in Lebanon* (Beirut: Center for Development Studies and Projects (MADMA), 2000).
Tawney, R. H., *Religion and the Rise of Capitalism* (London: J. Murray, 1926).
The Digest of Justinian, trans. C. H. Murno (Cambridge: Cambridge University Press, 1904), viii.
Thompson, Elisabeth, *Colonial Citizens* (New York: Columbia University Press, 2000).

Tibāwī, 'Abdul Laṭīf, *A Modern History of Syria* (New York: St. Martin's Press, 1969).

Toynbee, Arnold, *Turkey: A Past and a Future* (New York: D. H. Doran, 1917).

Traboulsi, Fawwaz, *A History of Modern Lebanon* (London: Pluto Press, 2018).

UNDP, *Toward a Citizen's State* (Beirut: UNDP, 2009).

UNESCO Institute for Statistics, *Global Education Digest* (Montreal: UNESCO Institute for Statistics, 2004).

van der Veer, Peter, and Lehmand, Hartmut, eds., *Nation and Religion: Perspectives on Europe and Asia* (Princeton: Princeton University Press, 1999).

Van Leeuwen, Richard, *Notables and Clergy in Mount Lebanon: The Khāzin Sheikhs and the Maronite Church, 1736–1840*, vol. 2 (Leiden: Brill, 1994).

Voltaire, *Philosophical Letters*, trans. Ernest Dilworth (New York: Macmillan Publishing Company, 1962).

Warda, Ibrāhīm, *Islamic Finance in the Global Economy* (Edinburgh: Edinburgh University Press, 2000).

Weber, Max, *The Protestant Ethic and the Spirit of Capitalism*, trans. Talcott Parsons with a foreword by R. H. Tawney (New York: Dover Publications, 2003).

Weiker, Walter, *Ottomans: Turks and the Jewish Polity* (Boston: University Press of America, 1992).

Wordsworth, William, *Complete Poetical Works by William Wordsworth* (London: Macmillan & Co., 1888).

Yārid, Nāzik Saba (Yared, Nazek), *Secularism in the Arab World* (London: Saqi Books, 2002).

Young, M., *The Ghosts of Martyrs Square: An Eyewitness Account of Lebanon's Life Struggle* (New York: Simon & Schuster, 2010).

Zamir, Meir, *Lebanon's Quest* (London: I. B. Tauris, 1997).

Zayn, Zayn N., *The Struggle for Arab Independence* (Delmar, NY: Caravan Books, 1960).

Ziyāda, Hanna (Ziadeh, Hanna), *Sectarianism and Intercommunal Nation-Building in Lebanon* (London: Hurst and Company, 2005).

Books in French

'Assaf, Raoul, ed., *Atlas du Liban* (Beirut: Saint Joseph University, 2003).

Bayḍūn, Ahmad (Beydoun, Ahmad), *Identité Confessionnelle et Temps Social chez les Historiens Libanais Contemporains* (Beirut: Publications d'Université Libanais, 1984).

Berger, Peter, *La Religion dans la Conscience Moderne* (Paris: Editions du Centurion, 1971).

Bonne, Emmanuel, *Vie Publique: Patronage et Clientèle* (Beirut: CERMOC, 1995).

Braudel, Fernand, *La Méditerranée et le Monde Méditerranéen a l'époque de Philippe II: La Part du Milieu*, vol. I, second edition (Paris: Armand Colin, 1966).

al-Bustānī, Fu'ād Afrām, *Le Problème du Liban* (Kaslik: C. R., 1976).

Chaigne-Oudin, Anne-Lucie, *Le France et les Rivalites Occidentales au Levant, Syrie-Liban 1918–1939* (Paris: L'Harmattan, 2006).

Châtelet, François, *Histoire des Idéologies* (Paris: Hachette, 1978).
Dāghir, Carole (Dagher, Carole), *Ces Hommes qui font la Paix* (Paris: Editions FMA, 1994).
Daḥdāḥ, Jean-Pierre, *Khalīl Gibran* (Paris: Editions Albin Michel S. A., 2004).
Farḥāt, Raymond, *Le Secret Bancaire: Étude de Droit Comparé (France, Suisse, Liban)* (Paris: Librarie Générale de Droit et de Jurisprudence, R. Pichon, 1970).
Gouraud, Philippe, *Le General Henri Gouraud au Liban et en Syrie* (Paris: L'Harmattan, 1993).
Jouplain, Paul, *La Question du Liban* (Paris: A. Rousseau, 1908).
al-KāḤī, 'Abdu, Boudjikanian, Aïda, and Khūrī, Joseph, *Orientations culturelles et Valeurs Religieuses au Liban* (Beirut: Centre d'Etudes et de Recherches sur l'Orient Chrétien [CEROC], 1991).
Khalīfa, 'Iṣām, *Des Etapes Décisives Dans L'Histoire Du Liban* (Beirut: Publications Beyrouth, 1997).
Labakī, Buṭrus, and Rjeily, Abū, *Khalil, Bilan des Guerres de Liban* (Paris: L'Harmattan, 1998).
Ma'lūf, Amīn (Maalouf, Amine), *Les Identités Meurtrières* (Paris: LGF, 2001).
Ma'lūf, Jamīl, *La Turquie Novelle et Les Droits de L'Homme* (Cairo: Dar al Hilal, 1906).
Massara, Antoine, *La Gouvernance D'un Système Consensuel* (Beirut: Librairie Orientale, 2003).
Mayla, Joseph (Maila, Joseph), and Masarra, Antoine, *Le Pacte Libanais: Le Message d'Universalité et Ses Contraintes* (Beirut: Librairie Orientale, 1997).
Monnier, Victor, *Bonaparte et les Suisses: L'Acte de Médiation de 1803* (Geneva: Bibliothèque Publique et Universitaire, 2003).
Murād, Nicolas, *Notice Historique Sur L'Origine de La Nation Maronite*, second edition (Paris: Libraire d'Adrien le Clere, 1844).
Naba, René, *Rafic Ḥarīrī: Un homme d'Affaires Premier Ministre* (Paris: L'Harmattan, 1999).
Qassīr, Samīr (Kassir, Samir), *Histoire de Beyrouth* (Paris: Fayard, Libraire Artheme, 2003).
Qurm, Jurj (Corm, Georges), *Le Liban Contemporain: Histoire et Société* (Paris: La Découverte, 2003).
Rabbāth, Edmond, *La Formation Historique du Liban Politique et Constitutionnelle* (Bierut: Librairie Orientale, 1973).
La Constitution Libanaise: Origines, Textes et Commentaires (Beirut: Université Libanaise, Distribution, Librairie Orientale, 1982).
Renan, Ernest, *Histoire des Origines du Christianisme* (Paris, 1863–1883).
Rousseau, Jean-Jacques, *Du Contrat Sociale* (Paris: Hachette, 1972).
Salām, Nawāf, *La Condition Libanais* (Beirut: Dār an-Nahār, 1993).
Sfayr, Antoine (Sfeir, Antoine), *L'argent Des Arabes* (Paris: Herme, 1992).
Shahnāwī, Nadā, *L'Occidentalisation de la vie Quotidienne à Beyrouth, 1860–1914* (Beirut: Éditions Dar an-Nahar, 2002).
Shāmī, Joseph G. (Chamie, Joseph G.), *Le Mémorial Du Liban* vols. I–V (Beirut: Chemaly & Chemaly, 2002).
Shiblī, Michel (Chebli, Michel), *Fakhreddine Ii Maan* (Beirut: L'Institut de Lettres Orientales de Beyrouth, 1946).

Shīḥā, Michel (Chiha, Michel), *Politique Intérieure* (Beirut: Editions du Trident, 1964).

Tabet, Jacques, *Pour faire du Liban la Suisse du Levant: apercu sur les conditions politiques, economiques et touristiques des deux pays* (Paris: Ramlot, 1924).

Volney, Constantin François, *Voyage en Egypte et en Syrie*, vol. 2 (Paris: Mouton, 1959 [1788]).

Yanoski, J., and J. David, *La Syrie ancienne et moderne* (Paris: Univers Pittoresque, Asie, t. VII, 1848).

Books in German

Bloch, Ernst, *Erbschaft dieser Zeit: Gesamtausgabe*, vol. IV, Werkausgabe edition Suhrkamp (Frankfurt am Main: Suhrkamp, 1977).

Bornkamm, Heinrich, *Luther's Geistige Welt* (Gütersloh: Bertelsmann, 1953).

Havemann, Axel, *Geschichte Und Geschichtsschreibung Im Libanon Des 19. Und 20. Jahrhunderts*, vol. 90, Beiruter Texte und Studien (Beirut: Ergon Verlag Wurzburg, 2002).

Junker, Beat, *Geschichte des Kantons Bern seit 1798: Helvetik, Mediation, Restauration*, vol. I (Bern: Historischer Verein des Kantons Bern, 1996).

Kuderna, Michael, *Christliche Gruppen im Libanon: Kampf um Ideologie und Herrschaft einer Unfertigen Nation* (Wiesbaden: Franz Steiner, 1983).

Lehmann, Hartmut, *Säkularisierung: Der Europäische Sonderweg in Sachen Religion* (Göttingen: Wallstein Verlag, 2004).

Lehmbruch, Gerhard, *Proporzdemokratie: Politisches System und politische Kultur in der Schweiz und in Oestereich* (Tübingen: Mohr, 1967).

Müntzer, Thomas, "Sermon to the Princes" in *The Collected Works of Thomas Müntzer*, ed. Peter Matheson (Edinburgh: T & T Clark, 1988).

Nesemann, Katrin, *Medienpolitik Im Libanon* (Hamburg: Deutsches Orient Institut, 2001).

Perthes, Volker, *Der Libanon Nach Dem Buergerkrieg: Von Tā'if Zum Gesellschaftlichen Konsensus?* (Baden-Baden: Nomos Verlag, 1994).

Rieger, Brigitte, *Rentiers. Patrone Und Gemeinschaft: Soziale Sicherung Im Libanon. Europaeische Hochschulschriften*, European PhD dissertations (Frankfurt: Peter Lang, 2002).

Rosiny, Stephan, *Der Islamismus Bei Den Schiiten Im Libanon* (Berlin: Das Arabische Buch, 1996).

Schenk, Bernadette, *Tendenzen Und Entwicklungen in Der Modernen Drusischen Gemeinschaft Im Libanon* (Berlin: Klaus Schwarz Verlag, 2002).

Schnittger, Otto, *Der Libanon im Kreuzfeuer* (Berlin: Arno Spitz, 1993).

Sichtermann, Siegfried, *Geschichte des Bankgeheimniss* (Frankfurt am Main: Knapp, 1953).

Plessner, Helmuth, *Die Verspätete Nation: Über die politische Verführbarkeit Bürgerlichen Geistes* (Stuttgart: W. Kohlhammer Verlag, 1959).

Suter, Meinrad, *Kleine Zürcher Verfassungsgeschichte 1218–2000*, Herausgegeben vom Staatsarchiv des Kantons Zürich (Zürich: Presse des Kantons Zurich, 2000).

Journal and Newspaper Articles

'Āad, Ḥanān, "Hādirat bi-Da'wa Min Markaz Al-Tawthīq Wa Al-Abhāth," *an-Nahār*, March 6, 2004.

'Abdul-Mālik, Anwar, "Orientalism in Crisis," *Diogenes* 44 (Winter 1963).

Abi Sa'b, Rūlā, "Shi'ite Beginnings and Scholastic Tradition in Jabal 'Āmil in Lebanon," *The Muslim World* 89.1 (1999).

Abū Ḥusayn, Abdul Raḥmān, "Problems in the Ottoman Administration in Syria during the 16th and 17th Centuries: The Case of the Sanjak of Sidon-Beirut," *International Journal of Middle East Studies* 24.4 (1992): 665–75.

Abū Shadīd, Kamāl, and Ramzi Nassar, "The State of History Teaching in Private-Run Confessional Schools in Lebanon: Implications for National Integration," *Mediterranean Journal of Educational Studies* 5.2 (2000): 57–82.

Al-'Adra, 'Jawād, "Neither Privatization nor Liquidation," *Ii-Monthly*, February 8, 2003.

"Corruption: The Lebanese Syndrome: Maintaining the System, Depleting the Resources," *Ii-Monthly*, October 25, 2005.

"Naturalization: In Defense and Opposition," *Ii-Monthly*, September 2, 2002.

"Crisis of Identity and the Role of the Zu'ama," *Il-Monthly*, May 2006.

Adūnīs, "Beirut Madina bila Madaniyyat," *as-Safir*, November 1, 2003.

"Risala Maftuha ila ar-Rais Bashar al Assad," *as-Safir*, June 14, 2006

"al-Khatf," *al-Hayat*, London, Feburary 24, 2010.

Ahmad, Eqbal, "Encounter with a Fighter," *Al-Ahram Weekly*, 388, July 30–August 5, 1998.

'Ajamī, Fu'ād, "The Summoning: A Reply to Huntington's 'The Clash of Civilizations?'" *Foreign Affairs* 72.4 (1993): 2–9.

Ajay, Nicholas Z., "Political Intrigue and Suppression in Lebanon during World War I," *International Journal of Middle East Studies* 5 (1974): 140–160.

al-'Alāylī, 'Abdullāh, "Hawl Kalimat 'Almana," *al-Āfāq*, 2, June 1978, 1–2.

'Amil, Mahdi "al-Ist'imar wa al-takhalluf," *al-Tariq*, 6 (1969), 48.

Anderson, Benedict, "Western Nationalism, Eastern Nationalism: Is There a Difference?" New Left Review, 9, 2001.

Anderson, Perry, "Internationalism: A Breviary," New Left Review, 14, 2002.

Anderson, Raymond, "Religious Balance in Lebanon Upset," *New York Times*, February 23, 1974

Arab Opinion Index 2012 (Doha: Arab Center for Research and Policy, 2012).

"Article I," The Washington Report on Middle East Affairs, XVI, December 1997, 4.

Arzūnī, Khalil, "Masa'lat al-ṭā'ifīya fī Lubnān," *as-Safir*, December 18, 2003.

'Assāf, Nayla, "Ouzai row draws fire onto handling of public funds," *Daily Star*, June 25, 2002, www.dailystar.com.lb/ArticlePrint.aspx?id=39377&mode=print, last accessed February 3, 2019.

Assouad, Lydia, "Rethinking the Lebanese Economic Miracle: The Extreme Concentration of Income and Wealth in Lebanon 2005–2014," WID.world Working Paper 2017/13.

'Atāllāh, Tony Jurj, "al-Mujannisūn fī Lubnān Mā Ba'd al-Harb," *al-Abhath* 45 (1997): 97–111.

Al-ʻAẓm, Sadek (al-ʻAER, Sādiq), "Orientalism and Orientalism in Reverse," *Khamsin* 8 (1981): 5–26.

al-'Aẓma, Azīz (al-Azmeh, Aziz), and F. Ṭarābulsī, "Aḥmad Fāris al-Shidyāq: Suʻlūk al-Nahḍa," al-Nāqid, 79, January 1995.

Barber, Benjamin R., "How Swiss Is Rousseau?" *Political Theory* 13.4 (November 1985): 475–495.

Barūdī, Sāmī (Baroudi, Sami), "Continuity in Economic Policy in Postwar Lebanon: The Record of the Ḥarīrī and Hoss Government Examined 1992–2000," *Arab Studies Quarterly* 24.1 (2002): 63–90.

de Borchgrave, Arnoud, "Syria Ignores Criticism as It Opts to Extend Lahhūd's Term," *UPI*, August 29, 2004.

Borger, Julian, "US Professors Accused of Being Liars and Bigots over Essay on Pro-Israeli Lobby," *The Guardian*, March 31, 2006.

Burgener, Louis, "Napoleon Bonaparte et la Suisse: Méthodes et Décisions," *The French Review* 45.1 (1971): 46–55.

Carlson, Richard W., "Mr. Harīrī Goes to Washington. The Prime Ministers Real Estate," *Weekly Standard*, May 12, 2003.

Chatterjee, Partha, "Secularism and Toleration," *Economic and Political Weekly* (1994): 1768–1777.

"Chirac to Sack Spy Chiefs for Probing Him," *Dawn*, March 11, 2012, www.dawn.com/news/44309/chirac-to-sack-spy-chiefs-for-probing-him, last accessed February 5, 2019.

Collet, Georges-Paul, "Some Aspects of Literary Relations between 'La Suisse Romande' and XIXth Century France," *The South Central Bulletin* 23.4 (1963): 46–50.

Corta, Francisco Salvador Barroso, and A. Joseph, "Lebanon Confronts Partition Fears: Has Consociationalism Benefitted Minorities?" *Contemporary Review of the Middle East* 5.1 (2018): 5–29.

Dagher, Carole, "With Lebanese President's Second Term, Democracy Suffers Severe Blow," *Washington Report on Middle Eastern Affairs*, December, 1995.

Davison, Roderic, "Turkish Attitudes Concerning Christian–Muslim Equality in the Nineteenth Century," *The American Historical Review* 59.4 (1954): 844–864.

Dekmejian, Richard Hrair, "Consociational Democracy in Crisis: The Case of Lebanon," *Comparative Politics* 10.2 (1978): 251–265.

Dennis, Mark, "If You Can't Beat'em, Buy'em," *Columbia Journalism Review* 33 (1994).

Denoeux, Guilain, and Robert Springborg, "Ḥarīrī's Lebanon: Singapore of the Middle East or Sanaa of the Levant?" *Middle East Policy* 6.2 (1998): 158–173.

Dīb, Kamāl, "Fashl al-Quwwāt al-ʻIlmāniya," *as-Safīr*, February 6, 2004.

Drucker, Jackie, and Abū al-Naṣr, Khalīl, "A Swiss in Lebanon," *Saudi Aramco* 26.4 (July/August 1975).

Dumont, Paul, "Le Franc-Maconnerie Ottomane et les idées françaises à l'époque des Tanzimat," *Revue des mondes musulmans et de la Méditerranée* 52.1 (1989): 150–159.

Economist Intelligence Unit, "Country Report: Lebanon – 3rd Quarter," 1996, 19.

Elazar, Daniel J., "Communal Democracy and Liberal Democracy: An Outside Friend's Look at the Swiss Political Tradition," *Publius* 23.2 (1993): 3–18.

Farha, Mark, "Global Gradations of Secularism: The Consociational, Communal and Coercive Paradigms," *Comparative Sociology* 11 (2012): 354–386.

"Searching for Sectarianism in the Arab Spring: Colonial Conspiracy or Indigenous Instinct?" *The Muslim World* 106.1 (2016): 8–61.

"Stumbling Blocks to the Secularization of Personal Status Laws in the Lebanese Republic (1926–2013)," *Arab Law Quarterly* 29 (2015): 31–55.

Findley, Carter Vaughn, "An Ottoman Occidentalist in Europe: Ahmad Midhat Meets Madame Gülnar, 1889," *American Historical Review* 103 (1998): 15–49.

Firro, Kais, "Lebanese Nationalism versus Arabism: From Būlus Nujaym to Michel Shīḥā," *Middle Eastern Studies* 40.5 (2004): 1–27.

Fisk, Robert, "Syria's Ally Stays in Beirut," *The Independent*, October 20, 1995.

"The Ghāzī Kana'ān I Knew Was Not the Sort of Man Who Would Commit Suicide," *The Independent*, October 13, 2005.

Frayḥa, Nimr (Freiha, Nemer), "Education and Social Cohesion in Lebanon," *Prospects* 23.1 (2003): 77–88.

Friedman, Thomas, "Obama on the World," *New York Times*, August 8, 2014.

"The Best Man for the U.N.," *New York Times*, April 27, 2005.

"Why is Trump fighting ISIS in Syria," *New York Times*, April 12, 2017.

Gambill, Gary, "With Syrian Backing: Saudi Prince Challenges Ḥarīrī," *Middle East Intelligence Bulletin* 4.9 (2002).

"Dossier, Rafīq Harīrī," *Middle East Intelligence Bulletin* 2 (2001), www.meforum.org/meib/articles/0107_ld1.htm, last accessed February 6, 2019.

"Dossier: Wafic Said," *Middle East Intelligence Bulletin* 5.2 (2003): 9–13.

Gambill, Gary, and Abdelnour, Ziad K., "Hezbollah: Between Tehran and Damascus," *Middle East Intelligence Bulletin* 4.2 (2002), www.meforum.org/meib/articles/0202_l1.htm, last accessed February 6, 2019.

Ghattas, Kim, "Read the Koran, Never Sing it," *International Press Service*, November 3, 1999, www.ipsnews.net/1999/11/rights-lebanon-read-the-koran-never-sing-it/, last accessed February 5, 2019.

Ḥaddād, Jurj M., "The Historical Work of Niqula El-Turk 1763–1828," *Journal of the American Oriental Society* 81.3 (1961): 247–251.

Ḥaddād, Maḥmūd, "The Rise of Arab Nationalism Reconsidered," *International Journal of Middle East Studies* 26.2 (1994): 201–222.

Ḥaddād, Simon, and Attitudes Toward Integrated Education"Palestinians in Lebanon: Towards Integration or Conflict?" *Journal of International Migration and Integration* 14 (2000), http://prrn.mcgill.ca/research/papers/hadda_000514.htm, last accessed February 4, 2019.

Haim, Sylvia G., "Islam and the Theory of Arab Nationalism," *Die Welt des Islams* 4.2/3 (1955): 124–149.

Ḥamdān, Kamāl, "Le Social dans la Reconstruction du Liban," *Maghreb-Machrek*, 169 (2000): 70–79.

Ḥamza, Nizār A., "Clientalism, Lebanon: Roots and Trends," *Middle Eastern Studies* 37.3 (2001): 167–178.

"Islamism In Lebanon: A Guide to the Groups," *Middle East Quarterly* 4.3 (1997): 47–54.

Ḥanna, Sāmī A., "The Egyptian Mind and the Idea of Democracy," *International Journal of Middle East Studies* 1.3 (1970): 238–247.

Hartman, Michelle, and Olsaretti, Alessandro, "The First Boat and the First Oar": Inventions of Lebanon in the Writings of Michel Shīhā," *Radical History Review* 86.1 (2003): 37–65.

Hatūm, Majdoline, "Harīrī's comments on citizenship issue provoke criticism," *Daily Star*, March 23, 2004.

Higonnet, Patrice, "Terror, Trauma and the 'Young Marx' Explanation of Jacobin Politics," *Past and Present* 191 (2006): 121–164.

Hourani, Guita, "Lebanese Diaspora and Homeland Relations," Center for Migration and Refugee Studies' First Meeting on Migration and Refugee Movements in the Middle East and North Africa, The American University, Cairo, 2007.

Information International, "University Students Survey (II)", *An-Nahar*, January 14, 1997, 10.

Jabbūr, Charles, "Interview with Salīm Al-Huss," *al-Masīra*, March 22, 2004.

Ja'ja', Antoine, "Al-Harīrī Fī Qalb Al-Hisār," *al-Massīra*, March 2004.

"Jalsa Majlis al Nuwwab," *An-Nahar* (Beirut), February 25, 2004, 2.

Jäschke, Gotthard, "Vom Osmanischen Reich zur Türkischen Republik: Zur Geschichte eines Namenswechsels," *Die Welt des Islams* 21 (1939): 85–93.

"Ehrenschutz Gottes und der Propheten in der Türkei," *Oriens* 15.1 (1962): 296–303.

Johnson, Michael, "Factional Politics in Lebanon: The Case of the 'Islamic Society of Benevolent Intentions' (Al-Maqāsid) in Beirut," *Middle Eastern Studies* 14 (1978): 56–75.

Katzenstein, Peter, "Capitalism in One Country? Switzerland in the International Economy," *International Organization* 34.4 (1980): 507–540.

Keddie, Nikki, "Secularism and Its Discontents," *Daedalus* 132.3 (2003): 14–31.

Khalīfa, 'Iṣām, "Lubnan lam yufsal 'an Suriya," *An-Nahār*, December 1, 2004, 12.

Khalil, Nevine, "Seeking Stability," *al-Ahram Weekly*, 540, June 28, 2001, http://weekly.ahram.org.eg/Archive/2001/540/re5.htm, last accessed February 6, 2019

Khashshān, Hilāl, "How Grantees Relate to Grantor: A Study on a Lebanese College Scholarship Foundation," *Research in Higher Education* 33.2 (1992): 263–73.

Khashshān, Hilāl, and Simon Ḥaddād, "Lebanon's Dramatic 2000 Parliamentary Elections: The Swooping Return of Rafiq Ḥarīrī," *Journal of South Asian and Middle Eastern Studies* 26.3 (2003): 1–22.

al-Khāzin, Farīd (al-Khazen, Farid), "Kamal Jumblatt, the Uncrowned Druze Prince of the Left," *Middle Eastern Studies* 24.2 (1988): 178–205.

Khidr, Jurj (Khudr, George), "al Almaniyya," *an-Nahār*, December 12, 1992.

"Naḥnu wa Al-Muslimīn [We and the Muslims]," *an-Nahār*, March 22, 2003.

"Huwwīyāt al-Lubnānīīn [Identities of the Lebanese]," *an-Nahār*, July 27, 2003.

Kisirwānī, Marūn (Kisirwani, Maroun), "Foreign Interference and Religious Animosity in Lebanon," *Journal of Contemporary History* 15.4 (1980): 685–700.

Kraydī, Marwān (Kreidi, Marwan), "State Control of Television News in 1990s Lebanon," *Journalism and Mass Communication Quarterly* 76.3 (1999): 485–498.

"Lebanon's 9th President," *United Press International*, November 6, 1989, www.upi.com/Archives/1989/11/06/Personality-Spotlight-Rene-Moawad-Lebanons-ninth-president/7924626331600/, last accessed February 5, 2019.

Leenders, Reinoud, "How the Rebel Regained His Cause: Ḥizballāh & the Sixth Arab–Israeli War," *MIT Electronic Journal of Middle East Studies* 6.2 (2006): 38–56.

Leibovich-Dār, Sara, "Taking Care of Family Business," *Haaretz,* April 17, 2004.

Lewis, Bernard, "Watan," *Journal of Contemporary History* 26.3/4 (1991): 523–533.

Lijphart, Arend, "Consociational Democracy," *World Politics* 21.2 (1969): 207–225.

Makīya, Kanan, "Secularism and Democracy are the Pillars of a New Iraq," *Wall Street Journal*, February 9, 2005.

Maktabī, Rania, "The Lebanese Census of 1932 Revisited: Who Are the Lebanese?" *British Journal of Middle Eastern Studies* 26.2 (1999): 219–241.

Mallāt, Shiblī (Mallat, Chibli), "Aspects of Shia' Thought from the South of Lebanon," Papers on Lebanon, 7, Centre for Lebanese Studies, Oxford.

Maqdisī, Usāma (Makdisi, Ussama), "The Modernity of Sectarianism," *Middle East Report* 26 (1996): 23–27.

"Corrupting the Sublime Sultanate: The Revolt of Tanyus Shahin in Nineteenth-Century Ottoman Lebanon," *Comparative Studies in Society and History* 42 (2000): 180–208.

"Ottoman Occidentalism," *American Historical Review* 107 (2002): 768–797.

"After 1860: Debating Religion: Reform and Nationalism in the Ottoman Empire," *International Journal of Middle East Studies* 34.4 (2002): 601–617.

al-Mawlā, Sa'ūd, "Al-Shī'a wa Lubnān," *al-Hayāt*, March 25, 2005.

McCallister, J. F. O., "Lebanon: A Bomb Aimed at Peace," *Time Magazine,* December 4, 1989.

Menemencioğlu, Nermin, "The Ottoman Theatre 1839–1923," *Bulletin (British Society for Middle Eastern Studies)* 10.1 (1983): 48–58.

Mermier, Franck, "Beyrouth, Capitale du Livre Arabe?" *Monde Arabe Maghreb-Machrek* 169 (2000): 100–108.

Mihyū, Sa'd (Mehio, Saad), "Harīrī: A Globetrotter Who Wants to Live History," *Daily Star,* December 12, 2002.

"Prime Minister Alwaleed bin Talāl?" *The Daily Star,* July 9, 2002.

Mubayyid, Sāmī, "Talāl: The Sad Story of the King of Jordan," *al-Mashriq* 4.15 (2005): 55–68.

Muhanna, Elias, "Lebanon's Confused Secularism," *The Guardian,* April 23, 2010.

"Muqabala," *as-Safīr*, April 27, 2006.

Murqus, Michel, "Muqabal ma' Jamil Al-Sayyid," *An-Nahār*, October 15, 1990.

Na'mī, Adīb, "Shughl al atfaal," *an-Nahār*, December 5, 2005.

Naqqāsh, Jurj, "Deux Négotiations ne font pas une Nation!" *L'Orient*, March 10, 1943.

Naṣr, Salīm, "Backdrop to Civil War: The Crisis of Lebanese Capitalism," *Middle East Report* 73 (1978): 3–13.

Naṣr, Vali, "Lessons from the Muslim World," *Daedalus* 132.3 (2003): 67–72.

Nassār, Salīm, "Al-Tamdīd Li-Lahhūd wa Al-Tajdīd Lil-Harīrī," *An-Nahār*, July 3, 2004.

O'Sullivan, Arieh, "Hariri: Hizbullah has right to attack Israel," *Jerusalem Post*, March 21, 2001.

Owen, Roger, "Using Present Day Notions of Imperialism: Globalization and Internationalism to Understand the Middle East's Late 19th Century Early Twentieth Century Past," *MIT Electronic Journal of Middle Eastern Studies* 3 (2003): 4–16.

Pannenberg, Wolfart, "How to Think About Secularism," *First Things* 64 (1996): 27–32.

Peres, Shimon, "One Region, Two States," *Washington Post,* February 2009.

"Post-Parliamentary Election Poll 2000," *Ii International,* September 23–October 5, 2000, 46.

Rampe, David, "Muslims and Europe," *International Herald Tribune*, July 7, 2006.

"Removal of Confession from Civil Registry Records," *The Monthly,* April 2009, 81.

Rizq, Yunān Labīb, "Looking Towards the Levant," *Al-Ahram Weekly,* September 20, 1999.

Rodinson, Maxime, "Aux Origines du 'Pacte National': Contribution à l'Histoire de la Crise Franco-Libanaise de Novembre 1943," *Die Welt des Islams* 28.1/4 (1988): 445–474.

Rondot, Pierre, "Lebanese Institutions and Arab Nationalism," *Journal of Contemporary History* 3.3 (1968): 37–51.

Rosiny, Stephan, "Power Sharing in Syria: Lessons from Lebanon's Taif Experience," *Middle East Policy* 20.3 (2013): 41–55.

Sa'āda, Anṭūn, "al-Mawārina Siryān Sūrīyūn," *al-Zawabi'a* 1 (1948), http://antoun-saadeh.com/works/book/book8/1264, last accessed February 6, 2019.

"Sacred Congregation for the Doctrine of the Faith-Declaration on Masonic Associations," *L'Osservatore Romano* (English Edition), December 5, 1983.

Sa'd Ghurayyib, Amal, "Factors Conducive to the Politization of the Lebanese Shia and the Emergence of Hizballāh," *Journal of Islamic Studies* 14 (2003): 273–307.

Salām, Nawāf, "The Emergence of Citizenship in Islamdom," *Arab Law Quarterly* 12.2 (1997): 25–147.

Salamey, Imad, "The Double Movement & Post-Arab Spring Consociationalism," *The Muslim World* 105.3 (2016): 187–203.

Salībī, Kamāl, "The Lebanese Identity," *Journal of Contemporary History* 6.1 (1971): 76–81.

"The Secret of the House of Ma'an," *International Journal of Middle East Studies* 4 (1973): 272–287.

"The Maronites' Historic Insight," *An-Nahār dossier*, 40, January 9, 1973.

Sālim, Latīfa Muhammad, "Levantine Experiences" *Al-Ahram Weekly*, 766, November 2005.

Salkind, Michael, and Trabulsi Fawwaz, "Organization for Communist Action," *Middle East Research and Information Project* 61 (1977): 5–8.
as-Sayyid, Radwān, "Mashrū'a Dawla," *Al-Mustaqbal*, February 13, 2007.
Shāmī, Joseph (Chamie, Joseph), "The Lebanese Civil War: An Investigation into the Causes," *World Affairs* 139.3 (1976): 171–188.
"Religious Groups in Lebanon A Descriptive Investigation," *International Journal of Middle East Studies* 11.2 (1980): 175–187.
Sharbil, Ghassān, "Muqabal ma' Jamīl as-Sayyid," *al-Hayāt*, July 13, 2005, 1.
Sheehi, Stephen Paul. "Inscribing the Arab Self: Buṭrus al-Bustānī and Paradigms of Subjective Reform," *British Journal of Middle Eastern Studies* 27.1 (2000): 7–24.
Sherman, Gorden E., "The Neutrality of Switzerland" *The American Journal of International Law* 12.4 (1918): 780–795.
Shīḥā, Michel, "Sur la révision de la Constitution," *Le Jour*, April 13, 1948.
"Des Résolutions! Des Actes!" *Le Reveil*, September 1, 1921.
Shihāb, Fuad, "Bayyān 'Uzūf Fu'ād Shihāb," *an-Nahār*, reprinted on March 11, 2004.
Shihāb, Hāfiz, "Reconstructing the Medici Portrait of Fakhr ad-Dīn al-Ma'ani". *Muqarnas* 11 (1994): 117–124.
Spagnolo, John P., "Mount Lebanon, France and Daud Pasha: A Study of Some Aspects of Political Habituation," *International Journal of Middle East Studies* 2 2 (1971): 148–167.
Stepan, Alfred, "Religion, Democracy and the Twin Tolerations," *Journal of Democracy* 11.4 (2000): 37–57.
Swartz, Mimi, "Cast Away," *Texas Monthly*, 32, 5, May 2004, www.texasmonthly.com/politics/cast-away/, last accessed February 6, 2019.
Tabak, Faruk. "Local Merchants in Peripheral Areas of the Empire: The Fertile Crescent During the Long Nineteenth Century," *Review (Fernand Braudel Center)* 11.2 (1988): 179–214.
Tanielian, Melanie Schulze, "Feeding the City: The Beirut Municipality and the Politics of Food during World War I," *International Journal of Middle East Studies* 46.4 (2014): 737–758.
Ṭarābulsī, Fawwāz, "al-Istiqlālān:'Asi'la ilā al-Tārīkh," *as-Safīr*, November 25, 2006.
"The Role of War in State and Society Transformation: The Lebanese Case," SSRC Paris, November 2–4, 1994.
"Tāriq Tarshīshī," *Al-Balad*, June 23, 2005.
Tassel, Janet, "The Global Empire of Niall Ferguson," *Harvard Magazine*, May–June 2007.
Tauber, Elieyer. "The Press and the Journalist as a Vehicle in Spreading National Ideas in Syria and the Late Ottoman Period," *Die Welt des Islams* 30 (1990): 163–177.
Tessler, Mark, "Arab and Muslim Political Attitudes: Stereotypes and Evidence from Survey Research," *International Studies Perspectives* 4.2 (2003): 175–181.
"Three Out of Four Iraqis Say Islam Should be Source of Law," *Agence France-Presse*, May 6, 2005.

Timn, T., "David Petraeus' Bright Idea: Give Terrorists Weapons to Beat Terrorists," *The Guardian*, September 2, 2015, www.theguardian.com/commentisfree/2015/sep/02/david-petraeus-bright-idea-give-terrorists-weapons-to-beat-isis.

De Tocqueville, Alexis, and Alexis Charles Henri Maurice Clérel Tocqueville, "The Old Regime and the French Revolution," *Anchor* 60 (1955): 11–13.

Toynbee, Arnold. "A Centenary View of Lenin," *International Affairs* 46.3 (1970): 490–500.

van Leeuwen, Richard, "Monastic Estates and Agricultural Transformation in Mount Lebanon in the 18th Century," *International Journal of Middle East Studies* 23.4 (1991): 601–617.

Wagner, Ewald, "Untersuchungen zur Sozialgeographie christlicher Minderheiten im Vorderen Orient (Beihefte zum Tübinger Atlas des Vorderen Orients. R. B: Geisteswissenschaften. Nr. 43) by Klaus-Peter Hartmann," *Zeitschrift der Deutschen Morgenländischen Gesellschaft* 132.2 (1982): 438.

Waldman, Peter, "Stepping Forward: Lebanese Premier Uses Own Resources to Spur Rebuilding of Beirut," *The Wall Street Journal,* March 29, 1994.

Walt, Stephen, and Mersheimer, John, "The Israeli Lobby and US Foreign Policy," *London Review of Books* 28.6 (2006): 3–12.

"Whispers," *The Economist*, August 31, 2000, www.economist.com/international/2000/08/31/whispers.

Whitney, Mike, "The Donald Trump Speech Nobody Heard" *CounterPunch*, January 19, 2017.

Wild, Stefan, "National Socialism in the Arab Near East between 1933 and 1939," *Die Welt des Islams* 25.1/4 (1985): 126–173.

Winter, Stephan, "The Ashraf and the Ashraf al-Niqabat in Egypt," *Asian and African Studies* 19 (1985): 17–41.

Wissa, Karim, "Freemasonry in Egypt 1798–1921: A Study in Cultural and Political Encounters," *British Journal of Middle Eastern Studies* 16.2 (1989): 143–161.

Yalman, Nur, "De Toqueville in India: An Essay on the Caste System," *Man* 4.1 (1969): 123–131.

"On Secularism and Its Critics: Notes on Turkey, India and Iran," *Contributions to Indian Sociology* 25.2 (1991): 233–266.

Yaqūb, Ghassān, "Istibiyan'", *As-Safīr*, January 28, 2005.

"You [Ḥarīrī] rejected all *Wikālāt al-Hasrīya*," *An-Nahār*, February 13, 2007, 1.

Young, Chris, "What Place of God in Europe?" *Christian Science Monitor*, February 21, 2005.

Young, Michael, "The Electoral System: A Modest Proposal," *The Lebanon Report*, 1 (1996).

"Targeting Harīrī", *Daily Star,* June 18, 2003.

Zarcone, Thierry, "La Franc-Maconnerie dans l'Empire Ottoman et dans la Turquie Contemporaine," *Les Cahiers d'Orient* 69 (2003): 75–86.

Zayani, Mohamed, "Al Jazeera's Complex Legacy: Thresholds for an Unconventional Media Player from the Global South," *International Journal of Communication* 10 (2016): 3554–3569.

Zisser, Eyal, "Syria, the Ba'th Regime and the Islamic Movement," *The Muslim World* 95 (2005): 43–65.

Articles in Edited Books

Abī-Ṣa'b, Rūlā Jurdī, "History and Self-Image: The 'Amili Ulema in Syria and Iran" in *Distant Relations*, ed. Houchang Shihābi (London: I. B. Tauris, 2006).

Abū Khalīl, As'ad, "The Longevity of the Lebanese Civil War" in *Prolonged Wars: A Post-Nuclear Challenge*, ed. Magyar Danopolous (Montgomery, AL: Mawell Air Force Base, 1994), 41–67.

Ahmad, Feroz, "The Special Relationship: The Committee of Union and Progress and the Ottoman Jewish Political Elite, 1908–1918" in *Jews, Turks, Ottomans*, ed. Avigor Levy (Syracuse, NY: Syracuse University Press, 2002).

Al-Azmeh, Aziz (al-'Azma, 'Azīz), "Nationalism and the Arabs" in *Arab Nation, Arab Nationalism*, ed. Derek Hopwood (New York: St. Martin's Press, 2000).

Berkes, Nizayi, "Historical Background of Turkish Secularism" in *Islam and the West*, ed. Richard Frye (The Hague: Mouton, 1957).

al-Birzī, Dalāl, "Al-Sulta Wa Al-Mujtama'" in *Al-Muwātnīya Fī Lubnān* (Beirut, 2000).

Bishara, Adel, "A Syrian Rebel: Gibran Khalil Gibran" in *The Origins of Syrian Nationhood: Histories, Pioneers and Identity* (New York: Routledge, 2011).

Chehabi, Houchang, and Mneimeh, Ḥassan, "Five Centuries of Lebanese-Iranian Relations" in *Distant Relations*, ed. Houchang Chehabi (London: I. B. Tauris, 2006).

"Iran and Lebanon in the Revolutionary Decade" in *Distant Relations*, ed. Houchang Chehabi (London: I. B. Tauris, 2006).

Dajānī, Nabīl, "The Changing Scene of Lebanese Television" in *The Mission: Journalism, Ethics, and the World* ed. Joe Atkins (Ames: Iowa State University Press, 2002).

Farha, Mark, "Historical Legacy and Political Implications of State and Sectarian Schools in Lebanon" in *Rethinking Education for Social Cohesion: International Case Studies*, ed. Maha Shuayb (London: Palgrave Macmillan, 2012), 64–85.

"Secularism in a Sectarian Society? The Divisive Drafting of the Lebanese Constitution of 1926," in *Constitution Writing, Religion and Democracy*, eds., A. Ü. Bâli and H. Lerner (Cambridge: Cambridge University Press, 2016).

"From Anti-Imperial Dissent to National Consent: The Formation of a Trans-Sectarian National Consciousness in Lebanon" in *The First World War and its Aftermath: The Shaping of the Middle East*, ed., T. G. Fraser (Chicago: Gingko/Chicago University Press, 2015), 91–110.

Flores, Alexander, "Die Anfange des Kommunismus im Nahen Osten" in *Der Nahe Osten In Der Zwischenkriegszeit* (Mainz: Franz Steiner, 1989).

Gelvin, James, "Secularism and Religion in the Arab Middle East" in *The Invention of Religion*, ed., Donald Peterson (New Brunswick, NJ: Rutgers, 2002).

Göle, Nilüfer, "Authoritarian Secularism and Islamist Politics: The Case of Turkey" in *Civil Society in the Middle East: Social, Economic and Political Studies of the Middle East*, vol. 50, ed., Augustus Richard Norton (Leiden and New York: Brill, 1995).

Güneş-Ayata, Ayşe, "Clientelism: Premodern and Modern" in *Democracy, Clientelism, and Civil Society*, eds., L. Roniger and Ayşe Güneş-Ayata (Boulder, CO: L. Rienner Publishers, 1994), 19–28.

Haddad, Robert M., "On the Melkite Passage to the Unia: The Case of Patriarch Cyril of al-Za'Im, 1672–1720," in *Christians and Jews in the Ottoman Empire*, eds., Benjamin Braude and Bernard Lewis (New York: Holmes and Meier, 1982), 67–90.

Ḥakīm, Carole, "Shifting Identities and Representations of the Nation amongst the Maronite Secular Elite" in *From the Syrian Land to the States of Syria and Lebanon*, Beiruter Texte und Studien 96, eds., Thomas Philipp and Christoph Schumann (Beirut: Orient-Institut, Ergon Verlag, 2004).

Hanioğlu, Şükrü, "Turkish Nationalism and the Young Turks: 1889–1908" in *Social Constuctions of Nationalism in the Middle East*, ed., Fatma Müge Göçek (New York: State University of New York, 2002), 85–99.

Hawrānī, Albert (Hourani, Albert), "From Jabal 'Āmil to Persia" [1986] in *Distant Relations*, ed., Houchang Shihābi (London: I. B. Tauris, 2006).

"Ideologies of the Mountain and the City" in *Essays on the Crisis in Lebanon*, ed., Roger Owen (London: Ithaca Press, 1976).

Hofman, Yitzhak, "The Administration of Syria and Palestine under Egyptian Rule (1831–1840)" in *Studies on Palestine during the Ottoman Period*, ed., M. Maoz (Jerusalem: Hebrew University, 1975), 323–333.

Hottinger, Arnold, "Zu'ama in Historical Perspective" in *Politics in Lebanon*, ed., Leonard Binder (New York: Wiley, 1966), 85–105.

al-Ḥuṣṣ, Salīm (Hoss, Salim), "Prospective Change in Lebanon" in *Peace for Lebanon: From War to Reconstruction*, ed., Deidre Collins (London: Lynne Rienner, 1994).

Isḥāq, Adīb, "Al-Ta'aṣṣub wa al-Tasāhul" in *Aḍwā' 'alā al-Ta'assub: Majmū'at mu'alifīn min Adīb Ishaq wa al-Afghānī* (Beirut: Dār Amwāj, 1993).

Issawi, Charles, "Economic Development and Political Liberalism in Lebanon" in *Politics in Lebanon*, ed., Leonard Binder (New York: Wiley-Blackwell, 1966), 69–83.

Jaafar, Rudy, "Democratic System Reform in Lebanon: An Electoral Approach" in *Breaking the Cycle: Civil Wars in Lebanon*, ed., Youssef Choueiri (London: Stacey International, 2007), 285–305.

Kafadar, Cemal, "The Ottomans and Europe" in *Handbook of European History 1400–1600*, vol. I (Leiden: Brill, 1994), 589–627.

Kedar, Mordechai, "In Search of Legitimacy: Asad's Islamic Image in the Syrian Official Press" in *Modern Syria: From Ottoman Rule to Pivotal Role in the Middle East*, eds., Ma'oz Moshe, Joseph Ginat, and Onn Winkler (Portland: Sussex Academic Press, 1999).

Lawson, Fred, "The Northern Syrian Revolts of 1919–1921 and the Sharifian Regime: Congruence or Conflict of Interests and Ideologies" in *From the Syrian Land to the States of Syria and Lebanon*, Beiruter Texte und Studien 96, eds., Thomas Phillip and Christoph Schumann (Beirut: Orient-Institut, Ergon Verlag, 2004).

Matar, Muhammad Farīd, "Hawl al-Fasād wa Subul Mukāfahatiha" in *Khayarāt Lilubnān* (Beirut: an-Nahār, 2004).

Ma'oz, Moshe, "Changing Relations between Jews, Muslims and Christians" in *Jews, Turks, Ottomans*, ed., Avigor Levy (Syracuse, NY: Syracuse University Press, 2002).

Mu'awwad, Yūsuf, "Jamal Pasha en Une Version Libanaise: L'Usage Positif d'Une Légende Noire" in *The First World War as Remembered in the Countries of the Eastern Mediterranean*, eds., Olaf Farschid, Manfred Kropp, and Stephane Daehne, Beiruter Texte und Studien (Beirut: Orient-Institut, Ergon Verlag, 2006), 425–446.

Naṣr, Salīm, "The New Social Map" in *Lebanon in Limbo*, eds., Theodor Hanf and Nawāf Salām (Beirut: Nomos Verlag, 2003).

Owen, Roger, "The Political Economy of Grand Liban: 1920–70" in *Essays on the Crisis in Lebanon*, ed., Roger Owen (London: Ithaca, 1976).

Piccard, Elisabeth, "The Political Economy of Civil War in Lebanon" in *War, Institutions and Social Change in the Middle East*, ed., Steven Heydemann (Berkeley: University of California Press, 2000).

Philipp, Thomas, "Image and Self-Image of the Syrians in Egypt" in *Christians and Jews in the Ottoman Empire*, eds., Benjamin Braude and Bernard Lewis (New York: Holmes and Meier, 1982).

Rāfiq, 'Abdul Karīm (Rafeq, Abul Karim) "Gesellschaft: Wirtschaft und Politische Macht in Syrien: 1918–1925" in *Der Nahe Osten In Der Zwischenkriegszeit* (Stuttgart: Franz Steiner, 1989), 440–481.

Reinkowski, Maurus. "Beyond the Mountain Refuge" in *From the Syrian Land to the States of Syria and Lebanon*, Beiruter Texte und Studien 96, eds., Thomas Philipp and Christoph Schumann (Beirut: Orient-Institut, Ergon Verlag, 2004).

Sa'āda, Khalīl, "Al-Ta'assub al-Dīnī fī al-Mashriq wa al-Sharqīīn" in *Aḍwā' 'alā al-Ta'assub: Majmū'at mu'alifīn min Adīb Ishāq wa al-Afghānī* (Beirut: Dār Amwāj, 1993).

Sa'āda, Ṣaffīya, "Basic Issues Concerning the Personal Status Law in Lebanon" in *Religion: Violence and Reconciliation*, ed., Thomas Scheffler (Beirut: Ergon Verlag, 2002).

Saba, Paul, "The Creation of the Lebanese Economy: Economic Growth in the Nineteenth and Early Twentieth Century" in *Essays on the Crisis in Lebanon*, ed., Roger Owen (London: Ithaca Press, 1972), 1–22.

Sachsenmaier, Dominic, Riedl, Jens, and Eisenstadt, Shmuel, eds., *Reflections on Multiple Modernities: European, Chinese and Other Interpretations* (Leiden: Brill, 2002).

Sa'd, 'Abdū, "Wāqa'i Mu'tamar bi-'Anwān Nahwa 'Itimād an-Nisbīya fī al-Intikhābāt," in *Abḥāth fī al-Qānūn al'Am*, vol. 1 (Beirut: Markaz Beirut lil Ma'lumaat, 2005), 24–37.

Sadowski, Yahya, The Evolution of Political Identity in Syria," in *Identity and Foreign Policy in the Middle East* (Ithaca, NY: Cornell University Press, 2002).

Salām, Nawāf, "Individu et Citoyen au Liban" in *Le Liban Aujourd'hui*, ed., Fādī Kiwān (Beirut: CERMOC, 1994).

Salamey, Imad, Abu-Nimer, Mohammed, and Abouaoun, Elie. "Comparative Post-Conflict Power Sharing Models for Syria" in *Post-Conflict Power-Sharing*

Agreements: Options for Syria, eds., Imad Salamey, Mohammed Abu-Nimer, and Elie Abouaoun (London: Palgrave Macmillan, 2018).
Ṣalībī, Kamāl, "Fakhr ad-Dīn al-Thānī wa al-Fikra al-Lubnānīya" in *Ab'ād al-Qawmīyā al-Lubnānīya* (Beirut, 1970).
Schatkowski, Linda, "The Famine of 1915–18 in Greater Syria" in *Essays in Honor of Albert Hawrānī*, St. Antony's Middle East Monographs 26, ed. J. Spagnolo (Reading: Ithaca Press, 1992), 229–258.
Schulze, Kirsten E., "Israeli and Maronite Nationalisms: Is a Minority Alliance 'Natural?'" in *Nationalisms, Minorities and Diasporas* (London: I. B. Tauris, 1996).
al-Solh, Raghid (al-Sulh), "Religious Identity and Citizenship" in *Peace for Lebanon?*, ed., Deirdre Collings (London: Lynn Rinner, 1994).
Strohmeier, Martin, "Muslim Education in the Vilayet of Beirut 1880–1918" in *Decision Making and Change in the Ottoman Empire*, ed., Caesar Farah (Kirksville, MO: Thomas Jefferson University Press, 1993).
"The Revolt of 'Alī Pasha Janbulad in the Contemporary Arab Sources and its Significance" in *Turk Tārīkh Kongresi: Kongreye Sunulan Bildirlir* (Ankara, 1983), 1515–1534.
Winter, Stefan, "The Nusayris before the Tanzimat in the Eyes of Ottoman Provincial Administrators, 1804–1834," in *From the Syrian Land to the States of Syria and Lebanon* eds., Thomas Philipp and Christoph Schumann (Beirut: Orient-Institut, Ergon Verlag, 2004): 97–112.

Report

Economist Intelligence Unit, "Country Report: Lebanon," 2006.

PhD Dissertations and Theses

Abū Khalīl, As'ad, "The Politics of Sectarian Ethnicity: Segmentation in Lebanese Society," PhD thesis, Georgetown University, 1988.
'Atīya, Nayla, "The Attitude of the Lebanese Sunnis towards the State of Lebanon," PhD dissertation, University of London, 1973.
Bray-Collins, Elinor Flora, "Sectarianism from Below: Youth Politics in Post-war Lebanon," PhD dissertation, University of Toronto, 2016.
Diller-Lybarger, Loren, "Between Sacred and Secular: Religion, Generations and Collective Memory among Muslim and Christian Palestinians in the Post-Oslo Period," PhD dissertation, the University of Chicago, 2002.
Elsaesser, Sebastian, "Die Theorie des Islamischen Aktivismus Bei Fathi Yakan," dissertation, Zentrum Moderner Orient, Berlin, 2005.
Faraḥ, Caesar, "The Problem of the Ottoman Administration in the Lebanon: 1840–1861," PhD dissertation, University Microfilms International, Ann Arbor, MI, 1977.
Farha, Philip, "Switzerland: Coherent Incoherence," BA honors thesis, Wesleyan University, 1993.

Ḥāmī, ‘Alī, “Khalīl Sa‘āda: L’Homme et L’Oeuvre 1857–1934,” PhD dissertation, Paris-Sorbonne University, 1986.
Ḥarīq, Ilyā F., “Political Change in a Traditional Society,” PhD dissertation, Chicago, 1964.
Haughton, Jonathan, “An Assessment of the Tax System of Lebanon,” Suffolk University, 2004.
Hawrānī, Najīb B. (Hourani, Najib), “Capitalists in Conflict: A Political Economy of the Life, Death and Rebirth of Beirut,” PhD dissertation, New York University, 2005.
Hilmī, Khālid (Helmy, Khaled), “The Contrasting Fates of Middle Eastern Politicized Islam & European Politicized Christianity: Historical Divergence in Configurations of Religious Contention and Democratization,” PhD dissertation, Harvard University, 2006.
Khalīfa, ‘Isām, “A La Récherce D’une Politique Ou D’un Concept De Secularisation Dans Le Liban Multiconfessionnel (1858–1975),” doctoral thesis, Paris-Sorbonne University, 1980.
Khūrī-Maqdisī, Ilhām (Khoury-Makdisi, Ilham), “Levantine Trajectories: The Formulation and Dissemination of Radical Ideas in and between Beirut, Cairo and Alexandria. 1860–1914,” PhD dissertation, Harvard University, 2003.
Jarūdī, Lāma, “The Palace of Beit ed-Din: Luxury and Status in a Society of Competing Notables,” A. B. honors thesis, the Department of Architecture, Havard University, 2000.
Rubin, Avi, “Ottoman Modernity: The Nizamiye Courts in the Late Nineteenth Century,” unpublished dissertation, Harvard University, 2006.
Shaery-Eisenlohr, Roschanack, “Constructing Shi’ite Nationalism,” PhD dissertation, University of Chicago, 2004.
Shmeil, Y., “La Sociologie du Systeme Politique Libanais,” PhD thesis, University de Grenoble, 1975.
Ṭarābulsī, Fawwāz N., “Identités et Solidarités Croisées dans les Conflits du Liban Contemporain,” PhD dissertation, Université de Paris VII, 1993.
Vloeberghs, Ward, “A Building of Might and Faith: Rafiq Hariri and the Muhammad Al-Amin Mosque: On the Political Dimensions of Religious Architecture in Contemporary Beirut,” Universite Catholique De Louvain, 2010.
Volk, Lucia, “Missing the Nation,” PhD dissertation, Anthropology Department, Harvard University, 2001.

Interviews

‘Ārif al-‘Abd (Beirut)
H. E. Abdullah bin Hamad al Attiyah (Doha)
Kamāl Abū Shadīd (Nabay)
Jawād ‘Adra (Beirut)
‘Adnān al-Amīn (Beirut)
Muhammad Sa‘īd Al-‘Ashmāwī (Cairo)
Muhammad ‘Alī al-‘Atāsī (Beirut)

Prof. Munīr Bashshūr (Beirut)
Prof. Ahmad Baydūn (Beirut)
Jurj Qurm (Beirut)
Prof. Mas'ūd Dāhir (Beirut)
Hānī Faḥṣ (Beirut)
Adīb Farḥa (Beirut)
Albīr Farhāt (Jarzī)
Prof. Nimr Frayḥa (Beirut)
Gregoire Haddād (Beirut, Bikffaya)
Haydar Hājj Ismā'īl (Beirut)
Yahyā Ḥakīm (Beirut)
Prof. Theodor Hanf (Byblos)
Hussein al Husseini (Ain al Tini, Beirut)
Arnold Hottinger (Zurich)
Guita Hawrānī (Notre Dame University)
SamāḤ Idrīs (Beirut)
Bishop Jurj Khidr (Brummana)
Sa'd Mihyū (Beirut)
Prof. Ṭāriq Mitrī (Beirut)
Tawfīq Muhanna (Beirut)
Ziyād Mūsā (Beirut)
Prof. Ahmad Mussalī (Beirut)
'Iṣām Na'amān (Beirut)
Maurice Nahrā (Beirut)
Prof. Nāsīf Nassār (Nabay)
Paul Sālim
Prof. Nawāf Salām (Beirut)
Salāh Salmān (Boston)
Rif'at as-Sa'īd (Cairo)
Prof. Radwān as-Sayyid (Beirut)
Prof. Hishām Sharābī (Washington, DC, Beirut)
Luqmān Slīm (Beirut)
Jubrān Tuwaynī (Beirut)
Ṣaffīya (Sophia) Sa'āda (Beirut)
Augarite Yunān (Beirut)
Walīd Slaybī (Beirut)

Newspapers and Journals:

Al-Ādāb
al-Āfāq
al-Afkār
al-Akhbār
al-'Ahd
Al-Balad
Elāph
Ha'aretz

al-Ḥayāt
Ii-Monthly – Information International
al-'Ijtihād
al-Jarīda al-Rasmīya (Official Gazette of the Republic of Lebanon)
al-Jinān
(L'Orient) Le Jour
Lebanon Report
Lisān al-Ḥāl
al-Kifāḥ al-'Arabī
Al-Ma'rad
Al-Mashriq
al-Masīra
Monday Morning
Al-Muqarnas
Al-Muwātinan-Nahār
al-Nāqid
an-Nūr (Cairo)
as-Safīr
ash-Sharq al-Awsat
Qadāyā
al-Watan al-'Arabī
al-Zawbi'a

Index